Christina Flotmann
Ambiguity in »Star Wars« and »Harry Potter«

Cultural and Media Studies

To Christoph

Christina Flotmann teaches English Literary and Cultural Studies at the University of Paderborn. Her research interests include contemporary popular culture and the Victorian era.

CHRISTINA FLOTMANN

Ambiguity in »Star Wars« and »Harry Potter«

A (Post)Structuralist Reading of Two Popular Myths

[transcript]

Bibliographic information published by the Deutsche Nationalbibliothek
The Deutsche Nationalbibliothek lists this publication in the Deutsche Natio-nalbibliografie; detailed bibliographic data are available on the Internet at http://dnb.d-nb.de

© 2013 transcript Verlag, Bielefeld

Cover layout: Kordula Röckenhaus, Bielefeld
Cover illustration: kallejipp / photocase.de (detail)
Proofread and typeset by Christina Flotmann
Printed by Majuskel Medienproduktion GmbH, Wetzlar
ISBN 978-3-8376-2148-8

Contents

Acknowledgements | 7

1. **Introduction: Structural Ambiguity** | 9

2. **Myth: Its Functions, Structure, and Workings**
   in Society and (Contemporary Popular) Culture | 25
2.1 Functions of Myth | 25
2.2 The Structure of Myth (As a Reflection
    of Human Consciousness) | 33
2.3 The Limitations of Structures and Mythical Ambiguity | 41
2.4 Myth as Ideology | 44
2.5 Myth and Popular Culture | 54

3. **The Superstructures of *Star Wars***
   and *Harry Potter* | 61
3.1 A Structural 'Star Wars' | 61
3.2 Dichotomised Frames: *Harry Potter* | 70

4. **The Mythical Ambiguity of *Star Wars***
   and *Harry Potter* | 83
4.1 *Star Wars's* Equivocal Messages | 83
4.2 *Harry Potter's* Ambiguous Intent | 95

5. **Evil Deconstruction** | 109
5.1 Questioning Dichotomies: The Emperor | 109
5.2 'Play With Security': Voldemort | 122

6. **Villainous Heroes and Heroic Villains** | 145
6.1 'Star-Cross'd' Choice-Maker: Anakin Skywalker /
    Darth Vader | 145
6.2 Villain-Type and Silent Hero: Severus Snape | 172

7. **Ideal Individuals** | 191
7.1 Unity in Duality / Duality in Unity: Harry Potter | 191
7.2 Type and Individual: Luke Skywalker | 214

8. Imperfect Ideals: The Women's Question | 229

8.1 Ambiguous Developments: Female Characters
in *Star Wars* | 229

8.2 Stasis and Play: Women in *Harry Potter* | 247

9. Individuals, Helpers, and Structural Necessities | 271

9.1 Good Nature Versus Evil Technology:
Humanoid Characters in *Star Wars* | 271

9.2 Structures and Formulas Promoting Social Equality (?):
Humanoids in *Harry Potter* | 287

**10. Structural Displacement: Ethnic Diversity
in *Star Wars* and *Harry Potter*** | 311

10.1 Token-Blacks and Evil Aliens: *Star Wars* | 311

10.2 19th-Century Conflicts and Social Awareness:
Ambiguous Otherness in *Harry Potter* | 322

11. The End(ings): Conclusion | 345

12. Works Cited | 371

Primary Sources | 371

Secondary Sources | 372

Internet Sources | 387

13. Appendices | 389

Appendix 1 | 389

Appendix 2 | 390

Appendix 3 | 391

Appendix 4 | 392

Acknowledgements

The success of this project would not have been possible without the following people whom I want to thank from my heart for their various ways of supporting me. Big thanks are due to my first supervisor Merle Tönnies for believing in me and my work, for valuable feedback throughout the writing process, for her patience, as well as constant moral support, and encouragement. I also thank my second supervisor Miriam Strube for her honesty and critical reading of my work. I am furthermore grateful to the following people from the English and American Studies Department at the University of Paderborn: Christoph Ehland, Nicole Schröder, Petra Tegtmeier, and particularly Scot Bell who proofread the manuscript. I thank my colleagues and ex-colleagues Joana Brüning, Heike Buschmann and Ina Grimm for their moral support, their help with formatting and the design of the graphics included in the thesis, as well as for the unforgettable party they organised for me on the day of my thesis-defence. Thanks are also due to Nele Reichert for her assistance with research. Furthermore, I want to thank my publisher transcript, especially Alexander Masch, Kai Reinhardt, and the Graphics Department for designing a great cover page. Last but not least thanks go out to the people closest to me who were essential to my success: my parents Cordula and Ulrich for making all this possible in the first place by financing my university degree and for their constant encouragement to pursue a difficult career path with an uncertain outcome. I also thank my brothers Matthias, Michael and Andreas, especially the latter who lent me his *Star Wars* DVDs, and my grandmother Eva who unfortunately did not see the completion of the project anymore, but who nevertheless took a keen interest in it during her lifetime. I am indebted also to my friends who lent their support in various ways, morally, as well as technically: Heiko, Katharina, Marianne, Mine and Silvia, thank you so much! Finally, my biggest thanks go to my partner Christoph for bearing with me through a time that was not always easy, for his support, his patience and his love.

November 2012   Christina Flotmann

1. Introduction: Structural Ambiguity

This thesis approaches the wide popular appeal of *Star Wars* and *Harry Potter* by reading the stories as myths. I assume that myths, most broadly defined as stories of origins,[1] have nowadays found their way into popular culture and survive in secularised form in what John G. Cawelti describes as formulaic fiction.[2] The two 'texts' I am dealing with in my thesis fit Cawelti's notion of formulaic stories well as each features stereotypical characters and events and follows a certain structural pattern. I will explore through *Star Wars* and *Harry Potter* in which ways myth attracts people, what it does for them, but also how it "distorts" 'reality.'[3]

To validate my reading of the stories as myths, I mainly resort to the ideas of Claude Lévi-Strauss and Roland Barthes, whose analyses of myth are different but also tie in with each other well. In a first step, Lévi-Strauss's "Structural Study of Myth" will be used to arrive at an understanding of the underlying patterns apparent in *Star Wars* and *Harry Potter* and the ways in which they generate meaning. In a second step it is then possible to apply Barthes findings from his study "Myth Today" and show how the familiar structures of formulaic stories help naturalise dominant-hegemonic assumptions and consolidate ideologies. The analysis and criticism of the tales' structures does not only rely on structuralist theories such as Lévi-Strauss's and Barthes's, but is also partly informed by poststructuralist approaches, such as Jacques Derrida's deconstruction. Both tales analysed not only allow deconstructivist readings, but also, because of the ambiguity inherent in popular cultural artifacts, themselves contain deconstructivist elements.

---

1   Cf. Kees W. Bolle, "Myth: An Overview," *The Encyclopedia of Religion*, Ed. Mircea Eliade (New York: Macmillan Publishing Company, 1987) 262.

2   Cf. John G. Cawelti, *Adventure, Mystery, and Romance: Formula Stories as Art and Popular Culture* (Chicago: The University of Chicago Press, 1976) 5.

3   Roland Barthes, "Myth Today," *Structuralism in Myth: Lévi-Strauss, Barthes, Dumézil, and Propp*, Ed. Robert A. Segal (New York: Garland Publishing, 1996) 21.

Lévi-Strauss notes binary oppositions and the attempt at balancing them as common to myths and folk tales and concludes that they lay bare a human desire to reconcile conflicting aspects of life.[4] The structurality of myth he identifies thus has a comforting function as it offers a secure frame for human experience and moral clarity. Order and clear ethical demarcations come at a price, however, as they facilitate the generation of ideology. Louis Althusser defines ideology as "the imaginary relationship of individuals to their conditions of existence."[5] Ideology operates largely unconsciously and is often characterised by rather narrow and one-sided assumptions as it works towards making the complexity of life bearable and manageable. Binary oppositions are at the root of much ideological thinking. Not only are the two terms of an opposition dependent on and constitutive of each other, they also always imply a hierarchy. One term is generally privileged before the other as Derrida notes.[6] This is problematic as it happens largely unconsciously so that people do not question it. The notion of hierarchy is at the basis of much ideological thought, as, for instance, when one group of people is seen as superior to the other. This ideological side to myth can become a dangerous tool if it is consciously employed to manipulate people into certain ways of thinking. Barthes criticises this use of myth which helps dominant hegemonic forces to remain in power.[7] When abused, myth becomes an instrument of suppression for some and promotion for others as it prevents actual discussion about important topics for the sake of both clarity and simplicity. Myth, and this will be one of the central aspects of my thesis, is thus ambiguous. It has both positive and negative effects, it comforts, provides order and security, but it also manipulates and "distorts."[8] These two sides will also be found in the tales studied.

The thesis is roughly divided into two parts. The first one uses the Lévi-Straussian analysis of myth to describe the binary structures found in *Star Wars* and *Harry Potter* and comment on the meaning(s) they yield. The second section deals with the ways in which the structures mainly focusing on the fight between good and evil, hero and villain, divert the attention from discourses of gender and ethnicity, topics that raise concerns in contemporary Western societies. The analysis

---

4   Cf. Claude Lévi-Strauss, "The Structural Study of Myth," *Structuralism in Myth: Lévi-Strauss, Barthes, Dumézil, and Propp*, Ed. Robert A. Segal (New York: Garland Publishing, 1996) 130.

5   Louis Althusser, "Ideology and Ideological State Apparatuses," *Literary Theory: An Anthology*, Ed. Julie Rivkin and Michael Ryan (Malden, MA: Blackwell Publishing, 2004) 693.

6   Cf. Jacques Derrida, *Positions* (Chicago: University of Chicago Press, 1972) 41.

7   Cf. Barthes 2.

8   Barthes 21.

will show that ambiguously, these 'real' issues are present in the two contemporary stories my analysis focuses on, but any 'true' discussion of them is avoided at the same time.

The second chapter directly following the introduction contains an overview of various theories of myth, chief among them of course the mentioned ones of Lévi-Strauss and Barthes. It links these readings of myth with *Star Wars* and *Harry Potter* via John G. Cawelti's definition of formulaic fiction, the catalogue of which comprises genres such as the Western, Romance, Gothic and Detective fiction, Fantasy and Science Fiction.[9] Tales of this kind have their largely binary set-up in common with myth in Lévi-Strauss's definition. The chapter further shows how the issues of gender and ethnicity treated in the thesis, used to have, and still have, much to do with binary oppositions. Both women and ethnic minorities have suffered (and suffer) from being Othered, i.e. being made subject to a hierarchy that posits them as inferior.[10] If discourses on gender and ethnicity have always had a structure similar to the one Lévi-Strauss described for myth, then myth and these discourses must somehow be closely related, a connection analysed in chapters eight to ten.

The third chapter of the thesis initiates the actual analysis of *Star Wars* and *Harry Potter* with a discussion of the tales' superstructures, i.e. the structures of all respective episodes of *Star Wars* and instalments of *Harry Potter* taken together. This is followed in chapter four by a more specific analysis of exemplary scenarios of binary oppositions and mediators as set up by Lévi-Strauss.[11] In the structural interplay between the characters making up the poles and filling the middle positions, light is shed on some of the most pertinent ideologies and concerns of the two series. Chapters five, six and seven belong together structurally. Their focus is on the close analysis of the protagonists from *Star Wars* and *Harry Potter* and the ways in which they relate to each other. The set-up of the three chapters foregrounds the structural focus of the thesis once more as the characters are analysed in a progression from evil, over mediator to good. The most mythical, i.e. static and formulaic characters, the Emperor from *Star Wars* at the evil end and Luke Skywalker, again from *Star Wars* at the side of good, constitute the frame of the three chapters, the discussion of the Emperor opening chapter five and the analysis of Luke closing chapter seven. Lord Voldemort, the chief evildoer from *Harry Potter* as slightly less one-dimensional than the Emperor, follows him. Anakin Skywalker / Darth Vader as well as Severus Snape are in the focus of the

---

9   Cf. Cawelti who describes and analyses many of these formulas in his work *Adventure, Mystery, and Romance: Formula Stories as Art and Popular Culture*.

10   Cf. also Derrida *Positions* 41.

11   Cf. Lévi-Strauss 130.

middle chapter six as the two most obvious mediating figures of the stories and Harry Potter, less formulaic than Luke Skywalker but still rather clearly good, is analysed before Luke in chapter seven.

It could be asked why a structural analysis focuses so much on the single characters of the thesis. First of all, as was just explained, the three chapters at the same time as discussing the characters, highlight the structurality of both tales being set up the way they are. Secondly, looking at the characters is in line with Lévi-Strauss's analysis of myth. The diagram he drew in his "Structural Study of Myth" of binary oppositions and mediator clearly shows that on the level of the mythical story opposing and mediating characters symbolically stand for the deeper structural conflicts between, for instance, life and death or good and evil.[12] The diagram further highlights the relationships between characters and by extension the relationship between the binary oppositions at the root of the tales. The interplay between the characters, e.g. the good and evil ones, makes clear the degree to which the two terms of binaries are dependent on each other for their existence. A good character would be rather pointless without an evil one to consolidate his or her goodness. Characters in mythical and formulaic stories are thus always carriers of meaning rather than realistic individuals. They carry out the deep-structural conflicts and support the themes the stories deal with. Incidentally, this reading is supported by an interesting statement eminent actor Sir Alec Guinness who played the role of Jedi Obi-Wan Kenobi in the original *Star Wars* trilogy, made on reading the script for the first time: "I thought the dialogue was pretty terrible and the characters fairly meaningless – but there was a story value."[13] The single elements of the tales such as dialogue or characters, do not matter as much as the story in its entirety. Another statement by Robert Ellwood is illuminating here: "Myth is symbol in narrative form."[14] Every element within the narrative has to conform to its symbolic purpose.

Still, the thesis will determine to which degree the two stories go beyond their structural focus and try to portray their characters as individual within the limits set by the structures. This is a question that is predominantly relevant for chapters eight to ten focusing on the discourses 'silenced' by the structures. Chapter eight looks at the ways women are treated in the tales and explores to which degree some of them are individual although their stories are definitely subordinated to those of the male heroes. Chapter nine discusses the various humanoid characters populating both

---

12   Cf. Lévi-Strauss 130.

13   Sir Alec Guinness qtd. in Steven A. Galipeau, *The Journey of Luke Skywalker* (Chicago: Open Court, 2001) 5.

14   Robert Ellwood, *Tales of Darkness: The Mythology of Evil* (London: Continuum, 2009) 7.

Star Wars and *Harry Potter* and analyses the functions they have as helpers of the protagonists on the level of the story but also on a meta-level as projection space for 'real-life' social issues of which an open discussion is shirked. Chapter ten finally analyses the treatment of ethnic minorities in the tales which ranges from almost total exclusion and 'making white' to at least an implicit awareness of their plight. Chapter eleven, the conclusion, makes use of the endings of both stories to focus and summarise the main findings of the thesis.

As the first *Star Wars* movies appeared in the late 1970s and early 1980s, much criticism was produced then which now appears a trifle outdated. The research on the films exemplifies the late 20th-century shift in focus to cultural studies and away from structuralism to poststructuralism. I believe the absolute nature of this shift and the accompanying utter rejection of structuralism is very harsh, and my thesis will show that structuralism can be a useful tool in the analysis of formulaic stories whose popularity, after all, is unbroken as is exemplified by the two objects of my study. Many of the books and articles written on *Star Wars* during the 1980s have a structuralist approach. They exploit the often-stressed connection between George Lucas and Joseph Campbell who had outlined the stages of the mythical hero's voyage in his influential work *The Hero With a Thousand Faces*.[15] Often, these structural analyses remain on the surface and do not yield any deeper insight than the fact that Lucas obviously did use the patterns defined by Campbell for his stories.[16] Several of the critics combine the structuralist with a psychoanalytic focus, interpreting Campbell's heroic journey as each individual's personal voyage to selfhood in the course of which initiatory thresholds need to be crossed and 'monsters' slain but which ends with the integration of all aspects of the personality and produces a complete human being who brings/is a boon for his/her society. Examples of this kind of analysis are Andrew Gordon's 1980 article "*The Empire*

---

15   Joseph Campbell, *The Hero With a Thousand Faces* (Princeton: Princeton University Press, 1949) 36-37.

16   The best example of this type of research on *Star Wars* was actually published in the late 1990s showing that Campbellian analysis of the movies had not even completely lost its appeal by then. Stuart Voytilla in his book *Myth and the Movies: Discovering the Mythic Structure of 50 Unforgettable Films* (Ventura: Wiese, 1999) 274-91 does nothing but describe the hero's journey as outlined by Campbell in the four movies existent at that point. Further literature highlighting the idea of *Star Wars* as myth, for instance, comprises Mary Henderson's catalogue accompanying the exhibition "*Star Wars*: The Magic of Myth" (Mary Henderson, *Star Wars: The Magic of Myth* (New York: Bantam Books, 1997)) as well as the Dorling Kindersley companion *Star Wars: The Power of Myth* (New York: Dorling Kindersley, 1999).

Strikes Back: Monsters from the Id,"[17] Martin Miller's and Robert Sprich's "The Appeal of *Star Wars*: An Archetypal-Psychoanalytic View,"[18] from 1981 as well as Marilyn R. Sherman's "*Star Wars*: New Worlds and Ancient Myths" (1979).[19] Although I also mention Jospeh Campbell in the course of the thesis, the approaches of these scholars differ from mine. First of all, I rely on Lévi-Strauss to analyse the stories' structures more than on Campbell. Secondly, while the works of these critics remain largely descriptive, I use structural analysis to explore the cultural meanings binary patterns create within the stories as well as potential effects they have on readers. Thirdly, I am not much interested in psychoanalytic readings which in my opinion restrict the meaning generated in the movies to a highly personal and internal level. I do not believe that the movies only reproduce each person's singular journey to fulfilment and rather interpret them as influencing a collective consciousness and dealing with wider social concerns, such as, for instance, questions of gender and ethnicity. The relevance of these latter topics and their partly problematic treatment can too easily be explained away by a psychoanalytic viewpoint.[20]

Later researchers justly criticise what they perceive as the intent behind the Campbellian analysis of *Star Wars*. They reproach the earlier critics of actually elevating the stories to a mythical level by their uncritical application of Campbell's theories and of playing to the interests of George Lucas and the merchandising machinery.[21] Fulfilling Campbell's criteria does not make the stories mythical according to these critics. They rather see mechanisms of manipulation similar to those Barthes finds in communication of any sort, at work, whereby films such as

---

17   Andrew Gordon, "*The Empire Strikes Back*: Monsters from the Id," *Science Fiction Studies* 7.3 (1980): 313-18.

18   Martin Miller and Robert Sprich, "The Appeal of *Star Wars*: An Archetypal-Psychoanalytic View," *American Imago* 38.2 (1981): 203-20.

19   Marilyn R. Sherman, "*Star Wars*: New Worlds and Ancient Myths," *Kentucky Folklore Record* 25 (1979): 6-10.

20   There are also more recent examples of psychoanalytic readings. Cf. for instance Alexander Cox, "*Star Wars:* Decoding the Spectacle of Myth," *Foundation* 92 (2004): 17-30. A rather insightful example is Steven A. Galipeau's 2001 *The Journey of Luke Skywalker: An Analysis of Modern Myth and Symbol*. Galipeau does a close reading of all episodes existent at the time of publishing and exposes the repeating archetypal symbolism informing the films (Steven A. Galipeau, *The Journey of Luke Skywalker: An Analysis of Modern Myth and Symbol* (Chicago: Open Court, 2001)).

21   In fact, George Lucas has openly avowed that in creating *Star Wars*, he intended to produce a myth (Cf. Laurent Bouzereau, *Star Wars: The Annotated Screenplays* (New York: Del Rey, 1997) 27).

the *Star Wars* episodes can be sold in such a way that some people immensely profit by it. Turning *Star Wars* into myth according to Daniel Mackay "is to obscure from whence comes the authority – 'the Force' – behind *Star Wars*. The authority behind the *Star Wars* story is not a universal mythic faculty within the human psyche, it is Joseph Campbell."[22] Similar tc me, Mackay looks at the downside of myth as tool of ideological manipulation. "Our mythology," he says "is the electronic archiving of quantified individuality according to scientific methods, and an implementation of this process in order to serve capitalism upon which our economy is based."[23] As this quote shows, his focus is largely on how myth shapes people to suit the demands of capitalist economy. My approach rather looks at social implications of ideology perpetuated by myth, such as views on matters of gender and ethnicity. Furthermore, Mackay has an entirely negative attitude toward myth and sees its sole use today in the furthering of economic interests. As my thesis will show, myth has a double function, it is ambiguous. It certainly has all the negative implications Mackay identifies but it also has positive sides: it creates community by stressing universal issues, it comforts and its moral simplicity helps people orient themselves in a complex world. In contrast to Mackay, I believe that *Star Wars* and *Harry Potter* for that matter *do* retain some "remnants of the old mythologies" which he claims "no longer carry weight in the way we live our lives today."[24]

The research conducted on the more recent instalments of the *Star Wars* saga is predominantly informed by contemporary cultural studies approaches to topics such as gender, ethnicity and 'race,' which are also part of my thesis. Three works need to be highlighted in this context. The first is a volume oᶠ essays on *Star Wars* called *Culture, Identities and Technology in the Star Wars Films: Essays on the Two Trilogies*, edited by Carl Silvio and Tony M. Vinci.[25] The editors' intention of moving beyond the mythical criticism of the films is already made clear by the heading of the book's introduction "Moving Away from Myth: *Star Wars* as Cultural Artifact."[26] The editors and the contributors obviously felt, similar to Barthes, that myth "distorts" and that therefore the mythical readings of the films

---

22   Daniel Mackay, "Star Wars: The Magic of the Anti-Myth," *Foundation* 76 (1999): 66.

23   Mackay 71.

24   Mackay 74.

25   Carl Silvio and Tony M. Vinci, eds., *Culture, Identities and Technology in the Star Wars Films: Essays on the Two Trilogies* (Jefferson: McFarland & Company, 2007).

26   Carl Silvio and Tony M. Vinci, "Moving Away from Myth: *Star Wars* as Cultural Artifact," Introduction, *Culture, Identities and Technology in the Star Wars Films: Essays on the Two Trilogies*, Ed. Carl Silvio and Tony M. Vinci (Jefferson: McFarland & Company, 2007) 1.

'naturalised' issues of gender and ethnicity and produced an undifferentiated and uncritical attitude towards them.[27] I agree with them, although I think it worthwhile, especially since *Star Wars* has so widely been associated with myth to more specifically analyse how exactly myth works in the films. This analysis can then be used as a basis for a discussion of the ways in which contemporary discourses such as the ones mentioned are veiled by mythical structures. I am not convinced that the concepts of 'myth' and 'cultural artifact' can easily be opposed. A myth *is* a cultural artifact as it comes into being in a certain culture at a certain (possibly trying) point in time and is perpetuated through ritual and retelling. It is, as mentioned before, restrictive to view myth completely negatively. The second well-researched collection of essays is Matthew Wilhelm Kapell's and John Shelton Lawrence's 2006 *Finding the Force of the Star Wars Franchise: Fans, Merchandise, and Critics.*[28] This book also deals with the issues of myth, religion, and spirituality in the films but also treats issues of sexuality, gender and 'race.' *Star Wars*, and this is something that my analysis will also show, very much moves between its naturalising mythical attributes and a more conscious ideologically critical stance. The third book in this vein is Kevin J. Wetmore Jr.'s *The Empire Triumphant: Race, Religion and Rebellion in the Star Wars Films* which contains excellent and ideologically critical analyses of the women, the characters with an 'ethnic background' as well as the humanoids of the stories.[29] His findings will be relevant for my chapters on gender, the humanoid characters and the treatment of ethnic minorities.

The last volume that needs to be mentioned with respect to *Star Wars* is Michael J. Hanson's and Max S. Kay's *Star Wars: The New Myth* from 2001 which obviously deals with questions similar to the ones my thesis raises. The brazen statement of the title "*The* New Myth" shows that Hanson's and Kay's interest lies in proving that *Star Wars* is indeed *the* new myth of our time, the story that, as they somewhat naively state in the conclusion to their work "best explains us as a people."[30] Basically, their work is in line with the earlier Campbellian and psychoanalytic readings, as they use C.G. Jung and Joseph Campbell for their scene-to-scene mythical analysis. Like the older works their book remains on a descriptive level at times. And although Hanson and Kay briefly analyse some of

---

27   Cf. Barthes 21.

28   Matthew Wilhelm Kapell and John Shelton Lawrence, eds., *Finding the Force of the Star Wars Franchise: Fans, Merchandise, and Critics* (New York: Peter Lang, 2006).

29   Kevin J. Wetmore Jr., *The Empire Triumphant: Race, Religion and Rebellion in the Star Wars Films* (Jefferson: McFarland & Company, 2005).

30   Michael J. Hanson and Max S. Kay, *Star Wars: The New Myth* (n.p.: Xlibris Corporation, 2001) 428.

the main themes of the films such as free will versus fate and look at particular characters which also feature in my analysis, the main difference between their approach and mine is that they expressly set out to prove that *Star Wars* is myth. This is not the main object of my thesis. I rather use theories of myth to shed light on the structures that shape and limit us as human beings and to find a possible explanation of why *Star Wars* and *Harry Potter* attract so many people in the way they do. In sum it can be said that the research on *Star Wars* has always moved between Campbellian mythical interpretations and analyses exposing the ideological level of the tales. My thesis links the two approaches as it offers a discussion of both the stories' structures and the ideological problems generated by them.

A much larger amount of research has been done on *Harry Potter* than on *Star Wars* and the phenomenon has spurred a miscellany of books and articles. In general it can be said that research on the novels is rather diverse. Criticism focuses on the characters, themes such as good and evil and free will / choice, fandom, the economic effects of the books and films as well as standard cultural studies themes such as gender and ethnicity, also treated in the more recent writings on *Star Wars*. Readings approaching the novels from a structural point of view are rare. The few examples I found provide a reading in the style of Campbell often coupled with a Jungian approach focusing on the hero's journey. M. Katherine Grimes's article "Harry Potter: Fairy Tale Prince, Real Boy and Archetypal Hero,"[31] as well as Julia Boll's "Harry Potter's Archetypal Journey"[32] are cases in point. To the best of my knowledge there is no analysis which focuses on the binaries informing the novels choosing a Lévi-Straussian approach and only Vandana Saxena in her 2012 study *The Subversive Harry Potter: Adolescent Rebellion and Containment in the J.K. Rowling Novels* actually mentions the anthropologist.[33] The results of my thesis thus complement and add to the structural analyses performed on *Harry Potter* so far.

Unfortunately, among the multitude of books published on the boy wizard, many remain on a merely descriptive surface level in their analysis. Prime examples are Sandy Andrea Kolbuch's *Mythische Elemente in der modernen Fantastischen*

---

31   M. Katherine Grimes, "Harry Potter: Fairy Tale Prince, Real Boy, and Archetypal Hero," *The Ivory Tower and Harry Potter: Perspectives on a Literary Phenomenon*, Ed. Lana A. Whited (Columbia: University of Missouri Press, 2002) 89-122.

32   Julia Boll, "Harry Potter's Archetypal Journey," *Heroism in the Harry Potter Series*, Ed. Katrin Berndt and Lena Steveker (Farnham: Ashgate, 2011) 85-104.

33   Vandana Saxena, *The Subversive Harry Potter: Adolescent Rebellion and Containment in the J.K. Rowling Novels* (Jefferson: McFarland & Company, Inc., 2012).

Literatur, erläutert am Beispiel von Joanne K. Rowling's [sic] Harry Potter,[34] Linda Jelinek's *Das Phänomen Harry Potter: Eine Literaturwissenschaftliche Analyse des Welterfolgs* from 2006,[35] Sandra Bak's 2004 *Harry Potter: Auf den Spuren eines zauberhaften Bestsellers*[36] and Claudia Fenske's M*uggles, Monsters and Magicians: A Literary Analysis of the Harry Potter Series* from 2008.[37] Other works, though non-academic prove to be insightful and valuable. Among them Travis Prinzi's book *Harry Potter and Imagination: The Way Between Two Worlds* (2009) needs to be specially mentioned.[38] Prinzi notices similar themes in the books that I do: he treats fear, evil, sacrifice as well as questions of 'race' and gender. However, while my analysis is based on a structural reading of the tales, i.e. on looking at how the themes described affect and are affected by the structures of the novels, Prinzi's discussion is character-based. This becomes obvious when he comments on Rowling's, as he believes, not entirely successful treatment of the figure of Snape in book seven, *Harry Potter and the Deathly Hallows*: "It is one of the rare places in an otherwise character-driven story where Rowling's plot demands trumped a character's action."[39] In fact critic Maria Nikolajeva, who has written a number of articles on *Harry Potter*, supports the character-driven view of the stories: "It is my conviction, shared by a number of critics and scholars that the attraction of the novels lies chiefly in the main character."[40] I strongly disagree with Prinzi and Nikolajeva and my thesis works from an assumption contrary to theirs: The stories are driven by the interplay between various binary oppositions which are of course mostly embodied by the characters. The characters in themselves,

---

34   Sandy Andrea Kolbuch, *Mythische Elemente in der modernen Fantastischen Literatur, erläutert am Beispiel von Joanne K. Rowling's [sic] Harry Potter* (München: AVM, 2010).

35   Linda Jelinek, *Das Phänomen Harry Potter: Eine Literaturwissenschaftliche Analyse des Welterfolgs* (Saarbrücken: VDM Verlag Dr. Müller, 2006).

36   Sandra Bak, *Harry Potter: Auf den Spuren eines zauberhaften Bestsellers* (Frankfurt a.M.: Peter Lang, 2004).

37   Claudia Fenske, *Muggles, Monsters and Magicians: A Literary Analysis of the Harry Potter Series* (Frankfurt a.M.: Peter Lang, 2008).

38   Travis Prinzi, *Harry Potter and Imagination: The Way Between Two Worlds* (Allentown: Zossima Press, 2009).

39   Prinzi 197-98.

40   Maria Nikolajeva, "*Harry Potter* – A Return to the Romantic Hero," *Harry Potter's World: Multidisciplinary Critical Perspectives*, Ed. Elizabeth E. Heilman (New York: Routledge, 2003) 125. There are further critics who perceive the *Harry Potter* series as character-driven. Cf. for instance Philip Nel, *J.K. Rowling's Harry Potter Novels: A Reader's Guide* (New York Continuum, 2003) 34.

however, as individual as Rowling tries to depict them, represent themes and ideas which are at the root of the tales. Certainly readers identify with Harry Potter, but they do not do so because he is such a wonderful individual but because he is *like* them, because he embodies their joys, worries and anxieties and thus presents a projection foil. This thesis is therefore adverse in outlook to the many critical pieces that focus on character.

A volume similar in focus to Prinzi's is Edmund M. Kern's *The Wisdom of Harry Potter: What Our Favourite Hero Teaches Us about Moral Choices* published in 2003.[41] Like me, Kern perceives the ambiguity of Rowling's stories.[42] However, he too works more on the level of characters and the story, while I try to expose how ambiguity shows itself in the structure and the interplay between binary oppositions. There are other scholars who have remarked upon or hinted at the ambiguity inherent in the novels. However, they usually focus on one particular instance of it while I try to draw attention to the way in which it is underlying the whole narrative. An example would be Patricia Donaher's and James M. Okapal's article "Causation, Prophetic Visions, and the Free Will Question in Harry Potter."[43] Donaher and Okapal comment the prophecies featuring in *Harry Potter* and the ambiguity they lend a narrative that otherwise clearly prefers choice.[44] Furthermore, Karin E. Westman discusses love and its ambiguous function in the books.[45]

One person who needs to be mentioned with respect to *Harry Potter* is John Granger, a rather prolific and non-academic commentator on the phenomenon. Granger alternately views the novels as Christian,[46] interprets them as following the alchemical process of creating a Philosopher's Stone,[47] and analyses them as

---

41   Edmund M. Kern, *The Wisdom of Harry Potter: What Our Favourite Hero Teaches Us about Moral Choices* (New York: Prometheus Books, 2003).

42   Cf. Kern 93-102.

43   Patricia Donaher and James M. Okapal, "Causation, Prophetic Visions, and the Free Will Question in Harry Potter," *Reading Harry Potter Again: New Critical Essays*, Ed. Giselle Liza Anatol (Santa Barbara: ABC-CLIO, 2009) 47-62.

44   Cf. Donaher and Okapal 53.

45   Karin E. Westman, "'The Weapon We Have is Love,'" *Children's Literature Association Quarterly* 33 (2008): 193-99.

46   John Granger, *Looking for God in Harry Potter: Is There Hidden Meaning in the Bestselling Books?*, (n.p.: Saltriver, 2006).

47   John Granger, *The Deathly Hallows Lectures: The Hogwarts Professor Explains Harry's Final Adventure* (Allentown: Zossima Press, 2008) 45-84.

postmodern.[48] While some of his ideas are intriguing, it is hard to take him entirely seriously academically, as he is, for instance, in the habit of using terms such as myth, postmodernism and poststructuralism without specifically defining them.[49] Contrary to my opinion, Granger believes the texts to be postmodern and poststructuralist rather than structuralist. Rowling's criticism of hegemonic institutions such as the government, the press, the legal and the educational system serve as justification for his viewpoint.[50] He also analyses Rowling's preoccupation with those on the fringes of society as postmodern.[51] My thesis will show that although there is certainly an awareness of these kinds of themes on the part of Rowling, a greater awareness in fact than Lucas shows in his *Star Wars* movies, the books are finally structuralist. They provide escape from exactly the themes Granger identifies as postmodern because they finally push them to the margins again. Inequality, for instance, is not abolished at the end of the novels. In fact, many issues that resemble real life ones are rather indirectly treated so that the impression arises that they are shirked to give readers a break. In this sense, Granger and I clearly differ in viewpoint and approach.

A reading that is closer to mine in its position on structuralism and poststructuralism is Luisa Grijalva Maza's in her article "Deconstructing the Grand Narratives in *Harry Potter*: Inclusion/Exclusion and Discriminatory Policies in Fiction and Practice."[52] Grijalva Maza sees the *Potter* novels as embodiment of the grand narrative of liberalism which in the novels as well as in real life often produces exclusion despite its professed openness and inclusiveness.[53] Although she approaches the novels from a poststructuralist and not a structuralist viewpoint, she, like me, comes to the conclusion that for their popularity the stories finally depend on structures and their limitations despite their urge to question them. While the scope of her paper only allows her to look into one grand narrative, I will argue that the novels and the *Star Wars* movies discuss and negotiate several ideologies (grand narratives) that appear to be constitutive of the Western mindset. Vandana Saxena, too analyses the structuralist and poststructuralist potential of the novels and to my knowledge is the only one apart from myself who explicitly evokes Lévi-

---

48   John Granger, *Unlocking Harry Potter: Five Keys for the Serious Reader* (n.p.: Zossima Press, 2007) 143-200.

49   Cf. for instance Granger on 'grand myths' in *Unlocking Harry Potter* 164.

50   Cf. Granger *Unlocking Harry Potter* 174-76.

51   Cf. Granger *Unlocking Harry Potter* 167-69.

52   Luisa Grijalva Maza, "Deconstructing the Grand Narrative in *Harry Potter*: Inclusion/Exclusion and Discriminatory Policies in Fiction and Practice," *Politics & Policy* 40.3 (2012): 424-43.

53   Cf. Grijalva Maza 426.

Strauss's structures of myth in connection with *Harry Potter*, albeit briefly.[54] Her specific focus, however, lies more on "cultural conceptualizations of growth and boyhood (...)"[55] and she explores particular features of the fantasy formula as well as the *Bildungsroman* and their "negotiation between subversion and containment (...)."[56]

A large amount of criticism on *Harry Potter* revolves around questions of 'race,' ethnicity and gender. There are several collections of articles that need to be mentioned in this respect. All of the following volumes contain essays on these topics also treated in my thesis: Lana A. Whited's collection *The Ivory Tower and Harry Potter: Perspectives on a Literary Phenomenon* (2002),[57] *Reading Harry Potter: Critical Essays* (2003),[58] edited by Giselle Liza Anatol and the follow-up *Reading Harry Potter Again: New Critical Essays* (2009)[59] as well as Elizabeth E. Heilman's *Harry Potter's World: Multidisciplinary Critical Perspectives* (2003)[60] and the consecutive *Critical Perspectives on Harry Potter* (2009).[61] It can be said that the contributors generally view the gender and 'race' questions in the novels more negatively in the volumes from 2002 and 2003, published before the *Harry Potter* series had actually been concluded. Examples of not entirely positive readings of, for instance, Hermione Granger and the house elves are Eliza T. Dresang's article "Hermione Granger and the Heritage of Gender,"[62] and Julia Park's "Class and Socioeconomic Identity in Harry Potter's England."[63] The

---

54   Cf. Saxena 35-37.

55   Saxena 166.

56   Saxena 25.

57   Lana A. Whited, ed., *The Ivory Tower and Harry Potter: Perspectives on a Literary Phenomenon* (Columbia: University of Missouri Press, 2002).

58   Giselle Liza Anatol, ed., *Reading Harry Potter: Critical Essays* (Westport: Praeger, 2003).

59   Giselle Liza Anatol, ed., *Reading Harry Potter Again: New Critical Essays* (Santa Barbara: ABC-CLIO, 2009).

60   Elizabeth E. Heilman, ed., *Harry Potter's World: Multidisciplinary Critical Perspectives* (New York: Routledge, 2003).

61   Elizabeth E. Heilman, ed., *Critical Perspectives on Harry Potter* (New York: Routledge, 2009).

62   Eliza T. Dresang, "Hermione Granger and the Heritage of Gender," *The Ivory Tower and Harry Potter: Perspectives on a Literary Phenomenon*, Ed. Lana A. Whited (Columbia: University of Missouri Press, 2002) 211-42.

63   Julia Park, "Class and Socioeconomic Identity in Harry Potter's England," *Reading Harry Potter: Critical Essays*, Ed. Giselle Liza Anatol (Westport: Praeger, 2003) 179-89.

completion of the *Potter* series in 2007 has allowed more balanced approaches to these topics in volumes published after that date. Well-grounded discussions on gender include Ximena Gallardo C.'s and C. Jason Smith's "Happily Ever After: Harry Potter and the Quest for the Domestic."[64] A good example of a thorough treatment of the house elves and the 'race' question is Brycchan Carey's "Hermione and the House-Elves Revisited: J.K. Rowling, Antislavery Campaigning, and the Politics of Potter."[65] A further very recent and extremely insightful and well-researched collection that needs to be mentioned is Katrin Berndt's and Lena Steveker's *Heroism in the Harry Potter Series* (2011).[66] The convincing articles of the two editors themselves must particularly be foregrounded. Steveker writes about Harry Potter's identity formation[67] and emphasises the "concept of unitary Selfhood" that the novels advocate, thereby hinting at the notion of mythical balance the structures propagate, without, however, explicitly linking the books with myth.[68] Katrin Berndt has contributed what is in my opinion the most profound, thorough and all-encompassing essay about the role of Hermione Granger written so far.[69] She analyses Hermione Granger as an individual and defends her against charges of anti-feminism from other critics. Although I still labour from the assumption that the characters are subordinated to the structures and to Harry's quest, Berndt's article makes clear how much Rowling tried to create individuals within the limited structural scope of the formulaic story she had at her disposal.

There is no substantial amount of research which treats both *Star Wars* and *Harry Potter*, a rather surprising fact given the many similarities between the stories and the huge success that unites both. The only book I could find that

---

64   Ximena Gallardo C. and C. Jason Smith, "Happily Ever After: Harry Potter and the Quest for the Domestic," *Reading Harry Potter Again: New Critical Essays*, Ed. Giselle Liza Anatol (Santa Barbara: ABC-CLIO, 2009) 91-108.

65   Brycchan Carey, "Hermione and the House-Elves Revisited: J.K. Rowling, Antislavery Campaigning, and the Politics of Potter," *Reading Harry Potter Again: New Critical Essays*, Ed. Giselle Liza Anatol (Santa Barbara: ABC-CLIO, 2009) 159-73.

66   Katrin Berndt and Lena Steveker, eds., *Heroism in the Harry Potter Series* (Farnham: Ashgate, 2011).

67   Lena Steveker, "'Your Soul is Whole, and Completely Your Own, Harry:' The Heroic Self in J.K. Rowling's *Harry Potter* Series," *Heroism in the Harry Potter Series*, Ed. Katrin Berndt and Lena Steveker (Farnham: Ashgate, 2011) 69-83.

68   Steveker 77.

69   Katrin Berndt, "Hermione Granger, or A Vindication of the Rights of Girl," *Heroism in the Harry Potter Series*, Ed. Katrin Berndt and Lena Steveker (Farnham: Ashgate, 2011) 159-76.

analyses both is Russel W. Dalton's *Faith Journey through Fantasy Lands: A Christian Dialogue with Harry Potter, Star Wars, and The Lord of the Rings*.[70] However, as the title suggests, it looks at the stories from a religious rather than a mythical or structural perspective. The exclusively Christian view of the tales which, for instance, Granger also propagates about *Harry Potter* is too narrow in my opinion, as there are countless ways of interpreting them quite free from any religious connotations. After all, there are a number of fans and followers of both *Star Wars* and *Harry Potter* who would not call themselves religious. Of course I do not deny that the stories have a moral message in accordance with Christian beliefs but just as it does not do to make myths of them unquestioningly, they should not be exploited to prop up Christianity in decline. In addition to Dalton's monograph, there are also a few internet publications which compare *Star Wars* and *Harry Potter*, for instance the essay "'The Chosen One:' Prophecy, Destiny, and Free Will in *Star Wars* and *Harry Potter*" by someone calling himself Matril.[71] As the title says, Matril (rather briefly) looks at the treatment of free will and fate and identifies it as central for the messages of both tales. I try to go beyond Matril's analysis in doing a close reading of especially Anakin Skywalker's / Darth Vader's development for which questions of fate, determination and choice are even more prominent than for Harry Potter's. Michael Valdez Moses comments on the tension between tradition and (post)modernity but predominantly compares the *Star Wars* and *Harry Potter* movies.[72] Obviously, so far comments on and articles about both *Star Wars* and *Harry Potter* are mainly to be found in online fan forums and internet journals and magazines.

In sum it can be said that much more research exists on *Harry Potter* than on *Star Wars* and almost none on the comparison of both phenomena. My work thus fills a gap when it comes to bringing the two stories together. The research on *Star Wars* was mentioned to be either rather uncritically informed by a Campbellian structural approach or by the perceived failings of George Lucas with respect to discourses of gender and ethnicity. For *Star Wars*, therefore my research builds a bridge between the older, mythical approaches and the more recent critical

---

70   Russel W. Dalton, *Faith Journey through Fantasy Lands: A Christian Dialogue with Harry Potter, Star Wars, and The Lord of the Rings* (Minneapolis: Augsburg Books, 2003).

71   Matril, "'The Chosen One:' Prophecy, Destiny and Free Will in *Star Wars* and *Harry Potter*," *Saga Journal* 2.8 (2006): n.pag. 5 Jul 2011 <http://www.sagajournal.com/mthechosenone.html>.

72   Michael Valdez Moses, "Back to the Future: The Nostalgic Yet Progressive Appeal of Wizards, Hobbits, and Jedi Knights," *Reason Magazine* (July 2003): n.pag. 7 Jul 2011 <http://reason.com/archives/2003/07/01/back-to-the-future>.

postmodern ones as it shows how much the (Lévi-Straussian) mythical structures contribute to the stereotypical way in which female characters, ethnic minorities and aliens are treated. It also demonstrates that both stories heavily rely on their binary structures and cannot be conceived of without them. The structuralist approach not only exposes ideological failings it also teaches us much about the ways in which formulaic fiction works. When it comes to *Harry Potter*, academic writing is particularly focused on similar social questions as treated by recent *Star Wars* researchers and the majority of books and articles is very character-centred. As my thesis focuses on structure and the way characters embody and perpetuate it, it presents a perspective opposite to the one prevalent in critical circles.

I would like to conclude this introduction with two general, important points about my thesis. Firstly, though I am aware of the fact that I am comparing films (*Star Wars*) and novels (*Harry Potter*), the thesis will not put much emphasis on the intermedial differences as my approach is predominantly semiotic, highlighting the similarities of both tales with respect to their storylines, characters, and above all, structures. Secondly, I know that my chosen structural focus will be considered unusual given the fact that structuralist approaches which have tended to categorise, classify, put up hierarchies and exclude, are thought to be out-dated by many academics. Still, I believe it is impossible to dismiss something (in this case a structuralist viewpoint) without looking at it thoroughly before. No one can deny that both *Star Wars* and *Harry Potter* largely depend on their familiar structures for their appeal. Thus, what I have tried to do is to combine a thorough description and analysis of the two tales' structures with a critique of them based on the hierarchies they establish. I believe that the approach I have chosen is highly profitable with respect to any kind of formulaic film or novel if one does not lose sight of the fact that structures provide comfort and security on the one hand but exclude and marginalise on the other. In short, structures, like myth, like S*tar Wars* and *Harry Potter*, like the following treatise, are ambiguous.

2. Myth: Its Functions, Structure, and Workings in Society and (Contemporary Popular) Culture

2.1 FUNCTIONS OF MYTH

Before I start expounding the theories of myth that will serve as a basis for this thesis, it is important to state that my understanding of myth is a broad one, incorporating the theories of several theoreticians of myth. Although the main focus of this thesis will be on two *stories*, *Star Wars* and *Harry Potter*, and the strictest interpretations of the concept 'myth' see it as a *narrative* of origins,[1] myth can also be understood differently. As will be seen, the various ways to view myth do not necessarily mutually exclude each other. On the contrary, the theories I will introduce are all significant and taken together will add something to the understanding of how myth works in society and in the human mind. Myths have always been special to people, they were not just any odd stories but they conveyed meaning and triggered action. Nowadays myths, as in stories of the earth, of gods and heroes seem to have lost their significance and died out. The phenomenal success of the two stories I will analyse and the important place they have in quite a number of people's lives raises the question whether some vestiges of the old myths have not survived till today, and, more importantly, whether people are not still in need of myths. If the latter is the case, what exactly is it humans draw out of them? To clarify the connection I see between *Star Wars*, *Harry Potter*, and myth, it is first of all important to define myth and its influence on people's lives.

---

[1]   Bolle, for instance, defines myth as "(...) a story concerning gods and superhuman beings." Furthermore, he says, "[a] myth is an expression of the sacred in words: it reports realities and events from the origin of the world that remain valid for the basis and purpose of all there is" (261).

Karen Armstrong starts her *Short History of Myth* with five important points about the workings and functions of myth within human society. The first one is that myth "is nearly always rooted in the experience of death and the fear of extinction."[2] As second point she mentions that it "is usually inseparable from ritual."[3] Thirdly, according to her, "myths are about extremity; they force us to go beyond our experience."[4] Armstrong goes on to say that a "myth is not a story told for its own sake. It shows us how we should behave."[5] "Finally," she holds that "all mythology speaks of another plane that exists alongside our own world, and that in some sense supports it."[6] Her five-point summary provides a general idea of what myth is about, although her points overlap in some instances. Her first and fifth claim, for instance, go together. Fear, especially of death and the seeming pointlessness of earthly existence, motivates people to invent stories that give their lives meaning and lift them up to a transcendent plane on which after death they continue to exist in the presence of some deity. Armstrong's first point then is the cause for people's propensity to tell stories while her fifth one refers to the outcome of the human fear of death.

Armstrong is not alone in attributing an escapist, fear-alleviating function to myth. Elemér Hankiss in his work *Fears and Symbols* perceives existential fears to be at the heart of human civilisation. To conquer these fears, Hankiss holds, people have developed two strategies, the 'Promethean' and the 'Appolonian strategy.'[7] The 'Promethean strategy' goes back to Prometheus, the mythical hero who brought fire to humankind and was severely punished for it. Hankiss sees Prometheus as a metaphor of external or material means of survival for human beings. Fire gave people warmth, security and new ways of preparing food. The 'Promethean strategy' thus refers to everything people do to feel externally secure in a universe in which many things such as natural catastrophes threaten their existence. They build houses and invent technology that is supposed to make their lives easier and smoother.[8] However, as Hankiss makes clear, this alleviation of external insecurities is not enough. People also have spiritual fears, as, for instance, the already mentioned one of death, which need to be relieved. That is where the 'Appolonian strategy' comes in. To conquer the fear that death destroys human

---

2   Karen Armstrong, *A Short History of Myth* (Edinburgh: Canongate, 2005) 3.

3   Armstrong 3.

4   Armstrong 3.

5   Armstrong 4.

6   Armstrong 4.

7   Elemér Hankiss, *Fears and Symbols* (Budapest: Central European University Press, 2001) 47.

8   Cf. Hankiss 48.

efforts and makes them seem vain, people began telling and believing in stories that lifted their own insignificant existence up to a higher plane and gave it meaning.[9] Creating myths, is one example of such an effort, different religions (which also often contain myths) another. After the most potent of these (mythical) stories have been told and retold for a while and after new generations have adapted them to their own times and anxieties, their origins become blurred and the human agency behind them tends to be forgotten. The stories turn into so-called grand narratives, which are not questioned for their original (human) construction and which in cases such as Christianity or Islam, sustain millions of people worldwide.[10]

The third point Armstrong makes about myth, namely that it forces us to go beyond our realm of experience, is also closely associated with myth's function of alleviating fear. To be able to overcome fears, people usually have to face them. Myth confronts human beings with their anxieties and offers some kind of solution to them. (One of these possible solutions will be introduced in the analysis of Claude Lévi-Strauss's work on myth later in this chapter.) The confrontation with fears also explains myth's closeness to ritual which Armstrong mentions as her second point. Indigenous peoples of many countries enacted and still enact this stepping beyond the realm of personal experience. Frequently, rituals accompany liminal periods in people's lives and are supposed to prepare human beings for their existence in some future stage.[11] Examples are the rituals adolescent boys undergo in many aboriginal societies to be initiated to manhood. The initiation to a new phase in life is always accompanied by anxieties which ultimately go back to the fear of crossing the threshold from life to death. In ritual these anxieties are symbolically faced and overcome so that the initiate emerges from his or her experience strengthened and ready to cope with the demands of adulthood. The close connection between myth and ritual also supports Armstrong's fourth point about myth, her claim that it has a didactic function and offers guidance on how people are supposed to behave. Ritual, as action, shows how myth invites people to act upon the principles it sets up. (What exactly these principles are will be elucidated later in the chapter, as well as throughout the thesis.)

All of Armstrong's five points about myth, the fear of death that informs it, the accompanying rituals, the transcendence of everyday life and experience, the didactic element and the elevation of human existence to the plane of some deity or other, are exemplified in the Egyptian myth of the god Osiris Sir James Frazer

---

9   Cf. Hankiss 49.

10   Interestingly, in this sense, Hankiss's analysis already points to the ideological quality and function of myth which will be expounded later in the thesis.

11   Cf. for instance Victor Turner, *The Forest of Symbols: Aspects of Ndembu Ritual* (Ithaca, NY: Cornell University Press, 1967) 93-95.

recounts in *The Golden Bough*. Osiris, originally one of the minor Egyptian gods, came to be famous as god of death. Initially, he was known for his beneficial behaviour towards the Egyptians whom he gave laws and taught how to cultivate the earth. His evil brother Seth murdered Osiris and threw his coffin into the Nile.[12] Osiris's wife Isis managed to locate the corpse of her husband upon which their enemies tore Osiris's body apart and scattered it all over Egypt. Isis was inconsolable. The sun god Ra took pity on her and sent the god Anubis who helped piece Osiris together again and revive him. Osiris then became the ruler of the underworld and the emblem of death and resurrection.[13] It is plain enough to see that the myth deals with people's fear of death and their hopes for an afterlife. Osiris represents the wish that they, too will be reborn to an existence that stretches beyond the physical death of the body. He unites the opposites of life and death and is therefore symbolically connected with different occasions on which life seems to die and be reborn. His association with agriculture, for instance, gained him a reputation as god of corn.[14] His death and rebirth then symbolise the dying and renewal of nature in the course of a year. His liminal experience of dying is finally beneficial for his society as he transcends death and promises new life.

Numerous rituals were performed in honour of Osiris and other gods. Animals and sometimes even people were sacrificed in the interest of some good allegedly proceeding from their death.[15] But other, less brutal action was taken, too. The death and rebirth of Osiris, for instance, were re-enacted by the Egyptians each year, as people believed that only if all the appropriate rites were properly observed, nature could regrow.[16] The rituals accompanying the Osiris-myth and many other mythical stories, thus make clear how myths have always incited action of some kind or other. In this sense, myth can be said to have a didactic function. Alluding to its ritualistic nature, Karen Armstrong adds that myth is "(...) an event which, in some sense, [has] happened once, but which also [happens] all the time."[17] What she hits upon here and what can be seen in the example of the Osiris myth and its ritualistic re-enactments, is a fundamental ambiguity of myth, which is significant for this thesis and will crop up time and again. In this case, the ambiguity pertains to myth being temporal and eternal at the same time.

---

12   Cf. Sir James Frazer, *The Golden Bough: A Study in Magic and Religion* [1890] (London: Wordsworth Reference Series, 1993) 363.
13   Cf. Frazer 366-67.
14   Cf. Frazer 370.
15   Cf. Frazer 370-71.
16   Cf. Frazer 373-76.
17   Armstrong 7.

The example of Osiris shows that myths very often deal with several topics that are intertwined and therefore mirror the complexity of life. Furthermore it demonstrates, that in most cases, a myth has one or more characters (be they mortal or divine) at its centre who have to take valiant action or sacrifice themselves to achieve certain aims. The principle of the mythical hero, who sets out to face tests and trials, is illuminated by Joseph Campbell in his work *The Hero With a Thousand Faces*. As the title already suggests, Campbell identifies a basic pattern for heroic action which can be found to underlie, albeit with slight possible variations, most stories of mythical heroes as well as more modern manifestations of heroic quests. The hero's movement, Campbell holds, is circular. The character in question is usually confronted with a task which he or she rejects at first.[18] After a while however, the task is accepted and the hero/ine sets out on his/her journey in the course of which s/he traditionally faces numerous trials.[19] When Campbell expressly identifies points on the hero's journey as 'crossings of thresholds,' it can be seen, that the stages of the hero's journey Campbell depicts, are congruent with what Armstrong says about myth taking people beyond their own experience. The hero/ine faces numerous liminal situations in which s/he has to prove that s/he is ready to advance to the next stage in his/her adventure and by extension his/her existence. The monsters s/he habitually encounters are threshold guardians that might make the ascension to the next level difficult and have to be overcome first. "The belly of the whale," one of the stages the hero/ine passes into according to Campbell,[20] is a metaphor of a situation in which s/he needs to enter unfamiliar territory, which is usually also associated with his/her own mind or soul and further advances him/her in his/her adventure.[21] This can be an actual belly of a whale as in the biblical story of Jonah, but it might also be a cave, a lake or sea the hero or heroine has to submerge him- or herself into, or in fact the land of the dead they need to enter to achieve their aims. While the heroic characters undergo these trials, they usually have help of some kind.[22] The helper figures who appear throughout myth and other related tales often have a didactic function showing that no one can go through life alone and that everyone needs somebody to rely on.

After having successfully navigated through all adventures, the hero or heroine is able to complete his or her task and return home with a boon for society.[23] Thus, the

---

18   Cf. Campbell *The Hero* 36.

19   Cf. Campbell *The Hero* 36.

20   Campbell *The Hero* 36.

21   Cf. Campbell *The Hero* 91.

22   Cf. Campbell *The Hero* 36.

23   Cf. Campbell *The Hero* 37.

mythical hero is always someone who benefits all society, as in the example of Osiris, and his adventures are circular, that is, he returns to where he came from. The death and rebirth of Osiris also perfectly embody this circularity. Obviously, Campbell's model of the hero's journey also serves as an extended metaphor of a person's psychological development, the monsters symbolising inner demons that have to be integrated and the thresholds difficult or transitional phases in life which have to be overcome. Campbell then goes on to lift the heroic mythical circularity to a higher plane, namely to what he calls the 'cosmogonic cycle.' This cycle represents the more general and greater gyrations of the cosmos that include the hero's circular journey, i.e. the (super)natural and situational factors that shape and create us as human beings. Campbell himself describes the cosmogonic cycle as follows:

The cosmogonic cycle is to be understood as the passage of universal consciousness from the deep sleep zone of the unmanifest, through dream, to the full day of waking; then back again through dream to the timeless dark. As in the actual experience of every living being, so in the grandiose figure of the living cosmos: in the abyss of sleep the energies are refreshed, in the work of the day they are exhausted; the life of the universe runs down and must be renewed.[24]

It can be seen that the cycle is supposed to be a picture for all the becoming and decay in nature. Examples would be the seasons, the waxing and waning of the moon, the alternation of day and night as well as that of life and death. The mythical hero's symbolic forays into caves, underground places or underwater and his re-emergences are encompassed by the cosmogonic cycle. The association of Osiris and his death and rebirth with dearth and the harvest season respectively, exemplifies Campbell's notion that the hero's journey is an attempt at metaphorically approaching phenomena and movements within nature and the cosmos. Campbell's view on the cosmogonic cycle also lays bare the similarities between his and Lévi-Strauss's theories. The hero's journey and the cosmogonic cycle are both highly structural and they focus on binary oppositions as much as Lévi-Strauss's theories do. Campbell uses sleep and waking here as the dichotomy to encompass and incorporate all others. It is important to note the difference between the two approaches, however. While Lévi-Strauss, as will be seen, gives most attention to the binaries themselves and the mediation between them, Campbell emphasises the circularity of myth and by extension life and nature. As will be seen with respect to *Star Wars* and *Harry Potter*, the two theories do not exclude but mutually reinforce one another.

---

24   Campbell *The Hero* 266.

So far, it has been established that myth helps mankind deal with existential fears and grow spiritually, caters to the human need for transcendence and functions as behavioural guide. Stories such as *Star Wars* and *Harry Potter*, I will argue, fulfil at least some of these functions, because they, too feature heroes who go through spiritual crises and through whom people can experience these crises themselves, one step removed from reality. Both stories, as will be seen, also offer moral guidance.

The myth of Osiris exemplifies a further theory of myth, put forth by René Girard. Girard assumes that violence instead of fear, is at the bottom of cultural and social achievement. He elaborates his theory by using examples from indigenous societies and from myth and tragedy. However, his findings concerning the sacrificial crisis and the scapegoating accompanying it can be observed in modern societies, too, albeit on a more indirect level. Culture, Girard holds, generates itself in the interplay between what he calls 'reciprocal' and 'unanimous' violence. Reciprocal violence exists between two or more individuals or groups of people in society. It is highly destructive and more often than not fuelled by desire of some kind.[25] Reciprocal violence produces the so-called "sacrificial crisis,"[26] i.e. it severely shakes the social equilibrium and thus needs to be ostracised. This is where the ritual of (human) sacrifice or scapegoating comes in. To rid themselves off evil created by reciprocal violence, people within a society unite to produce what is called 'unanimous violence.'[27] This kind of violence is not usually directed against the perpetrators of the social unrest but a chosen scapegoat, usually a person or group of people from outside the society, onto whom all evil the society is inflicted with, is projected. This individual or group of individuals as representative of evil is then ostracised or even killed by an act of unanimous violence on the part of the given society. The sacrificial ritual practised upon the unfortunate victim symbolises and is believed to enact the end of reciprocal violence and the restoration of the social order.[28] In contrast to the destructive nature of reciprocal violence, "(...) ritual violence [is thus] creative and protective (...)."[29] Girard summarises the process described above as follows: 'In the scapegoat theme we should recognize the very real metamorphosis of reciprocal violence into restraining violence through the agency of unanimity.'[30] He goes on to say that "[this] unique

25   Cf. René Girard, *Violence and the Sacred* (Baltimore: The Johns Hopkins University Press, 1977) 144, 145.

26   Girard 144.

27   Cf. Girard 96.

28   Cf. Girard 95.

29   Girard 144.

30   Girard 96.

mechanism structures all cultural values even as it conceals itself behind them."[31] This means that on the surface scapegoating is used to remedy an evil that society has been inflicted with. It seemingly has a moral tint. In fact, however, sacrificial rituals have a structuring function. "If the surrogate victim can interrupt the destructuring process [initiated by reciprocal violence], it must be at the origin of structure."[32] Girard's notions not only imply a structuring of society through crisis but also through Othering. Blame for certain crimes or social flaws is laid at the door of an Other so that society does not need to confront its own shortcomings. Thus, even before Lévi-Strauss has come into the picture, it becomes clear how closely structures are associated with binary oppositions. Girard's analyses show that structure is indispensable for people and that it is something they always strive for. Along with the interplay of opposites that is obviously part of myth, Girard's notion of societal generation through violence is important for my thesis, since the principle of order arising from chaos and the fact that some evil needs to be ostracised before order can be restored, are common structural features of stories of the kind I will analyse.

The notion of evil in itself is extremely important for the analysis that follows as much of the action of both stories is propelled by it. Evil is an extremely elusive and complex phenomenon but Terry Eagleton's discussion of it in his book *On Evil* will be helpful for narrowing down the concept in the chapters on the protagonists of *Star Wars* and *Harry Potter*. He makes clear that the use of the term 'evil' is often extremely ideological and serves distinct purposes. His example of two ten-year-old English boys killing a toddler and a policeman's reaction to the murderers, calling them evil, is a telling case in point. Eagleton says: "It [the policeman's reaction] was a preemptive strike against those who might appeal to social conditions in seeking to understand why they did what they did. And such understanding can always bring forgiveness in its wake. Calling the action evil meant that it was beyond comprehension."[33] Using the term 'evil' can thus have a distancing function. Evil mysteriously manifests itself in some people but does not have anything to do with the majority of humanity. This ideology is supposed to be comforting and provide relief, although it collapses at a closer look. The notion of evil and its functions for the two stories thus need to be analysed with care.

---

31   Girard 96.

32   Girard 93. (Michel Foucault expresses a similar view on structures arising out of catastrophic or chaotic situations in *Discipline and Punish: The Birth of the Prison* [1975] (New York: Vintage Books, 1995) 195-96.)

33   Terry Eagleton, *On Evil* (New Haven: Yale University Press, 2010) 2.

2.2 THE STRUCTURE OF MYTH
(AS A REFLECTION OF HUMAN CONSCIOUSNESS)

Many of the points that have been made about myth so far, have already implied what is central to myth and what will be elementary for my thesis. If the human fear of death as the 'big unknown' permeates myth, there has to be something that causes and nourishes this fear. This something is life, the opposite of death, which human beings generally cling to. Without their knowledge and love of life, there would be no fear of its opposite, death. The two extremes of life and death are, for instance, embodied in the death and revival of Osiris which in turn illustrate the dying of life in autumn and nature's renewal in spring. Girard's theory of myth confronts us with the opposites of chaos and order which are negotiated by the process of scapegoating and sacrificial rituals. Myth, thus, is always informed by and obtains its energy through binary oppositions which are part of life but contradictory and therefore pose a problem for humans. Binary oppositions as constitutive of myths are at the centre of Claude Lévi-Strauss's essay "The Structural Study of Myth" which contains the theories that form the basis of and point of departure for my thesis. Lévi-Strauss's essay will be used to describe the structures of *Star Wars* and *Harry Potter* but it will also be the starting point for a discussion of how structures can inhibit and limit certain discourses which run through the stories and are rather harmed by a binary approach.

In his structural analysis of myth, Lévi-Strauss holds that myths should not so much interest us for their superficial narrative content but for the deeper structural concerns they hide and oftentimes share. To prove his assumptions about mythical structure, the anthropologist looks at Greek myths as well as folktales from North America. Thus he very plainly interprets the term 'myth' as meaning story or narrative. The structuralist remarks that the similarity between myths of various regions and peoples is at odds with their apparent diversity on the level of content.[34] Their similarity, if not present on the superficial level of the narrative, must then manifest itself on the level of the myths' deeper structures. The way Lévi-Strauss proposes to look at myths, is to break them down into their smallest constituent units to see how the different elements of the mythical narrative function. He arrives at the conclusion that it is not the isolated units that constitute myth but the way in which these units group up with other units. The isolated smallest particles of myth thus form "bundles of relations."[35] Only in the interplay between these bundles, the myth acquires its meaning. The anthropologist then takes the Oedipus myth and its many variants to prove his theory. His elaborations on this particular

---

34   Cf. Lévi-Strauss 119.

35   Lévi-Strauss 121.

myth show how the bundles of relations very often comprise binary oppositions, the tension between whom furthers the production of meaning.[36] The contrasts which are at the heart of mythical structure tend to be similar to myths all around the world, since human anxieties are much alike. The connection between myth and existential human questions has already been established in this chapter. Therefore, mythical stories can look very different at first glance, but treat similar concerns if subjected to a more thorough scrutiny. The characters of myths can be different, for instance, but perform the same functions. Examples would be heroes in different shapes and disguises, as well as their adversaries and helpers who can also assume various forms. In one story, a magician or witch might appear to help the hero, in another, a magical object might present itself to the same purpose. The stories are dissimilar but the functions of the persons or devices are the same: to provide aid and advance the hero on his journey.

The characters of myth, indeed, are of great interest to Lévi-Strauss, too. Their set-up in a given myth, he believes, is revealing with respect to the myth's true concerns. The characters chosen for a given myth always represent certain concepts that oppose each other and feature one character, the trickster, who is able to bring these oppositions closer together. Lévi-Strauss formulates this as follows: "We need only to assume that two opposite terms with no intermediary always tend to be replaced by two equivalent terms which allow a third one as a mediator; then one of the polar terms and the mediator becomes replaced by a new triad (...).''[37] In its concern with binary oppositions, myth resembles and mirrors human thought which can only grasp concepts via its opposites. As Annemarie Schimmel affirms, "Polarity is essential to recognition: whatever is qualified with attributes can only be recognized because of polarity. Large and small, high and deep, sour and sweet – all such qualities are relative to an ordering system."[38] Therefore it can be taken for granted that myth is deeply entrenched with human thought and development, something, Lévi-Strauss tries to conclusively prove. The best way to understand his reasoning is to revert to the diagram he sets up for an exemplary North American myth which looks as follows and which shows what the character constellation of myth reveals about its deeper concerns:

---

36   Cf. Lévi-Strauss 123-34.

37   Lévi-Strauss 130.

38   Annemarie Schimmel, *The Mystery of Numbers* (New York: Oxford University Press, 1993) 42.

Initial Pair	First Triad	Second Triad
Life		
	Agriculture	
		Herbivorous animals
		Carrion-eating animals (raven; coyote)
	Hunt	
		Prey Animals
	War	
Death[39]		

Abstracting from the level of context of the given myth which features herbivorous animals, carrion-eating animals and prey animals as characters, Lévi-Strauss identifies a deep-set and largely subconscious layer of meaning. He believes that it illustrates people's fundamental grappling with the contradictory concepts of life and death, a mythical concern already established in this chapter. The two opposing terms he calls the *initial pair*. The animal characters of the story allow conclusions about the lifestyle of the people among whom the myth originated. The terms life and death are equated with agriculture and war. Agriculture is associated with life because of its nourishing function and war with death but the terms are less abstract and easier to grasp than those of the *initial pair*. The two abstract terms life and death are not only equated with simpler terms, but they are also joined by a mediating term, the hunt, which stands in between them. This substitution forms what Lévi-Strauss calls the *first triad*. He now argues that "one of the polar terms and the mediator becomes replaced by a new [*second*] triad (…):"[40] In the myth he uses as an example, the myth-makers have obviously replaced the positive term of agriculture and the mediating one of the hunt with the *second triad* consisting of the herbivorous animals, carrion-eating animals and prey animals. The herbivorous animals are animals living exclusively off plants (equating a lifestyle based on

---

39   Lévi-Strauss 130.

40   Lévi-Strauss 130.

agriculture), the carrion-eating ones animals that hunt other animals and feed on them (mirroring a lifestyle that is dependent on the hunt). In the diagram they are still closer to the term war. The middle ones are animals that feed off dead meat (mediators, equated with the average, neither completely good nor extremely evil human being). In this way the myth-makers have managed to exclude the completely negative notions of war and especially death. The prey animals hunt other animals or even humans and kill them but they do it to preserve life. They are already a step away from the concept of war, since killing in a war seems to be unnatural, whereas killing to be able to survive is less morally questionable.

The polar opposites of life and death are brought more closely together still, united in one figure, the carrion-eating animal, feeding on animals which have died from natural causes or which others have killed. The carrion-eating animal often inhabits regions of the earth where life is hard and only the fittest survives. It has to fight for its survival and feed off what it can get. In this sense, the existence of the carrion-eating animal resembles human life. It can also be characterised by periods of plenty and of scarceness. Humans, too have to take what they can get. The fact that the carrion-eating animal in fact does take what it can get and survives upon the scanty nourishment it finds, also presumes a certain cleverness. And in fact, the carrion-eating animals which are represented in the mythical stories Lévi-Strauss looks at, are more often than not the coyote or the raven, animals generally associated with intelligence. The carrion-eating animals not only symbolise the successful integration of death into life but also the clever acceptance of what is there and the skill to make the best of it. The mediator as a figure represents the ambiguity of myth. He is balanced, uniting binary oppositions but he is also hard to fathom. Since his character comprises two sides, he retains an unpredictable element.

It is rather interesting that the myth-makers chose carrion-eating animals to represent the mediating entity. They are certainly perceived as morally ahead of the prey-animals but are still closer to the morally lower side of the carnivorous animals than to the herbivorous animals that make up the side of the good and acceptable. A 'true' mediator-figure here might rather have been an omnivorous animal, since it would truly have stood between the two opposing groups of herbivores and carnivores. However, this fact only shows that the myth-makers understood much about life. A true balance between two extremes is hardly possible in an imperfect world. Since a perfect mediator always has a neutral character, or rather a personality which is balanced, he in a way suggests a transcendence of binaries. Slightly imperfect mediators hint at the fact that certain basic structures or dichotomies cannot finally be overcome by humans. This might also be an explanation of the fact that Lévi-Strauss does not set the entities in his diagram (for instance life, agriculture and herbivorous animals) on the same level. The *second triad* is contained within the limits of the first and both triads are embraced by the *initial pair*. The concepts are not equalised because they are not equal. The *first* and *second triads* can approach the concepts of life and death but can never fully grasp them.

Lévi-Strauss's diagram thus even contains a meta-mythical statement. It draws attention to myth's inadequacy at finally and exhaustively explaining the complexities of life. The particular myth's primary function, however, is to alleviate a deeply-set guilt about a certain lifestyle that necessitates the occasional killing of an animal or even a human being. Furthermore the myth allows people to position themselves. The middle position, held by the mediator, is considered to be the 'normal' one. Thus it is acceptable for people to be in between giving life and killing to sustain themselves, and by extension in between good and evil. It is interesting that Lévi-Strauss himself most probably did not intend the value judgements I interpreted into the diagram. However, the set-up of his schema with one part of the opposing pair (e.g. life) on top and the other (e.g. death) at the bottom implies a valuation. As Jacques Derrida holds, an ideological system which produces binary oppositions usually already sets them up in such a way that one of the terms, mostly the one first mentioned, is privileged.[41] In actuality, each of the poles only acquires meaning via its difference from the other and can only exist in relation to the other. This mutual dependence is inherent in our system of language and thought and cannot be broken down completely but only 'deconstructed'. The interplay between binary oppositions reveals a problem in human reasoning: the true nature of concepts such as, for instance, good or evil remains for ever elusive and we can only approach them via their opposite, i.e. by negative example. Lévi-Strauss's diagram shows how this metaphysical problem is addressed in certain types of stories.[42] In fact, thus, Lévi-Strauss's work contains the roots for its own Derridaean 'deconstruction.'[43]

Lévi-Strauss's diagram has highlighted the ways in which the character-constellation of myth can yield important insights into its deeper concerns. His analyses tie in with and enhance what the other theoreticians mentioned in this chapter put forth. Myths' preoccupation with binary oppositions such as the very basic and significant one between life and death underlines Armstrong's point about myth dealing with certain human fears, predominantly the one of death. Clearly, the mediator figure so commonly found in mythical stories represents an attempt at

---

41   Cf. Derrida *Positions* 41.

42   Cf. Jacques Derrida, *Of Grammatology* (Baltimore: The Johns Hopkins University Press, 1997) 47, 50. Cf. also Madan Sarup, *Post-Structuralism and Postmodernism* (New York: Harvester Wheatsheaf, 1993) 37.

43   Cf. Jacques Derrida, *Writing and Difference* (London: Routledge Classics, 2002) 354-57.

reconciling opposing ideas such as life and death. Myth is thus again shown as a palliative, alleviating human anxieties. Lévi-Strauss's analysis goes a step further than Armstrong's and Campbell's as it shows how exactly this palliative function of myth manifests itself and works on the structural level. It is similar to Girard's (also structural) approach, although in contrast to Girard who perceives the scapegoating ritual as a structure-giving restorative for a whole community or society, Lévi-Strauss in this particular analysis, highlights the effect of the mythical story on the individual. The characters of myth are of great significance in Campbell's as well as Lévi-Strauss's analyses. While Campbell draws attention to the structure and workings of a single, particular kind of myth, namely the one of the hero's journey, Lévi-Strauss identifies the underlying patterns of all myths and related stories such as folktales, as their similar preoccupation with binary oppositions. For both theoreticians the palliative function of myth in addressing and suggesting solutions for existential problems and fears, works via the mediating agency of its characters who make an identification possible for human readers/audiences. The didactic element that Armstrong describes is also present in Lévi-Strauss's analysis. His diagrams showing the structure of myth as an oscillation between and negotiation of binary oppositions, clearly suggest that myth advocates a middle position, a grey area for human beings to inhabit, and hold that this is all most human beings can safely do.

Lévi-Strauss's theories of myth have been harshly criticised on several grounds. The bases of criticism are astutely summarised by Alan Dundes in an article for the journal *Western Folklore*. One point on which reviewers have attacked Lévi-Strauss is that he, purposefully or from lack of knowledge, did not acknowledge the work of Russian formalist Vladimir Propp.[44] Propp already studied the structure of folktales on an empirical basis at the beginning of the 20th century, much earlier than Lévi-Strauss who wrote his major bulk of work during the 1960s and 70s. The formalist looked at a large collection of folktales, mainly from Russia and identified certain elements as common to many of them or only slightly varying. He then assigned functions to these elements, finding out which structural parts are indispensable in tales of the sort he studied.[45] Propp and Lévi-Strauss thus have certain interests in common, although their focal points differ. While Propp chose an empirical approach, Lévi-Strauss took single exemplary myths as his subject

---

44   Cf. for instance Alan Dundes, "Binary Opposition in Myth: The Propp/Lévi-Strauss Debate in Retrospect," *Western Folklore* 56.1 (1997): n.pag. <http://lion.chadwyck.co.uk/>.

45   Cf. Vladimir Propp, *Morphology of the Folktale* [1928] (Austin: University of Texas Press, 2005) 20-24.

matter. In contrast to Propp who looked at tales in their narrative linearity, the paradigmatic axis of a story was much more important to Lévi-Strauss.

These two points, Lévi-Strauss's non-empirical approach and his interest in paradigmatic relations between elements of a story, have also been the focus of criticism. Propp himself attacked Lévi-Strauss's non-empiricism in the following terms: "My model corresponds to what was modeled and is based on a study of data, whereas the model Lévi-Strauss proposes does not correspond to reality and is based on logical operations not imposed by the data ... [He] carries out his logical operations in total disregard of the material."[46] Lévi-Strauss has furthermore been charged with overemphasising the paradigmatic and lightly dismissing the syntagmatic dimension of stories.[47] Dundes himself criticises Lévi-Strauss for being "more of a comparativist than a structuralist" because he sometimes elucidates the complex meaning of one myth in comparison with another only.[48] In this his effort to find meaning in the structure of myth, Dundes goes on to say, Lévi-Strauss's comparisons are sometimes too far-fetched.[49]

Another point of criticism of Lévi-Strauss's works is that he "(...) analyzes both myths and folktales indiscriminately."[50] According to strict interpretations, as mentioned, a myth must needs be a sacred story of the origins of humankind and culture, and differs from a folktale. If approached from that angle, while Lévi-Strauss proposes to study myth, what he looks at for example in his famous "Structural Study of Myth" and "The Story of Asdiwal" are in fact partly folktales.[51] This seeming lack of knowledge about genre distinctions is especially piquant when taking into account that Lévi-Strauss expressly criticised Propp for studying folktales not myths on the grounds that "[tales] are constructed on weaker oppositions than those found in myths."[52] One point that can be made about Lévi-Strauss's 'incautious' use of the term myth and his criticism of folktales is that the concept of myth can be interpreted as infinitely broader than just a narrative of origin. As this chapter has already shown, myths can also be stories of gods, heroes and of transformation. What they all have in common, as Lévi-Strauss rightly identified, is their concern with binary oppositions, and possibly finally the one all-encompassing binary of life and death. However unwittingly, Lévi-Strauss seems to

---

46 Vladimir Propp, *Theory and History of Folklore* (Manchester: Manchester University Press, 1984) 76.
47 Cf. Dundes n.pag.
48 Dundes n.pag.
49 Cf. Dundes n.pag.
50 Dundes n.pag.
51 Cf. Dundes n.pag.
52 Propp *Theory and History of Folklore* 176.

already imply something in his essays that will form one of the bases of my thesis. He indirectly expresses the idea that folktales of whatever kind are similar to myths and have taken over functions that were first fulfilled by more all-encompassing myths but have over time become associated with the slightly more individual tales of different societies and groups of people. It is one of my assumptions that although many myths might have disappeared, their structures have continued to exist in different forms and nowadays find expression in popular tales.

This neatly leads me to and partly invalidates the next point of criticism Lévi-Strauss was faced with. Dundes remarks that other genres of folklore such as proverbs, riddles and curses contain binary oppositions, too and asks himself how binary oppositions can be used to define the nature of myth.[53] Funnily enough, he has given himself the answer to that question a few pages before in his paper where he says, almost as an aside "My own view is that Lévi-Strauss is not so much describing the structure of myth as he is the structure of the world described in myth."[54] That is exactly the point. Finally, Lévi-Strauss is not interested in arriving at a finite definition of the nature of myth. He is interested in what myth tells us about human beings, their social organisations and their coexistence. Vernon W. Gras supports this view when he says: "Ultimately, (…) binarism (...) is accepted as a general description of how the mind imposes order unconsciously and universally in all forms of social life. Lévi-Strauss illustrated the binary functioning of this unconscious mind in his studies of mythology."[55] The criticism that can be and has been levelled against Lévi-Strauss here, particularly by poststructuralists, is that he 'accepts' and does not question binarism. This criticism is a bit unfair, as one could, for example, just as well criticise the pioneers in the development of the computer for not instantly generating the type of PC we are using today. Showing the internal organisation of stories and by extension the human need for order and structure has paved the way for the poststructuralist questioning and exposing of this need and was thus essential for the development of poststructuralist thought.

Myth, for Lévi-Strauss is not an entity in itself but a powerful example of the ways humans think. In this fashion certainly other folkloristic genres such as riddles, curses and proverbs can also exhibit binary oppositions but myth as Lévi-Strauss has shown among others, is more universal and therefore offers a broader scope for analysis. It was also mentioned above that Lévi-Strauss seems to have been implicitly aware that binary structures are not restricted to myth. He does not claim that binaries cannot be part of any other folkloristic genre. Concerning Lévi-

---

53   Cf. Dundes n.pag.

54   Dundes n.pag.

55   Vernon W. Gras, "Myth and the Reconciliation of Opposites: Jung and Lévi-Strauss," *Journal of the History of Ideas* 42.3 (1981): 477.

Strauss's statement about folktales comprising weaker oppositions than myths, I believe, as does Dundes, that he is simply wrong. Binary oppositions are universal and appear in many different contexts. If they are present in a story, there is no degree to the strength of their presence. What is possibly varying in myths and folktales, are the contexts in which the binaries operate and therefore the meanings they obtain.

The universality Lévi-Strauss assigns binary thinking and the way in which he seemingly imposes his findings on his diverse material have possibly earned him the harshest criticism.[56] Certainly, this criticism is partly justified, too, since universalising always means simplifying at the expense of complexity. However, it also proves a point that is highly relevant for my thesis. If a lucid and ingenuous mind such as Lévi-Strauss's is prone to generalising and universalising, we all are. It cannot be denied that structures comprised of binary oppositions surround us and pervade our culture. They are simplifications but they are existent and, because it is easier to think in terms of binaries than to account for the complexity of the world, binary logic and reasoning are extremely tempting to adopt. Therefore, in this thesis I will not only look at the ways in which my two exemplary tales, *Star Wars* and *Harry Potter* are structured but also analyse what their binary organisation means for their complexity.

2.3 THE LIMITATIONS OF STRUCTURES AND MYTHICAL AMBIGUITY

The criticism of Lévi-Strauss becoming blind to diversity is thus one that can probably be transferred to many people and many situations in life in which it is easier to adopt a black and white view. For this reason, no matter how unduly universalist Lévi-Strauss might be, his approach is fitting for the analysis of cultural phenomena such as the ones I will look at as long as one takes structural analysis as a meta-phenomenon which at the same time as commenting on structurality also draws attention to the limitations structures impose on human beings. If employed

---

56   The critic who most strongly attacks him on these grounds is Clifford Geertz. In his work *Local Knowledge* he says of Lévi-Strauss: "For structuralists, Lévi-Strauss *cum suis*, the product side of thought becomes so many arbitrary social codes, diverse indeed, with their jaguars, tattoos, and rotting meat, but which, when properly deciphered, yield as their plain text the psychological invariants of the process side. Brazilian myth or Bach fugue, it is all a matter of perceptual contrasts, logical oppositions, and relation-saving transformations" (Clifford Geertz, *Local Knowledge: Further Essays in Interpretive Anthropology* (New York: Basic Books, Inc., 1983) 150).

with care, it helps to expose the constructedness of tales such as the ones I will analyse and many other cultural manifestations, and invites us to think beyond it. I believe that Lévi-Strauss is at least partly conscious of structuralism as simplification. The way I understand his approach to myth is that he acknowledges the fact that myth is ambiguous. On the one hand it provides guidance to people in a complex world but on the other hand it refers beyond itself and draws attention to the limitations inherent in binary thought. Myths employ the binary oppositions-mediator structure in an attempt at drawing attention to the problem of humanity being *caught* within certain structures of thinking. Thinking in binaries is always constricting since the two poles form a boundary which thought cannot transcend. Everything in thought and in language acquires meaning only with reference to something else. By employing dualisms, myth depicts the structures of human thought with all their advantages but also encourages reflection on their narrowness.

On an almost meta-mythical level, it thus alludes to the fact that all human thought is limited and finally "trapped in a kind of circle."[57] Even trying to destabilise certain concepts and their traditional associations usually means arriving back at exactly the terminology one wants to call into question. Jacques Derrida, takes metaphysics as an example and claims that

[there] is no sense in doing without the concepts of metaphysics in order to shake metaphysics. We have no language—no syntax and no lexicon—which is foreign to this history; we can pronounce not a single destructive proposition which has not already had to slip into the form, the logic, and the implicit postulations of precisely what it seeks to contest.[58]

By laying open the binary oppositions that govern human thought and life, mythical analysis as Lévi-Strauss proposes it, can at least allude to the problem of structure as not only ordering but also limiting. As Derrida and other poststructuralists see it, the trappings of structure are even stronger than that. Structures are not only limiting, they also conjure nostalgia for a point of origin, a wholeness, that in the eyes of poststructuralists is non-existent. Gras summarises this as follows: "[Lévi-Strauss] naturalized the reconciliation of oppositions so that mythology became an unconscious immanent aesthetic balancing the psyche with itself as well as the individual with his environment."[59] Myth, as seen by Lévi-Strauss nourishes the hope that there is a point at which binaries can be brought together, converge and create an inseparable wholeness or unity. Derrida notices this nostalgia for a fixed

57   Derrida *Writing and Difference* 354.
58   Derrida *Writing and Difference* 354.
59   Gras 483-84.

origin in Lévi-Strauss's works. He says that "one (...) perceives in his [Lévi-Strauss's] work a sort of ethic of presence, an ethic of nostalgia for origins."[60]

Derrida himself does not believe in this point cf origin which he calls the 'centre.' "[The] center", he says "[has] no natural site, [it is] not a fixed locus but a function, a sort of nonlocus in which an infinite number of sign-substitutions [come] into play."[61] A 'center' could, for instance, be a full and comprehensive understanding of the essential nature of 'life'. Since we can never arrive at this kind of understanding, we will never be able to find the 'center' in this matter or in others. In fact, we can only approximate what we understand by ideas such as 'life' and we usually create an identity for concepts via their negative. In the case of life that would be death. Derrida brings to our attention that the 'center' is not an actual presence but has a function in human discourse that is why it, or rather the nostalgia for it becomes visible in the various mythical attempts at reconciling binaries and arriving at a paradisical state of completeness. Its function is to fill a metaphysical void, abate an insecurity about the meaning of human life by producing a source or an origin. Derrida turns our attention to the fact that "[signifiers] and signified are continually breaking apart and reattaching in new combinations, thus revealing the inadequacy of Saussure's model of the sign, according to which the signifier and the signified relate as if they were two sides of the same sheet of paper."[62] Derrida calls the result of this "breaking apart" and "reattaching" of signifier and signified, this eternal "chain of signifiers"[63] 'play.'[64]

My analyses of *Star Wars* and *Harry Potter* will expose the tales' subconscious awareness of this nostalgia for origins and unity. While both stories cater to this nostalgia and human need, they try to break out of their structural corsets in places. How this works and what the results are will be seen in the course of the thesis. Binary oppositions of course must needs restrict Derrida's notion of 'play'. Because of the missing centre and the eternal "play of substitutions"[65] language and by extension all stories are subject to, the poststructuralist is suspicious of the assumption that fixed meaning can be generated in the interplay between signifier and signified. In this sense he also questions Lévi-Strauss's claim that the meaning of myths is generated through the friction between binary oppositions. Derrida is highly careful when it comes to them, especially because he perceives that one term, usually, the first one mentioned in binaries such as good-evil, or life-death,

---

60   Derrida *Writing and Difference* 369.

61   Derrida *Writing and Difference* 353-84.

62   Sarup 33.

63   Sarup 33.

64   Derrida *Writing and Difference* 352, 365.

65   Derrida *Writing and Difference* 365.

tends to be the one viewed more positively.[66] His deconstructivist aesthetics aim at exposing the ideological assumptions that lie hidden in the interstice between two opposing terms. This shows that the term 'post' in 'poststructuralism' does not only signify 'after' but also 'beyond.' Poststructuralism goes beyond structuralism by drawing attention to the fact that whatever meaning is generated by language is not necessarily innocent. For myths this means that apart from providing a palliative for certain human anxieties and direction through a fixed structural corset, they can also carry ideological, if not manipulative implications.

2.4 MYTH AS IDEOLOGY

The theoretician who most thoroughly expounds the idea of myth as ideologically laden is Roland Barthes. Barthes is alternately associated with structuralist and poststructuralist thought and can possibly be seen as writing on the threshold between the two significant movements. For him, "myth is a system of communication, (...) [with] a message."[67] As such it is associated with speech, and thereby with expression of some sort.[68] Barthes does not believe in an arbitrary and natural evolution of myth but sees it as "a type of speech chosen by history."[69] This statement on myth already makes clear that for Barthes, myth is something deliberately employed for whichever purposes. While both Lévi-Strauss's and Campbell's definitions basically start from the assumption that there is a phenomenon called myth which has to be described, Barthes works from an opposite angle. He begins by looking at real-life-discourses shaped by a certain society at a given point in history and draws attention to their mythical nature. These discourses can reside "not only [in] written [texts], but also [in] photography, cinema, reporting, sport, shows, publicity [etc.]."[70] Thus Barthes proposes a broader definition of myth than Lévi-Strauss and Campbell who basically see myth as story or narrative. Barthes wants to show how seemingly 'pure' language becomes myth in the minds of people. According to him, myth works on two levels. The first one is de Saussure's language level, made up of a sign consisting of a signifier and a signified. The language level is 'pure' in so far as it is not 'burdened' with any culturally received or ideological meanings, although the relationship between signifier and signified is already constructed. The language level describes the sound- or written image of a word (the signifier) and links it with a concept of this

66   Cf. Derrida *Positions* 41.

67   Barthes 1.

68   Cf. Barthes 1.

69   Barthes 2.

70   Barthes 2.

word which people have in their minds (the signified). Ideology, or myth, as Barthes calls it, comes in on the second level. On this second, mythical level, the language-level-sign "becomes a mere signifier."[71] It is almost impossible, Barthes believes, to separate the language-level-sign from certain associations that spring up in our minds as soon as we hear a word. Therefore, language is hardly ever truly 'pure.' The associations with the language-level-sign make up the signified on the level of myth. Together language-level-sign and associations form the sign on the level of myth. An example would be the term 'cross.' On the level of language, it is simply made up of the word or sound image *cross* and the mental image of a typical representative of this category. On the level of myth, associations such as Christ, death, resurrection, hope etc. are added. For the human mind, it is very hard to separate the two levels. Whenever we hear or read a word, associations will crop up immediately. Very often, these associations will be culturally received and not be questioned. They seem to be natural. In the case of the cross this means that other cultures might have associations with the concept that significantly differ from ours. It is now easy to see how the mental tendency not to separate mere language from its meanings and associations, can be exploited and how myth can be used to naturalise certain discourses. Barthes himself formulates it as follows: "We reach here the very principle of myth: it transforms history into nature."[72] In this sense, Barthes's view of myth comes very close to ideology, which also operates highly unconsciously, appears to be natural and often remains unquestioned.

Interestingly, Barthes's stance on myth makes explicit what Lévi-Strauss only implies in his study, namely the meta-function of myth. For Barthes, myth consists of "two semiological systems, (...): a linguistic system, the language (...); and myth itself, which [he calls] *metalanguage*, because it is a second language, *in which* one speaks about the first [his italics]."[73] Myth speaks about language and the limitations people are subject to because of language. However, what is more important for Barthes, is that myth is language which can be consciously employed in a certain manner. By listing all the areas in which myth plays a role, photography, cinema, written discourse, reporting etc., he makes clear that in all these fields it is common to tell stories beneath stories. Understood in this way, myth does not necessarily have a positive function. It can be used to veil truth or mask reality and to influence or even manipulate people through polarities which are more easily graspable than the complexity of reality but also more likely to produce certain (dangerous) ideologies.

---

71   Barthes 6.
72   Barthes 21.
73   Barthes 7.

In Barthes's view of myth as ideologically laden, ideology appears as something manipulative, potentially distorting. However, ideology is much more than that. To define it as simply a tool for powerful people to influence others, would be too one-sided. Ideology does not necessarily have to be bad or lead to horrible events such as World War II, but it can also be harmless or beneficial. First and foremost, ideology just is. It belongs to every person's life and even those who use it to manipulate are influenced by it. In his essay on "Ideology and Ideological State Apparatuses" Louis Althusser defines it as follows: "Ideology represents the imaginary relationship of individuals to their conditions of existence."[74] John Fiske points out that since "the idea of an objective, empirical 'truth' is untenable,"[75] each and every individual needs certain *beliefs* about what is true and find explanations for his or her particular situation in life. These beliefs are influenced by upbringing, family structure, surroundings, education and political views among other factors. It depends on the perceptiveness of a person whether he or she is able to question or go beyond some of the ideologies surrounding him or her. However, as astute as this person might be, he or she will never be able to completely step out of ideology. And very often, people do not want to question ideologies, either. They are comfortable and provide a certain security and guidance in a complex world. In this sense, they are reminiscent of and linked to the (sometimes too simplistic) meaning generated between binary oppositions in a Lévi-Straussian analysis of myth which also serves to comfort and reassure people. This quality makes ideologies beneficial and dangerous at the same time. They are helpful because people need 'truths' to cling to. If, out of complacency, fear or for other reasons, these ideologies are suddenly taken to be objective truths, they become dangerous. People seeking guidance and clinging to certain ideologies too firmly, are easy prey for others who exploit their fears for their own aims. An example would be the ideologies of the extreme right which have been exploited to gather massive numbers of followers in different countries in the course of the 20th century. The manipulative side to myth Barthes brings up, and its similarity to ideology in this sense is thus rather a consequence of the fact that ideology surrounds us and is hard to identify than an intrinsic feature of myth.

Barthes's view of myth as discourse that (subconsciously) influences us and the very similar definitions of ideology Althusser and Fiske give, in fact clearly emphasise the limitations of Lévi-Strauss's structuralist approach and explain the charges of simplification against it, mentioned above. "The Structural Study of Myth" is occupied with binaries and the meaning generated between them. This

---

74   Althusser 693.

75   John Fiske, "Culture, Ideology, Interpellation," *Literary Theory: An Anthology*, Ed. Julie Rivkin and Michael Ryan (Malden, MA: Blackwell Publishing, 2004) 1269.

meaning might incorporate mediator-figures as was shown in Lévi-Strauss's diagram, but it still comprises only three positions, the two extremes and something in between. This is, as critics have justly remarked a rather simplistic way of describing the world, and much of the complexity of societies and the dealings between human beings is lost if only these three positions are considered. Ideologies, as it were, are very often rooted in a binary approach to life and are naturalised by too narrow a focus on structures and the categorisation they necessarily bring with them. Therefore, taking a structuralist approach to stories always bears the danger of losing sight of other discourses which run below the surface but are muted by the dominance of the stories' binary organisation. Derrida hints at this problem of discourses 'silenced' by the structures when he remarks on the hierarchy always implied in a binary opposition.[76] "Myth," Roland Barthes says, "hides nothing and flaunts nothing: it distorts; myth is neither a lie nor a confession: it is an inflexion."[77] This statement for me, perfectly summarises the point I am trying to make. All kinds of different discourses are there, within myths, but it is in the nature of myth, or maybe in the nature of the 'reader' of myth, to channel the attention to some places while passing others by.

Structuralism has come to be regarded as problematic in connection with two areas of research especially, feminism and the discourse on ethnicity, which will also have a bearing for my thesis. Among the aims of representatives of the two fields it has been to question hierarchies derived from binary oppositions. Both feminist approaches and discourses on ethnicity have to deal with the constant Othering women and people from various ethnicities coming to 'western' countries are subject to. The most extreme form of Othering, the process of scapegoating, was analysed by René Girard and already mentioned in this chapter. It was shown that Othering frequently reveals more about those who 'other' and their problems than about those who are 'othered.' In many patriarchal societies women have constantly been set up as the Other of men. The relationship between men and women during the reign of Queen Victoria in 19th-century England, for instance, was dominated and regulated by binary oppositions. Men and women occupied what was called 'separate spheres,' men moving within the public and women within the private domain.[78] Furthermore, while men were associated with rationality, women, according to common belief, were sensitive and emotional. However, binaries were not only established between men and women but oppositional categories also appeared to differentiate between two opposing 'kinds' of women. As Sandra

---

76   Cf. Derrida *Positions* 41.

77   Barthes 21.

78   Cf. Miriam Strube, *Subjekte des Begehrens: Zur sexuellen Selbstbestimmung der Frau in Literatur, Musik und Visueller Kultur* (Bielefeld: transcript, 2009) 55.

Gilbert and Susan Gubar explain in their famous study *The Madwoman in the Attic*, women now have to confront a legacy of being either idealised or demonised which also largely goes back to the 19th century.

The picture of what the ideal woman should be like was greatly embellished by Coventry Patmore's narrative poem "Angel in the House" which portrays its heroine as beautiful, ethereal, gentle, meek, submissive, generous and loving, in short angelic. Genteel women during Victorian times would strain to achieve this ideal. As Gilbert and Gubar say, they would "[fast], [drink vinegar] and [subject themselves to other] cosmetic or dietary [procedures]" to attain the 'physical perfection' asked of them.[79] They would also sacrifice their own desires to those of their families, especially their husbands. In this sense, many of these women were dead in life, led "a posthumous existence in [their] own [lifetimes]."[80] Thus, the ideal and saintly woman was also always associated with death. Her selflessness and her pale beauty gave her an aura of the uncanny. Since she repressed all her desires and personal wishes, she was somewhat incalculable and inscrutable. Her very perfection and submission to an ideal thus contributed to the establishment of the other extreme of seeing her, the monster. It is no coincidence that so many beautiful, pallid female vampires populate Victorian fiction, for instance. The mysterious women in Poe's short stories are also somewhere in between angel and fiend. The demonic or fallen women in Victorian literature were often associated with female sexuality, something not acknowledged openly to exist.[81] Thus again, with respect to sexuality, Victorian society knew only two positions for women, the saint or the whore.[82] It is plain to see that these binaries created around men and women and also among women, are highly problematic, the worst being that many women came to incorporate and believe in these stereotypes themselves.[83]

The difficulty with this kind of categorisation is the same that was already hinted at several times in the course of this chapter. It makes the categorised easier to understand but naturally, it simplifies at the same time by leaving no space for diversity. Or, as Judith Butler puts it: "[The] subjects regulated by such structures

---

79   Sandra Gilbert and Susan Gubar, "The Madwoman in the Attic," *Literary Theory: An Anthology*, Ed. Julie Rivkin and Michael Ryan (Malden, MA: Blackwell Publishing, 2004) 817.

80   Gilbert and Gubar 817.

81   Cf. Strube 55.

82   Cf. Strube 57.

83   Miriam Strube exemplifies this by referring to the stereotypes set up around female black slaves and their treatment in literature. They were either depicted as nurturing and motherly or as voluptuous and sexualised. These stereotpyes, Strube says, have influenced the ways in which African American women perceive themselves (62-67).

are, by virtue of being subjected to them, formed, defined, and reproduced in accordance with the requirements of those structures."[84] The way Victorian women had to conform or willingly conformed to the ideals in circulation about them are a perfect example of what Butler means. The categories set up for women exerted power over them and helped keep them 'in their place.' The fact that women needed to be contained proves what was said about Othering at the outset of this part of the chapter. Othering implies fears and anxieties on the part of those who 'other.' Men, for instance, to put it simply, were afraid that their status in society and basically all areas of life would be contested if they allowed women free reign.

Butler further supports what has already been said about the limiting nature of structures and structuralism: "The poststructuralist break with (…) Lévi-Strauss refutes the claims of totality and universality and the presumption of binary structural oppositions that implicitly operate to quell the insistent ambiguity and openness of linguistic and cultural signification."[85] Butler is right when she stresses the important poststructuralist accomplishment of refuting 'totality and universality' and rejecting binary simplification. However, poststructuralism has not managed to refute the human *need* for binaries, nor has it diminished the presence of binary oppositions especially in popular culture. A structuralist approach does not do justice to the complexity of topics such as feminism or gender studies. Nevertheless, categorisation into binaries was and still is customary, so it is worthwhile choosing the structuralist approach to first expose, and then use poststructuralist readings to deconstruct it. Categorisation was common with respect to men and women. It was also used to differentiate various 'kinds' of women. The vestiges of it can still be seen in our culture today. If we look at a the film genre of romantic comedy, for instance, a very particular image of women is presented to us. Miriam Strube calls the type the "*good girl,* white, young (but not too young), with a body conforming to current standards of beauty, erotic, open, in search for Mister Right without being too promiscuous [my translation]."[86] Still, it seems, women are categorised, for example, according to their degree of attractiveness or what we would today call their current market value. This example from film is not completely random, since a part of my primary material comprises films.

In 1975 Laura Mulvey wrote about the role of women in film and used Freud's psychoanalytical theories to expose the influence of the 'patriarchal unconscious' on the structure of the mainstream Hollywood film. The spectator of this kind of cinema, she holds, is always constructed as male by way of the representation of the female in films. Women, she says, function "in patriarchal culture as signifier for

84   Judith Butler, *Gender Trouble* (New York: Routledge, 1990) 3.
85   Butler 54.
86   Strube 54.

the male other, bound by a symbolic order in which man can live out his phantasies and obsessions through linguistic command by imposing them on the silent image of woman still tied to her place as bearer of meaning, not maker of meaning."[87] Here, Mulvey also invokes a binary opposition, 'bearers of meaning' and 'makers of meaning.' It seems, that even for those who want to step out of the structuralist perspective which they perceive as harmful for feminist discourse in all its diversity, consciously or unconsciously fall back on binaries. The "silent image of woman" used as a projection foil for men, resembles the picture of the 'Angel in the House' of Victorian times. Cinema, Mulvey goes on to say, "poses questions of the ways in which the unconscious (…) structures ways of seeing and pleasure."[88] The structures of the mainstream film, she argues, subject women to the "male gaze."[89] Mulvey does not define what she means by mainstream film but I suppose that she is talking about films that follow a certain narrative pattern such as the romance or the western formula. (The term 'formula' will be explained later in this chapter.) Again, here is someone who holds that structures have the potential to subject, even suppress, if one thinks of Mulvey's statement concerning women as 'bearers of meaning.' The structures of the mainstream film make sure that women remain bearers and not makers of meaning. How exactly this works, Mulvey explains in the following: "The presence of women is an indispensable element of spectacle in normal narrative film, yet her visual presence tends to work against the development of a story line, to freeze the flow of action in moments of erotic contemplation. This alien presence then has to be integrated into cohesion with the narrative."[90] The heroine is not usually important for what she does but rather for what she means to the hero who is spurred to action and propels the narrative because of her.[91] Mulvey thus also criticises the power structures can have over their subjects, in this case women in the movies.

Mulvey's perspective, invoking structuralist categorisation has been criticised as reductive because it presupposes fixed and inflexible concepts of femininity and masculinity and similarly denies any diversity to 'the' spectator of mainstream films. He/she is taken as one body who assumes a 'male gaze' unreflected.[92] Some

---

87   Laura Mulvey, "Visual Pleasure and Narrative Cinema," *Literary Theory: An Anthology*, Ed. Julie Rivkin and Michael Ryan (Malden, MA: Blackwell Publishing, 1998) 586.

88   Mulvey 586.

89   Mulvey 589.

90   Mulvey 589.

91   Cf. Mulvey 590.

92   Cf. Barbara Creed, General Introduction, *The Sexual Subject: A 'Screen' Reader in Sexuality*, Ed. John Caughie and Annette Kuhn (London: Routledge, 1992) 5.

critics resolutely refuted Mulvey's thesis that the male is always presented in a position of power in mainstream filmic products. Both male and female subjects, they hold, can take up the 'male gaze.'[93] Jennifer Hammett goes one step further even and notes that "[few] today would argue that patriarchal texts invariably position spectators within ideologically complicit structures of identification and desire."[94] Cultural 'texts,' in this case films, can never presume a certain response from their 'readers.' Hammett here goes beyond a mere text-immanent criticism of female roles that posits the spectator as fixed and uncritically receptive of the dominant ideologies of the cultural text given. She sees the diversity of spectators as significant for the meaning-making process of a text. Thus again, the reductive quality and proneness for simplification of structures is attacked here. Diversity and multiplicity should be acknowledged.

Discourses of ethnicity have also been heavily influenced by binary categorisation. Before the term ethnicity became prominent to describe people who share a common social and linguistic background and possibly have the same skin-colour, the loaded term 'race' was used to describe different groups of people. Racial theory did not locate similarities between people in external factors such as common cultural traditions and language, but categorised people according to certain physical and genetic traits that they allegedly shared.[95] Within the theories of the 'races,' a hierarchy was implied which was set up by creating oppositions. One 'race,' the white or Caucasoid one, was supposedly better than the others which justified the imposition of 'white' culture and traditions on non-white people, something that was frequently done during the age of colonialism. A binary opposition between 'us' and 'them' was created and similar to the ways in which women were 'othered' by men during the 19th century, people who were non-white became the Other that had to be controlled and made alike. At the base of this Othering again lies a fear of people who are different externally and who might have notions of social organisation or morality that diverge from 'ours.' These Others might pose a threat or be hard to contain. Ian F. Haney Lopéz quotes Omi and Winant to explain the function of racial notions for societies. "Race becomes

---

93   Cf. Creed 5-6.

94   Jennifer Hammett, "The Ideological Impediment: Epistemology, Feminism, and Film Theory," *Film Theory and Philosophy*, Ed. Richard Allen and Murray Smith (Oxford: Clarendon Press, 1997) 245.

95   Cf. Bill Ashcroft, Gareth Griffiths and Helen Tiffin, *Post-Colonial Studies: The Key Concepts* (London: Routledge, 2000) 198.

'common sense' – a way of comprehending, explaining and acting in the world."[96] Notions of 'race' and the categorisation going along with them, obviously have a guiding function. They help people place themselves and others and keep a complex world structured and ordered, though obviously at the expense of certain people or groups of people. The quotation, however, not only explains why racial notions came into existence and are still virulent in modern societies. It also shows how closely notions of 'race' are connected to ideology. Many ideological assumptions consist of what people believe to be 'common sense,' namely that which is taken for granted and not questioned. Thus notions of 'race' are in some senses similar to the concept of myth that has been proposed here. They have an ordering and structuring function and they are closely linked to ideology.

The narrowly categorising and therefore problematic notions of 'race' are also part of the reason why the concept of assimilation is rejected when speaking about the relationship of a dominant social group and an ethnic minority today. The request to assimilate addresses people's fears of the Other by asking of newcomers to a society or country to become like the majority, to conform to the dominant group's expectations of proper citizenship and behaviour. Tariq Modood counters the concept of assimilation with that of multiculturalism. "Multiculturalism," he says "refers to (...) the forms of accommodation in which 'differences' are not eliminated, are not washed away but to some extend recognized."[97] And he adds: "Multiculturalism is characterized by the challenging, the dismantling and the remaking of public identities."[98] His definition recalls the aims of deconstruction. Similar to recent examples of feminist thought and theory, multiculturalism seeks to defy simplistic structuralist world views in a poststructuralist way. Assimilation is a highly structuralist concept. There is an 'us' and a 'them' and 'they' have to adapt to 'our' ways of life to be accepted and respected by 'us.' Multiculturalism as Modood sees it, takes into account the complexity of the world. For the concept to be successful, he believes, people have to challenge their 'common sense' or ideological notions of Self and Other and embrace broader and more inclusive concepts of their societies.

However, multiculturalist theories are not without fault. The gravest problem of multiculturalist policies is the fact that they distinctly focus on groups of people and

---

96   Ian F. Haney Lopéz, "The Social Construction of Race," *Literary Theory: An Anthology*, Ed. Julie Rivkin and Michael Ryan (Malden, MA: Blackwell Publishing, 2004) 966.

97   Tariq Modood, *Multiculturalism: A Civic Idea* (Cambridge, UK: Polity Press, 2007) 39.

98   Modood 43.

not on individuals.[99] This runs counter to most Western societies' constitutions, which are preoccupied with individual rights. Attempts at advancing a group of people must needs limit themselves to addressing problems common to all members of the group. Diversity among group members is not and probably cannot be taken into account. Binary structuring of one group against the other, 'us' versus 'them', is again paramount. Poststructuralist 'play' in the sense of individual difference is not encouraged. Homi K. Bhabha, another theoretician of culture, employs the picture of museum-galleries, connected via staircases to describe a fluid and equal society which takes the individual into account and does not stigmatise people for their (alleged) membership in certain groups:

The stairwell as liminal space, in-between the designations of identity, becomes the process of symbolic interaction, the connective tissue that constructs the difference betweeen upper and lower, black and white. The hither and thither of the stairwell, the temporal movement and passage that it allows, prevents identities at either end of it from settling into primordial polarities. This interstitial passage between fixed identifications opens up the possibility of a cultural hybridity that entertains difference without an assumed or imposed hierarchy.[100]

The stairwell is certainly a more apt picture to visualise complexity than Lévi-Strauss's mediator character. While the mediator blends both polarities and presents a perfectly balanced middle ground which is again rather static, the staircase symbolises complexity and diversity because there are various positions one can assume on it. It implies Derrida's notion of 'play' as it destabilises hierarchies. No one remains excluded from the upper galleries of the museum, in fact there is no hierarchy between lower and upper parts of it since both can contain fascinating exhibits. Going to a museum is furthermore primarily an individual and not a group experience. In this sense, the metaphor rejects a static, structuralist multiculturalism for a more fluid, 'hybrid' diversity that asserts the rights of all people alike, regardless of their skin-colour or ethnicity.

Both the discourse on female liberation and the one on 'race' and ethnicity are closely associated with binary categorisation and the problems and limitations arising from it. Theoreticians and others concerned have strongly rejected this, as they called it, simplistic, universalising structuralist approach in favour of a more open one, admitting diversity and complexity. My analysis of *Star Wars* and *Harry Potter* will show whether the universalist concerns of structures and their function of catering to a human need for spiritual or metaphysical reassurance, truly sacrifice

---

99   Cf. Christian Joppke, "Multiculturalism and Immigration: A Comparison of the United States, Germany, and Great Britain," *Theory and Society* 25 (1996): 449, 452.

100   Homi K. Bhabha, *The Location of Culture* (London: Routledge, 1994) 5.

diversity and complexity with respect to women and 'ethnic minorities' and 'subject' them to preformed categories which they cannot easily escape. It will be seen whether women are active agents, whether they serve as projection foils for male fantasies, or whether their position in the tales might be one in-between these two extremes, a Lévi-Straussian-mediator-position. Ethnic minorities, 'foreigners' and another group of characters possibly representing them and at the same time sublimating their very real concerns, the humanoids, will be looked at in a similar way. It needs to be found out whether the stance towards them is assimilationist and therefore finally binary, or more open and multiculturalist in the two stories.

2.5 MYTH AND POPULAR CULTURE

After the theoretical framework for the thesis has been established it remains for me to conclusively explain why I believe stories such as *Star Wars* and *Harry Potter* can be analysed as myths. The following traits were isolated as the most significant characteristics of myth: a structure based on binary oppositions and their negotiation, a certain universality, a tendency to reappear in different forms in various periods and countries, a penchant to address certain basic human fears and offer consolation, and, as the downside to structural simplicity, the perpetuation of cultural stereotypes and ideologies. There are scholars and critics who believe that mythical stories have died out in modern times and do not exist anymore. Postmodernism's belief in the death of grand narratives would be a case in point. I firmly disagree with such assertions. Although we live in a highly enlightened, rational age, in some respects, people have not changed much. They still find it easier to reduce the complexity of the world into schemes and the basic questions concerning life and death addressed in the old myths, have still not been answered. The need to face and if possible conquer these fears with the help of stories is thus not diminished. Since Greek myths have indeed lost much of their importance and validity for our culture, the principles and functions of myth enumerated have to find other expressions.[101] Popular formula stories perpetuate the structures of myth as detected by Lévi-Strauss and continue to present a certain (ideological) picture of the world. This view is shared by Mircea Eliade who remarks upon the heroic characters to be found in comic strips such as *Superman*, and the binary mythical

---

101   In fact there is an interesting cycle of stories to contradict the notion that Greek myths have lost their significance today. In his *Percy Jackson* series, American author Rick Riorden revives Greek mythology in a modern context, retells the old stories and adds new ones of his own invention, seasoned with a good portion of irony and meta-reflection. His works are an embodiment of the way mythical stories have always been perpetuated and rejuvenated through the ages by additions and adaptations.

structures constituting the detective novel.[102] Karen Armstrong also echoes the mythical relevance of popular culture, although she feels that something has been lost in the process.

We still long to 'get beyond' our immediate circumstances, and to enter a 'full time', a more intense, fulfilling existence. We try to enter this dimension by means of art, rock music, drugs or by entering the larger-than-life perspective of film. We still seek heroes. Elvis Presley and Princess Diana were both made into instant mythical beings, even objects of religious cult. But there is something unbalanced about this adulation. The myth of the hero was not intended to provide us with icons to admire, but was designed to tap into the vein of heroism within ourselves. Myth must lead to imitation or participation, not passive contemplation.[103]

Armstrong is partly right, however, there is a difference between one figure stylised into heroic proportions and a story. Ultimately, people do not need heroes on their own, they need heroes and their stories. Stories are important (for the western mind at least) to understand the world and come to terms with it, a view put forth, for instance, by Sarah Grochala.[104] Only hero and story taken together fill the human need for role models on whom to orient their behaviour and to understand certain facts of life. I will investigate the ways in which *Star Wars* and *Harry Potter* are indeed incentives to action and thus continue in the same vein as the old myths Armstrong alludes to.

The need for ideals and models who provide orientation Armstrong mentions is incorporated within formulaic stories. The term formula, according to John G. Cawelti, has two usages. "The first (...) simply denotes a conventional way of treating some specific thing or person."[105] As examples he mentions Homer's epithets "swift-footed Achilles" and "cloud-gathering Zeus."[106] The second usage of the term formula "refers to larger plot types."[107] Formulas thus either are characters or other elements of stories treated in conventional, well-known ways, or structural patterns that repeat themselves again and again in certain types of narratives. Examples of the latter would for instance be the romance, the Gothic, the western or

---

102 Cf. Mircea Eliade, *Myth and Reality* (London: George Allen & Unwin Ltd, 1963) 184-85.

103 Armstrong 135.

104 Cf. Sarah Grochala, "A Form of Ethics: The Disrupted and Misappropriated Story in the Monodramas of Mark Ravenhill," *Narrative in Drama: CDE Studies*, Ed. Merle Tönnies and Christina Flotmann (Trier: WVT, 2011) 142.

105 Cawelti 5.

106 Cawelti 5.

107 Cawelti 5.

the fantasy formula. Cawelti expressly mentions that binary oppositions are vital to these formulaic narratives and he also comments on their universal nature. "[Formulas] are ways in which specific cultural themes and stereotypes become embodied in more universal story archetypes."[108] Furthermore, he contends, these repetitive story patterns fulfil "man's needs for enjoyment and escape."[109] This brief definition of a narrative formula already contains most of the important points made about myths and their functions before. Like mythical stories, formulaic narratives tend to have a structure based on binary oppositions. A certain universality is attested to both. Both also appeal to emotions by confronting people with facts of life that are hard to reconcile. Finally, both expressly contain and perpetuate cultural stereotypes.

The new element Cawelti brings into play is the formulaic function of providing escape and enjoyment. These two functions have not been mentioned in any of the approaches to myth analysed so far and therefore seem to apply specifically to forms of popular culture and entertainment. Both *Star Wars* and *Harry Potter* are clearly formulaic stories according to Cawelti's definition. *Star Wars* contains elements of the science-fiction, the fantasy and the romance formula, while *Harry Potter* brings the fantasy, the detective and the Gothic formula as well as the boarding-school story together. It will be seen how the structures contribute to the satisfaction of escapist needs in the readers. The enumeration of formulas to be found in the two stories analysed, embodies another remark Cawelti makes about formula stories. For such a story to have any appeal at all, he says, "the individual version of a formula must have some unique or special characteristics of its own, yet these characteristics must ultimately work toward the fulfillment of the conventional form."[110] The stories must contain some new elements, maybe even disappoint the expectations with respect to certain points, but they must ultimately revert to the formula. By mixing different formulas, *Star Wars* and *Harry Potter* seem to achieve part of their unique appeal. Both stories also, as was mentioned during the discussion of Derrida, try to break out of their structural corset at times and return to it, a trait that possibly contributes to their popularity, too. The last quoted statement of Cawelti's also ties in with the ambiguity of Lévi-Strauss's view of myth. The structural approach to myth celebrates structurality as a means of ordering a complex world and providing direction for people, but at the same time it is conscious of the limitations structures impose. Similarly, the quote from Cawelti shows how formulaic stories are ultimately trapped within their own structurality. This structurality is positive as it provides enjoyment and escape for people but it is

---

108   Cawelti 6.
109   Cawelti 6.
110   Cawelti 10.

also limiting, since people's expectations only allow writers to go beyond the familiar structure to a certain degree but never to shatter it completely. The similarities between the 'structural study of myth' that Lévi-Strauss proposes and John Cawelti's view on formulaic fiction, justify the reading of stories such as *Star Wars* and *Harry Potter* as myths structurally.

By way of Cawelti's formulaic stories and my contention that they are modern myths, myth becomes associated with popular culture. Films and novels such as the ones I will analyse could only rise to their enormous success in today's popular cultural environment because they stir something within people and cater to their various needs of reassurance, enjoyment and escape. Incidentally, some of the proposed readings of items of popular culture such as film or literature, fall in with my theoretical analysis so far. The reading that is relevant for me is proposed by John Fiske in his influential work *Understanding Popular Culture*. Fiske starts by explaining Roland Barthes's notion of 'readerly' and 'writerly' texts, 'readerly' texts being texts which are easy to process and do not require much intellectual exertion on the part of the reader.[111] 'Writerly' texts on the other hand, are avant-garde texts, hard to understand and necessitating a high degree of intellectual involvement in the process of reading.[112] Fiske proposes to add a third category of texts. He suggests that popular texts which would mostly fall under the category of readerly texts, should henceforth be referred to as 'producerly texts.'[113] Reading popular texts, Fiske says, there is always a choice involved between simply reading them for pleasure and not investing much thought, and reading them critically, questioning them and identifying their blanks.[114] The term 'producerly' further suggests that there is a productive element to such a reading. It might open up new ways of looking at texts and generate insights which one would not have thought the texts to contain. It might even effect a creative reaction, as, for instance, the responses to various popular cultural manifestations in the form of fan fiction or filmic parodies show that can be found on the internet. The producerly reading is exactly the reading I will employ for my two primary sources. It is a reading which I believe gives popular texts the attention they deserve and does not dismiss them as unworthy of academic notice from the outset.

The producerly reading also again embodies the ambiguity that was mentioned several times with respect to Lévi-Strauss's view of myth. Tales with mythical structures can simply be viewed as organising and thereby facilitating human existence but they can also be seen as limiting because of the narrowness of their

---

111   Cf. John Fiske, *Understanding Popular Culture* (London: Routledge, 2006) 103.

112   Cf. Fiske *Understanding Popular Culture* 103.

113   Cf. Fiske *Understanding Popular Culture* 103.

114   Cf. Fiske, *Understanding Popular Culture* 104.

structures. In the same way, as Fiske says, popular texts can be read with a view to their dominant, most obvious codes but also with respect to their blanks and their subversive potential. In his article "British Cultural Studies and Television," Fiske summarises this in the following remark about TV programs, which is, however, equally applicable to other forms of popular culture:

The preferred reading theory proposes that TV programs generally prefer a set of meanings that work to maintain the dominant ideologies but that these meanings cannot be imposed, only preferred. Readers whose social situations lead them to reject all or some constructions of the dominant ideology will necessarily bring this social orientation to their reading of the program.[115]

The fundamental ambiguity of popular texts, and I am invoking a very broad notion of text here, which can include film or television programs, seems to be that they contain both preferred and subversive readings. This is also reminiscent of Derrida's notion of deconstruction which he proposes to apply to texts. It will be a challenge to identify both dominant and less dominant strands of meaning in the stories I propose to analyse.

Speaking of reading, it is necessary for me to say a few words about the way in which I will use the terms 'reader' and 'readers' in the course of my thesis. Generally, as was mentioned, I envisage a 'producerly' reader. This notion of the 'producerly,' critical reader is also in accordance with some stances within reader-response criticism, a school of criticism holding that the meanings of texts are not just pre-given or pre-formulated but that they only come into existence in the interplay between text and 'reader.'[116] Meaning does not simply reside in the text but needs to be made by the 'reader.' Wolfgang Iser especially holds that "the reader must act as co-creator of the work by supplying that portion of it which is not written but only implied."[117] This view of the reader ties in with much of what was elaborated upon in this chapter. Jennifer Hammett's stance in particular needs to be mentioned again here. Writing about cinema-audiences, she denies the notion of 'the' spectator as one body and alludes to the diversity and complexity of responses a film can evoke in different members of its audience which then also co-constitute the meaning of the particular film. Cultural 'texts' in all their different

---

115   John Fiske, "British Cultural Studies and Television," *What is Cultural Studies? A Reader*, Ed. John Storey (London: Arnold, 1996) 122.

116   Cf. Jane P. Tompkins, "An Introduction to Reader-Response Criticism," *Reader-Response Criticism: From Formalism to Post-Structuralism*, Ed. Jane P. Tompkins (Baltimore: The Johns Hopkins University Press, 1980) ix-x.

117   Qtd. in Tompkins xv.

manifestations are not autonomous but they are accorded significance by their 'readers.' Neither *Star Wars* nor *Harry Potter*, both of whom I read as cultural texts, would be as popular, if it were not for their millions of 'readers.' The 'readers' of myth are also alluded to by Barthes who focuses on the influential and even manipulative quality of myth. Those 'readers,' he contends, mostly do not separate 'pure' language and its culturally received and seemingly natural associations in their minds. Fiske has a more positive view of the 'reader,' as able to pass beyond the superficial level of what is there on a page to a level of hidden meaning, the text might not consciously wish to convey. Cawelti, though more implicitly than Fiske, has a similar notion of the 'reader' as essential for popular stories. On the one hand he or she is thoroughly familiar with the formulas used in popular stories, which enables a fast and superficial reading and understanding of the texts and makes recognition and therewith identification, enjoyment and escape possible. On the other hand, the 'reader,' Cawelti says, will only enjoy a text if it does not too slavishly follow a formula but adds something new. This posits the 'reader' as critical aesthetic judge. The 'reader' I think of when invoking the term in the course of the thesis is therefore a reader who has power over the text, who is critical and who does not easily fall prey to the simplicity of the familiar structures.

To sum this chapter up, four basic functions of myth can be extricated from the theoretical texts discussed. Firstly, by working with polarities, myth lays bare the structures of human thought. Secondly, it has a practical and didactic function, since it can provide direction for people, helping them address their fears and find a position in an increasingly complex world. This is usually achieved by a reconciliation of opposites such as life and death via a mediator figure. Lévi-Strauss mainly deals with these first two functions in his article on mythical structures. The third function of myth is only implied in his work as well as in that of Joseph Campbell. Myth is meta-language. It exposes the limitations of a closed language system, which cannot transcend binaries and ultimately finds itself in a circle. This problem is made explicit in Roland Barthes's and Jacques Derrida's treatment of the subject, which brings us to the fourth function of myth. The way Roland Barthes sees it, all discourse which has an obvious message and one or several hidden ones, is mythical. The people or institutions behind this sort of discourse frequently use myth to pursue certain aims. Myth is consciously employed to influence or even manipulate a larger mass of people. This makes the fourth function ambivalent at best.

Interestingly, the four functions partly contradict each other and are not easily reconciled. On the one hand myth supposedly exposes the way humans think and on the other it often veils things thereby manipulating people. It can have a *meta-*function but it also plays with the *sub*conscious. Again we seem to be left with binaries, which brings us back to the limitations of the human language system and mind, and the circularity we are ultimately caught in. Myth thus is fundamentally ambiguous.

The angry criticism structuralism, from which this thesis draws its foundations, has evoked, which is certainly justified to a large extend, seems to be very telling to me in one respect. Obviously, the harsh voices against structuralism and its ban from contemporary discourse on the grounds of its being antiquated and obsolete, represent the frustration about the fact that structuralist thinking is still present everywhere and cannot easily be rooted out. It predominantly exists in the parts of our knowledge we do not question and label as common sense. It therefore seems extremely productive to me to excavate the buried approach of structuralism and use it on two contemporary stories which have excited much attention in the course of the last 30 years. I do this with the view of analysing how exactly the binary structures work in these stories and how they manage to 'suppress' other discourses running through them. The popularity of *Star Wars* and *Harry Potter* makes them 'carriers of meaning' for many people. It will be interesting to do a 'producerly reading' and see how the narratives consolidate or question ideologies. The thesis will also finally offer a view on the degree to which the analysed stories can really be called modern myths.

3. The Superstructures of *Star Wars* and *Harry Potter*

3.1 A STRUCTURAL 'STAR'-WARS

Star Wars and *Harry Potter* though completely different stories at first glance, share structural characteristics which are typical of popular film and fiction. This chapter will be dedicated to the comparison of the six *Star Wars* films and seven *Harry Potter* novels on the level of their superstructure, i.e. the ordering principle underlying the complete series. A discussion of *Star Wars* with respect to its superstructure will open this chapter, to be followed by a discussion of the overall construction of *Harry Potter*. Both tales, as will be seen, strongly highlight the conflict between good and evil on a structural plane. The two sides are easy to identify for both moviegoers and readers. The *Star Wars* universe consists of the evil Empire and those fighting it trying to restore justice and equality, while the world of *Harry Potter* mainly consists of characters assisting the return of Lord Voldemort in order to impose an evil regime on the world, and those trying to prevent it. As will be seen, the construction of both tales, (and their storylines) strongly resemble Lévi-Strauss's analysis of binary oppositions in myths. *Star Wars* and *Harry Potter* are distinctly structured around the good-evil dichotomy as well as other binary oppositions closely related to it.[1]

---

[1] Without explicitly speaking of structures Joachim Polzer, too notes that the *Star Wars* movies are not so much about the pictures, the characters or external action as such but rather revolve around themes that resonate with each individual and thus have a universal appeal (cf. Joachim Polzer, "Die Selbstentdeckung der amerikanischen Identität und die Zerschlagung der europäischen Ambivalenz: 20 Jahre STAR WARS," *Weltwunder der Kinematographie: Beiträge zu einer Kulturgeschichte der Film- und Medientechnik* n4 (1997): 47).

There are six *Star Wars* movies, episodes four (*A New Hope*), five (*The Empire Strikes Back*) and six (*Return of the Jedi*), which were already completed in the early 1980s, and the prequel episodes one (*The Phantom Menace*), two (*Attack of the Clones*) and three (*Revenge of the Sith*) of 1999, 2002 and 2005 respectively. The latter contain the story preceding the original episodes, rounding off the cycle. In the first part of this chapter, the six movies are analysed in their chronological order rather than the order of their appearance. The number six has a strong symbolic value. "According to ancient and Neoplatonic systems, [it] is the most perfect number as it is both the sum and the product of its parts."[2] It can be divided equally, and with reference to the movies not only into the three older and the three newer parts, but also into three parts which are dominated by the evil Empire and three that focus on the freedom fighters representing the good principle. This means that already on the level of superstructure the dichotomies mentioned in the introductory part of the chapter are visible.

In episode one, (though the good win the big end-battle), the 'phantom menace' of evil is able to establish itself. This happens in a very subtle way and remains unnoticed by most of the characters. Nevertheless the presence of evil may be felt. The good side has managed to destroy a Sith warrior. The Sith are the upholders of the dark side of the Force, the polar opposite of the Jedi, who only use the light side of the mysterious energy field. Jedi master Yoda remarks, however, that "[always] two there are [sic] … no more… no less. A master and an apprentice."[3] Whereupon Jedi Mace Windu replies: "But which was destroyed, the master or the apprentice?"[4] This dialogue shows that there is a latent threat of evil still looming over the galaxy and a good deal of uncertainty remains despite the good side's victory. This is further emphasised by the camera angle directly after the mentioned dialogue. The camera moves around the faces of the various people attending Jedi master Qui Gon Jinn's funeral and comes to rest in a position where it shows Chancellor Palpatine's face, one side of which is cast in shadows. Lighting is used by the filmmakers to guide the identification of Palpatine as evil. Emphasising the presence of Palpatine in one of the last moments of the film hints at his importance for the propulsion of the story. It later turns out that he is the perpetrator of all evil and will become the Emperor in time. Therefore in episode one, the bad retain the upper hand in the end, albeit in a very subtle way. Palpatine remains undetected and can continue his scheming undisturbed.

---

2   Schimmel 122.

3   *Star Wars: The Phantom Menace* [German version: *Star Wars: Die dunkle Bedrohung*], dir. George Lucas, perf. Liam Neeson, Ewan McGregor, and Natalie Portman, DVD, LucasFilm Ltd., 1999, 2:02:49.

4   *Phantom Menace* 2:02:49.

Episode two ends with a huge victory for the good characters who have been able to turn an evil plan hatched by their enemies to their own advantage. The bad side is weakened, as the clone army the chief evildoers had intended for their own use, is enlisted by the good forces instead. It is clear, however, that the good have only won one battle and that final victory is far away because Count Dooku, one of the perpetrators of evil is able to escape in the end.[5] Generally though, hope is higher than in episode one that the good side may finally be able to destroy evil and restore balance to the Force. Episode three marks the lowest point in the story and the worst defeat of the good ones by the forces of evil. Anakin Skywalker, originally of the good side and a beacon of hope, is seduced by evil, turns into Darth Vader and becomes a powerful enemy who helps to seemingly destroy the Jedi order.[6] The fact that good and evil, and, as will be seen later in this thesis, possibly also mediation, are united in the person of Anakin/Vader, is an interesting variation of Lévi-Strauss's postulations about myth. While the dichotomies and the mediating instance are represented by distinctly separate characters in the material Lévi-Strauss analyses, here they become blurred, because they manifest themselves within one person. This deviation from Lévi-Strauss's 'norm' proves John Cawelti's notion that for formulaic literature to be of any interest and value, it has to renew itself within the limits of its fixed structure.[7] Anakin's fall from grace is

---

5   Cf. *Star Wars: Attack of the Clones* [German version: *Star Wars: Angriff der Klonkrieger*], dir. George Lucas, perf. Ewan McGregor, Natalie Portman, Hayden Christensen, and Christopher Lee, DVD, LucasFilm Ltd. 2002, 2:04:49.

6   Cf. *Star Wars: Revenge of the Sith* [German version: *Star Wars: Die Rache der Sith*], dir. George Lucas, perf. Ewan McGregor, Natalie Portman, Hayden Christensen, and Christopher Lee, DVD, LucasFilm Ltd, 2005, 1:10:08-1:21:38.

7   Cf. Cawelti 10. Deborah O'Keefe discusses the variations of these familiar patterns for fantasy literature at large. (Cf. Deborah O'Keefe, *Readers in Wonderland: The Liberating Worlds of Fantasy Fiction: From Dorothy to Harry Potter* (New York: Continuum, 2003) 167). Cf. also Kate E. Behr's highly illuminating article "'Same-as-Difference': Narrative Transformations and Intersecting Cultures in Harry Potter," *Journal of Narrative Theory* 35.1 (2005): 112-32, in which she discusses not only the transformations of Harry Potter in comparison to other similar stories but also those inherent in the story itself. The Potter-story, she argues, remains flexible because of changes and transformations within the characters and the relationships between them (cf. 117-18). M. Keith Booker confirms Cawelti's stance with respect to *Star Wars*: "All in all, while few specific elements of *Star Wars* may be particularly original, the film is unique in its effective combination of ingredients from so many sources" (M. Keith Booker, *Alternate Americas: Science Fiction Film and American Culture* (Westport: Praeger, 2006) 113).

brought about by chancellor Palpatine who secures his help with false promises. After saving Palpatine by killing Jedi Mace Windu, Anakin completes his transformation and murders all the Jedi at the Jedi temple. Evil dominates the movie and the only spot of hope is the birth of Luke and Leia at the moment of Anakin's final conversion into Darth Vader. The twins are promptly hidden by the good side so that they can grow up in relative peace and face their father and origin when they are ready for it.

Episode four again portrays victory for the good guys. They are able to destroy the evil Empire's Death Star, a lethal weapon of mass destruction, and bring about *A New Hope* for the galaxy.[8] As the movie-title suggests, in episode five, the Empire really does strike back, destroying a rebel base and setting a trap for the escaped rebel leaders. The hero, Luke Skywalker, Darth Vader's son, is nearly killed in his premature attempt at destroying his father. Thus again, the bad side dominates at the end, and the good (Luke Skywalker) is literally left precariously dangling above a bottomless abyss.[9] Although he is physically saved, he is severely shaken by the encounter with his father and the fears about his own (inate?) propensity for evil connected with it. In the last episode, the tide is turned at the very end and what seems to be a lost battle against a technologically almighty Empire, becomes victory because unexpected help turns up at the right moment. The end of the series therefore becomes a triumphant 'return of the Jedi', who had been believed extinct.[10] The basic line-up of the episodes thus illustrates and crystallises the polar opposites which, according to Lévi-Strauss are central to myth.

So far the series has been treated in its chronological order which exhibited an alternation of the good-evil dichotomy. In accordance with Lévi-Strauss's postulated dualisms, groups of two can be formed of movies one and two (evil-good), two and three (good-evil), three and four (evil-good), four and five (good-evil), as well as five and six (evil-good). However, the episodes of *Star Wars* also illustrate Lévi-Strauss's non-linear reading of myth. The anthropologist believes

---

8   Cf. *Star Wars: A New Hope* [German version: *Star Wars: Eine neue Hoffnung*], dir. George Lucas, perf. Mark Hamill, Harrison Ford, Carrie Fisher, and Alec Guinness, [1977], DVD, LucasFilm Ltd, Special Edition 2004, 1:52:20.

9   Cf. *Star Wars: The Empire Strikes Back* [German version: *Star Wars: Das Imperium schlägt zurück*], dir. Irvin Kershner, perf. Mark Hamill, Harrison Ford, Carrie Fisher, and Anthony Daniels, [1980], DVD, LucasFilm Ltd, Special Edition 2004, 1:50:00.

10   Cf: *Star Wars: Return of the Jedi* [German version: *Star Wars: Die Rückkehr der Jedi-Ritter*], dir. Richard Marquand, perf. Mark Hamill, Harrison Ford, Carrie Fisher, and Anthony Daniels, [1983], DVD, LucasFilm Ltd, Special Edition 2004, 1:57:16.

that myth should be read globally "as one complex pattern."[11] The dichotomies in myth are often very intricately and possibly unconsciously established. In this sense not only the good-evil pairings springing from the chronology of *Star Wars* belong together but it is also possible to group the episodes in a less obvious way, which is, however, in agreement with the titles of the single episodes. They reveal a lot more about the story's structure than is apparent at first glance. With the help of the titles, episodes one and four can be clustered together. *The Phantom Menace* and *A New Hope* imply the polar opposites evil and good. Both titles express very vague concepts only. From the title *The Phantom Menace* it is clear that the focus is on evil. A 'menace' denotes something negative and the attribute 'phantom' shows the vague and elusive nature of the threat. Like 'menace', 'hope' is an abstract noun and a concept which is not easy to grasp but it usually connotes something positive. These two form an opposing pair (bad-good) and start the new and the old episodes respectively.[12]

Things are not quite so obvious with the next coupling, namely episodes two and five, *Attack of the Clones* and *The Empire Strikes Back*. Here one can only infer from the content of episode two that the clones are used by the good side to fight the Empire, in which they succeed for the time being. Thus we have a good-bad pair, since of course, as the title suggests the Empire wins in episode five. The third and again quite obvious pairing of that sort can be found with episodes three and six. Since the two clusters before had the structure bad-good and good-bad, it is clear that this last pairing has to have the structure bad-good if one takes into account the happy ending of the series. Episode three is called *The Revenge of the Sith* while the title of episode six is *The Return of the Jedi*. In these titles alone there are two juxtapositions. The more obvious one relates to the Sith and the Jedi, the perpetrators of evil and the maintainers of good. The nouns characterising the actions of the Sith and the Jedi are also juxtaposed. 'Revenge' implies hatred, wrath and it also implies the possibility of atrocities being carried out, whereas 'return' suggests something more peaceful, namely that someone who has been away comes back. The latter noun conveys the idea that the Jedi are tough and not easily exterminated, no matter how terrible the *Revenge of the Sith* may be. It is interesting that at some point during the filming, episode six was titled *The Revenge of the*

---

11   Lévi-Strauss 122.

12   Anne Lancashire also comments on the structural interrelations between the Star Wars movies and especially compares *The Phantom Menace* and *A New Hope* which she says, effectively mirror each other structurally. However, while *A New Hope* "has a more comic, positive, and straightforward plot," *The Phantom Menace* is much darker (Anne Lancashire, "*The Phantom Menace*: Repetition, Variation, Integration," *Film Criticism* 24 (2000): 26).

Jedi.[13] It quickly became obvious, however, that revenge was a concept unfitting for a Jedi, which is also exemplified by the fact that Anakin Skywalker loses his status as a Jedi as soon as he decides for the evil side and commits murder. The Jedi are not active agents of evil (revenge), they rather react to the challenges they are faced with. Thus they merely 'return' which is actually a more powerful concept than 'revenge' because it shows that good has survived despite contrary assumptions. Obviously, the concept of 'return' also rounds off the story, because it implies that an original state is restored.

These structural features of *Star Wars* can be aptly visualised with the help of the geometrical figure of the hexagram. It consists of two triangles, one pointing upward, the other downward. Both are intertwined so that none dominates the other. According to Annemarie Schimmel "[the] hexagram could be interpreted in terms of polarities."[14] Therefore it is used here to symbolise the structural relationship between good and evil. The upwards pointing triangle reflects the positive and constructive while the downward triangle represents the negative, destructive aspects[15] of the *Star Wars* universe. The hexagram perfectly symbolises all the patterns of the movies' superstructure as described before. The triangles combine the three movies which are dominated by the good (upwards pointing) and the three films featuring evil victorious (downwards pointing), with the happily-ending episode six on top and its opposite movie three, containing the fall from grace of Anakin Skywalker and his betrayal of the Jedi as the lowest point. It furthermore parallels the contrasting episodes one and four, two and five as well as three and six. If one only considers the hexagram's points, it visualises the everlasting alternation between good and evil, hinted at in the movies' Manichean setup.[16]

---

13   Cf. Bouzereau 233-34.

14   Schimmel 126.

15   Cf. also Schimmel 126.

16   Manichaeism is a religion based on a dualism of good and evil. Good and evil clash as the realm of light is attacked by the forces of darkness. The realm of light tries to shift the fight to the realm of darkness by sending creatures of light to the land of darkness who are then eaten by monsters. By eating the good creatures, however, the monsters take up a grain of light and goodness, so that good and evil become mixed. Metaphorically, human beings are identified as the monsters, driven away from true knowledge of themselves and the light by their 'evil' physical drives. They may, however, be called back to the light if they strive to separate light from darkness in their life on earth, which practically means denying their physicality. Eventually, so Manicheans believed, there would be a complete return to the good state with people shedding their dark side altogether (cf. Sigfried G. Richter, "Gnosis und Manichäismus in Ägypten: Eine kleine Einführung," Arbeitsstelle für Manichäismusforschung,

Finally, the geometrical figure, if drawn precisely, displays a huge overlap of both triangles. Taken symbolically and in terms of the good-evil dichotomy, this means that there is an area where good and evil mix and where the clear-cut distinctions between the two separate entities become severely blurred. The grey area of the hexagram calls attention to Lévi-Strauss's assertion that myth is an attempt at mediation between seemingly irreconcilable opposites. It thus highlights myth's function of helping people find and come to terms with their position in life. People tend to organise the world into binary oppositions in order to reduce the complexity of life; however, in most cases it is not quite as simple as that. Myth in Lévi-Strauss's analysis, portrays human attempts at structuring as well as the final acceptance of elements that cannot be clearly attributed to one side. Furthermore, the grey area visualises the ambiguity of myth as on the one hand veiling certain discourses by focusing on binary oppositions (the outgrowths of good and evil in the points of the star), and on the other hand drawing attention to its own structures and the fact that there is something more than just extremes (the middle ground).

Institut für Ägyptologie und Koptologie, Westfälische Wilhelms-Universität Münster, 2009, n.pag., 15 Aug. 2012 <http://www.uni-muenster.de/IAEK/forschen/kop/mani/>). Richter's explanations about Manichaeism show how the victory over the forces of evil is rather a victory effected within humans, not one that completely and ultimately defeats evil. The implication is that people can always fall prey to evil again, something that is also hinted at in both of the stories analysed here. The allusions to Manichaeism are stronger in *Star Wars*, however, with its focus on the light and the dark side of the Force which can also compete in one person.

Fig. 1: The structural hexagram for Star Wars

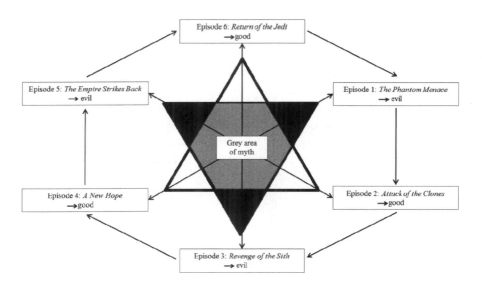

As a symbol of the superstructure of *Star Wars*, the hexagram is more fitting than the *cosmogonic cycle* which, according to Joseph Campbell visualises the eternal alternations between different states such as waking and sleeping, day and night, life and death, governing the cosmos and all life on it.[17] Both the cycle and the hexagram represent the mythical balance between different and even oppositional states. They draw attention to the fact that neither the good nor the evil state in the stories is fixed and eternal. As soon as the final point of extreme good in the *Star Wars* movies is reached, it is inevitable that a bad stage will follow in the logic of the cyclicality of Joseph Campbell's cosmogony. In fact, it is easily possible to imagine sequels to the galactic tales that deal with the resurgence of evil forces.[18]

---

17   Cf. Campbell *The Hero* 266. For an analysis of the relationship between George Lucas and Joseph Campbell and the way some of Campbell's ideas about myth were integrated in Lucas's work cf. for instance John Shelton Lawrence, "Joseph Campbell, George Lucas, and the Monomyth," *Finding the Force of the Star Wars Franchise: Fans, Merchandise, and Critics*, Ed. Matthew Wilhelm Kapell and John Shelton Lawrence (New York: Peter Lang, 2006) 21-33. Cf. also Hanson and Kay who use Campbell to analyse the movies and similarly conclude that "[t]he Cosmogonic Cycle is therefore an underlying theme for all six Star Wars films" (50).

18   This is something that has even been done, as there are countless novels by various authors inspired by the original *Star Wars* movies but also extending and going beyond them.

While with the cycle, the passage from one state to another is rather seamless and the circularity is emphasised, the hexagram visualises mythical ambiguity by stressing both circularity (Campbell) and structural closure (Lévi-Strauss). The circularity I am referring to here is not so much overtly present on the level of the story but rather implied by the structure, following Manichean principles (see also footnote 16). The fact that the saga ends with the victory-celebrations of the good side shows that the dominant reading privileges the good forces but it is not a sufficient criterion to dismiss the impression of structural openness and circularity. After all, the festivities also repeat themselves as we see the good side celebrate at the end of *The Phantom Menace* and *A New Hope*, too. Furthermore, other critics such as Christopher M. Brown, Konraad Kuiper and Anne Lancashire also perceive a sense of openness and possible continuation in the story.[19] The hexagram thus symbolises mythical circularity, shows Lévi-Strauss's mythical binaries as operative in *Star Wars* and stresses the preference of the first part of the dichotomies, in this case the good principle.[20] This visualises the ordering function

---

19   Christopher M. Brown also perceives the structural ambiguity of the *Star Wars* saga, hinting at the closure of the 'fairy-tale ending' while at the same time intimating that the cycle of alternating periods of good and evil might start again any time. (Cf. Christopher M. Brown, "'A Wretched Hive of Scum and Villainy': Star Wars and the Problem of Evil," *Star Wars and Philosophy: More Powerful than You Can Possibly Imagine*, Ed. Kevin S. Decker and Jason T. Eberl (Chicago: Open Court, 2005) 78-79). Koenraad Kuiper who interprets *Star Wars* as ideologically supporting imperial enterprises in the real world also implicitly comments on the structural openness of the movies: "A further consequence of the complex view of imperial ethics is that the enemy is redeemable. The enemy is not totally doomed since it [sic] has either given way to the forces of evil and can be converted to good; or is merely chaotic and can thus be turned to good by coming under the influence of the empire. Thus the battle against evil is never permanently won since the forces of evil can never be defeated" (Koenraad Kuiper, "*Star Wars*: An Imperial Myth," *Journal of Popular Culture* 21.4 (1988): 83). Thus it seems that some of the myths in the sense of Barthes which are generated or supported by popular stories only function with a certain narrative openness. Imperialism, for instance, legitimises its workings by assuming an evil which can never be fully conquered. Anne Lancashire, too offers a similar view when she says: "And there is also, with this second [prequel] trilogy focusing far more than the first on politics, a strong sense as well of repeating social and political patterns in human history more generally" (27).

20   Hal Colebatch, too implicitly refers to the ambiguity of *Star Wars* when he says that "[the] 'happy [ending]' promise[s] no everlasting Utopias" (Hal Colebatch, *Return of*

of structure but also, by featuring 'good' as the highest point, draws attention to the ways in which structures can be one-sided, limiting and prejudiced. The preference of good over evil is highly telling, because it demonstrates the structuralist prejudice of always favouring the first part of the binary opposition, which Jacques Derrida draws attention to.[21] The very set-up of *Star Wars's* superstructure thus makes it possible, even likely, that the tales are also prejudiced with respect to other binaries, an assertion that is examined in chapters six to eight. The hexagram embodies the contradictions inherent in myth as well as the structuralist and poststructuralist aims of this thesis: to thoroughly analyse the structurality of *Star Wars* and *Harry Potter* but also to look at its ideological implications.[22]

3.2 DICHOTOMISED FRAMES: *HARRY POTTER*

While the *Star Wars* series has six episodes, *Harry Potter* has seven. The significance of the number six, as a number of perfect balance, was already demonstrated with respect to *Star Wars*. From the mere fact that the *Harry Potter* series consists of seven books, one can deduce that potential dualities will not be as balanced as they are on the structural surface of *Star Wars*. According to Annemarie Schimmel, the number seven has both positive and negative connotations. The seven pillars of wisdom and the seven gifts of the Holy Spirit are instances of a positive valuation.[23] On the negative side, however, Christian faith knows seven deadly sins and the number is often associated with evil magical practices.[24] Rather neutrally, seven is frequently connected to certain stages in life. The seventh year is said to put a marriage to the test, for instance, and human

---

the Heroes: The Lord of the Rings, Star Wars and Contemporary Culture (n.p.: Australian Institute for Public Policy, 1990) 13).

21   Cf. Derrida *Positions* 41.

22   Christian Wessely, too draws up a structural visualisation of the original *Star Wars* trilogy emphasising the films' circularity. The three movies are represented by cycles surrounded by what he calls the "Metazyklus," (metacycle). (Christian Wessely, *Von Star Wars, Ultima und Doom: Mythologisch verschleierte Gewaltmechanismen im kommerziellen Film und in Computerrollenspielen* (Frankfurt a.M.: Peter Lang, 1997) 97). However, this attempt at structuring merely serves as an excursus for him and is thus only briefly discussed. Furthermore, as I have tried to show, I believe the star to be a more fitting symbol of the movies' superstructure and the single instalments than the circle, because it encompasses both openness and closure.

23   Cf. Schimmel 132, 135.

24   Cf. Schimmel 135, 131.

development is believed to occur in steps of seven years.[25] It is a number expressing a certain universality[26] and it is a rather powerful number, since connected to the astral deities Sun, Moon, Mars, Mercury, Jupiter, Venus and Saturn.[27] In mythologically-based stories, heroes often have to walk a sevenfold path or ascend through seven planetary spheres and their travel or quest might last for seven days or seven years.[28] The latter is the case in *Harry Potter*. The novels describe the hero's seven formative years at Hogwarts School of Witchcraft and Wizardry and the trials and adventures he lives through in the process of growing up. This process begins with his initiation into the wizarding world in book one. It includes his adolescent years in which he has to find out what kind of a person he wants to be, and ends with the victory over his archenemy and a definite decision for a particular kind of life and moral attitude in book seven. On the level of superstructure, there are similarities and differences between the *Star Wars* movies and the *Harry Potter* novels. The superstructure of the movies, as shown, displays an alternation of good and evil, with the two sides taking turns at defeating the respective other. In *Harry Potter* this alternating structure is not as clear. Usually, Harry wins the day at the end of the novels, though his victories become punctured as the dark side gradually rises to power. So what can be perceived is an intensification of evil and the growing resistance against it.[29]

Coupled with the slow rise of evil is a pairing similar, yet different to the one identified for *Star Wars*. In *Harry Potter*, both parts of the doublet are either predominantly focused on good or on evil while in *Star Wars* the pairs are constituted of opposites. The pairs of novels in the *Harry Potter* series form a frame-like structure, with the frames alternating between a focus on the good and the evil much like the episodes of *Star Wars*. Novels one and seven, two and six, and three and five belong closely together and book four marks the climax as the one filling the middle position.[30] In the first novel, Harry is introduced and his mysterious past is hinted at. The boy is confronted with his heritage by seeing his

---

25   Cf. Schimmel 129.

26   Cf. Schimmel 137.

27   Cf. Schimmel 142.

28   Cf. Schimmel 145-46.

29   Cf. also Gertrud Maria Rösch, "Wächst das Rettende Auch?: Die Konzeptionalisierung und Visualisierung des Bösen in den Filmen Harry Potter (2001ff.) und Men in Black (1997 / 2002)," *Der Fantastische Film: Geschichte und Funktion in der Mediengesellschaft*, Ed. Oliver Jahraus and Stefan Neuhaus (Würzburg: Königshausen & Neumann, 2005) 196.

30   Julia Boll comments on the 'mise en abyme' composition of the heptalogy but does not explain it (cf. 95).

dead parents in an enchanted mirror[31] and by having to face his enemy Voldemort for the first time.[32] Though one also becomes acquainted with the villain, the novel can nevertheless be subsumed under the heading 'Harry,' or 'the good.' Many of the important themes and secrets of the tale are established in novel one and taken up again or solved in novel seven.[33] Thus books one and seven form the first and most important narrative frame and they predominantly deal with Harry. The connection between the two novels and their focus on Harry becomes most apparent in the establishment of the themes of love and purity. Rita Singer, writing about psychomachia in *Harry Potter* and only alluding to the first frame puts it thus: "*Deathly Hallows* mirrors the theme of the first novel because the central virtue, charity, is constructed as the immaterial counterpart to largesse, the virtue presented in *Philosopher's Stone*. Charity and largesse serve as a frame for Harry's entire moral development."[34] The story begins with the sacrifice of Lily Potter, Harry's mother, who throws herself in front of her son when Voldemort casts the killing curse and thereby ensures Harry's survival.[35] This sacrifice is repeated by Harry in book seven when he lets Voldemort kill him without trying to defend himself so that no further harm comes to his friends.[36] Harry is thus able to impart the love he has been blessed with to his friends in return, which is an important factor in the destruction of the Dark Lord.

The other important factor has to do with the second fundamental theme of novels one and seven, innocence and purity of soul. In novel one, Harry shows that he is an extraordinary person when he manages to obtain the Philosopher's Stone

---

31   Cf. J.K. Rowling, *Harry Potter and the Philosopher's Stone* (London: Bloomsbury, 1997) 225-26.

32   Cf. Rowling *Stone* 309-18.

33   Kathleen McEvoy, too analyses the connection between the single books in the series. She does so with the intention of disproving Harold Bloom's claim that the books are "not well written" (Harold Bloom, "Can 35 Million Book Buyers be Wrong? Yes.," *Wall Street Journal* 7 Nov. 2000, 14 June 2011 <http://1xn.org/softspeakers/PDFs/bloom.pdf>). However, while rather extensively commenting on Rowling's "plant and pay off" strategy, McEvoy does not see the frame-like structure that can be generated from it. (Kathleen McEvoy, "Aesthetic Organization: The Structural Beauty of J.K. Rowling's *Harry Potter* Series," *Topic: A Journal of the Liberal Arts* 54 (2004): 15).

34   Rita Singer, "Harry Potter and the Battle for the Soul: The Revival of the Psychomachia in Secular Fiction," *Heroism in the Harry Potter Series*, Ed. Katrin Berndt and Lena Steveker (Farnham: Ashgate, 2011) 36-37.

35   Cf. Rowling *Stone* 316, 321-22.

36   Cf. J.K. Rowling, *Harry Potter and the Deathly Hallows* (London: Bloomsbury, 2007) 563-64.

despite the enchantments Dumbledore has cast to ensure its safety from Voldemort. Harry, who only thinks of preventing Voldemort from returning to power and keeping others safe from the evil wizard, does not seek any gain for himself by taking it. This is what makes him special and sets him apart from Voldemort and his power-hungry henchmen. The quest for the Philosopher's Stone foreshadows the much more important one for three magical objects, the Deathly Hallows in book seven. When found and united, the powerful regalia of Death help Harry win the final battle against Voldemort. Dumbledore makes clear just how important it is to be entirely altruistic in the search for the Hallows.

Maybe a man in a million could unite the Hallows, Harry. I was fit only to possess the meanest of them, the least extraordinary. I was fit to own the Elder Wand, and not to boast of it, and not to kill with it. I was permitted to tame and to use it. because I took it, not for gain, but to save others from it. But the [Invisibility] Cloak, I took out of vain curiosity, and so it could never have worked for me as it works for you, its true owner. The [Resurrection] stone I would have used in an attempt to drag back those who are at peace, rather than to enable my self-sacrifice, as you did. You are the worthy possessor of the Hallows.[37]

The third Hallow, Harry's Invisibility Cloak, is introduced early on in book one. However, at that time the readers do not know its true impact. The introduction of the Cloak in book one sets the scene for the introduction of the Hallows and is another link between the two books. A further connection between them is Dumbledore's past. On Harry's first ever journey to school it is hinted at in passing when Harry and his new friend Ron find Dumbledore on one of the cards that come with Chocolate Frogs, a sweet from the wizarding world.[38] A substantial part of the headmaster's history will be discovered and elaborately treated in book seven after his death.

The second frame consists of *Harry Potter* two and six. The two novels mirror each other in very striking ways, the second foreshadowing many of the sixth's incidents. In contrast to frame one which focuses on Harry, frame two foregrounds Voldemort and his secrets. Novel two introduces Voldemort's secret of immortality, though the readers only learn in novel six that the Dark Lord's diary, which Harry destroys in book two, is one of several Horcruxes which Voldemort has created to ensure his continued existence.[39] Thus the first and the second frame contain the most important secrets of the series, the Hallows and the Horcruxes. Both are

---

37   Rowling *Hallows* 576-77.

38   Cf. Rowling *Stone* 114.

39   Cf. J.K. Rowling, *Harry Potter and the Half-Blood Prince* (London: Bloomsbury, 2005) 467-68.

established in the same way, introduced and hinted at in novels one and two and explained and finally given a name in novels six and seven. The two novels of the second frame further contain important memories, mirroring and opposing each other. The memory in novel two is the one of the young Voldemort coming from the Horcrux diary. It is a memory that can act of its own accord and its actions are highly destructive.[40] In novel six, the memory of Potions Master Horace Slughorn, telling the student Voldemort how Horcruxes are made, helps Dumbledore and Harry find conclusive proof of Voldemort's secret.[41] It is thus constructive as it leads further to the heart of the mystery and to a knowledge of how to destroy the dark wizard. Another aspect that links novels two and four and establishes them yet more firmly as the second frame of the narrative is the fact that novel two foreshadows the irrevocable absence of Dumbledore through his death at the end of novel six. In book two, the school is afflicted by a Basilisk roaming the corridors and petrifying everyone who gets into contact with its eyes.[42] Dumbledore's apparent inability to account for the petrifaction of students, leads to the school governors suspending him from Hogwarts.[43] The characters thus get a first inkling of what school life without Dumbledore will be like. Eventually they will lose the headmaster for good in book six. A further link between the two novels is the introduction of Ginny Weasley to the story in book two. Harry has to save her from Voldemort.[44] This anticipates their closer relationship in book six when Harry finally starts requiting the love Ginny has felt for him from the start.[45] Book two also introduces the giant spider Aragog, one of Hagrid's monster friends.[46] This same Aragog dies in novel six, foreshadowing the more tragic death of Albus Dumbledore. Both appearances of the spider also coincide with important discoveries. In novel two Harry finds out that Hagrid has been falsely accused by the memory of Tom Riddle, and in book six he is able to coax the Horcrux-memory from Horace Slughorn.

The novels making up the third frame, three and five, are also connected through several elements and themes. One is the introduction of the inconsistencies and the scheming within the Ministry of Magic which can be exemplified by the politicians' reaction to Harry performing underage magic while at his relatives'

---

40   Cf. J.K. Rowling, *Harry Potter and the Chamber of Secrets* (London: Bloomsbury, 1998) 330-46.

41   Cf. Rowling *Prince* 462-70.

42   Cf. Rowling *Chamber* 312.

43   Cf. Rowling *Chamber* 283.

44   Cf. Rowling *Chamber* 330-48.

45   Cf. Rowling *Prince* 499.

46   Cf. Rowling *Chamber* 298-301.

home on two separate occasions in novels three and five. In novel three, Harry is not punished for inflating his aunt in anger.[47] While he really loses his temper on this occasion, Harry performs under-age magic again at the beginning of novel five to save himself and his cousin from Dementors.[48] Though it is permissible by wizarding law for under-age wizards to do magic in life-threatening situations, Harry is injustly suspended from school and has to attend a hearing this time.[49] The ministry's treatment of Harry's godfather Sirius, who is introduced in novel three and dies in novel five, thus forming another connection between the two novels, also is unfair. Sirius is still a fugitive at the end of novel three and his innocence is only known to Dumbledore and Harry and his friends.[50] In novel five, the ministry's irresponsibility and its final susceptibility to evil is carried to extremes in the figure of Dolores Umbridge, a ministry official who spies on the school and terrorises teachers and students alike.[51]

The other very important theme introduced in novel three and taken up in book five is the study of Divination and false and true prophecies. In book three, Harry and his friends take their first Divination lessons with a seemingly inapt teacher.[52] However, the readers get an inkling that there might be real prophecies after all when at the end of the novel Divination Professor Trelawney falls into a trance and tells Harry that the Dark Lord will return.[53] When Harry tells Professor Dumbledore about the prediction and asks him whether Professor Trelawney was genuine, Dumbledore says: "Do you know, Harry, I think she might have been. (...) Who'd have thought it? That brings her total of real predictions up to two."[54] Though nothing more is said about the second true prediction of hers, this statement sets the stage for it. True to a maxim that usually holds for short stories and detective fiction, most small details mentioned in the course of the *Harry Potter* novels become important at a later time and are taken up again. In book five, Harry and the readers find out about this second true prediction Professor Trelawney made concerning Harry and Voldemort which says that one has to kill the other.[55]

---

47   Cf. J.K. Rowling, *Harry Potter and the Prisoner of Azkaban* (London: Bloomsbury, 1999) 53-54.

48   Cf. J.K. Rowling, *Harry Potter and the Order of the Phoenix* (London: Bloomsbury, 2003) 21-22.

49   Cf. Rowling *Order* 29-30.

50   Cf. Rowling *Azkaban* 419-23.

51   Cf. Rowling *Order* 193.

52   Cf. Rowling *Azkaban* 112-19.

53   Cf. Rowling *Azkaban* 349-50.

54   Rowling *Azkaban* 458.

55   Cf. Rowling *Order* 741.

Prophecies, interestingly, play an integral part in both *Star Wars* and *Harry Potter*, emphasising the stories' preoccupation with the binary of free will and determination. The relevance of the prophecies for both tales and the different ways in which Lucas and Rowling treat them, will be analysed in the chapters dealing with the protagonists. The frame-like structure of the *Harry Potter* novels, however, gives us a hint already at Rowling's preferences with respect to the dichotomy. The first two frames deal with the existential choices of Harry and Voldemort, the former decides to sacrifice himself for his friends and the good, while the latter chooses to prolong his life with the help of the evil Horcruxes. As it is only the third frame which introduces the theme of prophecy and determination by fate, a frame that is contained within the first and second, the superstructure allows the assumption that free choice is valued more highly than the belief in destiny.

In the frame-like superstructure of the *Harry Potter* series, book four has a special position. *Harry Potter and the Goblet of Fire* links all the frames, containing elements and taking up narrative strands from its predecessors as well as introducing new ones to be expounded in its follow-ups. It brings novels one and seven even more closely together because it links Harry's first, unwitting defeat of the Dark Lord as a baby to his final and hard-fought victory over him in the duel after Voldemort's resurrection. The fight in book four foreshadows the one in novel seven but also shows that Harry is not strong enough yet to completely overcome the villain. The story of book four thus mediates between a Harry who is innocent and largely ignorant of the goings on in the wizarding world and a Harry who has grown up and learns to rely on himself and his own decisions. Book four also connects novels two and six. In all three of them the readers are exposed to important information relating to Voldemort's past, and the secret of his immortality is gradually revealed. In book two Voldemort appears as a memory out of an old diary and his power to inflict pain on others (Ginny Weasley and the victims of the Basilisk) is established. Novel four makes it genuinely clear to Harry for the first time what Voldemort is really capable of when he kills Harry's fellow student Cedric Diggory. This, however, is only the prelude to worse deeds to come in novels six and seven. So again, book four has a mediating function. It introduces Harry and the readers to the fact that Voldemort is capable of murder and prepares them for more atrocities in the subsequent books. With the proper return of Lord Voldemort, *Harry Potter and the Goblet of Fire* marks a climax or turning point in the series. It is interesting that the novel brings the powers of Harry and Voldemort together. In the graphic scene in which their wands connect, their similarities rather than their differences are made obvious. Good and evil (magic used defensively: Harry tries to disarm Voldemort, and magic used to inflict pain and assert power: Voldemort attempts to kill Harry) come together on an equal footing and produce something very beautiful. A fine-spun golden web encloses Voldemort and Harry and the sound of Phoenix song can be heard.[56] Novel four of *Harry Potter* is thus partly comparable to the grey area of the *Star Wars* hexagram. It takes up the mediating function Lévi-Strauss sees as so essential to myth as it features this collision and short-term equality of binaries.

It is interesting that both *Star Wars* and *Harry Potter* balance good and evil at least part of the time, *Star Wars* in the equal share good and evil is assigned in the line-up of the story and *Harry Potter* in this concrete scene from novel four. The dominant readings of both, however, finally morally favour the good, *Star Wars* by ending with victory for the good side and *Harry Potter* by letting Harry's will power dominate Voldemort's in the duel scenes of books four as well as seven. The bias in favour of good also becomes apparent in the fact that the frame associated with Harry and the Hallows embraces all the others and the central novel. The frame-like structure suggests that Harry and his way of vanquishing his antagonist with the help of the Hallows is preferred over Voldemort and his attempts at reaching immortality. This is of course a clear similarity to the superstructure of *Star Wars*, which though more balanced because of the series' six episodes, also favours the good side in the end. It indicates that in *Harry Potter*, too the structuralist bias of preferring one side of a binary opposition to the other is existent. It seems that it is very hard for people to bear the equality between the two parts of dualities, especially good and evil for very long.

Apart from the three frames and the central novel four, there is one further dimension to the superstructure of *Harry Potter*. While it illustrates the alternations in focus between Harry (the principle of good) and Voldemort (the principle of evil), it also leaves room for the inclusion of what I will call 'mythical prehistory' and 'continuation' to the actual story. In book one the readers learn in passing that Dumbledore defeated a dangerous dark wizard when he was younger.[57] Finally though, the headmaster dies in the course of the war against Voldemort. Thus an obvious parallel is established between Dumbledore and Harry. Travis Prinzi holds that by the end of book six, Harry "has taken his place as the next great hero of the Wizarding World."[58] However, although Harry defeats Voldemort and lives that does not mean that there will not be a new dark wizard sometime, whom Harry cannot match and who will require another hero to vanquish him.

There is even a hint at this kind of continuation of the cycle at the end of *Harry Potter and the Deathly Hallows*. Remus Lupin, one of Harry's father's oldest

---

56   Cf. J.K. Rowling, *Harry Potter and the Goblet of Fire* (London: Bloomsbury, 2000) 575-80.

57   Cf. Rowling *Stone* 114.

58   Prinzi 142.

friends and a friend and mentor to Harry, dies in the course of the final battle against Voldemort, together with his wife Tonks. However, the two had a child before. Little Teddy Lupin finds himself in almost exactly the same situation at the end of book seven as little Harry Potter at the beginning of book one. The parents of both died fighting Voldemort, thus both find themselves in one of the typical initial situations of a hero. Harry is also made Teddy's godfather by Lupin before his death. This mirrors the situation between Harry and Sirius. The connection is even evoked directly when Harry, before leaving for an especially dangerous enterprise, muses that "[he seems] set on a course to become just as reckless a godfather to Teddy Lupin as Sirius Black had been to him."[59] The notable difference is of course that Harry does not have a chance to live with his godfather Sirius because Sirius also loses his life in the fight against evil. Teddy Lupin, it is intimated in the epilogue to book seven, is a regular guest in the house of his godfather Harry and well loved by the whole family.[60]

Interestingly, Teddy Lupin's story is not only comparable to Harry's, but also to Neville Longbottom's, one of Harry's friends, and the only other boy to whom the prophecy Harry fulfilled could also have alluded.[61] Neville, like Harry, has suffered at the hands of Voldemort. His parents were tortured into insanity by the Dark Lord's supporters and as a result Neville grew up with his grandmother.[62] Teddy Lupin is also destined to be raised by his grandmother as both his parents and his grandfather die at the hands of Voldemort and his supporters. The mythical prehistory and -continuation indicate a Campbellian mythical circularity to the story of Harry Potter. Thus, similar to *Star Wars*, *Harry Potter* is ambiguous: at once circular and structurally closed, favouring the good side of the binary opposition between good and evil. However, the circularity is much less pronounced in *Harry Potter* than in *Star Wars*. The preferrence of good over evil is made more apparent structurally in the novels because of the unequal number of volumes as well as the important first frame focusing on Harry and his beneficial powers and embracing all the other novels.[63] The frame-like structure of the series with its centre, novel four as well as the possibility of pre-history and continuation can be visualised as follows:

---

59   Rowling *Hallows* 418.

60   Cf. Rowling *Hallows* 605.

61   Cf. Rowling *Order* 742.

62   Cf. Rowling *Goblet* 523.

63   John Killinger, too perceives circularity in the *Harry Potter* novels. However, he does not offer any proof of this cyclicality and fails to see that the stories are both closed and open at the same time. (Cf. John Killinger, *The Life, Death, and Resurrection of Harry Potter* (Macon: Mercer University Press, 2009) 65).

Fig. 2 The frame-like structure of Harry Potter

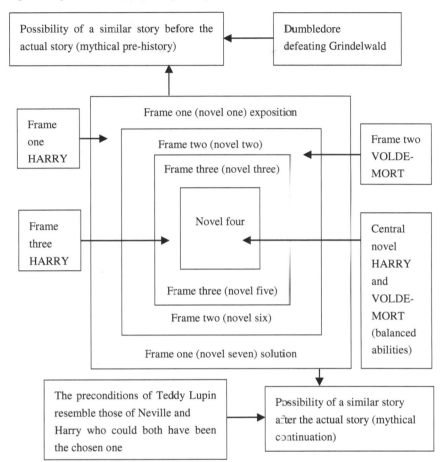

What becomes apparent from looking at the superstructures of *Star Wars* and *Harry Potter*, is that both stories deal with one fundamental binary, good versus evil. This proves the mythical nature of both tales, since myth, according to Claude Lévi-Strauss always deals with the negotiation between oppositions.[64] The superstructures also suggest that both stories contain a further function Lévi-Strauss assigns to myth, namely that myth not only sets up binary oppositions but also works towards a balance between them. For *Star Wars* this became visible in the symbol of the hexagram which shows a significant overlap of the two triangles standing for the three movies dominated by good and by evil respectively. The grey

---

64   Cf. Lévi-Strauss 130.

area which unites and combines good and evil is implicit only in the superstructure of the movies. The concrete instances of mediation will be discovered by the close analysis of the episodes and characters. For *Harry Potter* the mediating function of myth is already more apparent on the level of superstructure. In the frame-like way the narrative is set up, novel four sticks out because it is not directly part of any frame and presents the reader with however brief a spell of equality between the good and the evil principle. However, there are also subtle differences between *Star Wars* and *Harry Potter* on the structural level. *Star Wars*, though ending on the good principle, seems to be more open than *Harry Potter* as it allots an equal number of films to the depiction of good and evil and shows an alternation of both principles in the line-up of the movies. The star-like superstructure is reminiscent of Joseph Campbell's *cosmogonic cycle*.[65] The cycle can be seen as standing for the gyration typical of many processes in history, (human) life and even the cosmos and basically shows that things go on without end. This is also represented within the *Star Wars* hexagram with its alternating points of good and evil. Like the circle, the hexagram is closed and once orbited, the round can begin anew.

The *Harry Potter* series has an unequal number of instalments, four of which give prominence to Harry, the principle of good and only three to Voldemort, the principle of evil. Furthermore, the first narrative frame, made up of books one and seven and including all other novels focuses on Harry. Evil is thus embedded within good and good therefore the a priori state. Unlike *Star Wars* the good-evil dichotomy finally remains unbalanced in favour of the good in *Harry Potter*. The story does plant certain hints at mythical circularity represented by the possibility of mythical pre-history and -continuation mentioned before. Still, however, it is suggested that there always is and probably always will be good to vanquish evil. This is not only made amply clear by Harry's own experience but also by that of Dumbledore who defeated dark wizard Grindelwald in his youth. If another villain were to come, it is implied that another hero is probably already in the making to stand up to him. The character who serves as an example is Teddy Lupin, but it could also be any other. Ideologically, what is conveyed here is that there will always be people fighting evil, a very comforting message which also supports what John Cawelti says about the functions of formulaic literature. It seeks to provide escape and let people make certain experiences within the secure framework of a story instead of in real life.[66] Erin Munro argues that in *Harry Potter* this mainly works via the evocation of traditions and values within the framework of which the characters act. These traditions structure the characters'

---

65   Cf. Campbell *The Hero* 266.

66   Cf. Cawelti 6.

everyday lives and presuppose and thereby facilitate certain (moral) choices.[67] This creates the illusion of easy choices for the reader, too. The good ending also has a reassuring function and appeals to the good in all of us.

Both tales end with a victory for the good and are thus closed. However, as discussed above, they are also circular and open to possible continuation. The binaries of openness and closure exist side by side, more balanced in *Star Wars* than in *Harry Potter*, but definitely there in both tales. In this, the two stories reveal the fundamental ambiguity of myth, and thereby myth's own mediating function.[68] This interpretation runs counter to Martin Hall's analysis. Hall, who discusses myth and "the theory of international relations called Realism" in *Harry Potter*, also identifies two different movements within fantasy and science fiction as well as by extension in human history.[69] The "time's arrow" approach is a closed one. "In this type of story good defeats evil in the end."[70] In the "time's cycle" understanding "[e]vil is eternal and the terrors of history [are] intolerable since there is no meaning to them."[71] Hall goes on to say that "[i]n fantasy literature, the time's cycle understanding is supreme, whereas science fiction typically makes use of the time's arrow emplotment."[72] If one takes *Star Wars* to be science fiction and *Harry Potter* to be fantasy literature, Hall's premises seem to be reversed. As was mentioned,

---

67   Cf. Erin Munro, "Myth and Magic in the *Harry Potter* Series," *Xchanges* 2.1 (2002): n.pag. 7 Jul 2011 <http://infohost.nmt.edu/~xchanges/old_xchanges/xchanges/2.1/munro.html>.

68   To my knowledge, Edmund M. Kern is the only critic who has so far explicitly referred to the ambiguity respecting several themes in *Harry Potter*. (Others have only implied it.) However, in contrast to my approach, which tries to locate ambiguity in the overall construction of the novels and sees it as a purpose of popular fiction per se, Kern gives very specific examples of themes in the Potter stories which are treated equivocally. His four examples are "rule-following versus rule-breaking" (95-96), "emotion versus reason" (96-98), "inherited predisposition versus acquired adaptability" (98-100) and "fate versus free will" (101-102), the latter of which he believes to be subsuming all the other ambiguities. Destiny and free will and their interplay will also be a strong theme in this thesis, but I hope to be able to look at it more closely than Kern and discuss how it is interwoven with the structures of, incidentally not only *Harry Potter* but *Star Wars* as well.

69   Martin Hall, "The Fantasy of Realism, or Mythology as Methodology," *Harry Potter and International Relations*, Ed. Daniel H. Nexon and Iver B. Neumann (Lanham: Rowman & Littlefield, 2006) 177.

70   Hall "The Fantasy of Realism" 184.

71   Hall "The Fantasy of Realism" 184.

72   Hall "The Fantasy of Realism" 184.

Star Wars is structurally more cyclical than *Harry Potter*. Moreover, Hall also neglects to see that many of these kinds of formulaic stories are, to a certain degree, undecided about the 'time's arrow' and 'time's cycle' question.[73] My reading sees this kind of ambiguity as fundamental to the understanding of myth and also the two tales analysed. Binary oppositions must needs remain unresolved but it is the task of myth to make the tension between them as bearable for humankind as possible.

---

73   Christian Wessely similarly perceives the ambiguity of myth with respect to time. "[D]er Mythos ist demnach zeitlos, er ist ewig, aber zugleich durch seine zirkuläre Anlage in sich selbst gebunden, also ständig dem je eigenen Horizont verhaftet, was sich auch in lokaler Geschlossenheit der Mythenkreise zeigt" (69). ("Accordingly, myth is timeless, eternal, but at the same time restricted by its circular structure. Thus it is constantly bound up with its own horizon, something that also shows in the local closure of mythical circles. [my translation]").

4. The Mythical Ambiguity of *Star Wars* and *Harry Potter*

4.1 *STAR WARS'S* EQUIVOCAL MESSAGES

This chapter will present a closer discussion of the mediating and ideological spaces of *Star Wars* and *Harry Potter*. As the last chapter showed, the superstructures of both tales quite clearly mirror the complex interplay of binary oppositions at work in the stories. However, the superstructures do not only consist of binary oppositions; they also betray a certain unease about the categorical way in which these dichotomies are employed. First, each of the stories' superstructures offers a circular reading apart from the one strongly based on binaries. Second, both tales break through the pattern of the seemingly strict dualities by featuring grey areas where the opposing concepts overlap. These mediating spaces, as well as the dichotomies informing them, will be more closely examined in the present chapter. Their function of generating and simultaneously questioning ideologies needs to be discussed. The way I will go about this is by looking at the tales' character constellations to see the ways in which Lévi-Strauss's diagram of opposing poles and mediator figure applies to both stories. The basic and rather obvious binary opposition underlying the tales is the one between good and evil. However, it will be seen that there are other, less apparent dualities which are negotiated by the tales.

To illustrate the mediating processes at work in *Star Wars* and *Harry Potter* I will draw up diagrams in the fashion of those produced by Lévi-Strauss. They support my interpretation of the stories as mythical in the anthropologist's sense, as they reveal the close connection between character-constellation and deep-structural oppositions. Each of the diagrams stresses different points about the stories. The use of the plural (diagrams) already shows that the story cannot be reduced to one 'polar opposites-mediator' scenario. The exemplary six diagrams[1] I will present for

---

1   There are certainly even more possible diagrams.

Star Wars reveal the complexity of the series and, as will be seen, emphasise the basic ambiguity of myth and by extension popular culture. For instance, figures who are mediators in one scenario might become one of the poles in another. A close look at the diagrams shows the various ways in which popular cultural manifestations can be read and the different 'producerly' approaches they offer. The first exemplary diagram for *Star Wars* looks as follows (the second triad is numbered because of the ensuing alternative scenarios):

Initial Pair	First Triad	Second Triad (1)
Good		
	Light side of the Force	
		Yoda / Ben Kenobi
	People/creatures who are somehow associated with neither side or both sides of the Force	Anakin/Vader
	Dark side of the Force	the Emperor
Evil		

This first diagram already emphasises a number of points I would like to make about *Star Wars*. As with the Lévi-Straussian model, the first and second triad are embraced by the initial pair. However, I purposefully ordered the triads slightly differently from the way Lévi-Strauss did. The Emperor of the second triad is exactly on the same level as the 'Dark side of the Force' from the first triad. He is quite clearly allocable. There is nothing ambiguous about him, as he is primarily associated with seduction, manipulation and thus evil. Anakin/Vader is in the middle, because he unites good and bad characteristics. Yoda and Ben or Obi-Wan Kenobi are only nearly on the level of the 'Light side of the Force.' As will be seen in the chapters containing the close analysis of the characters, their 'goodness' contributes to Anakin's downfall, thus making the two complicit with evil, if in a very indirect way. The diagram reflects the fact that in the stories the poles of the good-evil dichotomy are treated unequally, good apparently being viewed less statically than evil. The first diagram thus invokes Derrida's recognition of the preference for one side to the binary over the other,[2] a realisation that is, as I

---

2   Cf. Sarup 39.

believe, already implied in Lévi-Strauss's diagram. By replacing "one of the polar terms [usually the top extreme] and the mediator" of the first triad with "a new [second] triad,"[3] one automatically excludes the bottom part of the initial pair. In Lévi-Strauss's diagram, the term thus ostracised is death, the one perceived more negatively. In the case of the *Star Wars* diagram, good is given preference by showing it to be more complex and interesting than evil. The mediating entity indicates how close good and evil are and how they actually constitute each other. The figure of Anakin/Vader makes this very clear, as he is influenced by both good and evil. The good Jedi contribute to his becoming the evil Vader, while evil in the shape of the Emperor finally makes him turn back to good and become Anakin once more. The first scenario, therefore, perfectly embodies the concerns of the poststructuralists about the structuralist approach: the hierarchical way in which we usually view binaries which makes us overlook the fact that one end of them would not exist without the other and that it acquires its identity only via its inverse. However, the scenario also serves as a starting point for an interpretation as it helps in identifying the fundamental concerns of the tales which can then be analysed for their cultural functions and significance.

In the following, I will present other possible Lévi-Straussian scenarios. It is assumed that the initial pair and the first triad as well as the position of the second triad in relation to initial pair and first triad remain the same.

Second Triad (2)	Second Triad (3)	Second Triad (4)
Anakin	Yoda/Ben/Anakin	Luke
Luke	Luke/Leia	Anakin/Vader
Vader	Vader/Emperor	Emperor

Second Triad (5)	Second Triad (6)
Yoda/Luke	Anakin
Ben	Anakin/Vader
Vader	Vader

---

3   Lévi-Strauss 130.

Scenario 2 is rather similar to scenario 1. As Anakin, the young protagonist is predominantly good. However, his fall from grace is a process, so that he already commits some evil deeds while he is still assumed to be generally good. Consequently, taking Anakin as the good pole again, suggests a gradation in goodness. Luke Skywalker can be seen as a mediator figure between the good and the evil half of Anakin. Being Anakin's son, it is intimated in the stories, he is prone to repeating his father's mistakes but he is also extremely good and always wants to do the right thing. Vader, as the lowest point of the diagram is quite unequivocal again.

While in his machine-like, evil state, he is not characterised by something that is present in his character but by a lack of, for instance, empathy and love. The same is true for the Emperor in scenario 1. Evil is thus characterised by an absence, not a presence. This invokes Derrida once more. A presence, or an origin as Derrida also calls it, would provide a reference point to explain the nature of something which is in this case evil. As this reference point is missing, however, all that can be done is eternally filling the absence of presence with different signifiers which might or might not approach the nature of the metaphysical phenomenon at hand. This is what Derrida speaks about when he refers to 'play.'[4] The true nature of evil can never be comprehended but only approached as it is ever shifting and changing. Filling an absence with various signifiers can be both beneficial and problematic. By filling the void which is the concept of evil with the pictures of certain characters such as the Emperor or Darth Vader, which then become the embodiment of evil in the stories, the movies make evil more comprehensible. As understanding usually helps acceptance, if, for instance, a person has experienced something horrible, this can be salutary. On the downside, representing evil in a certain way produces ideologies which can lead to mental inflexibility. Here again, the essence of mythical ambiguity is laid out before us: myth is by its nature a simplification of real life phenomena or circumstances. This helps people cope with the complexity of life but it also constrains them.

In diagrams 2 and 3, Luke, and Luke and his sister Leia respectively, stand as mediators between good and evil. They both fight for the side of the good but they also have to come into contact with evil as they fight for the soul of their fallen father Vader. Although Luke and Leia are good, evil is part of them by nature through their father. The good characters, Yoda, Ben, and Senator Organa who brings up Leia, are not blood-related to the twins but only serve as mentor figures from whom they learn. Good is therefore within them through their education, it is chosen. The question raised by the movies is whether good and evil are within people's nature or whether they are matters of personal choice. A further basic opposition is thus at

---

4   Cf. Derrida *Writing and Difference* 369.

work in the movies which is related to the good-evil one and which is perhaps even more significant. The movies structurally explore the binary of (natural/genetic) determination versus free will or choice. Apparently, this duality marks a challenge for Western societies, because it is a noticeable focal point not only of *Star Wars* but also, as will be seen, of *Harry Potter*, two of the most popular tales in recent years.[5] Luke and Leia represent the side of free will / choice, since evil is a natural part of them, but they decide for the good. They do so mainly because of the people they grow up with who shape their world views and notions about what is right and wrong. Scenario 4 interestingly rather implies a preference of natural disposition. Anakin/Vader is connected to the Emperor not through blood ties but through education; whereas, he is a blood-relative of Luke, the champion of good in this scenario. At the end of the series, Vader is turned into Anakin again by his son, representative of the good side to his nature. This would then support the claim that every person has a predisposition for good or evil.[6] The diagrams show that both positions, that of an inherent physiological or psychological bent for certain behaviour patterns, and that of personal temperaments being dependent on education, are held in the movies. Galipeau also perceives this ambiguity, although he only comments on it implicitly: "At issue here is the nature of the human personality: Can external forces alter the personality, or do such changes have to be generated from within

---

5   Hal Colebatch, who summarises some of the late 1970s and 1980s criticism of *Star Wars*, highlights the "dichotomy between power and freedom" as most relevant for the perception of the movies back then, due, no doubt, to a Cold War sensibility (90). Today the binary of choice versus determination seems to resonate more strongly, which appears to be, if equally political, more focussed on the individual. Catherine and David Deavel confirm individuality as a contemporary value when they say that "[i]n the modern West, choice itself is often conceived of as the highest goal. Libertarian freedom itself takes center stage as the Good" (Catherine Jack Deavel and David Paul Deavel, "Character, Choice, and Harry Potter," *Logos* 5.4 (2002): 53). These different readings are interesting since they serve as an example of the endurance of myth, which is read differently at various times.

6   Matthew Wilhelm Kapell argues that the whole Star Wars series is suffused by the elistist assumption that the value of a person is dependent on genetic inheritance. "[A] problematic message of the entire *Star Wars* saga is that rebellion against tyranny is less about choice and more about your genetic makeup" (Matthew Wilhelm Kapell, "Eugenics, Racism, and the Jedi Gene Pool," *Finding the Force of the Star Wars Franchise: Fans, Merchandise, and Critics*, Ed. Matthew Wilhelm Kapell and John Shelton Lawrence (New York: Peter Lang, 2006) 170). However, as my analyses will show, the movies give at least as much scope to choice and free will. As in many cases with popular cultural artifacts, it depends on how one reads them.

the individual?"[7] So once more, various readings are possible which seem to exclude one another. The true stance of the films is ambiguous.

Scenario 6 is possibly the most curious one presented as it significantly differs from the original Lévi-Straussian diagram. For the structuralist, the three different entities, polar opposites and mediator are strictly separated. Diagram number 6, however, sees the complete triad as embodied by the character of Anakin Skywalker / Darth Vader. Anakin's/Vader's mediating function as well as his embodiment of both extremes can be visualised with the help of the parallel structural movements the character makes within the movies. There are two scenes which are most significant for Anakin/Vader's development, namely his conversion to evil at the end of episode three and his return to the good side, concluding episode six. Both scenes involve triangular character constellations. In the third instalment, Anakin has to decide between good in the shape of Jedi master Mace Windu, and evil, represented by the Emperor. Since Anakin, soon to be transformed into Vader, decides in favour of the Emperor, the scene marks his moral low-point. The sequence at the end of episode six strongly mirrors and parallels the scene just described. Again, there are three main characters, Anakin/Vader, the Emperor and Luke Skywalker. And yet, again, Anakin/Vader has to make a choice and decide between the Emperor and Luke, his son. This time he chooses the good side, redeems his original fall from grace and reaches his moral highpoint. Visualisations of these movements can be found in Appendix 1.

It is important to note that this interpretation foregrounds Anakin's/Vader's choice between good and evil, while the role his original disposition plays was highlighted in the analysis of scenario 4. It can be seen that the contradiction between free will and determination not only exists between Luke/Leia and Vader but also within Vader himself. So again it is possible to see how the story is equivocal. Both sides of the binary are equally present. Two further points are interesting about this visualisation of Anakin's/Vader's structural movements within the story. Firstly, it is possible to see that both conversions are preceded by instability in the relationship between Anakin/Vader and the respective side he turns against. This instability will be the focus of the closer analysis of Anakin/Vader in chapter three. Secondly, the character constellations of the two triangles are significant. While the changing position of Anakin/Vader mirrors his occupation of both poles in scenario 6, the Emperor remains the only static entity in the two pictures. The representatives of the good side change, which illustrates a highly relevant quality of the freedom fighters and an advantage they have over the dark side. Good is much more diverse than evil. There are many different characters and creatures fighting for the good cause and they are even to be found in places

---

7   Galipeau 228.

where one would not expect them.[8] So the moment of surprise is decisive in the good side's fight against evil. This is a further hint which the tales provide as to how the viewers are supposed to understand evil. As was already shown with respect to diagrams 1 and 2, evil is characterised by a lack. Now, it becomes clear that it is also extremely static and inflexible. Formula stories seem to be especially prone to filling the essential void of concepts such as 'evil' with rather one-dimensional content. Readers and audiences are supposed to reject the ideologies the bad characters stand for. The simplistic depiction of evil, however, also furthers the generation of stereotypes and makes its identification as 'Other' possible. This is a point that M. Keith Booker explicitly makes: "For example, the imperial storm troopers (who are slaughtered en masse in the film) seem to be human, but the film intentionally dehumanizes them in ways that seem to invite us to ignore the humanity of those whom we have identified as enemies."[9]

Taken together, the two visualisations of Anakin/Vader's movements again form a hexagram and thus mirror the superstructure on a smaller scale. Despite the fact that the two triangles seem to show the greater diversity of good in comparison to evil, the star that can be formed from the two triangles suggests a certain equality of oppositions and is reminiscent of the more open, circular reading of the movies' superstructures. This balance is also a feature of diagram 6 in which Anakin/Vader embodies both the dualities and the middle position at once. The ambiguity characteristic of myths such as the one about Osiris, which emphasises the dualities of life and death and natural circularity at the same time, is thus at work in the superstructures as well as the character constellation of *Star Wars*.

The fifth scenario sees Ben or Obi-Wan, as he is called in episodes one to three, as the mediator between the good represented by Luke, and the bad represented by Vader. Obi-Wan knows both protagonists and plays a part in their education. He has influence on the young Anakin as well as Luke. His mediating position becomes apparent when it is taken into consideration that Obi-Wan's most

---

8   Cf. Colebatch who says that "[p]art of the heterogeneity, and the humanity, of the 'good sides' in these tales [*Star Wars* and *The Lord of the Rings*] is that the beings making them up have diverse interests, emphases and gifts" (19). Michael Valdez Moses also comments on the rebellion: "Luke and the other freedom fighters who oppose th[e] totalitarian menace are characterized by their relative independence (suggested by Han Solo's very name), their voluntary and negotiable participation in the great struggle, and their comparatively decentralized forms of resistance and military organization" (Michael Valdez Moses, "Back to the Future: The Nostalgic Yet Progressive Appeal of Wizards, Hobbits, and Jedi Knights," *Reason Magazine* (July 2003): n.pag. 7 Jul 2011 <http://reason.com/archives/2003/07/01/back-to-the-future>).

9   Booker 117.

important moments in the story occur in episodes three and four, and therefore in the middle part of the tale. He also shapes both protagonists, one, Anakin turning to evil, the other, Luke, to good. Obi-Wan's two most important scenes mirror each other structurally, much like Anakin/Vader's. They both feature Obi-Wan and two other characters in triangular relationships. The first scene I am referring to is the decisive one of Anakin's ultimate conversion to evil on the volcanic Mustafar system at the end of episode three. Obi-Wan shows himself at his morally lowest when he completely forsakes Anakin and even manages to further distance him from his wife Padmé. Obi-Wan's appearance leads to Anakin finally venting his rage on Padmé, killing her. This scene obviously contains Obi-Wan's moment of sinning. In episode four, he redeems himself in another triangular situation between himself, Darth Vader and Luke. By sacrificing himself so that Luke can escape to be able to continue fighting Vader, he has reached a moral highpoint again. By dying for Padmé's son Luke, Obi-Wan has atoned for playing a part in her death. Appendix 2 contains visualisations of these parallel structures. Yet again, taken together, the two movements form the six-pointed star. The two triangles make Obi-Wan's mediating function abundantly clear. Being once at the bottom and once at the top of the triangle establishes Obi-Wan as a fallible character and again reflects the fact that good is characterised as more complex than evil in the movies.

Interestingly, this view on the popular figure of Obi-Wan has only been made possible by the more recent three instalments, telling the story leading up to Luke's establishment as a hero. Something very similar can be noted with respect to Anakin/Vader. As the villain of the original trilogy, Vader is rather one-sided and the viewers do not truly get to know the motifs for his wrath and hatred. With the prequel episodes the figure of Anakin/Vader becomes more comprehensible and more human. The clear categorisation of characters such as Obi-Wan and Vader is thus severely questioned by the newer episodes. The dualities are not as strictly separated as Lévi-Strauss notes for the tales he analyses which indicates a certain poststructuralist awareness of the interdependencies between binary oppositions. To invoke John Cawelti again, it is obvious that the makers of *Star Wars* tried to revive the rather static and uninspiring formula of the fight between good and evil to generate fresh interest in their story. Cawelti also posits, however, that although surprising or new elements can rejuvenate formulas, the use of these elements must not be exaggerated. The basic formula needs to remain intact to make the popular tale work.[10] The reason for this is that formulas usually give readers or audiences

---

10   Cf. Cawelti 10. Cf. also Jann Lacoss, "Of Magicals and Muggles: Reversals and Revulsions at Hogwarts," *The Ivory Tower and Harry Potter: Perspectives on a Literary Phenomenon*, Ed. Lana A. Whited (Columbia: University of Missouri Press, 2002) 87.

the opportunity of making a clear decision for or against characters and thereby position themselves accordingly. So (how) does the formula work in the movies? In the case of the older *Star Wars* trilogies the audiences' sympathies are very clearly directed towards Luke Skywalker. It has already been demonstrated in the analysis of the diagrams that evil is depicted as rather static. That means that although good and evil are united in one person, Anakin/Vader, it is still quite clearly separated. The older trilogy shows the bad Darth Vader, while the newer episodes depict the good Anakin and his slow fall from grace. The clear-cut distinction between the two sides of the protagonist is also supported visually. The black-clad, masked and asthmatic Vader could not be more different from the cute little boy and handsome young man Anakin. When Anakin has finally fallen, there seems to be no trace of his goodness left till his re-transformation at the end of episode six. There is no good in evil. The representatives of the good side in contrast to that, as could also be seen in the diagrams, are hardly ever purely good.[1] Thus, until Luke appears who although he is shown the possibility of his own fall, never fails, it is very hard for audiences to know who to identify with.

However, it needs to be made completely clear that this confusion and the blurring of categories is entirely due to the newer trilogy.[12] If the original trilogy is watched on its own, there is the evil Emperor, evil Vader, good Obi-Wan, Leia and Luke: No problem to decide where one's sympathies should lie so far. As soon as all the six movies are watched in their chronological sequence, the difficulties begin. A good *and* an evil Anakin as well as a flawless and fallible Obi-Wan make it more difficult to take sides. The prequel episodes add depth to these two characters by pointing out their development but they also endanger the stability of the good-evil dichotomy and the familiar formula at work in the movies. They achieve this by blurring the boundaries between binary oppositions; but for me the makers also put the integrity and popularity of the older movies at risk because they made Anakin/Vader the most interesting figure and protagonist.[13] Luke becomes

---

11   These positions will be analysed more closely in the following chapters on the characters.

12   Cf. also Anne Lancashire who comments on the greater (moral) complexity of the more recent trilogy (33).

13   Tony M. Vinci supports the view that the new trilogy has a destructive effect on the older one. He argues that the audience's knowledge of the rather dysfunctional Republic through the prequels, produces disillusionment concerning the aims of the freedom fighters of the old trilogy, who wish to re-establish said Republic. (Cf. Tony M. Vinci, "The Fall of the Rebellion; Or Defiant and Obedient Heroes in a Galaxy Far, Far Away: Individualism and Intertextuality in the *Star Wars* Trilogies," *Culture,*

rather pale in comparison with his father. So for me it is at least questionable whether the identification with Luke which is so clearly desired in the older films, is still possible for people who have seen the newer trilogy before the original one.

So why did Lucas make the three new movies and tell audiences how Darth Vader came to be Darth Vader? Do they represent an error in judgement and destroy the integrity of episodes four to six or are there other, more positive ways of interpreting Lucas's attempt at completing the story? The prequel episodes seem to fulfil a very significant function for the tale as a whole and our understanding of it as myth. To explore their meaning, Lévi-Strauss's opposing poles-mediator diagram has to be taken to a meta-level, abstracting from the mere plane of the myth to include (an admittedly idealised concept of) human reality. The second triad on the level of characters would then have Anakin/Vader mediating between the rather ideal and flawless mythical hero Luke Skywalker and ourselves, the readers or viewers, the less than perfect individuals that populate the earth. Taken to the level of the first triad, Luke represents the older movies, Anakin/Vader the newer ones and we (as the audience) represent the reality of human life. The prequel episodes with their very human (anti)hero are thus mediating between the original and highly mythical trilogy with a perfect hero who always rises to the occasion and is supremely good, and our reality in which people are usually neither extremely good nor completely evil. The humanly more interesting story in the newer three movies has to function as link to our own and everyone's living reality. This position is supported by Laurent Jullier who says that "[i]t is our insecurities and the worries inherent in our zeitgeist, which have seeped into the magic world of the Jedi [my translation]."[14] Jullier goes on to comment on the way in which these anxieties are relieved when the six movies are watched in their chronological order, going from the more recent ones focussing on contemporary anxieties back to the older ones tapping into traditional values and painting the picture of the classical, individual hero who can set matters right.[15] In the Lévi-Straussian diagram set up to show the various functions of the two trilogies, the *initial pair* thus consists of the binary opposition between myth and reality.

Identities and Technology in the Star Wars Films: Essays on the Two Trilogies, Ed. Carl Silvio and Tony M. Vinci (Jefferson: McFarland & Company, 2007) 31).

14   Laurent Jullier, *Star Wars: Anatomie einer Saga* (Konstanz: UVK Verlagsgesellschaft mbH, 2007) 31.

15   Cf. Jullier 32. Cf. also Lincoln Geraghty, "Creating and Comparing Myth in Twentieth-Century Science Fiction: *Star Trek* and *Star Wars*," *Literature/Film Quarterly* 33.3 (2005): 196.

Initial Pair	First Triad	Second Triad
Myth		
	old movies	Luke Skywalker
	new movies	Anakin/Vader
	life on earth	audiences/viewers
Reality		

The extension of Lévi-Strauss's model gives a possible explanation of the existence of the prequel episodes and it offers a deconstructive reading of *Star Wars* and its significance. By making the newer movies less mythical and more human on the level of characters, Lucas draws attention to the fact that the older episodes are highly mythical and makes audiences question their applicability or validity with respect to their own lives. This interpretation is meta-mythical in the sense that it exposes the older episodes as constructed and ideologically charged. So once again, it is possible to read the production of the prequel episodes in two entirely different ways. On the one hand they destroy the clear-cut formula of the beloved older trilogy and make identification harder because of the many flawed characters. On the other hand, they show the protagonists as more human and thereby might just as well facilitate identification for people who reject Luke as too perfect.[16] The movies offer various, contradicting viewpoints which can be adopted by members of the audience according to their varying tastes and outlooks on life. This clash between different stances is inherent in much recent popular literature and film as such: Stories which seem to present a rather simple black and white world view often incorporate other viewpoints which are equally valid but less obvious and challenge

---

16   Cf. also Jonathan L. Bowen and Rachel Wagner, "'Hokey Religions and Ancient Weapons:' The Force of Spirituality," *Finding the Force of the Star Wars Franchise: Fans, Merchandise, and Critics*, Ed. Matthew Wilhelm Kapell and John Shelton Lawrence (New York: Peter Lang, 2006) who also hint at Anakin's role with respect to the audience: "One might even go so far as to suggest that such a savior [as Anakin] just might be more palatable than a wholly good savior, as we watch our own world crumble under the whims of men driven by impulse and desire and can only hope for their enlightenment" (90-91). Obviously, Bowen and Wagner also implicitly see Anakin as a mediator. Cf. furthermore Jullier 206.

the "dominant-hegemonic"[17] reading, a poststructuralist tendency of a genre which is otherwise predominantly structuralist.

The analysis of the Lévi-Strauss-like scenarios for *Star Wars* yielded several important points about the movies. Their set-up and order gave clues as to the way good and evil are seen in the films. Various characters occupy the pole of good in the second triads which shows that good is perceived to be manifold and dynamic. In contrast to this, evil is seen as rather static. True evil is only ever represented by the Emperor or Darth Vader. Furthermore, it obviously manifests itself in characteristics the villains lack rather than in attributes they possess. By showing good to be variable and evil to be static in the films, the diagrams also intimate a preference of good over evil, as good is treated in a more differentiated way. This invokes poststructuralist concerns with the hierarchies structuralists seemingly condoned. Much like the superstructure in the preceding chapter thus, the diagrams make clear that the movies are based on binary oppositions. Moreover, however, mediation between these binaries also becomes visible in the scenarios established. The mediating characters mirror the grey area of the *Star Wars* hexagram from chapter three. Scenario 6 featuring Anakin/Vader in all positions is highly relevant here, since it again is a visualisation of mythical ambiguity proper.[18] On the one hand it reveals the binary nature of the story. On the other hand, since Anakin/Vader fills both the two extreme poles and the middle ground, the diagram exhibits the same unity that also characterised the six-pointed superstructural star. Neither this diagram nor the star prefer any stance, they simply present balance. They also show how binaries such as good and evil can only exist in relation to each other. Like the superstructure, the diagrams offer various, diverse readings of the stories.

A further point that was established in this part of the chapter and will be highly relevant for the further course of this thesis, is the second important binary *Star Wars* obviously deals with, free will or choice versus determination. The scenarios allowed different readings of whether finally choice, shaped and furthered by education, or natural determination triumphs. In addition to the fact that ambiguity reigns once more, the binary of free will and determination itself is significant. It begs the question whether the mediation between good and evil is possibly only the smokescreen behind which one of the true issues that bother Westerners today is

---

17   Stuart Hall, "Encoding/decoding," *Culture, Media, Language: Working Papers in Cultural Studies*, 1972-79, Ed. Stuart Hall, Dorothy Hobson, Andrew Lowe, and Paul Willis (London: Routledge, 1980) 136.

18   Cf. also Nathaniel Van Yperen, "I Am Your Father: The Villain and the Future Self," *Essays on Evil in Popular Media: Vader, Voldemort and Other Villains*, Ed. Jamey Heit (Jefferson: McFarland & Company, Inc., 2011) 197.

negotiated. Good and evil is extremely hard to determine or pin down. In contrast to that it might be easier to speculate about people's motifs for something, about whether they are guided by a moral principle and choose their actions freely, or whether they are subject to internal or external constraints. Although this binary is as hard to resolve as the one between good and evil, it ultimately seems to be more interesting to people to find out why others commit evil deeds than to arrive at a true understanding of the nature of evil. This reinforces Sarah Grochala's assertion that people need stories to arrive at an understanding of others and the world.[19] It additionally puts the function of the newer trilogy of *Star Wars* films into perspective which seems to destroy the formulaic quality of the original movies and brings the characters closer to the audiences' reality. Viewers suddenly understand what motivates, for instance, Vader and Obi-Wan. The figure of Darth Vader without the explanation of its generation in episodes one to three seems a bit too static, almost boring.

Now obviously, the stories which are analysed here are longer and more complex than the tales Lévi-Strauss discussed in his "Structural Study of Myth." The diagrams reflect this complexity by offering various readings as to the characters and the oppositions in the tales. They give a first impression of how meaning is produced structurally in popular stories. Such stories are frequently based on binary oppositions which foreground a rather simple story of, for example, a fight between good and evil principles. However, it was established that the tales are also ambiguous and can be read in several ways. thus to a certain degree containing their own potential for deconstruction. The fact that a Lévi-Straussian analysis is productive in showing that the messages of popular entertainment and fiction are not pure and clear but are often ambiguous, should be enough to give the structuralist more prominence in the canon again.

4.2 *HARRY POTTER'S* AMBIGUOUS INTENT

Like *Star Wars*, *Harry Potter* is, on the surface, a story about the fight between good and evil, though as with *Star Wars* other dichotomies may be found. Therefore it seems likely that similar structures of opposing poles and mediator will be identifyable. A first scenario according to Lévi-Strauss's initial pair, first and second triads for *Harry Potter* could look as follows:

---

19   Cf. Grochala 142.

Initial Pair	First Triad	Second Triad (1)
Good		
	Magic used merely for defence	
		Dumbledore
		Harry Potter
	Magic used moderately / for good and evil purposes	
	Magic used to harm / acquire power	Voldemort
Evil		

As in the diagrams for *Star Wars*, the two diametrical opposites of good and evil form the initial pair which embraces the first and second triads. In *Star Wars*, the characters' souls and their moral attitudes are represented by the way in which they use the Force, while in *Harry Potter* the inner workings of a character are reflected by magic and the way in which it is employed. Therefore, the first triad is made up of magic used for good purposes, magic used to do harm or acquire personal power and, in between, magic used in both good and evil ways. On first glance at the diagram it becomes apparent that the difference between good and evil very much depends on the way characters act. Magic in the *Harry Potter* novels is something that is consciously employed, implying that its use is dominated by the dictates of reason and free will. Choice is thus established as an essential theme of the books. In the first diagram for *Star Wars* this theme was less apparent, although it is also prominent in the stories. The Force is much less defined than magic in *Harry Potter*. In the wizarding world everyone can do magic, with very few exceptions whereas mastery of the Force is not a widespread gift around the galaxy. Magic in *Harry Potter* is more concrete than the Force. It does not only help with the great and important tasks in life but also facilitates housework and small everyday chores. The Force, in contrast to that is never used for banal purposes. It is constantly established as something mysterious and sublime. Though of course decisions are important in the films, it is stressed throughout that the Force controls its practitioners as much as they control it. At Hogwarts emphasis is placed on learning to control magic. All this supports what the first diagram conveys: that the way people act is significant in the books about the teenage wizard.

The second triad in this first scenario, has Albus Dumbledore, Hogwarts headmaster at the top. Voldemort, the most fixed character in the novels constitutes the evil pole. Harry Potter stands as a mediator in this pattern. Though he is always on the side of the good, it cannot be denied that he has a connection with evil Lord Voldemort because of the part of the evil one's soul that is attached to Harry's.[20] It has to be noted that some of the characters are not exactly on the same level as the various uses of magic they reflect. Dumbledore, though the champion of the powerless and disenfranchised in the novels, dabbled in the dark arts in his youth, as reporter Rita Skeeter reveals after his death in book seven. Harry Potter embodies a middle position. He employs magic for the good in the majority of cases. However, he is also seen to be using magic against his enemies at times. Early manifestations are his attacks against Draco Malfoy,[21] more serious cases occur in novels five to seven, when he sometimes uses the spells of his opponents to achieve his aims.[22] Since he still mostly uses magic defensively and more importantly, usually has good intentions even when he casts dark spells, he is closer to the pole of good. Voldemort alone employs magic for evil purposes exclusively. Thus, as in *Star Wars*, evil seems to be less ambiguous than good. There are, however, characters in *Harry Potter* who can be considered wicked or mean but are not necessarily evil. Examples would be Draco Malfoy, Peter Pettigrew and the more interesting Severus Snape who is going to be analysed in chapter six. While the generally positive view of, for instance, Harry and Dumbledore is never fundamentally damaged by their forays into the territory of dark magic, the basically negative view of characters such as Draco Malfoy and Peter Pettigrew is never truly improved by the knowledge that they are simply mean or do not possess enough strength of character to resist evil. The readers' sympathies are very clearly directed towards certain characters and outlooks on life. This shows that our view on binary oppositions such as good and evil heavily relies on emotions which then lead to our hierarchisation of the terms in a dichotomy. Human feelings thus far more than rational facts are responsible for the generation of stereotypes via binary oppositions.[23]

In keeping with the analysis of the *Star Wars*-diagrams there are more Lévi-Straussian scenarios for the *Harry Potter* novels.

---

20   Cf. Rowling *Hallows* 550-51.

21   Cf. for instance Rowling *Prince* 489 where Harry, admittedly without knowing what exactly he is doing uses the potentially lethal Sectumsempra spell on Malfoy.

22   Examples are Rowling *Hallows* 428-29 where Harry uses the unforgivable Imperius curse and *Hallows* 477 where he employs the torture curse Crucio against a Death Eater.

23   Emotions also play an important role in the Othering of women and people from ethnic backgrounds different from one's own (compare also chapter two).

Second Triad (2)	Second Triad (3)	Second Triad (4)
Harry	The Order of the Phoenix (Harry, Dumbledore)	Dumbledore (Order)
Dumbledore/Snape	Snape	Harry/Ron/ Hermione
Voldemort	Death Eaters (Voldemort)	Voldemort (Death Eaters)

Second Triad (5)	Second Triad (6)	Second Triad (7)
Gryffindor	Harry/Dumbledore	Harry
Harry	Regulus Black	Kreacher
Slytherin	Voldemort	Voldemort

As with *Star Wars*, it seems to be possible to identify various poles and mediators. Harry, for instance, is found both representing good and filling the position of a mediator. It is merely Voldemort who is always found at the bottom of the diagrams. In that he is comparable to the Emperor of *Star Wars*.

In diagram 2, Dumbledore and Harry swap positions. Harry's natural goodness and his constant and conscious choices for the good side are stressed here. In scenario 1, the fact that Harry is partly determined from the outside is foregrounded. Voldemort forces himself and part of his nature upon him which accounts for some of the less endearing things Harry says and does in the course of the novels. In contrast to this there are many scenes in which he takes the conscious decisions which are morally right, and Dumbledore never tires of stressing Harry's natural goodness.[24] It is thus justified to identify him as the mediator in scenario 1 but it is equally possible to see him as the supreme good, as scenario 2 does. So as in *Star Wars*, a certain ambiguity reigns concerning the opposition between free choice and determination.[25] However, this ambiguity is not as pronounced as in the

---

24   Cf. for example Rowling *Prince* 477-78 and *Hallows* 571.

25   Gregory Bassham thoroughly comments on the questions of free will and determination in the *Harry Potter* novels in his article "The Prophecy-Driven Life: Fate and Freedom at Hogwarts," *Harry Potter and Philosophy: If Aristotle ran Hogwarts*, Ed. David Bagget and Shawn E. Klein (Chicago: Open Court, 2004) 213-26. He emphasises Rowling's final preference of choice (cf. 226) but fails to notice the underlying ambiguity with which the binary is treated in the novels. Bassham furthermore focuses on the kinds of choices made in Harry's universe in his article

tales of galactic strife. Looking at the scenarios set up for *Harry Potter*, many characters represented there make conscious decisions. Apart from Harry himself, who constantly decides for the good cause, Dumbledore (part of scenarios 1, 2, 3, 4, and 6) chooses to abstain from political power after erring in his youth. Snape (featuring in diagrams 2, and 3) also significantly decides to return to Dumbledore's side and to the fight against evil, after he has unwittingly turned Lily Potter over to Voldemort. Moreover, Ron (scenario 4) decides to rejoin Harry after leaving him out of frustration in book seven. Both Regulus Black and Kreacher of diagrams 6 and 7 make major decisions for the side of the good after brief stints with evil. Even Voldemort, part of almost all scenarios, can be said to have made a decision to be evil and to use his tremendous powers against people instead of for their benefit. Most of the people in the diagrams are thus associated with choices and decisions. This shows that free will is an even more important theme in *Harry Potter* than in *Star Wars*.

Additionally, it is crucial that the majority of the decisions are made for the good. Thus the *Harry Potter* novels seem to quite expressly favour the first mentioned terms of the binaries good/evil and free will / determination over the second. This greater degree of closure in *Harry Potter* in comparison with *Star Wars* was already mentioned in the chapter on the superstructures of the stories. *Star Wars*, though focussing on binary oppositions is also rather open because of its equal number of instalments featuring good and evil victorious and its star-like superstructure which suggests a circular movement with alternations between good and evil. *Harry Potter* implies the possibility of what I called pre-history and continuation but the structure of the seven novels does not make this explicit. The unequal number of instalments with the final one ending on Harry's grand victory and the fact that the most important and all-embracing frame consisting of novels one and seven focuses on Harry and the themes of love, selflessness and sacrifice, suggest a preference of choice and the good. However, it needs to be said that *Harry Potter* more than *Star Wars* was predominantly designed as a story for children for whom the triumph of good over evil is a comforting message. And the comforting aspect does not only hold for children reading the stories. Formulaic fiction, according to Cawelti, always has an escapist function.[26] Thus, adults who peruse tales of the formulaic kind also find relief within the confines of the formulas. To provide escape, stories such as *Harry Potter* need to have a good

---

"Choices Versus Abilities: Dumbledore on Self-Understanding," *The Ultimatel Harry Potter and Philosophy: Hogwarts for Muggles*, Ed. Gregory Bassham (New Jersey: Wiley, 2010) 157-71.

26   Cf. Cawelti 6.

ending to set them apart from reality which features equally harsh conflicts but often without a satisfactory solution.

Scenarios 2 and 3, featuring Snape as the mediator, are especially interesting since Snape goes through a development similar to that of Anakin/Vader. In the course of Harry Potter's story, Snape like Anakin makes a mistake and redresses it. Peter Appelbaum comes closest to interpreting Snape as a mediator. "Snape, in his unique multiple-agent role, is both in and out, the only Hogwarts teacher who maintains links to the real world. And, he is on the edge; he seemingly can go either way. He is liminal."[27] By betraying Lily Potter, the love of his life, to Voldemort before the start of the actual story he becomes one of the driving forces of the action. At the end of novel seven, he redeems himself by dying for the good cause. Visualisations of his structural movements which are similar to those of Anakin/Vader and Obi-Wan can be found in Appendix 3.

In scenario 3 Snape functions as the mediator between the two antagonised groups of the Order of the Phoenix under the leadership of Dumbledore and the Death Eaters who follow Voldemort's orders. Snape literally takes up the role of what Lévi-Strauss calls the trickster here.[28] He constantly tricks Voldemort by making him believe that he is on his side. No one from the good side, except Dumbledore, knows for sure whether Snape really is on their side and so they mistrust him. Snape must put up with this mistrust for his own safety and the security of the plans for bringing down Voldemort. With his unpleasant behaviour he therefore also tricks the good side. He remains an ambiguous character till the very end. Snape, as can be seen when looking at scenarios 2 and 3, not only functions as the mediator between Harry and Voldemort but also between the good and the evil sides at large. He does not only mediate between the ideas represented by hero and villain but also

---

27   Peter Appelbaum, "The Great Snape Debate," *Critical Perspectives on Harry Potter*, Ed. Elizabeth E. Heilman (New York: Routledge, 2009) 92. Both Travis Prinzi and Julia Boll describe Snape as a shapeshifter, a concept that also comes close to that of the mediator. However, Prinzi is more interested in the psychology of the character than in his structural function and Boll also emphasises a psychological reading by using Jungian archetypes to explain Snape. Her discussion of him furthermore remains rather brief (cf. Prinzi 195-96, cf. Boll 90). Maria Nikolajeva, too points to Snape's mediating function between Harry and Voldemort. However, she does not use the term 'mediator,' either (cf. Maria Nikolajeva, "Adult Heroism and Role Models in the Harry Potter Novels," *Heroism in the Harry Potter Novels*, Ed. Katrin Berndt and Lena Steveker (Farnham: Ashgate, 2011) 201). John Granger calls Snape a "critical or swing character," thereby also broaching the concept of the mediator (*Looking for God in Harry Potter* 19).

28   Cf. Lévi-Strauss 131.

between the very real people who fight for their respective sides in the story and is thus a mediator on the level of the story as well as on the level of the discourse presented in the good-evil dichotomy.

Scenario 4 again sees Dumbledore together with his Order of the Phoenix as the pole of good and Voldemort and his Death Eaters at the low point of evil. Harry and his friends Ron and Hermione qualify as mediators between the two groups because though they are essentially good characters, all of them have to fight demons within their own personalities. Furthermore they are the three characters who come almost as close as Snape to the dark side in the course of their attempts at bringing down Voldemort. Especially in book seven, they are tricksters in so far as they have to use dark magic, embody Death Eaters and perform illegal deeds to achieve their aims.[29] In many mythical and other formulaic stories it is indispensable that characters who want to restore the balance between two opposing forces are able to put themselves in the place of both sides. They are usually familiar with good as well as evil and understand both poles. Having experienced evil enables them to value what is good and to help preserve it. This is the role that can be attributed to Harry, Ron and Hermione here. The scenario also shows that on the level of the story Harry cannot defeat all the evil that is out there alone. He might be the representative of the good side in the fight, but he needs others who back him up. The same is true for Luke Skywalker who gets help from his sister Leia and his friend Han Solo in the decisive battles. This is something that clearly distinguishes the good side from the bad and further establishes the way good and evil are viewed both in *Star Wars* and *Harry Potter*. The good side is characterised by trusting in others and seeking alliances to achieve its aims. Evil does not trust. Its representatives recruit henchmen but because they are power hungry and want glory for themselves they are unable to form close ties, let alone friendships.

In scenario 5, the poles of good and evil are represented by ideas. Gryffindor and Slytherin are two of the four Hogwarts houses and they are named after the founders of the school, Godric Gryffindor and Salazar Slytherin. Gryffindor and Slytherin were friends originally but later became disenchanted with each other.[30] While Gryffindor wanted to teach young witches and wizards regardless of their origin, Slytherin preferred those who came from ancient wizarding families to half-bloods and muggle-borns.[31] Thus they can be said to stand for fairness and equality on the one hand and for injustice and inequality on the other. It is certainly significant that the two school founders used to be friends. Together with the other two founders Rowena Ravenclaw and Helga Hufflepuff they formed a unity in

---

29 Cf. for example Rowling *Hallows* 422-31.

30 Cf. Rowling *Chamber* 164-65.

31 Cf. Rowling *Chamber* 164-65.

which no interest of any single one of the four powerful witches and wizards was predominant. The founding of Hogwarts marks a harmonious origin, untouched by strife and discord which is looked back on with nostalgia. It is a utopia which could not hold for very long. Gryffindor and Slytherin, originally two sides of one coin, disagree and break apart, from which moment onwards the school becomes divided into houses, with Gryffindor and Slytherin the farthest apart. Harry presents the chance to bring the two adverse houses closer together again and reinstate a utopia. Since Harry indeed has connections to both houses, Gryffindor via his dead parents and his own leanings, and Slytherin through the dispositions Voldemort has transferred to him when he tried to kill him as a baby, he himself can be seen as a kind of utopian figure representing unity. And again, although Derrida rejects the longing for origins and the nostalgia that comes along with it, it cannot be denied that people do indeed have a desire for completion and wholeness.[32] Rowling caters to that desire. Despite the fact that Gryffindor's values win in the end, she inserts a Slytherin, Snape, who finally plays a big role and whom the readers ultimately are meant to admire. She also lets Harry tell his son in the epilogue that Slytherin is not all bad and that what kind of a person one is does not depend on the house one is sorted into. Thereby she manages to at least raise the readers' hopes that harmony is possible. This utopian element is not as pronounced in *Star Wars*, as the transformation is all within one character (Anakin/Vader) and the effects on society are not explicitly shown.

Scenarios 6 and 7 also exhibit this reconciliatory stance. Binaries are brought closer to each other. Again Harry and Voldemort function as the two poles of good and evil. In between there are Regulus Black (scenario 6) and Kreacher, the house elf (scenario 7). Regulus is Harry's godfather Sirius's brother. He joined Voldemort when he was sixteen and worked for him for a few years before finding out about the Horcruxes the Dark Lord had created to gain immortality. Then Regulus changed his mind and lost his life in an attempt to destroy one of the parts of Voldemort's soul.[33] Therefore he also has good and bad within him and is fit to bring the thoroughly bad (Voldemort) and the extremely good (Harry) more closely together. In scenario 7 this role is fulfilled by Kreacher, the Blacks' house elf. House elves are servants who work in big wizarding mansions. Most wizards believe that they are not worth as much as themselves and treat them badly.[34] Therefore the elves are usually highly attached to anyone who acts kindly towards them.[35] Kreacher does not like Sirius, since he treated the rest of his family –

---

32   Cf. Derrida *Writing and Difference* 369.

33   Cf. Rowling *Hallows* 159-62.

34   Cf. Rowling *Chamber* 19-21.

35   Cf. Rowling *Hallows* 163-64.

supporters of Voldemort – with contempt and left his home when he was only a teenager. Sirius has to pay for his unfriendly treatment of Kreacher when he is betrayed by the elf who sells him to Voldemort in book five.[36] This is Kreacher's bad deed. Harry, however, comes to understand the elf when he hears his story in book seven. Kreacher helped Regulus to whom he was highly attached, steal one of Voldemort's Horcruxes, witnessed Regulus's death on that occasion and spent years trying to destroy the Horcrux as Regulus had told him to do. He now helps Harry and his friends retrieve it and thereby redeems himself in Harry's eyes.[37] Thus Kreacher, too is fitting as mediator because he oscillates between the good and the evil side and finally helps tipping the scales in favour of the good. Visualisations of the elf's structural movements can be found in Appendix 4. Kreacher very obviously also functions as a mediator in the fashion of Obi-Wan, Anakin/Vader and Snape. The fact that both stories contain similar structural movements in characters who also have functions which are alike (two protagonists, Anakin/Vader and Snape and two mentors/helpers, Obi-Wan and Kreacher), shows that formulaic fiction depicts character change as a process that takes place openly, in the interplay with other characters. The change in the respective figures manifests itself in an alteration of their behaviour towards others, usually from bad to good. This is a clearly moral valuation of characters' actions and highlights the didactic function of myth.

It is not easily possible to draw up a meta-mythical Lévi-Straussian diagram which includes our own reality for *Harry Potter*. The reason is that the *Harry Potter* novels differ from the *Star Wars* tales in one important respect. They do not need mediators between their content and reality because they try to be as realistic as possible within the fantasy framework and the limitations posed by their structures. On the level of the story, they also already feature a comparison between the wizarding and our own (Muggle) world, albeit a highly satirical one. This mostly shows on the level of the characters who Rowling tries to depict as individually as possible, although they, too of course are subject to the formulaic structures. She even pays attention to minor characters. In *Star Wars* the characters more obviously fulfil functions for the story and are less individual. Story-wise, it seems, the *Harry Potter* tales are more open than the *Star Wars* movies while structurally, they are more closed. Apparently, if you choose to tell a formulaic tale that is rather closed structurally, there is scope for 'play' on the level of content, while if you write a formula story that is structurally more open, you need to include characters who are more static and who offer fixed points of identification or rejection for the readers or audiences.

---

36   Cf. Rowling *Order* 731.
37   Cf. Rowling *Hallows* 159-65, 180-83.

The diagrams set up for both stories show several similarities. Both tales are more complex in comparison with the stories originally analysed by Lévi-Strauss and thus leave much more room for interpretation and above all for ambiguous readings. *Star Wars* and *Harry Potter* are preoccupied with binary oppositions which have clear structuring functions. The good-evil dichotomy is the most obvious of them. However, as was seen in both tales, the duality of free will and determination is equally important. The question of which kinds of decisions humans take and how these decisions come about seems to be a pressing interest the stories explore. The diagrams of *Star Wars* as well as of *Harry Potter* furthermore embody Derrida's concern with the hierarchy existing between binary oppositions.[38] In *Harry Potter* this hierarchy is more apparent structurally (compare e.g. the frame-structure discussed in chapter three with the all-embracing frame one made up of novels one and seven foregrounding Harry as the good principle). *Star Wars* is more open structurally with an equal number of instalments featuring good and evil as victorious and also by showing Anakin/Vader as a character torn between two extreme positions. Although it is quite clear that the good side represented by Luke, Leia, Obi-Wan and Yoda is preferred, because the final instalment celebrates their victory, the case is not as clear for the binary of free choice and determinism. While the *Potter* novels favour free will, *Star Wars* lays prominence on the fact that both free choices and determining outward factors can shape a person's life. This becomes apparent when looking at the seemingly contradictory readings of scenarios 2/3 and 4 respectively: the former emphasises the choice to be good, while the latter raises the question whether individuals do not have a predisposition for either good or evil behaviour.

Maybe the most important point of the chapter is the ambiguity of both stories concerning various themes and characters. Myth is always ambiguous.[39] It

---

38   Cf. Sarup 39.

39   Alice Mills, who does a Jungian reading of the *Harry Potter* novels comes to a similar conclusion. However, she does not so much emphasise the positive potential of this ambiguity, the potential for harmonising, but stresses the shape-shifting qualities of Rowling's texts (cf. Alice Mills, "Archetypes and the Unconscious in *Harry Potter* and Diana Wynne Jones's *Fire and Hemlock* and *Dogsbody*," *Reading Harry Potter: Critical Essays*, Ed. Giselle Liza Anatol (Westport: Praeger, 2003) 8). Elaine Ostry, too analyses the ambiguity of *Harry Potter*, or what she calls the "ideological doubleness [of] the fairy tale, which is simultaneously radical and traditional." (Elaine Ostry, "Accepting Mudbloods: The Ambivalent Social Vision of J.K. Rowling's Fairy Tales," *Reading Harry Potter: Critical Essays*, Ed. Giselle Liza Anatol (Westport: Praeger, 2003) 90). Marc Bousquet who discusses the similarities of the *Harry Potter* novels with melodrama, also extensively comments on the ambiguity which he sees as

constantly tries to unite binaries which cannot be finally reconciled and it does so not only on the level of ideas such as good and evil or free will and determinism but also on a meta-plane. What this chapter has implied so far is that myth can function as a simplification of the complexity of life on the one hand but on the other it can also take up the role of mediator between simplicity and complexity as it constantly advocates balance and middle passages. Both positions are apparent, especially in *Star Wars*, where the original trilogy is mythical in the sense that it shows rather static characters without much scope for development. The more recent three films are mythical in a different way, as was depicted in the final diagram for *Star Wars*. They function as mediators between a complex reality and a simplistic rendering of it in the old trilogy.

Although the *Harry Potter* novels cannot be divided into two parts as neatly and easily as the *Star Wars* series, they allow similarly ambiguous conclusions about the function of myth. Maria Nikolajeva holds that "contemporary sophisticated fantasy contains a substantial amount of uncertainty and ambiguity, typical of postmodern thinking."[40] However, she sees fantasy works such as Philip Pullman's *Northern Lights* trilogy as much more ambiguous than *Harry Potter*.[41] On a surface level it might be true that there is more moral uncertainty in Pullman's books and that the characters are less easy to identify with. Still, the *Harry Potter* novels also contain ambiguity on a more implicit plane, as the following chapters will elucidate. The books feature rather one-dimensional characters such as Voldemort to facilitate access to certain themes. However, as was mentioned, they also contain many characters who are round and dynamic and undergo developments. In this sense, the novels like the *Star Wars* films make it easier for people to grasp difficult realities (myth in its simplifying function) but at the same time feature characters who the readers and audiences can identify with and who are not too far away from their own experiences (myth in its mediating role).[42] This can be visualised in the following Lévi-Straussian diagram which brings *Star Wars* and *Harry Potter* together.

---

inherent in the melodramatic genre. Melodrama and melodramatic structures, he holds, can be exploited as tools in the rhetoric of politicians to achieve certain aims. They can also, however, have a liberating function, true to their 18th-and 19th-century role of spurring the 'common man' to action against his aristocratic oppressors (cf. Marc Bousquet, "Harry Potter, the War Against Evil, and the Melodramatization of Public Culture," *Critical Perspectives on Harry Potter*, Ed. Elizabeth E. Heilman (New York: Routledge, 2009) 178).

40   Nikolajeva "A Return to the Romantic Hero" 136.

41   Cf. Nikolajeva "A Return to the Romantic Hero" 136.

42   Cf. also Suman Gupta who holds that *Harry Potter* contains three worlds, the magic and the Muggle world which openly feature in the text as well as our world which is

Initial Pair	First Triad	Second Triad
Complexity	Reality	readers/audiences (characters like Ron, Hermione, Petunia, Dumbledore, the Malfoys, Anakin/Vader, Obi-Wan, Han Solo)
	Star Wars / Harry Potter (myth as mediator)	Harry, Anakin / Vader, Snape, (Hermione)[43]
simplicity	myth as simplifier	static characters (Voldemort, the Emperor, Luke)

The initial and all-encompassing pair in this scenario is made up of complexity and simplicity. The first triad then consists of reality on the same level as complexity, and myth as simplifier on the same level as simplicity. Stories such as *Star Wars* and *Harry Potter* get the middle position here because they feature clear mythical structures but they also break them and show many different aspects of and characters from real life. They feature both simple mythical elements and mythical mediators which creates a balance between simplicity and complexity. The characters who most prominently embody this mediating position on the level of the second triad are Anakin/Vader, Snape and to an extent as will be seen, Harry Potter. They are linked with the audience/readers by their station in between extreme good and extreme evil. They exhibit feelings like love, hate, guilt, and envy, they are sometimes right, and at other times wrong, in short they are 'normal people' but also somehow larger than life because of excessive evilness in the case of Vader and equally extreme goodness exhibited by the child Anakin and Harry Potter.

---

implied through the other two. (Suman Gupta, *Re-Reading Harry Potter* (Houndsmills: Palgrave Macmillan, 2003) 85).

43   For this positioning of Hermione see Bryan Polk's idea expounded on the following page.

An idea worth mentioning with respect to the mediator scenarios comes from Bryan Polk. He sees the wizarding world as "a response to a world increasingly dominated by technology and impersonality,"[44] and the *Harry Potter* books "as a metaphor for the individual's struggle against the modern world."[45] He thus sets up a binary opposition between our (I would say postmodern) world and a simpler more traditional one with more direct human interaction and less reliance on technology. Viewed in this manner, Hogwarts advocates a return to and produces a certain nostalgia for values of 'the good old times.' In this scenario, Polk perceives Hermione as the prime mediator, although he does not use the word. Although she is a Muggle, she can still enter Hogwarts and the magical community. "If she can do this," Polk argues, "then so can we. (...) Like Hermione, we can choose to participate in a world *not* dominated by technology and not characterized by isolation and loneliness."[46] Hermione's double status as a Muggle and a witch thus makes her a mediating character almost as important as Harry, because she fulfils a bridging function between the Muggle reader and the wizarding world he or she enters. Polk, however, also makes clear that by entering the wizarding world, Hermione advocates the nostalgic position, the going back to a pre-postmodern world. Polk's ideas about Hermione thus support my general assumption that the *Harry Potter* novels finally rather reject postmodernism and poststructuralism instead of embracing it, as Granger believes.[47]

Apart from the mediating characters there are those figures who are mythical binary extremes. Voldemort and the Emperor are portrayed in a quite stereotypical way. Neither of them bring the stories closer to life. The characters mentioned on the level of 'reality' are the ones who are similar to everyone of us. Though they do not do everything right, and Darth Vader especially makes some seriously wrong decisions, they do what is morally correct in the end. Thus one can see that the mythical elements and structures in the two stories operate on different levels within the diagram. What is special about *Star Wars* and *Harry Potter* is that the stories contain all elements of the first and second triads. They unite the polarities and bring them more closely together in some of their figures who stand in between real life and myth. These figures challenge the one-dimensional and purely mythical figures and thereby make the stories more realistic. Both stories are full of the

---

44   Bryan Polk, "The Medieval Image of the Hero in the *Harry Potter* Novels," *The Image of the Hero in Literature, Media, and Society*, Selected Papers 2004 Conference of the Society for the Interdisciplinary Study of Social Imagery, Ed. Will Wright and Steve Kaplan (Pueblo: Colorado State University-Pueblo) 443.

45   Polk 444.

46   Polk 444.

47   Cf. for instance Granger *Unlocking Harry Potter* 167-69, 174-76.

ambiguity inherent in myth. They break the complexity of life down to simplistic categories and try to unite them but they also question the simplicity of this approach. This breaking down of complexity is also notable in the differences between Lévi-Strauss's diagram and the *Star Wars-* and *Harry Potter*-versions of it. The latter are significantly less complex. Quite obviously, they feature human characters instead of animals on the level of the second triad and it is not so much lifestyles which are contrasted in their first triad as moral attitudes and decision-making. The most basic binary pair that is negotiated in the two stories, good versus evil, also has clear moral implications, whereas this is not so much the case with Lévi-Strauss's initial pair of life and death. The human characters are easier to identify with than the animal characters and audiences as well as readers are certainly invited to take sides. Thus, Lévi-Strauss's (reasonably) neutral view on myth as a mediator reconciling opposing concepts such as life and death, develops into a much more biased one. The diagrams set up for *Star Wars* and *Harry Potter* expose the stories as ideology-ridden because of their more or less obvious preference for one side of the binaries. At the same time, as was mentioned, they also take up a mediating function because they question the ideologies they set up. The two stories exhibit a double function in this way: on the one hand they mediate between myth and reality and draw attention to the myth-making processes in our daily lives but on the other hand they quite clearly establish ideologies through their simplistic handling of certain characters and themes. It is the didactic and ideological purpose of both *Star Wars* and *Harry Potter* to show people that there are morally right ways of acting and reprehensible ones. The two stories clearly exhibit the mythical function of getting people to take action and emulate the morally correct behaviour represented to them.

5.   Evil Deconstruction

5.1   QUESTIONING DICHOTOMIES: THE EMPEROR

The present and the following two chapters will emphasise the importance of the diagrams presented in the previous part of the thesis. Three protagonists for each series will be examined, two representative of the extreme poles of the spectrum Lévi-Strauss set up as well as one filling the middle position. Proceeding in this way will once again underscore the significance of the diagrams analysed in the preceding chapter and show the manner in which the patterns Lévi-Strauss discovered in myths are predominantly embodied by the characters. The discussion will start with the unequivocally evil character of the Emperor and the slightly more ambiguous Lord Voldemort. From there, the analysis will proceed to characters who are both good and evil; heroes and villains, at some stage of the tales in the next chapter. These are Anakin Skywalker / Darth Vader for *Star Wars* and Severus Snape for *Harry Potter*. The final focus of this part of my thesis will be on the clear hero-figures of the stories, Harry Potter and Luke Skywalker. As a hero, Harry Potter still retains a hint of ambiguity whereas Luke Skywalker can rather unproblematically be placed on the side of the thoroughly good.[1] All of these characters will be compared for their functions in the respective tales and the implications of these comparisons will be discussed. The set-up of the present and two following chapters further emphasises the special middle position of Anakin/Vader. The usual order of the analysis is slightly changed here because in the final part of the chapter, Harry Potter is analysed before Luke Skywalker. So far, the *Star Wars* series has always been analysed first. This deviation does have a function: it makes perfectly clear that there are completely static and mythical

---

1   Hanson and Kay also see the rather static structural corset for *Star Wars* where, they say Yoda and Palpatine "stand at polar opposites, the enlightened good and the darkness of evil. All others, heroes or villains, fall somewhere in between where these two reside" (405).

characters such as the Emperor and Luke on both the good and the evil side and that there are characters in between, such as Anakin/Vader and the villain- and hero-figures of *Harry Potter*. The implications for the two stories, especially with regard to the good-evil binary and its co-dichotomy free will versus determinism, will be discussed in the course of the chapters. The natures of both oppositions need to be examined in more detail. The structuring of the chapters is supposed to mirror the fact that the individuality or propensity for development on the part of the characters is rather subjected to the structural corset of both stories.[2]

Since this part of the thesis starts with an analysis of the two supremely evil characters of *Star Wars* and *Harry Potter*, it would be prudent to define evil and the way it is understood in the two tales. Robert Ellwood in his *Tales of Darkness: The Mythology of Evil* understands evil as "that which causes suffering, which intrudes on what we think ought to be the rightful course of events, and maims or cuts short any life well before it has fulfilled its natural cycle."[3] His definition very clearly shows that evil is abstract, has many shapes and cannot easily be defined precisely. Ellwood's use of the words 'what we think' is extremely significant. Evil, he believes is not so much an absolute entity in itself but something that is made or created in our minds. Events or deeds that we 'feel' are evil become so for us. He himself formulates this in the summary of his book: "We begin to realize that myths of evil are actually not so much explanations of evil (…), as they are an inventory of varied ways of *feeling* about evil, of responding to it on other than purely rational terms."[4] Elwood's statement is in accordance with some of the functions of myth outlined in the theoretical chapter. Myth works as a guideline for people, helping them find their station in life by providing a playground for testing (moral) attitudes and feelings. This they can do by living out their own emotions through the triumphs and failures of fictional characters. (Apart from myth, this is also a principle of formulaic fiction where the readers' or audiences' sympathies are usually pushed heavily into one particular direction, which also often means that

---

2   This view is supported by Florian Kragl, who says of the characters in *Star Wars*: "The acting personae pass through this world like puppets on strings, every modulation of character is suppressed by the strictly binary organisation of the good-evil constellation [my translation]" (Florian Kragl, "Artus im 'Krieg der Sterne:' Zyklusbildung als Narratologisches Paradoxon einer Dynamischen Statik," *Neophilologus* 93 (2009): 284). Cf. also Andrew Gordon who holds that *Star Wars* is "populated with intentionally flat, archetypal characters" (Andrew Gordon, "*Star Wars*: A Myth for Our Time," *Screening the Sacred: Religion, Myth, and Ideology in Popular American Film*, Ed. Joel W. Martin and Conrad E. Ostwalt Jr. (Boulder: Westview Press, 1995) 73).

3   Ellwood 2.

4   Ellwood 143.

readers or audiences are 'fed' certain dominant ideologies). However, Ellwood's point does not sufficiently do justice to evil in myth. The 'modern myths' which are under analysis do indeed attempt to define evil; they might not be able to conclusively tell us what exactly evil is, but they do provide us with certain signs to look for when trying to distinguish evil from good. The attributes the stories assign might be stereotypical, prejudiced and simplistic but they are nevertheless there. Myth does try to make us respond to evil in a certain way by providing us with some fairly definite characteristics.

In addition to producing emotion, evil has a further and quite straightforward function. As Ellwood holds, "[it] exists, so to speak, not only as part of the story, but for the sake of the story."[5] This means that evil is vitally necessary to make the story a story in the first place. Without evil spurring the hero's or heroine's actions, there would be no heroic story. The antagonist thus, is as important as the protagonist, something also apparent from the Lévi-Straussian diagrams of the preceding chapter. Good and evil are in a dialectical relationship. They are equally present and create and inform each other, although there is often a bias toward good in stories such as *Star Wars* and *Harry Potter*. The following discussions will show if and how evil in *Star Wars* and *Harry Potter* fulfils the two functions outlined here: production of feelings and propulsion of the story. The Emperor of *Star Wars* as an entirely evil character will be the starting point of this analysis.

On a character scale from static to round, the Emperor would have to be placed rather far towards the static side. As could be seen in the diagrams of the preceding chapter he never changes his place in the binary opposition-mediator scenarios and always remains at the bottom. To be fair, the three more recent movies do show his development from senator to Chancellor of a small part of the galaxy and finally to ruler over his galactic empire. Nevertheless, this development is an outward one and not accompanied by any change in character. The Emperor remains the same evil person from beginning to end. In the first two movies of the series he is initially Senator then Chancellor Palpatine, a seemingly friendly and harmless advisor for both Padmé, then Queen Amidala, and Anakin Skywalker. However, the audience knows that he has abused his position during a political and economic crisis to enhance his power. By obtaining emergency powers in a semi-legal way, he has managed to become chancellor. This already indicates that he stops short of nothing to increase his influence. At the end of movie one when a close-up is shown of his partly overshadowed face at Jedi Master Qui-Gon Jinn's funeral it is suggested that the 'phantom menace' of the title alludes to Palpatine. The Senator, like many other stereotypical villains is the active force, while the 'good' side remains largely passive at first. In fact, the Jedi are the epitome of passiveness since they never take

---

5   Ellwood 3.

action till the eleventh hour. Thus, a further binary opposition can be identified in the movies, namely that of action versus passiveness. The implication here, as well as in many other works of formulaic fiction containing heroes and villains (for instance, 19th-century melodrama or Gothic fiction) is that reacting is valued more positively than acting. The rather negative valuation of acting, particularly acting to achieve one's own aims, made it possible to ideologically contain certain people or groups of people in their seemingly naturally allotted sphere (consider the role of women in 19th-century melodrama. Acting on their own behalf would have destroyed the Victorian ideal of the meek, passive and submissive middle-class woman who was content to place her husband's and family's needs before her own). One can thus see how stories are constructed to naturalise and keep social practices and patterns in place. In the ensuing chapter on Anakin/Vader it will be discussed in how far this strict moral judgement on action and passiveness is questioned in the movies, as passivity very specifically contributes to the development of evil. The purely negative valuation of action, as will be seen, is also attacked in the figure of Harry Potter.

Palpatine realises the importance of Anakin for his plans of ruling the galaxy and knows that he needs to get closer to the young man in order to feed him with a few of his ideas and notions. In film two, and even more so in film three, Palpatine thus becomes a father figure for young Anakin. While Obi-Wan represents the 'good' father, Palpatine obviously takes on the role of the 'bad' one.[6] And, as is so often the case in formulaic stories, eg. Gothic ones, inevitably the 'bad' father is initially more nurturing and offers more opportunities than the 'good' one. It is to Palpatine's advantage that the good side, represented by figures such as Yoda and Obi-Wan, fails to take care of Anakin properly, so that he has the opportunity to seduce the young man with evil. Again, as is the case with the action versus passivity opposition, the stance of the Jedi is questioned in the course of the movies, especially the more recent ones. It remains to be seen whether Obi-Wan is really unconditionally the 'good' father. Interestingly, only the 'good' pole of the opposition is ever genuinely called into question. It stays clear throughout that Palpatine is the 'bad' father for Anakin and that the kind of action he takes is evil. Evil, it seems is not even worth questioning while good acquires more weight and importance by being challenged. This treatment of evil is another indication of the fact that Palpatine / the Emperor is a rather static figure. The way he is presented makes it clear that evil is not supposed to appear in any way glamorous in the stories. What the tales convey here is the message that it is harder to be good than

---

6   Cf. Kate E. Behr, *The Representation of Men in the English Gothic Novel 1762-1820* (Levinston: Edwin Mellen Press, 2002) 114 for a definition of the 'good' father in Gothic fiction and 146 for an explication of the 'bad' one.

evil but possibly more rewarding in the end. Ideologically, leading the 'good life' mostly presupposes hard work and commitment but pays off at some stage. Choosing the simpler but bad path, as the story of Anakin shows, loses one love, family and friends, all that is worth living for in the ideological logic of the tales.

Though static the Emperor is rather clever. He understands the way the good and the evil sides influence and determine each other and in the first three episodes he is the only one who understands Anakin's needs, and how to play to them. He is aware of the young man's frustration about not being taken into full confidence by the Jedi Council and of his apparent weakness, his love for Padmé. His subtle manipulations almost always find their mark. When, for instance, it comes to finding and destroying the evil General Grievous, Palpatine says to Anakin: "I would worry about the collective wisdom of the [Jedi] Council if it didn't select you for this assignment. You're the best choice by far."[7] The statement does not attack the Jedi directly. Palpatine is careful not to turn Anakin against him by any remark that might anger the young man. Expressing his 'worry' is supposed to show that he cares for Anakin. More importantly, his statement firmly implants into Anakin the idea that none but he should go and destroy the evil general, a wish that Anakin himself has not explicitly expressed before this point. Thus Palpatine makes sure that the idea nags at Anakin, eats him from the inside and turns him against the Jedi, should they, as the Chancellor foresees, give the assignment to someone more experienced. His statement furthermore aims at assuring Anakin that Palpatine believes in him. He makes sure that Anakin will turn to him when the confidence of the Jedi Council is withheld. When indeed Anakin is not chosen for the mission to destroy General Grievous, Palpatine becomes more open in his remarks against the Jedi. After Anakin has informed him about the decision of the Jedi Council he says: "[The Jedi] don't trust you, Anakin. They see your future. They know your power will be too strong to control. You must break through the fog of lies the Jedi have created around you."[8] Here, the Chancellor's language becomes stronger but at the same time more vague. The 'fog of lies' is a very interesting metaphor in this respect. It sounds extremely powerful. However, what exactly does the 'fog of lies' the Jedi create mean? Palpatine here blames others and at the same time cleverly disguises the fact that it is he who has built up a 'fog of lies.'[9] The very unclear term 'fog' supports the vagueness of the whole statement. Evil in *Star Wars* is thus

---

7   *Revenge of the Sith* 00:39:05.

8   *Revenge of the Sith* 00:59:43.

9   Cf. also Shanti Fader, "'A Certain Point of View:' Lying Jedi, Honest Sith, and the Viewers who Love Them," *Star Wars and Philosophy: More Powerful than You Can Possibly Imagine*, Ed. Kevin S. Decker and Jason T. Eberl (Chicago: Open Court, 2005) 202.

not only active but also clever when it comes to exploiting the weaknesses of its opponents and those it wants to ensnare.

The main reason why Palpatine is essentially a static character and belongs at one end of the character spectrum for *Star Wars* and *Harry Potter* outlined in this and the ensuing two chapters, is that audiences do not get to know the true psychological motivations for his actions.[10] They are not shown his development from innocence to evil as they are Anakin's. It can, however, be assumed that his formation was achieved in a way similar to Anakin's since in the course of the movies, the audience learns about the organisation of both the Jedi and the Sith. To become either, one has to find a master, or Lord respectively, to provide the training. Both orders thus depend on a structure of interdependent mastery and apprenticeship. Hanson and Kay elaborate on this quoting from *Secrets of the Sith*: "[A] Sith named Darth Bane came up with a system that dictates that only two Sith may exist at a given time ... A master, and apprentice. The tension created between the two is aimed toward achieving their dark goals, for the apprentice shall be only as long as his master is his superior."[11] Though Palpatine alludes to a Sith Lord he has once known, the audience never conclusively finds out whether this was the Sith who turned Palpatine into what he is. The mystery that surrounds Palpatine and the fact that the audience only knows the Senator as an embodiment of evil without a definite idea where that evil comes from, support Ellwood's assertions about the nature of it. "[E]vil in the end is always the inexplicable. It is that which ought not to be, yet is."[12] The figure of Palpatine, however, also shows that myth is dedicated to producing feelings within its recipients. While Palpatine seems utterly boring and prosaic because he is so static, he still generates strong feelings of revulsion, but maybe also a certain fascination. For some it might seem admirable the way in which he manages to manipulate others and make them confer to his wishes. Anakin, who, as was already shown in the preceding chapter, can be seen as the character closest to all of us, mediating between myth as rather one-dimensional and simplistic story and reality, is certainly taken in by Palpatine. He is eaten up by the decision between Jedi and Sith and grows closer and closer to the seducer, while Palpatine seems to enjoy his life as an as yet hidden agent of evil.

The sole recognisable driving force behind Palpatine's actions is his hunger for power. For him, power justifies his behaviour and he believes it to possess an equalising force. This is proven by the following statement he makes: "All who gain power are afraid to lose it. Even the Jedi."[13] Anakin remarks that "[the] Jedi

---

10   Cf. also Jullier 24.

11   Hanson and Kay 323-24.

12   Ellwood 4.

13   *Revenge of the Sith* 00:43:27.

use their power for good" whereupon Palpatine replies: "Good is a point of view, Anakin. The Sith and the Jedi are similar in almost every way including their quest for greater power."[14] Obviously, Palpatine says these things to manipulate Anakin yet again but he also expresses his motivating philosophy. Both concepts, good and evil, are set against each other here showing once more that meaning is usually generated between the two poles of a dichotomy. The remark also quite bluntly exposes the ideology behind the discourse of good and evil that runs through Western societies. Ideologically, good and evil are always fixed with certain attributes and of course they are evaluated morally. Palpatine clearly states that good is a point of view, implying that evil is one, too. Ideology tends to veil the fact that good and evil are judged differently by different nations and by each and every person. Here, Palpatine in Derridaian fashion deconstructs the ideology that also runs through the movies themselves, because it is apparent that they also offer a certain view on what is good and what is evil. The movie deconstructs itself here and the ideologies at its core become exposed, even if only for a moment. The moment passes quickly, however, since contextually the Chancellor only exposes the Jedi as limited while at the same time he is careful not to expose his own side. So, on the surface, only the good side is questioned. The evil of the bad side remains evil exactly because Palpatine is not self-critical and only blames the good side. And, more importantly, since it is the evil side that questions the good one, the criticism of the good side, though it is justified in some respects, must needs be rejected by the audience as inappropriate. Ultimately, the deconstructive moment thus loses its potential, because what the villain says cannot be taken seriously. It rather functions as a reaffirmation of the clear line between good and evil for the viewers.

Palpatine's statement is further illuminating for his use of the term 'power'. He empties the moral terms of good and evil and substitutes them with the concept of power, thereby dispelling feelings of guilt, shame or any moral nature to justify himself and his doings. In the further course of the conversation between the Chancellor and Anakin it transpires that the difference between Sith and Jedi is that the Sith derive their power from negative emotions such as anger and hatred while the Jedi are rather dispassionate and selfless.[15] Anakin later on actually does summon all his negative emotions and acts on them, thus proving the derivation of Sith-power true. In the subsequent scene in which Anakin reacts furiously when Palpatine fully exposes himself as a Sith Lord the Chancellor says that his anger gives him strength.[16] However, this is exposed as a lie when the Chancellor's own

---

14   *Revenge of the Sith* 00:43:33.

15   Cf. *Revenge of the Sith* 00:43:52.

16   Cf. *Revenge of the Sith* 1:02:03.

conduct throughout the first three movies is taken into consideration. The most powerful Sith at that stage of the story, the Chancellor is clearly *not* governed by emotions of any kind at all. He rather obtains his power by manipulating the feelings of others while he himself is mostly calm and calculating. A large part of his power depends on well-chosen, adulating words and Anakin's credulity. The Chancellor certainly needs the far more physically powerful Anakin to cement his own power and he knows that he can only get him on his side by using his full range of persuasive skills. Power, in many of its variants, is an important driving force for evil in *Star Wars*. However, since power is as elusive a concept as evil, it is not very useful for explaining evil. Neither Palpatine's power based on cool and emotionally distanced reasoning and scheming, nor Anakin/Vader's power founded on an excess of emotions, however, are condoned in the stories. As with many of the other themes treated in the course of the tales, a balance between rationality and emotion seems to be necessary if one is to wield power wisely.

The most important hold Palpatine has over Anakin is his knowledge of the young man's love for Padmé and his fear of her death. And again, the Chancellor uses his verbal skills to forge an even closer bond between Anakin and himself. He makes Anakin believe that he has the power over life and death. This he does by telling the young Jedi the *legend* of Darth Plagueis, a Sith Lord who was able to prevent the death of loved ones by bending the Force to his will.[17] It is interesting to note that Palpatine explicitly states that the story of Darth Plagueis is a legend. Thus the audience can assume that its truth value is at least highly questionable. Furthermore, the Chancellor never directly says that he himself holds any such power. He assumes, correctly, that Anakin will infer as much. Palpatine here embodies the dangers Roland Barthes sees with myth. Myth can be consciously employed to manipulate people, to persuade them to take a certain direction, because it seems to be the natural one. This can be rather harmless as when people are influenced to buy a specific product through advertising, but it can also have grave consequences when people are indoctrinated into doing something that would normally be against their moral code. Palpatine uses a story to get Anakin to do his will, a story that later causes much harm and destruction. The ideological use of myth as understood by Barthes is identified as evil in *Star Wars* since it corrupts an otherwise promising and upright young man. The chancellor goes on to tempt Anakin:

Anakin, if one is to understand the great mystery one must study all its aspects not just the dogmatic narrow view of the Jedi. If you wish to become a complete and wise leader you must embrace a larger view of the Force. Be careful of the Jedi, Anakin. Only through me can

---

17   Cf. *Revenge of the Sith* 00:44:34.

you achieve greater power than any Jedi. Learn to know the dark side of the Force and you will be able to save your wife from certain death.[18]

This scene of seduction[19] is quite interesting because in part, Palpatine is right, of course. The most complete and wisest persons are those who know and have experienced both good and evil. They are also best equipped to get through life relatively unscathed. This is, for instance, true for many Gothic heroes and heroines who have to lose their perfect innocence in order to lead their lives safely and soundly.[20]

However, while seemingly saying that both or all sides are important, Palpatine totally denounces one side, the side of the Jedi as simply 'dogmatic' and 'narrow.' A complete and wise person is tolerant or at least neutral about all perspectives, so it becomes obvious here at the latest that Palpatine is not a good mentor who means well with Anakin. He clearly favours the dark side. Later in the quotation, Palpatine even specifically warns Anakin to beware of the Jedi, making it sound as though they were the evil ones. At the end of his short speech, he plays upon the two issues that are bothering Anakin. He is not satisfied with the way the Jedi treat him and wants more; and he is afraid of losing his wife, embodying a person torn between the search for (material) success and status and a quieter domestic life. Ideologically, it is implied that the two different desires do not go together. As will be seen in chapters six and eight, this holds for the figure of Anakin and also for his wife Padmé. In his speech to Anakin, once more Palpatine substitutes the word *evil* with the term *power*. Thus this statement is linked to his earlier one about good depending on the point of view. Later on he even warns Anakin not to "continue to be a pawn of the Jedi Council."[21] In fact he himself makes Anakin a pawn in his own greater schemes. The metaphor from chess is apt here since chess requires a player who determines the fate of the chessmen. Palpatine's remark implies that he sees Anakin as determined from the outside and not able to make up his own mind. It is quite ironic that a chesspiece that does not have its own will is supposed to

---

18   *Revenge of the Sith* 1:00:51.

19   There are several critics who point to the 'feminised' nature of Palpatine and the homoerotic subtext created by it (cf. for instance Veronica A. Wilson, "Seduced by the Dark Side of the Force: Gender, Sexuality, and Moral Agency in George Lucas's *Star Wars* Universe," *Culture, Identities and Technology in the Star Wars Films: Essays on the Two Trilogies*, Ed. Carl Silvio and Tony M. Vinci (Jefferson: McFarland & Company, 2007) 142, 147).

20   A good example of such a development from innocence to experience would be Emily St. Aubert, the heroine from Ann Radcliffe's *The Mysteries of Udolpho*.

21   *Revenge of the Sith* 1:01:42.

command life and death. The irony, however, is lost on Anakin and the superficial viewer. Evil, it can be said, determines and is determined. Palpatine determines Anakin and other minions. He in turn is determined by his longing for power.

Evil thus seems to be closely associated with determinism. Once more, as with the good-evil dichotomy, the terms in the one between free will and determinism inform and constitute each other. There would be no need to think about free choice if humans did not feel themselves to be influenced by factors outside their control which limit the freedom of will. Determinism would have no bearing on people if they did not consider themselves free beings, at least to a certain extent. Western, and particularly American, literature is suffused with questions about free will and determination. Thus the treatment of the binary in popular culture continues a long tradition. The preoccupation with matters of choice and determination goes back to the rise of Protestant forms of religion during the 16th century. In fact, Calvinism and Puritanism brought the terms of the binary closely together favouring, however, determinism. Adherents of these religious groupings believed that every human being's actions were predestined by God. Free choice for good or evil in life had little impact as you were either among God's elect or not. The reasoning was that if you were one of God's chosen people, your good acts would not be acts of your own free will but acts predetermined by the Almighty. If, however, you were not infused with God's grace, you could not gain that select position by choosing to do good. The highest power alone decided over your fate.[22] This belief in predetermination and divine grace has always had its supporters and detractors. It was a cosy belief for those who felt themselves to be among the elect, because it took final responsibility away from them and seemed to condone even their less ideal deeds. For those who were less sure about their status, it must have been a painful doctrine, because it was rather unforgiving, focused on arbitrary decrees of the Almighty and precluded a chance to reform through good deeds and thus gain a place among the blessed.

As I argue that popular stories such as the ones analysed by me, to a certain extent take over the functions of (religious) myths, it is not surprising that they deal with questions the old religions and myths also foregrounded. However, since strong religious belief is on the vane, it is no wonder, either, that in a world in which they partly replace religious texts, these popular tales advocate a more didactic stance oriented towards influencing and improving human behaviour. In a world in which an entity such as God is missing for many people, the stories have to create a strong picture of man who can rely on himself. This they cannot very well do by favouring a deterministic world view in which, after all, human agency

---

22   Cf. Perry D. Westbrook, *Free Will and Determinism in American Literature* (Cranbury: Associated University Presses, Inc., 1979) 3-4.

would be limited. They rather need to emphasise a world view based on personal choice and present role models to readers and audiences who take the good decisions. These good decisions are then even more clearly highlighted by the bad choices the evildoers make. Readers and audiences thus learn by positive and negative example. One such negative example, as will be seen, is the way Anakin lets the Chancellor interfere with his freedom of choice.

The moment the Chancellor has won Anakin over completely by a mixture of undermining his trust in the Jedi and playing to his fears about Padmé, the viewers learn that Palpatine never had the power over life and death and very likely never will have it. Padmé dies in spite, or in fact even because of Anakin's decision for evil and Palpatine does not stir a finger to help her. It is, after all, rather convenient for him to be rid of Padmé, who represents one of the only entities that still connect Anakin to the good side. With Padmé (and Obi-Wan) gone, Anakin will be all his. Palpatine's robbing Anakin of his friends and connections is a truly evil act. Terry Eagleton in his work *On Evil* says that "[h]uman beings can indeed achieve a degree of self-determination. But they can do so only in the context of a deeper dependence on others of their kind, a dependence which is what makes them human in the first place. It is this (…) that evil denies."[23] What Eagleton says here, is that human freedom and prosperity depend on people's relationships with others. Denying the necessity of human bonds leads to evil, as can be seen both in the case of the Emperor and Anakin/Vader.

With Anakin's conversion, Palpatine's status changes, too. He has managed to win over the person he believes to possess the power of extinguishing the Jedi order for ever and is paving his way to galactic rule. From the moment of Anakin's submission to his doctrine he becomes the master and the young man his apprentice. As soon as this happens, he puts on a cloak, draws back from Anakin and becomes remote. This seems a little inconsequential since he has met his young apprentice on a friendly and equal footing before. However, it falls in with Eagleton's assertion that evil renounces human contacts.[24] He now insists on being higher up in the hierarchy. Maybe his step is logical in the sense that the usual way the master-apprentice structure works is that at some stage the apprentice disposes of her/his master and becomes master her-/himself.[25] If interpreted in this way, Palpatine's retreat and his new aloofness are based in the fear of being overcome by his apprentice one day, too. He does well not to give Anakin too much ground for attack. Palpatine's change also dehumanises him. As Chancellor Palpatine he had a face and a human name, as the Emperor he is shrouded and he loses his name. He is

---

23   Eagleton 12.

24   Cf. Eagleton 12.

25   Cf. Hanson and Kay 323-24.

just the Emperor, the one who stands for and exerts infinite power and he becomes even more static than before. An Emperor is usually a person who holds largely unrestricted power. Thus the name, or rather title, is fitting because Palpatine has become the living embodiment of his dictum on power as making the value judgement of good and evil superfluous. Palpatine's name change alludes to a point about evil that will become more prominent in the discussion of Voldemort. Changing one's name is indicative of dissatisfaction with certain attributes or elements of one's existence. The name change points to a wish to be different, to acquire another identity. Thus a further characteristic of evil, which goes hand in hand with the striving for power is the dissatisfaction with the self. Evil, it is suggested, perhaps a little simplistically, is largely committed by people who are not at one with themselves who do not have a sufficiently balanced character. However simplistic, this view is supported by Eagleton who holds that "[t]he evil (…) are those who are deficient in the art of living."[26]

One other thing that changes with Palpatine's withdrawal, and his turning into an emblem of power, is that he discontinues his habit of talking. It was already mentioned that in the first three movies he talks rather incessantly and uses his command of language to win Anakin over. As soon as this is accomplished, words lose their importance. From the moment of Anakin's conversion onwards, the viewers only ever see the Emperor in short sequences in which he does not say much. Thus it is not only from Anakin that he withdraws but from the complete story. He becomes the principle of evil and is behind most of the mischief done in the stories. However, his role as the emblem of evil is rather static and one-dimensional. The final destruction of the Emperor is brought about because he, like Anakin, has one great weakness. It is funny that he manages to perceive Anakin's so clearly but is largely ignorant of his own. This weakness is that he sees Anakin's ability to love as a shortcoming and does not consider the positive power of this emotion. Love can produce fear of loss and in this function is responsible for Anakin's conversion into Darth Vader, however, it can also create fellow-feeling and strong bonds. In the end, one of the factors that make Vader change is his love for his son. The Emperor is only strong as long as his servant (Vader) is loyal to him. There seems to be a moment when the chief villain realises this and becomes anxious about Vader's loyalty. In *Return of the Jedi* Darth Vader approaches the Emperor about a small rebel force that has landed on the forest moon Endor, penetrating the dark side's deflector shield. He also tells the Emperor that "[his] son is with them."[27] The Emperor answers: "I wonder if your feelings on this matter are clear, Lord Vader." When Vader replies that "they are clear," the Emperor is

---

26   Eagleton 128.
27   *Return of the Jedi* 1:04:13

satisfied.[28] He even says that he has foreseen that Luke will come to Vader and that "[his] compassion for [Vader] will be his undoing."[29] The Emperor is much too sure of Vader's allegiance at this stage and acts very strangely. Almost in one breath he suspects Vader of unclear feelings about Luke but then just assumes that Luke's compassion will be his undoing. How can he doubt Vader and at the same time be sure of Luke's failure? Obviously his Frankensteinean arrogance has made the Emperor blind. He is too self-important to consider seriously that his creation, whom he believes to possess no self-will anymore, could turn against him. In the end of course, this is exactly what happens. The Emperor is defeated by his false evaluation of Anakin/Vader's 'weakness,' love. This fits in with another central ideology of Western discourse. Since love finally overcomes all evil in the movies, the ideology of love triumphant, love being stronger than everything else is transported here. Evil does not understand the power of and is unable to feel love.

Summing up, the Emperor can be described as a character whose only known motif for action is his hunger for power. He clearly functions as the seducer in the first three movies and the rather foggy principle of evil in the last three ones. As the former he has a human name but as the latter he sheds it and assumes one that fits his status as a concept. He is clever when it comes to achieving his aims but he overestimates his power and other people's fear of it and him. This combination of character traits aligns him with other rather stereotypical villains and can of course only lead to his downfall in the end. Although the Emperor is rather static, he is indicative of some of the things generally perceived to be evil. He is active in a clever and manipulative way, striving for the fulfilment of his aims. His actions, however, are only focused on his evil ends and his stasis as a character testifies to the fact that he does not have the ability to change or develop, supporting the tautology that evil, no matter in what a variety of forms it can manifest itself is always simply evil. Evil seemingly also has much to do with the wish to be almighty. Exercising power obviously fills a void, compensates the evil character for a dissatisfaction with him- or herself. It very conspicuously lacks the ability to understand and feel love. Finally, evil frequently seems to be driven and determined by the things it strives for. In turn it has to determine others to achieve its goals. Thus evil is strongly associated with the determination side of the free will - determinism binary. The discussion of the Emperor supports Ellwood's statements from the beginning of the chapter. Although evil itself basically lacks emotion, it produces feelings within those who fall prey to it and the audiences who watch the movies (see for instance the emotions Palpatine manages to stir within Anakin concerning Padmé and his relationship with the Jedi). Additionally, the analysis

---

28   *Return of the Jedi* 1:04:27.
29   *Return of the Jedi* 1:04:46.

also shows the inadequacy of Ellwood's interpretation. *Star Wars* quite distinctly presents us with the character traits of evil. Whether they are 'true' to reality or consistent with each and everyone's perception of evil or whether they are prejudiced and mirror a certain (Western) mindset is another question altogether. It is obvious, however, that the stories do wish to purport a particular image of evil. This trend of characterising evil is similarly visible in *Harry Potter*.

5.2 'PLAY WITH SECURITY': VOLDEMORT

Like the Emperor, Voldemort is only ever found at the bottom of the Lévi-Straussian diagrams for *Harry Potter*. Just like the Emperor in *Star Wars*, he is the constant evil principle in the novels. He is also similar to the Emperor with respect to the fact that he, too once had a human name which he shed for another when he acquired power. Voldemort's names, however, are much more metaphorical and less emblematic than those of Palpatine / the Emperor. This is a first indication that the Emperor rather serves as a type embodying all that is evil in his story, whereas Voldemort has a slightly higher degree of individuality. There are further points that differentiate the Dark Lord from the Emperor and show that he is not quite as static as the evildoer from *Star Wars*. Voldemort does not undergo any character development either but the readers are shown how he came to be the way he is. He was born Tom Marvolo Riddle, a name he never uses in the course of the story and one he does not want others to use.[30] It is a highly suggestive name. Thomas "comes from the Aramaic word for 'twin'" and thus again highlights the importance of dualisms for the story.[31] Tom Riddle will indeed find his 'twin' or good counterpart in Harry Potter. The term 'twin' is explicitly used with reference to Harry's and Voldemort's wands that share cores. The wonder of the 'twin cores' is highlighted in book four after Harry has escaped from the resurrected Voldemort and Dumbledore explains the magic Harry's wand performed on this occasion.[32] Both Voldemort's and Harry's wands contain a tail feather of Fawkes, Dumbledore's Phoenix and a symbol of supreme goodness. If Voldemort's and Harry's wands share cores this at least suggests that the power of both proceeds from the same source and that both initially had equal chances of using this power

---

30   Cf. Rowling *Chamber* 337.

31   Granger *Looking for God in Harry Potter* 48.

32   Since the two wands are brothers they do not work properly against each other. Harry's strength of will and force of mind are ultimately greater than Voldemort's and his wand forces the villain's one to reverse the last spells it has performed. This means that the shadowy forms of people Voldemort has murdered appear and help Harry escape (cf. Rowling *Goblet* 605).

for good or for evil. Tom Riddle's middle name Marvolo resonates with the English word 'marvel' and marks the evil wizard as special. The term 'marvel' has positive associations since it usually describes something good happening against all odds. The connotations of the name Riddle are quite obvious. Voldemort is and has been from his birth onwards, a mysterious figure. The Dark Lord's natural name then has several implications. First of all, it contains an allusion to the binaries which play an important part in the story. Secondly, it hints at Voldemort's strange and elusive character and thirdly, and rather surprisingly, it has a positive association to something extraordinary and good happening. Thus the name embodies the ambiguity of myth and its tendency to bring opposites more closely together. The Phoenix whose tail feather is at the core of Voldemort's wand is another symbol of this ambiguity since the mythical creature unites the ideas of life and death by dying in flames and being reborn from the ashes.[33] The name Voldemort bore as a boy therefore shows that a part of Riddle's original disposition at least seems to have been good and that he might have developed in a different way.

Riddle decides to shed his ordinary name early on, adopting the title of Lord and fashioning for himself the name Voldemort, "a name [he] knew wizards everywhere would one day fear to speak."[34] The aristocratic title he uses shows his firm belief in his high worth and in hierarchy. He clearly considers himself to be above other people. Since Voldemort is not aristocratic by nature, Rowling cleverly subverts the cliché of the evil aristocrat which is so common, for instance, in Gothic fiction and melodrama of the 19th century. Evil does not necessarily emanate from a certain class, though some of the evil figures in *Harry Potter* such as the Malfoys are aristocratic, but it springs from choices single persons make. Voldemort's self-fashioning as a Lord and the unusual name he chooses indicate that he is dissatisfied with himself and his situation, an inclination he shares with the Emperor. Voldemort wishes to be special and to be noticed for his outrageous deeds. He also wants to ascend the social ladder and acquire the prestige that members of the aristocracy hold. The actual name 'Voldemort' is very allusive. The French term vol-de-mort, meaning flight or wings of death, has negative connotations and hints at the fact that the Lord is the destructive principle in the

---

33   Cf. also Sarah E. Gibbons's insightful interpretation of Phoenix-symbolism in *Harry Potter*. Gibbons uses the Phoenix to illuminate the relationship between myth and commodity culture and argues that only by becoming commodified, i.e. being turned into popular culture can a myth truly unfold its symbolic power. (Sarah E. Gibbons, "Death and Rebirth: *Harry Potter* and the Mythology of the Phoenix," *Scholarly Studies in Harry Potter: Applying Academic Methods to a Popular Text*, Ed. Cynthia Whitney Hallett (Lewiston: Edwin Mellen Press, 2005) 87-88).

34   Rowling *Chamber* 337.

novels.[35] Voldemort, the name hints, is an agent of death for other people. His evil is thus clearly associated with death, a link that is strengthened by the villain's Horcruxes, his means of attaining immortality through murder. In contrast to Voldemort, the Emperor is not as immediately coupled with death, the reason for which is that, unlike Voldemort his activeness is limited to words rather than physical deeds. The Emperor is someone who predominantly talks others (especially Vader) into doing the dirty work.

Voldemort shares the Emperor's obsession with power though he is never really the tempter-figure for Harry that the Emperor alias Palpatine is for Anakin. It is interesting, though that in the movie-version of *Harry Potter and the Philosopher's Stone*, Voldemort, in the guise of Defence against the Dark Arts-Professor Quirrell, distinctly does take up the role of the seducer. He even tempts Harry with the same lies Palpatine manages to seduce Anakin with. Voldemort tells Harry, through Quirrell, that together they can bring Harry's dead parents back to life.[36] This is rather inconsistent with the novel in which it is quite clear that Harry would never choose Voldemort's side and offers without him having to explicitly affirm this. Possibly the producers of the movie had to make Harry's choice against evil more graphic, because films often tend to leave less time to focus on character development in more than a perfunctory fashion. In contrast to Anakin, Harry expressly does not let the bad events from his past influence him in favour of evil, so that Voldemort knows quite early on that Harry is a lost cause for him.

Nevertheless, he gives Harry and the readers an illuminating piece of information about his views on good and evil in book one. Professor Quirrell, whom Voldemort possesses, tells Harry that before he met the Dark Lord, he had been "full of ridiculous ideas about good and evil. Lord Voldemort showed [him] how wrong [he] was. There is no good and evil, there is only power, and those too weak to seek it."[37] This statement is very similar to Palpatine's on good being a point of view. The difference is that while Palpatine truly effaces the binary opposition between good and evil to supplant it with the concept of power, Quirrell upholds dichotomies. He replaces the opposing forces of good and evil with those of power and weakness. So, obviously for Voldemort, with Quirrell as his

---

35   Cf. also Yvonne Dreyer-Gehle, "'Harry Potter' im Schussfeld des Christentums," *Harry Potter im Quadrat: Der Unheimliche Erfolg eines Best- und Longsellers*, Ed. Peter Conrady (Oberhausen: ATHENA-Verlag) 22. (Cf. also Travis Prinzi's (152), John Killinger's (12) and Edmund M. Kern's (54) discussions of the name).

36   Cf. *Harry Potter and the Philosopher's Stone [German version: Harry Potter und der Stein der Weisen]*, dir. Chris Columbus, perf. Daniel Radcliffe, Robbie Coltrane, Richard Harris, DVD, Warner Brothers, 2001, 2:06:06.

37   Rowling *Stone* 313.

mouthpiece, a certain duality exists which equates his own evil deeds with power and the good side's efforts with weakness. While *Star Wars* through Palpatine's remark exhibits a meta-awareness of its own binary nature and thus slightly deconstructs itself, *Harry Potter* does not genuinely question its own binary set-up. One binary opposition is replaced with another. This is consistent with what has already been proved in the first two chapters: *Star Wars* is more open with respect to its binary structure than *Harry Potter*. Binaries are more clearly upheld in Rowling's novels.

However, another interpretation is possible. Palpatine's remark, though obviously devaluing binaries, comes from the evildoer and is therefore very likely to be rejected by most audience members who would protest that there are neutral criteria for establishing what is good and what is bad. This, as was mentioned, weakens the deconstructive moment. In *Harry Potter* it is the villain who affirms the existence of binaries, if only of the one consisting of power and weakness. Coming from the villain it might induce readers to ponder whether good and evil can really be equated with power and weakness, whether the villain's understanding of power and weakness is adequate, and whether there is not something in between these extremes. In this sense, the less deconstructive stance in *Harry Potter* might paradoxically even lead to a more critical attitude in readers than Palpatine's view on good as a point of view in *Star Wars*.

Voldemort's power, which he himself avows to so openly, strongly depends on violations of boundaries and moral norms. One of Dumbledore's memories of young Tom Riddle exemplifies how early this destructive penchant manifested itself in Voldemort. Back then, not yet headmaster, Dumbledore visits young Tom Riddle at the orphanage in which he has been raised to tell him about Hogwarts. The first account the readers get of Tom comes from the orphanage's manager. She confides Tom Riddle's strange behaviour to Dumbledore. "He scares the other children."[38] Obviously he has brought about the death of a pet rabbit and has unsettled two children in some way or another on a trip to the sea.[39] The first information Dumbledore ever gets about Riddle thus has to do with fear, destruction and death. Tom Riddle has not had a chance of developing his magical abilities in a favourable environment wherefore they seem to have grown out of hand already. When he learns that it is magic he can do he grows all excited and tells Dumbledore what he has done in that respect so far: "I can make things move without touching them. I can make animals do what I want them to do, without training them. I can make bad things happen to people who annoy me. I can make

---

38 Rowling *Prince* 250.

39 Cf. Rowling *Prince* 250-51.

them hurt if I want to."[40] He has also, it transpires, been stealing from the other children at the orphanage.[41] All this points to the fact that early on, Voldemort has discovered evil within himself and has not tried to quench it. It seems as if the boy already feels a certain entitlement, a right to take revenge on a society which he feels treats him badly. In the young Riddle's narration everything which will constitute the grown-up Voldemort is already laid out. He delights in dominating and hurting others, and, which is worse, even as a child without having gone through any magical training whatsoever and without knowing exactly what it is he can do, he uses his powers consciously to inflict harm, something Dumbledore also remarks on in his discussion of the memory with Harry.[42] This description of the young Voldemort leads to a definition of what is seen as specifically evil in Rowling's novels. Young Riddle, as well as grown-up Voldemort, are all transgression. They do not respect the property of others and they violate physical integrity. This transgressive element to evil was not apparent with the Emperor so much and it becomes obvious that as a character he is flatter than Voldemort. While the Emperor simply symbolises and embodies certain characteristics of evil, Voldemort is more of a character in his own right. Ellwood's first definition of evil which was quoted at the beginning of the chapter thus truly comes into play here for the first time. Evil is "that which causes suffering, which intrudes on what we think ought to be the rightful course of events."[43] Evil violates the way things should be and causes order and structure as we perceive it to collapse. It has a deconstructive function as it calls into question the structures we have set up for ourselves.

Voldemort's transgressions become clearer the older he gets. One of the most prominent examples of his manipulations given in the course of the novels is his treatment of Ginny Weasley in book two. By means of his old schoolboy's diary he has Ginny open the Chamber of Secrets and set a basilisk on several people. Finally, he even abducts her into the Chamber.[44] By the time Harry reaches the scene, Ginny is barely alive and the memory of Riddle contained in the diary has managed to leave the pages and act on its own. Riddle's explanation of Ginny's

---

40   Rowling *Prince* 254.

41   Cf. Rowling *Prince* 255.

42   Cf. Rowling *Prince* 259.

43   Ellwood 2.

44   For an illuminating analysis of Voldemort's diary, ideology and the implications it has for reading practices cf. Ryan Kerr, "Tom Riddle's Diary: How We Read Books," *Hog's Head Conversations: Essays on Harry Potter*, Ed. Travis Prinzi (Allentown, PA: Zossima Press, 2009) 127-39.

state is that "she opened her heart and spilled all her secrets to an invisible stranger."[45] He continues by saying that

Ginny poured out her soul to [him], and her soul happened to be exactly what [he] wanted. [He] grew stronger and stronger on a diet of her deepest fears, her darkest secrets. [He] grew powerful, far more powerful than little Miss Weasley. Powerful enough to start feeding Miss Weasley a few of [*his*] secrets, to start pouring a little of [*his*] soul back into *her*...[46]

This statement of Riddle's is relevant for more than one reason. Firstly of course it foreshadows some knowledge about Voldemort Harry and the readers only get full access to in book six. It alludes to the diary being a Horcrux and Riddle actually admits here that the journal contains part of his soul. Secondly the statement illuminates Voldemort's transgressions. He constantly escapes structures, crosses boundaries and even tries to do away with the latter completely. In this case he crosses boundaries in four ways. By leaving his 'frame,' the diary and turning from a mere memory into something more solid, he blurs boundaries of space and time as well as between the animate and the inanimate. Segregating part of his soul from his body, Voldemort defies the physical limitations humans are usually subject to. Finally, and most significantly, he blurs the boundaries of self and other when he possesses Ginny and forces her to open the Chamber of Secrets.

Another instance of this blurring of boundaries is identified by Lena Steveker as the strange connection between Harry's and Voldemort's minds. She analyses its relevance in Harry's identity formation. "Voldemort's presence within Harry is presented as a total collapse of the difference between self and other."[47] The notion of the unitary self, Steveker goes on to say, is challenged by the villain which is exemplified by so-called 'linguistic slippages' in the scenes in which Harry can partake of Voldemort's thoughts and feelings. These 'slippages' include the use of personal pronouns without clear identification of whether they refer to Harry or Voldemort.[48] The connection that Voldemort forces on Harry is interesting in several respects. As Steveker notes it questions the concept of a unitary identity. At the same time, however, it also re-establishes it. Emphasis is constantly laid on Harry's essentially good nature which shows itself ultimately unfazed by a loveless childhood with the Dursleys and the evil part of it in the form of Voldemort's Horcrux. Voldemort himself also reinforces notions of an essential identity. As much as Harry is fundamentally good, Voldemort's essentially evil nature is never

---

45   Rowling *Chamber* 332.
46   Rowling *Chamber* 333.
47   Steveker 78.
48   Steveker 75-76.

truly questioned. In this respect the stories are finally structuralist as fundamentals such as a thoroughly good and an entirely evil identity are reconstructed in Harry and Voldemort.

Still, Voldemort does temporarily endanger the stability of categories. His Horcruxes are the most prominent symbols of his transgressions. They defy space, time, and physical integrity, as well as, and most importantly, the binary of life and death, and place Voldemort somewhere outside structure because, at least until he regains his body, he is neither living nor dead and neither here nor there. In this shape he questions structure and symbolises 'play.'[49] Put more generally, Voldemort questions creation and its meaning as a whole, a stance that is also associated with evil by Eagleton.[50] A case in point is his preference of form over meaning, which is embodied by his Horcruxes maintaining his physical but not his spiritual existence. Voldemort, in short, is a poststructuralist as well as a postmodernist element to *Harry Potter*. Poststructuralists reject the meaning-giving quality of structures while postmodernists also question meaning in general. They are suspicious of authoritative concepts such as the author, the text, as well as grand narratives and express a general preference of "language games."[51] Obviously, these poststructuralist and postmodernist tendencies are rejected by Rowling. Voldemort, who lives them is clearly evil. Sarah E. Gibbons has an interesting take on this when she associates Voldemort with the postmodern obsession with youth:

In a cycle of motivation and consumption, citizens within commodity culture attempt to perpetually delay death, or at least old age, by surrounding themselves with purchasable representations of an ideal. Compared from such a perspective, Voldemort's wish to emerge from his own destruction renewed and powerful again is not abnormal. It links him both to the image of the phoenix and to the society beyond the legend, which pulls its totems of youth from fiction.[52]

John Granger also sees Voldemort as "the picture of postmodern man and a vignette-critique of the excess of our time."[53] Voldemort represents the downside to the postmodern existence. As was already mentioned, he is completely free in the sense that he does not have moral qualms and shuns human contact. His ultimate

---

49   Cf. Derrida *Writing and Difference* 352.

50   Cf. Eagleton 61.

51   Jean-François Lyotard, "The Postmodern Condition," *Literary Theory: An Anthology*, Ed. Julie Rivkin and Michael Ryan (Malden: Blackwell Publishing, 2004) 360. In this text Lyotard also defines the "crisis of narratives" (355).

52   Gibbons 90.

53   Granger *Unlocking Harry Potter* 208.

liberty, however, has also freed him from belief. He embodies the complete loss of a personal mythology, be it based in religious belief or other values. His inability to create meaning for himself leads to his fear of death which would put a stop to his entirely material life. If Voldemort can be associated with the postmodern man, he serves as a powerful critique via negative example of the loss of myths of any kind or grand narratives in contemporary society. The *Potter* series, intentionally or unintentionally, sets out to remedy this lack by creating "a new mythology"[54] which obviously resonates with a substantial number of people. In this sense it ties in with Eliade's ideas about how popular fiction and film are the mythology of today.[55]

John Granger in fact, goes further than simply calling Voldemort a 'postmodern man.' He claims that in general, Rowling's texts are truly postmodern in their attack of hegemonic institutions such as the government, the legal and educational system and the press.[56] Furthermore, he identifies as postmodern the novels' dedication to portraying the concerns of the marginalised, those who are oppressed by the 'myths' of our time.[57] I agree with Granger on the point that Voldemort is the vehicle displaying postmodern and poststructuralist tendencies in the text. However, there is much evidence (which has already been partly assembled in this thesis), that the series as a whole is rather more structuralist than poststructuralist. Many of the institutions Granger believes Rowling to attack are finally reformed and continue to exist in much the same way as before. The educational system, represented by Hogwarts is never truly called into question. After Voldemort's fall, the ideals of the school, e.g. the sorting, are perpetuated as if nothing had happened to challenge them. It remains to be seen how exactly the marginalised really fare at the end of the books. Voldemort, as a poststructuralist element is treated most mercilessly. In formulaic fashion the structural framework of the stories is finally re-established and Voldemort is prevented from becoming a true poststructuralist and postmodern element. The reactions of the wizarding community show that they do not want someone who might be able to possess them at any moment or someone who has come close to immortality, in short someone who symbolises what Derrida calls 'play.'[58] Under Voldemort's reign everything is insecure and unstable. Things can turn topsy-turvy from one moment to the other. It is no coincidence that in the final novel of the series, Voldemort has to be forced to exist only in the 'here' again by destroying his Horcruxes. He has to lose his superhuman qualities to fit into the wizarding world's order once more. As soon as the

---

54   Gibbons 91.

55   Cf. Eliade *Myth and Reality* 184-85.

56   Cf. Granger *Unlocking Harry Potter* 174-76.

57   Cf. Granger *Unlocking Harry Potter* 167-69.

58   Cf. Derrida *Writing and Difference* 352.

Horcruxes, his supernatural aides, are destroyed he is a man again and can be dealt with according to the standards of wizarding law.

In the character of Voldemort, Rowling does not joyfully affirm and embrace 'play' but focuses on the negative consequences it might have in a given society. Voldemort in power means chaos, destruction, and anarchy. By blurring boundaries, he makes a stable centre disappear. The villain is the entity that creates nostalgia in *Harry Potter*, nostalgia for the old order, for the once present boundaries and structures. Derrida also notices this nostalgia in Lévi-Strauss's works: "One (...) perceives in his work a sort of ethic of presence, an ethic of nostalgia for origins, an ethic of archaic and natural innocence."[59] Certainly, by portraying Voldemort in such an evil light, Rowling creates this nostalgia, this yearning for the good old times when life ran smoothly and when a structural corset with a secure centre defined human experience and existence. In this sense the treatment of Voldemort also strongly resembles Girardian scapegoating. 'Reciprocal violence' threatening the society has to be countered by 'unanimous violence,' a communal effort against an offender on whom all evil in society is projected.[60] And although Voldemort is by no means an innocent victim, the focus on him as the ultimate figure of evil does have something Girardian about it. For the 'good' wizards, the villain is the one who embodies all that is amiss in their society; among other things, Voldemort is racism personified. As the people Girard describes, who instead of punishing those who start the reciprocal violence, restore order by projecting evil onto an innocent third party, the wizards tend to forget or repress the fact that evil proceeds from their own midst. Racism can only exist because many people explicitly or implicitly support its ideologies, even some of those who count themselves among the 'good' side. (See also chapters eight to ten of this thesis for a closer analysis of these topics.) Were Voldemort the only adherent to racist ideas, he would not be able to make much difference in society. Still, he has to serve as scapegoat whose death reorganises the wizarding community. In this way, the novels certainly invite readers to relieve their (subconscious) guilt about their own stance on inequalities and other evils in society and their lives, by also projecting it onto Voldemort. Next to this villain they cannot be so bad. This is in line with the escapist function of formulaic fiction but it is also dangerous in the sense that it bars people from truly confronting naturalised assumptions and 'myths' (in Barthes's sense) they encounter every day.

To make absolutely sure that Voldemort is perceived as the Other of the wizarding society, he is not solely associated with evil, but also with 'madness,' which might be interpreted as *the* transgression par excellence. Foucault, for

---

59   Derrida *Writing and Difference* 369.

60   Cf. Girard 96, 144-45.

instance, identified madness as one of the chief ways in which the rules governing 'normal' behaviour can be violated, which is why it is usually treated in special hospitals or asylums away from 'normal' society.[61] The villain's connection with madness is emphasised in the way Dumbledore approaches young Tom Riddle when he first tells him about Hogwarts. "[T]he pair of them [look] rather like a hospital patient and visitor"[62] when Dumbledore sits down next to Riddle and the impression that the hospital alluded to is an asylum is strengthened by the fact that Riddle believes Dumbledore to be a psychiatrist sent for by the matron of his orphanage to check on him.[63] As a fully qualified wizard, Voldemort has the power of making people lose their sense of self, which could be qualified as spreading a kind of madness and which he demonstrates most prominently on Ginny Weasley in book two. He and his followers use the unforgivable Cruciatus curse to torture people into insanity[64] and Voldemort is closely associated with the soul-sucking 'Dementors' who leave their victims devoid of all happiness. Some of Voldemort's henchmen are raving mad, too, especially his most loyal adherent Bellatrix Lestrange, whose name is already telling in that respect and who shows marked signs of derangement in several situations.[65] In his connection to madness, Voldemort is feared as an infection on society; an element with the potential to make society ill. This is a further reason why his actions cannot be condoned. Thus Voldemort is doubly stigmatised: he is evil and he is mad to boot. No one could possibly identify with him.

His madness, however, can also serve as a narration to explain his evil. It is easier for people to come to terms with an evil deed, if they know why someone committed it. In a sense, Voldemort's madness thus makes him less frightening, because it offers a reason for his depravity. The Emperor is not associated with madness at all. The audience is not given any reason why he is evil, despite his greed for power. *Star Wars* and *Harry Potter* convey different messages about evil. In the figure of the Emperor it is not easily graspable and much less explainable. He is shown as having made a conscious choice for evil. Voldemort is more ambiguous in this respect. He is shown as entirely bad, but the link with madness also at least partly serves as an explanation for his villainy and possibly even slightly exculpates

---

61   Cf. Foucault 199.

62   Rowling *Prince* 252.

63   Cf. Rowling *Prince* 252-53.

64   Examples of victims would be Neville's parents who end up in the closed ward at St. Mungo's, the wizarding hospital (cf. Rowling *Order* 453-55).

65   One example is her behaviour at the Ministry of Magic, where she and her fellow Death Eaters try to take hold of the prophecy made about Harry and Voldemort in book five (cf. Rowling *Order* 689).

him. If he was mad from childhood, he is probably not fully responsible for his misdeeds. Gregory Desilet is correct when he criticises the ideological treatment of Voldemort: "No one, no thing, is purely evil and no conflict can be productively structured around the notion of radical evil – as that which is essentially defiled and corrupt."[66] A discussion based on such a concept of evil must needs return to and perpetuate structuralist dichotomies. Dustin Kidd argues in a similar vein when he stresses the normative function of the *Potter* novels: "Owing to their massive audience and broad appeal, the Potter novels are an extremely important source of social norms."[67] A one-sided treatment of villains in formulaic stories certainly does not promote a balanced and considerate approach with respect to delinquents in the real world. However, neither Desilet nor Kidd see the less dominant reading which might open up the possibility of a 'productively structured' discussion of evil.

The non-dominant reading of the madness-theme, which partly exculpates Voldemort, is supported by another, even more important discourse introduced to the story in book six when Harry and the readers learn about Voldemort's bad childhood. Why are the readers informed about certain periods from Voldemort's past? Are the snippets of information provided meant to arouse sympathy for a young man who did not have a good childhood and who has experienced much loss in his life? Or do they fulfil the human need for a story behind everything? It is hard for us to accept and comprehend evil without understanding where it comes from. With the Emperor, for instance, the reasons for his being evil remain largely enigmatic. This is why *Star Wars* needs a second character whose evil is explained and thereby normalised and integrated. This character is Anakin Skywalker / Darth Vader who will be in the focus of the next chapter. The need to know the reasons for something to be able to understand seems to be a motif for presenting Voldemort's story. Rowling obviously tries to show that "[v]irtue depends to some extent on material [and spiritual] well-being."[68] It can be seen that she, however slightly, questions the assumption of an essentially good or evil identity and concedes that external factors can have an influence in shaping a person. Still, she also believes in free choice. And free choice is an argument that defeats all others:

---

66   Gregory Desilet, "Deconstructing Harry Potter: The Hidden Cultural Costs of the Most Popular Children's Fantasy," *Transformative Communication Studies: Culture, Hierarchy and the Human Condition*, Ed. Omar Swartz (Leicester: Troubador Publishing Ltd., 2008) 175. See also Marc Bousquet who claims that "[t]he totalizing ethics of melodrama lean toward justification of violence – i.e. torture can be 'good' when employed against 'evil' people." (178).

67   Dustin Kidd, "Harry Potter and the Functions of Popular Culture," *Journal of Popular Culture* 40.1 (2007): n.pag. <http://lion.chadwyck.co.uk/>.

68   Eagleton 150.

despite a bad childhood, in spite of psychological problems, the good choices must always be made. In fact, Voldemort is quite a victimised character, paradoxical as that might sound: he has had a bad childhood, he is mad, he is lonely, unloved and evil and he cannot even expect sympathy. This is in stark contrast to the treatment of Anakin Skywalker / Darth Vader who is treated rather sympathetically as will be seen. This sympathy-question is extremely difficult and troubling, because it touches upon questions about choice and determination by circumstances that cannot easily be answered.[69]

One could say that we must believe in free will to be able to counter evil by punishment. As Eagleton says:

> If some people are really born evil, (…), they are no more responsible for this condition than being born with cystic fibrosis. The condition which is supposed to damn them succeeds only in redeeming them. (…) Those who wish to punish others for their evil, then, need to claim that they are evil of their own free will.[70]

Rowling's focus on free will is strengthened by the fact that the readers are also presented with a character, Harry, who is entirely the opposite of Voldemort, who also had a bad childhood but who significantly does not turn evil. The last sentence from the quotation by Eagleton, however, makes it crystal clear that the belief in free will has as many ideological connotations as the belief in (natural) determination. It serves as justification for certain opinions and acts, as much as the belief in determination. The notion that people who never try to fit in with society's norms and values remain outsiders and do not deserve our sympathy is not clearly contested by Rowling. "[She] seems to suggest that while nature determines certain aspects of one's character, it remains each individual's responsibility and choice to nurture themselves so they will become psychologically balanced and healthy

---

69   John Killinger, too brings up the question of whether Voldemort's evil is socially determined or innate but does not attempt to find an answer to it (cf. 55).

70   Eagleton 5-6. Ken Rothman directly applies this train of thought to Voldemort who he believes is unable to feel empathy with others. Instead he perceives them as objects which can be disposed of as soon as they are no longer needed (cf. Ken Rothman, "Hearts of Darkness: Voldemort and Iago, with a Little Help from Their Friends," *Essays on Evil in Popular Media: Vader, Voldemort and Other Villains*, Ed. Jamey Heit (Jefferson: McFarland & Company, Inc., 2011) 206). Rothman goes on to ask: "[S]hould persons without the capacity to recognize and weigh values be held responsible for the consequences of their actions?" (207).

individuals, like Harry Potter."[71] The information from Voldemort's past that is supposed to contextualise his evil and might create understanding is actually used to destroy him.[72] Voldemort is only ever presented through memories of 'good' characters. Although everyone knows that memory is highly subjective, we as readers trust Dumbledore, who we only know as a good character at that point in the story. His credibility is further cemented by the fact that the only memory Voldemort contributes to the story himself, the one in book two, is full of lies. Responses to Voldemort on the part of the other characters are always emotional. People either fear or hate him or are enthusiastic about his schemes. This, as Verena C. Seibold says, is one of the problems in our treatment of evil. We (understandably) allow it to be almost exclusively constructed via the feelings of those who suffer from it and neglect to take the history of and reasons for its generation into account.[73] This makes our view on it one-sided, mainly oriented towards value judgements and reinforces the Emperor's statement about good being a vantage point. The less dominant and more poststructuralist reading of Voldemort's history foregrounds the way in which binary oppositions constitute and reinforce each other. The good side establishes Voldemort's evil by presenting a rather limited version of the villain and his motivations and directing the feelings of the wizarding world and the readers in a certain direction. The implicit poststructuralist critique, however, does not go very far, as the biased treatment of Voldemort is more or less openly endorsed. The readers never once get to hear anything positive about Voldemort apart from the fact that he was a brilliant student. But since they know from Dumbledore, the supreme moral authority in the tales, that it is not abilities but moral decisions that define characters, this only tells

---

71   Karley Adney, "The Influence of Gender on Harry Potter's Heroic (Trans)Formation," *Heroism in the Harry Potter Series*, Ed. Katrin Berndt and Lena Steveker (Farnham: Ashgate, 2011) 190. Cf. also Sarah Fiona Winters who holds that "[i]n the world of Harry Potter, good and evil are manifested in external actions, not internal states of mind; it is conscious choice, not unconscious inclination, which makes a hero or a villain." (Sarah Fiona Winters, "Good and Evil in the Works of Diana Wynne Jones and J.K. Rowling," *Diana Wynne Jones: An Exciting and Exacting Wisdom*, Ed. Teya Rosenberg, Martha P. Hixon, Sharon M. Scapple and Donna R. White (New York: Peter Lang, 2002) 86.)

72   Cf. also Desilet 177.

73   Cf. Verena C. Seibold, "Noch nie war das Gute so böse – Warum auch gute Menschen böse handeln," *Noch nie war das Böse so gut: Die Aktualität einer alten Differenz*, Ed. Franz Fromholzer, Michael Preis, and Bettina Wisiorek (Heidelberg: Universitäts-verlag Winter, 2011) 93.

us that Voldemort obviously takes too much pride in his magical prowess. Dumbledore's treatment of the villain is also interesting as such.

In both *Star Wars* and *Harry Potter* it can be noted that those who develop into villains are to a certain extent neglected by the 'good' characters. There is some evidence of this for Voldemort and even more for Anakin Skywalker as will be seen in the next chapter. After re-emerging from the memory which Dumbledore shows Harry of Riddle at the Muggle orphanage, Harry asks the headmaster what he thought of Riddle upon meeting him for the first time. Dumbledore then makes some statements that are highly illuminating, though not so much about Riddle, but about himself. Or rather, his omissions reveal quite a lot about Dumbledore. It is interesting that the Hogwarts headmaster of all people, who always sees the good in others, should be so wary of Riddle from the beginning. Knowing all that Dumbledore does to nurture Harry and further the good in him, one could get the impression that he partly does it to make good his neglect of Tom Riddle. It is obvious that Tom Riddle / Voldemort has always wanted to rival Dumbledore rather than emulate his example. The wizened headmaster never explicitly tells Harry anything about how he treated Riddle after he had arrived at school but the readers can infer from the first encounter between Dumbledore and Riddle that the latter must have started his career at Hogwarts wary of the older wizard. In novel two *Harry Potter and the Chamber of Secrets* readers find out from Riddle's memory of fifty years back that the then headmaster of Hogwarts, Professor Dippet obviously held Riddle in high esteeem as a talented student and took pity on him for having to go back to the Muggle orphanage for the summer holidays.[74] Dumbledore confirms in book six that many of the teachers obviously liked Tom Riddle when he arrived at school and that it was mostly he himself who was careful with respect to the boy from the start.[75] Thus the good and righteous Dumbledore might have neglected to show Riddle the friendship and care he shows Harry. The wizened wizard must have known that Riddle, like Harry was special and since he bestows so much (positive) attention on Harry, he could have tried to win Riddle's trust and friendship.

The headmaster could have been the one to prevent Riddle from turning into Voldemort because he is the only one Riddle grudgingly respects and accepts as an equal from the start. In their first meeting at Riddle's orphanage, Dumbledore demands that the boy address him "as 'Professor' or 'sir'."[76] And, very unusual for Dumbledore, when Riddle asks him to prove that he is a wizard, he makes a demonstration of his powers and thereby exposes Riddle as a thief of his fellow

---

74   Cf. Rowling *Chamber* 263 ff.

75   Cf. Rowling *Prince* 337.

76   Rowling *Prince* 254.

orphans' property.[77] Up to this point in the story, the readers have hardly ever seen Dumbledore this demonstrative and strict. It seems as if the old wizard somehow already knows at this early stage in Riddle's career what the wizarding world will have to deal with. He seems to believe or feel that the only language Riddle understands is power and he establishes his power as a counter force to Riddle's from the very start. Dumbledore counters Riddle's commanding tone which foreshadows Voldemort's role as a none too benevolent master, by his request for respect. He furthermore makes clear that the way in which Riddle has so far employed his abilities is not condoned at Hogwarts. "At Hogwarts (…) we teach you not only to use magic, but to control it."[78] 'Control' is a very significant term to come up here. It associates the boy Tom Riddle with excess and is linked to the discussion of transgression and madness, establishing Riddle as the one with the power of destroying the secure structural frame of the wizarding world. Dumbledore senses potential transgression in Voldemort and instead of trying to counter it with kindness and understanding he answers it with demonstrations of power. Riddle, who has never experienced much understanding and kindness to begin with, now learns that exercising power is the way to get through life and that from Dumbledore of all people. Again, this could evoke sympathy in the readers, were it not for Harry, who also grows up neglected and unwanted but expressly does not develop in Riddle's direction. Nevertheless the question of how much influence the environment has on a person's development is raised here and Dumbledore, otherwise the perfect example of a leader who makes correct and wise decisions, is exposed as fallible in his relationship with the villain.[79]

I am aware of the fact that this is certainly not the dominant reading of the scene and that Riddle is definitely intended to be established as villain without feeling early on. Tammy Turner-Vorbeck identifies a similar dominant reading: "[T]hose not represented in the texts, those not living the good life, those being oppressed, persecuted, abused, neglected, or simply left behind by mainstream society must be somehow to blame. It is made inconceivable from this perspective that society itself

---

77 Cf. Rowling *Prince* 254-56.

78 Rowling *Prince* 256.

79 Travis Prinzi also takes this reading into account. "While 'choice' is presented as the primary difference between Harry and Voldemort, it is not as simple as just making the right choices, regardless of what you were born; it is possible that someone else can make choices for you – choices that permanently damage your own ability to choose" (159).

might be to blame."[80] She does not explicitly refer to Voldemort, but more to the treatment of different 'races' and ethnicities in the texts. However, her statement is useful, because Voldemort can be seen as the ultimate Other. The readers mainly get to know him through the eyes of others, he is seldom allowed to speak for himself. Furthermore, he is certainly less acceptable because he does not 'live the good life' and he also is a neglected child. Turner-Vorbeck strongly favours the hegemonic reading of *Harry Potter*, the one that reinforces social norms and punishes those deviating from it, which I also think is stronger in the novels than the more questioning, poststructuralist one. The treatment of Voldemort mirrors many contemporary (Western) societies in which individual merit and contributions have come to define society more than group solidarity and where individual blame is easier to assign and to punish.

However, the less dominant reading is inherent in the novels which again emphasises their ambiguity: Did Tom Riddle really have the same chances Harry has? As Travis Prinzi astutely puts it: "The question remains – and is never answered sufficiently – whether Voldemort ever had a choice to be anything other than what he was."[31] While Prinzi here implies the ambiguity of the texts, Jennifer Sattauer criticises what she perceives to be a too one-sided and black and white approach to the good versus evil binary. "Do underlying causes blur the definitions of 'good' and 'evil'?,"[82] she asks and goes on to state that "[i]n order to live up to their responsibilities as a mirror to our society and a safe-ground for vicarious empowerment, the Harry Potter novels need to address such questions."[83] Her conclusion is that they fail to do so.[84] I do not believe that it is as easy as that, although, as was mentioned, I too see the normative, structuralist reading as dominant. Questions of evil, where it comes from in a person and where the responsibilities for it lie, are extremely complex and impossible to answer conclusively.[85] If the function of popular fiction is firstly and foremostly to

---

80   Tammy Turner-Vorbeck, "Pottermania: Good, Clean Fun or Cultural Hegemony?," *Harry Potter's World: Multidisciplinary Critical Perspectives*, Ed. Elizabeth E. Heilman (New York: Routledge, 2003) 21.

81   Prinzi 60.

82   Jennifer Sattauer, "Harry Potter: A World of Fear," *The Journal of Children's Literature Studies* 3.1 (2006): 9.

83   Sattauer 9.

84   Cf. Sattauer 9.

85   Edmund M. Kern argues in similar fashion when he says that "[a]s literary myth, the Potter books suggest that evil is part of the human condition; it exists both intrinsically, in things that cannot be controlled, and instrumentally, in actions and decision that can

reinforce norms and to give people good examples of how to behave according to certain social values, then it makes sense for this kind of fiction to portray good and evil along clear-cut lines. It can then in a less obvious way, ask questions about the validity of these clear-cut definitions. By granting the readers (limited) access to Voldemort's past and also to Dumbledore's reactions to him, Rowling does subtly address the issues of social responsibility for evil. However, within the confines of formulaic fiction, authors have to walk a thin line between clarity and ambiguity.[86]

Another theme that needs to be addressed with respect to Voldemort, and one that should in fact induce even more pity in the other characters and the readers is fear. Fear is associated with Voldemort in two different ways. He manages to spread fear and embody the collective dread of the wizarding community. However, he has a further connection with this highly negative emotion which constitutes one of his great weaknesses. As much as he spreads fear, he is himself a scared person.[87] This is implied in his name which was partly discussed before. Vol-de-mort not only means flight or wings of death but also 'theft of death.'[88] Death does not have a completely negative quality in Rowling's works. It is certainly a sad and sorry affair when untimely brought about by Voldemort or his henchmen but apart from that it is constantly suggested that death is not the end of everything. Although Pennington uses the indecision about an afterlife in the *Harry Potter* novels to discredit them and their author – for instance, he accuses Rowling of not being "interested in serious speculation" and being mainly after "monetary success"[89] – the fuzziness of the novels' stance on death is just a further example of their general ambiguity. After all, they are realistic in a way, because they do not offer definite answers to problems that can never be ultimately solved. Voldemort essentially fears death and out of this fear has *stolen* it from himself. This is apparent in his creation of several Horcruxes, parts of his soul, split by murder, and stowed away in external containers. These Horcruxes preserve Voldemort but also leave him with a maimed

---

be" (213). He, too thus perceives the complexity of the issue in real life as well as in the *Harry Potter* novels.

86   A further point that would contradict Sattauer is raised by Nova Dahlén in a thesis written at Karlstad University, Sweden. She claims that Harry learns about good and evil in the interplay between Snape and Dumbledore, whose differences are emphasised in the first few novels while their similarities are foregrounded in the latter books (cf. Nova Dahlén, "Severus Snape and the Concept of the Outsider: Aspects of Good and Evil in the *Harry Potter* Series," Thesis, Karlstad University, 2009, 19, 7 Jul 2011 <http://kau.diva-portal.org/smash/record.jsf?pid=diva2:224466>).

87   Cf. Prinzi 66-67.

88   Dreyer-Gehle 22.

89   Pennington 92.

and fragmented soul. Evil is thus not only characterised by the spreading of fear but also by being fearful itself. Eagleton also draws this connection: "[E]vil is indeed all about death—but about the death of the evildoer as much as that of those he annihilates."[90] He goes on to explain that evil is afraid of death because it must cling to the physical existence it has established for itself as the only valid form of life. Since evil does not believe in the spiritual, the material is all it has. It cannot let physical existence go, cannot accept the fact of death.[91] Voldemort essentially embodies all this.

Apart from his fear of death, Voldemort is afraid of the prophecy about himself and Harry. Out of fear of what it bodes for him, he allows it to dominate all of his actions. First of all, this shows that the villain although seemingly free of all moral obligations is in fact driven and unfree. Secondly, and significantly, it is words that Voldemort follows so slavishly. In novel six, Dumbledore tries to make clear to Harry that the prophecy in itself does not mean anything at all. It only acquires meaning if someone makes it meaningful for his or her life. "But Harry, never forget that what the prophecy says is only significant because Voldemort made it so. (...) If Voldemort would never have heard of the prophecy, would it have been fulfilled? Would it have meant anything? Of course not!"[92] Voldemort's evil here is trusting someone else's word too much, taking it too literally. He never pauses to think about it, let alone question the content of a prophecy which to top it all, he has only heard half of. Prophecies are usually rather mysterious and no one knows why some people can seemingly see into the future. Furthermore, they are mostly quite vague. Thus it would be advisable to look at a prophecy very carefully to find out whether any truth value or any meaning for one's life can be obtained from it.[93] The

---

90   Eagleton 18.

91   Cf. Eagleton 24.

92   Rowling *Prince* 476.

93   The prophecy presents an interesting point of comparison with Shakespeare's *Macbeth* whose 'hero' also slavishly follows an oracle, because he is fascinated by the opportunities it seems to place before him. Rowling herself has hit on this connection between Voldemort and Macbeth in an interview (cf. Melissa Anelli and Emerson Spartz, "The Leaky Cauldron and MuggleNet Interview with Joanne Kathleen Rowling: Part Two," *The Leaky Cauldron*, 16 July 2005, n.pag., 7 Jul 2011 <http://www.accio-quote.org/articles/2005/0705-tlc_mugglenet-anelli-3.htm>). Terry Eagleton, too discusses Shakespeare's *Macbeth* and the evil emanating from the witches which is to "reject creaturely existence as a whole" (82). The witches through their fluidity and insubstantiality defy structures and meaning (cf. 80) and thus resemble Voldemort. Interestingly, it can then be said that Voldemort has traits of both,

evil that is represented by Voldemort's adherence to the prophecy is the evil of unquestioningly believing all one hears and reads, a meta-commentary on our society where many people allow themselves to be manipulated by myth in the sense of Barthes.

Voldemort's life of fear is made worse by the fact that it is also entirely loveless. The Horcruxes turn Voldemort into a terrible travesty of the phoenix at the core of his and Harry's wands.[94] Like the phoenix, Voldemort (seemingly) dies and returns. The phoenix usually returns from the flames in the shape of a baby bird.[95] It transcends death because it accepts when it is time to go or even gives itself up for others. Dumbledore's Phoenix Fawkes, for instance, does so at the end of novel five, when it swallows Voldemort's killing curse, which was intended for Dumbledore.[96] Voldemort, when he finally resumes a corporeal form in book four, looks like the travesty of a baby.[97] Though he tries to be like a phoenix, the Dark Lord lacks the essential qualities necessary for that: "undying love and loyalty."[98] His remorselessness in killing the innocent shows him to be without pity and incapable of human feeling. There are several instances in the course of the series that prove that he is not a faithful character either. He mercilessly kills even those who are on his side as soon as they have served their purpose. An example is Quirrell, whom he leaves to die at the end of book one.[99] So Voldemort has in common with the Emperor a total immersion in himself which prevents any thought of and for others. One important characteristic of evil which was already mentioned in chapter four, is a lack. It seems that the concept of evil is easier to grasp via the qualities it does not possess: love, empathy and loyalty.[100] Prinzi also identifies Voldemort's evil as devoid of these attributes and specifies it as dehumanisation. "[I]t is evil to *act* less than fully human, and in doing so, one *becomes* less than

---

the human and erring Macbeth and the supernatural witches. This, too seems to suggest that his case is not as easy or as one-dimensional as it is mostly depicted in the stories.

94   Cf. Gibbons 88.

95   Cf. Rowling *Chamber* 225.

96   Cf. Rowling *Order* 719

97   Cf. Rowling *Goblet* 555-56.

98   David Colbert, *The Magical Worlds of Harry Potter: A Treasury of Myths, Legends and Fascinating Facts* (London: Puffin Books, 2001) 93.

99   Cf. Rowling *Stone* 320.

100   Cf. David and Catherine Deavel, "A Skewered Reflection: The Nature of Evil," *Harry Potter and Philosophy: If Aristotle Ran Hogwarts*, Ed. David Baggett and Shawn E. Klein (Chicago: Open Court, 2004) 132, 133 and Deavel and Deavel "Character, Choice, and Harry Potter" 56.

human."[101] However, it is exactly the qualities the villain does not possess that defeat him time and again. Examples are the appearance of Dumbledore's Phoenix at the climax of novel two because of Harry's loyalty to the headmaster, the loyalty of Harry's friends in the fight against Voldemort and his henchmen, Harry's compassion for Wormtail and Sirius in book three as well as the love that makes Harry's parents, and ultimately Harry himself, sacrifice themselves for others. Not only does Voldemort lack these qualities; they can also become dangerous for him. They function as antidotes against the evil emanating from him.

Voldemort's predicament (he has never been loved, his life is dominated by fear, he is mad and he is evil) is one that can induce scorn on the part of the readers and Harry, who bravely faces death to protect his loved ones. However, it could also evoke pity. Certainly, the first option is the dominant one suggested by the books. But, if one takes into account the subtleties of the novels, the second one is indirectly invoked when Dumbledore says to Harry in the limbo place between life and death at the end of novel seven: "Do not pity the dead, Harry. Pity the living, and above all, those who live without love."[102] As Voldemort is the only character who truly qualifies for sympathy on these grounds, the pitying, forgiving stance even toward those who are unlike us, who do not 'live the good life' is implicitly advocated. Still, the fact remains that above all, Voldemort is depicted as a horrible, inhuman character who tortures and murders countless people simply because they are in his way. Despite the fact that the readers are offered some possible explanations of his behaviour he is not treated sympathetically. The reason for this is mostly the interplay of binary oppositions. If the story were only about Voldemort, readers would probably think about him and his motivations more intensely. However, Voldemort finds his counterpart in perfect Harry who represents the good, the better end of the binary opposition. Compared to Harry who has a similar start in life but who constantly takes the right decisions, Voldemort has no chance. Voldemort and Harry thus perfectly embody Derrida's notions about the hierarchy within binary oppositions.[103]

To sum up it can be said that Voldemort is a more round character than the Emperor. The latter mainly serves to embody the principle of evil and no explanations of his behaviour are given. The readers of *Harry Potter* do get glimpses of Voldemort's inner life but the explications offered do not entirely serve

---

101   Prinzi 73. Cf. also Jennifer Hart Weed, "Voldemort, Boethius, and the Destructive Effects of Evil," *Harry Potter and Philosophy: If Aristotle Ran Hogwarts*, Ed. David Baggett and Shawn E. Klein (Chicago: Open Court, 2004) 151.

102   Rowling *Hallows* 578.

103   Cf. Derrida *Positions* 41.

to arouse pity but rather to show that the villain truly is "beyond redemption."[104] In a way, it can be said that the Emperor is treated more fairly than Voldemort. The villain from *Harry Potter* is the personified evil with whom no true sympathy is possible. With the Emperor no pseudo-attempts at an explanation of his evil are made. He is left standing as an enigmatic, and as far as the audience knows, self-determined figure who does not act out of madness or a sad personal history. He is thus depicted as more independent than Voldemort which also fits with the fact that he is the one who severely shakes the opposition of good and evil, if only for a moment. Still, the fact that Voldemort's character, in contrast to the Emperor's opens up all the possibilities for discussion analysed above, makes him the ultimately more interesting and less static figure.

Voldemort as Harry's foil is finally a structural necessity. The Emperor functions as a tempter for Anakin Skywalker and he significantly shapes the young man and influences his later life and development. Voldemort neither tempts Harry nor really shapes him, except through being his absolute Other.[105] Both villains are highly powerful and both place power above any considerations of a moral nature. Each series questions binary oppositions in its villains in different ways. In *Star Wars* the character of the Emperor is rather static but the whole structural corset is more open than in *Harry Potter*. Palpatine's comment on good and evil being a point of view emphasises this structural openness. Voldemort's similar statement about the nature of good and evil is nevertheless different from the Emperor's as it ultimately upholds binary oppositions thereby leaving the structural framework of the novels intact. Instead of introducing ambiguity to the structures, Rowling uses it on her characters who are rounder than those from *Star Wars*. Finally, however, both the movies and the narratives, by using the villain figures to question binaries, also re-establish dichotomies. The notions of the evil side are always countered by the ideas of the good characters, who are, as will be discussed in greater detail, obviously presented as much more deserving of sympathy than the evildoers. In this way identification is directed towards the 'right' channels. Identification with the good characters is mainly made possible because the evil figures lack certain qualities perceived to be essential to human existence, especially love, respect and compassion. Furthermore the evil characters are rendered disagreeable by their arrogance and hubris. They constantly overrate themselves and their abilities. And, of course, they have powers that scare the other characters (and the audiences/readers alike).

---

104   Prinzi 161.

105   Cf. also the contrary and convincing readings by Karley Adney and Maria Nikolajeva (both in Katrin Berndt and Lena Steveker, eds., *Heroism in the Harry Potter Series* (Farnham: Ashgate, 2011) 177-92, 193-206.

The Emperor's and Voldemort's powers are very different and present different views on evil. The Emperor's power is mainly linguistic. He uses words to insinuate and manipulate. Voldemort does not talk very much in the course of the *Harry Potter* novels. His ways are not soft and cunning as the Emperor's. He often employs brute force to achieve his aims. His power and his ability to inspire fear lie in his constant transgressions, his violations of the wizarding society's rules and norms. He is dangerous because he threatens to produce chaos and disrupt the neat normative and ideological framework of the wizarding society. He is highly visible as a villain and all fears can easily be projected onto him. In the case of the Emperor this is impossible because he is less tangible. He remains in the background and lets others do the dirty work. He is dangerous for his talent in leading people astray and doing his bidding.

In the course of this chapter it has become clear that Rowling makes much more of an effort to define evil than does Lucas in his Emperor-figure. This effort means, however, that she is also more ideological, as she tries to give evil a 'story,' something that is commonly done to promote understanding of criminal acts in Western societies. Even the story she tells of Voldemort does not redeem him. With the negative example of Voldemort, she (probably unwittingly) exposes the ideology of self-responsibility and free choice as partly fallible. Voldemort is doubtless an evil character but his extreme evil onto which every single social evil can be projected stops people from reflecting their own part in social issues and by extension their own less than good sides. Let me repeat, in this context, the quotation by Robert Ellwood, I already included at the beginning of this chapter: "We begin to realize that myths of evil are actually not so much explanations of evil (…), as they are an inventory of varied ways of *feeling* about evil, of responding to it on other than purely rational terms."[106] What Ellwood alludes to here, the ideologies involved in discussions of evil, are exemplified in the treatment of Voldemort. Lucas, by showing different figures of evil (the Emperor and Anakin/Vader) makes the depiction of it a bit more multi-dimensional. Both Lucas and Rowling portray evil as active, clever and powerful but Rowling additionally underlines characteristics of evil that might shed some light on its origins. Evil for her is characterised by dissatisfaction and the wish for more as well as a proneness to remain alone. All this aligns evil with transgression of various kinds. Evil is determined by fears about one's own mortality and, as Rowling very implicitly suggests, is often aggravated by society which might to a certain extent account for its transgressions against society and its will to destroy structures that are essential for others. All this is the evil Voldemort embodies.

---

106   Ellwood 143.

Ultimately, although the Emperor is rather a type and as such an uninteresting character, his diffuse kind of evil is more frightening than Voldemort's because it is perpetrated in secret. If he can win over Anakin, he can win over more people. As Shanti Fader says:

[H]ow do we fight a Darth Sidious [the Emperor's Sith name]; how do we fight the evil that seduces rather than threatens us? In many ways, the wolves in sheep's clothing are far more dangerous than obvious foes – their work can be done quietly, unnoticed and unchecked. The knight with the shining sword may take down dragons, but is helpless against the rot eating away at the castle's foundation.[107]

Voldemort is not entirely persuasive. He does not promise glory, he does not treat his followers well. Some of them, such as the Malfoys, even seem to regret their entanglement with him at some stages of the story.[108] He is a single entirely evil person who wins quite a few followers but can be defeated. The Emperor, though he is also defeated in the end, perfectly embodies the way evil mostly works: it establishes itself in stealth and it very often has to do with persuasion, promises and raised hopes. And mostly it is not perpetrated by one person but by a whole bunch of people who collaborate to achieve certain aims, the principle behind this largely remaining in the dark.[109] The projection of fear onto a Voldemort-like figure is easier, because it takes responsibility for evil away from others but the way evil is represented in *Star Wars* with hopeful, power-hungry, wavering and doubting henchmen such as Darth Vader in focus is a much more potent image of the workings of evil in the real world. While the *Harry Potter* novels enquire into the nature of evil, the *Star Wars* films rather focus on the ways in which it establishes itself in a society and in a person. This is exemplified in Anakin Skywalker's development into Darth Vader which is going to be assessed in the following chapter.

---

107   Shanti Fader, "In Sheep's Clothing: The Face of Evil in *The Phantom Menace*," *Parabola: Tradition, Myth, and the Search for Meaning* 24.4 (1999): 90.

108   Voldemort himself suggests so at the beginning of book seven (cf. Rowling *Hallows* 15).

109   Cf. also Ken Rothman who believes that in *Harry Potter* "[t]he deepest horror of evil resides not in one particular villain but in numerous followers (possessed of varying degrees of self-awareness) and their actions" (213). This also, and perhaps even more obviously holds true for *Star Wars* where there is an even greater emphasis on masses and their propensity for evil (see for instance the droid army in *The Phantom Menace*, the clones turning against the good side in *Revenge of the Sith* and the masses of storm troopers in episodes four to six).

6. Villainous Heroes and Heroic Villains

6.1 'STAR-CROSS'D' CHOICE-MAKER: ANAKIN SKYWALKER / DARTH VADER

Anakin Skywalker / Darth Vader very often takes up the middle position in the Lévi-Straussian diagrams of chapter four because he is in between extremes such as good and evil as well as free will and determination. Consequently, he also assumes the middle position in this analysis of the characters, together with Severus Snape from *Harry Potter*. Their structurally central role and the importance they assume in their respective stories are based on one significant characteristic they share: both notably change in the course of their respective stories. This makes them special and sets them apart from the other protagonists. It is why, in contrast to the other characters who are analysed with respect to certain themes, Anakin Skywalker and Snape will rather be discussed in their chronological development. It will be seen which function exactly they fulfil in the stories and how they fit in with the overall structural framework of the two tales.

Anakin Skywalker / Darth Vader's most essential trait is his ambiguity, his oscillation between the poles of good and evil and the closely related extremes of free will and determination. His central position is also noted by Jonathan L. Bowen and Rachel Wagner as well as, incidentally George Lucas himself, whom they invoke: "George Lucas has said that Anakin is the ultimate protagonist of the films, and indeed, Anakin serves as a microcosm for the galaxy, so that his inner balance and spiritual well-being relate closely to that of the entire galaxy."[1] His two different names, one connected to his 'good' boyhood and the other to his 'evil' adult life in the service of the Emperor, are indicative of the rift in his nature. It is difficult to say where the name Anakin comes from. The only point that can safely be made about it is that it contains the term 'akin.' Since this means 'similar' or

---

1   Bowen and Wagner 75.

'related' one might see it as a confirmation of my theory concerning the mediating position of the more recent *Star Wars* movies which was expounded in chapter four. The latest films showing Anakin's fall from grace were seen as mediators between human reality and the original and rather formulaic ones. Anakin, containing both, good and evil; lovable and detestable traits, is the character most closely linked to the average cinema-goer.[2] The resemblance between him and most audience members does not extend to the fact that Anakin takes both sides of his nature to extremes. The radicality of his actions rather has a didactic function.

Anakin's last name, Skywalker, has both positive and negative connotations again emphasising the character's ambiguity. In a conversation with Jedi Qui-Gon in *A Phantom Menace*, young Anakin says that he wants to be the first one to see all the stars in the galaxy.[3] This shows his natural curiosity and his desire to develop and go beyond his little home planet. It is striking that he uses the concept of seeing to describe what he wants to do. His wish to *see* all the stars is in stark contrast to his later desire to *rule* the galaxy. Seeing is a peaceful concept, one that fits in with the Jedi ideals of knowledge and wisdom, whereas ruling is an aspiration associated with the Sith. However, Anakin's statement also gives the audience a first glance of the boy's ambition. A 'Skywalker' is always in danger of falling if he does not mind his steps. The name therefore also points to the fact that Anakin is a potential overreacher-figure.

The name which Anakin Skywalker is given as a Sith is as full of allusions as his boyhood name. 'Darth' immediately evokes rather negative images. It sounds similar to 'dark' while 'Vader' is reminiscent of the words 'invader' and 'father.'[4] The concept of invasion diametrically opposes the one of 'seeing' which the young Anakin had formerly embraced for his life, and alludes to the destructive nature of Darth Vader. In addition, Vader is the 'bad (dark) father' for his son Luke. (The good one is represented by Obi-Wan). The concept of the good and the bad father is rather common in formulaic stories such as, for instance, Gothic tales.[5] However, the term father is primarily positively connoted. It is associated with creation and thus productiveness. Therefore, a creative and productive element is implied within the otherwise rather negative name of Darth Vader. His 'good' son Luke is the embodiment of this positive element. The grain of good within evil also mirrors the

---

2   Cf. also Van Yperen who says: "Our ability, at times, to identify with Darth Vader makes him a potent character" (196).

3   Cf. *The Phantom Menace* 00:48:09.

4   Cf. Wessely who also associates the name with 'darkness,' as well as invasion and the concept of the 'father' (161-62).

5   A classic example would be Ann Radcliffe's novel *The Mysteries of Udolpho* in which St. Aubert serves as the heroine's 'good' and Montoni as her 'bad' father.

fact that the altogether more positive name of Anakin Skywalker nevertheless has negative implications (Skywalker as an overreacher). Thus the status of Anakin Skywalker / Darth Vader as a Lévi-Straussian mediator figure, uniting binaries in his nature is reinforced.[6]

Anakin Skywalker's name change links the hero-villain of *Star Wars* with the two villains already analysed in this chapter. Both the Emperor of *Star Wars* and Voldemort of *Harry Potter* change their rather common names into others exuding power. Both consciously choose to do so in order to intimidate other people and possibly also to legitimise their evil deeds in front of themselves. With Anakin Skywalker the name change works differently. He does not choose his new name Darth Vader himself but is dubbed thus by the Emperor after having sworn his allegiance to him. This already hints at the main difference between villains such as the Emperor and Voldemort, and Darth Vader and partly explains why the latter is treated with sympathy in the movies despite the fact that he constantly commits murder and other evil deeds.[7] Darth Vader is the only one of these villain-figures who is heavily manipulated into turning evil. His good core and talents are constantly abused and finally perverted. While the Emperor and Voldemort

---

6   Bowen and Wagner also focus on the "desire for balance (...) basic to Anakin's story" (76). They apply the concepts of religions such as Taoism to the movies, which also propagate balance of character as their chief value. In accordance with these mostly Eastern religions they identify an interrelatedness of good and evil in the movies which contradicts their simple reading as black and white and crystallises in the figure of Anakin (cf. 78).

7   The more recent trilogy is very interesting because it changes the status of Vader who is mostly known as one of the chief villains in the older films. Wessely states that Darth Vader is the embodiment of the Girardian scapegoat, an Other who is invested with all that seems negative in and worth eradicating from society (cf. 194). Showing Anakin, the human being and his fall from grace as well as the factors leading up to it, shows Vader in a different light and foregrounds his final redemption. Michelle J. Kinnucan, too reads the *Star Wars* films as strongly focused on what theologian Walter Wink calls 'The Myth of Redemptive Violence' (cf. Michelle J. Kinnucan, "Pedagogy of (the) Force: The Myth of Redemptive Violence," *Finding the Force of the Star Wars Franchise: Fans, Merchandise, and Critics*, Ed. Matthew Wilhelm Kapell and John Shelton Lawrence (New York: Peter Lang, 2006) 59). Violence is used in the movies, she suggests, to redress evil and reinstate a certain rightful order. "Violence rescues young Anakin from slavery; it frees Luke from farm life and family obligations; it reclaims the older Anakin/Vader from the Force's Dark Side; and, finally, it liberates the galaxy from Palpatine and his evil Empire" (65). This sense of certain (violent) sacrifices being necessary for things to run their good course is very Girardian.

doubtlessly have their reasons for turning bad, we see neither of them being actively manipulated by an agent of evil. Anakin Skywalker initially only seeks direction and a place for himself in the galaxy. Unfortunately he falls into the hands of the wrong sort of people. So quite contrary to the Emperor's and Voldemort's name changes which signal their (desire for) power, Anakin's forced name change shows his status as a slave to powers external to him. It can be seen already, that the binary of free will versus determination plays a big role for the character of Anakin/Vader.

Related to the notions of free will and determination is the discussion of destiny or fate which runs through the films and particularly manifests itself in the treatment of Anakin/Vader. However, when Hanson and Kay say that Anakin / Darth Vader is "a destiny-driven hero"[8] they are too narrow in their focus. First of all, he is not strictly speaking a pure hero, since his evil deeds qualify him as villain, too. Secondly, Hanson and Kay do not really clarify how they understand destiny. For them it is embodied in the concept of the Force, the rather vague and insubstantial energy influencing life in *Star Wars*.[9] They therefore see destiny as something impossible to grasp fully but nevertheless highly involved in shaping human life. Although they even remark upon the "[i]nterpretation of destiny"[10] on the part of the Jedi, they do not see that this 'interpretation' is relevant to the discourse on fate in the films. The common ideological understanding of destiny as something intangible and elusive is certainly invited by the concept of the Force but Hanson and Kay do not question it at all.[11] Fate in the movies is not entirely viewed as a force that cannot be influenced at all. On the contrary it is suggested that much of what is deemed destiny is in fact human doing. It is hard to say whether Anakin

---

8   Hanson and Kay 292.

9   Cf. Hanson and Kay 347.

10   Hanson and Kay 292.

11   Tony M. Vinci, for instance, remarks upon the close connection between the Force and destiny in the more recent trilogy. "[N]ot only can the Force be analyzed empirically in the prequel trilogy, but it is said to have a 'will.' Instead of being an 'ally,' the Force, through its own agency, becomes an oppressive energy equal to that of fate or predestination" (20). In contrast to that, Vinci holds, the Force is associated with individual agency in the older films (cf. 19). John Lyden similarly argues that the new films are more apocalyptic and therefore deterministic than the old ones (Cf. John Lyden, "Apocalyptic Determinism and *Star Wars*," *Culture, Identities and Technology in the Star Wars Films: Essays on the Two Trilogies*, Ed. Carl Silvio and Tony M. Vinci (Jefferson: McFarland & Company, 2007) 48). *Star Wars* seems to be at least ambiguous about Calvinist notions of predestination and the questions about personal responsibility they raise.

is truly a fated person or whether other people's belief in destiny turns him into one.[12]

Already as a child, Anakin is determined by other people. He and his mother Shmi are slaves to Watto, a junk-dealer. In contrast to this physical restriction, Anakin is a free-thinking child. His hopes and aspirations manifest themselves in the afore-mentioned statement about being the first one to see all the stars in the galaxy. Far from being oppressed, Anakin is friendly, curious and always ready to help others despite his own condition.[13] Thus he manages to help Qui-Gon and his entourage repair their damaged spaceship.[14] Ironically, at this stage of his life, he is freer than when he begins his training at the Jedi temple because although he has to do his work, he is not constantly watched and manipulated. His freedom of mind becomes apparent when upon first meeting Anakin, Padmé, the good-natured queen of Naboo asks him: "You're a slave?" Anakin indignantly replies: "I'm a person and my name is Anakin."[15] His answer makes obvious that initially he does have a strong sense of who he is. Padmé's assumption that he is not a free man is one of the first about him in the movies and it comes from the woman who will later become Anakin's wife and can firmly be placed with the good characters. Thus the good side's categorising of Anakin is established early on. Padmé's calling him a

---

12 Interestingly, discussions of fate and free will in the movies seldom revolve around the interpretation of fate on the part of humans and the fact that by assigning a certain 'destiny' to someone, it is possible that this particular destiny is brought about, nourished and even evoked. Analyses rather focus on the question of whether there is an all-knowing divinity guiding action and if that is the case, in how far the human being can be supposed to make his or her own choices within his/her limited range of freedom. Finally, usually the view of at least limited freedom is preferred (cf. for instance Jason T. Eberl, "'You Cannot Escape Your Destiny' (Or Can You?): Freedom and Predestination in the Skywalker Family," *Star Wars and Philosophy: More Powerful than You Can Possibly Imagine*, Ed. Kevin S. Decker and Jason T. Eberl (Chicago: Open Court, 2005) 7, 14).

13 Richard H. Dees argues that Anakin/Vader is not in fact that ambiguous because his loyalties are always clear. As a child he is good-natured and helpful whereas even in the second movie, before his actual transformation into Vader, "we never see the kind boy we met on Tatooine. Not once during the entire movie does [Anakin] show basic compassion: He's rude, arrogant, and ungrateful" (Richard H. Dees, "Moral Ambiguity in a Black-and-White Universe," *Star Wars and Philosophy: More Powerful than You Can Possibly Imagine*, Ed. Kevin S. Decker and Jason T. Eberl (Chicago: Open Court, 2005) 48).

14 Cf. *The Phantom Menace* 1:07:20.

15 *The Phantom Menace* 0:31:49.

slave might further foreshadow Anakin's later propensity of being a slave to his emotions.

The one to introduce the ideology of destiny as linked with the mysterious Force, is Jedi master Qui-Gon Jinn. When he finds out that Anakin's was a virgin birth, he instantly links this fact with the prophecy he has heard about one who will bring balance to the Force. In a conversation about Anakin with the boy's mother Shmi Qui-Gon says that "[their] meeting was not a coincidence. Nothing happens by accident."[16] In Qui-Gon's world picture, Anakin has a part to play.[17] He is not seen as a human being so much but as someone created by fate, someone who has to fulfil a destiny others have planned for him. This is not to say that Qui-Gon treats Anakin unkindly, he just does not believe in individual self-realisation as much as in the utility of a person within some greater scheme or plan. This is in line with the structuralist focus of this thesis. Seeing Anakin as the child of fate on the level of the story, serves to draw attention to the genre-typical way in which characters are treated in myth and formula fiction and film. Instead of round, individual characters, these kinds of stories focus on certain themes which they try to convey via the protagonists. The characters have metaphorical rather than truly individual value.

In contrast to Qui-Gon, Shmi sees Anakin's human potential. When Qui-Gon offers him the opportunity to leave Tatooine to be trained as a Jedi, the boy asks his mother if he can go. Shmi answers: "Anakin...this path has been placed before *you*. The choice is yours alone."[18] She very distinctly does not say: "This path is your destiny" or "This is what you should do" but stresses that it is one (of several possible) roads that he can follow and that it is a matter of choice for him to take this chance or leave it. Like Dumbledore in *Harry Potter* she advocates free will instead of dependence on a certain destiny. Qui-Gon and Anakin's mother Shmi thus represent diametrically opposed sides in the free will versus determination binary. By leaving his home planet to go with Qui-Gon, Anakin enters a worse sort of slavery than the one he has escaped from on Tatooine. His parting with his mother represents the parting with free will and his entry into the realm of the Jedi marks the onset of his determination by others.

---

16   *The Phantom Menace* 1:09:16.

17   In fact Hanson and Kay contradict themselves when they say that "there is validity in stating that Qui-Gon's will is what guided Anakin toward his future life of infamy" (92), and "[i]n many ways it is Obi-Wan who cultivates [the] seeds [of evil in Anakin]" (129) when at the same time they take Anakin/Vader to be "destiny-driven" (292). Their analysis, however, clearly highlights that the question of destiny and human agency is ambiguous in the movies.

18   *The Phantom Menace* 1:09:45.

From the start, Qui-Gon and his apprentice Obi-Wan argue about Anakin. Obi-Wan doubts that Qui-Gon should risk his standing on the Jedi Council for the boy. His lack of conviction in the matter is mirrored by that of the Council when told about Anakin. According to Qui-Gon's wish they test Anakin for extraordinary abilities and his worthiness to become a Jedi. In the process of testing "Anakin is treated more as a subject or patient than as a person."[19] This is comparable to the scene of Dumbledore's and Voldemort's first meeting which was also associated with a hospital environment. The possible villains incite a certain mistrust on the side of the good early on, their potential as Others is sensed. The Jedi are more interested in finding out whether Anakin fits in with their philosophy than in getting to know him as a person. His strong feelings especially put them off. Mace Windu tells him: "Be mindful of your feelings."[20] And Ki-Adi, another Jedi master says: "Your thoughts dwell on your mother." To this Anakin replies: "I miss her."[21] For a boy of eight missing his mother might be normal but the Jedi hold this emotion against him specially since their philosophy includes being dispassionate and disinterested. Yoda asks Anakin: "Afraid to lose her [the mother], I think, mmm [sic]?"[22] Upon this Anakin asks a little confusedly: "What has that got to do with anything?" And Yoda lectures: "Everything. Fear is the path to the dark side. Fear leads to anger. Anger leads to hate. Hate leads to suffering. I sense much fear in you."[23] Yoda's use of the stylistic device of a climax with three steps foreshadows the events to come and the fate that awaits young Anakin. He correctly identifies fear as Anakin's nemesis and anticipates his downfall.

Yoda's statement is revealing with respect to Anakin but also regarding the Jedi. It is asking much of the boy not to be afraid in this situation as he has just left his home, is among strange people and faces a test-situation. The 'good' and 'tolerant' Jedi do not try and accept the boy with all his emotions, good or bad, and teach him how to cope with them. They do not show much understanding for or patience with Anakin. For them he has to function like one of them and not like a child. They scare him by laying out a path for him which he must needs go down if he does not master his fears. They ask him to repress his emotions which almost as a principle makes them come to the fore with double force. Thus even here, the Jedi contribute to bringing about the 'fate' they fear for Anakin.[24]

---

19   Hanson and Kay 105.

20   *The Phantom Menace* 1:26:40.

21   *The Phantom Menace* 1:26:41.

22   *The Phantom Menace* 1:26:50.

23   *The Phantom Menace* 1:26:51.

24   Shanti Fader also deals with the less noble side of the Jedi. However, she does not so much focus on the mistakes the Jedi make with respect to Anakin but rather on the

At the heart of the problem lies Qui-Gon's belief in Anakin being the one to fulfil the prophecy about a person to come and bring balance to the Force. While Qui-Gon reduces Anakin to a role as 'the chosen one,' the other Jedi doubt whether the prophecy alludes to the boy and qualify him as too emotionally unstable to fulfil it. The prophecy polarises and leaves no room for balance in the Jedis' view of Anakin. In itself the oracle is rather shady and the audience never gets to hear the precise wording of it. In fact it is intimated that none of the characters really knows it, either.[25] Anakin, who is nevertheless associated with it straight away, is thus sacrificed for an idea or an ideal. This view is supported by a discussion the Jedi Council has about the prophecy in *Revenge of the Sith* in which wise Jedi master Yoda concedes for the first time that the prophecy "misread could have been [sic]."[26] In his words lie the doubts about a prophecy we never get to hear, doubts about Anakin but also doubts about the Jedi themselves who have possibly 'read,' that is interpreted the prophecy incorrectly. The possibility of a wrong interpretation of the prophecy might also imply a consciousness on Yoda's part of a possibly 'wrong interpretation' of Anakin.

Taken to another level Yoda's statement serves as a meta-commentary on language (of any sort), the human need to interpret what they see and hear and their propensity for misrepresentation. The prophecy, whatever its exact wording, is nothing more than a text that only acquires meaning when people make it meaningful through their interpretations. That language can be treacherous was already mentioned in the analysis of Palpatine / the Emperor, who uses it to manipulate and seduce Anakin. Anakin does not choose to let the prophecy reign over his decisions. Its meaning is forced on him, which makes him a victim as much as a perpetrator. Voldemort on the other hand, consciously models his behaviour on the prophecy made about him and Harry Potter. This reinforces and complements the difference between the true villains and Anakin with respect to their name changes. While the villains adopt other names consciously and voluntarily, Anakin is turned into Darth Vader by another. In the same fashion he

---

motives behind lying and truth-telling in the films. Although the Jedi lie at times, they mostly do it from higher and nobler motives (cf. "A Certain Point of View" 198) in contrast to the Sith who often tell significant truths which are, however "narrow" and "limited" and "only (...) serve their own purposes" ("A Certain Point of View" 202). Cf. also John Shelton Lawrence who attributes the failure of the Republic not only to "Anakin's furies" but also to Obi-Wan's "[bungled] (...) mentorship of Anakin" (27).

25   Cf. Matril n.pag.

26   *Revenge of the Sith* 00:39:05. Cf. also Hanson and Kay 292 who mention the "interpretation of destiny" with respect to the prophecy but do not further comment on it.

never chooses to become the incarnation of the prophecy. This again shows that he is not as pure a villain as the Emperor and Voldemort. In the conventions of other formulaic genres such as Gothic fiction and melodrama, the villains are the active and the victims the passive characters.[27] Anakin does not fit this binary scheme completely but unites the opposites of agent and victim in his nature.

The third *Star Wars* movie, *Revenge of the Sith* brings the ideas of destiny, free will and determination together. It portrays Anakin's fall from grace and good and evil united in one person. Arguably, it is in this movie as much as in *Return of the Jedi* that Anakin fulfils the mysterious prophecy and brings balance to the Force, not only by combining the two sides in his person but also by exposing just how similar the workings of good and evil sometimes are. The film shows the manipulations of the bad as well as the neglect of the good side which makes it hard for Anakin to withstand the allure of Senator Palpatine's seduction. The atmosphere of the movie is completely dominated by Anakin's unhappiness and fear which is underlined by the use of darkish, reddish colours and the fact that almost none of the scenes plays by daylight. The foremost of his anxieties is that his pregnant wife Padmé might die in childbirth, something he has repeatedly been dreaming of.[28] Anakin who still feels more inclined towards the good side at that point, consults Jedi master Yoda about these recurring visions but does not receive very helpful council. Like years before, when the boy was tested for his suitability to become a Jedi, Yoda's advice is vague.[29] Learning patience and acceptance is certainly important but at that time it does not really help Anakin when he is obviously in need of someone who can give him more substantial advice. The seed of frustration with the Jedi is thus sown. The scene shows Anakin as someone who has lost his ability to arrive at a solution by 'cool reason,' someone who finds it hard to trust himself and take his own decisions. The loss of his original identity is initiated and the determination by fear sets in, exactly as the Jedi have foreseen.

When Yoda cannot offer any sound advice, Anakin gets closer to the evil Chancellor Palpatine. Palpatine is cleverer than the Jedi, because he realises that with his potential and power, Anakin is a valuable ally and not desirable as an enemy. Palpatine does what the Jedi fail to do because they are too sure of Anakin's allegiance. He is kind, he listens, he comes up with seeming solutions to Anakin's problems. To win Anakin over he does not even have to do much, seeing that the Jedi Council does all the work for him by alienating Anakin ever further. The once

---

27 Cf. Merle Tönnies, "(En-)Gendering a Popular Theoretical Genre: The Roles of Women in Nineteenth-Century British Melodrama," Habilitationsschrift, Ruhr-Universität Bochum, 2002, 81.

28 Cf. *Revenge of the Sith* 00:29:15.

29 Cf. *Revenge of the Sith* 00:32:33.

promising Anakin is caught in a vicious circle. He wants to be a Jedi master with all that this implies but finds it hard to do. He violates several of the Jedi Council's rules, for instance, the one that Jedi are not supposed to marry or have children. He also feels that (maybe partly because of his rule-breaking) the Council does not entirely trust him. This drives him into the arms of the only person who seemingly cares for him, Palpatine, which again must increase the Jedis' mistrust. The fact that Anakin has married secretly shows that he still retains some vestiges of his former free spirit. He is not prepared to let his status as a Jedi interfere with his feelings and his individual plans for life. However, he also has to realise that his independence clashes with the ideals of the Jedi, abstinence, disinterestedness and aloofness. He is torn between his two lives and cannot figure out how to integrate one with the other.

His ambivalence even forces him into the role of a double agent. While Palpatine asks him to be his "representative" on the Jedi Council, the Jedi want him to spy on Palpatine.[30] This brings Anakin into conflict with his conscience because so far, he cannot see through the chancellor. Both the chancellor and the Jedi ask something dishonest and immoral of Anakin, and, what is more, both ask the same thing. This emphasises Palpatine's statement about the similar nature of good and evil which was analysed in the preceding chapter. The only difference between the two sides in this instance is that the Jedi are honest about their intentions and tell Anakin directly that they want him to spy on the chancellor whereas Palpatine wants Anakin as a 'representative.' This word sounds much more harmless, plays to Anakin's wish to be powerful (a representative is important) and generally mirrors the stealthy manner in which Palpatine cements his power. For both sides, Anakin only has a function to fulfil although Palpatine cleverly does not make him feel this. To the Jedis' demand of spying Anakin reacts accordingly: "You're asking me to do something against the Jedi code. Against the Republic. Against a mentor and a friend," he reproaches Obi-Wan.[31] Obviously, the good Jedi do not have any problem letting their charge do something against their code. They do not realise how this might corrupt his morals further.

It is also telling that Anakin calls Palpatine a mentor and a friend when it is Obi-Wan who should be this for him. Curiously Anakin's statement structurally mirrors Yoda's in episode one, about fear, anger, hatred and suffering. Anakin also uses a three-step climax to make his feelings about the Jedis' assignment clear. The rhetorical device foreshadows where Anakin's allegiance will eventually lie. He mentions the Jedi code first and the chancellor, his 'mentor' and 'friend' last, so it is obvious that his sympathies already lie with Palpatine. The statement also shows

---

30   *Revenge of the Sith* 00:34:51, cf. *Revenge of the Sith* 00:37:38.

31   *Revenge of the Sith* 00:38:21.

something about Anakin that goes deeper than his allegiance to Palpatine at that moment. It makes obvious the importance he attaches to people and bonds of love, trust and loyalty. The Jedi code, meaning the moral framework of the order, and the Republic are less important to him than the loyalty to his mentor. Anakin does not display this trait for the first time. Against the wishes of the Jedi he goes to free his mother in movie two and he marries Padmé and impregnates her without the knowledge of the Council.[32] These powerful feelings for other people are exactly what the Jedi deplore in him and the reason why they doubt that he will ever be a complete and wise representative of their order.

It is no coincidence that the villains of *Star Wars* and *Harry Potter* who were analysed in the preceding chapter lack exactly the qualities that Anakin possesses in the extreme. Obviously, characters in formulaic stories are either able to feel or they are not. If they are incapable of emotions they are completely evil, if they do feel love and can extend and inspire trust and loyalty, there is a certain gradation. On the one side there are characters such as Anakin who have problems with these emotions and cannot control or 'use' them properly. On the other side, there are those figures who are always perfectly aware of what is the correct thing to do; such as, for instance, Luke and Harry. They employ their emotions in exactly the right manner and thus benefit their society. Thus, love also has an ambiguous quality in both stories. And generally speaking, emotions seem to be important in judging characters and their moral behaviour. Since Anakin Skywalker can love, trust and be loyal, all hope is not lost, although he turns evil at some stage of the story. It is these feelings that will save him and bring him back to the side of the good eventually. His emotions also enable the audience to feel with him, which again cements his status as the character who brings the older, more formulaic movies closer to the viewers. They underline an ideology which is common to both *Star Wars* and *Harry Potter* and which holds that persons who are able to love, trust and be loyal cannot be completely evil, no matter how many bad deeds they commit. The propagation of this ideology is by no means unproblematic as it might easily play down the crimes of people who actually are 'not completely evil at heart.'[33]

---

32   In accordance with this, Hanson and Kay hold that in episode one, Anakin is not so much interested in the greater implications of the war against the Trade Federation but in helping the people who are closest to him at the time, his mother, Qui-Gon and Padmé (cf. 292).

33   Richard H. Dees also comments on the ideology of love in the movies. Love, he holds is only good as long as it creates a kind of universal fellow-feeling and compassion for others, maybe even those one does not particularly like or who are different from oneself in their outlooks on life. If love becomes possessive and is only focused on those closest to us it can become "the root cause of the intolerance that leads to too

However, there are also scientists and theoreticians who demand a discussion of evil that is less dominated by emotions and more focused on a neutral analysis of the generation of evil which might then lead to suggestions of how to prevent particular evils in the future.[34] One could argue that the filmmakers tried to choose such an approach that is more explanatory than judgemental with the role of Anakin/Vader in the more recent trilogy.

After Yoda's none too substantial advice on his dreams, Anakin's disappointment with the Jedi deepens. After failed attempts at opening his heart first to Obi-Wan and then to his wife Padmé, he grows ever closer to Palpatine, his attachment to the chancellor culminating in the scene of temptation which has already been analysed in quite some detail in the preceding chapter. Evil finally shows its true face and it is a marker of Anakin's strength of character that he is still not completely convinced and seeks the advice of the Jedi in this decisive situation. Since his master Obi-Wan is away on a mission, he approaches Jedi master Mace Windu, which is unfortunate for Anakin because Windu is one of those on the Jedi Council who mistrust Anakin most strongly.

Anakin: [The Chancellor] won't give up his [emergency] powers. I have just learned a terrible truth. I think chancellor Palpatine is a Sith lord.

Mace Windu: A Sith lord?

Anakin: Yes. The one we've been looking for.

Mace Windu: How do you know this?

Anakin: He knows the ways of the Force. He's been trained to use the dark side.

Mace Windu: Are you sure?

Anakin: Absolutely.

Mace Windu: Then our worst fears have been realized. We must move quickly if the Jedi order is to survive.

Anakin: Master, the chancellor is very powerful. You'll need my help if you're going to arrest him.

Mace Windu: For your own good, stay out of this affair. I sense a great deal of confusion in you, young Skywalker. There is much fear that clouds your judgement.

Anakin: I must go, Master.

---

many of the great crimes committed by humanity" (51). That love is at once a redeeming but also possibly dangerous force and therefore ambiguous is also an important theme in the *Harry Potter* stories, where Harry's rash action for love of Sirius in novel five leads to much harm, comparable to Anakin's rashness in avenging his mother and wish to ultimately protect Padmé from death.

34   Cf. Seibold 93.

Mace Windu: No. If what you've told me is true, you will have gained my trust. But for now remain here. Wait in the Council chambers until we return.
Anakin: Yes, Master.[35]

In this exchange, it becomes clear that Windu is not convinced of Anakin's integrity. He does not see his good intentions in telling him about the Sith Lord. Instead he confronts him with his insecurities yet again. One friendly word, a thank you, a reaffirmation of trust, might have finally won Anakin back to the good side. Mace Windu, however, makes his distance to Anakin clear from the start of the conversation. He calls him by his last name and carefully re-questions everything Anakin tells him. He also treats him condescendingly as "young Skywalker," making clear that he is the elder and wiser in the conversation. Most importantly, he does not give the young man the chance to come along to destroy the chancellor and thus the evil side within himself. Mace Windu certainly understands the enormity of the situation for the whole Jedi order but fails to comprehend its relevance for the individual standing before him. He does not see either that this individual might be decisive to the outcome of the events. Again, this is typical of the Jedi. They mostly think of the common good rather than of the individual's. Leaving Anakin alone with the confusion and fear he actually senses within him and taking away his chance to destroy the chancellor once and for all, Windu fails Anakin. By withholding his trust or making it dependent on certain conditions, he squanders the only chance of winning Anakin back to the good side.

In the ensuing fight between Palpatine and Mace Windu, it becomes clear that Windu is more powerful than Palpatine. The chancellor, however, derives his strength from Anakin, who finally rushes to his aid. Since Anakin feels that no help with his problems will come from the Jedi, he believes that his last chance to save Padmé lies with Palpatine. So he has to keep him alive at all costs. The Jedi in Anakin could easily have vanquished Palpatine but with the Sith in Anakin against him, Mace Windu has no chance, though he now tries to win the young man over. For the first (and last) time Mace Windu uses Anakin's first name, conscious now that only trust can win Anakin back for the good side. However, it is too late by then and Anakin kills him. After the deed, the young man still feels remorse, but Palpatine manages to convince him that from the chosen path there is no turning back: "You are fulfilling your destiny, Anakin. Become my apprentice. Learn to use the dark side of the Force."[36] It turns out that Palpatine, like the Jedi, has always seen Anakin as a puppet of destiny, a tool to help him carry out his schemes.

---

35   *Revenge of the Sith* 1:04:54.
36   *Revenge of the Sith* 1:12:20.

Anakin, however, is past caring and assents to everything Palpatine suggests.[37] It is apparent that he is fed up with being torn apart and tossed about. He has needed direction all along, which the Jedi – so much oriented on self-discipline, free will and independence from personal feelings – could not provide. Now he finally finds direction with the chancellor. The next thing he says sounds melodramatic but is also highly tragic for several reasons: "Just help me save Padmé's life. I can't live without her."[38] This plea shows that he is still not all bad at this point. He has retained his feelings for Padmé. Furthermore it indicates that he has ultimately converted because of Padmé, who, the audience later learns cannot live with his transformation. Finally, and most significantly, it is tragic because Palpatine reveals that he cannot defeat death and has lured Anakin into his service under false pretences. [39] Nevertheless Anakin enters his service. This does not happen because he is naturally evil like Voldemort who employs his powers to dominate and inflict harm from an early age, but because he is overcome by his emotions. Fear and desperation are what drive Anakin. His feelings have taken the upper hand, his decisions are not rational anymore. He has become imbalanced.[40] Still, while he shares the Emperor's and Voldemort's hubris and hunger for ever greater power, the significant difference between the true villains and Anakin is that in contrast to them he does have feelings, and feelings that not only centre on himself.[41] Anakin does not fear death for himself like Voldemort, but for his beloved Padmé. In this sense he is less egotistical than Voldemort and he is provided with an opportunity of redemption.

Upon Anakin's conversion Palpatine turns from friendly mentor into master, his first action being to give Anakin his new name of Darth Vader. By killing Mace Windu, Anakin has begun to kill the Jedi within him. Now he has to complete his transformation by exterminating his good side once and for all. Palpatine, now the Emperor, subtly pushes him in the direction he wants him to take:

Every single Jedi including your friend Obi-Wan Kenobi is now an enemy of the Republic...First I want you to go to the Jedi temple. We will catch them off balance. Do what

---

37   Cf. *Revenge of the Sith* 1:12:36.

38   *Revenge of the Sith* 1:12:45.

39   Cf. *Revenge of the Sith* 1:12:55.

40   Cf. also Bowen and Wagner 84.

41   This echoes Bowen's and Wagner's assertion that "the introduction of Palpatine alongside Anakin / Darth Vader calls viewers to carefully compare the two and hints at Anakin's more nuanced characterization as one who might challenge the reified categories of light and dark" (86).

must be done, Lord Vader. Do not hesitate. Show no mercy. Only then you will be strong enough with the dark side to save Padmé.[42]

Palpatine never actually tells Anakin/Vader directly to kill all the Jedi. Anakin and the audience infer that he wishes them to die from what he says. This lack of giving clear directions turns out to be something that Palpatine shares with the Jedi, though Palpatine himself certainly never considered points such as these when he mentioned their similarities. Anakin does not seem to realise the contradictions in what Palpatine says, and his complete and utter change of character and submission to the Emperor create a break in an otherwise credible story of inner struggle and transformation.[43] After Anakin's prolonged and agonising fight against his own demons, the combat between his free will and his supposed destiny, his final conversion into the concept of evil is too forced. Almost violently it seems, the filmmakers had to make the story of human Anakin fit with the following story of Darth Vader, the image of evil. This again supports the conclusion drawn here already of the more mythical nature of the older movies in comparison to the newer ones which seem to function as mediators between the original trilogy and human reality. It also suggests once more that themes, here the treatment of good versus evil, are finally more important than credible character development.

The showdown and final transformation into Darth Vader occurs after Anakin has killed all the Jedi in the temple, even the children and all other people and creatures who could potentially have become dangerous to the chancellor on his way to ultimate power. The latter has by now declared himself ruler of the "first Galactic Empire."[44] Anakin is on the Mustafar System, a volcanic planet, where he has killed some separatist functionaries. Padmé, very concerned about her husband, has followed him there, and unnoticed by her, Obi-Wan has hidden on her space cruiser. It is highly relevant that Padmé and Obi-Wan confront Anakin since they are Anakin's main and last connections to the good side. Padmé and Anakin have an intense and desperate conversation.

---

42   *Revenge of the Sith* 1:14:36.

43   Todd Hanson makes a similar observation when he comments on the assets and failures of *The Phantom Menace* and wonders that it does not include one scene in which Anakin's later evil is foreshadowed. The friendly, almost angelic child that is presented to the audience does not make the conversion Anakin undergoes entirely credible (Cf. Todd Hanson, "A Big Dumb Movie About Space Wizards: Struggling to Cope with *The Phantom Menace*," *A Galaxy Not So Far Away: Writers and Artists on Twenty Five Years of Star Wars*, Ed. Glenn Kenny (New York: Owl Books, 2002) 179).

44   *Revenge of the Sith* 1:31:52.

Padmé: Anakin, all I want is your love.

Anakin: Love won't save you, Padmé. Only my new powers can do that.

Padmé: At what cost? You're a good person. Don't do this.

Anakin: I won't lose you the way I lost my mother. I am becoming more powerful than any Jedi has ever dreamed of. And I'm doing it for you. To protect you.

Padmé: Come away with me. Help me raise our child. Leave everything else behind while we still can.

Anakin: Don't you see? We don't have to run away anymore. I have brought peace to the Republic. I am more powerful than the chancellor. I can overthrow him. And together, you and I can rule the galaxy, make things the way we want them to be.

Padmé: I don't believe what I'm hearing. Obi-Wan was right. You've changed.[45]

This highly emotionally charged exchange between the two makes two things very clear: one is that Padmé really loves Anakin, that she could even now forgive him for what he has done. The other is that Anakin is by now past all moderation and rational thought. He is completely subject to his (negative) emotions, the end of a development that started in movie one when little Anakin showed fear on leaving his mother and intensified in film two when Anakin the adolescent was too late to save his mother from her captors. When Padmé says that all she wants is his love and he replies that love will not save her, this shows that he has stopped believing in the power of love. This induces the final stage of his transformation. His ability to love and believe in love's power was his great strength which is gone now. All that is left to Anakin now are his enormous new powers. He is arrogant enough to believe that any human power, good or evil, can save someone from dying. In addition to his fear, which was already mentioned, this arrogance constitutes his 'tragic flaw' because his belief in his ability to save Padmé from dying is what finally leads him to convert – a serious error of judgement.[46] The ability to wield power and the consciousness of his might have replaced goodness, love and respect.

In their exchange, Padmé finally mentions Obi-Wan, the very last person who still stands in the way of Anakin fully turning into a Sith. Anakin reacts furiously, because he believes Obi-Wan has turned against him.[47] He feels alone, betrayed and forsaken by everyone, even those he believed to be his friends until now. He also has the irrational idea that Obi-Wan has stolen Padmé from him. Padmé's assertion that her behaviour has nothing to do with Obi-Wan but with Anakin's character

---

45   *Revenge of the Sith* 1:40:13.

46   Both *Star Wars* and *Harry Potter* show certain parallels with classical drama, predominantly in structure, but also with respect to characters as, for instance, in the case of Anakin Skywalker.

47   Cf. *Revenge of the Sith* 1:41:17.

change, her professions of love and her pleading with Anakin to come back to her go unheard, because Obi-Wan appears at exactly that moment. It is the appearance of good that finally brings about evil, thereby drawing attention to the ways in which binary oppositions are actually constitutive of each other once more. Anakin rages: "Liar! You're with him! You brought him here to kill me."[48] At that moment nothing is left of the earlier grandiose behaviour, when he claimed to be the most powerful person in the galaxy. He is hurt and scared and feels completely alone. He does not vent his rage on Obi-Wan but on Padmé, whom he throttles until she falls to the ground unconscious. When he blames Obi-Wan for his and Padmé's predicament, Obi-Wan calmly tells him that he has brought everything that has happened onto himself.[49] Anakin roars: "I see through the lies of the Jedi. I do not fear the dark side as you do. I have brought peace, freedom, justice and security to my new empire."[50] Obi-Wan is nonplussed: "Your new empire?", whereupon Anakin says: "Don't make me kill you."[51] This exchange shows that Anakin is past all rationality by now. Since *he* has broken the Jedi rule of sexual abstinence he expects that Obi-Wan has done so, too and has cuckolded him. His former master's calmness further enrages him.

All he can do now is react with violence or the threat of it. He does not have any true arguments for his case and cannot explain himself factually. Obi-Wan replies to Anakin's threat: "Anakin, my allegiance is to the Republic, to democracy!"[52] It is noteworthy that the Jedi master still calls him Anakin, which could be interpreted as an appeal to Anakin's former and original self. (Compare the use of the names 'Skywalker' and 'Anakin' by Jedi master Mace Windu which were analysed before.) Anakin's answer "If you're not with me then you're my enemy"[53] is highly revealing not only with respect to his character change. It also emphasises the discourse the director and producers obviously want to stage here. Obi-Wan's answer "Only a Sith deals in absolutes. I will do what I must"[54] while drawing his lightsabre tells us much about how the film-makers want the audience to see the world. Since the film came out in 2005, the political relevance of the statement after 9/11 cannot be overlooked. The two remarks are also interesting, because they directly suggest that thinking only in categories of black and white is too easy. This blunt and direct message is partly undermined by the deep-structures of the tales,

---

48   *Revenge of the Sith* 1:41:48.
49   Cf. *Revenge of the Sith* 1:42:19.
50   *Revenge of the Sith* 1:42:45.
51   *Revenge of the Sith* 1:42:15.
52   *Revenge of the Sith* 1:43:08.
53   *Revenge of the Sith* 1:43:14.
54   *Revenge of the Sith* 1:43:13.

however, which show that the stories heavily rely on absolutes in their generation of meaning. The statements themselves become more ambiguous when they are linked with Palpatine's statement in episode three about good and evil being a point of view. In fact, it is interesting that Obi-Wan accuses the Sith of 'dealing in absolutes,' while Palpatine, the supreme Sith, does not do so at all. His statement about the nature of good and evil is anything but absolute: it rather relativises both concepts. Palpatine, as was mentioned before, understands something about binary oppositions and the way they are used by people to establish hierarchies and obtain power. His superior knowledge, however, is rejected, since Palpatine is clearly evil. The movies' message is extremely ambiguous here. Neither Palpatine's sophisticated notion of good and evil nor Anakin's 'dealing in absolutes' are endorsed and, taking the two scenes together, it remains unclear which values the filmmakers want to propagate. At these two crucial points, the films contradict themselves without allowing the usual mythical ambiguity, as both concepts are rejected.

In *Harry Potter* no such rejection of structuralist and poststructuralist notions of good and evil occurs. In fact, Dumbledore, the epitome of goodness makes a statement similar to Anakin's at the end of novel four, right after Harry has informed him of Voldemort's return. Dumbledore tries to convince the blundering wizarding Prime Minister Fudge of the necessity to take steps against Voldemort. Fudge is not prepared to hear Dumbledore who finally says: "The only one against whom I intend to work (…) is Lord Voldemort. If you are against him, then we remain, Cornelius, on the same side."[55] The headmaster's words are a remarkable echo of Anakin's, but since in contrast to Anakin, Dumbledore is generally believed to follow a righteous and just path, they are not questioned. It seems that as long as one is on the 'right' side of the binary, everything is fine. This stance is extremely problematic, since Dumbledore, in his fight against evil does not always behave completely altruistically. He, too bends quite a few rules to achieve his aims and sacrifices people 'for the greater good,' most notably Snape.[56] These different and possibly largely unconscious approaches to binary oppositions, demonstrate how hard it is to integrate and deal wisely with these eternally existing dichotomies.

While Obi-Wan challenges Anakin, master Yoda confronts the newly styled Emperor, who is eager to get away from the powerful Jedi.

Yoda: If so powerful you are, why leave [sic]?

---

55   Rowling *Goblet* 615.

56   For a discussion of Dumbledore as a villain see Nikolajeva "Adult Heroism and Role Models" 199-200.

The Emperor: You will not stop me. Darth Vader will become more powerful than either of us.

Yoda: Faith in your new apprentice misplaced may be [sic]. As is your faith in the dark side of the Force.[57]

Yoda's statement about Anakin at the moment of his complete transformation to evil is highly relevant and echoes his earlier one about the prophecy that could have been misread. The Jedi have already misjudged Anakin once, the Emperor might make incorrect assumptions about him, too. The remark powerfully reinforces and extends Obi-Wan's earlier criticism of the Siths' black and white world-view by leaving room for doubt about Anakin's loyalties and refusing categorisation. While Yoda seems to have realised not only the difficulty of placing human beings according to binaries in general but also the unpredictable element in Anakin's nature in particular, Obi-Wan is less wise. In theory he knows and adheres to the Jedi philosophy of not 'dealing in absolutes,' however, in practice he still cannot see Anakin as a real person. He begins to fight his own apprentice and finally cuts off Anakin's legs. Thereby he literally finishes what the Jedi figuratively began when they took charge of the boy, namely pulling the rug out from under him. Taking Anakin's legs means that he will never manage to get up again on his own. The Jedi have finally taken away Anakin's self-confidence, his certainties, his good qualities and have made him completely dependent. Cutting off Anakin's legs is the Jedis' final contribution to turning him into the destiny-driven icon he has been for them from the beginning. Obi-Wan's cruelty goes even further. While the badly injured Anakin slides towards a lava-filled crate, his ex-master screams: "You were the chosen one. It was said that you would destroy the Sith, not join them. Bring balance to the Force, not leave it in darkness."[58] It is tragic that even at the moment when the audience can presume Anakin is dying, Obi-Wan does not see a person but 'the chosen one,' the prophecy and the Force.

The scene crystallises the Jedi's attitude toward Anakin in Obi-Wan, his mentor and teacher, the person who should be closest to him: the identification of Anakin with the prophecy of which no one knows the exact wording or meaning. Obi-Wan never considers that if one believes in the prophecy all that is happening might be part of the plan laid out for Anakin. Matril also considers the possibility that everything that happens is part of Anakin's destiny. He sees free choice as finally triumphing in the movies, arguing that the concept of destiny is mainly associated with the Emperor, who is quite clearly evil and claiming that ultimately things do

---

57   *Revenge of the Sith* 1:45:50.

58   *Revenge of the Sith* 1:55:02.

not turn out the way the chief villain has foreseen.[59] However, Matril undermines his own interpretation by referring to Obi-Wan's statement on Anakin having been the chosen one as "curiously fatalistic," thereby exposing the fact that not unlike the Emperor, the Jedi believes in destiny.[60] The binary of destiny and free will is completely blurred in the movies and it is very hard to decide which stance is finally endorsed. Even the wisest (here the Jedi), it seems, can never fully grasp the concept of destiny. (Compare also the analyses of the diagrams in chapter four.)

What the audience sees at the crucial moment of Obi-Wan's (temporary) victory over Anakin is something completely different from Obi-Wan. They see a human face contorted in pain, a face full of rage, but also fear and sadness. Anakin cries: "I hate you!" and Obi-Wan just turns to go with the words: "You were my brother, Anakin. I loved you."[61] By now sparks from the lava have ignited Anakin. Burning, he extends a hand to Obi-Wan in a gesture that could imply threat or simply helplessness but the 'good' Jedi just leaves him. The flames consuming Anakin can be interpreted in two different ways. Firstly they extinguish the old Anakin. They leave him so unrecognisable that when the Emperor rescues him from the flames, he needs a breathing device and other technical equipment to stay alive. Secondly, from Obi-Wan's point of view, the fire certainly has a purifying element to it. Clearly he wishes evil in the form of Anakin to burn to cinders and thus disappear. The moment of Obi-Wan's walking away completely unmasks the Jedi and their share in Anakin's transformation. It shows the Jedi, who are supposed to be selfless and help others, as people helping only those who are good and who think like them. It also perfectly embodies their policy of non-involvement. Obi-Wan's reaction mirrors Anakin's statement "If you're not with me then you're my enemy" and shows again that Obi-Wan does not really practice what he preaches about not dealing in absolutes. There is nothing selfless, nothing moral in his actions at that moment. Anakin's extended hand could have been a last plea for help ignored by Obi-Wan. The Jedi claims Anakin to have been his brother and to have loved him but his actions show nothing brotherly. He has no compassion for his apprentice in this situation. It was mentioned before that compassion is among the qualities both villains, the Emperor and Voldemort, lack. That Obi-Wan lacks compassion here shows him, if not exactly as a villain, at least as someone human and flawed who does not always act correctly. While the villains are stereotypical and never feel pity for anyone, Obi-Wan is a middle-character like Anakin, someone who is neither completely good, nor entirely evil but simply human. Like Anakin, Obi-Wan is brought closer to the audience by the new trilogy. In the old one, he is the

---

59   Cf. Matril n.pag.

60   Matril n.pag.

61   *Revenge of the Sith* 1:55:26.

rather stereotypically good, wizened old helper figure for the hero. The movie shows here how hard it is not to 'deal in absolutes' and find a balanced approach to life. It demonstrates that regardless of categories such as good and evil, everyone is first of all human.[62]

Finally, there are three factors which help turning Anakin into Darth Vader. The first is of his own doing. Undoubtedly the young man does evil by killing numerous people.[63] The second factor is Obi-Wan's leaving him maimed and unrecognisable. Obi-Wan's behaviour emphasises that it is partly the treatment of the good side that leaves Anakin burned, scarred and barely human. For dramatic reasons it was surely necessary to separate Anakin from Darth Vader visually. Otherwise Vader would still have been associated too closely with the handsome young man. The old concept of physiognomy comes in here: evil cannot be handsome, it has to be ugly, while someone handsome cannot be bad. The Emperor pulls Anakin out of the lava and makes his transformation complete as a third factor. He finally turns him into the concept he has always been for most of the characters. Anakin loses his individual name and his already scarred and broken face and body are hidden away behind a cloak and mask with an artificial breathing apparatus. This makes him breathe regularly and heavily, reminiscent of a machine but also of a very vulnerable person dependent on technology to stay alive. So again, even in his more stereotypical phase, Anakin is ambiguous. He is the fear-inspiring dark lord on the one hand, machine-like in appearance and horrible to behold, and the human being who has gone through terrible ordeals to be dependent on a breathing device on the other. As the latter he is to be pitied rather than abhorred. The last the audience sees of the newly completed Darth Vader in episode three is him having a tantrum over the fact that Padmé is dead. She obviously still carries some importance for him and that nourishes the hope that he will eventually regret his deeds and return to the good side. In this scene, Vader's wrath makes the whole room quake.[64] He is all power but at the same time it is made graphic that his power springs from the 'wrong' sources. It is not the wise and calm power master Yoda exudes but a power derived from hatred and fury. Quite plainly, this kind of power cannot lead to any good.

From the moment Anakin becomes Darth Vader he changes completely; from the headstrong boy to the subservient man, from the child unwilling to take orders to the man subjecting himself to the Emperor. This change is sudden but might in

---

62   Obi-Wan's actions also underline Palpatine's remark about the similarity of Jedi and Sith. Cf. also Hanson and Kay 322.

63   This, as Richard H. Dees correctly observes is not ambiguous but plainly morally reprehensible (49-50).

64   Cf. *Revenge of the Sith* 2:02:52.

part be explained by the hierarchical way in which the master-apprentice relationship is organised with the Sith. The apprentice can take over when his power exceeds his master's.[65] It can safely be assumed that in most cases there will be a violent takeover as the example of the already mentioned 'Sith legend' Darth Plagueis shows. The Emperor is also finally forcefully overthrown and killed by Darth Vader, his apprentice. As much as Anakin wanted to be master before, Darth Vader now subjects himself to the Emperor's teachings. It is ironic that he seems to have learned patience at last, especially when taking into account that he would not have had to wait long before the Jedi would have made him a master. With the Emperor he is now stuck in the role of second in command. Until almost the very end he is only an empty, if threatening shell that serves as foil for the good side, especially Luke. I disagree with Hanson and Kay who hold that "as a villain Anakin becomes more interesting."[66] The only interesting fact about him is that till the very end he is not even the ultimate villain and does not obtain unlimited power. Most striking about Anakin as a villain is his unimportance. The Emperor needs him to do the threatening and the dirty work for him and to inspire fear. By rejecting the role of a mascot the Jedi wanted to press him into, Vader has only achieved being pressed into another role, being a mascot for someone else. In every episode there is some governor or general who is higher in the hierarchy than Vader. When Princess Leia is kept prisoner on the Death Star in episode four she fittingly says: "Governor Tarkin. I should have expected to find you holding Vader's leash."[67] This indicates that Vader is indeed only the 'dog' of someone superior, someone whom he has to listen to and take orders from. A dog is also sometimes believed to be an animal that rather mindlessly follows his master's command. This association supports the fact that by turning into Darth Vader, Anakin has lost his ability to think freely and make his own decisions. Another point that becomes apparent from Leia's comment and the bold way she makes it, is that obviously Vader does not have the power to scare everyone, either. Leia, his daughter remains relatively unimpressed by his presence. She understands that it is not Vader himself who comes up with all the horrible ideas for destruction but the persons 'holding his leash.' It is not Vader, for instance, who has the idea of forcing Leia to reveal the hideout of the rebels by destroying her home planet of Alderaan with the Death Star. Governor Tarkin is responsible for this outrage.[68]

It is striking but also fitting that from the fourth episode onwards, the audience learns almost nothing about Vader's own feelings. In most decisive moments he is

---

65   Cf. Hanson and Kay 323-24.

66   Hanson and Kay 365.

67   *A New Hope* 00:54:56.

68   Cf. *A New Hope* 00:55:47.

rather seen through the eyes of other characters. Leia's statement which has already been mentioned, would be an example. A further example is the scene in which the Emperor confronts Darth Vader with Luke's presence and says: "I have no doubt this boy is the offspring of Anakin Skywalker."[69] The Emperor, it transpires, believes or wants to believe that Vader has completely severed ties with his old self, Anakin Skywalker. This is why he does not say: "I have no doubt the boy is your son." For the Emperor it is necessary to have the two parts of Vader neatly separated because he knows how dangerous Vader's good side could be to him. It is also consistent with the way the movies portray Anakin and Vader respectively. His two sides are always neatly split. The audience does not learn how Vader himself feels about Luke in this scene. The Emperor's command, however does not leave any doubts: Vader has to go and destroy Luke and his rebel friends. It is obvious why this has to be done. With Luke some small root of good, some part of Anakin remains within Vader. Only when this part of his nature is uprooted, the Emperor believes, will Vader really have torn down all bridges to his former self. Darth Vader seems to be willing to do the Emperor's bidding, though again, we never learn his true feelings on the matter and the true reasons why he himself decides to hunt down Luke.

All of Anakin's great purposes, such as seeing all the stars and bringing peace and freedom to the galaxy have evaporated and crystallised into his search for Luke and his rebel friends, which becomes the one and only reason for his existence.[70] Since the audience does not get to know Vader's motivations for the persecution of Luke, the villain's manic search can be interpreted in two ways. Either Vader truly seeks to destroy Luke, the unexpected last part of his former self that has appeared seemingly out of nowhere, or he is by now disappointed by the Emperor and his status and unconsciously looks for a reconciliation between his current and old nature. The latter interpretation does not seem completely far-fetched when Vader makes one desperate attempt at reintegrating rather than destroying his good side. He asks Luke to join him so that together they can "destroy the Emperor ... [and] rule the galaxy as father and son."[71] When Luke declines, however, Vader has to realise that a reintegration of this sort cannot work. His conflict about Luke shows that being evil does not pay off for him. He has not achieved any of his dreams and desires and is still dealing with his conscience, which is symbolised by Luke, his good side. It is much easier for Voldemort in *Harry Potter* to be evil, because he is never badgered by his conscience and never has any good side to start with. The tide begins to turn for Vader and Luke towards the end of *Return of the Jedi*. Luke

---

69 *The Empire Strikes Back* 00:51:16.

70 Cf. *The Empire Strikes Back* 1:03:34.

71 *The Empire Strikes Back* 1:47:17.

and the other rebels have landed on Endor, a forest moon and Vader approaches the Emperor:

Vader: A small rebel force has penetrated the [deflector] shield and landed on Endor.
Emperor: Yes, I know.
Vader: My son is with them.
Emperor: I wonder if your feelings on this matter are clear, Lord Vader.
Vader: They are clear, my master.
Emperor: Then you must go to the Sanctuary Moon and wait for him.
Vader: He will come to me?
Emperor: I have foreseen it. His compassion for you will be his undoing.[72]

While the Emperor still fears Vader's connection to Luke, Vader himself acknowledges Luke as his son for the first time. This is significant because obviously, Vader has accepted Luke as part of himself. To keep up suspense in this scene, the screenwriters have made Vader's answer to the Emperor's anxieties concerning Luke enigmatic. The Emperor wonders whether Vader's feelings on the subject of his son are clear and Vader says: "They are clear, my master." This might satisfy the Emperor but it does not tell us anything about the nature of Vader's feelings. While the Emperor assumes his answer to mean that Vader intends to pursue Luke further, the statement could also be read as the beginning of another transformation in Vader. Rather than killing Luke, he might have plans to overthrow the Emperor already then.

The fight between the Emperor, Vader and Luke that forms the showdown of film six is a fight between the competing ideas of fate and free will. The Emperor, who still speaks of "destiny,"[73] stands for the abuse of the person Anakin for an idea in the name of fate. Both Luke and Vader can be interpreted as standing for free will in this scene because both make conscious decisions, Luke against evil, and Vader for his son. The fact that Vader becomes re-associated with free will, and is not subject to destiny anymore, already heralds his conversion. Both *Star Wars* and *Harry Potter* associate free will with goodness and morally right decisions. By killing the Emperor, Vader kills the evil side within himself and becomes Anakin once more. This moment in the movie is a warning never to underestimate individual free will and never to assign too much power to fate. Fate is a concept that is hard to understand and most of the characters in the movies use it too lightly. Mostly what is deemed fate is really personal failure or triumph or someone's will which is consciously or unconsciously forced on others. The final battle makes

---

72   *Return of the Jedi* 1:04:05.
73   *Return of the Jedi* 1:32:33.

clear that even a small conscious decision can change or turn fate. Vader/Anakin can be said to have redeemed himself by saving Luke,[74] which is also apparent in the structure of the story (see the triangular visualisations of Anakin's fall and redemption in chapter two). However, as much as Anakin makes a conscious choice here, the element of natural disposition (his original good disposition represented by his son Luke) cannot be explained away. Steven Galipeau, who in fact chooses the interpretation foregrounding Anakin's free will in the final fight, also subtly undermines his own assertion. *"Luke's belief*, which was part perception and part hope – that there was still good in Darth Vader and that he could thus be turned to the Good Side, back to his true human self – eventually led to the transformation of evil energies [emphasis added]."[75] Luke's belief thus led to free choice, but it is also Luke's belief (Luke standing for Vader's originally good nature) that brings about the change in the villain. The mythical ambiguity of this situation cannot be resolved.[76] (Once more compare the discussion of the diagrams in chapter four.)

In sum it can be said that Anakin/Vader is the most important character in the movies. He presents a foil for the discussion of competing concepts such as good and evil, free will and determination as well as destiny. Fate in the stories can be read as heavily influenced by people. However, there is also the possibility to interpret it as simply there and unchangeable. It is rather interesting in this respect that by his two decisive choices for evil and for good, Anakin/Vader seems to affirm the validity of the fatal prophecy. Conscious choices stand equal to the workings of fate. Obviously the film-makers do not want to make too clear a decision on either free will or destiny. The fact that both are reinforced in the end shows that basically the two concepts are beyond human grasp. Tony M. Vinci claims that "the progressive themes of the original trilogy [e.g. focus on individuality] are conclusively over-simplified and subverted by positioning

---

74 Richard H. Dees perceives Anakin/Vader as most morally ambiguous at this point in the story. The fact that he still does not act out of wider feelings of love, compassion and responsibility but purely to save his son shows that he still only extends his love to those closest to him (like his mother and Padmé before). However, in contrast to the situation in which he avenges his mother in episode two and the one in which he turns against the Jedi in order to save Padmé in episode three, his action now (killing the Emperor) is beneficial since it restores peace and order. In this sense, Vader's action is morally ambiguous (cf. 52).

75 Galipeau 247.

76 Bowen and Wagner also hold that it is impossible to completely recategorise Anakin/Vader with the good side after the ultimate battle. "He is Anakin *and* Vader and remains both in the end, reclaiming his identity as Luke's father but unable to breathe for long without his black shell" (87-88).

individual autonomy as the direct cause of the tragic events that both *Star Wars* trilogy's [sic] are founded on."[77] This view is too narrow. I have tried to show how many different people and events influence Anakin to make his choice for evil. It is hard to say whether finally it is his free will, or fate, or both which prompt him to commit his evil deeds and the question is appropriately treated in a complex manner and finally left open. The opposition between choice and natural determination remains similarly unclear. How much of Vader's final conversion back into Anakin is due to his act of free will and how much of the good has actually been in his nature all along and comes to the fore anew with the appearance of his son Luke? The movies' stance remains ambiguous. Anakin/Vader, it seems, crystallises the mythical ambiguity that characterises popular entertainment and that was explored in the Lévi-Straussian diagrams of chapter four.

In addition to these equivocal patterns and Anakin uniting binaries, there are several ideologies that are underlying in Anakin's story, his fall from grace and his redemption. Firstly, it is very important that after his conversion to evil, so much changes for Anakin. His going from one extreme to the other has bearings on other parts of his life which also seem to change in the extreme. As Anakin he had a love life and friends: as Vader he has neither and is alone. The Jedi had almost made him master, whereas the Emperor basically uses him as a slave. As Anakin, many hopes rested on him. He was important because of his power and his ability to change the situation of the galaxy. When he is turned into Darth Vader he becomes a mere puppet and is really unimportant. His grand hopes and dreams remain unfulfilled and instead of being great he is not even able to breathe on his own. The Emperor exerts almost total control over him. The simple ideology behind all this, true to many fairy tale morals, is that evil does not pay off. This also shows in the fact that Vader's sole purpose becomes the search for his son Luke and thus the final extinction or reconstitution of his good side. Throughout the three original movies, Vader is still conscience-bitten and guilt-stricken. He needs to exterminate Luke, who reminds him of his good side and presumably makes him question his evil deeds. It is not worthwhile pursuing one's chosen path without any consideration for other people, and power alone does not make anyone happy. Patience rather than impatience is rewarded and sometimes the more difficult way is the better. This conventional message is fed to the audience of the movies.

There is another, even more relevant question that needs to be discussed with respect to Anakin/Vader which goes together with another ideology the movies support. Anakin Skywalker / Darth Vader has now been discussed at length and it has transpired that he is treated with much sympathy throughout. He is portrayed as an originally friendly, helpful and curious child who is taken out of his familiar

---

77   Vinci 28.

surroundings and is then constantly manipulated by the people around him and shaped according to their wishes. His turning evil, the movies seem to say, is almost inevitable because he is turned into a mascot in the name of destiny. However, although this is the dominant reading which the movies certainly invite, there is another, less sympathetic way of seeing his development. The movies neglect to draw enough attention to Anakin's own part in his fall and thereby direct the audiences' sympathy in too one-dimensional a way. One could see Anakin's history differently, after all: The child Anakin is freed from slavery by the Jedi. He has the opportunity to learn the ways of the Force, he comes to play an important role on the Jedi Council at an early age and is sent on decisive missions in the name of freedom. Not only does he have the favour and even friendship of many powerful Jedi, he also has the love of a powerful, intelligent and beautiful woman. So how come he throws all of this away to be with Palpatine / the Emperor? Why is he portrayed so sympathetically when he kills scores of people and creatures? He not only commits evil deeds when he is actively asked to by the Emperor and his henchmen. As early as movie two, he kills numerous people and other creatures to avenge the death of his mother, a scene that is rather quickly passed by as the one in which he murders all the Jedi at the Jedi temple, even the children in episode three. He also contributes to the deaths of his wife and Obi-Wan. The movies sell their audiences the ideology that even people who would by all social standards be called criminals and murderers, can be redeemed.

In one way that is a very appealing message. Everyone can change and everyone will be forgiven like Anakin, whose youthful apparition along with those of Obi-Wan and Yoda is finally hovering above the victory celebrations, smiling benignly on the revellers.[78] In another way, it is a dangerous ideology because it tends to play down the evil deeds of a criminal and forget the victims. The sandpeople who have to die because of the abduction of Anakin's mother and the young Jedi padawans are never spoken of again. Secondly it raises the hopes of second chances which are not always given in real life. Through one good deed, killing the Emperor, Anakin, it seems has redeemed hundreds of bad ones and is reintegrated into the society of the Jedi. I doubt whether things are that easy in real life. So in this way the movies trivialise evil and simplify the interplay of guilt and redemption. It needs to be said once more that the Emperor is not completely wrong when he says that the perception of good and evil depends on the point of view. Discussions on evil are certainly very often influenced by emotions, which frequently makes them less neutral and productive.[79] Still, it is impossible to completely factor out from these discussions those who have suffered from evil. A

---

78   Cf. *Return of the Jedi* 2:02:20.

79   Cf. Seibold 93.

middle way suggests itself here. This is again reminiscent of myth which always tries to work towards the reconciliation of extremes. In this sense, both readings are invited by the films, the more forgiving and dominant one which explains Anakin's fall and the less dominant one which assigns personal blame to Anakin and holds him accountable for his crimes.

All this makes Anakin a highly ambiguous figure and the different readings the text enables again show *Star Wars* to confer to the ambiguity found in myth and popular entertainment. As was mentioned already, Voldemort in *Harry Potter* is treated much less mercifully. His evil deeds are clearly foregrounded and countered by Harry's good ones. The victims are much more in focus. Although Voldemort has a bad childhood the readers do not truly feel sorry for him. There is a strong feeling running through the novels that the villain will have to account for his deeds at some stage, the horrible baby-like shape of the Horcrux split away from Harry's soul in novel seven gives a clear indication of what is to come for Voldemort.[80] In contrast to the ideology of guilt and atonement that is at work in *Star Wars*, *Harry Potter* propagates the ideology of crime and punishment. It is as simple an ideology but a more unforgiving one with a much more direct warning against pursuing the path of evil than in *Star Wars*. The movies only imply that Anakin loses everything by turning towards the evil side and represent this as his punishment. Voldemort cannot be reintegrated into society and has to die in the end without anyone feeling much sympathy for him. The movies and the novels thus present two different ways of dealing with guilt: redemption and punishment. In real life the two are not necessarily mutually exclusive.

6.2 VILLAIN-TYPE AND SILENT HERO: SEVERUS SNAPE

The character in *Harry Potter* whose role resembles that of Anakin/Vader most closely is Severus Snape. Though he does not play as big a part as Anakin/Vader in *Star Wars*, Snape is nevertheless an important character in the *Harry Potter* novels. Much like Anakin/Vader, he is one of the few characters in *Harry Potter* who undergoes a moral development. The Hogwarts Potions Master is arguably the most interesting figure in Rowling's novels and, as will be proved, he is a mediating character like Anakin. The one big difference between Anakin and Snape is that for the viewers of *Star Wars* it is made quite clear which side Anakin/Vader is on at any given time and there are only subtle signs that he might be ambiguous throughout the whole story. (See for instance the conversations between the Emperor and Darth Vader about Luke in *Return of the Jedi*.) Snape's moral development is similar though depicted differently. The readers of the *Harry Potter*

---

80   Cf. Rowling *Hallows* 566.

novels only learn about Snape's true character in the last quarter of the final novel.[81] Snape is not only distrusted by most of the characters in the novels but also by the readers because they see him almost exclusively through Harry's eyes.

So far, the names of all the characters discussed have been significant and each of the important figures had a name-change at some stage of the story. So, too does Snape. As we learn in novel six, as a student Snape assumed the name 'Half-Blood Prince,' which was supposed to emphasise his status as a half-blood and express a dissociation from his Muggle father. 'Prince' was his witch mother's maiden name, so he chose it to emphasise his wizard origins, which he was obviously proud of.[82] It is certainly no coincidence that 'Prince' is also a title much like Emperor or Lord. Snape, like Voldemort seems to have felt the need to distance himself from his common name as a teenager and assume another one more richly associative and powerful. However, unlike Voldemort and the Emperor and in concurrence with Anakin he resumes his original, ordinary name further on into the story. He does so much earlier than Anakin even, which shows that he has been humbled. This already marks him of as different from the villains of the stories and is an indicator of the fact that he is ultimately part of the good side.

His original name Severus Snape is telling in some respects, much like the names of those characters discussed already. His first name Severus is reminiscent of the word severe, meaning serious but also harsh or strict. All these attributes fit Snape, a character seemingly devoid of all humour, whose face is usually an inscrutable mask. He is also strict and at times even harsh with respect to the students, especially Harry. His first name is thus revealing concerning his character but it does not contain any ambiguity as did the names of Voldemort and Anakin. Severity in itself is neither good nor evil. The name hints at Snape's non-indulgent stance concerning Harry, which, although sometimes unfair, finally benefits the hero. His last name Snape calls forth associations with the terms 'snap' and 'snake'.[83] To snap something means to break it, a correlation that is quite fitting since Snape breaks two important connections in the course of his life – acts that heavily influence himself, Harry Potter and the wizarding world. He breaks his relationship with Harry's mother Lily because his Death Eater friends are more important to him at that stage and later on he breaks his allegiance to Voldemort by becoming a double agent for Dumbledore. The phrase 'to snap at someone' also fits

---

81   Cf. Rowling, *Hallows* 529-53.

82   Cf. Rowling *Prince* 593-94.

83   Cf. also for instance "Severus Snape," *Harry Potter Wiki*, 2012, 30 Aug. 2012 <http://de.harry-potter.wikia.com/wiki/Severus_Snape>, "Severus Snape: Data," *The Harry Potter Lexicon*, 2012, 30 Aug. 2012 <http://www.hp-lexicon.org/wizards/snape.html#name>.

Snape who often vents his rage on his students, especially Harry. The snake, a frequently used symbol in *Harry Potter* would align Snape with Voldemort and evil. His name's association with the term 'snake' emphasises the ambiguous status he has for Harry, the wizarding community and the readers throughout the novels. Harry usually refers to Severus Snape only by his last name, an attitude showing his dislike of and disrespect for the Professor. His last name being the more ambiguous one, this also contributes to the doubtful stance Snape has throughout the novels. Since it is Harry, a completely likeable orphan boy who guides the readers' sympathies, they have a hard time detaching themselves from his views. Until the end of book seven, the readers never really get Snape's own perspective but only see him through the eyes of other characters. This is crucial for the depiction and development of his character.

From the beginning, Snape is characterised negatively. He first appears during Harry's Sorting Ceremony after the little wizard's arrival at Hogwarts. The atmosphere in this scene is generally very pleasant. The students have all been sorted into the four school houses and a magnificent feast is just drawing to a close. Everyone is well-fed and sleepy. Harry suddenly notices Professor Snape, "a teacher with greasy black hair, a hooked nose and sallow skin."[84] This description of Snape in the midst of a happy and festive atmosphere qualifies him as a first-rate villain. He seems not very well groomed, is dark-haired, which in literary tradition, for instance Gothic fiction and 19th-century melodrama, is always a secure marker of a villain, and he does not meet the criteria associated with beauty. His appearance resembles that of a vampire, pale and bloodless. And directly after Harry has noticed him for the first time, something happens that associates him with evil far more clearly than his appearance. "It happened very suddenly. The hook-nosed teacher looked past Quirrell's turban straight into Harry's eyes – and a sharp, hot pain shot across the scar on Harry's forehead."[85] The pain in his scar, apparently caused by Snape's stare, is the first physical sign Harry gets that the relic of his encounter with Voldemort is not an ordinary scar and that it might be connected to secrets yet unknown and undreamed of. It seems fitting that someone who looks as evil as Snape can produce such an effect with just a look and thus the readers suspect him from the start. Interestingly enough, the scene provides clues as to the real nature of evil in the first novel. It later turns out that the villain of *Harry Potter and the Philosopher's Stone* is not Professor Snape, but Professor Quirrell, who has been hiding Voldemort under his turban all along. Quirrell is mentioned together with Snape in that scene, only in a much less conspicuous way. He seems to be jumpy and nervous but not particularly threatening. That is why in this first scene

---

84   Rowling *Stone* 138.

85   Rowling *Stone* 138.

featuring Snape all the suspicion naturally lies on the Potions teacher as the much more conspicuous figure. He gives Harry the feeling that he does not like him,[86] a very important first indicator of the relationship between the two, which is mainly characterised by mutual antipathy. When Ron's brother Percy tells Harry shortly afterwards that Snape "[knows] an awful lot about the Dark Arts" that does not help matters.[87] From that moment on Harry mistrusts the Potions Master. The basic misunderstanding alluded to here is the notion that someone who does not like him, or whom he does not like, necessarily has to be a bad person.

Evil in the first novel is established in an interplay between Quirrell as quite inconspicuous but definitely peculiar, and Snape as the rather obvious villain-type.[88] The two appear together most of the time but there are also scenes which feature them individually and usually the ones presenting Quirrell are much more harmless than the ones featuring Snape. The readers are manipulated into following Harry's judgement of events though they should actually be most careful at that point because the young wizard is new to Hogwarts and certainly cannot have a complete overview of the goings on. After the introductory scene with Harry's scar hurting, a whole chapter is dedicated to Snape. It is striking that the chapter is entitled "The Potions Master," attaching a label to Snape. The teacher is characterised through what he does: through his abilities. This has two implications, the first one being that Rowling makes sure the readers never forget that Snape is the Potions Master, however much he wants to be the Defence Against the Dark Arts teacher. The readers know that the position he fills does not satisfy him and they might suspect that brewing potions is not the only ability Snape has. His dissatisfaction naturally qualifies him as a potential villain seeing that the actions of the two evildoers from *Star Wars* and *Harry Potter*, the Emperor and Voldemort, are partly motivated by dissatisfaction. Snape's discontent also links him with Anakin who is impatient because he does not get what he wants soon enough. In retrospect and with the knowledge of every novel, the second interesting implication of the chapter title is that it runs counter to Dumbledore's dictum of book two. In his conversation with Harry, after the latter has rescued Ginny from the Chamber of Secrets and is worried about being similar to Voldemort, Dumbledore calms him down by saying: "It is our choices, Harry, that show what

---

86   Cf. Rowling *Stone* 138.

87   Rowling *Stone* 139.

88   Cf. Veronica L. Schanoes, "Cruel Heroes and Treacherous Texts: Educating the Reader in Moral Complexity and Critical Reading in J.K. Rowling's *Harry Potter* Books," *Reading Harry Potter: Critical Essays*, Ed. Giselle Liza Anatol (Westport: Praeger, 2003) 132.

we truly are, far more than our abilities."[89] Snape, however, is always defined with respect to his abilities. As I have already pointed out, the readers never learn much about his motives, feelings or choices in life until the final quarter of novel seven. Therefore, if one takes Dumbledore to be the authority on questions of morals and character, one might assume that Snape is characterised wrongly or unfairly or at least incompletely. It might also give readers a first clue that they need to be active in their reading and not judge by first appearances.

In the new students' first potions class Snape turns out to be even more unpleasant than Harry thought. He constantly taunts the young wizard and makes it obvious that he does not like him, though the readers never get to know the reason then. The first classroom scene with Professor Snape gives them another hint at the true personality of the teacher. "His eyes were black like Hagrid's, but they had none of Hagrid's warmth. They were cold and empty and made you think of dark tunnels."[90] Again, Snape is mentioned in the same breath as another character. This time he is contrasted with Hagrid, who is very clearly on the good side and has warm and friendly eyes, which once more makes Snape look like an evil character. Since the eyes are always an important hint at character in formula fiction because it is common ideology that they are linked to the soul, the importance of this statement cannot be overlooked. The coldness and emptiness of Snape's eyes thus only evokes negative associations at first sight. However, in the course of the novels the readers discover that Snape is an Occlumens, which means he can close his mind to penetration and hide his true thoughts and feelings.[91] This is a quality which makes him highly valuable in the good side's fight against Voldemort. In retrospect, one could thus interpret this little statement differently from the first reading. The simile of the tunnels Rowling uses to describe Snape's eyes is also striking. Dark tunnels are a common feature of Gothic fiction and are usually associated with the mind and all its recesses. They can be threatening because they are obscure and one does not know what might be lurking at the end of them but of course they might also contain good. They are, for instance, often the means of leading the heroine to freedom. The tunnels which Snape's eyes are likened to actually contradict the emptiness that is ascribed to them. Dark tunnels might be full of one thing or another, and the metaphor supports what was said about the teacher being mostly characterised by his abilities and not by his inner motives and feelings. It suggests that there is something more to Snape than meets the eye.

Since Snape is stigmatised as the villain in novel one, compared to Quirrell, the harmless stutterer, it is natural that Harry and his friends think it is Snape who

---

89   Rowling *Chamber* 358.

90   Rowling *Stone* 150.

91   Cf. Rowling *Order* 458.

"wants the [Philosopher's] stone for Voldemort."[92] It comes as a shock to Harry when he finally goes through the trapdoor hiding the stone and finds himself face to face not with Snape but with Quirrell. It seems to be almost harder for Harry to grasp that Snape is not the one who wanted to harm him all the time than to come to terms with the fact that Quirrell wants to kill him. The scene makes very clear that Harry has carefully nourished his dislike of Snape, has established him as the foe and is not prepared to let go of his notions easily. He says: "But I thought – Snape – " And Quirrell answers: "Severus? (...) Yes, Severus does seem the type, doesn't he? So useful to have him swooping around like an overgrown bat. Next to him, who would suspect p-p-poor st-stuttering P-Professor Quirrell?"[93] Quirrell's remark is meta-fictional since it draws attention to the way villains are usually constructed and placed in formula fiction. Furthermore, it holds up a mirror to the readers, raising their awareness of how easily they are prepared to accept the common stereotypical picture of the villain and make wrong judgements. It is interesting that despite the fact that Snape is innocent in the first novel readers are fooled into believing him to be one of the evildoers time and again in the course of the series. They are heavily influenced by Harry's view on the events and should have realised that his assessment of situations is rather limited when Quirrell reveals the true background to the events of book one.[94]

For the next few novels, Snape continues to be vindictive toward Harry and the readers dislike him ever more. Very often, however, at least at second sight, Snape's anger with Harry is completely justified from his point of view. When Harry and Ron fly a car to school in novel two, for instance, Snape's more mature understanding of what is at stake by an exposure of the wizarding world cannot be denied. In novel three Snape is again characterised in relation to another figure, namely that of Remus Lupin, the new Defence Against the Dark Arts teacher. He is mostly mentioned in connection with Lupin, and it is clear from the beginning that he loathes the other man.[95] The readers later find out that Lupin went to school with Snape and was part of a group of friends, among them, Harry's father James Potter, who constantly taunted Snape and did not leave him alone. So to a certain degree Snape's antipathy for Lupin is understandable, particularly when this person whom he despises also gets the job Snape has wanted for himself for several years. It is furthermore characteristic by now that Harry, Ron and Hermione always get to see Snape at the most unfavourable moments. When Dumbledore introduces Lupin to

---

92   Rowling *Stone* 281.

93   Rowling *Stone* 310.

94   Cf. also Schanoes 131-33.

95   Cf. Rowling *Azkaban* 104.

the school, Ron asks Harry to look at Snape and again the readers only get Harry's perspective.

Professor Snape, the Potions master was staring along the staff table at Professor Lupin. It was common knowledge that Snape wanted the Defence Against the Dark Arts job, but even Harry, who hated Snape, was startled at the expression twisting his thin, sallow face. It was beyond anger: it was loathing. Harry knew that expression only too well; it was the look Snape wore every time he set eyes on Harry.[96]

It seems as if the children only see what they want to see, and since it is stated directly that Harry hates Snape, he would hardly see any good in the teacher. Harry's enmity towards Snape increases in proportion to his growing friendship with Lupin. When it turns out that the latter is a werewolf, Snape exposes him out of revenge, certainly, but possibly also out of a desire to protect the students from a staff-related decision of Dumbledore's that he believes to be wrong. In the finale of novel three Snape again wants to protect Harry. His knowledge of events is restricted to the fact that one of James and Lily Potter's friends betrayed them to Voldemort and like everyone else he thinks it is Sirius Black.[97] Of course Snape is glad for the opportunity of revenge on Sirius Black, a person he hates, but he still also wants to protect Harry and his friends. And again the readers see him through Harry's eyes and to Harry he appears dangerous and mad to boot. He suddenly looks "quite deranged" and "there [is] a mad glint in Snape's eye that Harry [has] never seen before. He [seems] beyond reason."[98] This is interesting because here we have the evil-madness connection again. Many of the villains in *Harry Potter* are associated with insanity and Voldemort himself, as I have already demonstrated, does not have an entirely 'well-ordered mind.' Madness is an instance of the Other, it is unpredictable and therefore to be feared. So seemingly the villainous nature of Snape is established in this scene yet again. However, apart from the madness-connection, this is the first instance in the series in which Snape shows emotions, does not seem unfathomable and is not characterised by his skills alone. The dark tunnels of his eyes really seem to hide more than is apparent at first glance. Does a schoolboy's grudge against another person really justify his almost mad behaviour

---

96   Rowling *Azkaban* 104.

97   Funnily enough, though Snape and Sirius Black hate each other, both have something very important in common: they are severely misjudged by the people around them. The (false) judgement of persons and the reasons leading up to it are a large issue in the *Harry Potter* novels, as well as in *Star Wars*.

98   Rowling *Azkaban* 388.

or is it not a much deeper feeling (of hatred or something else) that is buried within Snape?

At this stage of the story the readers cannot know, but they suspect, that maybe Snape is more deeply involved in the story of Harry Potter than they have thought so far. When we consider the significance of emotions for the other characters discussed so far and for their classification as good or evil, Snape is an extremely interesting figure. As we have seen, the presence or absence of feelings such as love, compassion and loyalty are usually failsafe ways to judge character. We simply do not get to know, however, whether Snape loves anyone or whether he is truly loyal to Dumbledore until the end of novel seven. Rowling uses him to slightly break with the formula, a necessity if a writer wants to produce an original formulaic work according to Cawelti.[99] And, to a certain extent, she also uses him to expose formulaic conventions in the story.

In novel five we finally get a first, though very implicit, inkling of what exactly Snape's involvement with Harry's history might be or have been. Harry has to take Occlumency lessons with Snape to learn to close his mind to Voldemort. When teaching Harry, Snape uses the Pensieve, a device to store thoughts, to keep his most private memories from Harry because the lessons make him vulnerable to penetration of the mind, too. One day, Snape has to leave the office suddenly and Harry cannot resist plunging into Snape's memories stored in the Pensieve. The memory which Harry and the readers see and the way it is treated is interesting for several reasons. For one, it is the first instance ever that the readers get to see Snape's point of view. In the memory, Harry observes Snape, James Potter and his friends sitting one of their Ordinary Wizarding Level examinations. After they have finished Harry's father and his friends go outside, sit by the lake on the school grounds and start taunting Snape who at that moment has not done anything to provoke them.[100] Rowling, through her character Harry, still tries to direct the readers' opinion. Although "this [is] Snape's memory and Harry [is] sure that if Snape [chooses] to wander off in a different direction once outside in the grounds (…),"[101] he will have to follow, he keeps closer to his father, Sirius, Lupin and Pettigrew, thereby making clear which side he is on. Their hexing Snape, which the readers can assume has not been the first incident of the sort, partly explains the hatred Snape feels for James, Sirius and Lupin. It justifies Snape for the first time, and the readers, but also Harry, are forced to reconsider the roles of James Potter as the brave and flawless hero, and Snape as the villain.

---

99   Cf. Cawelti 10.
100   Cf. Rowling *Order* 568-72.
101   Rowling *Order* 567.

The fact that James is brought down from his pedestal at the same time also puts Snape's role and character into perspective. Rowling shows a complex world here, in which heroes are not completely flawless and those who appear to be villains not wholly evil. She can explore this grey area safely in between the extremes of the depraved Voldemort and the good Harry. The memory goes on to show something even more important. However, it gets rather lost among Harry's and the readers' disappointment in James. While James and the others torture Snape, Harry's mother-to-be intervenes on Snape's behalf. This gives clues as to the deeper meaning of Snape's hatred of James and already hints at a relationship between Snape and Lily which receives a serious blow when Snape shouts: "I don't need help from filthy little Mudbloods like her!"[102] Mudblood is a derogatory term for wizards with Muggle origins. Lily stalks off hurt. Predictably, Snape catches Harry prying into his memories and is furious. And, in line with the way he has been shown all through the previous novels, Rowling only has him comment on Harry's father, unpleasantly as ever, and let go the little hint at the relationship between him and Harry's mother. This potential connection would also, in retrospect, explain Snape's madness at the capture of Sirius Black in book three. If he liked Lily, he would naturally be very excited to find and to take revenge on the man he believes to be her betrayer and her downfall. But once again, the readers' attention is directed elsewhere. All in all the memory shows something essential to Snape's role and nature. He seems to be completely on his own, facing four opponents. Through his own stupidity, he also loses a person who seems to have been loyal to him, Lily. His loneliness certainly follows him through the years, and his unpleasant manners do not endear him to other people. It is, however, also essential to his later job as spy and double agent. Since he is not close to anyone he does not have such a hard time hiding information and feelings from other people. Loneliness, and a lack of personal connections, however, was also established as one of the markers of a villain, leaving the figure of Snape as ambiguous as ever.

The whole of book six, *Harry Potter and the Half-Blood Prince*, is more or less dedicated to Snape, although the readers only find out about this towards the end when it turns out that none other than Snape is the Half-Blood Prince. The book marks the absolute low point for the character of Severus Snape. The seemingly obvious facts are that he is involved in a conspiracy to bring Dumbledore down and is even the one who finally kills the famous and well-loved headmaster.[103] But again, the readers (and Harry) are only shown Snape's actions, not his choices and inner motivations so that he still remains ambiguous. The scene that raises severe doubts about Snape's stance as the evil one occurs when Harry pursues him after

---

102   Rowling *Order* 571.

103   Cf. Rowling *Prince* 556.

the murder and tries to engage him in wizardly combat. Snape, however, just runs away. When Harry screams: "Kill me like you killed him, you coward –," Snape charges back: "DON'T CALL ME COWARD!"[104] Snape decisively shows feelings here, and it seems to be important to him that people do not think him a coward, which considering what he appears to have done is quite a lot to ask. The capital letters also indicate the importance of the sentence for Snape, and the story. The readers can assume that Snape does have other hidden, and perhaps more noble, motivations. The feeling remains that Snape's tale and his role in the series are not at an end here.

And sure enough towards the end of novel seven, when the conclusion of the whole adventure is nearing, Snape's story is revealed to the readers. The teacher is finally killed by Voldemort because of complex entanglements concerning a powerful wand.[105] Harry witnesses the horrible scene and is present when Snape dies. The latter's final act is to leave the boy with certain memories that turn out to contain the key to the role Harry has to fulfil. The scene of Snape's death is remarkable because just as in one of the first scenes in which he appears, his eyes are mentioned. Snape asks Harry to look at him and "[the] green eyes [find] the black, but after a second something in the depths of the dark pair [seems] to vanish, leaving them fixed, blank and empty."[106] The difference from the first scene in which the teacher's eyes played a role is that it is now acknowledged that there has been something behind them after all. While before Snape's eyes were characterised as empty already in life, suggesting that a soul was missing, it is now stated that only after his death do his eyes become empty. This prepares the readers and Harry for the great revelations about the Potions Master in the chapter to come.

This chapter is entitled 'The Prince's Tale' and the term 'Prince' is employed in a different way here than in novel six. It does not now refer to Snape's mother's maiden name, his arrogance in youth or his seeming double-dealings, but is used as

---

104 Rowling *Prince* 564.

105 The Deathly Hallows of the book's title consist of the Invisibility Cloak in Harry's possession, a Resurrection Stone that has the power of fleetingly bringing back the dead and the Elder Wand, an unbeatable wand that can only be won in combat with the new owner defeating the old one. Voldemort has found out that Dumbledore was in possession of the Elder Wand and believes that Snape, who finished Dumbledore, must now be the true owner of the powerful magical object. However, Draco Malfoy disarmed Dumbledore before Snape killed him, so the wand's new master was really Malfoy and not Snape. Harry, in turn disarmed Malfoy after that which means that by the time Voldemort kills Snape, Harry is the Elder Wand's true owner. Killing Snape therefore gains Voldemort nothing.

106 Rowling *Hallows* 528.

the title 'Prince' and emphasises Snape's true nature and nobility. It is noteworthy that Snape alone, among all the characters in the stories who assume a title, is truly worthy of it, which is interesting given the fact that he is not a thoroughly good character. The chapter, even to its caption, thus reverses the first novel's chapter dedicated to Snape which is entitled 'The Potions Master.' It does not focus on Snape's abilities but hints at inner nobility and the fact that he has a story to tell after all. Harry leaves the dead man's side to delve into the memories Snape has left him, with permission this time. They contain Snape's life story and his unrequited love for Lily Potter, Harry's mother. Considering that Lily is one of the supreme principles of goodness in the stories, Snape's love firmly places him with the side of the good. The memories, however, also show another, slightly shady side to Snape. Already as a child, he exhibits a dislike for Muggles, which links him with the Death Eaters and Voldemort. He contemptuously calls Lily's sister Petunia "Muggle" twice and once even hurts her with a branch he causes to fall on her shoulder.[107] These are also usually the moments Lily draws away from him. She wants to be friends with Snape but not at all costs, something that becomes more pronounced later when Snape starts to spend time with the Death Eaters.

The memories of young Snape and Lily very clearly show that Snape is a mediating character. He is neither very good nor completely evil, but just a rather 'normal,' morose teenager who has strong likes and dislikes. He mistrusts Muggles, possibly because of his bad experiences with his own Muggle father.[108] However, he also likes Lily Potter, a Muggle, and thereby shows that he has a good core and that it is not just power but also people that are interesting for him. The importance of a woman in Snape's life who knowingly or unknowingly shapes many of his actions, connects him with Anakin Skywalker who is also driven by the love of and fear for a woman. For both characters, love is the motor for much of the action. This stands in notable contrast to the two fully-fledged villains of the stories, the Emperor and Lord Voldemort, both of whom completely lack the ability to love. Though Anakin and Snape commit evil deeds, their love for Padmé and Lily redeems them and shows that they are not the grand villains of the tales. However, arguably, Snape does more to redeem himself than Anakin. His memories show that he realised the mistake he made in joining the dark side rather early on and tried to redress it ever after. He constantly risks his life and finally sacrifices it for the good cause. His love for Lily also leads him to take much more rational decisions than Anakin, whose love rather makes him mad. Snape exhibits a balance of reason and

---

107   Cf. Rowling *Hallows* 534, 536, 538.

108   Only once during their Occlumency lessons does Harry manage to break through Snape's defences and penetrate a memory of Snape's. This shows him as a boy witnessing his parents' quarrels (cf. Rowling *Order* 521).

emotion. All this established, it seems rather unfair that Anakin/Vader is treated with much sympathy throughout the stories, while Snape is only rehabilitated towards the very end of the *Harry Potter* series, after his death. The two stories show two very different approaches to a similar phenomenon: a sinner who tries to be reintegrated into society. Anakin receives forgiveness in life and is ostensibly re-established as the good principle. Snape dies rather lonely and unforgiven, in fact, much as he has lived, unappreciated and misjudged. Travis Prinzi believes that, also in the light of excessive fandom surrounding Snape, Rowling should have made more of Snape's vindication.[109] Rowling's stance, however, seems realistic. People can be cruel and not very forgiving and virtue is not always rewarded. Character changes do not necessarily manifest themselves with a big bang as in Vader's case but rather come about gradually and silently as with Snape.

A memory showing Snape and Lily on the Hogwarts express on their first journey to school is interesting for several reasons. Firstly, Snape expresses his wish that Lily be in Slytherin house.[110] He himself is not prepared to be sorted into another house and is quite sure that he will be in Slytherin. His wish that Lily will go there also shows that he wants to have her nearby and expects them to continue being close friends. Secondly, straight after Snape has expressed his wish, there comes an interjection from another boy on the train compartment who meets the desire to be in Slytherin with disbelief. That other boy is James Potter. He in turn wants to be in *"Gryffindor, where dwell the brave at heart!"*[111] Slytherin and Gryffindor are established as the Houses among which the conflict between evil and good is carried out. The other two school houses Ravenclaw and Hufflepuff are never even taken into the equation. The readers are certainly expected to favour Gryffindor over Slytherin here, too. The preference for Gryffindor is expressed by James Potter, a character whom they have so far mostly experienced as brave and loyal. However, some readers might remember Snape's memory from book five in which he is harrassed by James and his friends. The scene is similar here. James and Sirius, who is quite logically also in the train compartment, start the argument about the school houses. Snape has not said anything to them and they are two

---

109 Cf. Prinzi 199. Snape is actually one of the most popular characters of the series and has incited much discussion and creative output on the web. Examples of websites dedicated to him or his movie alias Alan Rickman are: Lady Claudia, "Why Snape," 9 June 2002, 7 Jul. 2011 <whysnape.tripod.com>., *Professor-Snape.com*, 11 Aug. 2005, 8 May 2011 <professor-snape.com>.,Joomla!, "The True Story of Severus Snape," 2011, 8 May 2011 <severussnape.org>., and Snape fan fiction and fan art site Audrey, "Chock Full O' Sevy," 27 June 2011, 7 Jul. 2011 <www.sevysgal.com/home.html>.

110 Cf. Rowling *Hallows* 538.

111 Rowling *Hallows* 539.

against one. This memory and the one from book five taken together show that James and Sirius are not much better at that point than the Slytherin people they despise. They are childish and arrogant and they do not always judge situations correctly. On a smaller scale than in *Star Wars* thus, questions as to the nature of good and evil and the similarities between these opposing concepts are also present in the *Harry Potter* novels. Though they are much more elaborately treated in the figure of Anakin Skywalker / Darth Vader in *Star Wars*, it is striking that in *Harry Potter* these themes are explored with respect to Snape, the character who resembles Anakin most closely. It seems that in formulaic fiction it is easier to discuss the nature of such grand oppositions as good and evil and free will and destiny in relation to characters who are somewhat in between extremes and fulfil mediating positions.

The treatment of good and evil is closely linked to the binary of free will and determination or destiny which is also explored in this memory of Snape's first journey to Hogwarts. The narrator suggests that for some people it is easier to be good than for others. This is made clear by one statement he makes with respect to James Potter and Snape in the scene on the train. "Harry, whose attention had been focused entirely on the two beside the window, saw his father: slight, black-haired like Snape, but with that indefinable air of having been well cared for, even adored, that Snape so conspicuously lacked."[112] James, who is well-groomed and loved, obviously has the better basis to make morally right decisions than Snape, who comes about rather neglected and is more insecure about where he stands in life. It is certainly easier for Snape to be led astray by people who have the wrong values but who seem to provide a peer group for him. At one point during their Occlumency lessons, Harry manages to break into a memory of Snape's in which Snape's father is shouting at his wife.[113] It seems that Snape did not have an intact family and is looking for one in Hogwarts. He finds it in the Death Eaters but of course their suitability as family is at the very least questionable. The development of a moral sense which is strongly connected to free choice in the novels seems to have something to do with a person's socialisation. This is a stance that was already expounded in the analysis of Voldemort, who like Snape had a bad childhood.

However, the novels refute the notion that goodness and moral choice only depend on the upbringing and family background and they do so very notably in the figure of Severus Snape. And what claim could Voldemort have to be exculpated because of a miserable childhood when there are two figures, Harry and Snape, who make different choices under similar circumstances? Snape's choices are extremely decisive. By choosing Slytherin House and affiliating himself with a group of Death

---

112   Rowling *Hallows* 538.

113   Cf. Rowling *Order* 521-22.

Eaters, he alienates Lily. However, he never completely gives up on her. This becomes apparent when after relaying parts of the prophecy to Voldemort, he realises that Voldemort believes it to refer to Lily Potter's son. When Snape finds out that Lily is in danger he contacts Dumbledore and asks him to protect her. Dumbledore says to him: "If she means so much to you, surely Lord Voldemort will spare her? Could you not ask for mercy for the mother, in exchange for the son?" And Snape replies: "I have – I have asked him –"[114] Upon this Dumbledore says: "You disgust me, (...). You do not care, then, about the deaths of her husband and child? They can die, as long as you have what you want?"[115] After this Harry and the readers can see how much Lily still means to Snape when he croaks: "Hide them all, then, (...). Keep her – them – safe. Please."[116] But Dumbledore is still not satisfied: "And what will you give me in return, Severus?" Snape is surprised for a while but then he says: "Anything."[117] This scene stands in contrast to most of what Harry and the readers have learned about Snape so far and confirms the suspicions about the relationship between Snape and Lily. It finally proves that Snape is not the cold person Harry has experienced him to be. It also demonstrates that he has never stopped caring for Lily even after she turned her back on him. She is his link to the good side and the trigger which has to be pressed to reform him. She is for Snape what Luke is for Darth Vader. Snape selflessly and loyally loves Lily Potter to his end, even if he is never rewarded for it, even if most other people scorn him, believe him to be on Voldemort's side and do not understand why Dumbledore trusts him.

Snape is certainly one of the most tragic figures in the novels but he also, as Veronica Schanoes says, serves the function of teaching readers that morality is a complex issue.[118] Snape's love for Lily, which he was always able to preserve, is what distinguishes him from Voldemort, to whom he would otherwise be quite similar. Like Voldemort, he had a joyless childhood, like the Dark Lord he tried to win himself recognition via his magical abilities and like Voldemort he seems cold and heartless at first glance. However, unlike Voldemort he is able to love and it is the Dark Lord's mistake that he cannot understand love or distinguish real love from mere desire. The moment Voldemort kills Lily Potter he loses one of his most able and most dangerous allies, Snape, to the side of the good. And this is remarkable in itself since Lily's death could just as well have triggered Snape's further immersion with evil, as Padmé's death does Anakin's complete descent to

---

114   Rowling *Hallows* 543.

115   Rowling *Hallows* 543-44.

116   Rowling *Hallows* 544.

117   Rowling *Hallows* 544.

118   Cf. Schanoes 135.

villainy. Snape is shown as possessing great strength of character. When Lily is dead, he is remorse-stricken because he is aware that he played a part in her demise. This further distinguishes him from Voldemort, who is incapable of feeling remorse.[119] Despite his difficult childhood and his rather luckless life, Snape makes a conscious and highly significant decision to return to the good side at this stage. Thus, free will does not solely depend on socialisation or surroundings but seems to have more to do with inner resources and strengths.

Snape is the only character in both stories who makes a moral decision despite the fact that he is unloved and not well respected by most people. He decides to be good although he is never rewarded for it, is never the hero who gets all the glory.[120] Hal Colebatch who is actually discussing *Star Wars* makes an observation that is very fitting in this context: "[W]hile it seems the remembrance of a good father or other example is a good thing to have, those without it are not thereby excluded from virtue: indeed their ennoblement may be even more praise-worthy."[121] Snape who does not have any past or family honour he can cling to, has to make his own way in the world, which he finally does admirably. He is the figure who truly expresses Rowling's preference of free will over determination, of a free will that is not dependent on the approval of others. Peter Appelbaum confirms the importance of Snape with respect to the free will versus destiny question, when he says that "[b]ecause Snape took hold of destiny through his choices, rather than merely rising to the occasion like Harry, he seems to be the greater man."[122] However, it needs to be pointed out that this stance is highly idealistic and also ideologically charged. Freedom from social influences to the degree Snape exhibits it, is rather unrealistic and in this sense he is a model which is quite inaccessible for readers.

In sum it can be said that like Anakin Skywalker / Darth Vader, Severus Snape is a mediating character. Like Anakin, Snape undergoes a development in the course of the stories. Both go from good to bad and back to good. However, when they are compared, Anakin/Vader seems to be the more stereotypical character and

---

119 Before finishing him at the end of novel seven, Harry asks Voldemort to show some remorse, because it is the only thing that could slightly redeem him. Voldemort, however, is incapable of feeling what he has done and does not regret it (cf. Rowling *Hallows* 594).

120 Cf. also Appelbaum (90) and Catherine Jack Deavel and David Paul Deavel, "Choosing Love: The Redemption of Severus Snape," *The Ultimate Harry Potter and Philosophy: Hogwarts for Muggles*, Ed. Gregory Bassham (New Jersey: Wiley, 2010) 55.

121 Colebatch 16.

122 Appelbaum 91.

Snape the more 'realistic' one. While Anakin is nearly angelic as a child and turns into a fiend who murders countless people, only to be redeemed by the love of his son Luke, Snape is quite an ordinary child. His outward appearance is not very pleasant and he is neither extremely good nor completely evil. Later on he takes some wrong decisions which bring about the deaths of several people and set in motion the story but he is never the mass-murderer Anakin becomes. His conversion is not the big occasion that Vader's is. Only Dumbledore knows of it at the time and it is much later that Harry learns about it and restores Snapes' good name in front of the wizarding community. Snape's being a 'realistic' character is only a seeming paradox with what was said earlier about the 'unrealistic' ideological implications of choice independent from social recognition he embodies. On the level of character-depiction he is rather realistic. The ideology he sells is less so, which is problematic, because Snape's being a credible character, makes people eat the ideology he incorporates, too. Snape's more 'realistic' character is also in line with an afore-mentioned difference between *Star Wars* and *Harry Potter*. While *Star Wars* is generally more open structurally, *Harry Potter* strongly keeps up structures but tries to present characters as roundly as possible within their confines. Anakin, more strongly than the other characters in both tales, represents ideas, the themes of destiny, natural determination and free choice. This is even made clear on a meta-level in the movies themselves, since both on the level of structure and on the plane of the story, Anakin is reduced to the ideal of the prophecy by the Jedi.

All of the characters discussed so far have in common that they change their names at some stage of the story. The difference between the true villains and the mediators Anakin/Vader and Snape is that both middle characters regain or resume their original names. This emphasises the change in them and their recognition and acceptance of their failings. In contrast to the villains who never give up their high-flying assumed names, Anakin and Snape are humbled and their taking up their ordinary names once more signals that they are not as completely or irrevocably evil as the Emperor and Voldemort. Both Anakin and Snape are ultimately motivated by love which makes them better than the villains. Both stories thus adhere to the ideology that love has healing powers and brings out the good in people and that it is love that is most important in relationships between people. The most essential characteristic that the two figures share, however, is their entanglement with questions of free will and destiny. In the figure of Anakin Skywalker, the binary of free will and determination by some outward force, be it destiny or other, remains balanced out or unresolved. It is not clear how much of Vader's final conversion back to the good side rests on personal choice and how much simply emphasises his original nature.

With Snape the question of free will and determination is most definitely settled. Though he is imprisoned within structures that are not beneficial to him and categorised time and again, he is the character in the novels who can most clearly be allocated to the side of free will. He makes a choice for his Slytherin friends and against Lily, and he chooses to become a Death Eater and tell Voldemort of the prophecy. At the same time, however, he decides to mistrust Voldemort and appeal to Dumbledore for help when he feels that Lily might be in danger. And he makes a decisive choice of secretly following Dumbledore while pretending to still be loyal to Voldemort. He does not revoke this decision once it transpires that Dumbledore could not help Lily. Neither does he revoke it when he is faced with other people's mistrust and with the fact that he has to protect Harry, the son of his rival James Potter, the son that could possibly have been his had things gone differently. Anakin is never so level-headed. He mostly acts on his emotions and does not think very clearly. The dominant reading of the films also very much pardons the acts of cruelty Anakin commits during his fits of passion. For Rowling, more than for Lucas, it seems to be important to show individuals' active role in their fates. Contrary to a stance which sees people as biologically and socially determined, the *Harry Potter* novels highlight the power of people to shape their own destinies, a message whose ideological implications can also be a burden.

Terry Eagleton has an interesting point that helps us come to a conclusion on the treatment of evil in the stories. He contrasts the ways church fathers such as Thomas Aquinas see evil with the ones of the Manicheans. For Aquinas "[e]vil (…) is lack, negation, defectiveness, deprivation."[123] Note that this is exactly the way evil is defined in both stories analysed here. Eagleton goes on to describe the position of the Manicheans "who held the Gnostic theory that matter is evil in itself. For them, evil is a positive force or substance which invades us from the outside. It is the *science-fiction view of reality* [emphasis added]."[124] But is it really? Good science-fiction or formulaic fiction as such, it seems, takes a more differentiated view on the matter and rejects a stereotypical Manichaeism as Eagleton defines it. Both *Star Wars* and *Harry Potter* offer different ways of reading the generation of evil. With the Emperor it is simply there and no explanation is given of its origin. The villain functions as the tempter-figure in the movies, the external source of evil who poisons characters such as Anakin. So the Gnostic viewpoint is there. However, the films also suggest that the good side, too contributes a great deal to Anakin's transformation, which gives the Gnostic reading an edge. A contrary analysis might also see Anakin himself as culpable. Despite many blessings in his life he has a propensity for evil. The interpretation of evil in *Harry Potter* also remains ambiguous. It comes as an external force (Voldemort) but it is also within people and depends on their choices in life (Harry, Voldemort, Snape). The Gnostic

---

123   Eagleton 125.
124   Eagleton 125-26.

position sees evil as a structural given and thus takes responsibility for it away from people. Seeing evil as a lack within an individual is a more individual reading. It shows people to be morally responsible for their actions. Myth and formulaic fiction offer a balance between these two positions in the awareness that questions about the nature of good and evil can never be satisfactorily answered.

7.   Ideal Individuals

7.1   UNITY IN DUALITY / DUALITY IN UNITY: HARRY POTTER

After the discussion of the Emperor and Voldemort as the evildoers as well as Anakin/Vader and Snape as the mediating characters, this chapter is dedicated to the good side of the Lévi-Straussian scenario, namely the close analysis of Harry Potter and Luke Skywalker. The reversal of structure in dealing with the character from *Harry Potter* first is deliberate. Harry, as will be seen, is a rounder character than Luke. By treating Harry first and Luke later, the setup of this and the preceding chapters reflects the character constellation of the two series. The Emperor and Luke frame the analyses as the two most formulaic figures. Voldemort, as was seen, is at least a bit rounder than the Emperor but still of course pretty clearly belongs to the evil side. Anakin/Vader and Snape take the middle position in the discussion and Harry verges toward the completely good pole that is represented by Luke. Structuring the three chapters thus also reinforces the point made earlier about the greater flexibility in the characters of *Harry Potter* compared to the ones of *Star Wars*.

Harry Potter's story is set up as a novel of education. Harry goes through years of schooling to form his character and emerges as a fully grown man capable of taking his own decisions. What is significant, however, is that despite a development in terms of skills and character his essential nature does not change much, something that distinguishes him from Anakin/Vader and Snape from the outset.[1] He possesses all of the qualities that help him defeat Voldemort from the

---

1   Mary Pharr distinctly sees Harry as a developing hero (cf. Mary Pharr, "In Medias Res: Harry Potter as Hero-in-Progress," *The Ivory Tower and Harry Potter: Perspectives on a Literary Phenomenon*, Ed. Lana E. Whited (Columbia: University of Missouri Press,

start. These, we must assume are diametrically opposed to the characteristics of evil outlined in chapter three. Good is that which counters evil. Harry's advantages over evil include his ability to love, his compassion for others, a basic innocence and purity of soul and the acceptance of death. Harry incidentally is another Lévi-Straussian mediator in the stories although he is a more imperfect middle-character than Anakin/Vader in the sense that overall he can clearly be placed with the good while Anakin/Vader's story is rather equally divided into stretches of good and evil. Harry thus embodies Derrida's criticism of the human need for structures.[2] In a given structuralist setting, one part of the binary opposition is always favoured, something which is very much apparent in Harry. Still, the young wizard is also a mediator and the first binary he unites is development/change and consistency, since he develops and at the same time retains his most essential character. So on the one hand, Harry is comparable to Dickens's Oliver Twist, on whom Terry Eagleton comments as follows:

Goodness is sometimes thought to be free of social conditioning. (…) This is why Dickens's Oliver Twist remains untainted by the low life of criminal London into which he is plunged. (…) But this is not because Oliver is a saint. If he is immune to the polluting influence of thieves, thugs, and prostitutes, it is less because he is morally superior than because his goodness is somehow genetic, as resistant to the mouldings of cirmcumstance as freckles or sandy hair. If Oliver just can't help being good, however, his virtue is surely no more to be admired than the size of his ears.[3]

Virtue, Eagleton's quote makes clear, is something that essentially comes into existence in adversity. True goodness is not genetic but means choosing good despite experiences of evil, in spite of evil tendencies within the self. True virtue is not intrinsic; it is generated by resisting vice, once more exemplifying the way in which the opposing terms of binaries actually constitute each other. Harry, at least

---

2002) 54). However, for my analysis it is important to take into account his static side, too.

2   Cf. Derrida *Writing and Difference* 369.

3   Eagleton 9-10. In fact Drew Chappell argues in the opposite direction when he claims that Harry does not embody the fixed view on childhood presented, for instance, in *Oliver Twist*. Instead, in *Harry Potter*, "[t]he students are treated as 'becoming (…) rather than 'being' – a modernist construction" (Drew Chappell, "Sneaking Out After Dark: Resistance, Agency, and the Postmodern Child in JK Rowling's Harry Potter Series," *Children's Literature in Education* 39 (2008): 289). Rather, he says, "Harry Potter can be seen as a postmodern hero who engages with the complexities and ambiguities of the contemporary (adult) world" (283).

in the first books, is portrayed as naturally good, something that makes him a little boring at times. However, from the end of book four onwards, a dimension is added to his character.[4] His suffering and wrath after the deaths of his godfather and Dumbledore, show Harry struggling with evil, also the evil within himself and portray the development from frustration with fate to acceptance in novel seven. This means that goodness in Harry's case is a quality he naturally possesses to a certain extent, but also one he needs to develop through experience and the choices he makes.[5] From book five onwards, Harry has to fight his own demons, come to terms with personal catastrophes and learn that sometimes things do not turn out the way one wishes them to. All this helps him turn into the hero that is needed to rid the wizarding world off Voldemort, a hero who is prepared to make great sacrifices for others, one who is not simply dependent on chance and luck.[6] It will now have to be seen how stability and change of character are united with respect to Harry.

Harry's essentially unchanging character shows itself in his name which is significantly different from those of the characters already discussed because it is so

---

4   Cf. Travis Prinzi who divides the *Harry Potter* series into two distinct parts. The first four novels, he says, depict Harry as a rather stereotypical fairy-tale hero who always achieves his aims and wins the day. This kind of perfect hero, however, who does not succeed because of moral choices but because of luck, is the wrong sort, as Prinzi believes (cf. 126). Farah Mendlesohn, too sees Harry as a rather "passive" hero, although it needs to be said that her article appeared in 2002 when only four of the seven books in the series had been published (Farah Mendlesohn, "Crowning the King: Harry Potter and the Construction of Authority," *The Ivory Tower and Harry Potter: Perspectives on a Literary Phenomenon*, Ed. Lana A. Whited (Columbia: University of Missouri Press, 2002) 165).

5   John Granger also stresses the relevance of choice for the *Harry Potter* novels. However, he interprets this theme in a religious context (Granger *Looking for God in Harry Potter* 77-81). The exact nature of the particular choices Harry makes is also analysed by Lana A. Whited and M. Katherine Grimes who apply Lawrence Kohlberg's theories of moral development to the novels (Lana A. Whited and M. Katherine Grimes, "What Would Harry Do?: J.K. Rowling and Lawrence Kohlberg's Theories of Moral Development," *The Ivory Tower and Harry Potter: Perspectives on a Literary Phenomenon*, Ed. Lana A. Whited (Columbia: University of Missouri Press, 2002) 182-208).

6   Cf. Prinzi 126. Elaine Ostry after her reading of the first four books, similarly perceives Harry as "a static character like the fairy-tale hero" (97). Julia Pond, too sees the "transition from fairy tale into a mythological quest tale" that occurs after the fourth book of the series (Julia Pond, "A Story of the Exceptional: Fate, and Free Will in the Harry Potter Series," *Children's Literature* 38 (2010): 184).

decisively common. Neither his first name Harry, nor his last name Potter is in any way out of the ordinary or rare.[7] The name has nothing of the mystery of Tom Riddle's, nothing of the originality of Anakin Skywalker's and Harry is never an Emperor, a lord or a prince. The mere fact that the name is so ordinary in comparison with all the other exceptional names hints at Harry's being more humble than the other figures. While the others are shown to be special or at least give themselves a special status through their extraordinary names, Harry Potter is an everyman, someone who is distinctly common. Furthermore, what sets Harry apart from the others is that he never changes his name but retains his original one throughout. This shows him to be basically satisfied with who he is and confident about his identity in contrast to the Emperor, Voldemort, Anakin and Snape, who all either show insecurities about their identity or pretensions as to the status they think they should have. While all these characters are incomplete in some way or other, Harry seems to be whole despite bad experiences.

Apart from signalling that Harry is an everyman, the name has a positive edge. A potter is someone who creates things out of clay which he shapes according to his wishes. Thus the rather ordinary name of Harry Potter contains a hidden promise or possibility of constructive and beneficial behaviour. The biblical associations cannot be overlooked here. From the outset Harry is identified as the agency of creation, foreshadowing his world-building role at the end of the series.[8] In addition to its rather neutral connotation of an everyman, the name contains hope and the possibility for all everymen to actively shape the raw material of their lives. The Christian name Harry is a derivate of Henry, which in turn derives from the Germanic name Heimiric. This means "home ruler."[9] Harry it seems, apart from promising creativity and constructiveness, is also a possible leader.[10] Taken together with the productiveness of the potter, the name suggests that he can be an influential person though in a wise and beneficial way. These very positive connotations also contrast with the fact that all the other characters' names are ambiguous or downright destructive. Harry is the first one who has a completely unambiguous name calling forth only positive associations. Good, it seems, is accepting and being satisfied with who one is and not reaching beyond oneself.

The unity expressed by Harry's name in contrast to all the other names discussed before is significant because it exists in spite of or next to a fundamental

---

7   Cf. also Nikolajeva "A Return to the Romantic Hero" 131.

8   I am indebted to Merle Tönnies for this idea.

9   "Henry," *Behind the Name: The Etymology and History of First Names*, Ed. Mike Campbell, 10 May 2011, Jul 2011 <http://www.behindthename.com/name/henry>.

10   Cf. also Saxena who situates Harry in the tradition of "the heroes of English royalty in literature, like Shakespeare's Prince Hal and Harry Hotspur" (48).

duality in his nature that links him not only with the good side but also with Voldemort. This duality first finds expression in the wand Harry buys before starting at Hogwarts school. It turns out that the Phoenix whose tail feather is part of Harry's wand, gave one other feather which is contained in Voldemort's.[11] Harry's and Voldemort's wands are brothers, and as wands are an extension of their owners, the close relation between Voldemort and Harry is hinted at, evoking motifs such as the good and the evil twin, the doppelganger, and the alter ego. Since Voldemort's wand is powerful, it can be assumed that as its brother Harry's will be so, too. This means, as Ollivander rightly concludes that "we must expect great things from you, Mr Potter ... After all, He Who Must Not Be Named did great things – terrible, yes, but great."[12] Ollivander is the first person to directly link Harry with the evil Voldemort in this statement. However, at the same time, the wand associates Harry with great goodness in the form of the Phoenix whose tail feather is contained within it. The legendary bird itself contains the opposites of life and death within its nature. It is "a magical, eternal bird (...) [which] lives for centuries."[13] When its death is near it is said to build a funeral pyre and burn itself only to rise from the ashes rejuvenated. It has acquired many symbolic meanings and, for instance, stands for immortality, "undying love and loyalty."[14] All of these are qualities associated with Harry in the course of the stories. The phoenix is the unity behind the duality of good and evil and Harry's association with the bird which overcomes the opposition of life and death, suggests that he, too will have the power to balance out binaries. The connection with the phoenix-feather wand thus again establishes Harry as a potential mediator.[15]

The second instance that brings Harry's duality to the fore is the Sorting Ceremony upon his arrival at Hogwarts. The Hat who sorts the children into the four school houses obviously senses the qualities necessary for Slytherin House in Harry and wants to send him there. Harry, however, who has heard of Slytherin's bad reputation deliberately asks not to be put there and is sorted into Gryffindor instead.[16] Gryffindor and Slytherin Houses stand for opposing views of life. While Gryffindor is inclusive, accepting all students who are brave and resourceful,

---

11   Cf. Rowling *Stone* 96.

12   Rowling *Stone* 96.

13   Colbert 91.

14   Colbert 93.

15   Edmund M. Kern also notices the similarities between Harry and the phoenix and even explicitly calls Dumbledore's phoenix Fawkes "a mediating symbol, one situated (in a sense) between good and evil to serve as a reminder that, in the midst of devastation, hope may be found" (204).

16   Cf. Rowling *Stone* 133.

Slytherin is exclusive, predominantly taking students from pure-blood families. The Slytherins that the readers have met up to that point are rude and unpleasant without exception, whereas the Gryffindors are friendly and likeable.[17] Though Rowling is careful not to let anyone of the good characters look too flawless (see her treatment of James Potter and Dumbledore), their faults are forgiven and it always remains clear that the Gryffindors are basically good. The Sorting scene, despite stressing Harry's duality, also shows for the first time that Harry actively chooses good. Since choice and free will are very important in the novels and tend to be associated with the good side, Harry's position among those who wish to vanquish evil becomes even more cemented.[18] However, it is noticeable at this point already that free will is only good if it is employed correctly, i.e. if it manifests itself in decisions which are morally sound and display an awareness of other people's needs. If choices are made which only promote the self, as in the case of the Emperor or Voldemort, they are neither good nor free, because the person making them cannot abstract from his own desires and wishes nor empathise with others.

The exciting question with respect to Harry and his ability to make free choices is whether he can do it because of his freedom of mind or because of his originally good disposition. Harry, it seems, has both, the will to make choices that benefit rather than harm others and a basically good nature. Even before he knows that he is a wizard and despite all the hardship he has to endure with the Dursleys he never exhibits any inclination to become evil. This means that patience and a friendly disposition have already been parts of his character before he is initiated to the wizarding world. Harry's intrinsic, almost genetic goodness embodies what Derrida criticises as the longing for origins or essentials in structuralist thought.[19] This longing can also be perceived in the figure of Anakin Skywalker, though the idea of

---

17   Harry meets Draco Malfoy, a Slytherin-to-be in Diagon Alley before he starts his first year at Hogwarts and instantly dislikes him because he reminds him of his cousin Dudley (cf. Rowling *Stone* 88). In contrast to that the Weasleys who were, are, or in Ron's case will be in Gryffindor are all friendly, helpful and likeable. Mrs Weasley tells Harry how to get to platform nine and three quarters, Fred and George help him with his trunk and his and Ron's friendship is already established on that first train journey (cf. Rowling *Stone* 104, 105, 109-122).

18   James Potter and Dumbledore were mentioned as examples of good people with faults and weaknesses. James Potter bullied Snape at school but is nevertheless prepared to die to protect his wife and son. Dumbledore, who dabbled in the dark arts as a young man, realised after a family tragedy that he had chosen the wrong path in life. From that moment onwards he used his power to stand up for and protect the weak. Thus not only in the case of Harry, being good is associated with conscious moral decisions.

19   Cf. Derrida *Writing and Difference* 369.

an essential identity is more strongly called into question in *Star Wars* with Anakin turning to evil. Despite the evil within him, Harry is always clearly on the side of good.[20] Still he also functions as a mediator, someone who unites natural goodness and evil symbolised through Voldemort's Horcrux attached to his soul. He also mediates between determination by forces outside himself (Voldemort) and free will, mainly shaped at Hogwarts.

In connection with the binary of free will and determination which operates so strongly in the *Harry Potter* novels, the prophecy about Harry and Voldemort which was already briefly mentioned in chapter five, needs to be analysed in more detail. Harry and the readers eventually get to hear its exact wording which is the following:

The one with the power to vanquish the Dark Lord approaches ... born to those who have thrice defied him, born as the seventh month dies ... and the Dark Lord will mark him as his equal, but he will have power the Dark Lord knows not ... and either must die at the hand of the other for neither can live while the other survives ... the one with the power to vanquish the Dark Lord will be born as the seventh month dies ...[21]

The fact that Harry and the readers get to hear the prophecy stands in stark contrast to *Star Wars* where the oracle remains hazy and neither the characters nor the audience ever find out what or whom exactly it refers to. This shows that though both stories play with the ideas of fate directing human lots the theme is handled completely differently in the two tales. In *Star Wars* the prophecy stands above the whole story as the guiding idea that sets the events in motion and shapes their outcome. The idea of a person's allotted destiny that is linked with the prophecy does much harm in the movies. All, even the wisest and most intelligent characters rather mindlessly adhere to the prophecy for quite a long time and thereby mar Anakin Skywalker's life. Until very late no one questions the oracle and when they do, it is only the wisest of the Jedi, Master Yoda who suggests that the prophecy might have been misread.[22] However, it is telling that sagacious Yoda's comment only refers to the abilities of those deciphering the prophecy and does not question

---

20   Vandana Saxena contends that "(...) rather than focusing on [Harry's] innate goodness, Rowling's narrative portrays the adolescent quest as an active engagement with the external forces as they impinge on the constantly evolving self-hood" (53). This narrative strategy draws attention away from the basically structuralist search for a centre, in this case the unified self, and questions the concept of a stable identity.

21   Rowling *Order* 741.

22   Cf. *Revenge of the Sith* 00:39:05.

the actual oracle itself. This shows that the Jedi, however wise, are unable to rise above their belief in fate, in a human being's specially ordained place in the galaxy. With Harry Potter and the prophecy the case is different. The mere fact that Harry and the readers know exactly what it says diminishes its importance and the hold it has over the story. This also becomes clear when looking at the fact that Voldemort only knows half of it. His incomplete knowledge and the belief that the prophecy is significant beyond everything else, constitute the power it has over him. In Rowling's novels it is evil, not good that slavishly adheres to the word and believes in fate and determination by it. From Harry's point of view the prophecy is truly shocking at first because it suggests that he is 'the chosen one,' i.e. the one to either destroy or be destroyed by Voldemort. But, true to Dumbledore's dictum that fear of a name only increases fear of the thing itself,[23] which he repeats to Harry whenever it comes to saying Voldemort's name or not, clearly seeing and naming his potential fate through knowledge of the prophecy makes living with it much easier. As soon as the prophecy is heard and Harry has had some time to cope with it, it loses its importance and is hardly ever mentioned again.

A further difference between the prophecies and their treatment in *Star Wars* and *Harry Potter* is that while the Jedi never talk about the prophecy to Anakin, Dumbledore actually discusses its wording with Harry.[24] It turns out that he has a completely different idea of its significance for Harry's life than the Jedi. Dumbledore expressly says that it is up to Harry to follow the prophecy or turn his back on it and walk away. Thus in contrast to the Jedi, he takes the possibility of choice and Harry's individuality into account. However, he also mentions that sometimes it does not matter that one might have personally decided not to become involved in events. Now and again, the events just find one. It would be hard for Harry to turn away from the prophecy, because Voldemort has already decided to adhere to it. This means that he is going to pursue his supposed nemesis to the end of his life if Harry does not take action against him. The contents of the prophecy are thus forced upon Harry as is the part of Voldemort's soul that has attached itself to his. But, and that is the crucial difference from *Star Wars*, Harry always has the choice to follow the prophecy or walk away. He does not at first understand why Dumbledore diminishes the importance of the prophecy. "But sir," he says "it all comes to the same thing, doesn't it? I've got to try and kill him, or –"[25] And Dumbledore interrupts: "Got to? (…) Of course you've got to! But not because of the prophecy! Because you, yourself, will never rest until you've tried! We both know it! Imagine, please, just for a moment, that you had never heard that

---

23   Cf. Rowling *Stone* 320.

24   Cf. Rowling *Order* 741-44, *Prince* 477-79.

25   Rowling *Prince* 478.

prophecy! How would you feel about Voldemort now? Think!"[26] And Harry thinks of all the people Voldemort has murdered and the horrible things he has done and answers: "I'd want him finished. (…) And I'd want to do it."[27] He thus realises that it is not the prophecy that determines him but his knowledge that what Voldemort does is wrong and his love for some of the people who have died and those who are still threatened by the villain. Goodness is the wisdom to turn forces that one is allegedly determined by, into matters of choice and moral obligation.

Patricia Donaher and James M. Okapal come to a very similar conclusion about matters of choice and the prophecy in the novels. In fact they hold that the books advocate a stance in between what they call determinism, the belief that all events are somehow interconnected and dependent on one another, and libertarianism which views events as coming to pass independently and without inherent causality.[28] This middle position they call compatibilism. "Compatibilism is the view that current events (including *some* actions) are caused by antecedent events, but the antecedent events are not sufficient to determine only one possible future."[29] Dumbledore's reading of the prophecy is one example of compatibilism. Although it does determine Harry's immediate future, he does have an albeit limited amount of choice within the frame it sets, or, as Donaher and Okapal formulate it: "[P]rophecies describe what might come to be, given certain conditions, but are not descriptions of predetermined events."[30] This interpretation of a kind of 'third way,' uniting the seemingly mutually exclusive concepts of determinism and libertarianism perfectly fits my analysis of the stories as myth in the Lévi-Straussian sense. Although Rowling clearly favours choice, there is a certain ambiguity to her books, as they feature determinism (for instance with the prophecy and the fact that events take place almost exactly as it foresees in the end), too. Compatibilism functions as mediator balancing the binaries of free will and determination.

Dumbledore's discussion of the prophecy can be read as a Barthesian meta-commentary on the word and the dangers of human adherence to it. 'Keep your distance and assess words carefully,' he seems to say. 'Try to find out what your true motifs for an action are.' *Star Wars* goes to great lengths to show exactly what might happen if people set too much store by a prophecy and thus by words. The negative example of Anakin/Vader thus ultimately serves the same purpose of advocating free will as Dumbledore's positive one, albeit in a more indirect way.

---

26 Rowling *Prince* 478.

27 Rowling *Prince* 478.

28 Cf. Donaher and Okapal 48.

29 Donaher and Okapal 48. Cf. also Julia Pond (185) and Edmund M. Kern (107) for similar views on the question of free will and destiny in the novels.

30 Donaher and Okapal 52.

Still, although the preference of one side (free will) over the other (determination) is a very structuralist stance,[31] Rowling's treatment of the prophecy itself is rather poststructuralist. Dumbledore deconstructs the clearly ordained path the oracle seems to lay out for Harry and identifies the element of play (choice) still open to him within its limits. Donaher and Okapal support this view when they say that "[i]n particular, the structural and referential ambiguities of the prophecies [the one about Harry and the one about the Dark Lord returning] create the possibility of choice."[32] The prophecy in *Star Wars* is never deconstructed as clearly, although it leaves even more room for interpretation, since characters and audiences never even get to hear its actual wording. And although Yoda admits at some stage that it might have been misread,[33] Anakin's choice in the matter is never as clearly taken into account as is Harry's.

All in all, it can be said that the movies in contrast to the *Harry Potter* novels emphasise determinism more than choice, at least in their dominant reading. This becomes clear with respect to the figure of Anakin who is constantly determined by either fate, or the Jedi or the Sith. There is an element of choice in his final reconversion to the good side but, and that was already mentioned in chapters four and six, the movies' stance remains more ambiguous than the *Harry Potter* novels' as Anakin's conversion can equally well be interpreted as a return to his originally good nature represented by his son Luke. So when Russel W. Dalton, comparing *Harry Potter* and *Star Wars* says that "a clearly benevolent *purpose* drives certain events in [the] worlds [of the movies and novels],"[34] he is only partly correct. Both stories do focus on destiny and its role in a person's life. Both, however, also look at ways in which persons can shape their destinies through choice. As mentioned in chapter three already, *Harry Potter* more distinctly foregrounds the good, already in its superstructure and in this sense, it could be said that a 'benevolent purpose' runs through the novels that might help Harry make the correct choices.[35] *Star Wars*,

---

31   Cf. Derrida's notion of the hierarchy inherent in binary oppositions (Derrida *Positions* 41).

32   Donaher and Okapal 55.

33   Cf. *Revenge of the Sith* 00:39:05.

34   Dalton 21.

35   Jeremy Pierce also believes that the *Harry Potter* novels are destiny-driven to a degree. He specifically comments on the extraordinary quantity of luck the characters seem to have on their journey to eradicate evil. Many of the events simply come to pass because the protagonists learn about something that helps them on their way by chance. Pierce wonders whether so much luck is possible or whether there is some kind of agency propelling fate (cf. Jeremy Pierce, "Destiny in the Wizarding World," *The*

however, equally features good and evil. The Force is firstly and foremostly a neutral concept which can then be employed positively or negatively by people. The fact that the exact content of the prophecy is unknown in the movies, also indicates that although the stories are clearly destiny-driven, it is hard to speculate about the benevolence or malevolence of the purpose running through them from the outset. Particularly the more recent trilogy seems to be informed by a malevolent, rather than a benevolent purpose, if anything. Good and evil are rather balanced in *Star Wars*, not least structurally (see also the analysis of chapter three). The prophecy in *Harry Potter* is very specific in announcing a saviour, while the one in *Star Wars* only predicts that there will be someone to bring balance to the Force, which can mean many things. Thus, the 'benevolent purpose' first needs to be established, mainly through the behaviour and the decisions of the characters. The treatment of free will and destiny remains ambivalent in both stories, though still more so in *Star Wars*.

The prophecy that was made concerning Voldemort and Harry mentions power, or to be more precise it assigns Harry a power the Dark Lord does not have. This power clearly cannot lie in Harry's magical ability. Though he is quite a passable student, manages to master complicated spells such as the Patronus charm at an early age and can thus be assumed to become a skilled wizard at some stage, Voldemort's magic surpasses Harry's by far. The villain has advanced into areas of magic that Harry does not even dream of. However, if one accepts Dumbledore's dictum that it is "our choices (...) that show what we truly are, far more than our abilities,"[36] it becomes clear that Voldemort's magical skill cannot be everything. And so over time, Harry discovers that it is not so much skills he has that match the Dark Lord's but character traits that set him apart from the villain. One of these character traits is perseverance. Harry has a strong will and does not easily give up. The scene in which he defeats Voldemort at the end of novel four can serve as an example. At the same time that Voldemort utters the killing curse, Harry tries to disarm him. Since the two wands are brothers they do not work properly against each other. With enormous effort and will power Harry forces Voldemort's wand to reverse the final spells it has performed. Since all of these spells have been cast to murder people, the wand begins to regurgitate Voldemort's latest victims as ghostly presences who help Harry escape the villain.[37] These smaller acts of perseverance and strength of will help Harry later on when these qualities are really tested. This is most notably the case in novel seven when Harry has to fulfil two quests, one for

---

Ultimate Harry Potter and Philosophy: Hogwarts for Muggles, Ed. Gregory Bassham (New Jersey: Wiley, 2010) 48).

36   Rowling *Chamber* 358.

37   Cf. Rowling *Goblet* 577-79.

Voldemort's Horcruxes and one for the Deathly Hallows that will help him overcome death. Goodness, it seems is characterised by not giving up and retaining hope.

In the course of novel seven's two quests Harry's strength and perseverance are often tested, especially because all around him people are tortured and killed and he and his friends are also constantly subject to attack. What is hardest for Harry apart from hearing about the deaths of friends is the temporary betrayal of his best friend Ron, whose loyalty to Harry wavers for a short time due to the influence of one of Voldemort's Horcruxes.[38] Only with the return of the remorse-ridden Ron can the trio really resume their quests. Ron and Hermione are essential to Harry and constitute a great part of his power. The friendship of the three stands strong against opponents and through difficult times and even survives moments of disenchantment among them. Here, as in so many other mythical narratives, it is important for the hero to have friends. Lena Steveker, commenting on Harry Potter's identity formation says that "his identity as hero clearly depends on the personal relationships he sets up with the people surrounding him."[39] The heroes realise that they cannot do everything alone, an insight Harry finds hard to act upon sometimes.[40] The sharing of burdens and important tasks is the marker of the true hero because it shows that he gives others the chance to shine and is not egotistical and self-absorbed.

The villains in both tales only have followers but no true friends. Most people are afraid of them, others hope for a share of their power and sinister glory. Examples of the latter from both stories would be Governor Tarkin in *Star Wars* and Bellatrix Lestrange in *Harry Potter*. The problem is, however, that villains are never interested in sharing anything. They basically only abuse their henchmen for their own goals. Villains and their followers are mostly divided amongst themselves while the good side usually stands as one. This severely hampers the bad side's chances of success. Thus it is one of Harry's great strengths and part of his power that he is able to accept help and hold friends. Both Anakin Skywalker and Severus Snape lose their friends at some stage and start counting on the wrong people. However, since both originally have the ability to uphold friendships (Anakin with Padmé and Obi-Wan and Snape with Lily Potter) they manage to eventually regain

---

38   Cf. Rowling *Hallows* 254.

39   Steveker (69). Russel W. Dalton also comments on the importance of friendship in both *Harry Potter* and *Star Wars* (cf. 61).

40   Dumbledore's Army, the group of students whom Harry has trained in defensive magic in his fifth year at school, offers help at the end of book seven, after Harry has returned to school. It takes his fellows quite some time to persuade him that he does not have to do everything on his own (cf. Rowling *Hallows* 467-69).

the trust of the good side. The ideology as was mentioned before is that people who care for others can never be completely evil. Both also have at least one person who is loyal to them. For Anakin this person is his son Luke who tries to win him back for the good side and believes in him. For Snape this character is Dumbledore who knows that Snape deeply regrets what he has done and gives him a second chance. The importance of friendships and the trust in friends are thus essential messages of both stories. Of course, standing together and taking care of others instead of being egotistical is also a wider social ideology that is advocated as the way to success.

A further constituent of Harry's power is a certain wilfulness. This wilfulness, however, needs to be carefully balanced, something that Harry must gradually learn. Tom Morris summarises the Philosopher Aristotle's view of courage as follows: "[C]ourage is a midpoint between two extremes in our reaction to danger: the extreme of too little, which [Aristotle] characterizes as cowardice, and the extreme of too much, which he labels as rashness."[41] While Harry is not given to cowardice, he is prone to rashness. The best example of this, and one of the series' low points, is his not heeding Hermione's advice about the vision he has of Sirius being tortured in book five. Hermione fears that the vision is a fabrication by Voldemort who wants to manipulate Harry into entering the Ministry of Magic. Her judgement turns out to be correct and Harry's "saving-people-thing"[42] costs Sirius his life. Aristotle's definition of courage perfectly fits the mythical function of creating balance, presenting a middling position, visualised in Lévi-Strauss's diagrams. By the time Harry has come of age in book seven he has managed to unite 'cool reason' and emotion. His propensity for rash action has given way to more careful planning. A second thing, however, also happens. Harry begins to partly emancipate himself from the judgement of his overbearing mentor figures such as Dumbledore. So while he does trust others, he also eventually trusts himself and sometimes pursues the paths he thinks are right. Mostly his instincts prove correct. An example would be his decision to give in to the connection he has with the Dark Lord's mind once more. Though Hermione constantly tells him that Dumbledore wanted him to close his mind to it, Harry senses that he needs to use the knowledge of his opponent for his own ends.[43] It becomes clear here, that the Sorting Hat was not wrong when he said that Harry would do well in Slytherin. Especially in the final novel, Harry does indeed unite the bravery of Gryffindor and the cunning of Slytherin. The plans he and his friends hatch to get at the Horcruxes

---

41   Tom Morris, "The Courageous Harry Potter," *Harry Potter and Philosophy: If Aristotle Ran Hogwarts*, Ed. David Baggett and Shawn E. Klein (Chicago: Open Court, 2004) 13.

42   Rowling *Order* 646.

43   Cf. Rowling *Hallows* 192-93.

are worthy of Voldemort's cold intelligence. To finally defeat Voldemort, it seems Harry needs to emancipate himself from the good represented by Dumbledore to a certain extent. The power of the good side within him plus independence of mind and his own instincts of what he is supposed to do help Harry act with a balance of rationality and feeling. It is noteworthy that Anakin never achieves such a balance. In fact his acting purely out of emotion is his and many other people's and creatures' undoing.

A further part of Harry's power is his willingness to forgive. He, for instance, forgives Ron for doubting him when he is entered into the Triwizard Tournament against his will in book four.[44] And he also forgives Ron's more serious betrayal in novel seven.[45] Equally importantly, he is finally able to forgive Dumbledore for not telling him anything about his past entanglements with evil and he forgives Snape his part in James and Lily Potter's deaths.[46] Voldemort does not forgive as he himself asserts several times in the course of the stories and proves by the cruel treatment of people who have not fulfilled his orders in a satisfactory way. Forgiveness is thus clearly another quality that advances the good over the evil side.

The most important power Harry has, which makes him triumph over Voldemort in the end, encompasses all his other powers discussed before. This power is love. As early as book one Harry learns that he is a marked man, but not only in the negative sense. Apart from the scar caused by Voldemort's failed killing curse he has also been marked by his mother's love, which was so powerful that she was prepared to die for her son. These two marks, one the visible sign of evil that shows Harry's connection to Voldemort, the other the invisible sign of good, his mother's love, again allude to Harry's duality. However, the books make amply clear that his mother's sacrifice has left a deeper impression than the Dark Lord's murderous intentions. The love he has been blessed with which has kept him alive, paves the way for Harry's discovery of his own ability to love. He is always prepared to risk his life for the people he loves, for example Ginny in book two and Sirius in novel five. Notably, Harry also cares for the fates of creatures maltreated and distrusted by most of the wizarding world. He befriends Hagrid, the Hogwarts gamekeeper, who is half-giant, and gains the respect of some of the centaurs, humanoids who are otherwise rather wary of wizards. In novel two he makes friends with House Elf Dobby, the little servant of the Malfoys, who disobeys his masters to try and protect Harry from the horrors of the Chamber of Secrets.[47] Harry repays Dobby's friendship by ending his status as the Malfoys' slave, which earns

44   Cf. Rowling *Goblet* 313.

45   Cf. Rowling *Hallows* 308.

46   Cf. Rowling *Hallows* 577, 607.

47   Cf. Rowling *Chamber* 18-23.

him Dobby's eternal gratitude and devotion.[48] In novel seven Harry saves a goblin, another creature most wizards mistrust and some probably would have left to die.[49] The young wizard is furthermore always willing to extend a hand to those of his fellow students who are not as popular as he is. He befriends Neville Longbottom, the clumsy boy from his own House, and Luna Lovegood from Ravenclaw, who is an outsider because of her peculiar dress code and outlook on life. All this shows Harry's generosity, humanity and genuine care for others.

When Harry first learns that the power he possesses that Voldemort does not have is love, he feels a little let down.[50] He only completely understands at the end of novel seven how rich this ability makes him. The examples just given show Harry's own loving nature. However, he inspires love as much as he gives it. Voldemort and his Death Eaters are finally no match for all those who suddenly unite around Harry to help him bring down the forces of evil. Centaurs, house elves, hippogriffs, the giant Grawp, Hogwarts teachers, the Order of the Phoenix, fellow and former students and their parents, the people from the nearby village of Hogsmeade, and most importantly Hermione, Ron and the whole Weasley family make Harry strong against Voldemort.[51] However, as Karin E. Westman astutely remarks, the theme of love in *Harry Potter* has a dark underside and Harry has to learn how to "negotiate" his power correctly.[52] As Westman says "The desire to love and be loved can smother agency and purpose."[53] In book one, for instance, Harry is in danger of losing himself in front of the Mirror of Erised for love of his parents.[54] Westman also mentions Molly Weasley's extremely protective love that sometimes limits Harry's quest for knowledge as well as Bellatrix Lestrange's and Barty Crouch Jr.'s obsessive love for Voldemort which does much harm in the wizarding community.[55] The embodiment of good and less beneficial love is once

---

48   Cf. Rowling *Chamber* 362-64.

49   Cf. Rowling *Hallows* 393.

50   Cf. Rowling *Prince* 476.

51   Cf. Brycchan Carey, "Hermione and the House-Elves: The Literary and Historical Contexts of J.K. Rowling's Antislavery Campaign," *Reading Harry Potter: Critical Essays*, Ed. Giselle Liza Anatol (Westport: Praeger, 2003) 105.

52   Westman "The Weapon" 195.

53   Westman "The Weapon" 195.

54   Cf. Rowling *Stone* 229-31.

55   Cf. Westman "The Weapon" 194, 195. Edmund M. Kern, too remarks upon the ambiguous nature of love, especially in *Harry Potter and the Order of the Phoenix*, where Harry's ability to love both leads him to take rash and unreasonable decisions that harm people close to him, as well as finally saves him from Voldemort's possession (cf. 244).

more Harry himself who unites both sides: he uses love as an inspiration and a weapon. His love simultaneously *shields* others and *destroys* Voldemort. Again, Harry functions as mediator who brings the two extremes of protective and destructive love together.

In the course of the stories Harry proves countless times that he is willing to sacrifice himself for others. Mostly these others are his closest friends. At the end of book seven he makes a sacrifice that encompasses and surpasses all of the ones he made before. When he learns that a part of Voldemort's soul is attached to his own and Voldemort has to kill him to get rid of it, he bravely walks towards what he thinks is his own death. He does not defend himself when Voldemort utters the killing curse. By this time the battle against evil seems to be lost, he is tired of fighting and does not want any more of his friends and followers to die. With his willingness to lay down his life for his loved ones he repeats his mother's sacrifice. In the following Voldemort cannot touch or harm any of those fighting for Harry anymore.[56] Since Voldemort like the Emperor fails to understand the power of love because he himself is unable to feel affection, he simply cannot win. It is very hard not to see the Christian message that is behind the novels, as some religious fundamentalists choose to do.[57] Both stories, *Star Wars* and *Harry Potter*, as was already mentioned, heavily rely on the ideology of love overcoming hatred and evil, most prominently visible in the characters Anakin Skywalker, Luke Skywalker, Harry Potter and Severus Snape. Terry Eagleton makes a remarkable statement about the relationship between good and evil which, I think, explains a great deal about the *Harry Potter* novels but also about the function of formulaic fiction as such:

Virtue has hardly ever flourished in public affairs other than briefly and precariously. The values we admire—mercy, compassion, justice, loving kindness [i.e. all the values Harry (and Luke) embody] —have been largely confined to the private domain. Most human cultures have been narratives of rapine, greed, and exploitation.[58]

---

56 Cf. Rowling *Hallows* 591.

57 Several enraged parents tried to get the novels banned at American schools because they supposedly promote witchcraft and evil. See for instance "School Bans Harry Potter," *BBC News*, 29 Mar. 2000, 25 Jul. 2011 <http://news.bbc.co.uk/2/hi/uk_news/education/693779.stm>., David Usborne, "US Parents Want 'Evil' Harry Potter Banned," *The Independent*, 14 Oct. 1999, 25 Jul. 2011 <http://www.independent.co.uk/arts-entertainment/books/news/us-parents-want-evil-harry-potter-banned-743511.html>.

58 Eagleton 147.

By sacrificing his life, Harry Potter brings these values to the public sphere and has them counter 'rapine, greed, and exploitation' there. He shows that these virtues, although usually rather manifesting themselves in the private sector, are equally forceful as vice. His is not a Girardian sacrifice of a person being made to take upon him- or herself the sins of others, it is a voluntary sacrifice of someone who values love and fellow-feeling above everything else.[59] Eagleton's statement also makes something else clear once more. For good to appear, to show itself, evil is necessary. Only in the face of adversity can people show their true nobility of nature. Without occasional adversity people become complacent. Harry needs Voldemort to develop the way he does. As Martin Hall says: "In this sense, Voldemort *is* a tool for goodness. He strengthens his own opposition."[60] Thus although good and evil are clearly conceived of as separate categories in the novels, they can also be seen as constitutive of each other, something that is metaphorically rendered by the fact that Harry's and Voldemort's wands share cores.

It can be seen again that formulaic fiction on the one hand functions as a compensation for our often indefinitely rougher reality. True to Cawelti, it provides escape.[61] On the other hand, it stands in the tradition of myth which was always designed to get people to become active. Myth like formulaic fiction presents models who provide moral orientation for people. However, finally, it is not so much the models themselves who are important but the themes/ideals they embody. The example of Harry Potter very clearly shows once more that myth and formulaic fiction are fundamentally ambiguous. Harry's function in the sacrificial scene is essentially structural. The themes of sin and redemption, of love and its power are in the foreground rather than the character of Harry himself. Nevertheless Harry's

---

59   Nikolaus Wandinger discusses Girardian sacrifice in *Harry Potter* (Nikolaus Wandinger, "'Sacrifice' in the Harry Potter Series from a Girardian Perspective," *Contagion* 17 (2010): n.pag. <http://lion.chadwyck.co.uk/>). However, I do not find his article very convincing as he only introduces Girard's theory on sacrifice very briefly and does not truly apply it to the novels which he rather sees as suffused by a Christian notion of the concept. Girard does not specifically focus on Christian sacrifice but rather on the practice as carried out in pre-Christian societies.

60   Hall "The Fantasy of Realism" 188. Cf. also Christopher M. Brown who argues a very similar thing for *Star Wars*: "It may be that the Dark Side serves a good and necessary purpose: there would be no *genuine* goodness in the universe without the Dark Side as an impetus for noble action" (71). Cf. furthermore Jullier 222.

61   Cf. Cawelti 6.

character and his individual development are necessary to the sacrifice since it would not have come about without them.[62]

In addition to all the good character traits Harry has, he is also a great flyer. He manages to secure the most important position on the Gryffindor Quidditch team in his first year at Hogwarts. He plays seeker, the person who has to spot and get hold of the golden Snitch to end and usually win the game for his team. The search for the Snitch is a quest as the search for the way to destroy Voldemort. Quidditch prepares Harry for real life in a playful way. He can perfect his ability to see small things others would miss and he needs to fit in with a team. In Quidditch as in life it is important not to do everything alone. Terry Toles Patkin, too emphasises the symbolic function of Quidditch in the novels: "Games provide exercises in mastery: games of strategy related to mastery of the social system, games of physical skill associated with mastery of the self and environment, and games of chance linked with mastery of the supernatural. Quidditch clearly serves all three functions in Rowling's magical world."[63] The game shows Harry's special position early on. He flies amazingly well, never gives up and almost never loses a match. This might be taken as a metaphor for the whole story. With his combined skills and perseverance Harry will finally manage to accomplish his task of destroying Voldemort. Flying symbolises freedom and a certain security about what one is doing in life. In many popular songs, for example, persons are seen as flying if they have managed to be independent and happy in their lives in contrast to being stuck with old habits and fears.[64] Harry's flying thus foretells his ability to build up a happy, independent and fulfilled life. Incidentally, both Voldemort and Anakin/Vader are flyers, too. Voldemort's ability to fly without broomstick,[65] however, is as unnatural as the other things the villain does. His flying is extreme, another instance of his boundary-crossing. It does not symbolise freedom but represents a further instrument of bringing death and suffering. Thus even in the case of flying, there

---

62   Cf. also M. Katherine Grimes who holds that "[t]he true joy of the Harry Potter series is that the books' protagonist is both a bigger-than-life hero and a true-to-life boy, just as the books are both magical and realistic" (90). Edmund M. Kern concurs with Grimes's interpretation and holds that Harry's nature as 'real boy,' fairy-tale- and mythical hero makes the reading of Rowling's stories as "literary myth" possible (196-97).

63   Terry Toles Patkin, "Constructing a New Game: J.K. Rowling's Quidditch and Global Kid Culture," *Reconstruction* 6.1 (Winter 2006): n.pag. <http://lion.chadwyck.co.uk/>.

64   Examples would be R. Kelly's "I believe I can Fly," Vanessa Williams's "Open Your Eyes, You Can Fly," and Mariah Carey's "Fly Away," all of which associate flying with letting go of problems and insecurities and finding happiness.

65   Cf. Rowling *Hallows* 56.

are positive and negative ways of doing it. Harry, who accepts the limitations of even wizards in the air, uses a broomstick to fly, the ordinary tool people of his kind employ for the purpose. He mainly flies to work for a team, to bring a boon for his fellow players, as much as he does many of the other things he does for the benefit of his society. He also sometimes flies to thwart Voldemort or save other people.[66] His flying is therefore positively connoted. Anakin/Vader's flying abilities are variedly judged. While he is Anakin, he, like Harry flies to save others. An example would be the scene in *Phantom Menace* when he destroys the power generator for the droid army with his spacecruiser.[67] As Vader, he flies to bring death and doom to others and as such, his flying is obviously not condoned. He is defeated flying by his son Luke who manages to destroy the Death Star despite Vader's persistent persecution. Obviously, Vader has fulfilled the threat of the overreacher contained in his name and flown too high. The flying of the good side is portrayed as markedly better than that of the evildoers and it is solely the good characters whose flying symbolises true freedom.

As Voldemort's and Anakin/Vader's freedom is also restricted by their fears, most notably of death, it is worthwhile looking at the way Harry deals with this negative emotion. Unlike Voldemort and Anakin/Vader he is not consumed by fear. Instead of constantly running from something or other or working *against* certain factors, Harry rather works to build a good world, he works *for* a cause. This coincides with the creative and constructive associations with his name 'Potter' and diametrically opposes him to the villains. Rowling is realistic enough, however, to suggest that Harry's disposition is not easy to acquire or maintain and that it sometimes demands great strength of will to refrain from succumbing to one's fears and sadnesses. Even Harry sometimes has to cope with anxiety and grief. In novel one, for instance, he almost loses himself in front of the Mirror of Erised which shows him his heart's desire, to have his parents back.[68] The novel which is most openly dedicated to showing the reader how Harry copes with his fears is the third one. It is the book in which Harry encounters the Dementors, grizzly soul-sucking fiends guarding the wizard prison Azkaban. They are sent to patrol the entrances to

---

66   In book one, for instance, Harry and his friends use brooms to catch the key to a door that advances them in their search for the Philosopher's Stone which they want to reach before Voldemort (cf. Rowling *Stone* 301-302). At the end of novel six, Harry and Dumbledore use brooms to get back to school quickly after they have spotted the Dark Mark in the sky above Hogwarts (cf. Rowling *Prince* 543-45). And towards the end of the seventh instalment, Harry and Ron rescue Draco Malfoy and Goyle from the burning Room of Requirement on brooms (cf. Rowling *Hallows* 508-10).

67   Cf. *The Phantom Menace* 1:57:34.

68   Cf. Rowling *Stone* 225-32.

the school because alleged mass murderer Sirius Black has escaped from the legendary prison, a feat no one has ever managed before. The Dementors, by drawing breath, suck all joy and happiness out of their surroundings and leave people with only their worst memories, their fears and sadnesses.[69] Their ultimate weapon is the Dementor's kiss, which they administer to suck the soul out of people.[70] They are, in short, an image of the destructive and life-negating quality of depression, a metaphor which Rowling has confirmed herself.[71] Harry is affected by them worse than other people, because as Professor Lupin, his Defence Against the Dark Arts teacher in the novel tells him, he has had worse things happening to him than others.[72] Whenever a Dementor approaches him, Harry can hear the last moments of his parents' lives before they are killed by Voldemort. He regularly passes out when the Dementors come near him. In Professor Lupin's class the students are confronted with a Boggart, a creature that does not have a fixed shape but turns into what the person confronting it fears most. Lupin prevents Harry from tackling the Boggart because he is afraid that it will assume the shape of Lord Voldemort. However, Harry tells him that what he fears most are the Dementors. Lupin is impressed and tells the astonished Harry that this is rather wise because it "suggests that what [he fears] most of all is – fear."[73]

Harry does not really understand at that point but Lupin is right. Unconsciously, Harry seems to know that the Dementors are much worse than Voldemort. The Dark Lord can kill, but death might be better than the soulless existence brought about by the Dementors. Voldemort, after all, can be destroyed, despite all his efforts to remain tethered to life. In none of the novels, however, a way is shown to destroy the mysterious Dementors. They can be fended off but they cannot be completely defeated. They can always come back. Incidentally, they could probably destroy Voldemort as much as Harry. This is what makes them utterly frightening and horrible. The Dementors have the terrible power to make Harry worthless in the fight against Voldemort because they can take all the qualities away that distinguish him, loyalty, compassion, and most importantly, love.[74] The fact that Harry fears the Dementors more than Voldemort thus again shows something very essential about him which will become important later on: Harry is less afraid of physical

---

69   Cf. Rowling *Azkaban* 203.

70   Cf. Rowling *Azkaban* 268.

71   Cf. Ann Treneman, "J.K. Rowling, The Interview," *The Times* 30 June 2000, 5 Jul. 2011 <http://www.accio-quote.org/articles/2000/0600-times-treneman.html>.

72   Cf. Rowling *Azkaban* 203.

73   Rowling *Azkaban* 169-70.

74   Dalton also comments on loyalty, mercy and forgiveness in both *Star Wars* and *Harry Potter* (cf. 70, 95).

death than he is of a joyless, friendless and loveless life. Lupin teaches Harry to drive the Dementors away and thereby counter his fears. This can only be achieved by concentrating very hard on a happy memory. The formula 'Expecto Patronum' conjures a Patronus, made up of all the happy feelings sucked away by the Dementors. The Patronus takes the form of a silvery-white patron animal which, if powerful enough, can chase away hundreds of Dementors.[75] It is not a coincidence that on almost all the later occasions when Harry needs the Patronus, he does not concentrate on a happy memory but conjures up in his mind images of his best friends Ron and Hermione.[76] His friends and his love for them manage to help him even when they are not physically present. Harry's dealing with the Dementors, maybe his worst enemies after all, exemplifies his courage in overcoming not only Voldemort and death but also the hopelessness that could prevent his victory.

Harry's concrete fears have already been identified. He is afraid of losing all those who are dear to him, of leading a friendless, joyless and ultimately soulless life. There are also occasions on which he fears to become like Voldemort. The strange connection existing between the villain's mind and his own, frightens him most. These fears have in common that their causes can be fought. Harry can fight Voldemort and his henchmen in order not to lose his friends and all that makes his life worth living, he can also counter the Dementors who threaten to take his soul and he can decide for the good when required to make a choice. Voldemort's essential fear by contrast cannot really be countered as death is inevitable for everyone. Much as he tries to achieve immortality, he can never be sure that no one will find out his secret and destroy the Horcruxes. He is driven by this fear and it determines his whole existence. Harry is not driven and determined. Since he has experienced so many deaths in his life already he has come to accept mortality as part of existence. And because of his acceptance of death, he finally triumphs over it and survives Voldemort's killing curse for the second time.[77] It is thus not Voldemort, the powerful wizard who has "gone further than anybody along the path that leads to immortality"[78] who defeats death but Harry, the ordinary and at the same time not so ordinary boy. The scene of Harry's victory over death shows the boy's unity once more. As much as he unites good and evil, he unites life and death. It also shows that goodness is defined by the acceptance of one's own mortality. As Dumbledore says to Harry after his sacrifice: "You are the true master of death, because the true master does not seek to run away from Death. He accepts that he

---

75   Harry's Patronus is tested towards the end of the novel when hundreds of Dementors come for Sirius, Hermione and him (cf. Rowling *Azkaban* 414-15).

76   Cf. for example Rowling *Order* 22 and Rowling *Hallows* 449.

77   Cf. also Colebatch 17.

78   Rowling *Goblet* 566.

must die, and understands that there are far, far worse things in the living world than dying."[79]

Another important quality Harry has which fundamentally separates him from Voldemort is his innocence and purity despite the fact that he has one of Voldemort's Horcruxes inside him. Though his soul is obviously infested by something alien, it is still miraculously whole and complete. This is something that Dumbledore addresses several times. He also wonders why Voldemort who is so cunning and clever otherwise, does not notice the power that this gives to Harry. His purity enables him to procure the Philosopher's Stone in novel one, a wonderful and dangerous magical object which yields the elixir of life, making the drinker immortal. It is not hard to understand why Voldemort wants to possess the stone. Dumbledore in his wisdom has set up the best protection for the precious object. Only a person who wants "to *find* the Stone – find it, but not use it" will be able to take hold of it.[80] This same innocence also helps Harry in his quest for the Deathly Hallows in book seven. Harry thus unites a further binary: purity and impurity.

To sum up it can be said that Harry is a truly mythical character. Myth is characterised by a fundamental ambiguity. It is at once binary in nature and strives to overcome this duality. Joseph Campbell[81] confirms this when he says:

The mystery of life is beyond all human conception. We always think in terms of opposites – I and you, this and that, true and untrue – every one of them has an opposite. But mythology suggests that behind that duality there is a singularity over which it plays like a shadow game.[82]

In this sense Harry Potter perfectly embodies the nature of myth in a Lévi-Straussian sense. Many critics such as Jack Zipes who see Harry as purely a literary creation, miss this fundamental point about him. They take Rowling's hero too seriously as an individual character, which, as I have shown, he is, but only in one way. "[Harry] is a perfect model for boys because he excels in almost everything he undertakes. But this is also his difficulty as a literary character: he is too flawless

---

79   Rowling *Hallows* 577.

80   Rowling *Stone* 323.

81   For an analysis of Campbell's 'hero's journey' with respect to Harry Potter cf. Boll 85-104. Cf. also Katie L. Baker, "Harry Potter: A Hero of Mythic Proportions," Thesis, Buffalo State College, Dec. 2011, 6 Sept. 2012 <http://digitalcommons.buffalostate.edu/cgi/viewcontent.cgi?article=1000&context=english_theses>.

82   Joseph Campbell, *The Power of Myth*, Interview with Bill Moyers, Ed. Betty Sue Flowers (New York: Anchor Books, 1991) 57.

and almost a caricature of various protagonists from pop culture."[83] Zipes's reproach hits the mark. Harry is at times quite boring as a literary character. However, this is because he is not supposed to be very interesting as a figure but meant to embody timeless mythical themes and questions. He functions as a concept much more than as an individual. As this concept he transcends the binaries of good and evil and unites them. He also unites life and death by dying and being reborn like the Phoenix whose tail feather rests in his wand. Voldemort tries to transcend binary oppositions and does so in an obviously evil way by breaching countless boundaries. Harry, on the other hand, unites them and puts together again what Voldemort has made an effort to destroy. His position and role in the series makes clear that binaries are necessary and structures are needed to order human societies and thereby refutes a poststructuralist stance according to which structures are limiting and boundaries are unstable and fluent. His power to unite the opposition of good and evil resides in his consciousness of the evil within him and constant decisions for the good side. He unites the binaries of life and death by his acceptance of the latter.

Mythical ambiguity, however, is still paramount in the figure of Harry, because he not only unites binaries but he also re-establishes them, a seeming contradiction. By ridding his soul off the Horcrux, he shows that finally, he is Other than Voldemort, that despite the fact that he contains both good and evil parts, he has decided for the path diametrically opposed from the villain's. Finishing Voldemort who endangers the clear-cut structures of the wizarding world, is a further act of distinctly affirming binaries. The dead Tom Riddle on the floor is evil, Other, and therefore had to be vanquished for the good to reign once more. The person to question and blur boundaries is no more and the wizarding community can go back to their cherished order. To invoke Cawelti again, enjoyable formulaic fiction needs an element of the unpredictable, has to go beyond the clear-cut oppositions for a bit, to finally come back to them.[84] In Rowling's case it is Voldemort, the villain who to a large part makes the story interesting and to whom we owe the pleasure of reading. Without him, there would not be much need for Harry's exertions. In fact Voldemort is as ambiguous as Harry. His poststructuralist tendencies were already highlighted. He tries to destabilise structures, thereby of course also reaffirming them. However, as Kate Behr says "Harry resembles Voldemort partly because Voldemort inadvertently recreated some of his own powers in him, making them similar."[85] In this sense, Voldemort embodies one of the major attacks on popular

---

83   Jack Zipes, *Sticks and Stones: The Troublesome Success of Children's Literature From Slovenly Peter to Harry Potter* (New York: Routledge, 2001) 180.

84   Cf. Cawelti 10.

85   Kate Behr "'Same-as-Difference'" 121.

culture as 'making same.'[86] He thereby also calls forth echoes of theoreticians such as Barthes and Foucault. While Barthes highlights the influence of myth and ideology on people and the ways in which this influence can be abused by a hegemonic system, Foucault comments on the 'normalising' tendencies of society which also ultimately function to make people similar.[87] In this sense, Voldemort is extremely ambiguous as he embodies the 'same-making' function of popular culture as well as its tendency of subtly undermining structures that serve this end. By finishing the villain, Harry defeats both, his tendency to 'make same' as well as his poststructuralist strand. Both the dull machinery of popular culture with its repetitive story patterns *and* the poststructuralist fragmentation and loss of security are rejected to offer what exactly in their stead? To offer Harry, a supremely ambiguous character who stands for a 'post-poststructuralist' effort to create a traditional hero whom the readers can identify with on the one hand and a subtle undermining of old heroic patterns and mythic structures on the other; a truly utopian project.

7.2 TYPE AND INDIVIDUAL: LUKE SKYWALKER

Luke Skywalker is the counterpart to the Emperor and a completely good person, therefore he frames the characters analysed in the two preceding and the present chapter on the good side. As in the other cases the analysis will begin with a discussion of his name. His first name is pregnant with meaning. As Robert G. Collins remarks, it "means 'Light,' [and hints at Luke's function as] the visual life-nurturer of the cosmos."[88] It is also the name of one of the Evangelists, a person bringing his understanding of the truth about the divine grace to the people. Luke, by showing compassion and saving his father, can also be said to be a messenger of the true nature of the mysterious Force. The gospels might, as there is no scientifically provable truth about them, count as myths and Luke, the Evangelist is certainly a storyteller. This links him with George *Lucas*, the inventor of the *Star Wars* universe. The connection of the name with myth and storytelling is probably no coincidence and significant for the analysis of the original *Star Wars* trilogy.[89] The older three movies were analysed as more mythical because they are more

---

86   Cf. for instance Kidd n.pag.

87   Cf. Barthes 21, Foucault 183.

88   Robert G. Collins, "*Star Wars*: The Pastiche of Myth and the Yearning for a Past Future," *Journal of Popular Culture* 11.1 (1977): 3.

89   Christian Wessely also comments on these associations with the name. He, too believes in the connection between Luke and his creator George Lucas, but dismisses the connection with the Evangelist (cf. 161).

formulaic and morally clear-cut than the new instalments. The association of one of the main characters with biblical and mythical storytellers who spin grand narratives is therefore probably no coincidence. George Lucas admitted that by writing *Star Wars* he wanted to create a new myth.[90] Luke's name thus points to George Lucas' ambition behind the project of *Star Wars*. It also, however, draws our attention to a difference between the understanding of myths as stories of certain cultures and the series of movies. *Star Wars* has a very specific creator. For the myths of a people or society, the creator is usually unknown or it is believed that it had many creators and evolved through the centuries by people amending the story or adding to it. *Star Wars* is thus very clearly shown as a story constructed by a particular person, who had certain aims in producing it. This aligns it with Roland Barthes's concept of myth as a 'text' that has a strong potential of influencing or even manipulating people.[91] We have already seen some of the ideologies that run through *Star Wars* and will encounter more, especially in the following chapters dealing with women, humanoids and ethnic minorities.

Luke's last name, Skywalker has the same connotations that were already discussed for his father Anakin/Vader.[92] Luke Skywalker is not as common a name as Harry Potter, which shows that Luke does have a special status in the story from the start. It also sets itself apart from Harry's name because it is not as entirely positive. Luke's name already signals that he will have to face his father's heritage and hints at the possibility of Luke following in his father's evil footsteps. So Luke like Harry seems to contain a certain duality which for Luke is already made visible in his name. However, despite the ambiguity of his name Luke, like Harry never undergoes a name change. Both retain their original names throughout which shows that they do not have pretensions like the Emperor and Voldemort and do not take themselves too seriously.

When the audience gets to know Luke, he is an adolescent. His story, however, begins way before the events of *A New Hope* set in. This is the same for Harry

---

90 "I had a longtime interest in fairy tales and mythology, that sort of thing. I had decided that there was no modern mythology. The western was the last American mythological genre, and there had not been anything since then. I wanted to take all the old myths and put them into a new format that young people could relate to." (George Lucas qtd. in Bouzereau 27).

91 Cf. Barthes 2.

92 Wessely only perceives the positive side to the name 'Skywalker' and associates Luke with Helios, the god of the sun who replaces darkness with light (cf. 161). However, I believe the potential for overreaching is inherent in this telling name and becomes obvious when applied to the figure of Anakin Skywalker. Luke, too has a darker side which shows in the cave experience on Dagobah to be analysed later in this chapter.

Potter whom the readers get to know when he is eleven years old. The events that shape his life begin much earlier, too. Luke, again like Harry, lives with his aunt and uncle because his parents are supposedly dead. He is dissatisfied with his life and wants to get away from his home planet of Tatooine because there is nothing he can do there. "Well, if there's a bright centre to the universe, you're on the planet that's farthest from it," he says in answer to robot C-3PO's question where they are.[93] He wants to go to the Academy, a school where he can complete his education as a pilot, like his friends before him.[94] His uncle, however, is reluctant to let him go, not out of malice but because he needs him on his farm. Luke's aunt and uncle are not unkind but they, and especially Uncle Owen do not really want to see that Luke can do more than be a farmer. They have to die for Luke to be free to leave Tatooine with Obi-Wan Kenobi. This is different from the beginnings of Harry Potter's career as a wizard. While Luke achieves freedom through the death of his aunt and uncle rather early on, Harry has to return to his relatives each summer until he is seventeen and therefore of age by wizarding standards. The time he has to spend with Uncle Vernon, Aunt Petunia and cousin Dudley, though not pleasant, nevertheless does something important for Harry. The bad experiences he has there and the fact that in his relatives' household he is not treated as someone special, let alone famous, make him remain firmly grounded.

Luke is similarly disposed. Despite the slight threat of the overreacher in his name, he is never in any true danger of flying too high. The farming life with his relatives has humbled him. His wish to get away from Tatooine is not a burning ambition as it was for Anakin, who wanted to see all the stars in the galaxy. It rather comes across as the normal aim of a young adult who wants to build up a life for himself. And deep down Luke knows that his aunt and uncle mean well. By holding him back they want to protect him, as a conversation between them suggests. Aunt Beru says: "Luke's just not a farmer, Owen. He has too much of his father in him." Upon this Owen answers: "That's what I'm afraid of."[95] So in contrast to Harry's relatives they are well-meaning, and it can be assumed that they genuinely care for Luke and have brought him up with respect, teaching him what is morally right and wrong. Unlike Harry, Luke has people who care for him from the start. This makes him even less susceptible to the allure of evil.

Luke, too is the one who can finally defeat evil once and for all and like Harry he can do so because he has many qualities the evil side lacks. These qualities coincide with Harry's for the greatest part. The loss of his parents has not made Luke bitter. He is a friendly character who greatly cares for others. This first shows

---

93   *A New Hope* 00:19:26.

94   Cf. *A New Hope* 00:23:46.

95   *A New Hope* 00:24:24.

when his uncle buys the two droids, C3PO and R2D2, whom he treats kindly. When he sees parts of the message Leia has left in the bowels of R2D2 for Obi-Wan Kenobi, he is instantly worried because he suspects that she might be in danger.[96] On learning the importance of R2's message and finding out that stormtroopers have gone in search of the droids he races off to check his homestead because he is worried the Empire's henchmen might have traced the droids there. When he finds his aunt and uncle dead, he is shocked and furious.[97] He follows Obi-Wan on his mission to help Princess Leia, who is kept prisoner on Darth Vader's spaceship. Once they have entered Vader's ship he rushes to Leia's aid a little naively without having made any previous plans for escape, and Leia cannot help constantly nagging him about that.[98] Harry exhibits the same impatience and propensity to act without thinking. In both stories it is the female characters (Hermione and Leia) who confront the heroes with this shortcoming and advocate a reasonable and considerate way of dealing with events. This is very interesting and will be treated in greater detail in the following chapter on gender discourse. Both Harry and Luke have to learn to combine reason and emotion in the course of their stories. Luke's rescue mission, however, not only shows his deficiencies but also some of his strengths. It becomes clear that he is a selfless character who is prepared to help others without any thoughts for his own safety. Thus, like Harry, he is ready to make great sacrifices for others. His capacity for love matches Harry's and is part of his final victory over evil and the recovery of Vader for the good side. Further qualities that constitute his triumph are forgiveness and compassion, which also rank high with Harry. His compassion for Vader which the Emperor prophecies will be his undoing,[99] instead turns out to be the villain's end. Vader, it transpires, is finally moved by his son's faith in his good core and indeed re-discovers it within himself. Luke unconditionally believes in Vader, which means that he has forgiven him for his countless evil deeds and murders. His final task is a little different from Harry's, though both are Christ-like figures. While Harry sacrifices himself out of love for his friends, Luke forgives the sinner and leads him back to the light.

In further congruence with Harry, Luke has the ability to make true friends and win supporters. His counterpart, Vader, does not manage to do so because he is essentially fear-inspiring and threatens or even kills people who do not meet his

---

96   Cf. *A New Hope* 00:21:30.

97   Cf. *A New Hope* 00:38:59.

98   Cf. *A New Hope* 1:15:05.

99   Cf. *Return of the Jedi* 1:04:47.

wishes.[100] Luke, like Harry, has two friends who are closest to him, one male, the rogue Han Solo and one female, his sister Princess Leia. The relationships between the three are similar to those between Harry, Ron and Hermione, too. Like Ron, who is sometimes jealous of Harry because of his friendship with Hermione, Han Solo envies Luke because of his relationship with Leia.[101] This is, however, before he knows that Leia is Luke's sister and only loves him in a sisterly way. There is a similar situation in *Harry Potter and the Deathly Hallows* in which Ron's jealousy of Harry suddenly comes to light and Harry assures him that he has brotherly feelings for Hermione and believes Hermione to feel the same about him.[102] Like Ron and Hermione, Han and Leia end up as a couple. However, there is a slight difference in the friendships. While both pairs of friends stand selflessly by the heroes and help them wherever they can, Han and Leia seem to play more active roles than Ron and Hermione. Harry's best friends do heroic deeds but are never quite as much in the focus as Harry and his actions. They rather serve as an inspiration for the hero, who always conjures up their images in dangerous situations to remind himself why it is worth fighting. Han's and Leia's heroic roles and in addition the part of Lando Calrissian, another friend of the trio are much bigger in the final fight. This becomes clear because Luke's, Leia's and Han's, and Lando's heroics are shown in approximately equally long scenes.[103] While Luke has the task of facing Vader and the Emperor and possibly finishing them, there is still

---

100   When for example in *The Empire Strikes Back* Captain Needa fails to catch Han Solo's spaceship the Millennium Falcon, Vader kills him using the Force (cf. *The Empire Strikes Back* 1:10:30).

101   Cf. *Return of the Jedi* 1:18:34.

102   Cf. Rowling *Hallows* 308.

103   As the novels' narrative line always follows Harry, Ron and Hermione are never shown independent of him. That means that as soon as, for instance, they are back at Hogwarts for the final battle in *Deathly Hallows* and Harry goes his own ways to find the last Horcrux, we do not see the two anymore. While Harry locates the remaining fragment of Voldemort's soul, Ron and Hermione enter the Chamber of Secrets to destroy the one they took out of Gringott's bank. The readers do not see this but only learn about it, when the two tell Harry later on (cf. Rowling *Hallows* 500-501). Interestingly, one of the only felicitous scenes of *Harry Potter and the Deathly Hallows: Part Two*, the film version of the final novel is the mentioned one in the Chamber of Secrets. The filmmakers chose to actually show Harry's friends go down there and destroy the Horcrux, thus granting the two more independent agency (cf. *Harry Potter and the Deathly Hallows Part 2 [German version: Harry Potter und die Heiligtümer des Todes Teil 2]*, dir. David Yates, perf. Daniel Radcliffe, Helena Bonham Carter, Ralph Fiennes, DVD, Warner Brothers, 2011, 2:05:05).

the grand battle star the evildoers have constructed which needs to be destroyed. Han and Leia thus go to the forest moon of Endor and deactivate the deflector shield protecting the Death Star, while as soon as the shield is out of the way Lando and his crew of star fighters approach the battle station and destroy it by a well-aimed shot. Luke thus cannot do everything that needs to be done on his own.

The exact roles of the friends in the final battle of *Star Wars* are interesting. Luke is the emotional side of the victory. He needs to remain strong-minded and play to his capacities of love, compassion and forgiveness. Han, Leia and Lando take over the strategic and technical part. They need to have the abilities to plan and execute their plans under dangerous conditions. Thus, theirs is the rational side of the victory.[104] Emotion and ratio are brought into balance, exemplifying one of the core functions of myth. Luke and Leia redress their father's inability to display balance of ratio and feelings. Harry, too has to learn to unite reason and emotion. Much like Luke, he needs others to fight at his side but in his final heroic act of self-sacrifice he is very much alone as Jesus was when he marched towards his crucifixion. Thus in *Harry Potter* more emphasis is placed upon the single greatest heroic deed of one person while in *Star Wars* three, or even four heroes are almost equally important.

The two stories share the propagation of the ideology that you are stronger with others by your side than alone but they are once again different in their appreciation of character. Harry's finally facing Voldemort on his own stresses the contribution of the individual and is the climax of a development in the hero which is quite as much in the focus as the never-changing elements of his character. *Star Wars*, as was mentioned before, does not place as much importance on individuality, at least not on individuality in the sense of rounded character.[105] The protagonists'

---

104   Cf. also Christian Wessely who specifically comments on Luke and Leia symbolically belonging together (98).

105   Tony M. Vinci holds that the "valorization of the individual" is "one of the original *Star Wars* trilogy's most noticable thematic concerns" (11). This is not necessarily a contradiction to what I am trying to say. Individuality and individual contribution as a theme is emphasised in the films. However, the characters themselves are not really individuals, they rather represent mythic types, making clear to audiences the importance of individual action. "[T]he prequel trilogy," Vinci believes, "undermines the original trilogy's valorization of the individual" (12). I would argue to the contrary. Though one can say, as Vinci does, that Luke's individual action of redeeming Vader stresses the significance of individuality and that the prequel trilogy by placing more emphasis on destiny subverts this focus, one could also interpret the two trilogies differently. The older trilogy, as was already explained, is more mythical, because it contains more stereotypical characters who do not develop. The new trilogy, on the

characters do not develop to the degree those in *Harry Potter* do. The movies seem to rather foreground the joint, the social effort. This is also emphasised by the fact that *Star Wars* features more evil masses than *Harry Potter*. These agglomerations of bad people of course need to be countered by just as many fighting for the good course. In *Star Wars* fate and the grand scheme behind the universe are highlighted, in which every individual simply has a part to play. This is also supported by the titles of the movies. '*Star Wars*' alludes to the fact of the wars and does not highlight any individual contribution. Fittingly, the stars are often associated with fate in literature (see for instance Shakespeare's *Romeo and Juliet*), so that the titles clearly remind the viewers of the fatal component of the unfolding story. The titles of the *Harry Potter* novels are diametrically opposed, as they distinctly draw attention to Harry's role in the events and thus show the greater focus on individual character that Rowling displays.

It has been established so far that Harry and Luke share certain qualities which are essential to their victory over evil, such as compassion, loyalty and the ability to love and to forgive. Moreover, Luke is a great pilot, just as Harry is a superb flyer. Though Harry flies on a broomstick and Luke pilots spacecrafts of different sizes, the meaning of flying is similar for both. Only by flying does Luke get away from Tatooine and get to know the galaxy. The spacecrafts are his instruments to enlarge his horizon and follow his own goals and aims. Flying is furthermore crucial to the destruction of evil in *Star Wars*. Both lethal Death Stars are finished by pilots who manage to penetrate them with small spaceships and aim shots at their weak points. Incidentally, it is Luke himself who destroys the first Death Star in this way. Flying thus not only makes him free, as it does Harry, but is also an important weapon. For Luke, flying is already contained in his name. A 'Skywalker' suggests someone who is constantly moving between the various stars in the galaxy. Since in a galaxy as big as the one in *Star Wars* this is not possible by walking, flying is indispensable. Flying is associated with most of the important characters from both *Star Wars* and *Harry Potter* and can therefore be called a leitmotif of the stories. As much as choices are only deemed sound if they encompass the well-being of others and are made for the good cause, flying, too is closely associated with the good-evil dichotomy. Moving through the air is good as long as it is done for the good cause, humbly and respectful of human limitations. Voldemort's and Vader's flying for destruction is not condoned.

---

other hand, features more rounded characters such as Anakin Skywalker, with whom the audience can to a certain degree identify. Thus it seems that a focus on individuality produces types in the older movies, while an emphasis on destiny creates more individual heroes in the new trilogy.

As with Harry Potter, it is important to look at how Luke Skywalker deals with fear and the threat of death. Luke's process of growing up and facing his fears is much quicker than Harry's, who has seven years to learn how to act wisely. Since the focus of the movies is not on Luke alone, the producers did not have so much time to show what is going on within him. Therefore, Luke is a flatter character than Harry. His process of growing up, which like Harry's goes together with the facing of his fears, takes place in several days or weeks at most. And it is taken out of the context of the everyday and displaced to a location that is spatially removed from the planets where the main action takes place. Luke is ordered to go to the Dagobah system by an apparition of Obi-Wan Kenobi. There he is to find a certain Yoda, who is supposed to train him as a Jedi.[106] While approaching the planet, Luke talks to his droid R2 about it and says: "I'm not picking up any cities or technology. (...) Massive life-form readings, though. There's something alive down there."[107] Thus it can be seen that the place is not only spatially very far away from the main action of the movies but it also seems to be a natural location which stands in contrast to the highly technological cities and space stations Luke is used to. When Luke finally lands on the planet, it entirely consists of a kind of jungle with swamps all over. The life-forms that had manifested themselves on his computer monitors turn out to be mainly snakes and lizards.[108] Everything is covered in deep fog. The whole place is thus a metaphor and fits in with Joseph Campbell's ideas about the stages of myth in which the hero has to confront his own inner self and what is hidden there. Sometimes this process is symbolised by a journey up a mountain, to the bottom of the sea or even into the belly of the whale.[109] Here this far-away planet takes the same place and represents Luke's unconscious, which he has to penetrate to be able to understand his history and the way forward. The swamps are embodiments of something unfathomable and potentially dangerous, which is mirrored by the fact that Luke is confronted with his own dark side on the Dagobah system. In the same vein, the fogs suggest a sight which is (as yet) incomplete and probably has to be cleared. The jungle and the snake-like animals hint at something ancient and archaic and are symbols of human drives and instincts that usually remain hidden or repressed. (Snakes and lizards are very often part of Gothic stories and have similar symbolic functions there). In accordance with these interpretations Luke says to R2: "This place gives me the creeps. (...) Still... there's something

---

106 Cf. *The Empire Strikes Back* 00:12:37.

107 *The Empire Strikes Back* 00:39:12.

108 Galipeau even claims that "symbolically [Dagobah] is a very feminine landscape, (...) warm, and alive" (102).

109 Cf. Campbell *The Hero* 90-92.

familiar about this place."[110] This is reminiscent of Freud's description of the uncanny, which is fear-inspiring exactly because it is alien and at the same time unconsciously familiar.[111] When confronted with the uncanny, Freud says, we are subconsciously reminded of baser urges within our nature which we otherwise repress and which we most certainly fear.[112] It is interesting that the flatter the characters, the more richly suggestive the setting seems to be. Obviously, since the makers of *Star Wars* did not place so much attention on accentuated characters and their development, they needed to lend depth to the story, for instance with the help of the setting.

In Gothic fiction where uncanny atmospheres play a major role, the tension created by such settings usually persists and is not relieved. Here, however, in keeping with Joseph Campbell's observation that in myth a benevolent helper figure appears at some stage,[113] tension is relieved by the appearance of Yoda.[114] The Jedi master is at once strangely in keeping with the surroundings and totally out of place. He seems to be ancient like the place but is also different from every life-form we have seen there so far. At first Yoda seems to be very child-like and annoying. He rummages through Luke's belongings and speaks strangely. This is incongruous with the way in which he is depicted in the three more recent movies where he appears as a sage and powerful warrior without exception. One explanation of his slightly crazy behaviour appears to be the fact that he had to go into hiding when Anakin/Vader destroyed the Jedi Order. His long hermitage on a planet such as Dagobah could have contributed to his eccentric ways. The other would be that he 'puts an antic disposition on' to test the hero's patience, patience being an important quality for a Jedi. Yoda then serves Luke food,[115] a metaphor of the nourishing function helper figures in myth and fairy-tale usually have. They very often feed the heroes with new insights that help them win their battles. When Luke finds out that he is facing Yoda he is eager to start his training. Yoda, however, talking to the invisible Obi-Wan remarks that "the boy has no patience,"[116] thereby confirming my interpretation of his 'antic disposition' at the

---

110 *The Empire Strikes Back* 00:45:10.

111 Cf. Sigmund Freud, *The Uncanny*, [1919] (London: Penguin Books, 2003) 124.

112 Cf. Freud 148, 152.

113 Cf. Campbell *The Hero* 69.

114 It is no coincidence that the Campbellian view of myth manifests itself in *Star Wars*. George Lucas admits having read Campbell and expresses an admiration for the scholar's thoughts on the subject of myth. (Cf. for instance John Shelton Lawrence 21-33).

115 Cf. *The Empire Strikes Back* 00:52:36.

116 *The Empire Strikes Back* 00:53:21.

outset. Patience was what Anakin Skywalker also lacked, according to the Jedi, and sure enough the next thing Yoda says to Obi-Wan is: "Much anger in him, like his father."[117] And there it is yet again: the propensity of the Jedi to judge people according to destiny, their lineage or certain characteristics they allegedly possess. It transpires that Yoda has watched Luke from afar: "This one a long time have I watched [sic]. All his life has he looked away ... to the future, to the horizon. Never his mind on where he was [sic]. (...) What he was doing. Hmph. Adventure. Heh! Excitement. Heh! A Jedi craves not these things [sic]."[118] Both Luke and Harry obviously need to learn the lesson that for success it is important to be firmly grounded in the present. While Luke constantly looks to the future, Harry is prone to getting lost in the past as, for instance, when he detects the Mirror of Erised in book one. Dumbledore is much better in teaching that lesson than the Jedi. When he confronts Harry, who has sat in rapt silence in front of the Mirror for a few consecutive nights, he calmly explains to him his reasons for taking it to a new place where Harry cannot find it. He lets Harry understand why "it does not do to dwell on dreams and forget to live" and is very understanding of Harry's weakness.[119] In contrast to that the Jedi are always accusatory and impatient with the difficulties their charges have in following some of their highly idealistic and not very worldly dictums. Thus, while Dumbledore somewhat redresses the lack of trust he placed in Tom Riddle alias Voldemort from the start by expressly trusting Harry Potter, master Yoda is in danger of repeating the same errors the Jedi have made with respect to Anakin. The Jedi appear distanced and hard to please and their trust cannot be won easily.

Nevertheless, Yoda finally decides to train Luke. It is rather obviously part of the Jedi training to face one's fears. In contrast to *Harry Potter* where dealing with fears is a natural part of the process of growing up, in *Star Wars* it is a fixed constituent of the Jedi-education. Thus in *Harry Potter* the timing is more natural. Harry, it seems, is allowed to deal with fears, frustrations and aggressions exactly when he is ready for them, while in the process of becoming a Jedi, everything has its fixed place and the padawans are confronted with things they might not be ready for. Luke has to undergo such a test when Yoda tells him to enter a dark cave on the Dagobah system. The cave is of course another symbol of the unconscious and the dark recesses of the mind. Even before he enters it, Luke knows that "there's something not right here. I feel cold, death."[120] And Yoda answers: "That place ... is

---

117   *The Empire Strikes Back* 00:53:30.

118   *The Empire Strikes Back* 00:54:13.

119   Rowling *Stone* 231.

120   *The Empire Strikes Back* 1:00:07.

strong with the dark side of the Force. A domain of evil it is [sic]."[121] When Luke wonders what is in the cave, Yoda cryptically answers: "Only what you take with you."[122] And when Luke grabs his weapons he says: "Your weapons ... you will not need them."[123] In this scene, Luke approaches a territory that scares him. His going into the cave on the planet full of ancient creatures such as lizards and snakes, symbols of the irrational and of evil, mirrors Harry's descending to the Chamber of Secrets where he faces a Basilisk standing for his connection with evil in the form of Slytherin and Voldemort. When Yoda says that in the cave there is only what Luke takes with him, he also refers to Luke's very own fears which must be confronted and against which weapons, and be they as extraordinary as the lightsabre, will not help much. Apart from a rather short conversation about the dark side of the Force, Luke knows nothing about it. As always, the Jedi show themselves as cryptic and not very concrete here.

Thus Luke enters the cave unprepared, encounters Darth Vader, draws his lightsabre and cuts his head off. When he approaches the black helmet lying on the ground, the mask falls away and Luke, horror-stricken, sees his own face lying there before him.[124] So in this scene, Luke has done exactly what Yoda has warned him against. He has allowed his fear and anger to run away with him. Instead of facing Vader calmly, he has drawn his weapon and used the Force to attack and not to defend himself. Seeing his own severed head lying before him in Vader's helmet, Luke is confronted with the possibility of ending like Vader, the way he has acted in this situation being the first step on the way to the dark side. In short, Luke has to face something that he is utterly unprepared for: the fact that he, too has a shadow-side.[125] Steven A. Galipeau emphasises that "[i]n this movie [*Empire Strikes Back* and especially on Dagobah] Luke begins the transformation from hero (...) to *initiate*. The initiate learns that there is far more to life than heroic action and seeks knowledge and experience of life's deepest mysteries."[126] This view is similar to Travis Prinzi's about *Harry Potter*. Prinzi argues that Harry remains in the rather static fairy-tale hero tradition throughout the first four novels. From book five onwards, confronted with his darker side, he changes into a more mature hero who

---

121   *The Empire Strikes Back* 1:00:17.

122   *The Empire Strikes Back* 1:00:31.

123   *The Empire Strikes Back* 1:00:38.

124   Cf. *The Empire Strikes Back* 1:02:46.

125   Cf. also John Lyden, "The Apocalyptic Cosmology of *Star Wars*," *The Journal of Religion and Film* 4.1 (2000): n.pag. <http://lion.chadwyck.co.uk/>.

126   Galipeau 88. Cf. also Polzer (49, 51) who reads the movies not only as a story of individual growth but also as a metaphor of the realisation and actualisation of American identity.

combines heroic action with wisdom and love.[127] Both Luke's and Harry's heroism obviously goes beyond brave action. It includes a development in the course of which they need to come to terms with some of life's mysteries, surely one of the facts that makes them so attractive for movie audiences and readers. In the light of the *initiation* experience Luke has to undergo, Yoda's action here may also have something positive. In fact, not telling young people who have to learn much about life everything might just be a different but equally wise move as talking to them. Yoda lets Luke make his own experiences which sometimes works better than lectures. Luke will definitely never forget his encounter with Vader in the cave and Yoda certainly hopes that his future decisions will profit by this. Like other scenes mentioned before, this one is thus ambiguous. There is more than one way of reading it which is in accordance with the ambiguity often found in myth and formula fiction. However, it is still apparent that the Jedi do consider individuals as finally unimportant in the grand workings of the universe.

This is exemplified by the fact that Luke is definitely trained for the confrontation with Vader and the Emperor, not for himself. This becomes clear when Luke talks to Obi-Wan after Yoda has died in *Return of the Jedi*. Luke, who in contrast to the other Jedi believes in individuality and the possibility of change says about Vader: "There is still good in him."[128] Obi-Wan answers: "He's more machine now than man. Twisted and evil."[129] And Luke retorts: "I can't do it [destroy Vader], Ben."[130] In typical Jedi-fashion, Obi-Wan answers: "You cannot escape your destiny. You must face Darth Vader again."[131] Luke desperately repeats: "I can't kill my own father."[132] And Obi-Wan answers: "Then the Emperor has already won. You were our only hope."[133] This exchange shows several things. For one, Obi-Wan has not changed much and has not really learned from his experiences. He reacts to Luke's anxieties with the same stereotypical references to

---

127 Cf. Prinzi 126.

128 *Return of the Jedi* 00:45:03.

129 *Return of the Jedi* 00:45:07.

130 *Return of the Jedi* 00:45:12.

131 *Return of the Jedi* 00:45:15.

132 Wessely comments on the fact that Luke associates 'facing' Vader with 'killing' him (cf. 154). Luke has as yet, despite his Jedi training which is focused on mental and spiritual power, exhibited a deep rootedness in the materialistic side of existence. This is shown by the way he instantly draws his weapon each time he feels threatened, first in the cave on Dagobah (cf. *The Empire Strikes Back* 1:02:11), then in his first fight against Vader (cf. *The Empire Strikes Back* 1:36:57) and finally in the ultimate battle between him, Vader and the Emperor (cf. *Return of the Jedi* 1:41:02).

133 *Return of the Jedi* 00:45:25.

destiny as he once did to Anakin's. The conversation, however, also very clearly shows that the old Jedi order, which has by then died with Yoda, is truly dead and that a renewal in the form of Luke Skywalker is taking place. Luke does not accept the ideas about destiny which one cannot escape and which shapes one's life forever as easily as Obi-Wan does. He mixes his knowledge of the Jedi philosophy with genuine humanity, fellow-feeling and compassion. In fact his final conversion of Vader at least slightly questions the Jedi belief in destiny and everyone's preordained place in the universe as for Luke clearly, Anakin the individual is important.

Luke redeems his father by first of all breaking through the usual Jedi-disinterestedness and showing compassion and forgiveness for his father. Secondly, at the crucial moment he reverses Anakin's failure. He resists the constant temptations and threats of the Emperor and Vader. While at first he starts fighting Vader, he suddenly realises that hate and anger are indeed the path to the dark side and that he acts exactly as the Emperor wishes. When the latter says: "Good! Your hate has made you powerful. Now, fulfill your destiny and take your father's place at my side,"[134] Luke manages to do what he could not in the cave. He puts his lightsabre down.[135] The renewed mention of destiny has made him see sense. He not only wants to save his father but also to counter the constant predominance of fate. He is prepared to die rather than become evil and be turned into another mascot of destiny. Possibly this is also the moment when Vader fully realises what he has done and how he has gone wrong. When he sees that Luke has remained self-reliant and cannot be determined, he decides to become an individual again once more. Where Anakin fails, Luke succeeds. In this sense, *Star Wars* is a story of re-individuation.

Harry and Luke share traits that seem to be the markers of true heroes. They are selfless, loyal, compassionate, forgiving and they can feel true love.[136] They both fulfil a Christ-like role in their respective stories, Harry by sacrificing himself for the ones he loves and Luke by showing mercy and forgiveness for the sinner. It thus seems that a myth which wants to affect the audience needs a figure who goes against the grain, who is against the status quo, who transcends stereotypes and binary oppositions. However, the mere fact that these figures are a stock feature of myth makes them stereotypical themselves to a certain extent. Luke Skywalker is more stereotypical than Harry because he is treated more perfunctorily. Harry has seven years (seven rather large volumes) to develop an identity whereas Luke has

---

134   *Return of the Jedi* 1:48:59.

135   Cf. also Wessely 158. Luke has finally managed to break the pattern of violence and thereby completely embraces Yoda's teachings and becomes a Jedi.

136   Cf. also Lyden "The Apocalyptic Cosmology of *Star Wars*" n.pag.

considerably less time. While we get to see Harry's everyday interaction with his friends and his ordinary school days, Luke's development is presented to us in fragments and concentrates upon his task of confronting Vader. The fragmented nature of Luke's treatment is due to the fact that he is not the only important character in the fight against evil. He is not as much in the focus of his story as Harry is. Most times he appears he is singularly associated with the destruction of evil, which makes him more stereotypical than Harry who is also shown in contexts other than the pursuit of Voldemort. I am aware of the slight contradiction in describing Luke as a stereotypical character as it was mentioned before that he represents individuality. However, the individuality he represents is not a very personal one, it is rather the concept of individuality versus determination by some external force such as destiny. Some of the contradiction is left standing since ambiguity, as was already mentioned before, is part of the nature of myth. The binary of individuality versus stereotypicality is another one the two mythical stories bridge.

8.   Imperfect Ideals: The Women's Question

8.1   AMBIGUOUS DEVELOPMENTS: FEMALE CHARACTERS IN *STAR WARS*

The prominence of structures in the two series as well as the focus on white males as central to these structures, distinctly shows the downside to structuralism. Structures, which in the cases of *Star Wars* and *Harry Potter* are organised around the fight between good and evil and visualised in a few exemplary characters, hide other discourses from view which are also present in the stories. Michael Valdez Moses's rather naïve statement that "[i]n Lucas' future there exists amity and equality between white man and Wookie (…), between whites (Han, Luke, Obi-Wan) and blacks (Lando Calrissian and Mace Windu), between men and women (Princess Leia, Queen Padmé Amidala),"[1] needs to be looked at more closely in this context. The structures marginalise themes such as the treatment of women and 'ethnic minorities' as well as humanoids in the particular instance of *Star Wars* and *Harry Potter*, simply because audiences or readers concentrate on the three positions Lévi-Strauss identified in his diagram.[2] However, the vice-like hold these structures of the clash between extremes and the mediating efforts of a middle character have over popular narratives are also what might inspire Fiske's producerly readings.[3]

---

1   Valdez Moses "Back to the Future" n.pag.

2   Cf. Lévi-Strauss 130.

3   Cf. Fiske *Understanding Popular Culture* 103. On a more optimistic note, Janet Bergstrom suggests that "[t]he standard use of female identity to reinforce male (dominant, institutional) identity is no longer a regular pattern of narrative development" (Janet Bergstrom, "Androids and Androgyny," *Camera Obscura* 5 (1986): 40). It needs to be seen whether the structures truly privilege the male hero or whether there are subtle readings that emphasise a more 'female' narrative.

Precisely because narratives of the kind of *Star Wars* and *Harry Potter* seem closed, they produce numerous gaps and their dominant readings are often called into question by less dominant ones, as we have already seen in the preceding chapters. This chapter will explore one of these gaps, women and their role in the two popular series, while the following two parts of the thesis will deal with the approach of the stories to their abundance of humanoid as well as non-white characters. My agenda in doing a producerly reading of the two tales with respect to the three discourses just introduced, is not necessarily one of political correctness. I am primarily interested in the question whether the discourses are 'silenced' by the structures which have been widely discussed so far. In both stories it is noticeable that the advent of evil brings these themes to the attention of heroes and audiences/readers. Either the villains raise the awareness of injustice by dis-empowering those with little power further or they indirectly draw the attention to suppressed figures who challenged by evil suddenly rise up against it. It will be seen to which degrees the villains spotlight and influence the 'silenced' themes and whether the fact that it is the evildoers who stress them serves as a justification of 'silencing' them once more.

In keeping with my method of before I want to analyse the role of women in *Star Wars* first and then compare my findings to the treatment of women in the *Harry Potter* novels. A few general points can be made about the women in *Star Wars*. Most of the few women who play a role in the movies can be clearly categorised as either good or evil. Those whose disposition remains unclear do not play significant roles and there is only one woman who is on the side of evil. Since there are both good and evil men in the stories, equality would mean that the distribution among the women should be similar. The only evil woman in *Star Wars* is a bounty hunter called Zam, sent to kill Padmé Amidala, the former queen of Naboo. However, she only plays a minor role and is a little fish within the big machinery of evil dominating the galaxy which is obviously controlled by men. Her motifs for committing evil deeds are quite clearly pecuniary. Thus she does not resemble the male villains whose reasons for becoming evil are usually very foggy and mostly relate the the acquisition of greater power. Zam is not even completely human. She is a so-called changeling who can turn into a kind of monster. The producers of *Star Wars* seem to have been rather reluctant to portray women as evil. Since the bounty hunter appears in the second film of the more recent trilogy, she could even be seen as fulfilling a token role. The producers might have realised that they had portrayed women a little one-sidedly in the original movies and included an evil woman for 'political correctness.' If this were the case, however, they failed miserably, because Zam is neither important nor interesting as a villain, has only a five-minute appearance and is easily beaten by two men, Anakin Skywalker and Obi-Wan Kenobi. In formulaic stories, for instance Gothic ones or 19th-century melodrama, female villains are very often women who have simply risen above the constraints of their societies, do not conform to the social norms and are considered to be evil because of this. They are frequently demonised because people, especially men, fear their subversive potential and the threat they pose to patriarchy.[4] A perfect example is Lucy Westenra from the novel *Dracula*. After being turned into a vampire she becomes openly sexual and demanding, embodying male anxiety of women's realising and living out their desires. 'Evil' women in formula fiction are thus often more powerful than their meek and submissive 'good' counterparts but their power needs to be broken in the end and the women have to be ostracised or returned to their proper place. The fact that there is not even a truly powerful female villain in *Star Wars* is thus extremely telling. The stories obviously repress subversive female power and foreground male might.

As *Star Wars* often works with large groups of unnamed people which also feature some women, it can be said that the majority of women depicted is not of decisive importance for the stories. There are, for instance, some women among the Jedi but it is male masters Yoda, Windu and Obi-Wan who are constantly in the limelight. Not a single female Jedi stands out. There is also a number of victimised female characters not important enough to really get much attention in the stories. These women are for example held hostage by Jabba the Hutt who makes up quite some portion of the narrative of the old trilogy. They are frequently turned into objects of the 'male gaze.' Mulvey's phrase describes the fact that particularly popular cultural artifacts often serve male needs by objectifying women, portraying them as passive and submissive and not much of a threat to male hegemonic power.[5] Mulvey also identifies women as 'bearers' not 'makers of meaning' in popular entertainment.[6] Women are often there to incite action on the part of men rather than to act themselves. Jabba's female slaves are good examples of this. They are forced to wear bikinis and dance alluringly in front of their captor. As soon as he is fed up with them, he feeds them to one of his monsters. These women are turned into passive puppets and have to fulfil male commands.

On first looking it thus seems that female characters in the movies are very much determined by the structures of the narrative, which center on binary oppositions and largely male heroes. The women are categorised and one with subversive potential is missing. However, matters are not very different for the male characters, except for the fact that there are considerably more men than women in the story. The male characters, too are categorised and most are not very round (as was also already seen in the close analysis of the Emperor and Luke Skywalker). Thus one can say that overall, the characters in *Star Wars*, be they female or male

---

4   Cf. Gilbert and Gubar 819.

5   Cf. Mulvey 589.

6   Cf. Mulvey 586.

are rather dominated by the structures of the stories. The most prominent male example is Anakin Skywalker / Darth Vader who though rounder than most others is at the same time the epitome of objectification as the 'chosen one' supposed to bring balance to the Force. Still, all in all the structures are prejudiced in favour of the male characters, which confirms Derrida's suspicions about binary oppositions.[7] It will be seen what role some exemplary women play in the films and how they function within the structure predetermined by binaries.

Only three women in the movies are truly treated elaborately. Those three are the most important women in the stories and shall be analysed in detail. They have already been mentioned with respect to some of the male characters discussed in the preceding chapters and they are Anakin's mother Shmi, his wife Padmé and his daughter Leia. It is telling already that all of them are related to Anakin in some way which shows that he is the central figure around whom their narratives revolve. All the audience gets to know about Shmi is that she is a slave to Watto, the junk dealer who also owns Anakin. She has conceived Anakin without the participation of a man and is very supportive of her son. With respect to her slavery she is shown as brave and coping. Though she constantly looks worried, she does not express any thoughts or feelings about her own situation apart from her concern for her son. Thus she is presented as caring and selfless, the ideological image of the perfect mother. She is reduced to two defining characteristics: her love for and unfaltering belief in her son Anakin. When Anakin is freed by Qui-Gon and given the opportunity to become a Jedi, she does not think about herself or stand in his way. She very clearly represents free will when upon Anakin's question whether he might go with Qui-Gon she says: "Anakin, this path has been placed before you. The choice is yours alone."[8] Shmi is thus shown to fit into the binary corset of the stories. Her opinion clashes with that of Jedi Qui-Gon who firmly believes in destiny, the opposite to free will: "Our meeting was not a coincidence. Nothing happens by coincidence."[9] Since it is not Shmi's own role and feelings about being enslaved that are in the focus of the narrative but her function as virgin mother of Anakin and supporter of her son, it is clear that she is not a round character. She remains strongly within the confines of the fairy-tale structure, which very often stipulates a mother who loses her offspring to some kind of adventure and has to stay behind.[10]

After Anakin leaves Tatooine, the audience does not hear anything about Shmi for some time. Her fate is not in itself important for the story but only for the way in

---

7   Cf. Derrida *Positions* 41.

8   *The Phantom Menace* 1:09:45.

9   *The Phantom Menace* 1:09:25.

10   Cf. Propp *Morphology of the Folktale* 26-27.

which it influences Anakin. She retains some significance by constantly being in Anakin's thoughts. Eventually, she falls victim to the sand people, who capture and torture her. Shmi's victimisation and eventual death are necessary for the story because they spark off Anakin's move towards the dark side. Because of his strong love for his mother, he feels the urge to avenge her and kills all the sand people, men, women and children.[11] Shmi's role thus exemplifies Mulvey's analysis of women in popular films as 'bearers of meaning,' i.e. not actively propelling the story but rather symbolically functioning as incentives to action for men.[12]

One of the most important women of *Star Wars* is thus less a character in her own right than a stimulus to act for one of the protagonists, Anakin. All her life, Shmi is dependent on male characters: first on her owner Watto, then on the farmer Cliegg Lars, who buys her. On his mercy she is freed, however, does not walk away to lead her own life but marries him. So in a way, Shmi creates a new dependency for herself. However, the audience gets to know almost nothing about the circumstances of her marriage so that it is hard to say whether she acted out of gratitude, true love or other motives. The audience is informed about the nature of the marriage by Shmi's husband, her story after Anakin's departure from Tatooine as a child is thus filtered through a male point of view. Cliegg Lars characterises the marriage as good and Shmi as very loving.[13] This very sparse information surely serves the purpose of maintaining Anakin's idealised picture of his mother, which then makes Shmi worthy of her son's rescue and propels his action towards the unavoidable climax.

A few years into her marriage Shmi is victimised by male characters, the sand people and dies at their hands. For the greatest part of the story, Shmi is a victim of institutional and physical violence and determined by male characters. Gabriel S. Estrada summarises Shmi's role in the following terms: "An anti-feminist version of white womanhood appears in the image of the dead Shmi in the arms of her avenging son. (…) It is a pathetic end to a life showing no agency from this lowest-class woman, once a slave."[14] Shmi is, however, predominantly a victim of

---

11   Cf. *Attack of the Clones* 1:21:51.

12   Cf. Mulvey 589-90. Hal Colebatch echoes this view when he mentions that "[i]n [the story] women do little fighting, though some of the leaders on the 'good' side are women. This is an integral part of the chivalrous tradition" (20). This tradition also objectifies women and turns them into an incentive for action rather than portraying them as active themselves.

13   Cf. *Attack of the Clones* 1:23:00.

14   Gabriel S. Estrada (Nahuatl), "*Star Wars* Episodes I-VI: Coyote and the Force of White Narrative," *The Persistence of Whiteness: Race and Contemporary Hollywood Cinema*, Ed. Daniel Bernardi (London: Routledge, 2008) 78.

structural violence as it is plain to see how the structural framework which clearly centers around Anakin, his fall from grace and redemption, determines Shmi's role and reduces her to certain stereotypical female characteristics such as a caring nature and motherly love. In fact since she plays, however small a part in bringing about Anakin's fall from grace, she is not empowered by evil but helps furthering it by her very passivity and victimisation. Her story thus even constitutes a very subtle and probably largely unconscious undercurrent to the narratives that blames women for the evil that occurs.[15] Shmi is therefore not empowered but doubly victimised by evil. She is physically harmed and even dies at the hands of some of the bad characters and she is however subconsciously made partly responsible for what happens to Anakin. This and the stereotypical way in which she is turned into an icon show that overall, Shmi is not treated favourably by the producers and the story. However, her role could also be interpreted in a completely different way. Shmi could be seen, not as a victim but as someone who albeit subtly, holds quite a large amount of power. For a woman as powerless as she is, her loving and caring nature has a strong hold on Anakin and influences his and the story's development. Shmi incorporates the ideology of love's power.[16] However, this ideological viewpoint is dangerous, too. Solely defining women via their alleged power to love is not only a reduction of their complexity. Presenting love as women's 'power' might also gloss over the fact that many women, even today, do not have much actual social and political power. The two ways of interpreting Shmi's role coincide and once more emphasise the ambiguity of myth and popular fiction.

Padmé is the second important woman to enter Anakin's life. When the audience first meets her, she is part of an elaborate role game revolving around her job as the current queen of Naboo. *A Phantom Menace* begins with a difficult situation for the galaxy which features trade embargoes and small-scale skirmishes which the evil Senator Palpatine, later to become the Emperor, uses for his own sinister purposes. On Padmé's, then Queen Amidala's home planet of Naboo, the situation is especially precarious and the Queen who is known to stand up for the rights of her people is in danger of being assassinated. Two Jedi, Qui-Gon Jinn and Obi-Wan Kenobi are sent to escort her to the city planet of Coruscant to enable her to state her case in the galactic senate. However, they do not instantly reach Coruscant but are attacked by hostile starcruisers and have to land on the planet of

---

15   Cf. Gabriel S. Estrada, too notices this in the figure of Padmé (71).

16   However, since her love finally aids the corruption of Anakin, the image is also a negative one. See also Veronica Wilson who says: "Lucas posits this loving mother-son relationship, strangely enough, as a primary cause or source of the events that will gradually transform Anakin Skywalker into the terrifying Sith Lord Darth Vader" (137).

Tatooine to get replacement parts for their spaceship. Since Padmé is a queen, one could assume that she holds a powerful position in the narrative. In fact, her position is purely representative. This is already suggested by the queenly attire. It includes ornate, stiff and bulbous dresses, hairstyles and headdresses.[17] The stiff and heavy clothes and huge hats obstruct the queen's ability to move in a literal and symbolic way. The elaborate style of the clothes indicates that she predominantly fulfills a decorative purpose. Furthermore, the queen's face is always heavily made up. It is painted white with parts of the lips red, and little red marks on the cheeks. A large red gem adorns her forehead.[18] This makes her face look like that of a porcelain puppet, rather than that of a human being. Since a puppet is something to be played with, this alludes to the way she will be used by Palpatine.

However, her face is also a mask that hides the things going on behind it. And as a matter of fact, Padmé's function in the movies is not merely that of a figurehead and she cannot quite so easily be reduced to her dress and look. It was mentioned earlier that she is associated with role-play from the beginning. Padmé is highly conscious of the fact that as queen she does not have much actual power. Thus she exchanges roles with her handmaidens who look similar to her and heavily made up and dressed in the queen's garments can take over her part as representative while she can put on ordinary clothes and thereby attain more freedom to move. Queen Amidala is an example of how women's literal and figurative power to move can be limited by clothes. However, she is clever enough not to let herself be restricted by them. Not even Jedi Qui-Gon and Obi-Wan know that the person they take to be the queen's handmaiden is actually the queen herself. Padmé cleverly uses the protection granted by the powerful Jedi and his padawan to get out and see the world. This is how she meets little Anakin on Tatooine. For Anakin she instantly is an object of admiration. Upon meeting her he asks: "Are you an angel?"[19] As much as she stigmatises him with her question: "You are a slave?"[20] which was discussed before, he stigmatises and idealises her from the start. Despite this stigmatisation which foreshadows her unfortunate later role, she does have some power at that point in the story and is capable of independent thought and action. She, for instance, questions the wisdom of Qui-Gon's decision to let Anakin enter the podrace that will help them win the spare parts they need to repair their spacecraft.[21] She also takes up a lasergun and fights for her people

---

17   Cf. *The Phantom Menace* 00:07:49.

18   Cf. *The Phantom Menace* 00:09:10.

19   *The Phantom Menace* 00:31:11.

20   *The Phantom Menace* 00:31:49.

21   Cf. *The Phantom Menace* 00:42:38.

alongside her male security guards and the Jedi.[22] And she certainly does achieve some important aims for her home planet, most notably the peace and friendship with the Gungans, another people that lives on Naboo.[23] From the second movie onwards, after she has served her term as queen, she is a Senator on the galactic Senate which has at least nominal power to influence and govern the goings on in the galaxy. This position provides her with more actual power than her role as queen, because in the Senate she can speak whenever she has something to say. Her right to speak and address issues of some weight in front of many other important people, among them a number of males, makes Senator Padmé quite powerful. Powerful enough, in fact, to be the target of assassins once more.

Her power of speech does not coincide with a power to protect herself and she needs Jedi master Obi-Wan and his padawan Anakin to protect her, though against her will. She is definitely not the meek and submissive damsel in distress known from fairy-tales but she still cannot physically defend herself. In the decisive battles she also plays a subordinate role. Kevin J. Wetmore astutely analyses the battle scene at the end of movie one, in which the child Anakin outshines her heroics in every way by entering a small starfighter and accidentally destroying the power generator for the army of droids attacking the good side on Naboo.[24] It seems as if the filmmakers compromised with her role. Padmé is neither completely passive as she does have some political power, nor, however, can she finally take care of herself. The power that is granted to her is the power of the word, not the power of the sword. It is surprising how reluctant the filmmakers seem to portray a female warrior, especially after Leia, who will be analysed later in this chapter. In their eyes, obviously, women are not made to actively fight. Padmé's domestication coincides with her developing relationship with Anakin.

The more Padmé becomes involved with Anakin, the more she loses her interest in politics and an active life and becomes wife and mother-to-be. An important position in society *and* a role as wife and mother seem to be incompatible in the *Star Wars* universe.[25] Her emotional involvement makes her dependent and after her marriage to Anakin she cries more often and loses her active toughness. Like her husband, it seems, she fails to preserve her capacity for reason and gives in to unchecked emotionality. She unconsciously collaborates with Anakin in his obsession with her because she does not remain the pragmatic, reasonable, and

---

22   Cf. *The Phantom Menace* 1:42.25

23   Cf. *The Phantom Menace* 1:36:37.

24   Cf. Wetmore 147-48.

25   Cf. Estrada 87, and Philip L. Simpson, "Thawing the Ice Princess," *Finding the Force of the Star Wars Franchise: Fans, Merchandise, and Critics*, Ed. Matthew Wilhelm Kapell and John Shelton Lawrence (New York: Peter Lang, 2006) 115-16.

independent woman she once was.[26] In their arguments, when he confronts her with his fears, she reacts helplessly, governed by her own anxieties and emotions.[27] Furthermore as Anakin's lover, Padmé is suddenly sexualised. As the queen, the handmaiden and the senator she was always dressed formally without emphasising her femininity. These roles coincided with her strength of mind and independence. From the second movie onwards, whenever we see her together with Anakin, and increasingly whenever she appears, she wears flimsy and elegant dresses which leave her belly uncovered or show large portions of her back.[28] This reduces Padmé's to a sexual function and makes her even more of an icon of desirability or a fetish for Anakin. She is very clearly turned into the object of the 'male gaze.' The end of her active role as a politician and the beginning of her role as wife and mother thus coincides with a change in behaviour and outward appearance. The two spheres, work and home are neatly separated, which they should not be nowadays, and the latter especially is highly ideology-ridden.

Padmé's change also signals her fall. As an icon without any true link to real life anymore, she cannot help Anakin and her helplessness aggravates his problems. Her new passivity leaves her vulnerable and Anakin believes he has to protect her at all costs. Similar to Shmi before her, she acquires a function for the narrative and is not a character in her own right anymore. However, unlike Shmi, Padmé undergoes a development. She initially does have some independence and freedom of movement which however, she gives up for Anakin. Therefore, Padmé is an ambivalent character who is both a strong working woman negotiating the pitfalls of politics and an emotional and caring wife and mother. Still, since her development is from strength to weakness and from individuality to iconicity, Padmé's active role is clearly sacrificed to the story's structures focusing on Anakin. Simpson, also perceiving her iconic status argues that "[b]y virtue of their sex, Amidala and Leia carry a heavy mythic burden. They are the maternal progenitors of the resurrected Jedi Knights – for all intends and purposes, earth goddesses (…) – and as such ensure the galaxy's future."[29] Thus, according to him, Padmé is not only sexualised, she is allocated her place as mother of heroes to be, a function that completely takes away her individuality. The mothering function turns

---

26   Cf. Wilson (139) who sees Padmé's weakness and acquiescence with Anakin's evil as an extremely sexist portrayal of women.

27   Cf. *Revenge of the Sith* 00:31:06, 00:50:58.

28   Cf. also Simpson 122. Padmé, for instance, wears a dress revealing her belly when she and Anakin travel to Tatooine to rescue Shmi in *Attack of the Clones* (1:10:00) and a negligé leaving her back exposed at the beginning of *Revenge of the Sith* (00:28:15).

29   Simpson 117.

her into a structural necessity as she propels the story by producing the next great heroes.

Padmé does not manage to balance the binaries of work and private affairs the films ideologically re-establish which makes her a rather imperfect mythical figure. As an element within the structure of myth proposed by Lévi-Strauss, she is disruptive because she endangers balance, not only her own but also that of the hero. It is not surprising from the purely structural viewpoint that as such an unstable factor she is expelled from the story at the end of movie three. Her treatment in the movies on the whole is rather ambiguous. Since she does not have a leading role and rather functions as Anakin's incentive for action, she is subjected by the structures as 'bearer of meaning' in Mulvey's sense. Still, the films do not invite the audience to see her development from active politician to meek wife and mother as entirely positive. Their way of approaching the subject could also be seen as an indirect criticism of the imbalance in the relationship between Padmé and Anakin. While he constantly increases his power, she loses hers and her freedom in proportion and is destroyed by it. Anakin, too is severely changed after losing Padmé. The fact that their relationship mirrors the typical roles allotted to men and women for decades up to about the 1960s and that it does not work out and even ends catastrophically, justifies interpreting their situation as subtle criticism on taking away women's power and making them subject to male wishes and desires.

These male wishes and desires are extremely traditional. Padmé's role coincides with the Victorian ideal of the 'angel in the house' who was supposed to present the loving and caring counter-image to the hard working-reality for the man and turn the home into a sphere in which the husband could forget his troubles.[30] In a lucid article on Ginny Weasley, Harry Potter's wife-to-be, Gwendolyn Limbach calls one of the roles Ginny plays for Harry the "Beautiful Soul," referencing Hegel's *Phenomenology of Spirit*.[31] The image of the 'Beautiful Soul,' the woman idealised as provider of comfort for the male warrior,[32] is quite similar to the picture of the 'angel in the house'. Both images imply that the woman is not esteemed for herself but in her function of providing solace for the male hero. If Padmé is there to please her 'warrior,' then it becomes clear why she cannot be a fighter herself. Her role as comforter is in fact established early on, when she is still a strong and powerful young woman. When Anakin has to leave Tatooine and his mother in *Phantom Menace*, Padmé comes to be a substitute mother for him who talks to him and

---

30   Cf. Gilbert and Gubar 816.

31   Gwendolyn Limbach, "Ginny Weasley, Girl Next-Doormat?," *Hog's Head Conversations: Essays on Harry Potter,* Ed. Travis Prinzi (Allentown, PA: Zossima Press, 2009) 180.

32   Cf. Limbach 180.

shields him from the cold.[33] When she becomes Anakin's lover, Padmé continues to provide escape from his adventures as a warrior. The best example is the lovers' brief stint at Padmé's home planet of Naboo, a natural paradise.[34] Their stay on Naboo shows the possibility of their setting up a home together. Anakin and Padmé are constantly shown in beautiful interiors and exteriors: at a lavishly laden dinner table, near a cosy hearth-fire, or on a balcony overlooking a lake-panorama.[35] The setting on Naboo, however, not only shows the audience the possibility of Anakin's future life with Padmé, but also illustrates the ideal woman often stands for in formulaic fiction, termed the 'Beautiful Soul' by Limbach. It shows a woman, Padmé, creating home comforts for Anakin, which completely counter his experiences in the war against evil.

The problem is that Anakin is not allowed this counter-image in reality. It must needs remain an illusion which spurs his actions in spirit. However, Anakin wants the image to be real. He wishes to marry Padmé despite the fact that this is forbidden to him by the Jedi code. Ideal image and reality become blurred as Padmé is drawn more and more into Anakin's conflicts. The knowledge of their true situation (their illicit marriage, Padmé's pregnancy) shatters all illusions for Anakin and takes Padmé's role as comfort-giver away, as she herself needs to be consoled. Thus, again it could be said that the films at least partly subvert dominant gender-related stereotypes. By making the 'Beautiful Soul' become Anakin's true wife, Padmé's status as an ideal is diminished and she appears as a real woman with real needs. This convergence of real and ideal becomes problematic when Anakin, also true to gender-stereotypical practices wishes to protect Padmé (his ideal of innocence, beauty and home comforts). This wish turns into an obsession when he realises that he cannot keep her from dying. And while the ideal of the 'Beautiful Soul' should produce resolution and courage in the face of adversity in the hero, its reality creates exactly the excess of emotion in Anakin that the Jedi warn him against.

Padmé produces these emotions in Anakin and is thus, like Shmi, one of the people contributing to his downfall. On the one hand it could be said that it is completely in line with myth to caution against any kind of excess and advocate balance. On the other hand, subtly presenting two of the most important female characters as 'dangerous sirens,' leading men astray via the emotions they produce in them, is extremely interesting: Obviously, only the more dominant reading of the movies endorses the old ideal of heroism fed by the ideal of home comfort and pure female love. Still, the image of women is slightly disturbing at the same time. Both

---

33   Cf. *The Phantom Menace* 1:16:04.

34   Cf. for instance *Attack of the Clones* 00:45:54.

35   Cf. *Attack of the Clones* 00:50:49-00:53:59.

of the women treated so far appear in the more recent movies of the series. As the *Star Wars* films feature a significantly larger number of men than women we can conclude that we are dealing with films about male power and male anxieties. These anxieties come to the fore in the problematic roles Shmi and Padmé play. Men are supposed to stand strong and not fall to the temptations and promises of women, otherwise the galaxy goes to the deuce. Additionally and even more relevantly, men must not give in to emotions of any kind, otherwise they are weak. It seems that the movies subconsciously deal with the current male anxiety of acquiring too many female attributes.[36] As the 'good' Jedi warn against giving in to strong emotions, they can be seen as perpetuating a rather conservative ideal of manhood. The paradox is that this ideal obviously does not work very well, because repressed emotions cause much harm in the films.

Padmé is a highly ambiguous figure. On the one hand she is subordinated to the dominant male narrative of the movies as she becomes Anakin's 'Beautiful Soul' and at the same time an icon of sexuality and motherhood. These two roles clash as it is impossible for Padmé, as it would probably be for every women, to be both, ideal and real. And this is where a further possible reading of Padmé might set in, as on the other hand, the way the clash between ideal and reality is presented could be seen as a criticism of the pressures women were and still are subject to and the many different roles they are supposed to fulfil, especially in contemporary society. Padmé is fine as long as she is by herself and master of her own life. Her trouble begins with her love relationship and all the wishes and desires suddenly projected onto her. She becomes an embodiment of female objectification by men, and she tragically has a part in her own downfall as she tries to fulfil all the roles allocated to her. Her treatment thus might be read as sexist but it might also be viewed as a critique of female objectification and the pressures that come with being a woman today.[37]

How does the third important female character of *Star Wars*, Princess Leia Organa, fare? Her status as adoptive daughter of an important politician from

---

36 This reading is supported by Veronica A. Wilson who holds that Lucas "ultimately (…) [associates] femininity with darkness, deception, and moral decay" (134).

37 Diana Dominguez sees the treatment of Padmé as reflection on the changed reality of young women today who have many opportunities their mothers and grandmothers did not have, but who are also "coming of age in a more dangerous, sexualized and media-saturated culture. They face incredible pressures to be beautiful and sophisticated" (Diana Dominguez, "Feminism and the Force: Empowerment and Disillusionment in a Galaxy Far, Far Away," *Culture, Identities and Technology in the Star Wars Films: Essays on the Two Trilogies*, Ed. Carl Silvio and Tony M. Vinci (Jefferson: McFarland & Company, 2007) 126).

Alderaan, gives her a certain natural power. She is also actively involved in politics herself and leads the rebellion against the almighty empire. Viewed in this light, Steven A. Galipeau's Jungian interpretation of her seems one-sided. He perceives Leia as the "anima," the "enabler" of the male characters.[38] This principle can far more easily be applied to Padmé than to Leia who is quite as active as the men throughout. In fact, quite a few critics perceive Leia as a "confusing figure"[39] because she plays many roles such as "Goddess, Whore, Lover, Mother, Sister, and Castrating Bitch" at the same time. [40] Her playing these roles supports my structural reading, because they turn her into concepts, but there is decisively more to Leia. The confusion of the critics rather than being inherent in the portrayal of Leia, might well stem from these predominantly 1980s critics' own fears of female emancipation and power.

In fact there is much ground for viewing Leia as an empowered woman.[41] When the audience first meets her, her ship has been captured by the evil Lord Vader. On his huge battle station she is still on the run from his henchmen and we see her feeding little robot R2D2 with indispensable information about how to destroy the Death Star, a weapon of mass destruction the dark side has devised. So from the beginning Leia is shown as active and in motion. Before she is finally overpowered by Vader's stormtroopers, she bravely fights back, even using a laser gun. When she is brought before Vader, she shows no fear at all and is obviously not impressed by the presence of evil.[42] The contrast between Vader, who is clad in black, and Leia is emphasised by her white attire which suggests purity and goodness. Her dress is thus the only thing that countermands her strong and active appearance. It is long and floating, befitting a princess but certainly out of place on a mission to rescue the galaxy. Her hair is elaborately braided and coiled into snails on each side of her head. This makes her look child-like and cute and does not fit with her obvious toughness. Possibly the producers wanted to compromise between the new

---

38 Galipeau 72.

39 Andrew Gordon, "The Power of the Force: Sex in the *Star Wars* Trilogy," *Eros in the Mind's Eye: Sexuality and the Fantastic in Art and Film* (New York: Greenwood Press, 1986) 201.

40 Gordon "The Power of the Force" 196. Cf. also Hanson and Kay 384.

41 Diana Dominguez, for instance, sees Leia as a strong women and her role as transcending "the familiar fairy tale trope of (...) the silent but eternally grateful damsel in distress" (110).

42 Cf. *A New Hope* 00:07:20.

strong woman advocated by an upcoming feminism and the softer, feminine woman who would please a male audience.[43]

Leia, it turns out, is not only tough, she is also strong-minded. This is proved when, as Vader affirms, she resists his mind probe and refuses to betray the rebel alliance.[44] The Princess also has one big advantage over her mother Padmé. While Padmé succumbs to her negative emotions and finally dies broken by Anakin's change for evil,[45] Leia has emotions but also knows when reason is called for. When Governour Tarkin destroys her home planet of Alderaan and thus her adoptive parents, friends and everything she has grown up with, she is deeply shocked but shortly afterwards is able to refocus on the mission before her.[46] In this she resembles Luke who also quickly manages to regain control after the deaths of his aunt and uncle and the audience can see already that she, too qualifies as heroine. She unites emotion and rationality and exhibits a well-measured behaviour. She is thus the more perfect Lévi-Straussian mythical character than her mother Padmé. Apart from her balance of reason and emotion, Leia is also a strategist. When Han and Luke come to her rescue without any plan about how to get them out of Vader's battle station, she is highly impatient with them. While they pointlessly try to fight off Vader's huge advance guard, Leia takes action and opens the way into the garbage chute through which they can secure their escape with the help of R2D2.[47] Her obvious tactical and strategic ability which she also needs as a leader of the rebels, is in fact a trait usually associated with men. Leia, though wearing female clothes, is much more 'typically' male than Luke who represents emotions and intuition, attributes stereotypically associated with women. The fact that both their personalities and abilities are needed in equal measure becomes clear in *Return of the Jedi* and their ultimate fight against evil. While Luke deals with Vader and the Emperor which, as was mentioned, involves his emotional capacities for compassion and forgiveness, Leia and Han supply the tactical part to the good

---

43   Critics such as Philip L. Simpson suggest that in fact Leia, like her mother Padmé is constantly sexualised, her power is undermined and she is finally relegated to a role subordinate to males (cf. 120-21). I strongly believe that this is too one-sided a viewpoint, as I hope my analysis will demonstrate.

44   Cf. *A New Hope* 00:49:13.

45   Padmé's death resembles that of Merope Gaunt, Voldemort's mother who also dies of grief giving birth to her son. A mother, only just managing to give birth and then dying thus seems to be a common topos in fantasy and science fiction. Very often, the tale will then be about the way the child or children left alone will develop. In the case of Voldemort, this development is negative, with respect to Luke and Leia, it is positive.

46   Cf. *A New Hope* 1:34:50.

47   Cf. *A New Hope* 1:15:10.

side's victory. They manage to switch off the deflector shield protecting the second Death Star so that their starfighters can destroy the battle station.[48] It can already be seen that Leia, in contrast to Shmi and Padmé, does play an active part in the old trilogy, a part that almost equals that of her twin brother Luke Skywalker. She is also portrayed much more roundly than her grandmother and mother.

The clothes Leia wears for most of A New Hope were briefly discussed already. It was also mentioned that she, too is associated with the sexualisation that women in the Star Wars universe are partly subject to. When she is captured by Jabba the Hutt in Return of the Jedi, she has to wear a golden bikini and sit at the creature's feet on a leash that is wound around her neck.[49] The image of holding a woman on a leash which can be tightened around her neck at will, is a rather obvious one and symbolises the suppression of women by men and the fact that men have long had the power to do whatever they pleased with women. Jabba himself, a greedy, big slimy blob of a creature who constantly eats and keeps other women apart from Leia for pleasure stands for men's baser instincts. Leia is displayed as a sexy and decorative accessory in this (by now iconic) scene and is obviously displeased with the arrangement. Her face betrays how uncomfortable she feels.[50] Her attire suggests that not only is she kept against her will, but also exploited as a sex-object. As soon as help comes in the form of Luke and Lando who have come to free Han Solo, another prisoner of Jabba, Leia uses the general commotion created by Luke's entrance and manages to free herself. Again, she remains remarkably cool. To break free and be rid of Jabba at the same time, she winds her leash tightly around his neck and pulls until he suffocates.[51] She uses her seeming fragility and unimportance as an erotic toy to turn Jabba's own weapons against him.[52] The scene shows that Leia is neither prepared to be imprisoned nor to be turned into a sex-object for Jabba. Furthermore, she does not need direct help from the men for her escape. She manages to kill Jabba on her own. This scene reinforces what could be gleaned about Leia before: she is a strong and resourceful woman who takes independent decisions and is capable of managing her life without a man at her side. The fact that she actually kills Jabba also breaks through a stereotype concerning women: the assumption that they are solely loving, caring and peaceable and not capable of using violence. The way Leia is shown here puts her on an equal footing with the men around her, because it questions the binary of allegedly typical 'male' and 'female' behavior, and is thus rather progressive.

---

48   Cf. Return of the Jedi 1:50:05, 1:50:47.

49   Cf. Return of the Jedi 00:21:53.

50   Cf. Return of the Jedi 00:21:53.

51   Cf. Return of the Jedi 00:32:40.

52   Cf. also Dominguez 117.

Leia's independence is also indicated by the resistance she keeps up against Han's advances for quite a long time. Only at the end of the tales she gives in to him and by that time both have asserted their strengths and weaknesses and both have rescued the other once. (Leia is only captured by Jabba the Hutt because she wants to save Han who has been put into carbon freeze by Jabba's cronies.) At the end of *Return of the Jedi* Leia is even allowed to wear clothes that are more practical for a fighter, namely trousers and a jacket.[53] It seems that even the men have accepted by then that Leia has to be reckoned with. Philip Simpson disagrees on this point. He interprets Leia's rescue of Han as "[surrender of] her independent identity as leader of the Rebellion and [turn into] a passively suffering woman in a romantic tragedy."[54] I believe that this is really perceiving 'female identity' as too one-sided. Why is it that particularly men always assume that women can only be either committed to their jobs or romantically involved? (Not that Simpson's statement is in any way astonishing. The male producers of *Star Wars* also seem to have this opinion about women, as can at least be seen in their treatment of Padmé, who would be accurately described by Simpson's contention). Leia goes back to her role as rebel leader after rescuing Han. She shows that in contrast to Padmé she can successfully integrate both an actively political career and a fulfilled private life.

What can be said about Leia is that in contrast to her mother and grandmother she is truly empowered by evil. Only because the evil empire has taken over, Leia joins and even leads the rebel alliance. All her strengths such as tactical cunning and independence of mind are developed and sharpened by the rule of the Emperor. Leia is not subject to structural violence either. She is not passed by or turned into an icon by the structures of the tale as are Shmi and Padmé but is more important for her own actions and has a rounder character.[55] Leia and her brother Luke represent the oppositions of male and female and reason and emotion. Since, however, Leia as the female principle contains male traits and Luke as her male counterpart, shows characteristics associated with the female, both are mythical mediators in equal measure and thus almost equally important for the story. The qualifying 'almost' was used because the passages featuring Luke are still longer than those featuring Leia and his maturation and heroics are still the prime focus of the tales. His development and heroics are embodied by his Jedi training and later

---

53   Cf. *Return of the Jedi* 1:00:15.

54   Simpson 120.

55   Dominguez notes that Leia's "sassy personality is neither tamed nor punished, as is the case in traditional in [sic] fairy tales and most other stories featuring initially outspoken or strong women" (113). This stands in contrast to her mother Padmé.

transformation into a Jedi knight. Despite the fact that Leia, too is professed to be strong with the Force,[56] it is only Luke who is educated in the ancient tradition.

A further qualification needs to be made which concerns Leia and her relationship with Luke and Han. Gwendolyn Limbach has uncovered the way in which Ginny Weasley is objectified in *Harry Potter*. Male desire, Limbach says referencing René Girard's work *Deceit, Desire and the Novel*, often does not spring from pure interest in the woman herself but from the fact that the woman is also desired by another man. She becomes interesting, so to speak, because she is also admired by a rival.[57] This triangular scheme is, in Limbach's words "a trope that reduces female characters to property traded between men."[58] It is also highly structural and supports the assumption that in formulaic fiction and film frequently characters and their development only seem to be in the foreground when in fact they are used to enact and voice social anxieties. The triangular structure Limbach identifies with respect to Ginny, Harry and Ron (to be further analysed in the part of this chapter on the *Harry Potter* novels), can also be found in *Star Wars* where Leia is in the focus of attention of both Luke (who only learns that she is his sister rather late) and Han. A further triangle features Leia, Han and Lando Calrissian who also begins clamouring for Leia's attention as soon as he lays eyes on her.[59]

Despite all this, however, the viewers do not see Leia through the eyes of Han or Luke but are allowed to make up their own minds about her. Leia herself seems aware of the attentions of the men and plays with them when it serves her needs.[60] She also, as was mentioned, symbolically frees herself from the 'male gaze' and objectification by her victory over Jabba. One can thus say that despite the fact that men are more in the foreground in the movies, *Star Wars* primarily being a tale of male heroism, the producers of the older movies managed to include a strong female character who strives to free herself from her shackles and succeeds in great measure. There is a clear development in the female characters from Shmi, who is utterly victimised on all levels, over Padmé who turns from strong, independent woman to victim, to Leia who is strong throughout and who, it can safely be assumed will not let herself be dominated by Han Solo in a relationship nor be completely consumed by emotions. This chronological development of women in the movies, albeit briefly and stereotypically pictures female emancipation from total control by men over the negotiation of the different roles a woman can play in

---

56   Cf. *Return of the Jedi* 1:16:37.

57   Cf. Limbach 172.

58   Limbach 179.

59   Cf. *The Empire Strikes Back* 1:17:57.

60   Cf. for example *The Empire Strikes Back* 00:17:14 where Leia kisses Luke to annoy Han.

life, to a self-assured management of those various roles with a balance of attributes stereotypically associated with men and women.

However, if one considers the films in the order of their actual production an entirely different picture presents itself. Then Leia, the 'oldest' of the three characters is the most emancipated while those two who were created in the 1990s and 2000s have regressed to stereotypical female patterns of behaviour that seemed to have been overcome. Where the criticism of male chauvinism was rather open with Leia who actively ridiculed the men for their slowness and thoughtlessness, it was pushed to the margins in the newer movies. Rather than giving the audience a positive example of a strong woman like Leia the producers of the more recent trilogy used the negative example of a woman (Padmé) who loses her independence in marriage. The question is whether this regression from rather active to passive criticism actually mirrors a cultural development in the Western world with respect to the role of women or whether feminist ideas were just not as present anymore in the 1990s and 2000s as they were during the 1970s. It is a question that is hard to answer and I suppose that both is true to some extent.[61] Gabriel S. Estrada also perceives this development in the movies and finds an economic explanation for it: "George Lucas' anti-classist, anti-sexist, and anti-racist representations predictably fade throughout the *Star Wars* series. As he gains production power and money he abandons the working-class male heroes of *Episodes IV-VI* and creates a prequel trilogy I-III starring elite heroes."[62] His statement seems to imply that one always supports most what one currently associates oneself with and that economic privilege does have a bearing on political sympathies.

To sum up it can be said that all of the important women in *Star Wars* depend on the structures of the stories to varying degrees. Leia as the strongest, is still part of them as one pole of several binaries. Furthermore, on the whole, she is rather outshone by her brother. *Star Wars* is very obviously the story of Anakin's fall and redemption, the latter mainly helped along by Luke. Shmi and Padmé are victimised by the structures. They do have a certain power, Padmé more so than Shmi, but finally it is not a power that reinforces them as individual characters but one that is

---

61   Dominguez asks a very similar question and also sees several possibilities of interpreting this regression. She, too considers the possibility of it being "an unconscious reflection of the vocal and often virulent backlash against feminism (...) in the past few years" (124).

62   Estrada 69. Concerning Leia and Padmé, Estrada believes that their roles both regress and that both go from active to passive (cf. 84). I completely agree with him with respect to Padmé but think that his verdict on Leia is too strict. As my analysis shows, she remains a strong, active and self-determined woman throughout who plays a large part in the rebellion's victory.

only important as far as it influences the central character Anakin. This power, emotional influence, is extremely ambiguous in itself as it leads to Anakin's downfall and takes away their true political and social power. Emotions are female characteristics, the films seem to say, which men have to beware of so as not to become unbalanced and feminine. However, apart from turning Shmi and Padmé into icons or in fact by doing so, the films can also be seen to be criticising the objectification of women.

8.2 STASIS AND PLAY: WOMEN IN *HARRY POTTER*

The most striking difference between *Star Wars* and *Harry Potter* with respect to women is that there are just many more female characters in Rowling's novels. So there is a chance that among this larger number will be some who are not as rigidly categorised and objectified as the few in *Star Wars*. Many characters, whether male or female only gain their importance through their relationship with Harry who is as central to the novels as Anakin/Vader is to the movies.[63] In this sense Elizabeth E. Heilman is right when she says that "the *Harry Potter* books feature females in secondary positions of power and authority."[64] Harry is certainly the most important character and he is male. However, it was already mentioned that Harry is a structural element, like all of the other characters. Looked at from this angle, there is a certain equality between men and women, as both sexes and their individual representatives are subordinated to the series' structures. Connected to that it can be said, for example that both the female and the male fellow Gryffindors and students from other school houses who are mentioned in the course of the novels and are not

---

63   Cf. also Michele Fry, "Heroes and Heroines: Myth and Gender Roles in the Harry Potter Books," *New Review of Children's Literature and Librarianship* 7.1 (2001): 161, who goes on, however, to argue that Hermione is an exception to the mythical pattern which naturally foregrounds the hero (cf. 162).

64   Elizabeth E. Heilman, "Blue Wizards and Pink Witches: Representations of Gender Identity and Power," *Harry Potter's World: Multidisciplinary Critical Perspectives*, Ed. Elizabeth E. Heilman (New York: Routledge, 2003) 222. In her 2009 second edition of the *Critical Perspectives on Harry Potter*, Heilman is still convinced that "women [in the novels] are marginalized, stereotyped, and even mocked" (Elizabeth E. Heilman and Trevor Donaldson, "From Sexist to (Sort-of) Feminist: Representations of Gender in the Harry Potter Series," *Critical Perspectives on Harry Potter*, Ed. Elizabeth E. Heilman (New York: Routledge, 2009) 140). I find her second evaluation rather unconvincing since she does not change her first article much and simply incorporates those bits of new data from the final three novels that fit her original argument.

closely related to Harry, are unvaryingly irrelevant for the stories. Furthermore Harry has two equally important best friends, Ron and Hermione, one male and one female. He also has two other friends whom he sets great store by, Luna Lovegood and Neville Longbottom, also female and male. Luna might even be a trifle more important to Harry than Neville because she supplies emotional support and manages to reach Harry in times in which he finds it impossible to talk to his other friends.[65] Then there is also Ginny who plays a significant part in Harry's life and also at times joins the circle of friends. So with respect to Harry's closest friends there is a near balance between male and female, maybe even a slight overbalance towards the female. It can also be said that there is an emphasis on female talent in the stories. Lily Potter's, Hermione's, Ginny's, Minerva McGonagall's, Mrs Weasley's and even Bellatrix Lestrange's magical prowess is specifically mentioned repeatedly, something that cannot be said for many of the male characters where only Dumbledore's and Voldemort's powers are ever accentuated.[66] Three further women who influence Harry are his mother Lily, his substitute mother Molly Weasley and the evil Bellatrix Lestrange. These three as well as Ginny Weasley and Hermione Granger will be analysed with respect to their roles and functions for the plot and the structural framework.

Basically, as Ximena Gallardo C. and C. Jason Smith hold, most women in the novels have nurturing functions, and can be seen in what they call the "good wife and good mother tradition."[67] Apart from the obvious nurturers, Lily and Molly, Hermione, Luna and Ginny would also fall under this category, Hermione mainly providing intellectual support while Luna and Ginny are emotionally sustaining. Still, particularly the three latter characters cannot be reduced to this function as will be seen in the course of this chapter. Lily Potter is certainly the ultimate nurturing mother, who goes as far as giving her life for her child. She is also importantly absent, which means that Harry has to find her again.[68] In her selfless sacrifice she embodies the angelic part of what Gilbert and Gubar describe as the ideal Victorian woman.[69] Thus she is very like Shmi Skywalker. Whenever she appears (in a magic mirror, as a ghost-like presence in the reverse spell effect, and brought back for a short time by the resurrection stone) she has a sustaining and

---

65   Cf. for instance Rowling *Order* 760-61, and Rowling *Hallows* 521-22.

66   Cf. for instance Slughorn's and Snape's assessment of Lily Potter, née Evans in *Prince* (71) and *Hallows* (535), the praise Ginny receives from Slughorn (cf. *Prince* 139, 141), Harry's awed reaction to Mrs Weasley's dueling power and his remark on Bellatrix's skill (cf. *Hallows* 589).

67   Gallardo and Smith "Happily Ever After" 92.

68   Cf. Gallardo and Smith "Happily Ever After" 97.

69   Cf. Gilbert and Gubar 817.

protective function. Harry's mother is one of the only characters who is allowed to remain on the pedestal she is put on by Harry and other characters.[70] He never loses his idealistic vision of her. While his father's memory is slightly tarnished when Harry finds out that he and his friends bullied Snape when they were at school, his mother retains her integrity. Most things we learn about her come from people who held her in high esteem, especially from Severus Snape who loved her. In his memories which date back to their shared childhood, she is pretty, curious, clever and loyal to him as well as her sister.[71] She is also very clear in her choices for the good side. (She turns away from Snape when he starts hanging out with Death Eaters).[72] These early decisions are reinforced by her sacrifice for Harry which turns her into the ideal of pure selfless goodness.

Lily Potter is an icon, an ideal rather than an individual and her individuality is sacrificed for the structural set-up of the stories. Thus like Shmi from *Star Wars* Lily Potter is a character truly out of a fairy-tale. She is too good to be real. She embodies an image of women which is at the same time traditional as it includes the loving care for children and stereotypical since it reduces woman to the love for their children and excludes other aspects of their personalities and lives. Lily Potter is victimised by evil but her victimisation constitutes her empowerment at the same time. Her freely chosen death at Voldemort's hands and her decision to sacrifice herself for her child, make her immortal and cement her status as an ideal of goodness which shines like a beacon above everything Harry does. Despite no longer being physically present and existing as an ideal only in the memories of people, she is one of, if not the most powerful female presence in the stories. Her sacrifice and her bravery form a guide to Harry's behaviour leading up to his own sacrifice towards the end of the story. She also functions as a guiding principle for Severus Snape, the other character apart from Harry who is crucial in Voldemort's final downfall.[73]

However, at the same time, Lily is easily the most one-sided female character in the novels and her individuality is clearly sacrificed to the structural opposition between good and evil. Her portrayal conforms to the way women were presented in Victorian times and is thus extremely conventional. However, she embodies only one part of the angel-demon dichotomy identified by Gilbert and Gubar. This is not surprising since unlike *Star Wars* with Anakin/Vader, *Harry Potter* rather neatly separates the binary oppositions in the characters, Harry being a slight exception. Nevertheless it is revealing, since the more threatening, sinister, less rationally

---

70   Cf. Prinzi 274.

71   Cf. Rowling, *Hallows* 531-42.

72   Cf. Rowling *Hallows* 542.

73   Cf. also Gallardo and Smith "Happily Ever After" 99.

graspable side to women symbolised by the image of the demon or vampire, is missing in Lily Potter, arguably *the* female principle in the novels. This is reminiscent of the almost complete lack of evil female figures in *Star Wars* and seems to reflect an effort in contemporary popular fiction and film to repress women's less ideal sides. Like Shmi and Padmé, Lily also embodies the 'Beautiful Soul' image laid out by Limbach.[74] She represents an ideal of home and a family Harry has never experienced but constantly wishes for.[75] Still, the novels do not remain one-sided with respect to the depiction of the good mother. They simply have the good and the evil side manifest themselves in clearly separated characters. A good mother, Gallardo and Smith say, can also be one who becomes active and does things that seem to be reserved for men. An example of this is Tonks. "[H]er death challenges expected roles: when she joins the final battle against Voldemort, we are to understand that her active role in the fighting is appropriate even though she is a new mother."[76] Sarah Zettel similarly assesses Lily Potter's attitude of remaining in the Order of the Phoenix and continuing to fight while she was already pregnant with Harry and affirms that this "raises Lily above a simple cliché."[77] Thus although there is a strongly traditional element to Rowling's depiction of mothers, she also subverts it at times. Obviously, she tries to make two very different pictures compatible.[78]

While there is no noteworthy evil female character in *Star Wars*, Lily Potter does have an evil counterpart in the *Harry Potter* novels, the infamous Bellatrix Lestrange. So while evil is missing from Lily's own character it manifests itself in Bellatrix. Lord Voldemort, like Harry has two adherents he trusts most, one male, Severus Snape, and one female, Bellatrix Lestrange. Bellatrix is characterised negatively throughout the novels. Her name Lestrange bears associations with the words 'strange' and 'estranged' and clearly marks Bellatrix out as Other. At the same time her first name is Latin and translates 'female warrior.'[79] She constitutes a "presence of phallic aggression in the female body."[80] Her strangeness is

---

74   Cf. Limbach 180.

75   Cf. also Amy H. Sturgis, "When Harry Met Faërie: Rowling's Hogwarts, Tolkien's Fairy Stories, and the Question of Readership," *Hog's Head Conversations: Essays on Harry Potter*, Ed. Travis Prinzi (Allentown, PA: Zossima Press, 2009) 90.

76   Gallardo and Smith "Happily Ever After" 94.

77   Sarah Zettel, "Hermione Granger and the Charge of Sexism," *Mapping the World of the Sorcerer's Apprentice*, Ed. Mercedes Lackey (Dallas: Benbella Books, Inc., 2006) 89.

78   Cf. Donaher and Okapal 52.

79   Cf. Gallardo and Smith "Happily Ever After" 95.

80   Gallardo and Smith "Happily Ever After" 95.

emphasised by her mad and dangerous behaviour. Part of her 'abnormality' also derives from the fact that she "does not display the motherly feelings commonly associated with women."[81] This is interesting, because in fact she thereby transcends one of the most pertinent stereotypes in circulation about women. The readers first meet her in person at the end of book five. With the help of the resurrected Voldemort, she has escaped from prison and now assists the villain in his quest for the prophecy. She is obsessed with apprehending Harry and bringing him before her master and would do anything for the Dark Lord. This is what makes her so dangerous. When Harry and the readers first see her in the depths of the Ministry of Magic her face is described as "alive with a feverish, fanatical glow."[82] She is prepared to use Ginny Weasley as a means to put Harry under pressure to give up the prophecy.[83] Bellatrix's attempt at torturing Ginny is only the first of many atrocities she will commit in the further course of the story. The fanaticism which Harry instantly detects in her face deprives her of any human feeling. Hers as well as Voldemort's character exemplify Terry Eagleton's impression that evil is that which ultimately abhors meaning and nihilistically seeks to destroy it.[84] Both the male and the female villain's lives lack something that makes them meaningful. Neither Voldemort nor Bellatrix truly love, neither has children, neither has a task to fulfil them. The only thing they are interested in is destruction. In a story that sets much store by the elements that give meaning to life, namely love, friendship, family, fulfilling jobs, and hobbies, villains who question and endanger all this cannot possibly come to any good.

Bellatrix is a victim of the stories' structures like Harry's mother and as her counterpart. She is the bad mother who wants to destroy structure and order itself and of course cannot be left alive when structure and order are re-established. She, like Voldemort exemplifies Derrida's contention that in our treatment of binary oppositions we always prefer one of the terms of the opposition while the other has to be contained, explained away or destroyed in some way.[85] It is noteworthy that the female villain of *Harry Potter* is characterised by exactly the same features as the male villain. It was mentioned already that she displays male or phallic power. Her treatment is therefore ambiguous. It could be argued that her expulsion from the story in the end reflects an expulsion of more active, male traits in women. But this, I think, would be too narrow a view. In fact, it was already seen, that active women are not condemned in the novels, if they use their resources for the 'right'

---

81   Gallardo and Smith "Happily Ever After" 96.

82   Rowling, *Order* 691.

83   Cf. Rowling *Order* 691.

84   Cf. Eagleton 60-61.

85   Cf. Derrida *Positions* 41.

purposes. Bellatrix's similarity to Voldemort rather shows that it is not active male traits in women that need to be eradicated but active male traits in men *and* women which harm society. Anne Collins Smith offers an analysis that neatly ties in with this view. She argues that love in the novels is actually used in quite a feminine way as it is never displayed aggressively but always manifests itself as a counter-force to Voldemort's evil.[86] In contrast to Westman who interprets love as Harry's most important 'weapon,'[87] Collins Smith claims that Harry never *consciously* uses his ability to love as such.[88] As an example she mentions the scene in which Harry frees himself from possession by Voldemort through his love for Sirius at the end of novel five.[89] Love is thus a strong but non-violent force which does not "[participate] in and implicitly [promote] the masculine structure."[90] In this sense it is diametrically opposed to Bellatrix's and Voldemort's 'phallic power.' Love does have its dangers but it is rendered as mostly hazardous to those who cannot feel or extend it and beneficial for the good side, in contrast to *Star Wars*, where its aggressive/obsessive potential destroys the protagonist.

Since Harry's real mother cannot be there for him in the flesh, his substitute mother is Molly Weasley, a woman who has seven children of her own and a big heart. Like Lily, she is treated stereotypically almost to the end of the story. Her main characteristics are her motherly kindness and care and she manages the large Weasley household with resolute strength while her husband goes to work at the Ministry of Magic. Of course, the readers only ever meet her in relation with Harry. In the first novel she is the one who tells him how to get to platform nine and three quarters to reach the Hogwarts Express.[91] The barrier between the platforms is a kind of threshold Harry has to cross which initiates him to a new phase in his life. His childhood with the Dursleys is over and his life at Hogwarts about to start. Mrs Weasley, truly the substitute mother, functions as a Campbellian helper figure here who enables Harry's entry into this new world. She shows kindness and understanding for the as yet unknown child who asks for her help. In the course of most of Harry's subsequent visits to the 'Burrow' we see Mrs Weasley in the role of the housewife. She makes breakfast and dinner, washes socks and reminds her

---

86   Cf. Anne Collins Smith, "Harry Potter, Radical Feminism, and the Power of Love," *The Ultimate Harry Potter and Philosophy: Hogwarts for Muggles*, Ed. Gregory Bassham (New Jersey: Wiley, 2010) 80.

87   Cf. Westman "The Weapon" 195.

88   Cf. Collins Smith 88.

89   Cf. Collins Smith 88.

90   Collins Smith 91.

91   Cf. Rowling *Stone* 104.

children to clean up their rooms.[92] Molly thus plays a traditional female role. She is sustainer and nurturer physically as well as emotionally.

However, *Harry Potter* ends with a change in her role. In the final battle for Hogwarts, she actively fights for the good side and thus shows that there is more to her than household spells. Evil in the form of another woman, Bellatrix Lestrange, the bad mother, finally empowers her and makes her use all the powerful magic she has. When in the very final stages of the fight, only Voldemort himself and his most loyal servant Bellatrix are powerful enough to withstand their attackers, Mrs Weasley does not care that Voldemort is beside them. She rushes to the aid of her daughter Ginny, Hermione and Luna, who are battling Bellatrix. Her cry "NOT MY DAUGHTER, YOU BITCH!"[93] printed in capital letters shows her mighty fury. The fact that she uses language she has always forbidden her children to use, indicates that she knows that ultimately there are more important things than manners. The duel between the two witches is formidable and Harry watches "with terror and elation as Molly Weasley's wand slashed and twirled, and Bellatrix Lestrange's smile faltered, and became a snarl."[94] Molly Weasley here not only opposes the witch who threatens her daughter, but also Bellatrix's nihilism and denial of meaning as well as her misanthropist ways. Like Harry in his final battle against Voldemort, Molly epitomises the meaning of the world she fights for: love, solidarity and family, not only in the restricted sense of blood-relations but also in the figurative sense of brotherhood between all people. "It is fitting, then," Gallardo and Smith say, "that Lestrange's final duel is against the super-mom of the series, Molly Weasley."[95] It becomes obvious that Harry, the other onlookers and Bellatrix Lestrange did not expect anything like this from Molly Weasley, who finally kills her opponent. The use of Mrs Weasley's full name in the quote registering Harry's astonishment shows respect for a brave woman who has transcended her usual role and is, like Harry's mother, prepared to die for her child. In the other scenes which feature her, she is mostly referred to as Mrs Weasley and her first name is not mentioned. This appellation is thus associated with her role as wife, housewife and mother. The use of her first name, Molly, makes her somewhat more individual.

Molly Weasley does not fight and kill for fun as the Death Eaters do but she does it out of necessity and expressly to protect her loved ones, represented by her

---

92 Mentioning of her household chores can be found in novels two, four, five, six and seven. In book five it is a matter of course that she cooks for the whole Order of the Phoenix assembled at Grimmauld Place (Examples: Rowling *Chamber* 41, Rowling *Goblet* 55-56, Rowling *Order* 78, Rowling *Prince* 82-83, Rowling *Hallows* 101).

93 Rowling *Hallows* 589.

94 Rowling *Hallows* 589.

95 Gallardo and Smith "Happily Ever After" 97.

daughter Ginny here. So in one way, it could be said that Molly does not so much transcend her role in this scene. She just takes her caring, protective and nurturing nature to the extreme. However, as in countless other instances before, a further interpretation is possible here. By letting her fight and kill Bellatrix, the Dark Lord's most powerful ally, Rowling implicitly shows that Molly's role as housewife and mother of seven was a choice and that Mrs Weasley is a powerful witch who could have done something different. Molly transcends her role by showing the readers that she took a decision out of her own free will. Rowling clearly supports the ideology of strong family bonds but she also does something else. In the role of Molly Weasley, she honours housewives who are often looked down upon. Molly Weasley's final appearance is a warning never to underestimate them. As Sarah Zettel contends:

For an author to show that only traditional male power and place matter is to discount and belittle the hard and complex lives of our peers and our ancestresses. The best way to do it is what Rowling does – to show the traditional role as one possibility among many, and to show it as both negative and positive according to the choices of the person playing the role.[96]

Ginny Weasley is one of the important women in Harry's life. She is the girl he loves and his wife to be. So that is a similarity between her and Padmé who is Anakin's wife. However, in contrast to Anakin, Harry consciously tries not to involve Ginny into his business, though he does not always succeed. While Anakin fails Padmé, Harry continues to be protective about Ginny. This, Limbach attributes to Rowling's use of the 'Beautiful Soul' stereotype. Harry separates the spheres of his life that have to do with the war against Voldemort and his love for Ginny, because for his heroism the ideal of love and home comfort waiting for him at the end, needs to remain intact.[97] Ginny literally helps maintaining the only place Harry has ever called home, Hogwarts, in his absence during novel seven.[98] So Ginny very clearly has the function of providing comfort, and ultimately, the family Harry has always wished for. In this sense, she, too fills a nurturing, motherly function.

Still, she does undergo an important development in the course of the novels and thus further exemplifies the fact that despite having written clearly structural novels which rather foreground themes such as love and choice, Rowling also sets great store by her characters. For Ginny it is love at first sight when she sees Harry. Harry, on the other hand, needs time to realise that he loves her. In the first scenes that feature Ginny, we get to know her as a typical little girl. On platform nine and

---

96   Zettel 92.
97   Cf. Limbach 180.
98   Cf. Limbach 182.

three quarters shortly before Harry's and Ron's first journey to Hogwarts, she complains that she herself cannot go yet and is told off by her mother.[99] In book two when Harry is staying with Ron's family for the first time, Ginny acts like a teenager with a crush. When she sees Harry, she squeals and runs away and her brothers confirm that she has been talking of nothing but him all summer.[100] The novel comprises Ginny's first year at Hogwarts and she comes to play a rather important role. It finally turns out that it has been her who opened the Chamber of Secrets but that she has been tricked into doing so by one of Voldemort's Horcruxes. When Mr Weasley chides her with the words: "Haven't I taught you *anything*? What have I always told you? Never trust anything that can think for itself if *you can't see where it keeps its brain*," she appears gullible and easily impressible.[101] In the course of the novel she is completely objectified first by Lucius Malfoy who slips her the diary and thus uses her to achieve his aims of purging the school off Muggle-borns and discrediting Arthur Weasley, and secondly by Voldemort himself.[102] She has to be rescued from Voldemort's clutches by Harry like any naïve fairy-tale princess. Her childishness and naivité do not make her very attractive for Harry who is only one year older than her but seems much more grown up.

Ginny largely disappears through novels three and four and makes her re-entry to the story in book five more grown-up. Significantly, she is not the passive princess to be rescued anymore but becomes active herself. She accompanies Harry, Ron, Hermione, Neville and Luna to the Ministry of Magic to rescue Sirius and fights Death Eaters along with them. In book six she finally gets together with Harry after she has dated some other guys and Harry through jealousy has discovered his feelings for her. As with Leia in *Star Wars*, interest in Ginny is generated in triangular relationships. When Harry realises his feelings for Ginny she is in a relationship with Dean Thomas, Harry's fellow Gryffindor. After Ginny has split up with Dean, she becomes a contended object between Harry and Ron. Limbach notes how Ginny's authority is taken away by Harry who does not grant her the decision to be with him, but needs the approval of Ron, who functions as a representative of the Weasley patriarch here.[103] Ginny is not the only female character who is thus subjected to the male discourse of the stories. Harry's first girlfriend Cho Chang is similarly introduced as the object of desire for both Harry

---

99   Cf. Rowling *Stone* 103.

100   Cf. Rowling *Chamber* 42.

101   Rowling *Chamber* 353-54.

102   Cf. Limbach 168-70.

103   Cf. Limbach 179. Cf. also Saxena who comments on the triangular relationships between the teenagers, too (62-63).

and Cedric Diggory who not only compete for her attention but also the Triwizard Cup in novel four.[104]

Further such triangles not mentioned by Limbach include Ron's awakening romantic interest for Hermione in the light of the attention she gets from Victor Krum. In true formulaic and mythic fashion, Rowling slightly questions these triangular structures by reversing them. As Limbach also mentions, in novel five, it is Harry who becomes the object of Cho's and Ginny's rivaling attention. Both are repeatedly mentioned together, always presenting Ginny in a better light than Cho. Early on thus Cho is rejected as not the right girlfriend for Harry while Ginny gradually advances to the limelight.[105] It is rather interesting that Rowling seems to equally subject male and female characters to the 'male gaze.' There are two other instances which show Harry's status as an object of desire. The first scene is Harry's using the Prefects' bathroom in novel four spied on by the female ghost Moaning Myrtle who admits to sometimes watching the Prefects bathing, too .[106] Here, it is Harry who becomes the object of Myrtle's glances, the 'bearer of meaning.' In the movie version of *Harry Potter and the Goblet of Fire* this scene is milked for all it is worth. We see a well-built Harry Potter lowering himself into the water and Moaning Myrtle obviously trying to flirt with him while he tries to assemble as much foam as possible in front of his privates. Although a six-packed Harry Potter is a bit of a stretch since the narrator in the novels frequently mentions his skinniness, the scene can be read in this sexualised way even in the book. It demonstrates Barbara Creed's claim that the 'male gaze' does not necessarily presuppose a male perpetrator. The phrase rather stands for an objectifying view that can be taken by both men and women.[107]

Rowling presents a counter image to *Star Wars* where it is exclusively women who are subjected to the 'male gaze.' This is also supported when in novel six Harry becomes the object of female desire once more. Fellow Gryffindor Romilda Vane chases after him, finally even trying to feed him a love potion.[108] However, although Rowling turns the situation from *Star Wars* around and subjects men to the 'male gaze,' the girls who do the gazing are not really presented as strong, desiring subjects but rather as immature and shallow, only interested in Harry because of his fame. Romilda Vane's last name is telling in this respect. So while one could say that by objectifying men in these instances, the novels create a certain equality, they also at the same time render the 'gazing' girls stereotypically. This

104   Cf. Limbach 172-74.

105   Cf. Limbach 176.

106   Cf. Rowling *Goblet* 401.

107   Cf. Creed 5-6.

108   Cf. Rowling *Prince* 286-87, 289.

assessment is supported by Sarah Zettel who holds that not "all the portrayals of women in the Harry Potter series are nuanced or fair," but goes on to say that neither are those of the men.[109] "This balance," she says, "matters with regards to the charge of sexism."[110] It does, too concerning my argument that the stories are predominantly structural. All characters, be they male or female are less important than the themes and ideas they stand for. Still, finally, the story is focused on Harry and focalised through him. As Limbach puts it: "because this is Harry's narrative, he sees himself only as the subject who desires, not as the object who is desired by another."[111] And although Ginny and Cho are much more important to the narrative than Myrtle and Romilda, their individuality is also subordinated to the dominant narrative of the hero. Another such triangle involving Ron as well as Hermione and Lavender Brown, who compete for his love in novel six, is at least a bit different. As with Cho and Ginny, Lavender and Hermione are constantly compared and the girlish and absurd Lavender comes even worse off than Cho.[112] The readers are invited to see Ron a little more detachedly than they see Harry, which is also due to the fact that they share Harry's perspective and Harry can watch Ron's affairs with more distance than his own. Ron, too seems to be more aware of his status as object of desire than Harry in book five.[113] Still, however, he does not much care and enjoys the attentions of Lavender as long as they satisfy him.

The reading of Ginny as part of several triangles rather makes her a structural feature and takes away her agency. However, there is also another possibility of reading her role which takes into account her individuality. It seems that Harry only begins to take an interest in her when she stops being childish, naïve and impressible. When Ginny becomes an independent and free-thinking young woman she is suddenly much more desirable for him than as the little princess. This says a lot about the way Rowling sees the role of women. Harry, the hero of the stories whom the readers follow through his adventures and whose judgement they very often accept, prefers a woman who is independent-minded and active for his girlfriend. This is confirmed when at the beginning of book seven, he muses about

---

109   Zettel 98.

110   Zettel 98.

111   Limbach 176.

112   Lavender is constantly presented to be using absurd pet names for Ron such as 'Won-Won' (Rowling *Prince* 332). She also gives him a 'romantic' heart-shaped necklace for Christmas which Ron is naturally extremely enthusiastic about (cf. Rowling *Prince* 316-17).

113   Ron, for instance, ponders about how to break up with Lavender and says that "the more [he hints he wants] to finish it, the tighter she holds on. It's like going out with the Giant Squid" (Rowling *Prince* 421-22).

Ginny's qualities and thinks that "one of the many wonderful things about Ginny [was that] she was rarely weepy."[114] Weeping is usually considered a predominantly female inclination, one which throughout literary history has often rather hindered than helped female characters in their development.[115] Since Ginny is not prone to crying, she is not considered the traditional woman. In this sense she is juxtaposed with Cho Chang who is highly emotional and weepy, something Harry cannot handle very well, wherefore they split up.[116] Extreme emotionality is thus neither endorsed in *Star Wars* nor in *Harry Potter*, although the dangers of it are not as clearly depicted in the latter series and it is rather rendered as slightly comic in the context of adolescent drama.

Ginny is allowed to undergo a development and emerge as an active, self-determined young adult. Although she is not allowed equal status as Harry who only takes Ron and Hermione on his quest in book seven, she does have some degree of individuality. As Limbach notes, she constantly challenges Harry's request for her to stay out of the fight and shows herself to be a powerful witch.[117] After her abuse by Voldemort in book two, she learns from her mistakes and emerges from her toils more grown up and resolute. In this sense it can be said that Ginny, too is empowered by evil. At the same time, however, she is empowered by her own growing sense of self, her choices and her abilities, for example in the field of Quidditch. In fact, Ginny is not the only female character Harry likes and makes friends with for her independence of mind. Luna Lovegood, another close friend of his is not an insecure girl either but a serene young woman with a free will who actively choses the good side and remains loyal to Harry to the very end. Harry, who is more impressed by characters such as Ginny, Luna and Hermione than by passive girls, thus at least implicitly supports female emancipation and strength. This reading is slightly undermined by the fact that Harry tries to keep Ginny out of the final battle against Voldemort, thereby denying her agency and an active role in the fight.

The reading of Ginny thus once more underlines the ambiguity of the series and of popular fiction. Ginny is comparable to Leia who also appears as the object of male desire. While both Ginny and Leia are depicted as rather strong characters, only Leia manages to free herself from her objectification in her symbolic victory

---

114 Rowling *Hallows* 99.

115 As an example, Ann Radcliffe's *The Mysteries of Udolpho* can be given once more. Emily, the heroine is prone to crying which leaves her weak and unfocused. She has to largely overcome her sensitivity to emerge as a balanced and grown up woman at the end of the novel.

116 Cf. Rowling *Order* 496.

117 Cf. Limbach 184-85.

over Jabba. Ginny resists male dominance but is still more subjected to it, especially to her role as Harry's 'Beautiful Soul' than Leia. In yet another twist, however, it needs to be said that female characters are not the only ones objectified. Both the protagonist of *Star Wars* and *Harry Potter* are subject to other people's wishes, projections and desires as much as the girls just analysed. Anakin and Harry are the 'chosen ones' onto whom the wish for freedom of their respective worlds is projected. Thus it finally becomes clear again that ultimately it is not the characters who are important in the two series but rather the themes they embody. In this sense, a certain equality between men and women is noticeable.

The last and unarguably single most important female character in the *Harry Potter* novels to be analysed is Hermione Granger. Much has been said about her and her role in the books. A recent and extremely convincing study of her character is presented by Katrin Berndt who rebuts many of the charges laid against Rowling's depiction of Harry's best female friend. Berndt confirms my claim that sexuality is not of major importance in the novels. Although Hermione's development is filtered through Harry's eyes, which shows that her story is subordinated to Harry's, the readers do not see her as a sexual object because Harry never has any romantic interest in her.[118] This is a notable contrast to Ginny. In this sense Hermione is not reduced to the stereotype of female attractiveness. Berndt goes on to state that her physical features are not considered very important at all, as she is never outwardly described in great detail.[119] Instead, Hermione's inner strengths are foregrounded which are much more essential to the fight against evil than her looks.

Like Harry, Hermione develops in the course of the stories. When we first meet her, her most noticeable characteristic is her correctness. She reminds Ron that he has got "dirt on [his] nose" which shows that she cannot stand disorder and likes everything to be in its proper place.[120] Hermione continues in this vain for some portion of novel one by criticising Harry's and Ron's proneness to rule-breaking. After a few weeks in Hogwarts, Harry and Ron save her from a mountain troll who has been let loose in the school. In the aftermath Hermione, who decides that she rather wants to have friends than keep up her correct, law-abiding attitude, relents a trifle and tells the horrified teachers that their encounter with the troll was her fault. "From that moment on," the narrator tells us, "Hermione Granger became their friend."[121] Already at that early point she manages to set aside her correctness and love for rules for her friends. She knows that there are more important things than

---

118   Cf. Berndt 161.
119   Cf. Berndt 162.
120   Rowling *Stone* 122.
121   Rowling *Stone* 195.

rules and she achieves a balance between her belief in certain laws and the persons enforcing them, in this case the teachers, and her knowledge that rules are there to be broken at times. Hermione never acts unthinkingly and always considers rules and the consequences her actions might have for others, but she also from a very early stage onwards, achieves a certain critical distance from the society she moves in. Partly this is made possible by her status as Muggle-born which gives her an in-depth knowledge of the Muggle world and thus an opportunity of comparison. Her critical distance helps Hermione see injustice and inequality within the wizarding community, a feat she achieves much earlier than the other major characters.[122]

The troll-scene, despite showing Hermione's growth has also particularly been charged with sexism by many critics.[123] It needs to be said, however, that most of the articles lamenting Hermione's role appeared while only the first four books of the series were published. Much of the criticism that was published after the completion of the series especially highlights Hermione's development. Apart from the already mentioned Katrin Berndt, June Cummins and Karley Kristine Adney offer positive interpretations of Hermione, too. Cummins specifically addresses the disputed troll-in-the-bathroom scene. She does not see Hermione as solely the passive damsel in distress who needs to be rescued by men but claims that the scene is one of transformation for her. In Gothic fashion, she argues, "elements of Horror or the Grotesque" are often associated with female development.[124] The troll, she believes stands for Hermione's 'monstrous' side (her bossiness, her extreme law-abiding, her know-it-all attitude) which she needs to shed in order to become

---

122 Cf. Berndt 170. Cf. also the mediating function Hermione takes up according to Bryan Polk as discussed in chapter four. Gregory Bassham commenting on education in Hogwarts makes its "narrow vocational education" responsible for the wizarding world's racial bias (Gregory Bassham, "A Hogwarts Education: The Good, the Bad, and the Ugly," *The Ultimate Harry Potter and Philosophy: Hogwarts for Muggles*, Ed. Gregory Bassham (New Jersey: Wiley, 2010) 220). Hermione is equipped to see beyond her society's structures because she has a wider perspective.

123 See for instance Christine Schoefer, "Harry Potter's Girl Trouble: The World of Everyone's Favorite Kid Wizard is a Place Where Boys Come First," *Salon* 13 Jan. 2000. 10 June 2011 <http://www.salon.com/books/feature/2000/01/13/potter>, and Natasha Whitton, "Me! Books! And Cleverness!: Stereotypical Portrayals in the Harry Potter Series," *WomenWriters* 15 May 2004. 10 June 2011 <http://www.women writers.net/summer04/reviews/HarryPotter.htm>.

124 June Cummins, "Hermione in the Bathroom: The Gothic, Menarche, and Female Development in the Harry Potter Series," *The Gothic in Children's Literature: Haunting the Borders*, Ed. Anna Jackson, Karen Coats, and Roderick McGillis (New York: Routledge, 2008) 178.

friends with Harry and Ron.[125] She needs to leave the bathroom, a space as Cummins claims, typically inhabited by adolescent girls and associated with menarche and menstruation to be able to become active and powerful.[126] "[O]nce she gets past this scene," Cummins says, "[Rowling] no longer needs to position Hermione as a Gothic character or her story as in the Gothic mode."[127] Thus for Cummins, the bathroom scene is one of transformation from 'girly-girl' to strong, active young woman.

Karley Adney remarks on the strong role Hermione plays especially in novel five of the series, *Harry Potter and the Order of the Phoenix*, where she is the most effective agent in the fight against Dolores Umbridge who debars the students from proper knowledge of how to fight the Dark Arts.[128] It is Hermione who constantly questions Umbridge's teaching methods in a way that Umbridge cannot counter. It is also Hermione who comes up with the idea for Dumbledore's Army, the student group practising defensive spells on their own.[129] Furthermore, she advances the enlightenment of the wizarding community about Voldemort's return by setting up an interview between Harry and journalist Rita Skeeter, thereby countering the Ministry of Magic whose representatives are in denial about the the villain's rebirth.[130] Hermione, who early in the series usually seeks to advance her own knowledge, thus becomes the educator of her school fellows as well as the entire wizarding community in book five, which makes her extremely important and powerful.

Hermione has many advantages over Harry and Ron. She is better at school and knows more, because she constantly reads. From the start she is established as an ambitious and well-educated young woman. She can perform spells the other two only dream about and manages complex feats of magic like brewing difficult potions long before they are taught in class. Some people in the novels find that the more surprising because Hermione does not have what they deem the 'proper' wizarding ancestry. She is Muggle-born and Rowling shows herself politically correct in her case since she makes clear that background does not necessarily have

---

125 Cf. Cummins 180.

126 Cf. Cummins 179.

127 Cummins 187.

128 Cf. Karley Kristine Adney, "From Books to Battle: Hermione's Quest for Knowledge in *Harry Potter and the Order of the Phoenix,*" *Topic: A Journal of the Liberal Arts* 54 (2004): 108. See also Janet Brennan Croft, "The Education of a Witch: Tiffany Aching, Hermione Granger and Gendered Magic in Discworld and Potter World," *Mythlore* 27.3-4 (2009): 135.

129 Cf. Adney "From Books to Battle" 109.

130 Cf. Adney "From Books to Battle" 110.

any bearings on development and skills. Hermione's knowledge and ability to reason often helps the trio of friends out of sticky situations. She manages to break through Snape's defensive enchantment guarding the Philosopher's Stone in book one which involves a logical riddle.[131] She also solves the mystery of the Chamber of Secrets in the second book.[132] In their friendship it is definitely Hermione who supplies the brains that are as necessary in their triumph over evil as Harry's emotional abilities. She has to teach the rash Harry patience several times. After Harry has had a vision of Sirius being tortured, she is not convinced that they should all rush off to the Ministry of Magic to save him. She says: "Voldemort knows you, Harry! He took Ginny down into the Chamber of Secrets to lure you there (…), he knows you're the – sort of person who'd go to Sirius's aid! What if he's just trying to get *you* into the Department of Myst—?"[133] At this point she is interrupted by an impatient Harry. She also tries to convince Harry not to go to his birthplace Godric's Hollow in book seven, because she is sure that Voldemort will be expecting them to come there.[134] Once more, she is proved right.[135]

Her ability to reason has not made Hermione a cold person, however. On the contrary, she is always there to help Harry in his adventures and shares his moral ideals. Her emotional support becomes clearest when, against her better judgement, she accompanies Harry to Godric's Hollow in novel seven. When Harry cries at his parents' grave, Hermione just takes holds of his hand and conjures up a wreath of Christmas roses for him to put on it.[136] This shows how close she is to him emotionally. Harry confirms this to a jealous Ron some time later when he says: "She's like my sister. (…) I love her like a sister and I reckon she feels the same way about me. It's always been like that."[137] Hermione is a perfect mythical element since she unites reason and emotion. However, as some critics argue, this balance does not exist from the start. In the first three novels, Hermione frequently embodies gender-related stereotypes as Eliza T. Dresang notes. "Repeatedly Rowling has Hermione 'shriek,' 'squeak,' 'wail,' 'squeal,' and 'whimper,' verbs never applied to the male characters."[138] As time goes by, Hermione lays aside this

---

131　Cf. Rowling *Stone* 306-08.

132　Cf. Rowling *Chamber* 312-13.

133　Rowling, *Order* 647.

134　Cf. Rowling *Hallows* 87.

135　Cf. Rowling *Hallows* 278-79.

136　Cf. Rowling, *Hallows* 269.

137　Rowling *Hallows* 308.

138　Dresang 223. Elizabeth Heilman, too sees Hermione as depicted negatively (cf. Heilman "Blue Wizards and Pink Witches" 227). Marion Rana also shares this negative view on the representation of women in the books (cf. Marion Rana, *Creating*

slightly hysteric attitude and becomes more sober. Katrin Berndt parries Dresang's charge by suggesting that these "so-called weak attributes" rather show Hermione, whose rationality is often stressed, as a balanced character, "a girl who neither feels compelled to suppress her emotions (...) nor is reluctant to act upon them."[139] Much like Harry, and in the fashion of a true mythical mediator she unites stereotypical male and female attributes such as reason, tactical understanding, loyalty and the ability to love.[140] Hermione's depiction thus tries to break free from stereotypical assumptions about the way women are supposed to be, or, as Berndt puts it: "The heptalogy does not show [Hermione] overcoming habits rendered unemancipatory but suggests overcoming the gendered rendering of certain habits."[141] I completely agree with Berndt here. Why is a woman showing her feelings always perceived negatively by feminists? It strongly seems as if the feminists reading *Harry Potter* here advocate 'manly' women who hide or suppress emotions to achieve greater equality. Sarah Zettel has an opinion on Hermione similar to Berndt's: "Hermione does nothing, ever, just because the boys would like her better for it. She does what she does because her own judgement tells her it is right."[142] This, Zettel concludes makes "Hermione Granger (...) a feminist."[143]

Her role resembles Leia's in *Star Wars* as does the whole constellation of the three friends. There are two pairs of brothers and sisters (Luke and Leia who are actually related and Harry and Hermione who are as close as siblings) and a third character who is distinctly jealous but finally wins the female sibling's love (Han Solo in the case of *Star Wars* and Ron in *Harry Potter*). Three, a similarly magical number as seven, seems to be frequent in formulaic stories. Since common sense tells us that three is always a difficult number for a friendship as one could feel left

---

Magical Worlds. Otherness and Othering in Harry Potter (Frankfurt a.M.: Peter Lang, 2009) 78-82).

139   Berndt 166.

140   Cf. also Natalia Gómez Pascual who suggests that "the role subversion of the characters in the novels and the potential dual nature – active/passive – of the Harry/Hermione duo are intended to question behavioural models socially validated." She goes on to ask: "May J.K. Rowling be providing the audience with a conception of the two characters as interchangeable and, therefore, possessing the same heroic qualities?" (Natalia Gómez Pascual, "A Bridge Between Two Different Worlds: On the Reflection and Fracture of Stereotypes in the Harry Potter Novels," *Anuario de Investigación en Literatura Infantil y Juvenil* 5 (2007): 106).

141   Berndt 166. For a discussion of Harry as a "psychologically androgynous hero" see Adney, "The Influence of Gender" 177-91.

142   Zettel 95.

143   Zettel 95.

out, it adds additional tension to the tales as it opens the possibility of one of the party leaving. This is what both Han Solo and Ron do twice in the course of their respective stories only to come back and complete the trios again. Back together the trios can then successfully tackle evil. Hermione's character also resembles Leia's. Like Leia, Hermione contains many attributes that are traditionally associated with men, an analytic mind and a rational take on the world. Harry, on the other hand, like Luke, has many traits that are commonly considered feminine: a big heart and a caring and protective nature. Both stories thus seem to value the fact that a complete human being contains both masculine and feminine attributes. By endowing their male heroes with conventionally female characteristics, the creators of both stories show that they set much store by these traits, at least when they are reasonably employed. After all, the seemingly feminine features like the ability to love, feel compassion and loyalty are the redeeming characteristics of both stories and bring about final victory.

Hermione is essential to Harry's development.[144] Some of her rational abilities seem to have rubbed off on Harry by the time of books six and seven. It is noticeable that she still contributes to the action but she does not solve the riddles alone anymore. Harry partly takes over that function. He tries to find out what Malfoy is up to in book six, for instance, largely without Hermione's help. In novel seven he also contributes as much to their plans to get at the Horcruxes as Hermione. One could thus say that some of her power is taken away from her in the course of the narrative.[145] However, *both* Ron and Hermione lose some of their importance for the actual encounters between Harry and Voldemort when Harry realises that he is the chosen one and has to finish the villain. The fact that already in books one to three, though Ron and Hermione help him, it is always Harry who has to do the final step to solve the mystery on his own, foreshadows his role as single and ultimate destroyer of Voldemort. In the sense that it is Harry, the hero who has to perform the final heroics, Hermione and her power are partly sacrificed to the structures of the story.[146] Maria Nikolajeva, too emphasises Hermione's role as "'merely' Harry's helper – in a Proppian or Campbellian sense" and states "that

---

144 Examples would be the mentioned criticism of Harry's jumping to conclusions after his vision of Sirius in the Department of Mysteries and her telling him off for using the Sectumsempra-curse on Malfoy in book six (cf. *Order* 647, *Prince* 495-96).

145 Both Katrin Berndt (169) and Travis Prinzi, however, emphasise Hermione's resourcefulness at the beginning of book seven, where, as Prinzi says "Harry and Ron are utterly clueless about the way in which to begin the Horcrux hunt" while "Hermione has things well-planned" (268).

146 Cf. Prinzi who says that "[e]ven Hermione's considerable talent and strength are only worth anything insofar as they help Harry's quest" (260).

her special qualities are nothing but the extension of the hero."[147] Mimi R. Gladstein, however, makes an interesting statement about equality in Rowling's novels: "In the world Rowling has created, sex is, as it should be, irrelevant to the question of one's moral fiber."[148] Her view ultimately supports the argument that the woman's question is not as important in the novels as other issues such as moral integrity which is constantly foregrounded in the hero and his friends. In this sense, as was already mentioned, *Star Wars* is a trifle more emancipated, since Luke's friends Leia and Han have more equal shares in the victory over evil compared to Luke than Ron and Hermione in comparison with Harry.

The best example of Hermione's power is that Rowling lets her do something autonomous. When Hermione learns about the injustice with which house elves are treated she decides not to remain silent about it but react. She forms the Society for the Promotion of Elfish Welfare and tries, albeit rather unsuccessfully, to recruit more members.[149] This is astonishing because it is the only action by anyone in the novels that is not in some way or other connected to Harry and does not directly contribute to the solution of a riddle or achievement of a goal. Hermione does not care what Harry and Ron think and that most of her fellow students ridicule her, she carries on with her society and even considers to "take S.P.E.W. further" after she has finished school.[150] Though we never find out what Hermione really does in later life, her commitment to S.P.E.W. at least indicates her independent behaviour and shows that she is likely to model her life the way she wishes. With Hermione's efforts for the house elves, Rowling shows her to have an autonomy even from Harry that other characters do not have. By letting her act independently, Rowling for once and briefly leaves aside the binary structures so much centred on Harry. Katrin Berndt calls this Hermione's very own brand of heroism. Her efforts for the elves show her to be the "only heroic character who confronts the evil *within* the good order,"[151] something that makes her special and sets her apart from other main figures. The fact that she recognises and fights the evil that lies within, makes her powerful because she has a knowledge that others have not. She understands that for Voldemort to perpetrate his evil it needs others who condone it or even have a share in it.[152] She transcends the structures of the wizarding world by looking

---

147   Nikolajeva "A Return to the Romantic Hero" 131.

148   Mimi R. Gladstein, "Feminism and Equal Opportunity: Hermione and the Women of Hogwarts," *Harry Potter and Philosophy: If Aristotle Ran Hogwarts*, Ed. David Baggett and Shawn E. Klein (Chicago: Open Court, 2004) 59.

149   Cf. Rowling *Goblet* 197-98, 210.

150   Rowling *Order* 206.

151   Berndt 172.

152   Cf. also Rothman 213.

through them.[153] As the underlying racism of the wizards' society is a factor that heavily contributes to Voldemort's rise, Hermione has a truly important function in first drawing attention to the problem.[154] She is thus not a character who is completely subjected to the structural framework of the novels. Of course most of her action depends on Harry but it becomes clear that she does have her own ideas about her life and the readers can imagine that she will be successful even without her powerful friend Harry Potter.

When we look at the female characters from *Harry Potter* who were analysed we can also see a development similar to the one depicted for the women in *Star Wars*. The older Mrs Weasley is the one with the more traditionally female role as housewife and mother which however, she transcends, if briefly, at the end of novel seven. The younger female characters Ginny, Luna and Hermione are more active and self-assured. They combine a healthy sense of self which manifests itself in an active stance towards life with 'typically' feminine emotional qualities. It is this mixture Rowling sees as successful for young women. In this sense all of the young female characters analysed fulfil mediating positions and are allowed to survive in the end. In contrast to them the character of Bellatrix Lestrange who is simply egotistical, follows her own aims and is therefore one-sided, cannot succeed.

In certain ways women in both stories are subjected to the structures as male characters take most of the shine. Rowling is more considerate in her depiction of women than Lucas because her tales simply feature more women and depict them as more individualistic, self-contained and active. Both Lucas and Rowling try to emphasise that traits deemed typically masculine *and* traditionally feminine are indispensable and especially stress the importance of traditionally feminine traits such as love, compassion and loyalty by endowing their male heroes with them. This could be read as a message to men saying that to get through life nowadays it is not necessary to become more traditionally masculine, i.e. tougher, harder and more efficient but rather to assume a few traditionally feminine traits such as the ability to feel with others. However, as was mentioned earlier in the chapter, the popular stories also negotiate the anxieties that go along with a change of the masculine role. It seems that as with so many other points analysed so far, 'feminine traits' such as emotionality need to be adopted with care. Balance and not excess is the magic word.

One final point needs to be made concerning women in the novels, however. Quite a few critics have mentioned that Harry himself represents many attributes

---

153   Cf. also Saxena 94-95.

154   Cf. Grijalva Maza 431.

traditionally associated with women.[155] Gallardo and Smith comment on the way in which Harry's story resembles that of Cinderella, and therefore embodies a rather feminine narrative.[156] They point out that Harry even makes a choice in the end of the novels that reinforces this emphasis on the importance of the feminine in the hero. He symbolically rejects male/phallic power when he gives up the Elder Wand and chooses a domestic life instead.[157] It is worthwhile to briefly look at the theme of domesticity as it is also present in *Star Wars*. In contrast to Harry's, Anakin's quest to establish familial bonds is frustrated which Michael Valdez Moses comments in the following way: "Perhaps it will be the visible signature of the post-9/11 epoch that the political and social conflicts that beset the popular hero inevitably frustrate his profound and persistent desire for domestic tranquility."[158] The recent *Star Wars* trilogy emphasises the difficulties and insecurities that are associated with the topic today but by doing so also presents marriage and family as values which are still important and desirable. The older trilogy shows us working family relationships (Leia and Luke as sister and brother and Leia and Han as husband and wife to be) as well as family relationships repaired (Luke and Anakin/Vader), thus cementing the family as a social value. When watching the films in their chronology, they therefore send the reassuring message that family, which is after all ideologically perceived as micro-society, is still functional and provides the basis for personal growth and happiness as well as social prosperity.

The *Harry Potter* novels similarly stress the significance of family by having their hero who searches for true familial ties all through his youth, find domestic bliss in the end and be happy and content with it. The meaning of his name, 'home-ruler' that was discussed in chapter seven acquires another significance in this context, because it not only highlights his potential to rule but also a domestic side to him. Giving up the Elder Wand and thereby rejecting adventure, Rowling finally places greater importance on a quiet, happy and fulfilled life and merges qualities that are stereotypically male (heroism, adventurousness) and female (domesticity)

---

155   Cf. for instance Susanne Gruss's and Karley Adney's essays in Katrin Berndt and Lena Steveker, eds., *Heroism in the Harry Potter Series* (Farnham: Ashgate, 2011) 39-54, 177-92.

156   Cf. Ximena Gallardo-C. and C. Jason Smith, "Cinderfella: J.K. Rowling's Wily Web of Gender," *Reading Harry Potter: Critical Essays*, Ed. Giselle Liza Anatol (Westport: Praeger, 2003) 195.

157   Cf. Gallardo and Smith "Happily Ever After" 104.

158   Michael Valdez Moses, "Blockbuster Wars: Revenge of the Zeitgeist: What Bruce Wayne and Anakin Skywalker Can Tell Us About America's Political Mood," *Reason* (Sept. 2005): n.pag. 15 Jul. 2011 <http://reason.com/archives/2005/09/30/blockbuster-wars-revenge-of-th>.

in her hero. As Casey A. Cothran says: "Rather than sexist, [Rowling's] work struggles to articulate and define the nature of a positive masculinity."[159] Domesticity, often identified as a cliché associated with traditional womanhood, gets a positive ring in both stories, as *male* heroes (Harry, Anakin, Han) are associated with the search for it. Especially in the *Harry Potter* novels it is validated as something that both men and women can aspire to and shape together. Needless to say that the propagation of family and domesticity finally also serves ideological purposes. This is wonderfully illustrated by George Lucas himself who in an interview with Bill Moyers said the following: "Ultimately Vader is redeemed by his children and especially by having children. Because that's what life is all about – procreating and raising children, and it should bring out the best of you."[160] A statement such as this makes one wonder whether Tom Carson is not correct when he says about Lucas that "[his] relationship to his own material's dark side is unwitting, if not stubbornly ignorant. (...)Very little matters to him except his own product, and like a good salesman, he believes in it absolutely."[161] The 'dark side' of the material obviously is its ideological underpinnings of which the propagation of family is one of the more harmless.

Once more, the characters finally have a function in the structure, sell an ideology or prop up certain value systems. As much as Rowling and Lucas attempt to make them credible and round, their efforts are limited by the structures of the stories which by their very nature use characters as vehicles to present certain themes and ideas.[162] Still, some women are rounder, more independent and

---

159   Casey A. Cothran, "Lessons in Transfiguration: Allegories of Male Identity in Rowling's *Harry Potter* Series," *Scholarly Studies in Harry Potter: Applying Academic Methods to a Popular Text*, Ed. Cynthia Whitney Hallet (Lewiston: Edwin Mellen Press, 2005) 131. Mimi R. Gladstein similarly believes, that gender roles are to a certain extend subverted in the novels. "In something of a reversal of the popular stereotype that the male is rational and the female is emotional, Harry and Ron are sometimes masses of emotions, while Hermione is the calm voice of reason." (55).

160   George Lucas, Interview with Bill Moyers, "Cinema: Of Myth and Men," *Time Magazine* 26 Apr. 1999, 16 Jul. 2011 <http://www.time.com/time/magazine/ article/0,9171,990820,00.html>. See also Koenraad Kuiper who says: "Almost all the major episodes in the *Star Wars* trilogy embody imperial myths. The Skywalker family is the nuclear family which is the social unit on which an empire is based" (79).

161   Tom Carson, "Jedi Uber Alles," *A Galaxy Not So Far Away: Writers and Artists on Twenty Five Years of Star Wars*, Ed. Glenn Kenny (New York: Owl Books, 2002) 165-66.

162   This position is supported by Meredith Cherland who applies poststructuralist theory to the gender question in *Harry Potter*. Female characters according to her are caught up

emancipated than others. It seems common in formulaic fiction and film for female characters to embody certain stereotypes such as the 'Beautiful Soul' or the 'angel in the house' or represent ideologies foregrounding the power of love. Examples from *Star Wars* and *Harry Potter* are Shmi, Padmé, Lily, and Ginny. However, true to Cawelti's dictum that the formula needs to be spiced up a bit[163] to keep it interesting, there are female characters who stretch the structural frame, most notably Leia from *Star Wars* and Hermione from *Harry Potter*. Both are remarkably emancipated, also from the male heroes, Leia because she combines romance and political action and is never punished for the latter,[164] and Hermione, because of her important social engagement on the part of the house elves which shows her superior awareness of problems in the wizarding world.

---

in traditional roles such as the temptress, "the achiever" (Meredith Cherland, "Harry's Girls: Harry Potter and the Discourse of Gender," *Journal of Adolescent and Adult Literacy* 52.4 (2008/2009): 277), "the helpful," "the clever," "the just" (278). Hermione, Cherland claims "serves as foil for Harry." (278) an argument that backs up my own about the subordination of discourses such as the one of gender to the heroic quest motif.

163   Cf. Cawelti 10.
164   Cf. Dominguez 113.

9. Individuals, Helpers, and Structural Necessities

9.1 GOOD NATURE VERSUS EVIL TECHNOLOGY: HUMANOID CHARACTERS IN *STAR WARS*

This chapter will explore the roles and functions of humanoid characters in the two stories. Humanoids are taken to be creatures who share certain physical or mental features and/or abilities with humans but on the whole differ significantly from them in looks and/or behaviour. As before, the characters from *Star Wars* will be treated first, followed by a discussion of those from *Harry Potter*. In each story-cycle there is one interesting point which unites the humanoid characters. The humanoids in *Star Wars* are closely associated with the binary opposition between nature and technology whereas those from *Harry Potter* share a precarious social position. These points will serve as basis for the analysis, because they already hint at the fact that once more, characters in the stories are used to emphasise certain themes rather than exist as individuals. It remains to be seen to which degree single or groups of individuals fit in with these structures or transcend them.

Most of the humanoid creatures in the movies are rather unequivocally good or evil. The good humanoids are mostly associated with nature, whereas the bad ones are linked to or dependent on technology. There are a few notable exceptions, though. The Tuskan Raiders or Sand People, for instance, are evil but rather connected to nature as they live in the deserts of Tatooine. There are also exceptions on the other side. The two robots R2D2 and C3PO are staunch supporters of the good side. Five humanoids are particularly significant for the story, as well as two groups, the clones who play a particularly large role in episode II and the Ewoks who help the freedom fighters in their final battle against the Empire in episode VI. The five important individuals, Jar Jar Binks, Yoda, R2D2, C3PO and Chewbacca are 'good' characters without exception. Apart from these individuals, *Star Wars* features masses of humanoid characters predominantly fighting for the evil side (e.g. the armies of battle droids and the storm troopers). These large groups are also closely associated with technology, do not think for themselves and are controlled by the Emperor. This reflects an almost programmatic post-World-War-II suspicion of masses, their proneness to manipulation and their power to inflict harm on a large scale.[1] It can be inferred that once more, *Star Wars*, more strongly than *Harry Potter* focuses on the collective side to evil, the way in which everyone can contribute to its dissemination. The discussion of the major characters already showed that the protagonists of *Star Wars* are less individual than those of *Harry Potter*. While *Star Wars* is thus preoccupied with themes such as the spreading of evil and the determination of people through fate or outward forces, *Harry Potter* broaches the nature of evil and individual responsibility in its generation.

One of the most curious groups of humanoids featuring in *Star Wars* is the clone army. The fascination the clones excite is probably due to the fact that cloning has become a very real possibility in our society and that the clones thus relate to our dreams and fears of what technology can do. This fascination with and anxiety over cloning finds expression not only in *Star Wars* but also in countless other contemporary science fiction novels and movies, even crossing the boundaries of popular entertainment.[2] The clones are ambivalent characters as they change their allegiance midway through the story. The only character who shares this status is Anakin Skywalker / Darth Vader, which assigns the clones some importance as a group and merits a closer look at them. In addition to the clones, Yoda, Jar Jar, Chewbacca, the robots and the Ewoks will be analysed to see whether my thesis that they are subject to the structural corset and evoke binary oppositions such as good – evil, nature – technology, as well as free will – determinism will prove true.

Jedi-master Yoda is a small, green creature with big ears, sparse hair and kindly eyes. In the more recent movies the audience mainly sees Yoda as an important part of the Jedi council. He is the wisest of the Jedi and usually the one to finally take decisions, the one all others look up to. Furthermore, he is calm and level-headed and never needs to raise his voice. Still, he is also a great warrior. At the end of movies two and three, the audience sees him fighting two of the major villains, Count Dooku and the Emperor. On both occasions he does not manage to defeat

---

1   Cultural critic Raymond Williams explains the origin of the term 'masses' and describes how it is employed today, analysing the prejudices implied in the use of the word as well as the bourgeois fears associated with the 'mob' (cf. Raymond Williams, *Culture and Society 1780-1950* [1958] (Harmondsworth: Penguin Books, 1966) 287-89).

2   Examples are the 2005 novel *Never Let Me Go* by Kazuo Ishiguro, recently turned into a film, and the 2005 movie *The Island* directed by Michael Bay.

evil. This is not so much because Yoda's powers are too weak, but because the villains flee, which emphasises his status as thoroughly good. The villains usually only engage those in a fight whom they deem inferior in skill or susceptible to manipulation. Yoda, they have to realise, is neither. He is the one character in the series who is completely stable, who will never be turned away from the good side. This makes him the antithesis of the fickle Anakin and the fixed centre around which the Jedi gravitate. His stability is caused by the balance within his character, another indicator of his being good. It was already mentioned that he is wise, i.e. contemplative, as much as active if necessary. He does not use his power to fight unless it is essential and therefore displays an equilibrium of passivity and activity. Furthermore, he constantly tries to teach his padawan learners humility, calm and acceptance in the face of what life has in store for them.[3] He himself practices this attitude towards life, which aligns him with characters such as Harry Potter and Luke Skywalker and further marks him as truly good.[4] Yoda remains humble and stoic through all the suffering portrayed in the movies. He never condemns even Anakin's horrible deeds of the third film and usually merely comments on events, though some obviously pain him. He indicates this by slowly closing his eyes and lowering his head.[5]

In the older movies, Yoda, who as one of the only two remaining Jedi had to go into exile, has become a hermit on the Dagobah system. When he first appears to Luke, his solitude seems to have made him a little peculiar though one could argue that with his strange behaviour he wants to test Luke's patience which, as he later laments, is not extensive.[6] The scenes on Dagobah show the little green fellow as closely associated with nature, and in a figurative sense, human nature.[7] Yoda is a fitting resident of Dagobah and guide to Luke there, because as the powerful Jedi he is, he knows people's minds and tries to form them. The scenes show that despite his hermitage and solitude Yoda is still exceedingly powerful. They also graphically point out that his power is mainly a mental one and derives from inner resources such as his free will and belief in the Force. He very literally and a little simplistically shows that you can move big things if you only believe in yourself

---

3   Cf. *Revenge of the Sith* 00:32:48.

4   The chapter on Harry Potter and Luke Skywalker analysed the correlation between acceptance, especially of one's own mortality, and goodness and showed that the lack of this kind of acceptance mostly leads to evil.

5   Cf. *Revenge of the Sith* 1:14:05, *The Empire Strikes Back* 1:07:13.

6   Cf. *The Empire Strikes Back* 00:53:22.

7   For an analysis of the Dagobah scenery as an image of the human mind and soul, see chapter seven.

and have enough will power.[8] The scene in which he uses the Force to lift Luke's spacecraft out of the swamp, a device that is at least thirty times his size and weight, shows that his freedom of mind helps him achieve his aims. In a world which is populated with archaic creatures such as snakes and lizards and geographically characterised by swamps and caves, features metaphorically linked with human instincts and drives, Yoda seemingly easily shows how these instincts and drives can be controlled and even bent to one's will.[9]

One of the curious aspects about the figure of Yoda is that despite his power he is, in a sense, powerless. He never manages to destroy evil himself and all he can do is try and impart his philosophy to others. On what they make of it, he never has much influence. It is hard to teach powers which are difficult to comprehend and even more complicated to learn. Many, even of the greatest and most powerful Jedi, fail to completely attain Yoda's wisdom. So while Yoda's power resides in his own strength of will, his powerlessness lies in the fact that he cannot truly influence the ways his philosophy and knowledge will be used by his disciples. Even Obi-Wan cannot completely overcome his resentment and disappointment. And though he becomes wiser with age, he never quite reaches Yoda's pure, stoic acceptance, which is, for instance, shown by the fact that Obi-Wan strongly condemns Anakin/Vader even in the original trilogy when the events of the more recent one lie far in the past.[10] In his accepting attitude to life, Yoda thus stands out.

This is not the only characteristic his singularity hinges upon, however. It is further cemented by the fact that the movies do not feature any other creatures like him. He seems to be without origin. We do not even get to know what tribe or people Yoda belongs to. All the other humanoids (and the human characters, too) have a home planet and some kind of tribe or group they belong to. The planets and the tribes are always named. Yoda is a mystery. As the antithesis to the divided Anakin, he symbolises unity and the transcendence of binary structures. He is obviously meant to represent the supreme spiritual entity of the stories. Yoda partly functions as the centre, the notion of which Derrida identifies as predominant before postmodernism. "Thus it has always been thought that the center, which is by definition unique, constituted that very thing within a structure which while

---

8   Cf. *The Empire Strikes Back* 1:08:58.

9   Galipeau expresses Yoda's binary and at the same time unitary nature in the following way: "Mythologically, because of his close relationship to water, vegetative life, and animals, [Yoda] is closely linked to the symbolism of the Great Earth Mother the elemental, archetypal feminine principle. Yet Yoda also clearly reflects the masculine principle of spirit" (118).

10   Cf. *Revenge of the Sith* 1:55:05.

governing the structure, escapes structurality."[11] Derrida's postulation does not hold completely here because Yoda is part of the structure as very obviously good and exercising the power of his free will. It proves true in other ways, however. The little green creature rises above binaries such as activity and passivity, power and powerlessness, and, more importantly, curiously eludes structurality by its lack of origin and relations, which makes it impossible to place. Yoda seems to be the source of much that happens because he has taught some of the evil (Dooku) as well as some of the good (Qui-Gon, Obi-Wan). His influence, however, as was mentioned, is limited and depends on how his pupils use his teachings. The full ambiguity of myth comes to the fore again in Yoda. He is central in that his teachings form the supreme moral codex of the world of *Star Wars* but he is marginal at the same time, because his philosophy naturally does not reach everyone. Yoda at the same time influences and does not influence the structures of the tale. He is the perfect example of the fact that original unity is boring. He needs to bring both good and evil on its way for the story to exist at all.

As he is the mystical centre of the tale, it is easy to see why Lucas chose him to be represented as a humanoid. A human being would have been less mysterious, there would have been others of his kind and he would have had a traceable and graspable origin. To invest Yoda with his power and simultaneous powerlessness over the story and give him an almost god-like presence, he had to be humanoid and thus fantastic. Yoda's counterpart in *Harry Potter* is Albus Dumbledore, who, in contrast to him is clearly a human being with origins and human flaws despite his tremendous magical skills and wisdom. Dumbledore, though brilliant, is not surrounded by the same aura of mystery as Yoda. Though he is the moral centre of the novels, his being human, i.e. prone to mistakes after all, means that he can more easily be replaced than Yoda, whose complete and flawless wisdom dies with him. In sum, though with Yoda a humanoid has an important position in the movies, his status as a humanoid is also in a way exploited, because it is not an end in itself but has a clear function for the story.

Each of the two trilogies features one single further rather important humanoid character. In the newer one he is called Jar Jar Binks, while in the older movies his name is Chewbacca. Jar Jar, the Gungan is introduced to the audience at the beginning of *Phantom Menace*. He is instantly recognisable as an amphibian kind of creature and indeed it turns out that the Gungans live in an under-water city. Jar Jar is not exactly beautiful nor is he cute or cuddly as Yoda. He has long, flapping ears and large goggly eyes. We meet him in a scene in which he is fleeing from attacking imperial troops and almost running over Jedi Qui-Gon Jinn, who then saves his life. The scene perfectly establishes his character. He is good-natured,

---

11   Derrida *Writing and Difference* 352.

though a little cowardly and, most importantly, he is extraordinarily clumsy. This is something he even acknowledges himself and a character trait that has led to his expulsion from the Gungan society.[12] When he opens his mouth to talk to Qui-Gon, it becomes apparent that he speaks "the most peculiar dialect."[13] The fact that he does not have the correct grasp of the standard language the humans speak, makes him appear infantile and a little ridiculous. It emphasises Jar Jar's status as not quite human, and his flailing arms additionally mark him off as a jester. Some critics have even gone so far as to suggest that Jar Jar's pidgin variety of English shows him to be a parody of an African American.[14] For Kevin J. Wetmore this is aggravated by the fact that Jar Jar's voice and movements are supplied by a black actor.[15] I would not go so far as to see Jar Jar as such a parody, but still, Wetmore's contention raises one important point: obviously, there is a tendency in the films to displace discourses of ethnicity, diversity and multiculturalism and transfer them to humanoid characters. (More on this in the following chapter on the treatment of ethnic minorities in the films and novels). Even if Wetmore's judgement on Jar Jar is too harsh, the Gungan is not taken entirely seriously as an individual. This notion is strengthened by Qui-Gon's treatment of him, which is highly condescending.[16] Apart from infantilising Jar Jar, however, Qui-Gon's behaviour does not let the Jedi appear in a good light as the upholders of peace in the Republic are usually above expressing derision for 'lesser' creatures. This reading slightly undermines the one that is critical of the Jar Jar figure, as it exposes the snobbish ways of the 'superior' white males and makes audiences wonder whether the behaviour of those in power is adequate.

Despite all this, the fact remains that Jar Jar is not treated as an individual in the stories but as a type, someone providing comic relief. He stumbles through much of the action of *Phantom Menace*. In the final battle of the movie, his awkwardness is again used to introduce some comedy into the story. Jar Jar actually defeats many of his droid opponents, though not through valour and decisive action but because of his blundering. He is presented as a coward who rather runs away than putting

---

12   Cf. *The Phantom Menace* 00:16:53.

13   *The Empire Strikes Back* 00:48:19 (C3PO on communicating with the Millennium Falcon).

14   Cf. Wetmore 142, cf. also Estrada 83, Esther Godfrey, "'To be Real:' Drag, Minstrelsy and Identity in the New Millennium," *Genders* 41 (2005): n.pag. 16 Jul. 2011 <http://www.genders.org/g41/g41_godfrey.html>, and Patricia J. Williams, "Racial Ventriloquism," *The Nation* 5 Jul. 1999, 15 Jul. 2011 <http://www.thenation.com/article/racial-ventriloquism>.

15   Cf. Wetmore 143.

16   Cf. *The Phantom Menace* 00:10:56.

himself in the line of fire. Thus he throws adversaries off balance, and catches his foot on one of the battle droids lying on the floor so that its gun goes off and blasts some other droids apart.[17] These are only a few of the stunts he performs. His actions are shown alongside Padmé's and little Anakin's and Wetmore is right when he says that compared to Anakin, Jar Jar as well as Padmé look rather lame and tame.[18] While Padmé is in the midst of action but needs male help to achieve her aim of capturing the viceroy of the trade federation and Jar Jar bungles through much of the battle, accidentally destroying a few enemies, Anakin is the true hero of the scene. Though he is only a child he takes decisive action as soon as he finds himself within the spacecraft. Much of what he does in the scenes happens by accident, too but in contrast to Jar Jar, Anakin actively faces the situation and makes the most of it. He manages to destroy the trade federation's main reactor so that they cannot operate their droids anymore, certainly the good side's most significant step towards victory. The battle scenes from *Phantom Menace* thus already give a very clear indication as to the importance of the various characters. We see Anakin, a white male human and one of the most essential characters of the movies, Padmé, a woman and Jar Jar, a humanoid. Very obviously, Anakin is the most active and effective here. Even as a child, he beats the female and the humanoid characters. The scenes clearly show that *Star Wars* is a series of movies focused on a male human hero and that many of the other characters, though valuable for him to varying degrees, are ultimately of secondary importance. In these scenes, they are even used to enhance and emphasise Anakin's resourcefulness.[19]

Jar Jar Binks is eventually offered a job in Padmé's service. After she has served her term as queen she becomes a senator and Jar Jar her assistant. This is a bit inconsequential since Jar Jar was always deemed rather stupid before. When Padmé has to go into hiding in *Attack of the Clones* because of the attempts on her life, Jar Jar becomes her representative on the senate. The scene in which Padmé tells Jar Jar this, makes obvious that the main characters still do not take the Gungan entirely seriously. When Jar Jar verbosely thanks her for trusting him with this important task, Padmé cuts him short by saying: "Jar Jar, I don't wish to hold you up. I'm sure you have a great deal to do."[20] This in fact translates as: "Jar Jar, don't hold me up, I have a great deal to do." Certainly, in what follows, Jar Jar is not exactly depicted as clever and cunning. Palpatine, later to become the Emperor, exploits the fact that Padmé is gone to stage a vote of no confidence against the

---

17   Cf. *The Phantom Menace* 1:48:56.

18   Cf. Wetmore 147-48.

19   Cf. Wetmore 148.

20   *Attack of the Clones* 00:26:29.

present chancellor and secure himself more powers. Jar Jar is easily persuaded to call for this vote in the name of Padmé. He is in a way empowered by the rise of evil because he becomes involved in politics, but his empowerment ultimately only serves the evil side. From the moment of this vote onwards, Jar Jar does not have any significant scenes anymore. His ascent to the political stage seems to have made him less important than he was when he was accompanying the main characters on their journeys, where he could at least show his kindheartedness and sympathy. Introducing him to politics seems to have been a feeble attempt by the filmmakers to make his role appear more serious and less ridiculous. It seems likely that the producers were influenced to change Jar Jar's role by audience reactions to the humanoid after *The Phantom Menace* was released. The majority of these responses was negative, if not outright hostile.[21] Obviously, the filmmakers were not prepared for such strong reactions to a character they had probably intended as a provider of comic relief. Turning him into a politician is quite an ironic move as it seems to propagate the ideology of the bungling political figure and invites the projection of a general frustration with politicians throughout the Western world. Instead of giving Jar Jar a career in politics the screenwriters might just as well have written him out of the stories completely. Jar Jar is very obviously subjected to the overall structures. His individuality is sacrificed to his comic function. The comedy he provides is supposed to boost the more recent trilogy, which is otherwise quite grave and heavy and lacks the humour of the original one. Jar Jar is never supposed to function as an individual but as a foil for the other characters. As he shows how not to behave, he emphasises the protagonists' bravery and decisiveness.

The original trilogy features the character of Chewbacca, a very tall and hairy humanoid with a dog-like snout who communicates with howling and barking sounds also reminiscent of a dog. And indeed, he is the faithful sidekick to Han Solo, rogue and friend of Luke and Leia. Chewbacca, the Wookie does not speak any intelligible language but like the little robot R2D2, who whistles and bleeps to communicate, Chewie's meaning can be inferred from the situation and from the way he makes the sounds. Chewie is not exactly the character to pick a fight but if

---

21   Cf. for instance a website dedicated to the character with the rather direct title *The Death to Jar Jar Binks Home Page*. 2 Aug. 2011 <http://www.mindspring.com/~ernestm/jarjar/deathtojarjar.html>, and a video uploaded to YouTube entitled "Jar Jar Binks Must Die" (mechayamcha, "Jar Jar Binks Must Die," *YouTube* 2 Aug.2011 <http://www.youtube.com/watch?v=LFcs9hIn_Qs>). Although maybe not without irony these internet reactions might nevertheless have induced those responsible for the movies to change the role of the humanoid and then slowly let him disappear from the story completely. Critic Todd Hanson has also expressed his dislike of Jar Jar (cf. 190-91).

he has to, he fights bravely and loyally. This loyalty and his sympathy for Han, Luke and Leia mark him off as a good character. He is also quite an intelligent humanoid since he is a good pilot and mechanic.[22] In decisive moments the good side would often be worse off without him because his technical knowledge frequently saves the day.[23] Although Jeffrey A. Weinstock interprets Chewbacca as a similarly "nasty racist [stereotype] of black men"[24] as Jar Jar, I believe he is treated better than the Gungan. He is granted intelligence and the power to really help the good characters. He also seems to voluntarily follow Han Solo, while Jar Jar is bound to the Jedi by a life-debt[25] and has something of the noble savage. We never get to know how Chewie and Han met but it is obvious that they are genuine friends. Though Chewie serves as a sidekick to the protagonists, as a true friend he is more equal than Jar Jar. Nevertheless, he, too is subject to the structures as he embodies the nature-technology binary. The audience gets a brief impression of the planet the Wookies originate from in *Revenge of the Sith* when the Wookies serve as a target for the Empire and Yoda rushes to their aid. Although they come from a very natural star, the Wookies are obviously warriors. They constantly wear ammunition belts and carry laser guns. However, as Chewbacca shows, they are essentially peaceful and only fight when they are attacked.

It could thus be said that the Wookies, especially Chewbacca, function as mediators between nature and technology. They are close to nature, which is emphasised (a little simplistically) by the fact that they do not wear clothes,[26] but they are also associated with technology, signalled by their weapons and especially by Chewbacca's mechanical and piloting qualities. In fact, all the good peoples the audience meets in the course of the three movies seem to have maintained their connection with nature and balance a natural with a technological lifestyle. The Gungans, too, though they live in a highly technological city under water and use blasters and laser weapons in battles, return to nature when in danger. As Jar Jar

---

22   Cf. *A New Hope* 00:47:48, *The Empire Strikes Back* 1:26:02.

23   An example would be *Return of the Jedi* 1:41:49. With the help of two Ewoks, Chewbacca enters one of the imperial walkers attacking the good side, defeats the pilots and uses it to destroy further imperial machinery.

24   Jeffrey A. Weinstock, "Freaks in Space: 'Extraterrestrialism' and 'Deep-Space Multiculturalism,'" *Cultural Spectacles of the Extraordinary Body: Freakery*, Ed. Rosemarie Garland Thomson (New York: New York University Press, 1996) 331.

25   As Qui-Gon has saved his life, Jar Jar has to follow him and do his bidding according to Gungan law.

26   Steven A. Galipeau argues that Chewbacca "represents instinctive qualities that Luke still has to come to terms with in himself" (38). The point he makes is congruous with Chewie's closeness to nature and his appearance which resembles an animal.

tells the Jedi and the people from Naboo, who want to find Gungan Big Boss Nass, "When in trouble, Gungans go to sacred place."[27] Chewbacca, although he is treated sympathetically, does not play a major role, predominantly functions as helper for the protagonists and embodies the dichotomy of nature and technology. In this sense, he is a structural feature more than an individual character.

From the more natural humanoids, let us turn to those who are predominantly associated with technology. The clones which feature in the newer *Star Wars* trilogy are curious characters. I would group them as humanoids because although they look like humans and derive their hereditary material from a human, they are technologically created, act according to the wishes of their manufacturers and therefore lack an independent mind. However, this does not identify them as bad from the outset, which is interesting, because usually being determined by another entity/being is a sure sign of evil in the stories. The way the clones are depicted shows that the equation of determinism with evil and free will with good is subtly problematised in the stories. Determination does not necessarily have to be evil; its moral appraisal depends on the way in which someone is influenced. The clones are alternately directed to support the good and the evil side.

On the whole, however, the clones are also used to emphasise free will by negative example. As clones they are humanoid creatures who are completely exploited, whether for good or for evil. They are created as an army for the Republic and used by the good side to fight evil in *Attack of the Clones*. As the cloners tell Obi-Wan, the clones are fabricated so as not to ask questions and fulfill every order unthinkingly.[28] It is astonishing that the Jedi are prepared to use them at all, since first of all, their intelligence should have told them that as the clones act unquestioningly, they are also prone to do the bidding of someone less well-meaning. Secondly, the Jedi themselves preach freedom of mind and attach much importance to strength of will.[29] However, as was already seen in their treatment of Anakin, even they cannot always practice what they preach. Their use of the clones,

---

27   *The Phantom Menace* 1:35:29.

28   Cf. *Attack of the Clones* 00:44:41.

29   Mark T. Decker also wonders about this fact and concludes that part of the evil derives from the fact that "the Jedi [believe] more and more that they need the products of industrial society and [think] in more and more one-dimensional terms" (Mark T. Decker, "They Want Unfreedom and One-Dimensional Thought? I'll Give Them Unfreedom and One-Dimensional Thought: George Lucas, *THX-1138*, and the Persistence of Marcusian Social Critique in *American Graffiti* and the *Star Wars* Films," *Extrapolation* 50.3 (2009): n.pag. <http://lion.chadwyck.co.uk/>). He goes on to say that "the triumph of industrial society over the more humane power of the Force also leads to a political dictatorship with the broad consent of the governed" (n.pag.).

though seemingly made necessary by the desperate situation of the galaxy, is despicable because they actually exploit creatures without will power for their purposes.

As is to be expected, the Jedi's plan backfires. The evil Senator Palpatine, a.k.a. the Emperor to be, has foreseen their use of the clones and has had them outfitted with a special command centre over which he alone has control. In the big fight between the defenders of the Republic and the imperial troops, he tells the clones to fulfill a certain executive order which has them ambush and kill all the Jedi. Of course, they do so unquestioningly.[30] The clones cannot really be made morally responsible for this act of cruelty. They are not created with a conscience. They do not think, they execute orders. Thus, they themselves are not necessarily evil but still constitute another very graphic example of the importance of free will. The masses of clones created to serve a purpose as well as the storm-troopers of the older movies are also supposed to be reminiscent of the masses of people who unquestioningly followed Hitler's regime in the 1930s and 40s. It is not quite clear in the movies, whether the clones become the storm-troopers but in any case, the storm-troopers do not seem to have much of a will of their own, either. Like the clones, they mindlessly do their masters' bidding. While the clones all look the same, their one face representing the unanimity with which an enormous number of people condoned cruelties during the Third Reich, the storm-troopers, whose name is highly allusive, are masked and wear the same uniforms. This also suggests like-mindedness and uniformity of purpose. The clones / storm troopers could be analysed as poststructuralist freedom from structure taken to its extreme. They are completely free from moral conscience which is usually generated by setting up good from evil, a structuralist practice.

Estrada makes another important point respecting the clones that shows the degree to which audience sympathies are directed in the movies: "The dark hordes of dead indigenous cloned men [indigenous because they are played by a Maori

---

30   It is also a common feature of *Star Wars* and *Harry Potter* that whenever the good side does anything that is morally questionable, they pay for it some time later. This is the case with the Jedi's use of the clones. In *Harry Potter* it can, for instance, be noted when Fred and George Weasley stuff a Slytherin into a broken Vanishing Cabinet towards the end of novel five (cf. Rowling *Order* 552).They certainly think that this is fun and just want to get rid of an opponent but their behaviour has grave consequences. The Vanishing Cabinet, it turns out, opens up a connection between Hogwarts, which is supposed to be impenetrable from the outside, and a shop of dark artifacts in Knockturn Alley. Through Fred's and George's action, the Death Eaters find out about this connection and manage to penetrate the school in book six (cf. Rowling *Prince* 548).

actor] are not moaned because they suffer through no ethical struggles as they battle for whatever side controls them. Lucas fails to show that pain is felt by people of all races in war."[31] Like Wetmore before, Estrada sees questions of ethnicity transferred to the humanoids. It seems a little far-fetched to assume that the casting crew consciously chose a Maori actor to fill the role of the clones simply to discriminate against the Maori or any other indigenous peoples. However, Estrada still has a point. The large mass of clones, all looking the same does not invite audience sympathies. Although the clones are dying in large numbers (also for the good side), their deaths are passed by. Since they are all the same, their deaths are not as detrimental as the deaths of any of the individual characters, such as, for instance, Obi-Wan and Yoda. In this sense, the clones stress the importance of individuality and the danger of starting to consider human beings as expendable when there is a possibility of technically producing them in great numbers.

In a way, the clones unite the extremes of determinism and its opposite freedom. They are designed to do someone else's bidding but they are also completely free from the disturbing influence of emotions and moral qualms. Ideology is not necessary anymore to make them pliable. They are ultimately manipulated by technology to buy each and every ideology their employers sell them. Their uniting of binaries is of course completely dystopian and presents the antithesis to, for instance, Harry Potter's way of bringing oppositions together. Harry, too unites determination (the Horcrux within him) and freedom. His mediating qualities are utopian, however, because they include conscious and free decisions. Comparing the clones and Harry, the significance of free will is emphasised once more.

The clones are also a large, if not the main component of the nature vs. technology binary, which is very important in the treatment of the humanoids. While Yoda is completely free and in control of his own nature, the clones are entirely determined from the outside. They are a wonder of technology, a technology which can either be used for good or for evil. The clone wars are a warning against unchecked technological progress. Even the makers cannot always foresee every consequence their creations can have or every use they might be put to. The clones are mediators between a good and an evil way of using technology. Importantly, they show that it is not technology itself that stands on the evil end of the opposition; it is rather technology employed in an evil way. This is reminiscent of the treatment of free will which in itself is not necessarily good and can also be used for evil. Since they belong to the genre of science fiction the six *Star Wars* movies of course abound with technology. The good side uses it as much as the bad side. The Jedi and their adherents, like the Sith fly through space in state-of-the-art

---

31   Estrada 83.

spacecruisers. Like the evil side, they use laser guns and other weapons to fight their enemies. And by taking over the clone army in film two, they accept the use of creatures that can be programmed and manipulated to their wishes, similarly to the droid armies the evil side employs. The technology that is defeated by nature in the form of the Ewoks in the finale of the sixth film is the technology of the evildoers, their speeders, their imperial walkers etc. Ultimately, it is especially the dehumanising use technology can be put to that is criticised in the movies.[32] Thus the clones fulfill a (didactic) purpose. They are supposed to alert audiences to the dangers inherent in technology, even when it initially seems harmless enough. So like Yoda, the clones are exploited for a certain purpose. Humans, because they are not inherently associated with technology, would not have made good examples of the misuse of it.

Instances of the fact that technology is not seen as entirely negative in the movies are the two robots R2D2 and C3PO. I would group them among the humanoids, as their bodies resemble those of humans, though 3PO's more so than R2's. R2, however, still has a trunk, something that resembles a head, as well as arms and legs. C3PO is "fluent in over six million forms of communication,"[33] can think for himself, at least to a certain degree, and take his own decisions. R2 also has a kind of language, though none we can directly understand. His hooting and whistling sounds are mostly translated by C3PO. However, since his whistling is different in quality depending on the situation, the audience can usually infer whether R2 expresses happiness, satisfaction, sorrow, grief or fear. In fact what best qualifies the two droids for the category of humanoids is their ability to 'feel' with the humans and their loyalty to them. Again, their empathy characterises them as good. It can be seen that there are no exceptions to the patterns established for the main characters in chapters five to seven. They apply for the humans as well as for the humanoids.

The two robots even exhibit rather human character traits. While C3PO is not very adventurous and prefers the comfort of home to flying across the galaxy, R2D2 is brave and always willing to be part of an adventure. They are among the only characters who feature in every one of the six films and they are very obviously mediators between the opposing poles of nature and technology. Their sympathetic dispositions make them appear almost human but at the same time both are obviously technical, which is often advantageous for the protagonists, as 3PO and especially R2 help them out of sticky situations numerous times.[34] R2 can, for instance, log into every computer, also on enemy-territory and break codes for the

---

32   Cf. Dalton 92.

33   *Return of the Jedi* 1:08:09.

34   Cf. Sherman 9.

good side. He manages to stop the garbage chute in *New Hope*[35] and when he is attacked, he always has a few surprises in store for his opponents.[36] Hanson and Kay state that "[t]here is a great deal of irony within this role of the droids, because they bring about compassion, humor, and familiarity, without being human themselves!"[37] They come to the conclusion "that humanity is not a physical quality, but a state of mind, and that it is a trait that must be preserved as technology continues to become a part of our daily lives."[38] In the robots, the main qualities that constitute a hero are emphasised once more. It does not matter so much who or what one is, it is important how one treats other people. Both *Star Wars* and *Harry Potter* place communality and cooperation with others in the focus, which seems especially important in times of postmodern alienation.

The droids always accompany the human characters and usually come in when human know-how does not suffice anymore to solve a problem or escape a difficult situation. Thus, as essential as these two humanoids are for the story, they still only function as helper figures for the human characters. It is always very clear who the true heroes are. The robots sometimes take independent action but this is usually focused on helping or saving 'their humans.'[39] Thus the droids, too are dependent on their human 'masters.' Their main function in the story is to destabilise the simplistic 'nature equals good while technology is evil' equation. The Sand People from Tatooine play a similar, though not as important role in the tales. They live in the deserts of their home planet and have a close connection with nature. This does not mean, however, that they are good, too. In fact, they are rather vicious and therefore reinforce the message of 3PO's and R2's roles in reverse. Closeness to nature does not necessarily imply goodness of disposition.[40]

---

35   Cf. *A New Hope* 1:21:10.

36   Cf. for instance *Attack of the Clones* 1:35:19, *The Empire Strikes Back* 1:44:09.

37   Hanson and Kay 417.

38   Hanson and Kay 417.

39   Cf. for example *A New Hope* 1:19:28, *The Empire Strikes Back* 1:44:09, *Return of the Jedi* 1:38:31.

40   Estrada even goes so far as to state that "[w]hile *Episode II* shows that both technologically advanced Republic and 'primitive' tribal cultures can descend to 'savagery,' the film naturalizes the assumption that semi-nomadic indigenous people are more prone to do savage acts" (79). This is correct in a sense, as the Sand People's savagery is depicted as inbred. The audience is not presented with any reason for them to abduct Anakin's mother. They seem to be doing it out of sheer malice. If their cruelty is genetic, however, the question is whether the Sand People can be blamed for their actions. By comparing their atrocities with Ankin's the viewers are led to question the white man's behaviour towards the indigenous population of Tatooine.

A final example of humanoids embodying the opposition between nature and technology are the Ewoks. It is highly relevant that they appear at the very end of the series and that they, unlike the Gungans and the Wookies, do not exhibit a balance between nature and technology. The small Ewoks who help the freedom fighters in their final battle in *Return of the Jedi* are very close to nature and know nothing of imperial technology until the Empire invades their planet. They live in tree huts, carry self-made spears as weapons and worship the golden C3PO as a god immediately upon seeing him.[41] Technology enters their lives in a hostile manner when the Empire starts using their planet as base for generating the energy shield that protects their Death Star. Their aid for the protagonists proceeds as much from a desire to help them as from a wish to protect themselves and their beautiful natural territory. The weapons they use against the highly technological Empire are tree trunks rolling down slopes and off-balancing imperial walkers, stones thrown at the storm-troopers and ropes used to arrest the flight of the enemies' speeders.[42] The Ewoks and their victory over the seemingly almighty galactic Empire are a powerful final image of the films, summing up the debate on the binary of nature and technology which runs through the treatment of the humanoid characters. It is not a coincidence that the Ewoks do not, like the Wookies or the Gungans, use technological weapons. Clear delineations are finally re-established. Nature, and true and pure nature, has to win the battle against technology. However, we need to be precise here. The final battle reinforces what was already said above concerning the nature-technology opposition: It cannot simply be read in terms of good nature and evil technology. The binary is treated in a more differentiated way in the movies. Technology is not viewed as evil per se but its beneficial or harmful consequences strongly depend on the way it is used.[43]

In this light, the final image of the last movie remains: good nature beats bad technology. This strongly reinforces the most important moment of the series, Anakin/Vader's return to the good side, the 'return of the Jedi' in him. Anakin/Vader, too is a mediator between nature and technology, not least because he is half human and half machine, which would even qualify him as a humanoid.

Anakin's mass murder of them is shown to be out of proportion and morally unjustifiable. Anakin's evil is definitely not inbred. He can take moral decisions, which makes his deeds worse.

41   Cf. *Return of the Jedi* 1:07:51. This leads Weinstock to conclude that the Ewoks "play on [a] stereotypical construction of the 'primitive' African pygmy tribe living in the jungle, astounded by the white man's technological 'magic' and too simple to be devious" (333).

42   Cf. *Return of the Jedi* 1:42:47-1:43:22

43   Cf. also Hanson and Kay 331.

In the end, his good nature, too defeats his evil machine shell. This finally makes crystal clear why the humanoid creatures are subjected to the nature-technology dichotomy. In effect throughout the series this binary becomes a metaphor for an opposition within human nature. It reflects a struggle between the better instincts, morals, compassion, love and loyalty on the one hand and greed, hunger for power, hatred and cruelty on the other. The nature versus technology opposition and its final resolution issues a warning not to let oneself become mechanical and hard-hearted.[44] At the same time the end is highly reassuring, true to formulaic fiction, because the victory of good nature comes on two fronts, through the Ewoks on the more general level and through Darth Vader on the more personal one.

Thus one can see that overall the humanoids in the movies and their individuality are sacrificed to structural considerations finally reinforcing (didactic) ideas. However, ultimately, even Anakin/Vader, the originally human character, is subject to them. In this sense, inequality between humanoids and human characters perhaps only exists on a rather superficial level. On the deeper, structural plane of the story, the humanoid and human characters alike often simply stand for ideas. There is another way of perceiving the situation of humanoids in the movies which shows a certain dynamism as opposed to my rather structural reading of them. Christopher Deis sees the Othering of 'aliens' as he calls them, happening as a kind of development. Looking at the chronology of the movies, the newer trilogy features a myriad of alien creatures. The cityscape of Coruscant, perceived as the political centre of the galaxy throughout the new trilogy is teeming with different life forms.[45] These aliens are, however, according to Deis, more and more relegated to the margins of society.[46] "By *A New Hope*, the alien Other has been removed from the center of galactic civilization and literally, as well as symbolically, 'ghettoized' to the hinterlands of the Galactic Empire."[47] Deis's point gives rise to two different interpretations of the treatment of humanoids. Reading the films in

---

44   Cf. also Sherman who says: "There are no mechanized monsters that gain control and victimize mankind, and there are no evil scientists who have perverted humanity. Man's imperfections are exactly that. (...) The terror of a dystopia ruled by a technology run amok is replaced by an image of the real villain – the dark side of man" (9).

45   The Jedi Council with its diverse members is a case in point (see for instance *Revenge of the Sith* 00:35:30).

46   Cf. Christopher Deis, "May the Force (Not) Be With You: 'Race Critical' Readings and the *Star Wars* Universe," *Culture, Identities and Technology in the Star Wars Films: Essays on the Two Trilogies*, Ed. Carl Silvio and Tony M. Vinci (Jefferson: McFarland & Company, 2007) 81-84.

47   Deis 84.

their chronological order, one could say that the gradual and subtle relegation of these characters to the fringes of society naturalises their position as Others. This interpretation would corroborate the one in which the filmmakers rather mindlessly use the 'aliens' to prop up binary oppositions and the themes they want to express through them. When watching the films in the order of their appearance, another interpretation suggests itself. The more recent movies are the ones showing more diversity among humans and aliens and depicting the humanoid characters as natural parts of society. This reading would foreground a move from Othering to a more broad acceptance of diversity and would therefore criticise a binary world view. It is interesting that the two readings of the movies (chronological and in the order of the episodes' appearance) with respect to humanoids and women yield contrary results. While watching the films in the order of their appearance makes the treatment of humanoids look less biased, it is the other way around with the women's question, where the chronology features the strongest woman (Leia) at the end. This shows which social issues are in the focus of attention at a particular time but also once more underlines the mythical ambiguity pervading the films.

9.2 STRUCTURES AND FORMULAS PROMOTING SOCIAL EQUALITY (?): HUMANOIDS IN *HARRY POTTER*

In *Harry Potter* the situation concerning humanoids is different from *Star Wars*, although the novels also contain quite some groups of them, including the giants, the half-giants, the centaurs, the house-elves, the goblins, and the werewolves. The binary between nature and technology does not apply in *Harry Potter*, because technology plays such a marginal role. However, the humanoids in the novels have something in common, too. Nearly all of them are not well respected by the majority of the wizards. They are thus part of a social conflict between dominant hegemonic and dominated group. There seems to be a greater awareness of the social issue of equality with respect to the humanoids than there is in *Star Wars* where at least on the level of the story inequality does not play much of a role. In *Harry Potter* the humanoids are taken as characters in their own right to a greater extent. Inequality is acknowledged already on the level of the narrative. It remains to be seen whether the awareness of inequality stretches to the deep-structures of the novels or whether, as in *Star Wars*, a structural reading will show that the stories elide discourses of equality between wizards and humanoids. In order to find out, the novels' most important humanoids will be discussed. Rowling introduces the readers to at least one exemplary representative of most of the groups mentioned in the course of the stories, which also hints at the fact that she does have a certain agenda with respect to them. In the following Hagrid the half-giant, Winky, Dobby and Kreacher the house elves, as well as Lupin the werewolf will be analysed for the roles they play in the narrative. By acquainting the readers with one representative from each respective humanoid group the narrator manages to bring the plight of these characters, especially with respect to wizards, to the readers' consciousness.

Hagrid, the half-giant is one of the most important humanoid characters in the novels. The only thing that physically distinguishes him from the wizards is his greater size. His full name is Rubeus Hagrid but he is usually called by his last name only. Hagrid does not seem to mind. He is not used to people calling him anything but 'Hagrid,' which becomes apparent when he is angry with Harry in novel six and calls him 'Potter.' Thereupon, Harry resorts to calling him 'sir,' which surprises Hagrid so much that he forgets his crossness.[48] Even Professor Dumbledore uses only Hagrid's last name when referring or talking to him. Although Hagrid does not seem to wish this to be otherwise, it still shows that he commands less respect than the teachers, who are all addressed as 'Professor.' This is remarkable given the fact that he himself is appointed Care of Magical Creatures Professor in Harry's third year. Apart from his teaching duties, Hagrid is the Hogwarts gamekeeper, which means he is responsible for the school grounds and the creatures living in the Forbidden Forest. He loves his job and especially the more ferocious magical animals. Although they are feared by most wizards, Hagrid constantly emphasises that they are simply misunderstood creatures.[49] His commitment to and sympathy with them probably spring from the awareness that as a half-giant he, too is likely to be misjudged by wizards. His care for and compassion with these creatures, but also humans, predominantly Harry, Ron and Hermione, shows Hagrid to be a thoroughly good character.[50]

Since the half-giant lives in a small hut close to the Forbidden Forest, grows his food himself and has no electricity, he, like some of the *Star Wars* characters, is associated with nature in a highly positive way. However, the fact that he lives in a hut without many comforts, wears patched clothes and has a wild and tangled beard also makes him appear slightly primitive especially to characters such as Draco Malfoy and his father.[51] His way of speaking, which does not exactly meet Oxford English standards, adds to that impression.[52] Speech and the proper command of it hence seem to be standards by which the intelligence and social level of certain

---

48   Cf. Rowling *Prince* 215.

49   Cf. for instance Rowling *Order* 394 (Hagrid about the Thestrals).

50   Saxena notices how Hagrid by caring for his magical creatures and also for the children, even acquires motherly characteristics which aligns him with characters such as Mrs Weasley (cf. 55, 149).

51   Cf. Rowling *Stone* 88, *Chamber* 283.

52   Cf. Mendlesohn 166.

characters are judged. Hagrid is viewed sympathetically but is still marginalised. This was already found to be true for Jar Jar Binks from *Star Wars*. In addition Hagrid is not a fully trained wizard, a fact that increases the condescension with which some wizards treat him. In his third year at Hogwarts he was hoodwinked by Tom Riddle, a.k.a. Lord Voldemort, expelled from school and forced to snap his wand in two.[53] This means that Hagrid is in fact disempowered by evil. However, he does not let Voldemort's lie destroy his life. He seems to like his job as Hogwarts gamekeeper and he is not forced into passivity by Voldemort's act. On the contrary, he is an ardent supporter of the good side and fights to the end. Still, his origins and history lead some wizards to believe that they are better than Hagrid.

His status as a half-giant of course adds to this. Harry and Ron only find out about Hagrid being a half-blood in novel four when at the Yule Ball they overhear a conversation between him and Madame Maxime, the other half-giantess in the stories. This conversation is very telling with regard to the standing of half-giants. First of all, while Hagrid is honest about his origins, Madame Maxime, on being asked about her heritage, indignantly claims that she has "big bones" and rushes off.[54] Obviously, being a half-giant in the wizarding community is not easy and Madame Maxime rather denies this truth. In this situation readers are definitely not led to empathise with Madame Maxime. Since she treats Hagrid, a likeable character in a very unfriendly way here, readers do not tend to think highly of her at that moment. The text does not directly ask them to stop and consider that it might be society at large that forces her to deny her heritage. This wider view, however, going beyond Hagrid's and Madame Maxime's personal situations, is quickly evoked by Ron's telling reaction to the revelation. While Harry does not care about the fact that Hagrid has a giantess as a mother, Ron echoes the wizarding community's prejudice about giants: "Well, they're ... they're... (...) not very nice."[55] The readers are thus directly confronted with the stereotypes about giants by the fact that even Ron, whom they like and who is friends with Hagrid, seems to mind the fact that Hagrid is 'different.' As Karin E. Westman says: "Making her target the formation and replication of ideology rather than prejudice per se provides Rowling with the opportunity to show how contemporary cultural opinion becomes naturalized as truth."[56] Ron has imbibed all the ideologies at the root of the

---

53   Cf. Rowling *Stone* 69, *Chamber* 299-300.

54   Rowling *Goblet* 373.

55   Rowling *Goblet* 374.

56   Karin E. Westman, "Specters of Thatcherism: Contemporary British Culture in J.K. Rowling's Harry Potter Series," *The Ivory Tower and Harry Potter: Perspectives on a Literary Phenomenon*, Ed. Lana A. Whited (Columbia: University of Missouri Press, 2002) 315. Cf. also Steven W. Patterson, "Kreacher's Lament: S.P.E.W. As a Parable

wizarding society and he repeats them unthinkingly even while knowing Hagrid's character, showing the extend to which these prejudices are 'naturalised' in the sense of Barthes.[57] Before this scene, the category of 'half-giant' has never been invoked. Readers might have briefly asked themselves at the beginning of the story why Hagrid is so extraordinarily big but quickly pass this question by and take him for granted as a friendly and benevolent character. It is a trick of Rowling's to first of all introduce the readers to Hagrid's good character before confronting them with the truth about his origins. Hagrid is given the chance to show all his good traits before he is stigmatised. When he is, it does not much matter anymore. Even Ron quickly forgets Hagrid's status and good Harry is not very interested in it in the first place, since he clearly sees Hagrid as a friend rather than someone belonging to a certain category.

Rowling's depiction of Hagrid and Harry's reaction to him make two points clear. First, Hagrid underlines Harry's sporting nature. His unquestioning acceptance of Hagrid, especially compared to other characters, who are not as tolerant, establishes Harry as a behavioural model. His goodness is emphasised through Hagrid.[58] This is problematic to a certain extent as Harry's incomplete understanding of social conflicts and their bearings for the larger war they are fighting, distracts readers' attention from them, too. So Harry's attitudes and conduct can only be praised on a rather personal level. Secondly, Rowling prefers persons to be judged according to their behaviour with respect to others and their choices rather than their origins or blood. Her approach to the gamekeeper supports her negative view of the racial ideologies advocated by Voldemort and his cronies. While the evil characters believe that 'racial' or genetic markers influence a person's character, Rowling's treatment of Hagrid refutes this theory. His origin as a half-giant has no bearing whatsoever upon his character and his friends know that he is good by the time they find out about his heritage. Thus, his parentage plays no, or in Ron's case, at least no lasting role in their evaluation of him. In this sense, Hagrid is treated differently from, for example, Jar Jar in *Star Wars*. While Jar Jar is presented as a clown throughout and his ineptitude is emphasised, Hagrid is

---

on Discrimination, Indifference, and Social Justice," *Harry Potter and Philosophy: If Aristotle Ran Hogwarts*, Ed. David Baggett and Shawn E. Klein (Chicago: Open Court, 2004) 113-17 for a logical analysis of why discrimination is often at the root of bigger problems in society.

57   Cf. Barthes 21. Cf. also Saxena 99.

58   Cf. Mendlesohn 166, and Marion Rana, "'The less you lot have ter do with these foreigners, the happier yeh'll be': Cultural and National Otherness in J.K. Rowling's *Harry Potter* Series," *International Research in Children's Literature* 4.1 (2011): 46.

allowed to prove himself as loyal and brave time and again.[59] Thus Rowling treats her characters more justly than Lucas by advocating an attitude of seeing the best in people rather than the worst.

This is one side to the depiction of Hagrid, the one that makes clear that character is not supposed to be judged according to its flaws, 'racial' or genetic make-up. The other side to his treatment, however, basically shows that Hagrid is not equal to the wizards. He is not a fully trained sorcerer, he does not have a 'proper' house, does not speak 'proper' English and he very literally lives outside the inner circle of the Hogwarts society on the edge of the Forbidden Forest. All the other characters who appear during the time when Harry is at school live at Hogwarts and are therefore part of the school's community. Though Hagrid appears within the school building once in a while and also takes part in the banquets, he is somewhat marginalised. Even if his post is upgraded to include teaching, he is notably different from the other teachers who are almost all depicted as highly skilled, well-dressed and outfitted with authority. In concurrence with this, it is obvious that Hagrid, as individually as he is pictured, does have certain functions within the narrative that mainly revolve around the hero Harry.

Hagrid's cabin is not only placed close to the Forbidden Forest to show Hagrid's slightly marginalised position. The forest on the Hogwarts grounds represents the Other to the wisdom and rationality that reign within the school. In the forest, the characters are often confronted with their deepest fears. Harry, for instance, faces Voldemort there twice, once in his first year and once in novel seven.[60] Ron, who is afraid of spiders, meets giants arachnids in there.[61] Apart from evil, the forest also hosts good creatures, such as the unicorns, the thestrals and the centaurs. Similar to the planet Dagobah in *Star Wars*, the Forbidden Forest thus stands for the human mind and all its nooks and crannies. Hagrid is a character who travels both worlds, the rational one of the school and the rougher, more emotional one of the forest. He lives on the threshold of the worlds and functions as a mediator between both. He sometimes even accompanies the children into the forest, for example in novel one, when they have to do a detention in there,[62] thus helping them on their way to confronting and defeating their fears. This makes Hagrid's role partly resemble Yoda's who also serves as a guide in the symbolic

---

59   At the end of novel five, for instance, Hagrid tries to defend Professor McGonagall against Dolores Umbridge and her henchmen from the Ministry (cf. Rowling *Order* 635-36). In book seven, he helps getting Harry safely away from Privet Drive (cf. Rowling *Hallows* 51-57).

60   Cf. Rowling *Stone* 277-78, Rowling *Hallows* 563-64.

61   Cf. Rowling *Chamber* 296-301.

62   Cf. Rowling *Stone* 268-81.

landscape of Dagobah. Hagrid's closeness to the animals in the Forbidden Forest also fits this interpretation and symbolises his association with the more instinctive, animal parts of human beings. Fittingly, it is furthermore the case, as Julia Eccleshare states, that Hagrid's cabin presents an emotional refuge for the protagonists, who very often come there to escape the crowdedness of the school for some hours or because they need a respite from the taunts of their classmates.[63] Problems such as the children's worries about the Philosopher's Stone, Hermione's status as a muggle-born as well as trouble with their friends, find expression in Hagrid's hut.[64] And although Hagrid might not always have a solution to their quandaries, he listens and offers comfort when necessary. He is the adult they are closest to at school, because Hagrid is not as forbidding as Professor McGonagall and not as remote as Dumbledore. Thus, Hagrid is not only a mediator between reason (the realm of the school) and emotion/instinct (the forest) but also between the children and the adults.

The ambiguity of myth comes through again with respect to Hagrid. On the one hand, by telling Hagrid's individual story, the narrative does draw attention to the problems of minorities, and makes clear what Rowling believes to be the correct way of treating other people. On the other hand, Hagrid, despite all his individuality, is subjected to the structures of the tale, because he has clear functions with respect to Harry, the main and most important character. While he is there to underline Harry's goodness and righteousness, his own importance as an individual is limited.

Another group of creatures that is not well treated by most wizards, is the group of the house elves. They are positively enslaved by wizards and cannot leave their masters' service unless they are given clothes.[65] Most elves, however, dread such a situation because it is deemed shameful to lose one's job in that way.[66] Furthermore, the elves to whom this happens, do not seem to really know what to do with themselves and their freedom and are lost in a world they cannot navigate on their own. Only very old and rich wizarding families 'own' elves.[67] As a matter of fact, the three exemplary elves the readers meet in the course of the novels, belong to some of the most unpleasant families the stories feature. Dobby, the first house elf the readers get to know, belongs to the Malfoys, Winky works for Mr Crouch, an overly correct and bossy person, and Kreacher and his ancestors have

---

63   Cf. Julia Eccleshare, *A Guide to the Harry Potter Novels* (London: Continuum, 2002) 60.

64   Cf. Rowling *Stone* 250-52, *Chamber* 127, *Azkaban* 297.

65   Cf. Rowling *Chamber* 193.

66   Cf. Rowling *Goblet* 124.

67   Cf. Rowling *Chamber* 36.

served the Black family for ages. Most of the members of these families are snobbish and look down on others. Thus it is only logical that they 'own' servants who take care of their household duties and whom they can boss around. The families who keep house elves are also all so-called pure-blood families. The fact that it is these high and noble families who enslave other creatures is not a coincidence. They are the same ones who also look down on Hagrid and other half-bloods. By their hierarchical notions and belief in blood-status as a marker of good breeding and character, they justify their foul treatment of others. Rowling strongly condemns these racial ideologies and the consequences they have for other people and creatures, notably through her depiction of humanoid characters such as the house elves.

The three house elves introduced in the novels all suffer different fates. Winky of novel four serves her master loyally. Her ancestors have been in the Crouch household for decades and she considers it an honour to work for him. However, when Winky does not meet Crouch's expectations, he fires her and leaves her desperate and inconsolable. He only thinks about his own good name and does not spare one thought for the elf and her further life, while Winky still remains loyal to him.[68] Indeed, she finally lands at Hogwarts but is unhappy and takes to drinking.[69] The school, readers learn in novel four, keeps over 200 house elves who prepare the sumptuous meals and clean the students' rooms. The irony of this is not lost upon Hermione, who makes sure that the readers notice the incongruence between what Hogwarts stands for under Dumbledore, namely free choice and goodness, and the fact that scores of creatures are enslaved in its bowels.[70] The fact that the good and enlightened Hogwarts keeps house elves, and even in great numbers, shows that the relationship between good and evil is never simple in Rowling's novels. The readers never finally learn what becomes of Winky and whether she manages to overcome her addiction to butterbeer. In fact it is curious that the only one of the three exemplary house elves whose fate is not resolved and who persistently resists her freedom, is female, whereas Rowling depicts such strong women among the humans.

In comparison with Dobby and Kreacher, who will be analysed next, Winky appears weak and pathetic. She is the example of a truly victimised house elf who has been brainwashed and is henceforth unable to live her own life. However, her story has an important function. It triggers the sole plot strand in the novels which is not directly connected to Harry and his fate. Hermione, the novels' strongest woman, takes pity on Winky and after hearing about the house elves at Hogwarts

---

68   Cf. Rowling *Goblet* 331.

69   Cf. Rowling *Goblet* 466.

70   Cf. Rowling *Goblet* 161-2.

forms the Society for the Promotion of Elfish Welfare.[71] The fact that the only action that Harry is not directly part of and that is not performed because of him, is an act of social awareness, is highly significant and makes clear how important fellow feeling and the fight against injustice and inequality are for Rowling. As Brycchan Carey suggests, Rowling contrasts two ways of dealing with social problems as exemplified by the elves: Harry's rather personal involvement with individual elves on the one hand and Hermione's public espousal of their cause on the other.[72] Jackie C. Horne expresses a similar opinion. She links Harry's personal commitment to single house elves to 'multiculturalism,' an "approach to antiracism [that] focuses on individuals learning about others and about their own biases."[73] Hermione's more political activism she holds, is similar to 'social justice antiracism,' the realisation "that racism lies not only in individuals, but also in institutions that grant privileges and power to certain racial groups in a society, and restrict other racial groups from the same."[74] Horne goes on to say that "[i]ntriguingly, one can find traces of *both* a multicultural *and* a social justice approach, as well as the tensions between them, in the seven books."[75] Thus, she, too perceives the ambiguity underlying Rowling's works with respect to many of their important themes. Once more, a binary – the one between public and private – is operative on the structural level and again Harry finally functions as Lévi-Straussian mediator when he brings personal and public spheres together in his ultimate fight against Voldemort. However, one might say that Harry remains an incomplete mediator in this respect. As was mentioned before, Harry's personal approach to tolerance and acceptance is still favoured. The problem this generates is that structural racism is not fully recognised by most of the protagonists and thus the readers.

House-elf Winky, whose individual fate is not important enough to be mentioned again after triggering Hermione's action, is finally subordinated to the structures of the novels as she is to the structures of the wizarding world, since she does not stand as a character in her own right. Her function is to help bring the discourse on justice and equality running through the novels to the readers' attention. Ron, who is not at all convinced by Hermione's commitment to the liberation of house elves, mentions several times that the elves "*like* being

---

71   Cf. Rowling *Goblet* 198-9.

72   Cf. Carey "Hermione and the House-Elves" 105.

73   Jackie C. Horne, "Harry and the Other: Answering the Race Question in J.K. Rowling's Harry Potter," *The Lion and the Unicorn: A Critical Journal of Children's Literature* 34.1 (2010): 79.

74   Horne 79.

75   Horne 80.

enslaved."[76] This shows again that good and evil is not a simple matter. Those who enslave the creatures and deny them respect are certainly evil. But what about those who silently acquiesce in their treatment and repeat the stereotypes in circulation about them such as Ron who is definitely not a bad character? (Note that he is also the one who perpetuates the prejudices about giants). Hermione, on moral high-ground in this case, decisively answers this question by saying that "it's people like *you*, Ron (…) who prop up rotten and unjust systems, just because they're too lazy to –," at which point she is interrupted.[77] Terry Eagleton would not be too hard on Ron. In his work *On Evil* he differentiates the truly wicked from those who contribute to evil through a lack of knowledge or the belief that they are acting for the best. The latter, he believes are influenced by "forms of wickedness (…) built into our social systems" whose ideologies they might not completely see through.[78] Both Hermione and Ron have important functions for the story in this sense. While Ron stands for the unquestioning continuation of stereotypes representing the uncritical mass of society and thus a largely unwitting form of evil,[79] Hermione embodies social responsibility and political consciousness. Since in many cases throughout the novels, Hermione's judgement and appraisal of situations is sounder than Ron's, the readers are inclined to think about her exertions for the house-elves, despite Ron's best efforts to ridicule her.

The destinies of Dobby and Kreacher, the other two important house elves, are different. Dobby is a special elf from the start. He is introduced to the readers as early as novel two and reappears in books four, five, six and seven. Doubtlessly, he is one of the humanoid creatures treated with most warmth and sympathy in the stories. When Harry first meets Dobby in his bedroom at 4 Privet Drive, the elf warns Harry of evil things about to happen at Hogwarts the following year and urges him not to return to the school.[80] For telling Harry this, Dobby has to punish himself by banging his head against the wall. The bonds with the wizarding family he serves are very strong and elves are not supposed to divulge their masters' secrets.[81] When Harry meets Dobby again in the hospital wing at Hogwarts, he learns that the little elf has tried to prevent him from returning to school with all his might. Even when he has already arrived for his second year of schooling, Dobby

---

76   Rowling *Goblet* 198.

77   Rowling *Goblet* 112.

78   Eagleton 144-45.

79   Cf. Rothman's contention that the worst evil in the novels does not emanate from Voldemort but from those who follow and support his ideologies, wittingly or unwittingly (213).

80   Cf. Rowling *Chamber* 22.

81   Cf. Rowling *Goblet* 331.

attempts to get him home again. Harry is not happy about this but Dobby tells him that he is "too great, too good to lose"[82] and that because of his triumph over Voldemort he means hope to the house elves, too.[83]

The two scenes are highly revealing concerning Dobby's character. First of all, he is protective and caring, even about someone (Harry) he has never met before. This aligns him with other good characters from both *Star Wars* and *Harry Potter* who exhibit compassion and an urge to help fellows in need such as, for instance, C3PO, R2D2 and Hagrid. Secondly, Dobby is obviously aware of and averse to the socially unjust treatment of the elves. This becomes clear when he acknowledges Harry's importance as the vanquisher of Voldemort even for the enslaved and brainwashed creatures. Dobby leaves no doubt about the fact that he does not like the family he works for and is unhappy with his life, even though he has to punish himself for acknowledging this.[84] The third, and most significant thing the readers learn about Dobby in Harry's first two encounters with him, is that despite his status as a slave and in contrast to, for instance, Winky, the elf is capable of free and independent thought and action. Seeking Harry out costs Dobby much as he will have to punish himself for it, to say nothing of the chastisements that await him if his family ever finds out. Along with his empathetic nature, this connection to free will employed for the good, cements Dobby as a benevolent character even further. Nevertheless and in spite of his individuality, the house elf is still subjected to the structures of the narrative. Dobby's story in *Harry Potter and the Chamber of Secrets* follows a well-known fairy-tale pattern: a poor and enslaved creature helps a powerful person and is in turn rewarded for his help. Harry finally frees Dobby from the Malfoys' clutches.[85]

His role has a further purpose, however, which closely resembles one of the functions Hagrid has for the story. Dobby is another of the characters who help to set Harry up as irrevocably good. When the house elf first comes to Privet Drive to warn Harry of the danger of returning to Hogwarts, Harry, not heeding the fact that he will be in trouble if Uncle Vernon finds out about Dobby, asks the elf to sit down and make himself comfortable.[86] Dobby's rather noisy sobs of gratitude and his exclamations that he has never been offered a seat by a wizard, emphasise Harry's benign nature. All the same, it seems as if Rowling exaggerates this scene a little. Dobby is a bit too awe-struck by Harry, a twelve-year-old boy after all, and his hero-worship is blown up out of proportion. Ostry contends that Dobby's "slavish

---

82   Rowling *Chamber* 22.

83   Cf. Rowling *Chamber* 194.

84   Cf. Rowling *Chamber* 19-20.

85   Cf. Rowling *Chamber* 362-63.

86   Cf. Rowling *Chamber* 19.

adoration of Harry is played for laughs and underscores his essential slave nature."[87] I strongly disagree. The elf's profuse admiration is not so much comic as a little uncomfortable. Dobby, hence, has a leveling function. He grounds Harry who is embarrassed by Dobby's excessive reverence and at the same time gives the readers a chance to distance themselves from the hero's role to a certain degree. What, in fact has Harry done yet, especially for the house elves, to merit Dobby's devotion? Dobby, as can be seen, is presented with the ambiguity typical of myth in novel two. On the one hand, he is a free-thinking individual but on the other hand he has a few clearly defined structural functions. The end of the second book, however, is not the end of his actual story. From book four onwards, Rowling lets the readers see what happens to Dobby after his happy ending in novel two and thus breaks through the fairy-tale pattern established for him. In fact not everything is 'happy ever after' for Dobby who finds it hard to get a job after being freed from the Malfoys.[88] When he finally lands at Hogwarts, the other elves are wary of him, because he demands pay and a few days off a month for his services.[89] Once more, the story slightly questions the structural corset it is itself set up around. What has begun as a fairy-tale ends in real life.

Despite this structural break, Dobby then acquires a fairy-tale role once more. In the course of novels four, five and six he makes the odd appearance but very obviously serves as a structural feature. He leaves his own fairy-tale and enters Harry's. From the moment Harry sets him free, Dobby becomes his voluntary servant and a typical fairy-tale helper figure.[90] In book four he provides Harry with Gillyweed which helps him succeed in the second task of the Triwizard Tournament.[91] When Harry and his friends do not know where to practice Defence Against the Dark Arts so that Professor Umbridge does not find them in the fifth novel, Dobby comes up with the idea for a room.[92] And in novel six, he assists Harry in finding out where Draco Malfoy, whom Harry suspects of doing mischief, is disappearing to.[93] Finally, in the last instalment of the series, Dobby does something that encompasses and surpasses his former acts of kindness. He actually sacrifices his life to rescue Harry, Ron, Hermione, Luna, Dean and the goblin

---

87   Ostry 96. Marion Rana shares Ostry's negative evaluation of the elves' representation in the novels (cf. *Creating Magical Worlds* 48).

88   Cf. Rowling *Goblet* 329.

89   Cf. Rowling *Goblet* 329-30.

90   Cf. for instance Campbell *The Hero* 69-73 who describes the role of the 'supernatural' helper in myths.

91   Cf. Rowling *Goblet* 425-27.

92   Cf. Rowling *Order* 342-43.

93   Cf. Rowling *Prince* 422-24.

Griphook from Malfoy Manor where they are about to be handed over to Voldemort. Structurally, he thereby becomes the ultimate helper figure. However, he also finishes his own little heroic tale within the tale. Dobby is quite as much the hero as Harry and is prepared to go through with his adoration for 'the boy who lived.' Harry in fact acknowledges this by burying Dobby without magical assistance and by thinking that he should have had a funeral as pompous as Dumbledore's.[94]

In this sense Dobby's story in a way rivals Harry's because up to that point, Harry has been in mortal danger but has not yet faced a situation in which he truly had to consider sacrificing himself. When the time comes, Harry needs to summon the same courage and be as selfless as Dobby. This means that the elf's story also mirrors and foreshadows Harry's own, as Harry, too will eventually have to take the decision to sacrifice himself for his loved ones.[95] It is obvious that Dobby is closely entangled with the stories' structures. Foreshadowing Harry's sacrifice and closely mirroring the young wizard's heroics, Dobby's story serves to emphasise one of the most important themes of the novels: sacrificial love. However, Dobby's final act of coming back to his old masters' house, of ultimately shedding his fear of and dependence on the Malfoys, is also and very predominantly an act of great bravery, strength of character and independence of mind which partly disproves Ostry who holds that Dobby is ultimately a slave.[96] Thus at the same time as completing Dobby's story in correspondence with a typically heroic structural pattern, in his last minutes, Rowling also shows him as an individual who has finally triumphed over determinism. Brycchan Carey who sees Dobby as "merely a commodity whose life is expendable, a statistic in a wider struggle, whose mind-forged manacles prevent him from truly acting as a free agent,"[97] is thus only partly right. Dobby is a structural entity but he is also a heroic and ultimately free individual. This is in line with the mythical ambiguity of the story and truly connects the elf with some of the most important characters of both stories, such as Anakin Skywalker, Luke Skywalker, Obi-Wan and Harry Potter.

House elf Kreacher's story is very different again and it involves Harry almost as much as Dobby's. Kreacher and all his ancestors were house elves in the Black family. The readers get to know him in book five, when the Order of the Phoenix moves into Sirius' house at number 12 Grimmauld Place to use it as headquarters.

---

94   Cf. Rowling *Hallows* 387-88.

95   Travis Prinzi also argues that Dobby's death is one of the strongest transformative moments for Harry, that prepares him for the role he will have to play at the end of the novel (cf. 96).

96   Cf. Ostry 96.

97   Carey "Hermione and the House-Elves Revisited" 167.

Kreacher is a highly unpleasant character, constantly muttering insults under his breath to the "mudbloods and bloodtraitors" who have infiltrated the house of his "poor mistress."[98] Sirius treats him with contempt and Harry and the others do not like him either. Only Hermione feels pity for him, despite the insults he throws at her. Thus, interestingly, the figure of Kreacher shows that Harry is not always the wonderful boy that characters such as Hagrid and Dobby suggest he is. He does harbour grudges and dislikes as much as any other person. Like Dobby, Kreacher thus obviously has a levelling function. To become a perfect hero, Harry needs to overcome his egotism. He cannot only be a hero for those who like Dobby respect and admire him but also has to reach those who are not favourably impressed by him such as Kreacher. This interpretation is strengthened by the similarities between Dobby's and Kreacher's actions. Both leave their employers for a while to serve those who possess their true loyalty, the difference being that Dobby leaves the bad Malfoys to help Harry, whereas Kreacher initially chooses the side of evil over good.[99] Structural movements thus clearly play a role in the treatment of the elves and they partly have an educating function for Harry and the readers.

At the end of book five Kreacher plays a part in the conspiracy that leads to Sirius's death. Therefore, when Harry inherits his godfather's house and Kreacher at the beginning of novel six, he expresses his dislike of the elf and rejects him. He sends him to work in the Hogwarts kitchens without second thoughts about Kreacher's feelings.[100] In this instance Harry's actions do not differ much from Mr Crouch's who sends Winky away without considerations for her wellbeing. It is implicitly suggested that Harry needs to change this attitude and learn to pity all creatures ('Kreachers'). Meanwhile, Kreacher unsurprisingly keeps up his hostile attitude towards Harry, when he is summoned to spy on Draco Malfoy. Of course, he is unwilling to tell on "the Malfoy boy," who represents the pure blood-line Kreacher so admires, which angers Harry even further.[101]

In novel seven, however, there is a turning point in the relationship between the two. Harry, Ron and Hermione return to Grimmauld Place to start their search for the Horcruxes. When they realise that while cleaning the house two years earlier, they saw a locket which qualifies for one of the Horcruxes but unknowingly threw it away, Harry summons Kreacher to question him about it. Kreacher breaks down and tells them the horrible tale of how he saw his beloved master Regulus Black,

---

98   Rowling *Order* 101-102

99   Cf. Kathryn N. McDaniel, "The Elfin Mystique: Fantasy and Feminism in J.K. Rowling's *Harry Potter* Series," *Past Watchful Dragons: Fantasy and Faith in the World of C.S. Lewis*, Ed. Amy H. Sturgis (Altadena: The Mythopoeic Press, 2007) 199.

100   Cf. Rowling *Prince* 55.

101   Cf. Rowling *Prince* 423.

Sirius's brother, die while trying to destroy one of Voldemort's Horcruxes.[102] Watching Regulus die made Kreacher almost mad with grief. When Harry wonders why Kreacher was prepared to betray Sirius to Voldemort, Hermione interjects and graphically explains how the bonds between master and elf work. The elves do not care for the ideologies their masters might advocate. They are loyal to those who treat them kindly. Regulus was kind to Kreacher, and the Death Eaters whom he approached to tell on Sirius must have been so, too.[103] Sirius, who did not like the elf, though he certainly had his reasons, reaped the reward for his behaviour towards Kreacher. Hermione goes on to suggest that Kreacher did not even fully understand that Regulus tried to bring down the Dark Lord. Regulus did not tell him any details to protect him and his family.[104] This ideological enslavement of the elves is indeed problematic, because, as Farah Mendlesohn points out it denies the elves "self-liberation" and "absolves them from responsibility."[105] This in some ways aligns them to the clones from *Star Wars* who also unquestioningly do their respective masters' bidding. The elves are utterly dependent on the kindness or caprices of their owners. Suman Gupta stresses the implication of this dependence: "[T]he anti-racism and tolerance that exists in our world [would be] essentially due to the charity and altruism of those belonging to superior races. There are superior and inferior races and the latter are necessarily at the mercy of the former."[106] It can thus be said that Rowling's treatment of the elves is ambiguous. On the one hand, she clearly shows (through Hermione) that enslavement of people or species is wrong. On the other hand, however, the elves' basic nature lets their status as slave appear naturally given and therefore reinforces a world view built upon the inequality between peoples and creatures.

All the three elves who appear in the stories stand for different parts of the rather sick relationship between them and their masters. Winky shows how the elves are at the mercy of their 'owners' and how dependent they are made in the course of their service. She also exemplifies how their own lives and sense of selves are taken away from them and how many of them go to pieces when they are sacked. Dobby is an example of an elf who wants freedom. His masters are unkind and cruel and he wishes to break away from them. The novels tell the readers about his bid for freedom, the problems he encounters and his final success, when he manages to break free from the Malfoys' unholy influence. Kreacher is as interesting as Dobby. He most clearly lays bare the ideological implications of the

---

102   Cf. Rowling *Hallows* 159-63.

103   Cf. Rowling *Hallows* 163.

104   Cf. Rowling *Hallows* 163.

105   Mendlesohn 178-79.

106   Gupta 109.

relationship between master and elf. His story shows that most elves are so dependent on their masters in mind and body that they simply "[parrot] their beliefs" and do not question them.[107]

The impressive scene which occurs directly after Kreacher's tale, shows that both Kreacher and Harry in fact possess great strength of mind. Harry slowly manages to overcome his dislike, forgive Kreacher his involvement in the plot surrounding Sirius and develop understanding for the elf who is clearly devastated. It is interesting, however, that it needs a certain story for Harry to pity the elf, a story explaining Kreacher's behaviour. Without that story, possibly nothing would have changed in the relationship between the two. This shows Harry to be an incomplete savior-figure, because he does not really pity people and creatures for the sake of pitying only. The elf, too sees Harry differently when he tells him that they want to complete the work Regulus started. Harry shows Kreacher that he trusts him now by giving him an important task that sets them on the tail of the Horcrux. From this moment onwards, Kreacher changes towards Harry and even shows respect for Hermione, whom he always called 'mudblood' before. This is really an achievement, given how Kreacher was brainwashed and prone to repeat his old masters' pure-blood ideologies. It shows that Kreacher has a mind as strong as Dobby. This notion is reinforced when in the final battle for Hogwarts, Kreacher leads the other elves into the fight against Voldemort's regime.[108] The elf, it seems, has finally not only freed himself from his old masters' beliefs, but also becomes active. And, what is more, he even manages to enlist the other elves and gets them to stand up and fight against their suppression by people such as the Malfoys. This is something that even Dobby does not effect, and all that Hermione wishes for. Like Dobby, Kreacher achieves a good kind of freedom and both elves' significance for the story shows how important individuation and emancipation, not

---

107   Rowling *Hallows* 163. Rivka Temima Kellner even interprets the house elves with their submissive stay-at-home roles and their ideological enslavement as "representations of unemancipated and unempowered women of the past" (Rivka Temima Kellner, "J.K. Rowling's Ambivalence Towards Feminism: House Elves – Women in Disguise in the 'Harry Potter' Books," *The Midwest Quarterly: A Journal of Contemporary Thought* 51.4 (2010): 367). While Kellner views the house elves' representation as largely negative, Kathryn N. McDaniel, who also likens the elves to house-wives, evaluates Rowling's treatment as complex and aware of the problems of second-wave feminism. In fact, she accuses Rowling's critics of "wish[ing] she were more 'fantastic' in depicting the world as they believe it should be and not in the full light of its real paradoxes and contradictions" (204).

108   Cf. Rowling *Hallows* 588.

only of the main characters but also of the humanoids are to Rowling.[109] A less dominant reading would be to ask whether the elves actually fight against their suppression by the structures of the wizarding world in the end or whether they simply fight for Harry who has treated them kindly. The latter reading would be supported by Kreacher's battle-cry: "Fight! Fight! Fight for my master, defender of house-elves! Fight the Dark Lord, in the name of brave Regulus! Fight!"[110] Once again the text is ambiguous.[111]

Kreacher resembles several other characters from *Harry Potter* as well as *Star Wars*. The fact that he is both good and evil at certain stages of the story aligns him with Severus Snape but also with Anakin Skywalker. All three go back to good from evil and can therefore be seen as Lévi-Straussian mediators. Kreacher's mediating function is rather clear. (See also the two visualisations of his structural movements in chapter four.) He helps Harry arrive at an understanding of the relationship between wizards and elves, of Regulus and even of Sirius, whom he adored unquestioningly before. His story and behaviour also make Harry understand that kindness is something that needs to be shown all people and creatures without distinction.

Kreacher and especially Anakin Skywalker also share the experience of manipulation by different sorts of people and show how difficult it is to get rid of beliefs and practices that someone has instilled and nourished in one for a long time. Both their stories thus demonstrate the dangers of manipulation and determination from the outside and advocate a free mind. Kreacher's tale, however, is a stronger bid for freedom of mind than Anakin's. The level of manipulation he is subject to is much higher than Anakin's. It almost resembles that of the clones in *Star Wars*, who are also alternately good and evil because they are used by the various sides and are not constructed to question the orders they get nor their own

---

109 For Prinzi the scene featuring the house elves joining battle does not go far enough. He argues that depicting them as attacking their opponents with cleavers and kitchen knives, borders on the comic and belittles the elves who, as is established before in the novels, have their own powerful kind of magic (cf. 255). However, he contradicts himself in this instance, as in the chapters preceding the one on the house elves, he has very rightly argued that the novels favour a gradual approach to social change (cf. eg. 221-43). After all, the house elves have been physically and psychologically enslaved for centuries and it is a big step for them to enter the fray at all.

110 Rowling *Hallows* 588.

111 Cf. also Horne 97, and Saxena 157. According to Rana this scene emphasises the fact that the house-elves are completely dependent on a human master for their survival and that none of them truly overcomes this dependency ("'The less you lot have ter do with these foreigners (…)'" 54).

actions. While the dilemma of the clones is simply presented, leaving audiences to make up their own minds about it, Kreacher's tale has a clear solution. Rowling, again, is much more decisive than Lucas and distinctly shows the position she favours. The fact that Kreacher achieves freedom of mind at last, at least partially, proves once more that this is of great importance to her. It also demonstrates her strong belief that people can in fact be free. Kreacher is more favourably treated than Anakin and the small elf whom many wizards would deem unimportant, is stronger than the former Jedi who only overcomes evil at the very last moment.

All in all it can be said that the elves have a mirror-function. They reflect the fates of some of the main characters and thus serve to put more emphasis on important themes such as free will versus determinism and the development from good to evil and back to good, explored in the two tales. In this way the fact that Rowling introduces the readers to exemplary members of each 'race' in her stories, which was seen positively before, can also be viewed as less good. Since the elves only stress certain ideas and themes of the novels, the focus is shifted from the fate of their enslaved 'race' to the few individuals' personal growth. The problem of their slavery is not really solved and still existent at the end of the series. Harry, otherwise always the champion of the oppressed, does not seem to care to end slavery either, although he likes Dobby, Kreacher and Winky. "[B]y the end of the Potter series, an exhausted Harry is thinking only about sleep in his 'four-poster bed … and wondering whether Kreacher might bring him a sandwich there.' Thus, the closing line of the main body of the novel – and the body of the seven-book saga – embraces slavery, rather than firmly rejecting it."[112] Once more, the novels are curiously ambiguous.[113] However, there is one charge against Rowling which I believe I have proved wrong with my analysis of the house-elves. Julia Park finds that "the author's depiction of an enslaved class as something to entertain her reader is reprehensible."[114] As my analysis has shown the elves are by no means used for comic relief. They function as helper figures for Harry and are often essential to his success. They ground him and shape his notion of himself as a hero. Furthermore, the three elf-representatives the readers get to know, are individualised as much as the story allows and their emancipation process is outlined alongside Harry's. On the whole, the reader is not supposed to laugh about the elves but to pity them and understand both Harry's and Hermione's action on their behalf.

---

112   Giselle Liza Anatol, "The Replication of Victorian Racial Ideology in *Harry Potter*," *Reading Harry Potter Again: New Critical Essays*, Ed. Giselle Liza Anatol (Santa Barbara: ABC-CLIO, 2009) 113.

113   Brycchan Carey also sees the role of the house-elves in the novels as highly ambiguous ("Hermione and the House-Elves Revisited" 165).

114   Park 185. Farah Mendlesohn also believes that Dobby is a "figure of fun" (165).

The final humanoid from *Harry Potter* who needs to be looked at more closely is Remus Lupin, the werewolf. Being a werewolf of course means that most of the time, Lupin is and looks like a 'normal' human being. His condition only comes to the fore at the full moon, once a month. Then he usually drinks the wolfbane potion which makes him stay harmless.[115] If he did not take the remedy, he would be dangerous and go after humans. Lupin is an unusual werewolf because he fears his condition and the consequences it can have for other people. Fellow werewolves the readers get to know in the course of the story, most notably the vicious Fenrir Greyback, are highly bloodthirsty and enjoy killing.[116] Obviously thus, Lupin does not simply embrace a condition that has the potential of harming others but chooses not to give in to his baser instincts.

Lupin is very important for Harry at a time that is difficult for the young wizard and remains loyal to him ever after their first meeting. This already suggests that Lupin is another character who is subjected to the structures mainly dealing with Harry's story. A friend of Harry's parents, he is the one who teaches Harry to fight his own demons, the Dementors in novel three. So he is obviously at school as a Defence Against the Dark Arts teacher because Harry needs him. The Patronus charm that Lupin teaches Harry, is one of the most important skills Harry has, because it helps him preserve his mental sanity through all the dark and difficult times he faces. Lupin also provides Harry with much craved information about his past and his parents. In these senses the werewolf functions as a helper figure.

As many of the other humanoids, however, he is also introduced to the reader as a human being and an individual. Lupin, very clearly a good character because of his empathetic behaviour, is extremely ashamed of his affliction and tries to hide the fact that he is a werewolf. As the other humanoids analysed so far, werewolves are feared and disrespected by most wizards. Lupin's case thus raises the same social issues of mutual respect among all people and creatures as do the other cases of humanoids. Werewolves are considered evil per se and almost no one makes the effort to find out whether there are differences amongst them. Their treatment opens up the 'race' issue again. The contamination of their blood is believed to affect their character. Again Rowling makes crystal clear that for her it is not blood that effects a person's behaviour but choice. Lupin by taking the wolfbane potion and keeping

---

115   Cf. Rowling *Azkaban* 380.

116   In this sense, Lupin also functions as a mediator between the realms of reason and instinct; his werewolf persona stands for the fulfilment of desires, whereas his guilt-ridden everyday personality embodies rationality (Cf. also Amy M. Green, "Interior/Exterior in the Harry Potter Series: Duality Expressed in Sirius Black and Remus Lupin," *Papers on Language and Literature: A Quarterly Journal for Scholars of Language and Literature* 44.1 (Winter 2008): n.pag. <http://lion.chadwyck.co.uk/>).

away from humans at the time of the full moon, has decided for a course of action beneficial to others. Fenrir Greyback, his vicious counterpart, by contrast derives pleasure from harming others and freely indulges in his desire for human blood.

By telling Lupin's story, Rowling indirectly asks readers to question stereotypes and make differentiations. Harry and the readers do not know of Lupin's status when they first meet him. Thus Rowling employs the same strategy for him as she does for Hagrid. Harry and the readers get to know Lupin as a sympathetic human being and excellent teacher who takes special care of students who lag behind or are timid in some way. When Harry and the readers finally find out that Lupin is a werewolf in a dramatic scene towards the end of novel three,[117] the readers are not much inclined to believe evil of Lupin. As Lupin is the second figure who is treated thus by Rowling, it becomes obvious that she has an agenda of dispelling prejudices. Harry also experiences other magical creatures of whom the wizarding community disapproves as benevolent, such as the centaurs, represented by Firenze, the hippogriffs, exemplified through Buckbeak and the Thestrals, who take him to London on the night he quickly needs to get to the Ministry of Magic to rescue Sirius. Lupin obviously functions as an incentive for Harry, the wizarding community at large and the readers to break with prejudices and practice tolerance and understanding.

There is still more to the treatment of Lupin, however. Rowling also suggests that there is always more than one side to stories such as his. Lupin himself, it seems, is equally to blame for the fact that he is not accepted. In his stories about his childhood and youth, it transpires that from an early age onwards Lupin tried to hide his condition rather than accept it as part of himself and openly admit to it.[118] After all, being bitten by a vicious werewolf is nothing he can be blamed for. Lupin does not even tell his best friends at school, for fear of losing them.[119] As they are clever Sirius and James Potter, they find out soon enough and do not leave Lupin but help him make his transformations easier. They become animagi, wizards who can turn into animals to be able to roam the school grounds with him at the full moon. Equally, Dumbledore extends a hand towards him, trusts him and takes him on as a teacher at the beginning of novel three. This should have taught Lupin that the people who really matter, will not let him down. All the same, he continues with his secrecy. When he arrives at Hogwarts to teach, no one is supposed to know of his condition because he fears that people will not accept a werewolf as teacher for their children. As soon as Snape, out of anger, tells his students of Lupin's

---

117   Cf. Rowling *Azkaban* 372.
118   Cf. Green n.pag.
119   Cf. Rowling *Azkaban* 381.

predicament, Lupin resigns and leaves the school.[120] Lupin simply never manages to face people about his condition and to present himself self-confidently. He rather remains shabby and poor because he assumes that no one will give him a job anyway.

Some critics have read Lupin, his association with 'contaminated' blood, and his reluctance to 'come out' as an embodiment of a homosexual.[121] Christopher Wrigley, for instance, attacks Rowling for "not being entirely 'correct'" in her treatment of him, presenting "his condition [as] both pitiable and dangerous."[122] However, only the irresponsible handling of Lupin's 'condition' is depicted as dangerous in the novels as the werewolf Fenrir Greyback shows who hunts and bites for pleasure. Lupin is always portrayed as a sensible person and good mentor for Harry. It does seem strange to compare a potentially dangerous werewolf to a homosexual and I do not think that Rowling intended this connection. In 'enlightened' societies surely very few people believe that homosexuals are aggressive predators who are exclusively focused on 'infecting' others with their 'condition.'

Tison Pugh and David L. Wallace's analysis makes more sense in this context. They liken the prejudices about 'contaminated' blood, Lupin has to deal with in the wizarding community to the difficulties homosexuals, especially gay men, often encounter. The affliction Lupin suffers from resembles the problematic of AIDS which is highly contagious like the werewolf bite and transmitted via the blood.[123] The metaphorical link with AIDS is more apt, because it comes closer to the nature of the stereotypes against homosexuals (gay men) today. People are not so much afraid of gay people spreading their homosexuality but of them transmitting diseases such as AIDS. Again, then, Rowling shows the reality by contrasting Lupin and Greyback. There are people who handle diseases (in this case the werewolf gene) responsibly and there are others who do not. Once more, it does not matter what the person is, but rather what s/he makes of his condition. Choice is again foregrounded with respect to Lupin and his existence as a werewolf. And in

---

120 Cf. Rowling *Azkaban* 456.

121 Cf. also Michael Bronski who reads the complete *Potter*-series as a tale of coming-out, equating the adventures of the hero who literally needs to come out of the Dursley's cupboard under the stairs and realise and acknowledge his 'difference' with the experience of homosexuals (Michael Bronski, "Queering Harry Potter," *Z Magazine Online* 16.9 (2003): n.pag., 5 Jul 2011 <http://www.zmag.org/zmag/viewArticle/13675>).

122 Christopher Wrigley, *Return of the Hero* (Lewes: The Book Guild Ltd., 2005) 20.

123 Cf. Tison Pugh and David L. Wallace, "Heteronormative Heroism and Queering the School Story in J.K. Rowling's *Harry Potter* Series," *Children's Literature Association Quarterly* 31.3 (Fall 2006): n.pag. <http://lion.chadwyck.co.uk/>.

fact, though social discrimination against Lupin's kind is existent in the novels, it is never foregrounded. Those characters who matter most all hold Lupin in high esteem. No one, for instance, actually asks him to leave the school once he is 'outed,' he decides to go of his own free will. In fact he avoids every situation in which he might have to face the prejudices of the larger wizarding community. Thus is is partly he himself who propagates the stereotypes because he has internalised them to such a high degree. If there is a problematic point about the depiction of Lupin then it is this, that the blame for the way people deal with his condition is partly shifted to him. However, Rowling never says that there are no true prejudices against werewolves and that it is all in Lupin's head, she just, once more, focalises her narrative through Harry who is accepting and tolerant and cannot know what Lupin truly faces 'out there.' Rowling's message with respect to Lupin, but also, for instance, Hagrid and Madame Maxime is clear: she asks people not to hide their true selves but to try others out. Maybe their reaction is not as bad as feared.

Lupin's fears become most pronounced when in book six, it becomes clear that Tonks, a fellow member of the Order of the Phoenix, has fallen in love with him. His self-loathing, however, makes it hard for him to accept the fact that he is worth loving. Even when the two finally marry at the beginning of novel seven and Tonks becomes pregnant, Lupin remains unhappy. He actually decides to leave his wife. Because of him, he fears, she and their unborn child will face the same derision and rejection that he does. Lupin even wishes that he had never begot the child.[124] At this stage Harry, always the champion of the suppressed, starts telling Lupin off. He makes clear to Lupin that what his child could be ashamed of, is not Lupin's condition as such but the cowardice with which he runs away from it.[125] And although Lupin is severely offended at first, he later forgives Harry and tells him that he was right.[126] He goes back to his wife and is extremely happy when his little son is born. When he dies in the final battle against Voldemort and Harry brings him, his parents and Sirius back to life with the resurrection stone for a few minutes, Harry apologises to Lupin. Lupin admits that he is sorry not to see his son grow up but that he wanted to help create a better world for him.[127] This shows that he, like Kreacher, has learned something. He has accepted himself and started to fight for his recognition. Lupin, too thus undergoes a development which shows that recognition and acceptance are hard work sometimes and cannot come from one side alone. He is a foil for Harry because he shows how difficult life can be if

---

124   Cf. Rowling *Hallows* 175.

125   Cf. Rowling *Hallows* 176.

126   Cf. Rowling *Hallows* 358.

127   Cf. Rowling *Hallows* 561.

one does not accept oneself. When we think back to chapter seven on Harry Potter and Luke Skywalker, acceptance is one of the chief abilities the hero needs to finally defeat Voldemort. It includes the acceptance of death but also the admission of the fact that sometimes there are things within the self that are hard to understand but nevertheless need to be integrated to be able to live freely. Lupin shows what Harry's story could have been, had he, for instance, given in to his fears concerning the dark side within him represented by the Horcrux. He, too is thus a mirror-figure. And although his story is also subordinated to Harry's, much like Dobby and Kreacher, he is also an individual and thus mythical ambiguity applies to his story, too.

In sum, it can be said that Rowling's treatment of humanoids is much more differentiated than Lucas's. This was already noticeable throughout the chapter, because it was much harder to find similarities and points of comparison between the creatures from the two tales, than, for instance, for the main characters such as the Emperor and Voldemort, Harry and Luke. Despite the fixed structural corset, which, as was shown in the chapters on the protagonists, applies to both stories, Rowling manages to treat even minor characters fairly and with a love for detail. Although their stories mostly relate to Harry's in some way or the other, they are also depicted as individuals undergoing developments and usually changing for the better in the course of the narratives. Lucas mainly includes humanoids as fairy-tale helper figures whose backgrounds the audience does not get to know. Some also provide comic relief. Most of the humanoids in *Star Wars* are in fact subject to the nature versus technology dichotomy which is also negotiated in the figure of Anakin Skywalker / Darth Vader. Therefore, many of the creatures only embody a conflict played out in Anakin/Vader and are thus very much subjected to the structures of the tale. *Star Wars* also presents a rather balanced distribution of humanoids. Those who are feeling creatures are mostly good, while the robots and droids are evil with a few exceptions. In *Harry Potter,* most of the important humanoids, especially Hagrid, Lupin and Dobby, are good which shows that Rowling feels a need to demonstrate that otherness is not necessarily evil. It is also significant that in *Harry Potter* the readers are always presented with at least one good and one less good example from each humanoid group. There is Hagrid who accepts his status as a half-giant and Madame Maxime who at first denies it and thereby temporarily loses Hagrid's friendship. On the level of the house elves Dobby serves as the example of freedom while Winky and Kreacher cling to their old bounds, (although the latter is also an instance of the fact that old dependencies can be overcome). The same pattern can be found with Lupin and Greyback, the former rejecting and the latter embracing his role as werewolf. Instead of echoing the Death Eaters' belief in the importance of blood for a person's development and character, Rowling constantly emphasises the importance of choice and behaviour towards others.

All in all it can be said that *Star Wars* by featuring more masses of evil people focuses on the generation of evil through structures that have many (witting or unwitting) followers. *Harry Potter* foregrounds the individual and its way of dealing with evil and (social) injustice. However, the humanoids' plight is primarily focalised through Harry who adopts a sporting, empathetic attitude.[128] This might detract readers from the structural violence these creatures are faced with on a larger social scale. In this sense my thesis that the structures of heroic tales limit, hide and distort other discourses such as the one on social justice for minorities, is proved to be true.

---

128   Cf. also Horne 83.

10. Structural Displacement: Ethnic Diversity in *Star Wars* and *Harry Potter*

10.1 TOKEN-BLACKS AND EVIL ALIENS: *STAR WARS*

Both *Star Wars* and *Harry Potter* are distinctly 'Western' tales. The overwhelming majority of the main human characters are white and Western-European-looking. Examples from *Star Wars* include Anakin, Shmi, Padmé, Qui-Gon, Obi-Wan, Senator Palpatine, Luke, Leia and Han-Solo.[1] In *Harry Potter* this does not look much different. The protagonists, among them Harry, Ron, Hermione, Dumbledore, the Weasleys, Lupin, Sirius, Neville and Luna are white and English without exception. Thus 'foreignness' in the tales is defined against these backgrounds. The origins of Lucas's characters are not always clearly delineated and by using space and imaginative planets as setting, the filmmakers have made an effort to distance the characters and events of the movies from the real world. In *Star Wars* thus only the looks of most of the human protagonists reveal the Western context in which the tales originate.

The question of ethnicities and diversity has two levels in the films. First, the characters who are obviously non-white need to be analysed. Second, another look has to be taken at the humanoids, who, approached from an angle additional to

---

1   Cf. Estrada who strongly criticises the *Star Wars* films for what he perceives to be their classism, sexism and racism (69). On the subject of white dominance in the movies he says: "Fueled by miscegenation fears, *Star Wars* focuses on the protection of white lives and loves through white male agency" (76). Cf. further Stephanie J. Wilhelm, "Imperial Plastic, Republican Fiber: Speculating on the Post-Colonial Other," *Finding the Force of the Star Wars Franchise: Fans, Merchandise, and Critics*, Ed. Matthew Wilhelm Kapell and John Shelton Lawrence (New York: Peter Lang, 2006) 175, and Peter Lev, "Whose Future? *Star Wars*, *Alien*, and *Blade Runner*," *Literature/Film Quarterly* 26.1 (1998): n.pag. <http://lion.chadwyck.co.uk/>.

those which were already applied in the preceding chapter, shed further light on the treatment of ethnicities in the films. For *Harry Potter* it will be interesting to analyse what exactly is contended through the treatment of minorities which basically consist of three groups in the novels. There are Harry's non-white fellow students, 'foreigners' from other parts of Europe, as well as the minority of the half-bloods and "mudbloods" within the dominant hegemonic group of the predominantly white English wizards and witches. Do the books express an awareness of these groups' problems and rights, which would by extension show an awareness of tensions between different social groups in British society? It needs to be seen to which extent, if at all, the films and the novels incorporate Homi Bhabha's museum-gallery-stairwell-approach to cultural diversity[2] which seems to me to be the most equal and individual, the fairest but also the most utopian. The assumption is that since both stories are extremely structural, they will have a hard time overcoming an 'us' versus 'them' mentality.

Minorities are defined as "historically disadvantaged or oppressed groups" within a so-called dominant society.[3] "The notion of minority refers to more than merely a numerical relationship, but to one characterized by unequal power and cultural incompatibility between majority society and minority group."[4] The characters representing ethnic minorities for *Star Wars* are easily identified. In films one and two of the more recent trilogy, Padmé has a black head of security each and in *Phantom Menace* Anakin's friend Kitster is from an Asian, possibly Pakistani background. However, while all three are presented as good and benevolent, they are not of much consequence for the stories. Kitster is there to be happy for the 'wonderful' Anakin when he wins the podrace and the two security officers serve as guards for the 'precious white' lady.[5] There are only two characters, the Jedi Mace Windu and the 'scoundrel' Lando Calrissian who are non-white and have some importance in the tales. It is curious that despite all the diversity that is simulated by the inclusion of countless different humanoid peoples, the stories feature almost no human diversity. It still seems to have been important to the filmmakers to include one representative black person in each the older and the more recent films. Possibly this was done for reasons of political correctness. Other ethnicities such as Hispanics do not appear. In the following, the black Mace Windu and Lando Calrissian need to be analysed in detail to see how they function within the movies. Mace Windu, as a Jedi knight, is certainly highly powerful. He appears in all movies of the prequel trilogy and very often alongside Jedi master Yoda. On the

---

2 Cf. Bhabha 5.

3 Joppke 451.

4 Joppke 451.

5 Cf. *A Phantom Menace* 00:09:22, 1:06:41; *Attack of the Clones* 00:03:05.

Jedi Council he sits to the left of Yoda and frequently functions as speaker who announces decisions.[6] He is also seen to join Yoda in his solitary meditations and is usually present in decisive situations conferring with Yoda and Obi-Wan.[7] His closeness to Yoda certainly shows Windu to be powerful, something Anakin confirms when he talks about his mentor Obi-Wan to Padmé and says that he is "as wise as master Yoda and as powerful as master Windu."[8] The three most important Jedi of the newer trilogy are very different in character. While Yoda is the patient, friendly and accepting one, and Obi-Wan the youthfully rash, Mace Windu has the role of the severe and strict one who seriously doubts Anakin from the moment he sets foot in the Jedi temple in *Phantom Menace*. He never smiles, always looks grave and stern and at times treats Anakin condescendingly. His demeanour, and doubts about the cute child Anakin with whom the audience feels because he has just had to leave his mother and looks very forlorn among the Jedi, do not endear Windu to viewers. The films show the audience a human, non-perfect side to Mace Windu only when it is too late, namely in his fight against Palpatine at the end of *Revenge of the Sith*. There, he finally acknowledges Anakin's importance and starts appealing to him, suddenly even using his first name.[9] By partaking in this fight, Windu ultimately and conclusively becomes part of Anakin's story. Chapter four and appendix 1 show him as part of the first of the two triangles that visualise Anakin's fall from grace and redemption. Windu symbolically marks the beginning of Anakin's destruction of the Jedi, literally and figuratively. Helping to kill Mace Windu initiates a chain of other murders, most noticeably those of all the Jedi, even the young padawans at the temple. It thus starts the destruction of the actual Jedi order. However, it also sets off the destruction of the Jedi within Anakin which can be seen when shortly after the murder, the young man fully subscribes to the Emperor's ideology.[10]

It is therefore apparent, that, like many of the other characters already analysed, Mace Windu, though powerful and seemingly important, ultimately has a structural function. He helps propel Anakin's story by being implicated in his fall from grace. The suggestion that his importance is structural, rather than individual, is also supported by the fact that after his death, he completely disappears from the story while other Jedi remain present even after their demise. The original trilogy shows who the truly important Jedi are: the surviving Obi-Wan and Yoda as well as the redeemed Anakin. They are the ones who hover above the victory-festivities of the

---

6   Cf. for example *The Phantom Menace* 1:21:17.

7   Cf. *Attack of the Clones* 00:25:33, 00:55:06; *Revenge of the Sith* 00:38:44.

8   *Attack of the Clones* 00:27:18.

9   Cf. *Revenge of the Sith* 01:10:46.

10   Cf. *Revenge of the Sith* 01:13:13.

good side, as one with the living Force, even after death.[11] No one ever refers to Windu or cares to communicate with him through the Force after his murder. His function in the duel with Palpatine and Anakin is to stand in for Obi-Wan and Yoda, both of whom cannot die at that point because they appear in the (already present) original movies and are still needed. Mace Windu has to be sacrificed for Yoda and Obi-Wan to remain in the story. And since unlike Yoda and Obi-Wan he is not depicted as especially friendly or congenial, he is expendable for the audience.

It is important to explicitly state again at this point how *much* and how *well* audience sympathies are focused on Anakin. The term 'much' refers to audiences' own share in the focusing process as they themselves are engrossed in Anakin's development. The word 'well' was used to make clear how much of this process of audience-identification is guided by the filmmakers and the way the story is constructed. Mace Windu originally is quite an independent character. Unlike some of the other Jedi, most notably Qui-Gon, he is not taken in by Anakin's sweet and innocent appearance. He reserves the right to make his own judgements concerning the situation, see it differently from other Jedi and openly say so. It should be noted that this makes him a very free-minded and therefore good character by the standards established for both the *Star Wars* movies and the *Harry Potter* novels before. The audience, however, does not take into account that Windu's assessment of Anakin might be correct, because he is not a particularly likeable character. It thus seems, that even if characters show independence of mind and clearly belong to the good side, they are only viewed sympathetically if they in turn are sympathetic towards the hero or heroine.

Snape in *Harry Potter* is in a similar situation as Mace Windu. He sees a side of Harry the readers and incidentally Harry himself do not (want to) see, as it often shows the hero as an ignorant and arrogant adolescent. Snape gives Harry the opportunity to learn not only to 'love' his friends but also those who do not like him. The readers of *Harry Potter* are taught this lesson along with Harry and Snape is vindicated. In *Star Wars* no such learning process is started as the unlikeable Windu is expunged from the story without further ado. As soon as Windu's fate becomes entwined with Anakin's, he very literally loses his independence and becomes determined by Anakin. This is made palpable by his begging for Anakin's support in his fight against Palpatine.[12] The contradiction implied in this is highly significant for my analysis. Windu becomes truly important for the story (even if only for a few minutes) and wins the audience's sympathy, only at the moment his and Anakin's paths cross and he loses his freedom and ultimately his life. Mace

---

11   Cf. *Return of the Jedi* 2:02:20.

12   Cf. *Revenge of the Sith* 01:10:46.

Windu is thus one of the best examples of how most of the minor characters, be they black, white, or humanoid, are clearly subjected to the dominant narrative, which is that of Anakin/Vader and finally of good and evil principles at war with each other.

What does all of this mean for the treatment of one of the only non-white characters in the stories? Was it necessary at all to cast Windu as a black person? On the one hand it could be said that it was not and was only done for reasons of political correctness, which then are undermined by the fact that Windu is not treated sympathetically, dies and is quickly forgotten by the other characters and the audience. Esther Godfrey supports such a reading when she calls the two blacks who appear in the prequel trilogy, Mace Windu, and the much less important Captain Panaka "naturalized black men" who "lend authenticity to the film's seeming multiculturalism."[13]

However, as was often the case before, mythical ambiguity is at work here again, as on the other hand, possibly casting Windu as a black has very good reasons and shows an equal handling of black and white actors. Clearly, the figure of Windu is not supposed to draw attention to the problems that black people are generally assumed to have. The actor Samuel L. Jackson just plays a role that any other (white, yellow, green or orange) actor could also have played. A black actor plays, not a sympathetic character, whom the audience particularly likes, but a none too likeable figure. This could be interpreted as an embodiment of equality. Exclusively casting blacks as good and likeable characters would betray a slightly condescending stance or one implying a certain guilt on the part of white filmmakers. It would introduce a structure, a hierarchy once more. Since blacks were often treated badly by whites in the past, such an approach would create the impression that whites now have to redeem themselves by exclusively portraying blacks as 'good guys.' Thereby they would not take diversity among blacks into account and would very likely stigmatise blacks as 'the good guys' as much as they stigmatised them as 'the slaves,' 'the bad guys,' or the 'faithful sidekicks' before. This invokes what Stuart Hall calls "politics of representation."[14] These grew out of a fatigue with what he labels "politics of resistance" against white racism, which, as much as they were justified in calling attention to the existence and perpetuation of discrimination, also led to the white majority perceiving blacks as one

---

13   Godfrey n.pag. Tom Carson argues that the introduction of two token-blacks to the series was actually pointless, because the issues of diversity and multiculturalism are played out on the field of the humanoid characters anyway (cf. 167).

14   Stuart Hall, "New Ethnicities," *Black British Cultural Studies: A Reader*, Ed. Houston A. Baker, Jr., Manthia Diawara, and Ruth H. Lindeborg (Chicago: University of Chicago Press, 1996) 165.

homogeneous group.[15] The 'politics of representation' then focused on bringing black diversity into representation and expressly encouraged portraying blacks from within the group, thereby loosening their dependence on an external, white perspective. In this sense the casting decision of the makers of *Star Wars* could be seen as aware of the diversity within the large group of black people all over the world. Blacks and whites (as well as people of further skin-colours and ethnicities), it would say, can portray both good and evil characters as well as those in between. It would also question the assumption that just because a black actor is cast for a particular role, his part has to somehow accommodate 'black problems.'

In sum, I believe that both positions are inherent in Mace Windu's role. He can be seen as sacrificed to the structures of the heroic quest but his casting for a part that does not deal with 'black social issues' also exhibits a certain equality. However, the fact remains that in contrast to other protagonists who die at the beginning or in the course of the story, he is largely forgotten soon after his death. Furthermore, it should be remembered that he is one of only two somewhat significant black figures in the tales. Thus, his role and casting might just as well be a sham and they remain ambiguous at the least.[16]

The other black character, Lando Calrissian, is introduced in a highly ambiguous way oscillating between a depiction as unreliable and suggestions of his trustworthiness. He is Han Solo's buddy, but someone even the roguish Han does not place entire confidence in.[17] However, in a way, Lando's trustworthiness is established before the audience even sees him. In his conversation with Leia about Lando, Han describes his old pal as a "scoundrel."[18] In itself, the term does not have positive connotations. But since the audience is already familiar with Han who

---

15   Hall "New Ethnicities" 163.

16   Interestingly, the Wikipedia page on Mace Windu, cautious as one needs to be with sources like that, indirectly suggests that Samuel L. Jackson who plays the Jedi, himself might have had some (unconscious?) misgivings about the role, although he had obviously expressed a wish to work with George Lucas before the offer came. According to Wikipedia, Jackson requested "that his character die in a spectacular fashion, rather than being killed off ingloriously." Wikipedia goes on to inform the reader that in David Letterman's Late Show of 13 May 2005, Jackson commented on the unusual purple colour of his lightsabre as "a way of making the character unique and easily distinguishable" ("Mace Windu," *Wikipedia*, 2011, 5 May 2011 <http://en.wikipedia.org/wiki/Mace_Windu>). If Wikipedia tells the truth, we can assume that Jackson was at least subconsciously aware of the ways in which his role could be problematic.

17   Cf. *The Empire Strikes Back* 1:12:40.

18   *The Empire Strikes Back* 1:12:22.

himself qualifies as a scoundrel and is called one by Leia on several occasions, they are inclined to be cautious with respect to Lando but not necessarily meet him with negative feelings. Han, too seems to be untrustworthy at first and turns out to be one of the protagonists' most loyal friends. Expectations are high that this pattern will be repeated with Lando. When he is finally introduced, he seems to be genuinely happy to see Han and his entourage and turns out to be a charmer when it comes to women. With his attentions to Leia, he instantly becomes a rival for Han who desires her, too.[19] This echoes old stereotypes about the sexual potency of black men inducing white men to be on the guard against them.[20] The audience, sympathising with Han, will view Lando with caution at this point. From the first it is made clear, however, that the black man will not get the pure, white maiden. When Lando tries to make a pass at Leia, Han looks worried and instantly tells him off.[21] Leia herself is also highly suspicious of Lando and ensures that the audience remains guarded about him.[22] This mistrust turns out to be justified when Lando betrays Han and Leia to Darth Vader.[23]

Still, a qualification needs to be made here. Very obviously, Lando has no love for the Empire and has tried to avoid contact with imperial troops before Han and Leia unwittingly led them to his small mining operation. He is responsible for his enterprise as well as quite a number of people living in cloud city, therefore it is at least partly understandable that he selfishly sells Han and Leia to Vader in order to carry on with his business in peace. He even explains this and apologises to the two protagonists.[24] Steven A. Galipeau views Lando as an everyman in this situation, meaning that Lando is used to show how in everyday life, people tend to take practical decisions based on their own well-being and that of those closest to them, instead of making noble and self-sacrificial choices. "The everyday demands of life limit what we can do for others, even when we care to do more."[25] In the further course of the action, however, the audience's expectation that Lando is a 'good' scoundrel like Han, are fulfilled and the figure of Lando comes to represent the possibility of heroic nobility in an everyman. Lando is not impressed when Vader orders Han to be frozen in carbon and still less when the evildoer reneges on his

---

19   Cf. *The Empire Strikes Back* 1:18:05.

20   Cf. Wetmore 132.

21   Cf. *The Empire Strikes Back* 1:18:13.

22   Cf. *The Empire Strikes Back* 1:17:36.

23   Cf. *The Empire Strikes Back* 1:24:47.

24   Cf. *The Empire Strikes Back* 1:25:05. Cf. also Richard H. Dees who argues that Lando takes a "*utilitarian* decision" which places the safety of the multitude he is responsible for before that of one buddy he has not seen for a long time (43).

25   Galipeau 152.

promise that Leia and Chewbacca can remain in cloud city. He manages to free Leia and Chewie and escape with them. And together, the three even rescue Luke, who is left maimed by his encounter with Vader.[26]

From this time onwards, however, Lando changes utterly and a little inconsequentially. The heroics of Han, Leia and Luke seem to have made him 'see sense.' He stops being selfish and discontinues his habit of making passes at Leia. He drops all that made him individual and slightly interesting to completely subordinate himself to the ways of the white heroes. The 'white path' seems to be entirely justified, while Lando's own interests do not count for much. Tellingly, the audience does not get to know what happens to Lando's mining colony, since he himself manages to leave it in time. The black man who used to be different and independent from the heroes, is 'tamed' and assimilates himself to their wishes.[27] Compared to this, the treatment of Mace Windu in the prequel episodes is more differentiated, since he at least is allowed to retain his individuality almost through to the end.

In *Return of the Jedi* Lando is part of the heroes' every mission. The first thing they do in movie six is to rescue Han from the clutches of Jabba the Hutt. As Kevin J. Wetmore correctly observes, Lando is ridiculed in the ensuing fight with Jabba and his entourage.[28] Leia, half-naked and in chains, as well as Han, still suffering from the after-effects of his time frozen in carbon, are much more effective in the fight than Lando who is not incapacitated in any way. Leia manages to kill Jabba as was analysed in chapter eight while Han, whose eyesight is diminished as a consequence of the carbon, accidentally finishes off the dangerous bounty hunter Boba Fett. In the meantime, the first and unspecified charging attacker throws Lando off balance and brings him within inches of death.[29] This again, as Wetmore also asserts, establishes the superiority of the white heroes[30] and shows that Lando is in fact doubly victimised. First he has to change his former nature to assimilate to the heroes. Then he is even shown as less good or effective when his first test of heroic courage arrives. The scene of the fight against Jabba also mirrors the battle scene from movie one, *The Phantom Menace*, where the child Anakin is shown to be more effective than the woman Padmé and the humanoid Jar Jar taken together (see chapter eight). Both scenes establish the supremacy of certain characters over others. In the case of the battle scene in movie one, Anakin's importance as hero is

---

26   Cf. *The Empire Strikes Back* 1:49:51.

27   Cf. Wetmore 133.

28   Cf. Wetmore 136.

29   Cf. Wetmore 134; Cf. *Return of the Jedi* 00:31:50-00:34:15.

30   Cf. Wetmore 133.

cemented while the discussed scene from movie six emphasises the superiority of the white heroes Luke, Leia and Han.[31]

Lando's status as secondary to the other heroes is further underlined in the scenes of the final battle against evil. While Luke needs to confront and overthrow Vader and the Emperor, Han and Leia switch off the Death Star's deflector shield on Endor. Lando is assigned the task of destroying the Death Star. At a first glance it looks as if the tasks were distributed equally among the heroes. However, it quickly becomes obvious that Han's and Leia's as well as Luke's missions get far more attention than Lando's. After all, the audience has already seen the destruction of one Death Star in A New Hope. While Luke, back then, was celebrated for his heroics, Lando's achievement in destroying the second Death Star, probably as difficult if not more so than the demolition of the first one, is passed by.[32] It is not as important anymore because Luke has already vanquished the Emperor before and brought Vader back to the good side and Han and Leia have managed to defeat all the troops on Endor with the help of the little Ewoks. Thus, it can be seen that Lando is very much subjected to the structures of the heroic quest. He loses the independence and self-sufficiency he had achieved in cloud city as Darth Vader invades the mining colony, which means that he is severely disempowered by evil.

Comparing the two representative black characters of Star Wars, it can be seen, that the treatment of Lando Calrissian, though he is allowed some heroics and survives in the end, is worse than that of Mace Windu. Although Windu is sacrificed to keep other more important characters in the story, the Jedi is at least shown as independent and powerful through to his final scene, in which despite the fact that he is defeated by the Emperor in the end, he fights bravely, his powers matching those of the villain until Anakin joins the fight. Unlike Lando, he is not ridiculed as less potent than the white characters. With respect to the depiction of ethnic minorities in the movies, the time that elapsed between the first and the prequel trilogy was beneficial. Issues of equality have come to people's consciousnesses more and more and the increasing amount of research on popular culture has contributed to unearthing the inequalities present in the structures and makings of popular tales since. The fact, however, that the portrayal of Windu is simply ambiguous instead of downright prejudiced, shows that there is still much work to do in the arena of equality and diversity in popular film.

The analysis of actual representatives of ethnic minorities in Star Wars needs to be followed by a closer look at the role of the movies' diverse humanoid population as a fictional representation of ethnic diversity. A large variety of peoples and

---

31 Estrada also remarks on the secondary importance of Mace Windu and Lando Calrissian (cf. 76).

32 Cf. also Wetmore 136.

creatures are featured in the movies who seem to more or less coexist peacefully. The way the dealings between humans and humanoids are described in the stories, is obviously meant to purport that all characters are equal. Thereby the very real issue of tensions between predominantly white majorities and ethnic minorities is deferred and sublimated. As was already shown, the humanoids are finally very much subjected to the heroic quests of the human heroes and to the exploration of ideas of good and evil, free will and determination. Their treatment is thus not as equal as the movies wish to make their audiences believe. It was already implied that some of the humanoids recall stereotypical renderings of certain ethnic minorities in various subtle ways. One example that was given, was Jar Jar Binks, whose way of speaking, Wetmore claims, resembles pidgin varieties of English which are predominantly spoken by black Africans.[33] A further example of the fact that some of the humanoids are not used innocently but are (consciously or unconsciously) loaded with meaning would be Watto, the junk dealer Anakin works for on Tatooine. With his shrewd face and crooked nose he calls forth old stereotypes about Jews.[34] His cunning, mercenary nature which cannot be fooled by Jedi mind-tricks[35] further corroborates his association with clichés about Jewishness. If interpreted in this way, the demonstrative innocence with which the humanoid creatures are treated, takes on a perfidious edge, and as Wetmore says, subverts the anti-colonial narrative.[36] Ethnic stereotypes are sold to audiences, not by actually portraying the people they supposedly characterise, which might induce audiences to view them critically. They are depicted in creatures who on first sight have nothing to do with the ethnic groups portrayed. Thus distanced from their actual object the stereotypes are not recognised easily, nor questioned, remain virulent and are transformed into ideology. This displacement is especially dangerous and objectionable since the movies have reached a large audience over the years and continue to be powerful in popular culture.

Ideology is also at work when one looks at the ways in which the portrayal of evil in the movies subtly brings ethnic minorities and humanoids together. Some of the minor evil characters, such as the 'humanoid' viceroys of the trade federation in *Phantom Menace* speak English with an accent that does not sound Western-European but rather Arabian. Given the fact that the newer trilogy originated in the context of Islamic fundamentalist terrorist threats, this is somewhat unfortunate as it adds fuel to prejudices against Arabs and other ethnicities stereotypically associated with terrorist activities. A conflict of an old, Euro-centric order represented by a

---

33   Cf. Wetmore 143.

34   Cf. Wetmore 173.

35   Cf. *The Phantom Menace* 00:32:52.

36   Cf. Wetmore 159.

democratic state apparatus, and a newer, foreign threat from the outside, represented by the separatists, is hinted at here. However, it should not be forgotten that Palpatine or the Emperor-to-be is behind all of the unrest establishing itself at the beginning of *Phantom Menace* and deepening through *Attack of the Clones* and *Revenge of the Sith*. He, a white, Western character, not some humanoids with Arabian-English accents, is the main bully in the playground, a fact that establishes the movies as at least superficially anti-colonialist. The Emperor embodies the contribution of the West to conflicts with, for instance, Islamic fundamentalists. In this context it is significant that all the helpers of evil in the old trilogy, are as white and Western-looking as the protagonists. Some, by their way of speaking, can clearly be identified as British, others as American.[37] This would suggest that on some fronts the filmmakers were sensitive to, and possibly wanted to create an awareness of the ways in which mainly white Westerners have controlled the world in the past and still do so today.[38] This ambiguous message concerning good and

---

37   Cf. for example *A New Hope* 00:35:30-00:37:25.

38   M. Keith Booker also perceives this ambiguity in the depiction of good and evil. The Empire, at least in the original trilogy, he says, can certainly be associated with the Soviet Union and "the galactic political situation portrayed in the film[s] draws upon the rhetoric of the Cold War" (116). However, the clear demarcation between West and East cannot really hold, because "the forces of the Empire, with its advanced technology and superior resources, clearly have much in common with the capitalist West, while the rebel forces often resemble less well equipped anticolonial forces, such as the Viet Cong in Vietnam or the National Liberation Front of Algeria" (116). Booker even goes further, likening the rebel alliances in the movies to Al Quaida terrorists and their successful attack on the Death star in *New Hope* to the destruction of the World Trade Centre in 2001 (cf. 118). He believes that by subtly undermining the seemingly clear-cut line between good and evil the films "[remind] us that perspectives different from ours do exist and might perhaps be perfectly legitimate" (119). In a similar vein, Tom Carson remarks on the more sinister side to the Jedi exposing their rather "authoritarian mystique" (161). He goes on to say that "eligibility for the club [the Jedi Order] is a matter of superior bloodlines; not the most democratic notion" (162) and concludes "that one of the things [the movies] offer us an escape from is democracy" (164). Michael Valdez Moses also hints at the problematic nature of the good-evil opposition in the movies drawing attention to the similarities of the final scene of *New Hope* and the "Nazi propaganda film *Triumph of the Will*" ("Back to the Future" n.pag.). For a close analysis of Eastern influences to the Jedi and the rebellion cf. Walter (Ritoku) Robinson, "The Far East of *Star Wars*," *Star Wars and Philosophy: More Powerful than You Can Possibly Imagine*, Ed. Kevin S. Decker and Jason T. Eberl (Chicago: Open Court, 2005) 29-38.

evil corroborates the Emperor's statement from episode three about good being a point of view.

White domination, exploitation of others and self-righteous belief in their entitlement to power are depicted in the rule of the Emperor and his henchmen. At the same time his role as chief villain has a reassuring touch. He still falls within most of the audiences' social backgrounds, perspectives and frames of mind. He is finally calculable and predictable and thus a hero from the same cultural background (i.e. white Western) can vanquish him. This once more shows the ambiguity that myth and formulaic fiction share.

The treatment of ethnic minorities in *Star Wars* makes obvious that the concerns of non-white people were not highest on the agenda of the filmmakers. There is even a contradiction between the way (imaginary) humanoids are included into the story to create a world that looks diverse and the manner in which actual minorities are treated. The presence of innumerable humanoids compared to the near-absence of non-white characters, suggests a displacement of the very real problems between ethnicities. These are seemingly addressed by the inclusion of the humanoids, the majority of whom peacefully coexists with the human characters. Thus, the true difficulties between ethnicities are eschewed, as again, the structures of the heroic quest prevail.[39] Showing the co-existence with the humanoids as unproblematic, the filmmakers trivialise a very real problem, make it easier for the audience to forget troubles related to their everyday life and emerge into a world that is less complex and more binary than their own. Ethnic stereotypes are naturalised in the humanoid characters.

10.2 19TH-CENTURY CONFLICTS AND SOCIAL AWARENESS: AMBIGUOUS OTHERNESS IN *HARRY POTTER*

In the *Harry Potter* novels the issue of diversity is more multi-layered than in *Star Wars*. While in the movies 'foreignness' has to be defined against an unspecified white, European or Western background, *Harry Potter* has white and distinctly English characters as its reference points. As Mary Pharr puts it: "[T]he wizarding world seems an Anglo-Saxon colonial construct dominated by action-oriented white men."[40] This makes the frame of reference much narrower still for *Harry Potter* than for *Star Wars*, as mainly English values are celebrated. There is significantly more diversity in *Harry Potter* than in *Star Wars*. Still it can also be seen that

---

39   Wetmore 140.

40   Mary Pharr, "A Paradox: The *Harry Potter* Series as Both Epic and Postmodern," *Heroism in the Harry Potter Series*, Ed. Katrin Berndt and Lena Steveker (Farnham: Ashgate, 2011) 10.

unlike *Star Wars* where all of the characters exemplifying diversity have different skin-colours, *Harry Potter* additionally features characters as 'foreign' who are from other more or less westernised European countries. Three different levels of Otherness present in the stories of the teenage wizard need to be looked at and analysed. The first is the level of ethnic minorities in the Potter-universe. The second level deals with European characters who do not look significantly different from the white English characters but are set apart explicitly by their not being English. The third level is also the most difficult one to grasp. Otherness seems to be most present on the plane that distinguishes pure-blooded wizards from so-called half-bloods and Muggle-borns. My discussion will start with the way ethnic minorities in the strictest sense are presented and will go on to deal with the treatment of the European Other and the obsession with blood-status in the novels.

In her representation of people with ethnic backgrounds differing from the white English one taken as basis, Rowling tries to be as diverse as the actual British society. The tales explicitly mention five black-, two presumably Indian- and one supposedly Chinese-British character. It is striking, however, that Blacks seem to be in the majority as in *Star Wars*. I do not want to go too far with my interpretation but it seems as if white Western guilt were strongest with respect to black people and that this (internally very heterogeneous) group's demand of equality has come to the consciousness of the average Westerner more than issues relating to, for example, Asian minorities. It is important to note, however, that although all of these ethnicities are present in the *Harry Potter* novels, most of the characters representing them are rather insignificant. The slight exception is Kingsley Shacklebolt, black Auror, member of the Order of the Phoenix and staunch supporter of Harry. At the end of the story it is even hinted that Kingsley will become Minister for Magic, heralding a new regime of respect and equality.[41] Thus he is a powerful wizard with quite some influence in the wizarding community and even beyond, as one important statement on him suggests. Uncle Vernon, when confronted with the danger he and his family are in at the beginning of novel seven, asks why they cannot have Kingsley, whom he has seen on one or two previous occasions, as protector. Kingsley, it seems, has something very reassuring about him and, what is more important for Uncle Vernon, manages to dress like Muggles.[42] Already at the beginning of the last instalment, Kingsley thus implicitly suggests himself as a good candidate for the mandate of Minister for Magic, which also involves dealings with the Muggles every now and then. He obviously qualifies as a mediator between the two worlds, if even Uncle Vernon, one of the 'worst sort of Muggles' there is with prejudices against everyone who does not fit

---

41   Cf. Rowling *Hallows* 596.
42   Cf. Rowling *Hallows* 34.

into his world picture, exhibits something close to trust in and respect for Kingsley Shacklebolt. In endowing a black person with the most important political post the wizarding world holds, Rowling exhibits political correctness. She shows that in her world, skin-colour does not have the significance it still unfortunately has in some places in actual societies. Making a black man Minister for Magic carries the implicit assumption that because as a black person he himself is possibly aware of inequality and ill-treatment, he will make a difference during his term in office. The new regime that starts with Harry's victory over Voldemort is thus suggested to be entirely different from the previous ones which is embodied in the skin-colour of the new Minister.

Still, it has to be said that Kingsley's appearances in the stories are easily countable and that he does not have many speaking lines. His actions are often focussed on Harry, but at the same time, he is one of the more independent characters in the novels. He has a function in the wizarding community that is not aligned with Harry. As bodyguard to the Muggle Prime Minister he makes sure that social structures (also in the world of the Muggles) are upheld no matter how much mayhem Voldemort causes. His respectful and protective stance towards the Muggles does him credit. Kingsley is the embodiment of moderation and balance also because he is not empowered by evil. He is depicted as calm and powerful from the moment the readers first get to know him in book five. Throughout the action, he remains calm and powerful. His stoic bravery and power are Dumbledorish qualities which show him to be an important character for the wizarding world if not so much for the novels.

By portraying her new Minister for Magic as a black man, Rowling, as mentioned, has her readers assume that he will make a difference because of an awareness for inequality and injustice inherent in his status as a Black. This is very interesting because in fact the novels never broach the issue of problems between different ethnicities. No one in the novels is ever disadvantaged for his or her colour of skin, while many are discriminated against and insulted because of their blood status. Similar to *Star Wars* where inequality between different ethnicities is virtually non-existent as a problem and the more or less peaceful coexistence of different human and humanoid characters is supposed to suggest equality, the *Harry Potter* novels obviously displace the very real problems of discrimination and ethnic tensions. None of the other 'coloured' characters of *Harry Potter* play major roles in the story. Most of them are likeable and the majority, such as Lee Jordan, Angelina Johnson, Parvati and Padma Patil, as well as Cho Chang, are staunch supporters of Harry. Blaise Zabini who briefly appears in book six, is disagreeable, not because he is black but because he is a Slytherin.[43] Members of that house are

---

43   Cf. Rowling *Prince* 137.

hated by Harry and his friends almost on principle. Characters from ethnic minorities, it seems, are not seen as Other because of their skin colour or other markers of their social status, but rather only when their moral values do not match Harry's. As this holds true for all characters of the novels, there is a certain equality implied here. The downside to this seeming equality, however is the suggestion that the Other is perceived as 'good' only as long as it conforms to the values and norms of the dominant hegemonic group and assimilates itself. Following this logic, difference in moral outlook would lead to Othering, because the Emperor's (true) claim that good and evil can be perceived very differently by various people would be ignored.

This rather fits in with the treatment of the other characters 'of colour' in the novels. They are not treated differently from the rest of the wizarding society and no problems with their origins and skin-colours are mentioned. Lee Jordan, a black boy, is the Weasley twins' best friend. He is involved in much of their mischief-making and is the clever (and very partial) commentator of the Quidditch matches.[44] During Voldemort's reign in novel seven, Lee broadcasts a critical radio programme and is therefore constantly in danger of being caught by Death Eaters.[45] Angelina Johnson, another black girl, is chaser on the Gryffindor Quidditch team and supposedly quite a beauty. In novel four she tries for Triwizard Champion and in book five becomes Quidditch captain.[46] She is loyal to Harry, attends every meeting of Dumbledore's Army in novel five and reappears to fight for Hogwarts at the end of novel seven.[47] Parvati Patil of Gryffindor and her twin sister Padma of Ravenclaw are minor characters who appear every now and again, most notably to accompany Harry and Ron to the Yule Ball in book four. Otherwise Padma is not mentioned often and Parvati, Harry's fellow Gryffindor rather appears as a typical giggly teenager.[48] Both, however, stand by Harry in the battle for Hogwarts.

The probably Chinese Cho Chang is Harry's first girlfriend for some portion of novel five. Although her Asian looks are mentioned, the attraction she has for Harry very clearly does not lie in their ethnic differences but in her beauty, her skills as Quidditch seeker on the Ravenclaw team and her being a year older than him and going out with his rival in the Triwizard Tournament Cedric Diggory.[49] She is responsible for some smooching and teenage drama in novel five and Harry finally breaks up with her because he feels annoyed by her emotional ups and downs and

---

44   Cf. for instance Rowling *Stone* 205.

45   Cf. Rowling *Hallows* 355.

46   Cf. Rowling *Goblet* 230; Rowling *Order* 202.

47   Cf. Rowling *Hallows* 485.

48   Cf. for example Rowling *Goblet* 350.

49   Cf. Rowling *Goblet* 339.

her theatricality.[50] As was mentioned in chapter eight she does come off worse than Ginny Weasley who is introduced as the 'proper' girlfriend for Harry in book five.[51] This could be interpreted as a prejudice in favour of the white English girl. It is, however, the only instance which could be seen as less than neutral with respect to a character of an ethnic minority. At the end of book seven, Cho, like countless others, loyally fights for Harry and Hogwarts and their differences are obviously forgotten. In this sense she is dependent on Harry and the structures of his heroic quest anyway.

The character representing an ethnic minority in Britain who is mentioned most often is Dean Thomas, another black boy and Harry's fellow Gryffindor. He is Harry's rival for the affections of Ginny Weasley in book six. Now this could be constructed as a triangle which instead of having Ginny and Cho contest for Harry's attention, has Harry and Dean fight for Ginny's love. As Harry wins Ginny in the end, she, too obviously needs to be outfitted with a white English man. However, this interpretation, which would see Dean as disadvantaged because of his skin colour, does not really hold. Ginny has other white boyfriends before Dean and Harry. Thus it is not the black boy who is ditched for the white but rather all former boyfriends have to make way for the hero and one true lover. Rather than an ethnic prejudice, the love triangle is structurally determined. Mostly Dean is shown as Harry's loyal follower. He displays a degree of independence because he joins Harry's Defence Against the Dark Arts Club in book five, despite the fact that his best friend Seamus Finnigan mistrusts Harry and stays away. This shows that Dean is capable of taking decisions on his own, which, if we think back to the close analysis of the main characters, aligns him to the side of the good. Dean is also one of the few fellow students who reappear for a fraction of novel seven, before the protagonists actually go back to Hogwarts to fight their final battle there. Harry, Ron and Hermione learn that Dean who is not sure whether he might be Muggle-born because his father left the family before his birth, flees the persecution of the Death Eaters and is on the run like the trio of friends.[52] Once again, note how Dean does not have to escape the dark side because of his skin-colour but because of his unknown blood-status. As soon as he as well as Harry, Ron and Hermione are caught by Snatchers[53] and brought before the Death Eaters, Dean's independence vanishes and is subordinated to Harry's, Ron's and Hermione's bravery and

---

50   Cf. Rowling *Order* 496.

51   Cf. Limbach 176.

52   Cf. Rowling *Hallows* 243.

53   People who wish to profit financially by the difficulties some people have under Voldemort's regime. The Snatchers work for the Death Eaters and are paid by them but are not a part of their organisation.

resourcefulness. It is the latter three with the help of house elf Dobby, who rescue everyone from the clutches of the Death Eaters at Malfoy Manor. During the time the friends spend at Bill and Fleur's home Shell Cottage, Dean does not have a true function and becomes rather unnecessary.

It is striking that obviously all of the characters just introduced have a certain kind of independence from the hero Harry. This distinguishes them from most of the people who are close to Harry and whose existence in the story seems to very much depend on him. Lee Jordan commentates the Quidditch games and has his own radio show later on, and Angelina Johnson and Cho Chang are both successful Quidditch players, date and lead relatively normal students' lives. Even the Patil twins and Blaise Zabini do their own things. Those who do come into closer contact with Harry seem to lose their independence through it. Cho is reduced to a constantly crying teenager in emotional chaos and Dean does not take initiatives anymore as soon as he gets into contact with Harry and his friends who take over instantly. The characters representing ethnic minorities in Britain seem to be dependent on Harry to a lesser degree than the humanoids introduced in the last chapter. Though most of them are not very important for the story, they are allowed to lead independent lives.

Very definitely, *Harry Potter* does not give a differentiated account of social diversity, the main reason again being that the tales are focused on Harry, the white, male English protagonist. On the one hand, one could say that it is refreshing, also for the minorities represented themselves, not to be stereotypically portrayed as having to struggle with certain problems which are then transferred to their whole community.[54] Their existence is simply taken for granted and they are characterised as no different from the white British majority in the main. On the other hand, this non-differentiating approach undermines the awareness of social inequality that is raised by figures such as the house elves. Assimilation, i.e. complete adaptation to the host-culture is believed to be an outdated model in theoretical discussions on immigration and ethnic minorities.[55] As Elaine Ostry says "[C]urrent multicultural theory views 'color-blindness' as naïve and unintentionally harmful, glossing over – or whitewashing – cultural differences instead of trying to understand and appreciate them."[56] By adopting this 'colour-blind' approach, Rowling provides

---

54 For an analysis of this problematic representation of, specifically blacks, in a dramatic context, see Deirdre Osborne, "How Do We Get the Whole Story? Contra-dictions and Counter-narratives in debbie tucker green's Dramatic-Poetics," *Narrative in Drama*, CDE vol. 18, Ed. Merle Tönnies and Christina Flotmann (Trier: WVT, 2011) 181-206.

55 Cf. for instance Joppke 454.

56 Ostry 94. Cf. also Rana *Creating Magical Worlds* 76, Rana "'The less you lot have ter do with these foreigners (...)'" 50-51, and Saxena 96-97.

escape true to the dictates of formulaic fiction.[57] Making the Other English means making it comprehensible, predictable and therefore less frightening and threatening. Reading *Harry Potter* people can forget for a while the very real social problems that might exist in their neighbourhood. Readers can identify with Harry Potter the 'good' white English hero who does not look down on people from other ethnic backgrounds. And although none of the characters representing minorities is among his very close friends, he treats them sportingly and accepts them the way they are. The picture that is painted here in fact is quite a colonial one: happy people from the former colonies seamlessly blending with the mother country and its values, next to the genial Englishman, feeling a trifle superior but playing the gracious host. While this might be interpreted as weakening the argument for equality put forth through the treatment of many of the humanoids, it could also be seen as a displacement of the problem that actually makes sense. Rowling banks on the fact that sometimes the removal of themes from a realistic background to a realm of fantasy, makes readers more inclined to think about them. Thus she uses creatures such as the house elves and the werewolves to suggest that inequality is still widespread and needs to be countered, which in turn again shows that the humanoids rather have a certain function for the stories and are not so much characters in their own right.

The second level of characters that needs to be discussed comprises the figures from other European countries. It is in novel four, *Harry Potter and the Goblet of Fire* that the children get to know most 'foreign' wizards. They first visit the final of the Quidditch World Cup where they get the opportunity to see witches and wizards from other countries, and realise that their ways might be different from their own. The second chance the Hogwarts students get at making contact with foreign witches and wizards, is the Triwizard Tournament that takes place throughout the school year directly following the World Cup. The tournament traditionally involves three wizarding schools, Hogwarts, Beauxbatons from France and Durmstrang from Bulgaria. The treatment of the delegations from the two foreign schools is rather stereotypical.[58] Both make a special entrance when they arrive at Hogwarts. The Beauxbatons students and their headmistress travel in a large flying carriage drawn by Palomino horses.[59] The delegation from Durmstrang pops out of the lake on the Hogwarts grounds in a big sailing vessel.[60] These, their

---

57   Cf. Cawelti 6.

58   Cf. Elizabeth E. Heilman and Anne E. Gregory, "Images of the Privileged Insider and Outcast Outsider," *Harry Potter's World: Multidisciplinary Critical Perspectives*, Ed. Elizabeth E. Heilman (New York: Routledge, 2003) 254; Eccleshare 81.

59   Cf. Rowling *Goblet* 213.

60   Cf. Rowling *Goblet* 216-17.

first appearances already link Beauxbatons with beauty and elegance and Durmstrang with rather sinister literary tropes such as the Flying Dutchman.[61] The names of the foreign schools have a highly suggestive ring to them, too. Beauxbatons, loosely translatable as beautiful wand, sounds rather pleasant and suggests elegance as do the carriage and the winged horses, whereas Durmstrang sounds dark and threatening, thus also mirroring the appearance of the delegation in the sailer. Both schools are further represented and embodied by their heads. Beauxbatons' headmistress Madame Maxime, a half-giantess Hagrid falls in love with, is beautiful, well-dressed and graceful despite her size.[62] Igor Karkaroff, headmaster of Durmstrang, whose name already has an unpleasant sound, is a sly character, whose smile, Harry instantly notices, does not reach his eyes.[63] The students from the two schools also conform to this stereotypical picture in the main. Those from Beauxbatons, mainly girls, are all beautiful, especially Fleur Delacour who is to become Triwizard champion.[64] The Durmstrang students all look grumpy and forbidding in their thick fur coats.[65]

It is certainly no coincidence that the two delegations come from France and Bulgaria respectively. The introduction of them and the accompanying stereotypes ring with a certain nostalgia for former times in which English conflicts were relatively clear and easy to name.[66] The two schools and their rivalry with Hogwarts echo and take up the concerns of predominantly 19th-century Gothic fiction and

---

61   The almost immediate impression of Durmstrang as threatening and dark is intensified in the movie version of *Harry Potter and the Goblet of Fire* where the ancient schooner emerging from the lake in the dusk has an extremely forbidding quality (cf. *Harry Potter and the Goblet of Fire [German version: Harry Potter und der Feuerkelch]*, dir. Mike Newell, perf. Daniel Radcliffe, Robbie Coltrane, Ralph Fiennes, Blu-ray, Warner Brothers, 2005, 00:16:18).

62   Cf. Rowling *Goblet* 214.

63   Cf. Rowling *Goblet* 217. Cf. also Rana *Creating Magical Worlds* 69.

64   Cf. Rowling *Goblet* 222.

65   Again, the movie version exploits this stereotypical picture and milks it for all it is worth. The Beauxbatons girls introduce themselves to the Hogwarts students in lavish dresses that emphasise their shapely figures and dance into the Great Hall bowing and sighing. (An association of the French with sexual licence is thus much more obvious in the films than in the novels). The Durmstrang students, all male, tall and muscular enter the Great Hall performing acrobatic acts which at the same time appear extremely martial (cf. *Harry Potter and the Goblet of Fire*, Blu-ray 00:18:36).

66   Cf. Giselle Liza Anatol, "The Fallen Empire: Exploring Ethnic Otherness in the World of Harry Potter," *Reading Harry Potter: Critical Essays*, Ed. Giselle Liza Anatol (Westport: Praeger, 2003) 172.

melodrama which often set the English, representing the West, up against an evil East, embodied by countries such as Romania or Bulgaria.[67] In addition to or instead of this conflict between West and East, sober and proper England, was often contrasted with France which was seen as immoral and decadent. Conflicts and problems within the 'real' contemporary England, for instance respecting ethnic minorities, are sublimated and projected onto these old frays which have lost much of their acuity today.[68]

The stereotypical perception of the 'foreigners' continues when the guests have sat down for their first sumptuous feast in Hogwarts. The protagonists notice how the French are extremely particular with respect to the food and complain about the cold.[69] Ron, who in accordance with the trope of French beauty has instantly fallen for Fleur Delacour, has only eyes for her and ignores everything else. Hermione, so intent upon fairness on other occasions, makes her dislike of Fleur known in an unusually sharp tone.[70] As much as Ron is devoted to Fleur, he admires Victor Krum, the Bulgarian Triwizard champion who is also a famous Quidditch player. He therefore represents a rather unquestioning but non-hostile attitude, while Hermione is simply annoyed by Victor's presence because all the girls run after him

---

67   Wolfgang Hochbruck, Elmo Feiten and Anja Tiedemann specifically analyse the construction of the delegation from Durmstrang as 'Eastern,' i.e. "the unwanted, the dangerous and the non-British." (Wolfgang Hochbruck, Elmo Feiten and Anja Tiedemann, "'Vulchanov! Volkov! Aaaaaaand *Krum*!': Joanne K. Rowling's 'Eastern' Europe," *Facing the East in the West: Images of Eastern Europe in British Literature, Film and Culture*, Ed. Barbara Korte, Eva Ulrike Pirker, and Sissy Helff (Amsterdam: Rodopi, 2010) 234). They differentiate between the "Romantic convention (…) in which wilderness and lack of civilisation increase exponentially with distance from the British Isles" (237) and a cold war-based understanding of 'Easterness' (238). Both notions, according to them, can be found in the novels. In similar fashion Marek Oziewicz discusses the construction of 'Englishness' via the East vs. West binary. (Marek Oziewicz, "Representations of Eastern Europe in Philip Pullman's *His Dark Materials*, Jonathan Stroud's *The Bartimaeus Trilogy*, and J.K. Rowling's *Harry Potter* Series," *International Research in Children's Literature* 3.1 (2010): 1-14). Ulrike Kristina Köhler also analyses the stereotypical depiction of the French and Bulgarian delegations and their function of corroborating Harry's heroics as well as reinforcing English superiority (Ulrike Kristina Köhler, "Harry Potter – National Hero and National Heroic Epic," *International Research in Children's Literature* 4.1 (2011): 19-20). Cf. also Rana "'The less you lot have ter do with these foreigners (…)'" 46-50.

68   Cf. Anatol "The Fallen Empire" 172.

69   Cf. Rowling *Goblet* 219-20.

70   Cf. Rowling *Goblet* 221.

like groupies. When she finds out that Victor actually lounges around the library to see her, she is flattered and consents to go to the Yule Ball with him.[71] This in turn makes Ron who really likes Hermione, though he does not admit it to himself at that stage, prejudiced against Krum. The triangular situation between Ron, Hermione and Victor Krum resembles the one in *Star Wars* between Han, Leia and Lando. In both cases, the white, male, Western hero finds a rival for the attentions of a woman in a 'foreign' character. Obviously, this is another common trope in formulaic film and fiction and in both cases it displays an unconscious 'white' fear of people who are different or Other, and especially of these Others taking taking away white women. In both cases these fears of miscegenation are alleviated as Han gets Leia and Ron gets Hermione in the end and 'racial purity' is guaranteed.

This is an example of how the seemingly harmless relationships between couples in formulaic fiction and film can have quite alarming undertones. This unconscious effect is (seemingly) balanced by the fact that on a conscious level the story is critical of racist thought, predominantly in the figure of its hero. When Ron confronts Hermione about Victor by saying that she "fraternis[es] with the enemy,"[72] Harry finds this notion unconvincing and tells Ron so. In fact, Harry himself maintains an observant attitude towards the strangers and in accordance with his respectful and just nature, refrains from too harsh judgements of them. Thus to a certain extend the old stereotypes concerning France and Eastern Europe are questioned in his person. However, his attitude is certainly also used to firmly place him as the good character once more.

In addition to the stereotypes already mentioned. Rowling treats the 'foreigners' contrary to, for instance, Hagrid or Remus Lupin In the chapter on humanoids it was shown that the readers are given the chance to get to know both Hagrid and Lupin as essentially good and benevolent characters before it is revealed that they are half-giant and werewolf respectively. With Fleur and Krum as the representatives of their schools and countries it is the other way around. Their treatment abounds with stereotypes from their introduction onwards, so that at least readers who approach the novels in 'readerly' fashion, have an ambivalent, if not rather hostile attitude towards the two from the start which is aggravated by the fact that they are competing against Harry. Fleur is characterised as arrogant. She looks down on Harry, the youngest and involuntary Triwizard champion[73] and does not even heed Ron when he asks her out for the Yule Ball.[74] She is also the one who is constantly weakest in the challenges the champions face. She comes last in the first

---

71   Cf. Rowling *Goblet* 367.
72   Rowling *Goblet* 367.
73   Cf. Rowling *Goblet* 271.
74   Cf. Rowling *Goblet* 347.

task, emerges from the lake without having rescued her sister who has been taken prisoner by the merpeople in the second task, and she has to be saved from the labyrinth before the third task is finished.[75] Thus, though she is shown to be brave by entering the tournament at all, it is also suggested very stereotypically that as a beautiful girl she cannot be too brainy and capable at the same time.

Victor, used to success as a fabulous Quidditch seeker, is shown to be absorbed in himself, constantly wearing a brooding, grumpy expression.[76] It is also repeatedly mentioned that he does not seem to be as secure on the ground as in the air,[77] suggesting a hidden wish to find flaw with someone who has achieved much and saying more about the observer than about Victor himself. Madame Maxime and Igor Karkaroff are not treated very sympathetically, either. The Beauxbatons headmistress toys with the affections of the good-natured Hagrid who does everything for her and is shown to be in denial of her heritage as a half-giantess at the Yule Ball.[78] Professor Karkaroff, who tellingly is almost constantly referred to by his last name only, is characterised as highly unpleasant on the whole. He does everything to find out the tasks for the champions beforehand[79] and is afraid of Auror Mad-Eye Moody, which makes him suspicious.[80] Furthermore, all of the four characters' limited knowledge of the English language is repeatedly emphasised.[81] This embodies the anglophone arrogance about the English language as universally important. It is never even mentioned that none of the Hogwarts students speak either French or Bulgarian. It also firmly establishes and re-affirms the stoutly English background of the novels and at the same time reveals an underlying insecurity about the stability of this background.

Three of the four 'foreign' characters are 'redeemed' in the course of the novels. Fleur is shown to care genuinely for her little sister when she effusively thanks Harry for saving her after the tournament's second task.[82] Beneath her arrogance, obviously a loyal and caring person lurks. (It should be remembered that people who can love in both *Star Wars* and *Harry Potter* can never be truly bad

---

75 Cf. Rowling *Goblet* 315, 437, 542.

76 Cf. for example Rowling *Goblet* 240.

77 Cf. for instance Rowling *Goblet* 104.

78 Cf. Rowling *Goblet* 372-73.

79 Cf. Rowling *Goblet* 289.

80 Cf. Rowling *Goblet* 227.

81 Cf. Rana *Creating Magical Worlds* 77 and Rana "'The less you lot have ter do with these foreigners (…)'" 48. For Fleur's pronunciation of certain English words cf. for instance Rowling *Goblet* 222, for Hermione lecturing Krum on how her name is pronounced, cf. Rowling *Goblet* 364.

82 Cf. Rowling *Goblet* 437-39.

characters.) At the end of book four Fleur falls in love with Bill Weasley, Ron's eldest brother, and thus becomes aligned with 'proper' Englishness. She reappears at the beginning of book six, when she visits Bill and the Weasley family to improve her English. Although especially the Weasley women find her affectations extremely annoying,[83] she finally proves herself worthy at the end of book six when she sticks by Bill and re-confirms her love for him even after he has been bitten and disfigured by a werewolf.[84] In the final instalment she has found her place in English society. She marries Bill and moves to a small quintessentially English cottage by the seaside with him. There she mainly cares for the household while Bill carries out errands for the Order of the Phoenix. She shows herself a staunch and loyal supporter of the good side, the troublesome times causing her to lose much of her former egotism. The excrescences of evil have turned a wayward French girl into a good English housewife. Her redemption thus cannot be seen entirely positively, since it comes at the expense of her original verve and brings about her domestication and assimilation to the English customs. Thus although she, too comes from a white Western background, she needs to be made to fit in with English culture, similar to the characters from ethnic minorities who are presented as assimilated from the start.[85] Englishness is constantly naturalised as the standard by which everything else and all other people are measured.

Victor Krum redeems himself by liking the bookish, not very attractive and therefore often slighted Hermione and preferring her before all the other girls he could have. The readers meet him again at Fleur's and Bill's wedding in novel seven, where he additionally shows himself as thoroughly opposed to evil.[86] This, however, also means that he is not really estimated for what he is, a Bulgarian Quidditch player with a rather morose nature, but for his associations with the main characters and the opposition between good and evil. We never find out why he is so grumpy and insecure in spite of his fame and success which should endow him with a good sense of self. As with many of the other characters, a more round picture of him is thus sacrificed to the structures of the tales. Madame Maxime ultimately accepts her association with the giants and accompanies Hagrid on a mission to win them over for the good side. On this occasion, Hagrid later tells Harry, Ron, Hermione and the readers, the giants take offence and Madame Maxime rescues him. This means that like Victor Krum, she only redeems herself

---

83   Cf. Rowling *Prince* 90.

84   Cf. Rowling *Prince* 581.

85   Cf. also Gallardo and Smith "Happily Ever After" (92) who do not so much focus on Fleur as having to be assimilated to English values but on her being pressed into a traditional female role in the final novel.

86   Cf. Rowling *Hallows* 123-24.

because she acts beneficially with regard to an important English character and supports the good side. She, too is thus subjected, first of all to the English perspective of the novels and secondly to their binary structures.

Igor Karkaroff is the only one of the four characters who never exhibits any good traits. It turns out that he was once a Death Eater but when apprehended after Voldemort's first fall, wriggled himself out of the clutches of justice by giving the authorities the names of other, more important followers of the Dark Lord.[87] The end of novel four sees him fleeing from his old buddies and at the beginning of book six, the readers learn that he has been found murdered, presumably by his former fellows.[88] Thus the Bulgarian Karkaroff is established as a fickle and cowardly character who only seeks his own gain. Though he turns his back on the Death Eaters he is not brave enough to join the good side and stand up against his former friends. Therefore he is not worthy of the good side's efforts but he is not even a true and threatening villain which would have given him some authority. He is just not important enough to be either.

It can be seen that the European 'strangers' who come to Hogwarts in book four are treated as more foreign than the ethnic minorities living within the Hogwarts community. The blacks or Asians have been 'integrated' into the mass of 'the English' in order for other conflicts to be highlighted, namely the old ones between France and England and between East (Romania, Bulgaria etc.) and West (England).[89] This shows a certain nostalgia for the old and rather clear conflicts in light of an ever more complex world. Thereby the choice of 'strangers' reflects an escapist attitude towards some of the actual problems of English society. Obviously, and a little sadly, the treatment of the 'foreigners' represents one of the weaknesses of the narrative which is otherwise at pains to be as differentiated as possible within its structural framework.[90] But then again, this framework is what limits truly progressive stands. As Giselle Liza Anatol says: "One possibility for why racial identity *cannot* be mentioned in Rowling's texts is that the works wobble between seeking a way out of the imperialist agenda and experiencing a certain nostalgia for the safety and security attributed to the empire."[91] She makes two decisive points here which both support my reading of *Star Wars* and *Harry Potter*. First, the *Harry Potter* novels try to find a way out of the structures imperialism prescribes but they are also determined by them. This is reminiscent of

---

87   Cf. Rowling *Goblet* 511-13.

88   Cf. Rowling *Prince* 103.

89   Cf. also Andrew Blake, *The Irresistible Rise of Harry Potter* (London: Verso, 2002) 109 about the old enmity between France and England.

90   Cf. also Heilman and Gregory 242.

91   Anatol "The Fallen Empire" 174.

the poststructuralist tendencies I found within an otherwise highly structural text. Second, Anatol very clearly stresses the (mythical) ambiguity of the novels, allowing for one reading or the other.

Instead of portraying true diversity, Rowling constantly emphasises common human traits and values. An example would be the appearance of Voldemort's Dark Mark in the sky at the World Cup and the Death Eater activity on that occasion. Both make the World Cup a unifying experience rather than one of diversity. All witches and wizards present are united under the threat Voldemort poses to their *shared* values as human beings. Rowling lets Dumbledore, her main spokesman when it comes to the morals of the books, summarise her call for unity as follows at the end of book four: "The Triwizard Tournament's aim was to further and promote magical understanding. In the light of what has happened – of Lord Voldemort's return – such ties are more important than ever before. (…) [We] are only as strong as we are united, as weak as we are divided."[92] Stressing shared values is a typical mythical stance, as myth very often places the depiction of human nature before the portrayal of individuals. It also falls in with the goals of formulaic fiction which usually sets out to depict ideas at war with each other, embodied in some character or other, and finally reconcile them. The emphasis on unity also mirrors the structuralist longing for a stable centre or origin which precludes true diversity.

This does not just hold for *Harry Potter* but also for *Star Wars*. Again, it has to be noted that there are similarities to the treatment of 'strangers' in both tales. Although *Star Wars* does feature two rather important black characters, while *Harry Potter* plays out certain conflicts on a level once removed by making the 'problematic' characters French and Bulgarian instead of black or Asian, the handling of the figures from both stories is surprisingly congruous. Mace Windu and Lando Calrissian, as well as Fleur and Victor are not treated very sympathetically. Mace Windu is strict and forbidding, Lando is introduced as a betrayer. Fleur exhibits a certain arrogance and egotism while Victor is morose and grumpy and does not live up to his qualities as a Quidditch seeker. Audiences and readers do not particularly like these characters. Only when they either seek for the protagonists' forgiveness in the case of Windu and Lando, or redeem themselves by acts that are beneficial to the main characters, as for instance Fleur, Victor and Madame Maxime do, are they finally accepted. All of these characters also have in common that they are not as important as the protagonists and are subjected to the dominant narrative of the 'white' Western heroes in some way or other. Windu paves the way for Anakin's fall from grace, Lando's heroics are constantly superseded by those of the white heroes, Fleur is turned into an English housewife, and Karkaroff is sacrificed to stereotypical notions of evil as weak, cowardly, and,

---

92   Rowling *Goblet* 627.

most importantly, coming from Eastern Europe. Both stories, thus very clearly have a problem incorporating the Other if it takes human form.

There is, however, a third group of characters that needs to be looked at in the context of ethnic diversity and 'foreignness' in *Harry Potter*, which is the group of those deemed to have 'unclean' blood. These characters do not necessarily belong to an ethnic minority, nor are they strangers to England. Nevertheless, they are discriminated against and persecuted under Voldemort's reign. They are important because projected onto them are problems members of different ethnicities have in England and elsewhere. This group is subject to taunts and sneers already when Voldemort is still in hiding, which is most graphically exemplified by Hermione, whose parents are both Muggles and who therefore has a difficult status within the wizarding community. Fellow students such as Draco Malfoy constantly pick on Hermione's parentage and call her "Mudblood,"[93] a derogatory term for witches and wizards with Muggle origins. As turns out in the course of the novels, Hogwarts alone has seen repeated campaigns against 'Mudbloods.' One of the school's founders, Salazar Slytherin himself, was against accepting Muggle-born witches and wizards at Hogwarts. The resulting quarrel with the other founders induced him to leave the school, but not before he had included a device that, if handled correctly, assured the 'cleansing' of the school from Muggle-borns. This device was the Chamber of Secrets of the so-entitled second novel.[94] Voldemort, when at Hogwarts, had found out about the Chamber, opened it and had the Basilisk within it kill a Muggle-born student.[95] When the said Chamber is reopened in book two, several Muggle-borns are petrified, although this rather happens by accident, since Voldemort who is behind it once more, is more interested in getting at Harry than killing 'Mudbloods' at that stage.[96]

The hostility towards Muggle-borns and Muggles for that matter, is not limited to the school. In the outside world, during Voldemort's first reign, many Muggle-borns and Muggles were killed as some of the Order members affirm.[97] When the villain finally moves into the open after his return at the end of novel five, he instantly resumes his Muggle-huntings. Matters have become worse by novel seven, in which the Ministry of Magic begins to collaborate with Voldemort. Muggles are killed and Muggle-born witches and wizards rounded up and brought to the Ministry for questioning. They have to give up their wands and are threatened with incarceration as they are now perceived as "thieves of [the wizards'] knowledge and

---

93   Rowling *Chamber* 123.
94   Cf. Rowling *Chamber* 164-65.
95   Cf. Rowling *Chamber* 335-36.
96   Cf. Rowling *Chamber* 336.
97   Cf. Rowling *Goblet* 127-28.

magic."[98] The slogan "Magic is Might" on a statue of a witch and a wizard sitting on the emaciated forms of a great number of Muggles in the grand hall of the Ministry sums up Voldemort's ideology and accords Muggles and Muggle-borns their 'rightful' place.[99] Although the villain's violent way of bringing about wizard-dominance is condemned in the books, at the same time there is a subtext telling the readers that being a wizard is in fact much more desirable than being a Muggle. Not only are the Dursleys, the only Muggle family the readers truly get to know, decisively unlikeable and boring, but Harry and Hermione, the two characters raised by Muggles are depicted as trying hard to integrate into the wizarding world.[100] Thus again, the narrative sends conflicting messages here.

The pure-blood mania and racism which includes a hatred of half-bloods such as centaurs and werewolves, largely emanates from one group of people within the wizarding world, namely upper-class witches and wizards who belong to the old aristocratic families and have the greatest hegemonic power. As Travis Prinzi says: "Race is socially constructed. By whom? By the people who are advantaged by the oppression of others."[101] Examples of those advantaged would be the Malfoys who live in a large manor house and employ house elves, Bellatrix Lestrange and her husband, the former being Mrs Malfoy's sister, and the Blacks, who own a grand town house full of expensive silverware and dark artifacts. These families are all interrelated and like to keep to themselves. Members who do not fulfil the family's expectations are ousted, as, for instance, Sirius Black who did not conform to his parents' ideologies, Andromeda Black who married a Muggle-born, and Andromeda's daughter Tonks, who is positively hated by her relatives for marrying werewolf Remus Lupin.[102] In the eyes of these families, wizards stoop beneath their station by marrying Muggles and lose some of their grandness and importance. Wizards marrying Muggles endanger the ideology of the greater desirability of the wizarding world. However, as Grijalva Maza holds, this desirability can only be established and held up in opposition to the Muggle world.[103] Thus as with evil being needed for the production of good, the Muggle world is necessary to emphasise the special status of the wizarding community. The old aristocracy's contempt for Muggles and Muggle-born witches and wizards is based in fear. The members are afraid of disintegrating as a class and losing power and desirability by slowly mixing with people of different social origins. Traditional rules and

---

98   Rowling *Hallows* 18.
99   Rowling *Hallows* 198-99.
100   Cf. Grijalva Maza 428-29.
101   Prinzi 249.
102   Cf. Rowling *Hallows* 16-17.
103   Cf. Grijalva Maza 429.

privileges have to be kept at all costs. "A subtle example of institutionalized racism in the Wizarding World – one that maintains pureblood advantage – is the enforcement of the restriction against underage wizardry."[104] Since in a household comprising several wizards it is impossible to determine who exactly performed magic, the law "can only be enforced upon Muggle-borns," meaning that all other underage wizards and witches can theoretically practice magic over the holidays while Muggle-borns can not.[105]

What the likes of the Malfoys do not realise, and what has been mentioned before, is that they are disintegrating from within and need 'new blood' to regenerate. Many members of the old families the readers encounter in the course of the story, are extremely strange, their behaviour bordering on lunacy. Bellatrix Lestrange, her last name being telling in that way, and Mrs Black, Sirius's mother who out of pure spite has ensured her continued existence after death in a picture shouting insults at the "Filth! Scum! By-products of dirt and vileness! Half-breeds, mutants, freaks (...)" who enter her house, are cases in point.[106] The association of the mostly racist old wizarding families with inbreeding and madness are no coincidence according to Giselle Liza Anatol who observes that "Rowling (...) connects racism to regression, not progress."[107] Their belief in pure-blood has led to sterility and stasis and we see many of the old family-lines such as the Gaunts' and the Crouchs' extinguished by the end of the series. Mixing of blood is essential for renewal as Ron affirms as early as book two: "Dirty blood, see. Common blood. It's mad. Most wizards these days are half-blood anyway. If we hadn't married Muggles we'd've died out."[108] It is interesting that it is Ron who voices this point here, as he is otherwise shown to be frequently and rather mindlessly repeating the stereotypes in circulation, for instance, about house-elves and giants. One explanation of this lies in the obvious fact that Ron's father, who works in the Ministry of Magic, espouses Muggle rights. Thus through his upbringing Ron is simply more sensitive to the problems between wizards and muggles than to those between wizards and other magical creatures. He has been taught the politically correct attitude by his father. Another explanation is that once more, an individual approach to social diversity is espoused by Rowling here. Ron utters his disgust not so much as a general comment on his society's discriminatory politics but as a reaction to the way Malfoy treated Hermione, his friend. It is easier for him to recognise injustice when it concerns someone close to him. The characters, and

---

104   Prinzi 250.

105   Prinzi 251.

106   Rowling *Order* 74.

107   Anatol "The Replication of Victorian Racial Ideology" 110.

108   Rowling *Chamber* 127-28.

with them the readers, very often learn about social issues in the novels, because they are demonstrated on one exemplary character. This was shown with respect to the humanoids in the preceding chapter and here applies to Hermione and her status as muggle-born. And as in many similar situations, his statement does not lead to a general discussion about the injustice of the system but to denigrating Malfoy and morally boosting Hermione.[109] Strictly speaking, Malfoy, though more viciously, simply repeats the prejudices he has grown up with in a manner similar to Ron. The social is relegated to the personal level here.

Those who the racists pursue, for the most part are not aristocratic but what they would call 'upstarts' like Hermione Granger whose parents are Muggles but who outshines her grand, aristocratic fellow students in each and every exam. Here we have another reason why the old aristocracy which numerous Death Eaters are members of, is afraid of Muggle-borns. They do not understand how they come to have magical powers and what they cannot explain scares them. It is hard for them to see that 'Mudbloods' like Hermione and half-bloods like Harry, beat them in many relevant areas of life, including school-work and Quidditch. They just cannot stand other people prospering while they lag behind.[110]

Obviously, fear of difference or the Other often has to do with fear of departing from the status quo, of losing the hegemonic power and the privileges one's family has held for centuries. Funnily enough, it is often people who are not even part of these privileged classes by birth who stir those fears. Voldemort himself is not a pure-blood and though his father was aristocratic he was also a Muggle, and therefore despised by the villain. So the agitators frequently seem to come from the outside. In this sense Voldemort moves within aristocratic circles, even forms the head of them, but at the same time remains an outsider. His ancestors lived in filth and, as Harry remarks, he has not inherited wealth and does not have a vault at Gringotts, one of the institutions at the centre of wizarding traditions.[111] In this sense it could be said that Voldemort instead of guarding a class in itself, is guarding a desire, something he never had but wishes to obtain: the full admittance to the circles of the Malfoys with everything that goes with it. This is a further instance of his breaching boundaries. He is in a way, classless, not really belonging to the upper class but not belonging anywhere else, either. He is unique and remains outside the class structure. It is extremely important for him to forge himself an

---

109   Cf. Rowling *Chamber* 127-28.

110   This of course begs comparison with the situation in Nazi Germany, a connection which has often been made by critics (cf. for instance Connie Neal, *The Gospel According to Harry Potter: Spirituality in the Stories of the World's Most Famous Seeker* (Louisville: Westminster John Knox Press, 2002) 68 and Köhler 23-25).

111   Cf. Rowling *Hallows* 397.

identity mainly based on the heritage of his mother, which, as he finds out, goes all the way back to Salazar Slytherin. This is his legitimation for moving among people such as the Malfoys, but it exists only on paper and does not show in anything substantial or material like money or estates. The persecutions of Muggle-borns thus reveal that he wants to kill the Muggle part within himself so as to fully belong with the pure-blooded wizards and their aristocratic circles.

All their scheming and persecutions turn on Voldemort's circle in the end. The wizarding aristocracy is shown as thoroughly corrupt and rotten and is overthrown, many of its Death Eater members being killed in the final fight against evil, or landing themselves in prison. In a near-utopian gesture, all those who are hated or persecuted by Voldemort's regime, unite to bring it down, Rowling's answer to her own and Dumbledore's earlier call for unity. The new triumphs over the old, a new moderate middle is established with people such as Kingsley Shacklebolt returning justice to the Ministry. The grand finale thus makes very clear that there are characters who "struggle against the limitations of their world,"[112] something that, for instance, Hermione has done throughout. However, it also reinforces the big oppositions that are explored throughout the series as even the struggle between the Death Eaters and the other members of the wizarding society, is liable to the rules of the binary structures: 'Mudbloods' against pure-bloods, new versus old, innovation counter tradition, and, again very clearly, good versus evil and free will against determinism. All the binaries can finally be reduced to these latter two. The aristocracy represented by the Death Eaters is decadent at best if not outright evil, while those fighting against it are good. Voldemort and the Death Eaters stand for determinism as they are ultimately not free but determined by their fears of the Other and the disintegration of their class. And of course, they also try to dominate and determine everyone else. As was already shown Harry Potter and many of his followers in contrast to that exhibit freedom of mind and are therefore able to triumph.

By establishing this class conflict, Rowling once more uses an old fray which has lost some of its acuity by the beginning of the 21st century. Again, class questions were very often addressed in the literature of the late 19th and early 20th centuries by which time English society began to shift and the established upper classes lost much of its power and significance. Gothic fiction once more has to be named as an example of class-consciousness, as its villains, like Rowling's, frequently come from aristocratic backgrounds. In the sense that problems between the white English majority and ethnic minorities are not verbalised but projected onto the struggle between pure-blooded and Muggle-born witches and wizards, they are sublimated and need not be addressed directly. Anatol sees this displacement of a

---

112   Pharr "A Paradox" 10.

real issue as problematic: "In the end, I believe that [Rowling's] inconsistent rendering of what it means to be an other to society's hegemonic forces weakens the explicit anti-racism theme of the books."[113] It is indeed a little confusing for readers to have the problem of racism addressed on three different planes. Distancing issues such as this, however, can also sometimes help to make them appear in a clearer light.

Rowling might furthermore have decided to displace the problems out of political correctness. It is not Black- or Asian-British people who suffer because of their skin-colour but all people, black or white who do not have the 'right blood.' In this way, the black Dean Thomas is as much affected by Voldemort's politics as is the white Hermione Granger. This idea does not specify one group of people as victims but unites different ethnicities in suffering and finally triumph, again emphasising the idea of unity. While on the one hand this can be read as promoting equality, it again eradicates differences between people and eschews real social problems for the more simple conflict between good and evil. Still, the fact that it is mainly white people who discriminate against others shows that whiteness is by no means connoted very positively throughout the novels. As Anatol mentions, it is often associated with Voldemort and takes on an "eerie and disturbing" quality.[114] Myth, after all, is supposed to have a universal appeal and the myth of Harry Potter in particular fulfils this criterion in being extremely pliable and allowing various readings from different perspectives. Still, and this is mythical ambiguity at work again, one could also argue the other way around and say that this displacement of problems between white majority and ethnic minorities further marginalises these groups within society and diminishes their visibility. This it does in the novels, for as was shown, none of the characters belonging to different ethnic groups, such as Lee, Dean, Angelina, Cho or Kingsley, finally are of central importance to the stories. This is yet another example of how popular fiction and film can very often be read in opposing ways. Anatol, too sees this ambiguity in Rowling's depiction of 'race.' She takes Harry's scar as "metaphor for race: an obvious physical trait, like the color of one's skin (...) that makes one the object of others' gazes and assumptions, whereas one's actual experiences tend to be ignored."[115] However, quite frequently, being 'different' is a burden for Harry and he wishes to be able to blend in with the crowd.[116] This then is a conflicting message for people who are notably 'different' and ties in with Rowling's depiction of real ethnic diversity in characters such as Cho Chang, Lee Jordan and Parvati Patil. Harry's wish to be one

---

113   Anatol "The Replication of Victorian Racial Ideology" 109.

114   Anatol "The Replication of Victorian Racial Ideology" 110.

115   Anatol "The Replication of Victorian Racial Ideology" 111.

116   Cf. Anatol "The Replication of Victorian Racial Ideology" 111.

among many echoes her assimilationist stance with regard to the various ethnicities portrayed.

Although *Star Wars* and *Harry Potter* seem very different in their treatment of Otherness and 'foreignness' and surely are in many respects, the tales have one thing in common: both shirk a true discussion of social and ethnic diversity and displace it to other planes. In the case of *Star Wars* the fact that only two representative and reasonably important black characters are included, shows that the filmmakers were aware that they needed to tend to issues of political correctness but did not wish to get in too deep. The struggle between different kinds of peoples is shifted to the level of the imaginary humanoids so as not to let it come too close to the audiences' consciousness. In *Harry Potter*, the displacement is even more artful as it happens on several planes. For reasons of political correctness, characters of ethnic minorities are included but assumed to be an inconspicuous part of mainstream society. The very real struggles for recognition these people often have to face in their societies, are sublimated to struggles between England and France, England as a representative of the West and Bulgaria as embodying the East, which are mostly resolved today. Furthermore, they are shifted to conflicts between different social classes, which have also lost some of their poignancy. The makers of *Star Wars* paint the (utopian) picture of a world in which troubles between different people and peoples as such do not exist. The sole problem of the galaxy is the fight between good and evil in which characters, no matter whether they are human or humanoid, meet and are either on the one or the other side, a rather dangerous and reductionist ideology. *Harry Potter* at the same time glosses over the real problems and assures readers that conflicts can be solved, as is the case with the old clash between East and West and the different social classes. Rowling also offers the utopian and highly mythical idea that people should resort to what they have in common rather than what differentiates them. In unison, every crisis can be resolved. In *Star Wars* this idea also appears, albeit less explicitly. At the end of *Return of the Jedi* different peoples unite to finally defeat the Emperor's regime of evil. Both stories thus to a certain extend try to bypass the fact that there are differences between people. 'Foreigners' are assimilated to Western lifestyle and thought or ostracised. It is worthwhile to cite John Granger here, once more who says:

The alchemical idea of 'harmony and balance' (...) that is (...) the underlying cosmology of (...) a large part of the story's ending (...) is the 'structure' Ms. Rowling offers as her poststructuralism. Instead of conventional structures that are necessarily exclusive and oppressive qua metanarratives or Grand Myths, Ms. Rowling gives us love, harmony, and balance as transcendent principles that inform profane reality and the successful pursuit of which are the answer to all natural strife.[117]

Two points need to be made about his claim. First of all, the narrative attempt at harmonising or arriving at a balance is by no means a poststructuralist characteristic. It is, on the contrary, extremely structuralist. Lévi-Strauss has shown that "mythical thought always works from the awareness of oppositions towards their progressive mediation."[118] So myth, a concept by the way, that Granger frequently uses without specifying it, and which he repeatedly says postmodernism seeks to overcome, does exactly what he states in the above quote: it balances, but often only seemingly. In this context, Girard also needs to be mentioned again. In his cultural theory of violence and scapegoating, harmony within a community is restored by projecting blame for a failing within the community onto a person or group of persons external to it.[119] Voldemort, it can be argued, is scapegoated because he is blamed for the problems within the 'good' wizarding community. The persecution of him veils the racial issues and inequality within the wizarding world, i.e., the structural discourse of good versus evil overlays other alarming trends and tendencies within the 'good' wizarding order which very much resemble real-world issues. Scapegoating does nothing but restore structure and order (harmony) to a society, often neglecting to root out the real evil (scapegoats are hardly ever personally responsible for the problems they are (mis)used to solve). This is not to say that Voldemort is not an extremely iniquitous character who commits quite an amount of evil deeds but to state that he, too is used to camouflage another evil, namely the silent corroboration of injustice out of ignorance. Attempts at harmonising thus always finally serve structures which refutes Granger.

The second point about his statement, which further shows him to be partly incorrect lies in the figure of Harry Potter himself. Harry Potter is all as wonderful as Granger says and he is certainly a role-model teaching us harmonising courage and love. However, he is also a white, English hero. Therefore, despite Granger's assumption that Rowling questions structuralism in her criticism of institutions and her assessment of the treatment marginalised characters receive which she certainly does to a point, she also finally stipulates that it is a white European hero who overcomes differences and binary oppositions. In this sense it could be said that the grand narrative of western supremacy remains unchallenged. This becomes especially apparent in her treatment of 'foreigners' which is surprisingly less sensitive than that of humanoids.

---

117   Granger *Unlocking Harry Potter* 231.

118   Lévi-Strauss 130.

119   Cf. Girard 95.

True diversity which celebrates difference and attempts to avoid thinking in binary categories of us and them, does not exist in the universes of *Star Wars* and *Harry Potter*. Homi Bhabha's stairwell model which is not hierarchical and leaves space for difference and play does not apply[120] to the stories which are still hierarchical and binary in nature. Uniting different people under the ideologies and narratives dominant in Western societies makes difference seem less threatening and pushes the actual problems between various ethnic groups to the side. It is noteworthy in this respect that none of the stories features any character with a Muslim background. Both tales rather provide escape for (especially Western) audiences and readers who, while watching the films or reading the novels, want to forget the political and social troubles of their day. Still, *Harry Potter* more so than *Star Wars* does show an awareness of social problems, but the conflicting and ambiguous way in which these are handled, demonstrates that these issues are not easily solvable, not even in science fiction and fantasy and even less so in the real world.

---

120   Cf. Bhabha 5.

11. The End(ings): Conclusion

Both *Star Wars* and *Harry Potter* end with a Girardian restoration of 'good' order. In an act of unanimous violence,[1] social evil has been identified in and projected onto two (three) figures, the Emperor, (Darth Vader) and Lord Voldemort. These characters have successfully been killed off which finishes the reciprocal violence.[2] The Girardian reading of the endings emphasises the two main points of this thesis, the first of which being that both tales are very clearly structural and the second that they are highly ideological. The structurality of Girard's approach is apparent as the interplay between reciprocal and unanimous violence forms a repeating and therefore circular pattern which is reminiscent of Joseph Campbell's cosmogonic cycle.[3] This cyclical rotation between two binary states was emphasised in the third chapter of the thesis looking at the superstructures of both *Star Wars* and *Harry Potter*. The circularity of *Star Wars* was visualised in the picture of the hexagram which apart from displaying the equal share of good and evil episodes, showed the alternation between the two poles from one film to the next. The final victory of good in *Return of the Jedi* made up the uppermost point of the star, closely followed by the descent to evil depicted in episodes one to three. The celebration of the good side bringing seeming closure cannot hide the fact that there are still evildoers out there who might one day rise to be the next Emperors, as everyone is prone to evil to a certain extent. This is made particularly clear in the figure of Anakin / Darth Vader, an originally charming and loveable boy who turns into a mass murderer spreading fear throughout the galaxy.

Harry Potter is not as open structurally as *Star Wars*, because it obviously favours the good side. In the frame-like superstructure I drew up for the novels with three frames consisting of novels one and seven, two and six, and three and five, as well as a central book, four, it is plain to see that first of all, more novels focus on

---

1   Cf. Girard 96.

2   Cf. Girard 144-45.

3   Cf. Campbell *The Hero* 266.

Harry and his story than on Voldemort, and secondly, that the all-embracing frame of first and seventh book very clearly foregrounds themes such as love and purity of soul, the character traits and abilities that ensure Harry's victory. In contrast to *Star Wars*, which ends with the festivities of the good side, *Harry Potter* does not stop with the victory celebrations. Rowling constructed an epilogue, relaying the 'happily ever after' of the main characters. More than Lucas with *Star Wars*, she therefore breaks the cyclical structural patterns of myth and fairy tale, one of the slight modifications of the formula that according to Cawelti are necessary to make a popular story interesting.[4] Still, Rowling, too includes hints at circularity by telling the readers that before Harry's story begins, Dumbledore has already defeated a dangerous dark wizard. Patterns, therefore, obviously repeat themselves. She also introduces the character of Teddy Lupin whose initial situation resembles that of Harry and Neville Longbottom, the two boys to whom the prophecy whose contents Voldemort later forced on Harry, could have alluded. Teddy's parents, like Harry's are killed in the fight against Voldemort (Neville's parents, too are permanently incapacitated by the evil side). Like Neville, Teddy grows up with his grandmother. These similarities are no mere accidents. The readers are supposed to ponder whether Teddy is not a new hero in the making which would, like Dumbledore's feat against Grindelwald, hint at a certain mythical continuation.

Star Wars is more open than *Harry Potter* structurally but both stories to different degrees oscillate between openness and closure. This is also the first instance of their ambiguity, which is inherent in myth as "mythical thought always works from the awareness of oppositions towards their progressive mediation."[5] The short quote by Lévi-Strauss makes the equivocality of myth abundantly clear. It is centred around binaries and 'works towards' their reconciliation but can never truly balance them. Therefore, the dichotomies will be left standing and myth will constantly teeter between them. The ambiguity that this undulation leads to was analysed in chapter four. Looking at the Lévi-Straussian diagrams set up for *Star Wars* and *Harry Potter*, one can see that both stories though structured around oppositions, are rather complex, because they do not just feature one possible mediating scenario. Several characters can be found in different positions of the schemas at various points in the stories. This means that within the fixed structural corset, the tales offer a certain flexibility. Solely the evildoers are constantly at the bottom of the diagrams. The inflexibility of evil underlines the stories' structurality and embodies Derrida's criticism of structuralism in general and binary oppositions in particular. Oppositions, far from neutrally coexisting, are always set up

---

4   Cf. Cawelti 10.

5   Lévi-Strauss 130.

hierarchically, one term being privileged.[6] This is already visible in Lévi-Strauss's diagram where the initial pair, life and death, is arranged so that life is at the top and death at the bottom.[7] By portraying evil as static and those truly evil as beyond redemption, it is clear that with respect to the good and evil binary, *Star Wars* and *Harry Potter*, too are hierarchical and prejudiced. In both stories, the ultimate villains are vanquished in the end and evil is condemned and ostracised while good stands strong. Evil cannot be condoned. There cannot truly be a moral approximation of good and evil.

So how do matters finally stand with the second very significant binary opposition underlying both tales, free will or choice versus determination (by fate or nature), which was also first identified in the character constellations of chapter four? The movies and the novels are equivocal with respect to the dichotomy between free will and determinism. The protagonists Luke and Harry are shown to be determined by evil to a certain extent. Luke's father is the villain Darth Vader while Harry contains a part of his arch-enemy Voldemort's soul. The ways in which people can be influenced by fate are also highlighted metaphorically through the prophecies featuring in both stories. Still, the tales additionally stress the free choices people can make within their various limitations by nature, circumstances or destiny. Both, Luke and Harry take conscious decisions for good despite their connection with evil. Choice is thus clearly foregrounded for both of these characters and ultimately preferred. Still, the questions of whether someone is naturally good or evil, whether goodness or villainy is written in a person's genes or whether it is a matter of choice, are never satisfactorily answered, as they cannot be in real life.

Rowling is more explicit in her preference of free will than Lucas. In the final novel she presents the readers with numerous choices characters make, predominantly for the good. Examples are Dumbledore's renunciation of power, Dobby's return to the house of his old masters to help Harry, Kreacher's embracing of Harry's cause, Narcissa Malfoy's lying to Voldemort, Harry's own sacrifice for his friends as well as Snape's betrayal of the Dark Lord for love. Free will, and this was also established in the course of the thesis, is only endorsed as long as it is used for the good of others and not for egotistical reasons. Voldemort's choosing evil is unacceptable under these terms which is also made clear by the pitiless treatment he receives. Someone who takes the wrong decisions cannot expect lenience or mercy. In this sense, when obviously advocating free will, but only if employed for the good cause, the books are as prejudiced as with reference to the good-evil binary.

---

6   Cf. Derrida *Positions* 41.

7   Cf. Lévi-Strauss 130.

Again *Star Wars* is more open with respect to the dichotomy between free will and determinism, as it was also more open concerning its superstructure and the distribution of good and evil. In fact, because of the more recent trilogy one could even say that there is slightly more emphasis on determinism through the prophecy that shapes young Anakin's life and consequently the lives of so many others. The old trilogy clearly emphasises personal choice in Luke Skywalker who resists Vader's and the Emperor's temptations and decides for good, despite the fact that his father believes it to be Luke's destiny to join him in his cruel exploits. Still, the fact remains that with the three new films taken into the equation, the overall story is far more Anakin Skywalker's / Darth Vader's than Luke's. With respect to Anakin/Vader the matter of choice and determinism remains unresolved to the end. It is not clear whether Vader truly thinks of everyone's good when he destroys the Emperor or whether he egotistically saves his son.[8] His act might equally be a free decision or his naturally good side (represented by his son) come to the fore again. With respect to *Star Wars* it was pointed out in chapter four that the more recent trilogy seems to be mediating between the old films and audiences as the more realistic one, as it shows that it is not always easy to take the right decisions. The circumstances under which a person grows up as well as the people who influence that person help shape the choices this person makes. It cannot finally be determined how much share free will, natural disposition, circumstance and something as elusive as destiny have in the development of a human being. *Star Wars* is more realistic (pessimistic) about people's ability to make the right choices than *Harry Potter*. Finally, one could ask how free a will truly is which is so much focused on doing good and taking the right decisions for others. Is not the way Harry acts which is mostly driven by love, rather determined, too? And is not Voldemort who nihilistically denies meaning as such, freer than Harry in some respects? Free will is only condoned as long as it is determined by a benign principle, a way of thinking that goes back to 16th-and 17th-century Calvinist doctrines and shows us how much the two terms in binary oppositions depend on and constitute each other.

In chapters five, six and seven the most significant and convincing Lévi-Straussian binary oppositions-mediator scenario of each respective tale was chosen and thoroughly analysed. For *Star Wars* the Emperor embodies the pole of extreme evil, Anakin/Vader serves as the mediator and Luke stands for the ultimate good. Voldemort on the evil side, Snape as the intermediary element and Harry as the good make up the triad for *Harry Potter*. The analysis of these characters was ordered according to their realistic or mythical potential. The Emperor and Luke frame the analysis as the most mythical, i.e. static and clearly allocable of the

---

8   Cf. for instance Dees 52.

characters while all the others are assembled in between those two, Voldemort closest to the Emperor, Anakin/Vader and Snape in the middle and Harry as slightly less one-dimensional than Luke, before the latter. The set-up of these chapters alone demonstrated once more that the stories are not particularly flexible as regards their characters and are clearly dominated by their binary structures. However, the three chapters' outline also already hints at the fact that the characters from *Harry Potter* are slightly more individual than those from *Star Wars*.

In the closer analysis of depravity in the figures of the Emperor and Voldemort, two different positions on evil crystallised themselves. The Emperor is a rather mysterious figure and the audience does not get any clear explanation of where his evil comes from. The simple reason that is given, if that is a reason at all, is his hunger for power. In the end, the Emperor is mercilessly dealt with: he is thrown into the electric core of his own Death Star. His cruel end is possible because the Emperor is never humanised. Not once is his evil ever brought closer to the audience by giving it a story. What is more, while it is not explained *why* he is evil, it is clearly established *what* constitutes his depravity. His evil is described as a kind of lack. Rather than qualities the villains possess, their evil is defined via attributes they do not have, such as the abilities to love, be loyal, or trust. Voldemort resembles the Emperor in this sense. However, in contrast to the viewers of *Star Wars*, the readers of *Harry Potter* get to know the story of Voldemort's evil, his sad childhood at the Muggle orphanage and desertion by his parents. Thus, here evil gets a story and readers are given reasons for the villain's behaviour. Still, Voldemort's end is similar to that of the Emperor. Although Harry half-heartedly tries to get him to repent and Voldemort in fact kills himself without meaning to through his own backfiring curse, he nevertheless needs to be disposed of, just like the Emperor. The implications of Voldemort's case are rather interesting. Although the readers get to hear his story, no true pity for him is evoked, clearly because he makes evil instead of good choices. In both cases, evil is beyond redemption. Neither of the two scenarios, evil that establishes itself in stealth and without clear reasons and is seductive and manipulative, and evil that is partly generated through desertion and negligence by society, can be condoned. Both need to be punished, and even a story behind evil cannot necessarily generate understanding. In Voldemort's case it is quite clear that the focus is on punishing the evildoer and not so much on trying to find ways of preventing his kind of evil in the future. This prevents a true debate about social responsibility. The Emperor's kind of evil, it was concluded, seems a bit more realistic in terms of contemporary life. Much evil nowadays is hard to pin down as, for instance, the horrible example of the Norwegian assassin Anders Breivik shows. This elusiveness makes it desirable in turn to project evil onto certain figures or groups of people, since this seems to be easier than to try and understand the complex connections between world politics, economics and other factors that often further evil and which make the Emperor's statement that "good [and evil are] a point of view" true.[9] The rather emotional Girardian attitude of projecting evil onto single individuals or groups of individuals is certainly endorsed in both *Star Wars* and *Harry Potter*.

As chapter six explores, *Star Wars* also presents us with a character who partly attenuates the harsh judgement passed on the Emperor and who functions as mediator in the sense of Lévi-Strauss. With Anakin Skywalker / Darth Vader the audience gets the whole picture: his original goodness despite slavery, furthered by his loving mother, his ambition, his loneliness and discontent in his Jedi training, the neglect of the Jedi, his seduction by evil in the shape of Senator Palpatine later to become the Emperor, his mass murder (including women and children), his pettiness as a villain who needs to do the Emperor's bidding and his final conversion and recovery for the good side. Again the more recent movies can be seen to be mediating between the older ones and reality. While the old films feature extreme good and irredeemable evil, the more recent ones show the propensity for evil even in the best of persons. Determination through fate (manifesting itself in a prophecy), the negligence of the good Jedi as well as the active seduction of evil (Palpatine) and an excess of emotions clearly dominate Anakin/Vader's story. By using him as a negative example, *Star Wars* similarly to *Harry Potter* though not nearly as explicitly, emphasises choice and condemns exclusive and blind adherence to fate. However, it could be argued that the way Anakin/Vader is treated in episodes one to three is a little too apologetic as it creates much sympathy in the audience for the character who we quite literally see murdering more people than the Emperor and Voldemort together. At the end of *Return of the Jedi* he is allowed to become one with the Force like good Obi-Wan and Yoda. His allotted mission of bringing balance to the Force which he has finally accomplished by killing the Emperor, seems to have redeemed him and absolved him from his crimes. Fate thus serves as justification here. Extending forgiveness is certainly an admirable act in accordance with Christian values, but the films and the finally ambiguous treatment of Anakin raises the question (and does not answer it) of how far forgiveness can actually go.

Snape is the character who closely resembles Anakin/Vader in *Harry Potter*. He, too goes from good to bad, and back to good in the course of the story. There is, however, a clear difference between the two: Snape returns to the good side much earlier than Anakin and truly tries to protect others, even people he does not particularly like, from Voldemort. Furthermore, unlike Anakin, he dies without being forgiven by the protagonist. Harry only learns Snape's true story after the latter's demise. Ultimately, Snape is the more admirable character than Anakin. Despite a bleak childhood, unloving parents, the loss of the love of his life, and the

---

9   *Revenge of the Sith* 00:43:33.

fact that none of the 'good' characters likes or trusts him, he reverses his earlier, wrong decisions. He is possibly the freest character depicted in both stories but it seems sad that he embodies the ideology of virtue not rewarded and emphasises the fact that freedom can make one rather lonely. Where Anakin gets too much sympathy, Snape surely gets too little. Obviously, while taking the right decisions is seen as good, it does not guarantee one the recognition of others. Both Anakin/Vader and Snape as mediating characters force viewers and readers to ask questions such as to what extent we can truly know other people, whether we do not sometimes pass judgement too quickly, and to what degree circumstances can pardon the actions of a person. The two characters show that despite the strict structural framework which they are subject to like all of the other characters, the stories do not have a completely simple and one-sided view on evil. Nevertheless it is notable that all of the evil characters as well as the mediators die in the end. This is then an attempt at finally clearing matters up and making them less complex. Evil in the shape of the Emperor and Voldemort as well as the middle characters who resist a clear categorisation, is expelled from the stories. Only good remains, sending the comforting message that all grey zones and complexities are eradicated and clarity reigns. However, this message can only be superficially comforting and is undermined by the fact that Anakin/Vader and Snape remain standing as possibly the most interesting characters of the two series. The questions about them are surely not answered by their deaths. The two stories are structuralist (preferring one side to the opposition of good and evil, free will and determination) as well as poststructuralist (questioning the hierarchy implied in dichotomies through Anakin/Vader and Snape).[10]

However, there still is a subtle difference in the way the good – evil binary is treated in both stories. As Verena C. Seibold holds, deeds which are considered to be evil are mostly handled in an extremely emotional way, for instance by the press, which is (understandably) predominantly focused on the victims. Seibold now argues that the emotionality with which evil is usually viewed prevents us from looking at it in a more neutral way, trying to figure out how a crime could come to be perpetrated, which factors influenced the delinquent(s) and what can be done to prevent a similar deed in the future.[11] Harry Potter is very much emotionally centred on the victims of Vodemort's crimes. It is emphasised throughout how much Harry has lost through the villain's murder of his parents and the readers share his pain about the deaths of Cedric Diggory, Sirius Black, Dumbledore, his owl Hedwig, Mad-Eye Moody, Dobby, Fred Weasley, Lupin and Tonks. Voldemort's story is told, but not with the intention of creating sympathy or a sort

---

10   Cf. Derrida *Positions* 41.

11   Cf. Seibold 93.

of understanding for the villain. He is presented to have made evil choices for which he himself is entirely to blame. The novels focus very much on the individual and personal. The wider social implications of evil and discrimination finally remain largely in the background. Thus what propels the story is the defeat of the particular evil represented by Voldemort and the protagonists do not much think about what the villain's story can teach them about the generation of evil and possible ways of preventing it before it comes to pass.

Star Wars goes a step further into the direction that Seibold suggests as it conflates good and evil within one of the protagonists, Anakin / Darth Vader. It does not focus as much on the victims as Harry Potter and depicts all the circumstances that lead to the generation of evil using Anakin/Vader as an example. Although the story, too is focused on the individual (Anakin/Vader), the viewers still get a slightly wider social perspective. They are shown what is amiss in the educational system of the Jedi and what would need to change to better incorporate difficult individuals such as Anakin. In fact Luke, the last remaining Jedi and the one to presumably resurrect the Jedi order, redeems his father Vader through his compassion, a trait Jedi such as Obi-Wan and Yoda partly lacked in their upbringing of Anakin. It can be assumed that Luke will renew the Jedi order in this respect. Harry Potter, though he frees the wizarding world from Voldemort, is not one to really change the wider social order. Thus the two stories are different in their take on evil. While Star Wars shows its generation, Harry Potter is more interested in its nature, however sketchy our understanding of it must remain.

The free will – determinism dichotomy is closely linked to the contentions Seibold makes about evil. If we consider people to be free to choose the way they act, we focus very much on their individual responsibility and not so much on the influence wider social factors could have on their behaviour. The belief in free will is what makes people punishable by law for their crimes. If people could not control their actions through their choices, how could we hold them accountable for crimes? Free choice is usually preferred before determination, although it is only the 'good' choices that are condoned, as can be seen, for instance with respect to Harry and Voldemort. The fact that free will is held in such high and determinism in such low esteem, also in the popular cultural artifacts of our time, is partly responsible for the development that Seibold laments in the debate about evil. If we only consider the free choice of persons in the committing of crimes, then we cannot sufficiently take into account the part circumstances or society might play in the generation of evil. So focusing exclusively on free choice or determinism in the handling of crimes shows less about the true nature and circumstances of the crime than about the way certain hegemonic institutions such as the press, the police or the law want the crime to be perceived. The hierarchy Derrida perceives in the treatment of binary oppositions makes a balanced viewpoint difficult.

The two supremely good characters Harry and Luke are the complete opposites of the evil ones. They are innocent in the sense of non-egotistical, loyal and brave. In contrast to the villains they can make friends, trust, forgive and most importantly, love. The two are the only ones of the protagonists analysed who retain their original names throughout. The villains undergo name-changes which signal their pretensions and hunger for power, while the mediating characters, too alter their names but return to their original ones after their recovery for the good side. Names thus have much to do with identity and the heroes' identities are stable. Neither Harry nor Luke is ever truly tempted by evil. This lack of vice makes them a trifle boring as characters. It is no coincidence that Luke is part of the frame of the three chapters dedicated to the protagonists of the stories as one of the most static figures.

Both heroes are used to impart themes that Lucas and Rowling consider important. Harry embodies choice, purity of soul, loyalty and love while Luke predominantly stands for forgiveness and individuality.[12] Luke represents the ideology of the American Dream: every individual can achieve great things and a single person can be extremely important for the fate of quite a number of people and whole countries. After the Vietnam war and with the Cold War in full swing during the 1970s and 80s this was a hopeful message for Americans.[13] This partly glosses over the other side to the medal, namely the fact that masses of people can do horrible things together. The way in which masses are prone to manipulation and evil is shown in *Star Wars* but the collective depravity of the masses of droids and storm troopers is still outshone by the heroes' individual action. Stasis and individuality in Luke's character are not so much a contradiction. Individuality is not perceived as free self-realisation but as heroic choice and greatness of action for the benefit of others. Understood in this way, individuality must needs be static as the kind of heroism depicted in *Star Wars* but also in *Harry Potter* is not particularly singular. This is underlined by *The Hero with a Thousand Faces* in which Joseph Campbell identifies similar heroic patterns in different stories through the ages. Still, the conjunction of stasis and individuality in Luke's character makes him a trifle ambiguous, too.

Harry Potter is a rather utopian character since he unites many binaries: good (via his parents and his own decisions) and evil (the Horcrux attached to his soul), free will (his good choices) and determinism (represented through the prophecy), stasis (his consistently good nature) and development (his learning and overcoming of resentment) as well as most importantly life and death. One of his most utopian qualities is expressed by what Eagleton says about the nature of good:

---

12   Cf. for instance Vinci 11.

13   Cf. Booker 115

Virtue has hardly ever flourished in public affairs other than briefly and precariously. The values we admire—mercy, compassion, justice, loving kindness—have been largely confined to the private domain. Most human cultures have been narratives of rapine, greed, and exploitation.[14]

Good, which has rather flourished in the private domain is brought to the public by Harry who sacrifices himself not only for those most dear to him but also for all the people who fight for his side with the goal to finish evil. In this sense he is larger than life. A further utopian characteristic is that he unites many of the different 'races' of the wizarding world. In the final battle, centaurs and house elves come to his aid and together they manage to withstand the onslaught of the Death Eaters and defeat them. The question is whether this utopian moment is upheld. Are the centaurs more respected afterwards? Are the house elves freed? Was their decision to fight in the final battle a choice to stand up for their own rights or was it rather born from their loyalty to Harry? The readers simply do not get to know. The epilogue set at King's Cross is all about the wizards and their most precious and important institution, Hogwarts. House elves and centaurs are not mentioned. The final sentence of the actual story before the epilogue has Harry wondering whether Kreacher might bring him a sandwich up to the dormitory. This sentence, as Giselle Liza Anatol has also remarked, gives rise to the assumption that good, utopian Harry who is a chance for the wizarding world, has not completely understood the structures of his society and the ways in which the suppression of creatures such as the house elves has contributed to the evil rampant in society for so long.[15] Harry does not quite fulfil his utopian potential in this sense and oppressive structures persist which also shows the limits of the individual.[16]

Apart from uniting the various 'races' of the wizarding world, Harry also brings all the school houses together, literally and figuratively. Students from Gryffindor as well as Ravenclaw and Hufflepuff fight for him and there are single Slytherins who also finally take Harry's side, most notably Snape, Horace Slughorn and Narcissa Malfoy. In the epilogue it is mentioned that Harry even reaches a certain degree of cordiality with Draco Malfoy. Harry also unites the most important qualities of all houses: Gryffindor's bravery, Ravenclaw's wit (especially emphasised in his quest for the Horcruxes and Hallows in book seven), Hufflepuff's loyalty and Slytherin's cunning (the will to use unusual, sometimes even illicit means to achieve an end). This means that Harry restores the peace and harmony originally embodied by the four Hogwarts founders which was then disturbed by

---

14   Eagleton 147.

15   Cf. Anatol "The Replication of Victorian Racial Ideology" 113.

16   Cf. also Saxena 111, 134-35.

Slytherin. He embodies an ideal and harmonious origin which according to Derrida is extremely structuralist.[17] This kind of origin, Derrida says cannot be traced and remains elusive and ultimately an ideal upon which then prejudice and exclusion is built.[18] The founding of the school, as is intimated throughout the novels was never as perfect as many of the characters wish to believe, thus, ideal origins do not exist.[19] That Harry creates at least an inkling of them or a nostalgia for them, makes him a rather utopian character.

Rowling makes sure, once more, that finally, borders remain intact and four (school founders) do not become one. Nineteen years after Harry's victory over Voldemort, when the readers see Harry's and Ginny's and Ron's and Hermione's children leave for Hogwarts, the tradition of sorting is still upheld, the different school houses are still existent. Obviously, Harry's feat has not had a lasting effect on the wizarding world, or people would have advocated the abolition of the four houses and the fusion of all students into just one school. After all, the sorting contributes to much of the harm done in the novels. Still, the frankly dubious practice of assigning fixed and inflexible identities to students at as early an age as eleven, has been kept up despite the novels' wary stance with respect to determinism of any kind. Much as Harry himself on his first journey to Hogwarts, his son Albus Severus now fears that he will be in Slytherin. And although Harry has named his son after a famous Gryffindor and a Slytherin, both of whom did not consequently embrace the ideologies of their houses all through their lives, he only calms his son's fear on the surface. He tells him that it does not matter to him and Ginny if he is sorted into Slytherin and that "Slytherin house [would gain] an excellent student" in him.[20] Finally, however, he tells Albus that after all, if being sorted into Gryffindor is so important to him, he can choose and that "[t]he Sorting Hat takes [his] choice into account."[21] He also tells his son that *he* did indeed choose Gryffindor over Slytherin and that the Sorting Hat indulged him. By emphasising his own choice, a choice that led to much good, Harry betrays the fact that he actually does prefer Gryffindor to Slytherin. His choice will now surely influence his son's. Harry's utopian mediator qualities have not brought about any

---

17   Cf. Derrida *Writing and Difference* 369.

18   Cf. Derrida *Writing and Difference* 369.

19   Cf. for instance the scene in *Deathly Hallows* in which Harry, Ron and Hermione are talking to goblin Griphook about Godric Gryffindor's sword which Griphook claims the school founder has stolen from goblins (Rowling *Hallows* 409).

20   Rowling *Hallows* 607.

21   Rowling *Hallows* 607.

true change but rather initiated a re-establishment of structures, true to formulaic fiction.[22]

This also becomes apparent when looking at one final and significant point the thesis established about the heroes and the villains of the stories. Both villains in different ways function as deconstructive elements questioning the structures of the institutions represented, and in meta-mythical fashion of the tales themselves. The Emperor bluntly exposes good and evil as relative concepts, remarking that "good is a point of view."[23] This small and significant statement challenges the ideological assumption that good and evil are fixed and unvarying categories in every possible context, an assumption that leads to many rash judgements, stereotyping and Othering. It makes clear that different people might see the oppositions differently and that after all, the way they are viewed is influenced by personal beliefs and feelings as well as the respective cultural background. The Emperor's statement calls into question the very structuring of the films itself, where the Jedi are posited as the ultimately good and the Sith as the supremely evil. The Emperor draws attention to the similarities between Jedi and Sith and this thesis has indeed discussed some of the failings of the Jedi, for instance with respect to Anakin. Their elitism and authoritarianism, qualities running counter to diversity and freedom established as good in the tales, have also been remarked upon.[24] Once more, it is fitting that it is the newer trilogy which destroys the rather secure and comfortable moral dualism of the older one and is thereby closer to a 1990s and 2000s reality. (Palpatine, the Emperor to be, makes the statement to seduce Anakin in episode three). Voldemort is an even more poststructuralist element than the Emperor. He calls binary oppositions into question by his transgressions against them. He violates the boundaries between here and there, past and present, self and other as well as life and death. In fact, it could be said that he is an evil mediator, since the binaries he tries to bring together are better not united. While Harry balances binaries in a good way, Voldemort is completely destructive. He destabilises many of the secure structures the wizarding society has built up for itself. His worst transgression is his attempt at cheating death which identifies him as the postmodern man, afraid of old age, physical decay and demise.[25]

In both *Star Wars* and *Harry Potter* it is the evildoers who draw attention to the limitations of structure and the ideological prejudices it creates. This brands the otherwise legitimate poststructuralist critique of structures as 'evil' and advocates a return to structurality. The heroes Luke and Harry function as counter forces to evil

---

22   Cf. Cawelti 10.

23   *Revenge of the Sith* 00:43:33.

24   Cf. Carson 161-62.

25   Cf. Gibbons 90, and Granger *Unlocking Harry Potter* 208.

in this sense as much as in the ways described above. Both finally stand for moral clarity and re-establish binaries. Luke frees Anakin/Vader from the morally dubious state between loyalty for the Emperor and affection for his son by turning him back to the good side. Harry rids the wizarding community of a character who endangers its physical, mental and ethical integrity. By finishing Voldemort, he recreates the boundaries between life and death which the villain threatened as well as all the other binaries Voldemort invalidated. Once again *Star Wars* is more open than *Harry Potter*. The latter is a linear story about the ascension of evil, the threat it poses to the values and norms of the wizarding community and its vanquishing by a morally sound hero. The poststructuralist tendencies are rather clearly rejected. *Star Wars* can be read in two different ways. If one watches the films in their chronological order from episode one through to episode six, a picture similar to that of *Harry Potter* presents itself. Poststructuralist evil threatens the galaxy and a static, thoroughly good hero brings it down and thereby re-establishes clear moral categories. In this reading the Emperor's 'poststructuralist project' is not endorsed. If, however, one watches the films in the order of their actual appearance, the case is more interesting. Then, the secure, morally unambiguous movies come first and those questioning clear-cut divisions and categorisations follow. In this reading, the poststructuralist critique would remain standing. No interpretation is privileged and it is up to the audience to decide which understanding they prefer. This balanced approach invokes the six-pointed star of chapter three again, which once more shows itself to be an apt symbol of the movies.

To come back to the Girardian reading of the stories' endings invoked at the beginning of this chapter, the second important point about my thesis that it highlights is the ideological nature of myth. The fact that social evils are projected onto a scapegoat who then stands as the ultimate image of evil makes clear first of all that an undifferentiating black and white world-view is easier for humans to uphold and secondly that cultural texts such as *Star Wars* and *Harry Potter* facilitate the generation of ideology by presenting such a rather simplistic outlook on life. As Roland Barthes says, myth used as a manipulating tool by dominant hegemonic groups "naturalises" assumptions about reality that might not in fact be natural at all.[26] Some of these ideologies have already been discussed with respect to the major characters of the movies and novels, one of the most significant being the belief that good and evil are fixed categories and that the evaluation of what is good and evil does not vary from person to person. Structures based on binary oppositions are very often conducive to the formation of ideologies. The thesis has shown how the two stories analysed are dominated by those characters directly representative of the opposing poles in their structural corset. This structural focus

---

26   Barthes 21.

then, as Barthes says "distorts" rather than "hides" other discourses.[27] These discourses are there beneath the surface but are not brought to consciousness and therefore can be used to consolidate stereotypes and prejudices. Chapters eight to ten looked at the ways in which the stories treat topics and discourses less obvious in heroic narratives and attempted to find out to which degree the binary structures help suppress and ideologically encode questions of gender and ethnicity.

The treatment of women in both novels and films is ambivalent. The stories present us with the most glaring stereotypes as well as with women who are depicted rather individually, at least as individually as the structures allow. In *Star Wars* there are only three women who play substantial roles at all and all of them are depicted differently. They all have a connection to Anakin/Vader which is significant as it hints at the fact that they are structurally subordinated to him and his story. Shmi, Anakin's mother is a flat character standing for motherly love and care. She is the ultimate victim, first enslaved and later abducted and murdered, but also, perversely, she is depicted as one of the sources of Anakin's fall from grace as her murder triggers his mighty fury and first killing spree. She is thus doubly victimised: a supremely good, patient and passive character whose goodness still leads to evil. Her role in that respect once more emphasises the way in which binaries, in this case good and evil, constitute each other. Shmi is very obviously used as a structural element, an incentive for Anakin's actions which propel the story. Padmé, Anakin's wife to be is not as completely one-sided. In contrast to Anakin's mother she undergoes a development. When the audience gets to know her she is queen of her planet, a rather powerful figure and active politician who fights for the rights of her people. The more she becomes associated with Anakin, the more she loses her active toughness and becomes passive. As the two marry and Padmé becomes pregnant, she is turned into an icon of home comfort and motherhood. She changes from active, rather individual young woman to passive incentive for Anakin's actions. As with Shmi, there is a subtle suggestion that she contributes to Anakin's evil by not setting anything against it and by triggering his strong emotions. As I said in chapter eight, however, her story can also be read as a critique of the way women have been and still are sometimes sacrificed to the 'male heroic quest,' i.e. male advancement and fulfilment. Padmé literally loses her life at the end of episode three, suffocated by her husband Anakin in his striving for power, an apt image of female subjugation.

The third important woman of *Star Wars*, Leia, is also the most emancipated and individual one. She is part of the male quest throughout, resists the advances of the men around her for quite some time and contains not a few characteristics that are stereotypically associated with men, such as resourcefulness, bravery and a

---

27   Barthes 21.

rational, practical and tactical mind. In an iconic scene she resists the suffocation that killed her mother Padmé when she frees herself from the clutches of Jabba the Hutt who has put a chain around her neck and keeps her for his (erotic) amusement. She uses her very chain to throttle Jabba, turning his own (male) weapons against him. Still, of course, Leia is finally subordinated to the male heroic quest. The story of her brother Luke who is trained to become a Jedi knight and face his evil father Darth Vader is obviously in the foreground of the original *Star Wars* trilogy. Nevertheless, Leia is an important character and attains quite a degree of emancipation from the men. It is rather interesting that once more, the perspective on women in the movies depends on how the films are read. Watched in their chronological order, they show a development from a completely passive woman (Shmi), over a reasonably active one, Padmé until she does not manage to balance her job and private life anymore, to a self-confident and emancipated young princess (Leia). Viewed in the order of their appearance, there would be a regression from active to passive female roles. It is possible that the respective points in time of the films' appearances are partly responsible for that shift. With third-wave feminism in full swing young women were confident in the early 80s, ready to make their mark on the world. Nowadays women have to live up to this legacy, have to grab hold of the opportunities their mothers and grandmothers fought for them to have. Many women find it hard to fulfil all the expectations and to balance a successful career, a family and a private life. It is thus once more possible to interpret the movies as critical of the roles incidentally both women and men have to play nowadays. The new trilogy brings the story closer to reality. If the balanced Leia is the ideal, women need to be careful not to take wrong turns like Padmé.

Harry Potter essentially tries to establish equality by featuring more female characters, also in relation to the male ones. As in *Star Wars* different kinds of women are depicted. Some of them are types, such as Harry's mother Lily, who embodies the absolute good which is never sullied or taken down from her pedestal. Lily is clearly a structural feature, the 'good' mother, a protective principle who serves as incentive for action, guides the hero through all his adventures and finally has to be emulated. Bellatrix Lestrange is her evil counterpart and as such as clearly structural as Lily. Her uncaring and non-nourishing ways which are destructive instead of creative and run counter to the healthy continuation of society, need to be ostracised. She is finally killed by Mrs Weasley, the maternal archetype who establishes family values and love above aggressive phallic power. Mrs Weasley defeating Bellatrix could be read as a conservative stance on Rowling's part: the 'traditional' housewife winning over the active, powerful new woman. But it is not as easy as that. Female activeness is not condemned in the books (see for instance Hermione and Tonks). It is merely rejected if it becomes destructive and harms others. This kind of active destructiveness, however, is not simply a feature of the female but also of the male villains and is unacceptable for women and men, thus creating a certain equality. Mrs Weasley's feat advocates a caring and kindly stance towards others, on the part of women as well as men. The ideology underlying this is the one of 'agape,' brotherly love. This ideology runs through the stories and feeds all of the relevant binaries: good is preferred over evil, good choices over evil ones, determination by good causes over determination by evil, good actions over bad ones. The principle thus advocated is charity and the search for it as a unifying, moral guiding principle in a world in which other moral instances such as God have receded to the background, again emphasises the finally structuralist thrust of the tales. By trying to go back to a centre (in this case charity) which does not truly exist in itself but only comes into being in adversity with greed, unkindness and evil, the stories betray their structuralist nostalgia.

The depiction of Ginny Weasley, Harry's wife to be, is ambiguous. On the one hand, she, too is a structural feature as she functions as Harry's 'Beautiful Soul,' an image of home comforts and love he needs to sustain him through his final adventure.[28] On the other hand, she is allowed to undergo a development from fairy tale princess who needs to be rescued by prince Harry in novel two to strong, independent woman who fights alongside the good. The fact that Harry actually prefers her when she has outgrown her status as fairy tale princess is a sign that female individuation and fulfilment is endorsed, at least by the protagonist. Hermione Granger, the most important woman in the *Harry Potter* novels is also the most independent one. While she is at times associated with female stereotypes such as shrieking and weeping in the early novels[29] she undergoes a development and plays quite a significant role, not only in book five, where she fights for the acquisition of knowledge and the enlightenment of the wizarding world about Voldemort's return,[30] but also in novel seven, where without her and her superior skills and knowledge, Ron and Harry would quite often be lost. Hermione is also the only character in the novels who is allowed to take any action that does not immediately have to do with Harry's quest, an astonishing fact and one that privileges her even before Ron, Harry's other best friend. Hermione's actions against the suppression of house elves show that she has identified the racism permeating wizarding institutions and the society at large.[31] In contrast to Harry she fully understands the significance of the house elves' and other 'races'' plight for the struggle between good and evil.

28   Cf. Limbach 180.

29   Cf. Dresang 223.

30   Cf. Adney "From Books to Battle" 108-10.

31   Cf. for instance Berndt 172.

In the end, Hermione is married to Ron and both she and her husband and Harry and Ginny perpetuate the ideology of the significance of the family for society. The readers do not get to know whether Hermione and Ginny are housewives or whether they are working mothers. As with the house elves and centaurs, Rowling leaves these questions open. However, she also does so with respect to the male characters, as we do not learn what Harry and Ron do for a living, either. In this sense, once more, a certain equality is apparent. Still, on the whole it is noticeable that there is no direct mention of inequality between women and men in the novels. And if something is not brought to the readers' consciousness it 'naturally' seems as if it were not there. Obviously Rowling shirks a direct approach to this theme.

Awareness of inequality is raised for the humanoid characters of *Harry Potter* analysed in chapter nine, whose treatment is more balanced than that of the aliens in *Star Wars*. The movies frequently use them to either displace and perpetuate racial stereotypes (examples are Jar Jar, junk dealer Watto and the leaders of the trade federation) or to convey and compound themes that are important to the heroic quest of the main characters. All of the humanoids in the films are, for instance, clearly allocable to one or the other end of the nature versus technology opposition. Most of those associated with nature are good while those associated with technology are evil. There are important exceptions, however, for example R2D2 and C3PO, the two droids who are highly technological and good, and the Sandpeople who are close to nature and evil. These exceptions prove that the main theme of the movies, as technological as they might be, is in fact not nature versus technology, but good nature versus bad nature. Technology is not evil per se but only becomes so if it is employed in a way that harms others. It becomes noticeable once more that all binaries can finally be traced back to the good versus evil one, and 'good' use of something is always preferred. This principle is in operation in both stories.

The humanoid creatures in *Star Wars* are therefore very much subordinated to the structures as they merely function as helpers to the heroes or embody themes deemed important. The most individual of them is Yoda who in fact has a utopian function similar to Harry's. He is a unique creature without known origins. As the moral centre of the films he unites binaries such as activeness and passivity, power and powerlessness as well as reason and emotion. He creates nostalgia for a primal state of harmony and unity, although he, too is somewhat demystified by the more recent trilogy in which he is shown as fallible like the rest of the Jedi. Yoda, as the other humanoids is ultimately a structural feature. He functions as helper of Luke's development and fixed point on which the hero can orient himself.

Rowling creates more of an awareness for the humanoids' situation by drawing attention to the fact that each and every non-wizard group or 'race' is disadvantaged in the wizarding community. She introduces her readers to at least one main representative of each humanoid people as a means of evoking understanding and sympathy. One of her strategies is to acquaint the readers with the individual before letting them know what 'race' this individual belongs to and which kinds of stereotypes are usually associated with it. She does this, for instance, with Hagrid, the half-giant and Lupin the werewolf. In this way prejudices are dispelled. Most of the humanoids are still subject to the story's structures, however. All relate to Harry, most are helper figures for him. They for example teach Harry important lessons (eg. Lupin) and emphasise his integrity as he is usually the sporting one who accepts and respects them all. Focusing on Harry stresses the individual approach to problems such as discrimination. As was repeatedly mentioned, this focalisation through Harry, who does not always understand the wider social implications of the battles he fights, becomes difficult if it debars readers from a more overarching perspective.

Like the aliens in *Star Wars* the humanoids in *Harry Potter* also stress important themes. Dobby mirrors the love and self-sacrifice which Harry primarily stands for by becoming the ultimate helper figure, rescuing Harry, Ron, Hermione and some others from Malfoy Manor in book seven and being killed in the process. House elf Kreacher undergoes a structural movement from sinning to redemption similar to those of Obi-Wan, Anakin/Vader and Snape analysed in chapter four and visualised in appendices one to three. All in all, it can be said that although the humanoids are structural entities they are treated more fairly by Rowling than by Lucas.

The final chapter of the thesis dealt with the treatment of ethnic minorities, a topic that is much more multi-layered in *Harry Potter* than in *Star Wars*. As was mentioned, in *Star Wars* the issue of diversity is largely displaced onto the humanoids who function as the Other and are generally subordinated to the main white male characters. On the level of human diversity, there are only two blacks, both of whom are less important than the white characters in the final analysis. Mace Windu of the more recent films, though a powerful Jedi and almost equal to the Emperor, is killed by Anakin and quickly forgotten. Lando Calrissian, rogue and friend to Han Solo is initially shown as the independent and individual administrator of a mining operation, only to lose his independence as soon as the white heroes' path crosses his. He is subordinated to the white heroes' quest and is constantly shown as inferior to them and their heroics.[32] Both Windu and Lando can clearly be identified as token inclusions on the part of the filmmakers. Apart from them no true diversity exists on the level of humans. The films rather propagate a colonial ideology of the strong, righteous white man who has a natural right to rule.

In *Harry Potter* ethnic diversity is treated on three levels. The first one is the level of actual characters from various ethnic backgrounds. All of these are minor

---

32   Cf. Wetmore 133.

characters and completely assimilated to English society. They are never discriminated against because of their skin colour, they just blend in and are made same. This is an extremely problematic stance. Assimilation is not considered a valid approach in theories on diversity and multiculturalism anymore since it naturalises the ideology of a seamless integration.[33] Rowling's attitude seems strange considering the social awareness she showed with respect to the humanoid characters but then the issue of gender inequality is not directly broached either. Obviously, real life problems tend to be displaced in the books.

The second level on which Rowling discusses diversity, is the one of characters from various European backgrounds who come to Hogwarts to compete in the Triwizard Tournament in book four. The depiction of heads and students from a French magical school as well as a Bulgarian one, is highly cliché-ridden. While the French are beautiful, sexy and haughty, the Bulgarians are sullen, grumpy and sinister. This echoes the stereotypes of the French as libertines and Eastern Europeans as rough and slightly dangerous that were already virulent in 19th-century melodrama and Gothic fiction. Conflicts between sober and proper England and licentious France and a modern, technological, progressive West (represented by England) and a traditional, undeveloped and wild East (e.g. Bulgaria, Romania) are not so much in discussion anymore today.[34] However, they serve the purpose of formulaic fiction well, because they are clearly binary in nature and thus rather simple in comparison with the true and more complex problems existing between different ethnicities today. The treatment of non-English people is the main weakness of Rowling's novels. While the books take pains to introduce representatives of the humanoids such as Hagrid and Lupin as benevolent before they are actually exposed as half-giant and werewolf respectively, they constantly emphasise the fact that the French and Bulgarian students are Other from the start. Ultimately, the non-English 'foreigners' are treated in a way similar to the characters of actual ethnic minorities and also to Lando Calrissian of *Star Wars* who becomes 'white' in the course of the adventures. They are assimilated to the ways of the English. They make up for their arrogance or grumpiness by falling in love with someone English (eg. Fleur Delacour and Victor Krum) or helping one of the heroes (for instance Madame Maxime). It is hard to believe that Rowling who shows acute social awareness on the level of the humanoids, is blatantly ignorant when it comes to the European Other depicted. The most benign interpretation of this would be that the treatment of the European 'foreigners' is a displaced critique of how societies approach the issues of diversity and multiculturalism.

---

33   Cf. Joppke 454.

34   On the treatment of these Eastern stereotypes cf. for instance Hochbruck, Feiten and Tiedemann, and Oziewicz.

The final level on which Rowling approaches difference is the level of actual racial segregation. Voldemort's war is in fact a war for the purity of wizarding blood. For him and his henchmen, all wizards who do not have a pure-blood heritage are inferior and need to be hunted down and eradicated. The issue of class also plays a role in this context as most of those who deem themselves superior are aristocratic. Fear of the new, of the erosion of old values and privileges is at the root of the Death Eaters' struggle. Rowling makes it crystal clear that she does not endorse this kind of racism. Finally then, on this level once removed from real social problems, she does take a stand and rejects the elitist notion that some are better than others. Only if all work together as equals can a good order be created and upheld, an order in which everyone will be respected. Ron the pureblood, Hermione the Muggle-born and Harry the half-blood who jointly free their community from Voldemort are the best example that cooperation does the trick, Harry again functioning as mediator in between the two extremes of 'pure' and 'dirty' blood.

All in all it can be said that *Star Wars* though more open than *Harry Potter* structurally, is much narrower and generally more prejudiced in the treatment of its characters. J.K. Rowling makes an effort to depict her characters as individually as possible within the confines of the structures and although she displaces matters of inequality she at least makes clear that the Death Eaters' notions of superiority are not to be accepted. Both stories completely follow Cawelti who holds that "the individual version of a formula must have some unique or special characteristics of its own, yet these characteristics must ultimately work toward the fulfillment of the conventional form."[35] They slightly break the formula only to come back to it at the end but they employ different strategies. *Star Wars* show greater flexibility on the level of structure, therefore it seems, the stability and immobility of formulaic fiction needs to be transmitted via the characters in the movies. Both the Emperor and Luke are rather static and even for Anakin it is mostly clear what side he is on at a given moment. Most of the female and humanoid characters are not individuals either, but propel the action by being incentives for heroic action or convey ideas important for the story. The two token blacks are rather subordinated to the dominant white male discourse.

Harry Potter is more closed structurally with its uneven number of instalments, the majority of which focus on Harry, the good principle. Still, within this frame, Rowling tries to give characters as much individuality as possible, the sad exception being the figures from other European countries portrayed in novel four. Although all of the characters depicted relate to Harry somehow and of course acquire their importance through him and are therefore subordinated to the hero's quest, they are also individuals and develop. Examples are Dobby, Kreacher, Lupin and Snape.

---

35   Cawelti 10.

Compared to Lucas, Rowling is more politically correct, because she subtly alludes to issues such as discrimination and inequality, although as was mentioned, the wider social perspective is often distorted by the focalisation through Harry. Structurally, Lucas's tales exceed hers in elegance, the depiction of characters is more successful in Rowling's works.

To conclude it can be said that both stories are definitely myths in the sense of Lévi-Strauss and Barthes. They clearly exhibit the structural patterns of extreme poles and mediator and they show a tendency to prefer the parts of the oppositions that seem more desirable. Good behaviour is finally advocated as all oppositions are reducible to the good-evil one. There are good and evil choices, good and evil ways of being active, as well as sound and unhealthy modes of dealing with one's mortality. The treatment of these binaries shows how much both stories are fixed on the search for the unifying principle of charity. The treatment of discourses which are not directly relevant to the heroic quest and thus overshadowed by the structures of the stories, is ideological and invokes Barthes's view of myth as texts of any sort used to legitimate the authority of the dominant hegemonic group.[36] Both tales, for instance, propagate the desires of a predominantly white, male and in the case of *Harry Potter* English 'elite' which echoes colonial interests of establishing supremacy and legitimating white rule. A further ideology that both tales adhere to is the one of the stable and functioning family as the backbone of society. *Star Wars*, apart from the more obvious heroic quest, is also a story of repairing and reuniting a family with Luke and Leia discovering their status as siblings and Luke recovering and reintegrating their lost father. Han completes the trio as prospective son- and brother-in-law and symbolises the promise of the family's continuation. Harry Potter, too is constantly in search of a family and his, Ron's and Hermione's conventional marriages of the epilogue even support the ideology of the traditional family more directly than the 'familial' structures of *Star Wars*.

As an area of further research it would certainly be rewarding to apply Lévi-Strauss's and Barthes's theories of myth to a more extensive pool of narratives (films or novels) with similar structures and mythical intent. Such an analysis would provide us with more profound evidence of the basic similarity of formulaic tales and would probably yield an almost empiric overview of the values deemed important in Western societies and propagated and perpetuated in these kinds of stories. In complementary fashion, it might also prove worthwhile to look at tales originating from non-Western backgrounds such as stories of indigenous peoples. According to Lévi-Strauss they should deal with similar binary oppositions but it would be interesting to see which kinds of values they finally advocate. I am aware of the fact that this thesis, too was written from a Western perspective, so it would

---

36   Cf. Barthes 21

be fascinating to learn about the reception of phenomena such as *Star Wars* and *Harry Potter*, which after all, are written to support Western values, in non-Western countries. There are some examples of such research but the field could certainly be extended.[37]

To sum up this chapter and the thesis I would like to come back to Karen Armstrong's functions of myth outlined at the beginning of the dissertation and conclude by trying to answer the question of whether *Star Wars* and *Harry Potter* fulfil all the criteria she sets up. While the Lévi-Straussian and Barthesian readings decribe the structure and some of the intents of myth well, they might not quite hit at the true core of myths as narratives of the numinous such as, for instance, the Osiris myth. Firstly, myth for Armstrong "is nearly always rooted in the experience of death and the fear of extinction."[38] Secondly, it "is usually inseparable from ritual."[39] Thirdly, "myths are about extremity; they force us to go beyond our experience."[40] Fourthly, myth is didactic[41] and last but not least, it contains an element of the divine.[42] Her first characteristic of myth is clearly fulfilled in both *Star Wars* and *Harry Potter*. Fear of death is exemplified in Anakin/Vader and even more so in Voldemort and has terrible consequences in both cases. The two characters' wrong ways of dealing with their fear of death need to be countered by the heroes who exhibit bravery in the face of it (Luke and Harry) and accept the fact of their mortality thereby mastering death. A life of love and fellow feeling is advocated as the remedy to fear of death in both tales. Armstrong's third criterion is also fulfilled. The treatment of extremity is visible in the Lévi-Straussian structure of myth which both stories show. Myth has a cathartic aim in taking us through situations and letting us live out emotions which we would not usually encounter in real life. We escape to the formula for a while, are entertained and emerge relieved of extreme emotions. The events of *Star Wars* and *Harry Potter* are obviously on that mythical plane. How many people in Western societies have actually experienced a war for the last sixty years? Who of us has ever been faced by a prophecy telling us that we have a special mission in life? How many are persecuted by evil madmen, who of us can race through the galaxy in state-of-the-

---

37 Cf. for instance Gabriel S. Estrada for a Nahuatl perspective as well as Hollie Anderson, "Reading Harry Potter with Navajo Eyes," *Harry Potter's World: Multi-disciplinary Critical Perspectives*, Ed. Elizabeth E. Heilman (New York: Routledge, 2003) 97-108.

38 Armstrong 3.

39 Armstrong 3.

40 Armstrong 3.

41 Cf. Armstrong 4.

42 Cf. Armstrong 4.

art spaceships or do magic? The experiences of the two stories, as of myth in Armstrong's sense are extreme and by their very extremity reinforce the 'normality' of our everyday life as audiences and readers are ultimately relieved that they do not have to fight the battles of hero or heroine.

Certainly, both *Star Wars* and *Harry Potter* also embody the didactic function of myth. We are invited to emulate the behaviour of the heroes in extending the hand of friendship to others, no matter whether they are like or unlike us, trusting others and ourselves, being loyal and loving. The ways of the heroes, although often difficult, are made more desirable to us by the utter depravity of the villains. In this sense, didactically and ideologically readers and audiences are not given a choice of who to imitate. The villains are rotten to the core and no one would wish to be like them. Armstrong's second criterion, myth's inseparability from ritual is, I believe, partly fulfilled. The fan meetings, conferences and parades for both phenomena as well as the incessant re-viewing and re-reading of the stories do contain an active element and acquire an almost ritualistic nature. The fan culture surrounding both *Star Wars* and *Harry Potter* incidentally is a phenomenon that would merit further research, especially in connection with the stories being viewed as myths. Of particular interest in this respect would be the analysis of the profusion of fan fiction on the web, ranging from rewrites and continuations of the stories to romances about single characters, which are sometimes explicitly sexual. Myths only became myths because they were perpetuated through the ages, changed and amended for the purposes of particular people or societies. *Star Wars* and *Harry Potter*, too seem to be 'eternalised' in such a way, the internet playing a great role in their continuation. The field of fan activity and fiction merits a further book that exclusively focuses on this, for lack of a better word, phenomenon as it would have gone beyond the scope of this thesis.[43]

Armstrong's last function of myth needs to be briefly explored. Do *Star Wars* and *Harry Potter* tell stories of a higher plane of being, of the numinous? I do not think they finally do. They are ultimately worldly and present guides for earthly life. Both Harry and Luke, for instance, are incomplete Christ-like figures. Harry represents the loving Christ who sacrifices himself for others (though notably for those he loves and not so much for the sinners).[44] Luke complements Harry's

---

43   Constantin Gillies's non-academic volume on *Star Wars* fan activity presents many curious and enjoyable anecdotes and oddities in connection with the movies (Constantin Gillies, *Die Macht mit uns: Star Wars und die Folgen* (Reinbek: Rowohlt Taschenbuch Verlag, 2003)).

44   Cf. also Vandana Saxena who says: "The persistence of the problems of race, bloodlines and violence, even in the post-Voldemort magical community, deconstructs the reading of Harry's sacrifice only in terms of Christian narrative [sic] of redemption.

sacrifice by being the redeeming Christ who forgives the sinner (Vader). Although Harry, too achieves a degree of understanding, even forgiveness for people who sinned and personally disliked him (Kreacher, Snape), he only does so after they have changed towards him. While Luke is more forgiving (he believes in Vader's goodness throughout), he never needs to make as cold-blooded a sacrifice as Harry. The stories, although they certainly fulfil a quasi-religious function as popular myths, can never truly achieve the status actual salvific histories have. Their heroes simply fall short of the complete and all-encompassing goodness of, for instance, a Jesus Christ. They retain human flaws. Dumbledore who is established as the wise principle of goodness through novels one to six, turns out to be human, too and make mistakes in book seven. Yoda is also destabilised by the more recent trilogy where he is not shown as the wise and passive sage who leads a hermit's life on a lonely and distant planet but as an active warrior and a flawed individual who does not manage to read the prophecy and Anakin correctly.

The Force and magic, too are interesting in this respect. Magic is not so much a spiritual force in *Harry Potter* as an expression of the individual's strength of mind. With the Force it is a bit different. In the original trilogy it is depicted as a kind of spiritual energy which connects all living beings and also links them with the inanimate. Those who practice its ways are in harmony with (their) nature. In the more recent trilogy, the Force, as so many of the other aspects and characters of the older films, is demystified. It is scientifically explained as an aggregation of midi-chlorians and becomes measurable in the blood of a person.[45] It is also shown to be a somewhat elitist energy as not every human or creature in the galaxy is endowed with its powers.[46] Magic, too, is reserved for some individuals. In this sense, neither the Force, nor magic resembles Jesus's grace, for instance, which is not only lavished upon a select few. Both *Star Wars* and *Harry Potter*, although they are mythical in the sense of Lévi-Strauss and Barthes, the prime theories my thesis is based on, cannot be called myths in the sense of tales of the numinous which take up a quasi-religious role. Thus despite the fact that stories such as the ones analysed have taken over some of the functions of myths and religious tales and have

---

His sacrifice, though it saves the community from immediate destruction, does not solve the problems in the long run. Historical grounding of the narrative prevents it from being an absolute allegory of Christ's story: unlike Christ's sacrifice, which succeeds in redeeming man, Harry's sacrifice merely succeeds in showing the way" (134).

45   Cf. John Perlich, "'I've Got a Bad Feeling About This...:' Lucas Gets Lost on the Path of Mythos," *Sith, Slayers, Stargates, + Cyborgs: Modern Mythology in the New Millennium*, Ed. David Whitt and John Perlich (New York: Peter Lang, 2008) 21-22.

46   Cf. Perlich 23.

certainly partly supplanted them nowadays, they can never completely replace the comforting and all-encompassing nature of true (numinous) myths.

Finally, it can be said that the endings of both *Star Wars* and *Harry Potter* are as ambiguous as the rest of the tales. Evil has been vanquished and a quasi-utopian condition reigns, albeit briefly, when all the different human and alien/humanoid characters celebrate together. The final emphasis in *Star Wars* is on good, sugarcoating the fact that structurally, the circular movement between good and evil could instantly start anew. The movies thus have a hopeful ending, leaving audiences as euphoric as the characters. This kind of ideological fairy-tale ending is both soothing and dangerous. It is comforting, because moral clarity makes life easier, yet dangerous, because in real life, matters are hardly ever simple and disappointment must inevitably follow as life catches up with members of the audience once more. In *Harry Potter* the preference for good is made even clearer than in *Star Wars*. There are seven novels which means that in contrast to *Star Wars* one part of the binary opposition (good) is given preference on the level of the superstructure. Still, the narrative does not stop with the euphoria of the victory over Voldemort and the Death Eaters. It takes the readers back to the calmer, less extreme, even contemplative atmosphere of the epilogue. Fans and scholars alike have been puzzled by this epilogue but maybe it does have a function after all. It brings the reader back to reality, grounds him or her, after the excitement of the stories, and in a figurative sense, after the hype around the whole Harry Potter-phenomenon. The reader sees a family saying good-bye to their children who are off to boarding school. There is all the joy and the anxiety connected to such an event. The reader has reached the realm of the everyday once more. However, the family who is presented is not quite as 'normal' as other families and the platform in King's Cross Station from which the school train goes is not an ordinary one. And the reader knows that the train will take the children to an all but ordinary school. Thus, even if life cannot be all dragon- or Voldemort-slaying and the euphoric times of victory cannot persist, Rowling seems to say, there is still magic in everyday experience.

12. Works Cited

PRIMARY SOURCES

Harry Potter and the Deathly Hallows Part 2 [German version: *Harry Potter und die Heiligtümer des Todes Teil 2*]. dir. David Yates. perf. Daniel Radcliffe, Helena Bonham Carter, Ralph Fiennes. DVD. Warner Brothers, 2011.

Harry Potter and the Goblet of Fire [German version: *Harry Potter und der Feuerkelch*]. dir. Mike Newell. perf. Daniel Radcliffe, Robbie Coltrane and Ralph Fiennes. Blu-ray. Warner Brothers, 2005.

Harry Potter and the Philosopher's Stone [German version: *Harry Potter und der Stein der Weisen*]. dir. Chris Columbus. perf. Daniel Radcliffe, Robbie Coltrane, Richard Harris. DVD. Warner Brothers, 2001.

Rowling, J.K. *Harry Potter and the Deathly Hallows*. London: Bloomsbury, 2007.

---. *Harry Potter and the Half-Blood Prince*. London: Bloomsbury, 2005.

---. *Harry Potter and the Order of the Phoenix*. London: Bloomsbury, 2003.

---. *Harry Potter and the Goblet of Fire*. London: Bloomsbury, 2000.

---. *Harry Potter and the Prisoner of Azkaban*. London: Bloomsbury, 1999.

---. *Harry Potter and the Chamber of Secrets*. London: Bloomsbury, 1998.

---. *Harry Potter and the Philosopher's Stone*. London: Bloomsbury, 1997.

Star Wars: Revenge of the Sith [German version: *Star Wars: Die Rache der Sith*]. dir. George Lucas. perf. Ewan McGregor, Natalie Portman, Hayden Christensen and Christopher Lee. DVD. LucasFilm Ltd, 2005.

Star Wars: Attack of the Clones [German version: *Star Wars: Angriff der Klonkrieger*]. dir. George Lucas. perf. Ewan McGregor, Natalie Portman, Hayden Christensen and Christopher Lee. DVD. LucasFilm Ltd, 2002.

Star Wars: The Phantom Menace [German version: *Star Wars: Die dunkle Bedrohung*]. dir. George Lucas. perf. Liam Neeson, Ewan McGregor and Natalie Portman. DVD. LucasFilm Ltd, 1999.

Star Wars: Return of the Jedi [German version: *Star Wars: Die Rückkehr der Jedi-Ritter*]. dir. Richard Marquand. perf. Mark Hamill, Harrison Ford, Carrie Fisher and Anthony Daniels. [1983]. DVD. LucasFilm Ltd, Special Edition 2004.

Star Wars: The Empire Strikes Back [German version: *Star Wars: Das Imperium schlägt zurück*]. dir. Irvin Kershner. perf. Mark Hamill, Harrison Ford, Carrie Fisher and Anthony Daniels. [1980]. DVD. LucasFilm Ltd, Special Edition 2004.

Star Wars: A New Hope [German version: *Star Wars: Eine neue Hoffnung*]. dir. George Lucas. perf. Mark Hamill, Harrison Ford, Carrie Fisher and Alec Guinness. [1977]. DVD. LucasFilm Ltd, Special Edition 2004.

SECONDARY SOURCES

Adney, Karley. "The Influence of Gender on Harry Potter's Heroic (Trans)Formation." *Heroism in the Harry Potter Series*. Ed. Katrin Berndt and Lena Steveker. Farnham: Ashgate, 2011. 177-91.

---. "From Books to Battle: Hermione's Quest for Knowledge in *Harry Potter and the Order of the Phoenix*." *Topic: A Journal of the Liberal Arts* 54 (2004): 103-12.

Althusser, Louis. "Ideology and Ideological State Apparatuses." *Literary Theory: An Anthology*. Ed. Julie Rivkin and Michael Ryan. Malden, MA: Blackwell Publishing, 2004. 693-702.

Anatol, Giselle Liza, ed. *Reading Harry Potter Again: New Critical Essays*. Santa Barbara: ABC-CLIO, 2009.

---. "The Replication of Victorian Racial Ideology in *Harry Potter*." *Reading Harry Potter Again: New Critical Essays*. Ed. Giselle Liza Anatol. Santa Barbara: ABC-CLIO, 2009. 109-26.

---, ed. *Reading Harry Potter: Critical Essays*. Westport: Praeger, 2003.

---. "The Fallen Empire: Exploring Ethnic Otherness in the World of Harry Potter." *Reading Harry Potter: Critical Essays*. Ed. Giselle Liza Anatol. Westport: Praeger, 2003. 163-78.

Anderson, Hollie. "Reading Harry Potter with Navajo Eyes." *Harry Potter's World: Multidisciplinary Critical Perspectives*. Ed. Elizabeth E. Heilman. New York: Routledge, 2003. 97-108.

Appelbaum, Peter. "The Great Snape Debate." *Critical Perspectives on Harry Potter*. Ed. Elizabeth E. Heilman. New York: Routledge, 2009. 83-100.

Armstrong, Karen. *A Short History of Myth*. Edinburgh: Canongate, 2005.

Ashcroft, Bill, Gareth Griffiths and Helen Tiffin. *Post-Colonial Studies: The Key Concepts*. London: Routledge, 2000.

Bak, Sandra. *Harry Potter: Auf den Spuren eines zauberhaften Bestsellers*. Frankfurt a.M.: Peter Lang, 2004.

Barthes, Roland. "Myth Today." *Structuralism in Myth: Lévi-Strauss, Barthes, Dumézil, and Propp.* Ed. Robert A. Segal. New York: Garland Publishing, 1996. 1-29.

Bassham, Gregory. "Choices Versus Abilities: Dumbledore on Self-Understanding." *The Ultimate Harry Potter and Philosophy: Hogwarts for Muggles.* Ed. Gregory Bassham. New Jersey: Wiley, 2010. 157-71.

---. "A Hogwarts Education: The Good, the Bad, and the Ugly." *The Ultimate Harry Potter and Philosophy: Hogwarts for Muggles.* Ed. Gregory Bassham. New Jersey: Wiley, 2010. 212-25.

---. "The Prophecy-Driven Life: Fate and Freedom at Hogwarts." *Harry Potter and Philosophy: If Aristotle Ran Hogwarts.* Ed. David Bagget and Shawn E. Klein. Chicago: Open Court, 2004. 213-26.

Behr, Kate E. "'Same-as-Difference': Narrative Transformations and Intersecting Cultures in Harry Potter." *Journal of Narrative Theory* 35.1 (2005): 112-32.

---. *The Representation of Men in the English Gothic Novel 1762-1820.* Levinston: Edwin Mellen Press, 2002.

Bergstrom, Janet. "Androids and Androgyny." *Camera Obscura* 5 (1986): 36-65.

Berndt, Katrin and Lena Steveker, eds. *Heroism in the Harry Potter Series.* Farnham: Ashgate, 2011.

Berndt, Katrin. "Hermione Granger, or A Vindication of the Rights of Girl." *Heroism in the Harry Potter Series.* Ed. Katrin Berndt and Lena Steveker. Farnham: Ashgate, 2011. 159-76.

Bhabha, Homi K. *The Location of Culture.* London: Routledge, 1994.

Blake, Andrew. *The Irresistible Rise of Harry Potter.* London: Verso, 2002.

Boll, Julia. "Harry Potter's Archetypal Journey." *Heroism in the Harry Potter Series.* Ed. Katrin Berndt and Lena Steveker. Farnham: Ashgate, 2011. 85-104.

Bolle, Kees W. "Myth: An Overview." *The Encyclopedia of Religion.* Ed. Mircea Eliade. New York: Macmillan Publishing Company, 1987.

Booker, M. Keith. *Alternate Americas: Science Fiction Film and American Culture.* Westport: Praeger, 2006.

Bousquet, Marc. "Harry Potter, the War Against Evil, and the Melodramatization of Public Culture." *Critical Perspectives on Harry Potter.* Ed. Elizabeth E. Heilman. New York: Routledge, 2009. 177-95.

Bouzereau, Laurent. *Star Wars: The Annotated Screenplays.* New York: Del Rey, 1997.

Bowen, Jonathan L. and Rachel Wagner. "'Hokey Religions and Ancient Weapons:' The Force of Spirituality." *Finding the Force of the Star Wars Franchise: Fans, Merchandise, and Critics.* Ed. Matthew Wilhelm Kapell and John Shelton Lawrence. New York: Peter Lang, 2006. 75-93.

Brennan Croft, Janet. "The Education of a Witch: Tiffany Aching, Hermione Granger and Gendered Magic in Discworld and Potter World." *Mythlore* 27.3-4 (2009): 129-42.

Brown, Christopher M. "'A Wretched Hive of Scum and Villainy:' *Star Wars* and the Problem of Evil." *Star Wars and Philosophy: More Powerful than You Can Possibly Imagine.* Ed. Kevin S. Decker and Jason T. Eberl. Chicago: Open Court, 2005. 69-79.

Butler, Judith. *Gender Trouble.* New York: Routledge, 1990.

Campbell, Joseph. *The Power of Myth.* Interview with Bill Moyers. Ed. Betty Sue Flowers. New York: Anchor Books, 1991.

---. *The Hero With a Thousand Faces.* Princeton: Princeton University Press, 1949.

Carey, Brycchan. "Hermione and the House-Elves Revisited: J.K. Rowling, Antislavery Campaigning, and the Politics of Potter." *Reading Harry Potter Again: New Critical Essays.* Ed. Giselle Liza Anatol. Santa Barbara: ABC-CLIO, 2009. 159-73.

---. "Hermione and the House-Elves: The Literary and Historical Contexts of J.K. Rowling's Antislavery Campaign." *Reading Harry Potter: Critical Essays.* Ed. Giselle Liza Anatol. Westport: Praeger, 2003. 103-15.

Carson, Tom. "Jedi Uber Alles." *A Galaxy Not So Far Away: Writers and Artists on Twenty Five Years of Star Wars.* Ed. Glenn Kenny. New York: Owl Books, 2002. 160-71.

Cawelti, John G. *Adventure, Mystery, and Romance: Formula Stories as Art and Popular Culture.* Chicago: The University of Chicago Press, 1976.

Chappell, Drew. "Sneaking Out After Dark: Resistance, Agency, and the Postmodern Child in J.K. Rowling's Harry Potter Series." *Children's Literature in Education* 39 (2008): 281-93.

Cherland, Meredith. "Harry's Girls: Harry Potter and the Discourse of Gender." *Journal of Adolescent and Adult Literacy* 52.4 (2008/2009): 273-82.

Colbert, David. *The Magical Worlds of Harry Potter: A Treasury of Myths, Legends and Fascinating Facts.* London: Puffin Books, 2003.

Colebatch, Hal. *Return of the Heroes: The Lord of the Rings, Star Wars and Contemporary Culture.* n.p.: Australian Institute for Public Policy, 1990.

Collins, Robert G. "*Star Wars*: The Pastiche of Myth and the Yearning for a Past Future." *Journal of Popular Culture* 11.1 (1977): 1-10.

Collins Smith, Anne. "Harry Potter, Radical Feminism, and the Power of Love." *The Ultimate Harry Potter and Philosophy: Hogwarts for Muggles.* Ed. Gregory Bassham. New Jersey: Wiley, 2010. 80-93.

Cothran, Casey A. "Lessons in Transfiguration: Allegories of Male Identity in Rowling's *Harry Potter* Series." *Scholarly Studies in Harry Potter: Applying Academic Methods to a Popular Text.* Ed. Cynthia Whitney Hallet. Lewiston: Edwin Mellen Press, 2005. 123-34.

Cox, Alexander. "*Star Wars:* Decoding the Spectacle of Myth." *Foundation* 92 (2004): 17-30.

Creed, Barbara. General Introduction. *The Sexual Subject: A 'Screen' Reader in Sexuality*. Ed. John Caughie and Annette Kuhn. London: Routledge, 1992. 1-11.

Cummins, June. "Hermione in the Bathroom: The Gothic, Menarche, and Female Development in the Harry Potter Series." *The Gothic in Children's Literature: Haunting the Borders*. Ed. Anna Jackson, Karen Coats, and Roderick McGillis. New York: Routledge, 2008. 177-93.

Dalton, Russel W. *Faith Journey through Fantasy Lands: A Christian Dialogue with Harry Potter, Star Wars, and The Lord of the Rings*. Minneapolis: Augsburg Books, 2003.

Deavel, Catherine Jack and David Paul Deavel. "Choosing Love: The Redemption of Severus Snape." *The Ultimate Harry Potter and Philosophy: Hogwarts for Muggles*. Ed. Gregory Bassham. New Jersey: Wiley, 2010. 53-65.

---. "A Skewered Reflection: The Nature of Evil." *Harry Potter and Philosophy: If Aristotle Ran Hogwarts*. Ed. David Baggett and Shawn E. Klein. Chicago: Open Court, 2004. 132-47.

---. "Character, Choice, and Harry Potter." *Logos* 5.4 (2002): 49-64.

Decker, Mark T. "They Want Unfreedom and One-Dimensional Thought? I'll Give Them Unfreedom and One-Dimensional Thought: George Lucas, *THX-1138*, and the Persistence of Marcusian Social Critique in *American Graffiti* and the *Star Wars* Films." *Extrapolation* 50.3 (2009): n.pag. <http://lion.chadwyck.co.uk/>.

Dees, Richard H. "Moral Ambiguity in a Black-and-White Universe." *Star Wars and Philosophy: More Powerful than You Can Possibly Imagine*. Ed. Kevin S. Decker and Jason T. Eberl. Chicago: Open Court, 2005. 39-53.

Deis, Christopher. "May the Force (Not) Be With You: 'Race Critical' Readings and the *Star Wars* Universe." *Culture, Identities and Technology in the Star Wars Films: Essays on the Two Trilogies*. Ed. Carl Silvio and Tony M. Vinci. Jefferson: McFarland & Company, Inc., 2007. 77-108.

Derrida, Jacques. *Writing and Difference*. [1967]. London: Routledge Classics, 2002.

---. *Of Grammatology*. [1967] Baltimore: The Johns Hopkins University Press, 1997.

---. *Positions*. Chicago: University of Chicago Press, 1972.

Desilet, Gregory. "Deconstructing Harry Potter: The Hidden Cultural Costs of the Most Popular Children's Fantasy." *Transformative Communication Studies: Culture, Hierarchy and the Human Condition*. Ed. Omar Swartz. Leicester: Troubador Publishing Ltd., 2008. 161-89.

Dominguez, Diana. "Feminism and the Force: Empowerment and Disillusionment in a Galaxy Far, Far Away." *Culture, Identities and Technology in the Star Wars Films: Essays on the Two Trilogies*. Ed. Carl Silvio and Tony M. Vinci. Jefferson: McFarland & Company, Inc., 2007. 109-33.

Donaher, Patricia and James M. Okapal. "Causation, Prophetic Visions, and the Free Will Question in Harry Potter." *Reading Harry Potter Again: New Critical Essays*. Ed. Giselle Liza Anatol. Santa Barbara: ABC-CLIO, 2009. 47-62.

Dresang, Eliza T. "Hermione Granger and the Heritage of Gender." *The Ivory Tower and Harry Potter: Perspectives on a Literary Phenomenon*. Ed. Lana A. Whited. Columbia: University of Missouri Press, 2002. 211-42.

Dreyer-Gehle, Yvonne. "'Harry Potter' im Schussfeld des Christentums." *Harry Potter im Quadrat. Der Unheimliche Erfolg eines Best- und Longsellers*. Ed. Peter Conrady. Oberhausen: ATHENA-Verlag. 13-50.

Dundes, Alan. "Binary Opposition in Myth: The Propp/Lévi-Strauss Debate in Retrospect." *Western Folklore* 56.1 (1997): n.pag. <http://lion.chadwyck.co.uk/>.

Eagleton, Terry. *On Evil*. New Haven: Yale University Press, 2010.

Eberl, Jason T. "'You Cannot Escape Your Destiny' (Or Can You?): Freedom and Predestination in the Skywalker Family." *Star Wars and Philosophy: More Powerful than You Can Possibly Imagine*. Ed. Kevin S. Decker and Jason T. Eberl. Chicago: Open Court, 2005. 3-15.

Eccleshare, Julia. *A Guide to the Harry Potter Novels*. London: Continuum, 2002.

Eliade, Mircea. *Myth and Reality*. London: George Allen & Unwin Ltd, 1963.

Ellwood, Robert. *Tales of Darkness: The Mythology of Evil*. London: Continuum, 2009.

Estrada, Gabriel S. (Nahuatl). "*Star Wars* Episodes I-VI: Coyote and the Force of White Narrative." *The Persistence of Whiteness: Race and Contemporary Hollywood Cinema*. Ed. Daniel Bernardi. London: Routledge, 2008. 69-90.

Fader, Shanti. "'A Certain Point of View:' Lying Jedi, Honest Sith, and the Viewers who Love Them." *Star Wars and Philosophy: More Powerful than You Can Possibly Imagine*. Ed. Kevin S. Decker and Jason T. Eberl. Chicago: Open Court, 2005. 192-204.

---. "In Sheep's Clothing: The Face of Evil in *The Phantom Menace*." *Parabola: Tradition, Myth, and the Search for Meaning* 24.4 (1999): 88-90.

Fenske, Claudia. *Muggles, Monsters and Magicians: A Literary Analysis of the Harry Potter Series*. Frankfurt a.M.: Peter Lang, 2008.

Fiske, John. *Understanding Popular Culture*. London: Routledge, 2006.

---. "Culture, Ideology, Interpellation." *Literary Theory: An Anthology*. Ed. Julie Rivkin and Michael Ryan. Malden, MA: Blackwell Publishing, 2004. 1268-273.

---. "British Cultural Studies and Television." *What is Cultural Studies? A Reader*. Ed. John Storey. London: Arnold, 1996. 115-46

Foucault, Michel. *Discipline and Punish: The Birth of the Prison*. [1975]. New York: Vintage Books, 1995.

Frazer, Sir James. *The Golden Bough: A Study in Magic and Religion.* [1890]. London: Wordsworth Reference Series, 1993.

Freud, Sigmund. *The Uncanny.* [1919]. London: Penguin Books, 2003.

Fry, Michele. "Heroes and Heroines: Myth and Gender Roles in the *Harry Potter* Books." *New Review of Children's Literature and Librarianship* 7.1 (2001): 157-67.

Galipeau, Steven A. *The Journey of Luke Skywalker.* Chicago: Open Court, 2001.

Gallardo C., Ximena and C. Jason Smith. "Happily Ever After: Harry Potter and the Quest for the Domestic." *Reading Harry Potter Again: New Critical Essays.* Ed. Giselle Liza Anatol. Santa Barbara: ABC-CLIO, 2009. 91-108.

---. "Cinderfella: J.K. Rowling's Wily Web of Gender." *Reading Harry Potter: Critical Essays.* Ed. Giselle Liza Anatol. Westport: Praeger, 2003. 191-205.

Geertz, Clifford. *Local Knowledge: Further Essays in Interpretive Anthropology.* New York: Basic Books, Inc., 1983.

Geraghty, Lincoln. "Creating and Comparing Myth in Twentieth-Century Science Fiction: *Star Trek* and *Star Wars.*" *Literature/Film Quarterly* 33.3 (2005): 191-200.

Gibbons, Sarah E. "Death and Rebirth: *Harry Potter* and the Mythology of the Phoenix." *Scholarly Studies in Harry Potter: Applying Academic Methods to a Popular Text.* Ed. Cynthia Whitney Hallett. Lewiston: Edwin Mellen Press, 2005. 85-105.

Gilbert, Sandra and Susan Gubar. "The Madwoman in the Attic." *Literary Theory: An Anthology.* Ed. Julie Rivkin and Michael Ryan. Malden, MA: Blackwell Publishing, 2004. 812-25.

Gillies, Constantin. *Die Macht mit uns: Star Wars und die Folgen.* Reinbek: Rowohlt Taschenbuch Verlag, 2003.

Girard, René. *Violence and the Sacred.* Baltimore: The Johns Hopkins University Press, 1977.

Gladstein, Mimi R. "Feminism and Equal Opportunity: Hermione and the Women of Hogwarts." *Harry Potter and Philosophy: If Aristotle Ran Hogwarts.* Ed. David Baggett and Shawn E. Klein. Chicago: Open Court, 2004. 49-59.

Gómez Pascual, Natalia. "A Bridge Between Two Different Worlds: On the Reflection and Fracture of Stereotypes in the Harry Potter Novels." *Anuario de Investigación en Literatura Infantil y Juvenil* 5 (2007): 91-108.

Gordon, Andrew. "*Star Wars*: A Myth for Our Time." *Screening the Sacred: Religion, Myth, and Ideology in Popular American Film.* Ed. Joel W. Martin and Conrad E. Ostwalt Jr. Boulder: Westview Press, 1995. 73-82.

---. "The Power of the Force: Sex in the *Star Wars* Trilogy." *Eros in the Mind's Eye: Sexuality and the Fantastic in Art and Film.* New York: Greenwood Press, 1986. 193-207.

---. *"The Empire Strikes Back*: Monsters from the Id." *Science Fiction Studies* 7.3 (1980): 313-18.

Granger, John. *The Deathly Hallows Lectures: The Hogwarts Professor Explains Harry's Final Adventure*. Allentown: Zossima Press, 2008.

---. *Unlocking Harry Potter: Five Keys for the Serious Reader*. n.p.: Zossima Press, 2007.

---. *Looking for God in Harry Potter: Is There Hidden Meaning in the Bestselling Books?* n.p.: Saltriver, 2006.

Gras, Vernon W. "Myth and the Reconciliation of Opposites: Jung and Lévi-Strauss." *Journal of the History of Ideas* 42.3 (1981): 471-88.

Green, Amy M. "Interior/Exterior in the Harry Potter Series: Duality Expressed in Sirius Black and Remus Lupin." *Papers on Language and Literature: A Quarterly Journal for Scholars of Language and Literature* 44.1 (Winter 2008): n.pag. <http://lion.chadwyck.co.uk/>.

Grijalva Maza, Luisa. "Deconstructing the Grand Narrative in *Harry Potter*: Inclusion/Exclusion and Discriminatory Policies in Fiction and Practice." *Politics & Policy* 40.3 (2012): 424-43.

Grimes, M. Katherine. "Harry Potter: Fairy Tale Prince, Real Boy, and Archetypal Hero." *The Ivory Tower and Harry Potter: Perspectives on a Literary Phenomenon*. Ed. Lana A. Whited. Columbia: University of Missouri Press, 2002. 89-122.

Grochala, Sarah. "A Form of Ethics: The Disrupted and Misappropriated Story in the Monodramas of Mark Ravenhill." *Narrative in Drama*. CDE vol. 18. Ed. Merle Tönnies and Christina Flotmann. Trier: WVT, 2011. 141-54.

Gupta, Suman. *Re-Reading Harry Potter*. Houndsmills: Palgrave Macmillan, 2003.

Hall, Martin. "The Fantasy of Realism, or Mythology as Methodology." *Harry Potter and International Relations*. Ed. Daniel H. Nexon and Iver B. Neumann. Lanham: Rowman & Littlefield, 2006. 177-94.

Hall, Stuart. "New Ethnicities." *Black British Cultural Studies: A Reader*. Ed. Houston A. Baker, Jr., Manthia Diawara, and Ruth H. Lindeborg. Chicago: University of Chicago Press, 1996. 163-72.

---. "Encoding/decoding." *Culture, Media, Language: Working Papers in Cultural Studies, 1972-79*. Ed. Stuart Hall, Dorothy Hobson, Andrew Lowe, and Paul Willis. London: Routledge, 1980. 128-38.

Hammett, Jennifer. "The Ideological Impediment: Epistemology, Feminism, and Film Theory." *Film Theory and Philosophy*. Ed. Richard Allen and Murray Smith. Oxford: Clarendon Press, 1997. 244-59.

Haney Lopéz, Ian F. "The Social Construction of Race." *Literary Theory: An Anthology*. Ed. Julie Rivkin and Michael Ryan. Malden, MA: Blackwell Publishing, 2004. 964-74.

Hankiss, Elemér. *Fears and Symbols*. Budapest: Central European University Press, 2001.

Hanson, Michael J. and Max S. Kay. *Star Wars: The New Myth*. n.p.: Xlibris Corporation, 2001.

Hanson, Todd. "A Big Dumb Movie About Space Wizards: Struggling to Cope with *The Phantom Menace*." *A Galaxy Not So Far Away: Writers and Artists on Twenty Five Years of Star Wars*. Ed. Glenn Kenny. New York: Owl Books, 2002. 172-202.

Hart Weed, Jennifer. "Voldemort, Boethius, and the Destructive Effects of Evil." *Harry Potter and Philosophy: If Aristotle Ran Hogwarts*. Ed. David Baggett and Shawn E. Klein. Chicago: Open Court, 2004. 148-57.

Heilman, Elizabeth E. and Trevor Donaldson. "From Sexist to (Sort-of) Feminist: Representations of Gender in the Harry Potter Series." *Critical Perspectives on Harry Potter*. Ed. Elizabeth E. Heilman. New York: Routledge, 2009. 139-61.

Heilman, Elizabeth E., ed. *Critical Perspectives on Harry Potter*. New York: Routledge, 2009.

---, ed. *Harry Potter's World: Multidisciplinary Critical Perspectives*. New York: Routledge, 2003.

---. "Blue Wizards and Pink Witches: Representations of Gender Identity and Power." *Harry Potter's World: Multidisciplinary Critical Perspectives*. Ed. Elizabeth E. Heilman. New York: Routledge, 2003. 221-39.

--- and Anne E. Gregory. "Images of the Privileged Insider and Outcast Outsider." *Harry Potter's World: Multidisciplinary Critical Perspectives*. Ed. Elizabeth E. Heilman. New York: Routledge, 2003. 241-59.

Henderson, Mary. *Star Wars: The Magic of Myth*. New York: Bantam Books, 1997.

Hochbruck, Wolfgang, Elmo Feiten and Anja Tiedemann. "'Vulchanov! Volkov! Aaaaaaand *Krum*!': Joanne K. Rowling's 'Eastern' Europe." *Facing the East in the West: Images of Eastern Europe in British Literature, Film and Culture*. Ed. Barbara Korte, Eva Ulrike Pirker, and Sissy Helff. Amsterdam: Rodopi, 2010. 233-44.

Horne, Jackie C. "Harry and the Other: Answering the Race Question in J.K. Rowling's Harry Potter." *The Lion and the Unicorn: A Critical Journal of Children's Literature* 34.1 (2010): 76-104.

Jelinek, Linda. *Das Phänomen Harry Potter: Eine literaturwissenschaftliche Analyse des Welterfolgs*. Saarbrücken: VDM Verlag Dr. Müller, 2006.

Joppke, Christian. "Multiculturalism and Immigration: A Comparison of the United States, Germany, and Great Britain." *Theory and Society* 25 (1996): 449-500.

Jullier, Laurent. *Star Wars: Anatomie einer Saga*. Konstanz: UVK Verlagsgesellschaft mbH, 2007.

Kapell, Matthew Wilhelm and John Shelton Lawrence, eds. *Finding the Force of the Star Wars Franchise: Fans, Merchandise, and Critics.* New York: Peter Lang, 2006.

Kapell, Matthew Wilhelm. "Eugenics, Racism, and the Jedi Gene Pool." *Finding the Force of the Star Wars Franchise: Fans, Merchandise, and Critics.* Ed. Matthew Wilhelm Kapell and John Shelton Lawrence. New York: Peter Lang, 2006. 159-73.

Kellner, Rivka Temima. "J.K. Rowling's Ambivalence Towards Feminism: House Elves – Women in Disguise in the 'Harry Potter' Books." *The Midwest Quarterly: A Journal of Contemporary Thought* 51.4 (2010): 367-85.

Kern, Edmund M. *The Wisdom of Harry Potter: What Our Favourite Hero Teaches Us about Moral Choices.* New York: Prometheus Books, 2003.

Kerr, Ryan. "Tom Riddle's Diary: How We Read Books." *Hog's Head Conversations: Essays on Harry Potter.* Ed. Travis Prinzi. Allentown: Zossima Press, 2009. 127-39.

Kidd, Dustin. "Harry Potter and the Functions of Popular Culture." *Journal of Popular Culture* 40.1 (2007): n.pag. <http://lion.chadwyck.co.uk/>.

Killinger, John. *The Life, Death, and Resurrection of Harry Potter.* Macon: Mercer University Press, 2009.

Kinnucan, Michelle J. "Pedagogy of (the) Force: The Myth of Redemptive Violence." *Finding the Force of the Star Wars Franchise: Fans, Merchandise, and Critics.* Ed. Matthew Wilhelm Kapell and John Shelton Lawrence. New York: Peter Lang, 2006. 59-72.

Köhler, Ulrike Kristina. "Harry Potter – National Hero and National Heroic Epic." *International Research in Children's Literature* 4.1 (2011): 15-28.

Kolbuch, Sandy Andrea. *Mythische Elemente in der modernen fantastischen Literatur, erläutert am Beispiel von Joanne K. Rowling's [sic] Harry Potter.* München: AVM, 2010.

Kragl, Florian. "Artus im 'Krieg der Sterne:' Zyklusbildung als Narratologisches Paradoxon einer Dynamischen Statik." *Neophilologus* 93 (2009): 279-94.

Kuiper, Koenraad. "Star Wars: An Imperial Myth." *Journal of Popular Culture* 21.4 (1988): 77-86.

Lacoss, Jann. "Of Magicals and Muggles: Reversals and Revulsions at Hogwarts." *The Ivory Tower and Harry Potter: Perspectives on a Literary Phenomenon.* Ed. Lana A. Whited. Columbia: University of Missouri Press, 2002. 67-88.

Lancashire, Anne. "*The Phantom Menace*: Repetition, Variation, Integration." *Film Criticism* 24 (2000): 23-44.

Lawrence, John Shelton. "Joseph Campbell, George Lucas, and the Monomyth." *Finding the Force of the Star Wars Franchise: Fans, Merchandise, and Critics.* Ed. Matthew Wilhelm Kapell and John Shelton Lawrence. New York: Peter Lang, 2006. 21-33.

Lev, Peter. "Whose Future? *Star Wars, Alien*, and *Blade Runner*." *Literature/Film Quarterly* 26.1 (1998): n.pag. <http://lion.chadwyck.co.uk/>.

Lévi-Strauss, Claude. "The Structural Study of Myth." *Structuralism in Myth: Lévi-Strauss, Barthes, Dumézil, and Propp*. Ed. Robert A Segal. New York: Garland Publishing, 1996. 118-34.

Limbach, Gwendolyn. "Ginny Weasley, Girl Next-Doormat?" *Hog's Head Conversations: Essays on Harry Potter*. Ed. Travis Prinzi. Allentown: Zossima Press, 2009. 167-87.

Lyden, John. "Apocalyptic Determinism and *Star Wars*." *Culture, Identities and Technology in the Star Wars Films: Essays on the Two Trilogies*. Ed. Carl Silvio and Tony M. Vinci. Jefferson: McFarland & Company, Inc., 2007. 34-52.

---. "The Apocalyptic Cosmology of *Star Wars*." *The Journal of Religion and Film* 4.1 (2000): n.pag. <http://lion.chadwyck.co.uk/>.

Lyotard, Jean-François. "The Postmodern Condition." *Literary Theory: An Anthology*. Ed. Julie Rivkin and Michael Ryan. Malden: Blackwell Publishing, 2004. 355-64.

Mackay, Daniel. "Star Wars: The Magic of the Anti-Myth." *Foundation* 76 (1999): 63-75.

McDaniel, Kathryn N. "The Elfin Mystique: Fantasy and Feminism in J.K. Rowling's *Harry Potter* Series." *Past Watchful Dragons: Fantasy and Faith in the World of C.S. Lewis*. Ed. Amy H. Sturgis. Altadena: The Mythopoeic Press, 2007. 183-207.

McEvoy, Kathleen. "Aesthetic Organization: The Structural Beauty of J.K. Rowling's Harry Potter Series." *Topic: A Journal of the Liberal Arts* 54 (2004): 14-23.

Mendlesohn, Farah. "Crowning the King: Harry Potter and the Construction of Authority." *The Ivory Tower and Harry Potter: Perspectives on a Literary Phenomenon*. Ed. Lana A. Whited. Columbia: University of Missouri Press, 2002. 159-81.

Miller, Martin and Robert Sprich. "The Appeal of *Star Wars*: An Archetypal-Psychoanalytic View." *American Imago* 38.2 (1981): 203-20.

Mills, Alice. "Archetypes and the Unconscious in *Harry Potter* and Diana Wynne Jones's *Fire and Hemlock* and *Dogsbody*." *Reading Harry Potter: Critical Essays*. Ed. Giselle Liza Anatol. Westport: Praeger, 2003. 3-14.

Modood, Tariq. *Multiculturalism: A Civic Idea*. Cambridge, UK: Polity Press, 2007.

Morris, Tom. "The Courageous Harry Potter." *Harry Potter and Philosophy: If Aristotle Ran Hogwarts*. Ed. David Baggett and Shawn E. Klein. Chicago: Open Court, 2004. 9-21.

Mulvey, Laura. "Visual Pleasure and Narrative Cinema." *Literary Theory: An Anthology*. Ed. Julie Rivkin and Michael Ryan. Malden, MA: Blackwell Publishing, 1998. 585-95.

Neal, Connie. *The Gospel According to Harry Potter: Spirituality in the Stories of the World's Most Famous Seeker*. Louisville: Westminster John Knox Press, 2002.

Nel, Philip. *J.K. Rowling's Harry Potter Novels: A Reader's Guide*. New York: Continuum, 2003.

Nikolajeva, Maria. "Adult Heroism and Role Models in the *Harry Potter* Novels." *Heroism in the Harry Potter Novels*. Ed. Katrin Berndt and Lena Steveker. Farnham: Ashgate, 2011. 193-205.

---. "*Harry Potter* – A Return to the Romantic Hero." *Harry Potter's World: Multidisciplinary Critical Perspectives*. Ed. Elizabeth E. Heilman. New York: Routledge, 2003. 125-40.

O'Keefe, Deborah. *Readers in Wonderland: The Liberating Worlds of Fantasy Fiction: From Dorothy to Harry Potter*. New York: Continuum, 2003.

Osborne, Deirdre. "How Do We Get the Whole Story? Contra-dictions and Counter-narratives in debbie tucker green's Dramatic-Poetics." *Narrative in Drama*. CDE vol. 18. Ed. Merle Tönnies and Christina Flotmann. Trier: WVT, 2011. 181-206.

Ostry, Elaine. "Accepting Mudbloods: The Ambivalent Social Vision of J.K. Rowling's Fairy Tales." *Reading Harry Potter: Critical Essays*. Ed. Giselle Liza Anatol. Westport: Praeger, 2003. 89-102.

Oziewicz, Marek. "Representations of Eastern Europe in Philip Pullman's *His Dark Materials*, Jonathan Stroud's *The Bartimaeus Trilogy*, and J.K. Rowling's *Harry Potter* Series." *International Research in Children's Literature* 3.1 (2010): 1-14.

Park, Julia. "Class and Socioeconomic Identity in Harry Potter's England." *Reading Harry Potter: Critical Essays*. Ed. Giselle Liza Anatol. Westport: Praeger, 2003. 179-89.

Patterson, Steven W. "Kreacher's Lament: S.P.E.W. As a Parable on Discrimination, Indifference, and Social Justice." *Harry Potter and Philosophy: If Aristotle Ran Hogwarts*. Ed. David Baggett and Shawn E. Klein. Chicago: Open Court, 2004. 105-17.

Pennington, John. "From Elfland to Hogwarts, or the Aesthetic Trouble with Harry Potter." *The Lion and the Unicorn: A Critical Journal of Children's Literature* 26.1 (2002): 78-97.

Perlich, John. "'I've Got a Bad Feeling About This...:' Lucas Gets Lost on the Path of Mythos." *Sith, Slayers, Stargates, + Cyborgs: Modern Mythology in the New*

Millennium. Ed. David Whitt and John Perlich. New York: Peter Lang, 2008. 9-29.

Pharr, Mary. "A Paradox: The *Harry Potter* Series as Both Epic and Postmodern." *Heroism in the Harry Potter Series*. Ed. Katrin Berndt and Lena Steveker. Farnham: Ashgate. 2011. 9-23.

---. "In Medias Res: Harry Potter as Hero-in-Progress." *The Ivory Tower and Harry Potter: Perspectives on a Literary Phenomenon*. Ed. Lana E. Whited. Columbia: University of Missouri Press, 2002. 53-66.

Pierce, Jeremy. "Destiny in the Wizarding World." *The Ultimate Harry Potter and Philosophy: Hogwarts for Muggles*. Ed. Gregory Bassham. New Jersey: Wiley, 2010. 35-49.

Polk, Bryan. "The Medieval Image of the Hero in the *Harry Potter* Novels." *The Image of the Hero in Literature, Media, and Society*. Selected Papers 2004 Conference of the Society for the Interdisciplinary Study of Social Imagery. Ed. Will Wright and Steve Kaplan. Pueblo: Colorado State University-Pueblo. 440-45.

Polzer, Joachim. "Die Selbstentdeckung der amerikanischen Identität und die Zerschlagung der europäischen Ambivalenz: 20 Jahre STAR WARS." *Weltwunder der Kinematographie: Beiträge zu einer Kulturgeschichte der Film- und Medientechnik* n4 (1997): 45-51.

Pond, Julia. "A Story of the Exceptional: Fate, and Free Will in the Harry Potter Series." *Children's Literature* 38 (2010): 181-206.

Prinzi, Travis. *Harry Potter and Imagination: The Way Between Two Worlds*. Allentown: Zossima Press, 2009.

Propp, Vladimir. *Theory and History of Folklore*. Manchester: Manchester University Press, 1984.

---. *Morphology of the Folktale*. [1928]. Austin: University of Texas Press, 2005.

Pugh, Tison and David L. Wallace. "Heteronormative Heroism and Queering the School Story in J.K. Rowling's *Harry Potter* Series." *Children's Literature Association Quarterly* 31.3 (Fall 2006): n.pag. <http://lion.chadwyck.co.uk/>.

Rana, Marion. "'The less you lot have ter do with these foreigners, the happier yeh'll be:' Cultural and National Otherness in J.K. Rowling's *Harry Potter* Series." *International Research in Children's Literature* 4.1 (2011): 45-58.

---. *Creating Magical Worlds: Otherness and Othering in Harry Potter*. Frankfurt a.M.: Peter Lang, 2009.

Robinson, Walter (Ritoku). "The Far East of *Star Wars*." *Star Wars and Philosophy: More Powerful than You Can Possibly Imagine*. Ed. Kevin S. Decker and Jason T. Eberl. Chicago: Open Court, 2005. 29-38.

Rösch, Gertrud Maria. "Wächst das Rettende Auch?: Die Konzeptionalisierung und Visualisierung des Bösen in den Filmen *Harry Potter* (2001ff.) und *Men in Black* (1997 / 2002)." *Der Fantastische Film: Geschichte und Funktion in der*

Mediengesellschaft. Ed. Oliver Jahraus and Stefan Neuhaus. Würzburg: Königshausen & Neumann, 2005. 187-97.

Rothman, Ken. "Hearts of Darkness: Voldemort and Iago, with a Little Help from Their Friends." *Essays on Evil in Popular Media: Vader, Voldemort and Other Villains.* Ed. Jamey Heit. Jefferson: McFarland & Company, Inc., 2011. 202-17.

Sarup, Madan. *Post-Structuralism and Postmodernism.* New York: Harvester Wheatsheaf, 1993.

Sattauer, Jennifer. "Harry Potter: A World of Fear." *The Journal of Children's Literature Studies* 3.1 (2006): 1-14.

Saxena, Vandana. *The Subversive Harry Potter: Adolescent Rebellion and Containment in the J.K. Rowling Novels.* Jefferson: McFarland & Company, Inc., 2012.

Schanoes, Veronica L. "Cruel Heroes and Treacherous Texts: Educating the Reader in Moral Complexity and Critical Reading in J.K. Rowling's *Harry Potter* Books." *Reading Harry Potter: Critical Essays.* Ed. Giselle Liza Anatol. Westport: Praeger, 2003. 131-45.

Schimmel, Annemarie. *The Mystery of Numbers.* New York: Oxford University Press, 1993.

Seibold, Verena C. "Noch nie war das Gute so böse – Warum auch gute Menschen böse handeln." *Noch nie war das Böse so gut: Die Aktualität einer alten Differenz.* Ed. Franz Fromholzer, Michael Preis, and Bettina Wisiorek. Heidelberg: Universitätsverlag Winter, 2011. 91-106.

Sherman, Marilyn R. "*Star Wars*: New Worlds and Ancient Myths." *Kentucky Folklore Record* 25 (1979): 6-10.

Silvio, Carl and Tony M. Vinci, eds. *Culture, Identities and Technology in the Star Wars Films: Essays on the Two Trilogies.* Jefferson: McFarland & Company, Inc., 2007.

---. "Moving Away from Myth: *Star Wars* as Cultural Artifact." Introduction. *Culture, Identities and Technology in the Star Wars Films: Essays on the Two Trilogies.* Ed. Carl Silvio and Tony M. Vinci. Jefferson: McFarland & Company, Inc., 2007. 1-8.

Simpson, Philip L. "Thawing the Ice Princess." *Finding the Force of the Star Wars Franchise: Fans, Merchandise, and Critics.* Ed. Matthew Wilhelm Kapell and John Shelton Lawrence. New York: Peter Lang, 2006. 115-29.

Singer, Rita. "Harry Potter and the Battle for the Soul: The Revival of the Psychomachia in Secular Fiction." *Heroism in the Harry Potter Series.* Ed. Katrin Berndt and Lena Steveker. Farnham: Ashgate, 2011. 25-38.

Star Wars: The Power of Myth. New York: Dorling Kindersley, 1999.

Steveker, Lena. "'Your Soul is Whole, and Completely Your Own, Harry:' The Heroic Self in J.K. Rowling's *Harry Potter* Series." *Heroism in the Harry*

Potter Series. Ed. Katrin Berndt and Lena Steveker. Farnham: Ashgate, 2011. 69-83.

Strube, Miriam. *Subjekte des Begehrens: Zur sexuellen Selbstbestimmung der Frau in Litertur, Musik und Visueller Kultur*. Bielefeld: transcript, 2009.

Sturgis, Amy H. "When Harry Met Faërie: Rowling's Hogwarts, Tolkien's Fairy Stories, and the Question of Readership." *Hog's Head Conversations: Essays on Harry Potter*. Ed. Travis Prinzi. Allentown: Zossima Press, 2009. 81-101.

Toles Patkin, Terry. "Constructing a New Game: J.K. Rowling's Quidditch and Global Kid Culture." *Reconstruction* 6.1 (Winter 2006): n.pag. <http://lion.chadwyck.co.uk/>.

Tönnies, Merle. "(En-)Gendering a Popular Theoretical Genre: The Roles of Women in Nineteenth-Century British Melodrama." Habilitationsschrift. Ruhr-Universität Bochum, 2002.

Tompkins, Jane P. "An Introduction to Reader-Response Criticism." Introduction. *Reader-Response Criticism: From Formalism to Post-Structuralism*. Ed. Jane P. Tompkins. Baltimore: The Johns Hopkins University Press, 1980. ix-xxvi.

Turner, Victor. *The Forest of Symbols: Aspects of Ndembu Ritual*. Ithaca, NY: Cornell University Press, 1967.

Turner-Vorbeck, Tammy. "Pottermania: Good, Clean Fun or Cultural Hegemony?" *Harry Potter's World: Multidisciplinary Critical Perspectives*. Ed. Elizabeth E. Heilman. New York: Routledge, 2003. 13-24.

Van Yperen, Nathaniel. "I Am Your Father: The Villain and the Future Self." *Essays on Evil in Popular Media: Vader, Voldemort and Other Villains*. Ed. Jamey Heit. Jefferson: McFarland & Company, Inc., 2011. 189-201.

Vinci, Tony M. "The Fall of the Rebellion; Or Defiant and Obedient Heroes in a Galaxy Far, Far Away: Individualism and Intertextuality in the *Star Wars* Trilogies." *Culture, Identities and Technology in the Star Wars Films: Essays on the Two Trilogies*. Ed. Carl Silvio and Tony M. Vinci. Jefferson: McFarland & Company, Inc., 2007. 11-33.

Voytilla, Stuart. *Myth and the Movies: Discovering the Mythic Structure of 50 Unforgettable Films*. Ventura: Wiese, 1999.

Wandinger, Nikolaus. "'Sacrifice' in the *Harry Potter* Series from a Girardian Perspective." *Contagion* 17 (2010): n.pag. <http://lion.chadwyck.co.uk/>.

Weinstock, Jeffrey A. "Freaks in Space: 'Extraterrestrialism' and 'Deep-Space Multiculturalism.'" *Cultural Spectacles of the Extraordinary Body: Freakery*. Ed. Rosemarie Garland Thomson. New York: New York University Press, 1996. 327-37.

Wessely, Christian. *Von Star Wars, Ultima und Doom: Mythologisch verschleierte Gewaltmechanismen im kommerziellen Film und in Computerrollenspielen.* Frankfurt a.M.: Peter Lang, 1997.

Westbrook, Perry D. *Free Will and Determinism in American Literature.* Cranbury: Associated University Presses, Inc., 1979.

Westman, Karin E. "'The Weapon We Have is Love.'" *Children's Literature Association Quarterly* 33 (2008): 193-99.

---. "Specters of Thatcherism: Contemporary British Culture in J.K. Rowling's Harry Potter Series." *The Ivory Tower and Harry Potter: Perspectives on a Literary Phenomenon.* Ed. Lana A. Whited. Columbia: University of Missouri Press, 2002. 305-28.

Wetmore Jr., Kevin J. *The Empire Triumphant: Race, Religion and Rebellion in the Star Wars Films.* Jefferson: McFarland & Company, Inc., 2005.

Whited, Lana A., ed. *The Ivory Tower and Harry Potter: Perspectives on a Literary Phenomenon.* Columbia: University of Missouri Press, 2002.

--- and M. Katherine Grimes. "What Would Harry Do?: J.K. Rowling and Lawrence Kohlberg's Theories of Moral Development." *The Ivory Tower and Harry Potter: Perspectives on a Literary Phenomenon.* Ed. Lana A. Whited. Columbia: University of Missouri Press, 2002. 182-208.

Wilhelm, Stephanie J. "Imperial Plastic, Republican Fiber: Speculating on the Post-Colonial Other." *Finding the Force of the Star Wars Franchise: Fans, Merchandise, and Critics.* Ed. Matthew Wilhelm Kapell and John Shelton Lawrence. New York: Peter Lang, 2006. 175-83.

Williams, Raymond. *Culture and Society 1780-1950.* [1958]. Harmondsworth: Penguin Books, 1966.

Wilson, Veronica A. "Seduced by the Dark Side of the Force: Gender, Sexuality, and Moral Agency in George Lucas's *Star Wars* Universe." *Culture, Identities and Technology in the Star Wars Films: Essays on the Two Trilogies.* Ed. Carl Silvio and Tony M. Vinci. Jefferson: McFarland & Company, Inc., 2007. 134-52.

Winters, Sarah Fiona. "Good and Evil in the Works of Diana Wynne Jones and J.K. Rowling." *Diana Wynne Jones: An Exciting and Exacting Wisdom.* Ed. Teya Rosenberg, Martha P. Hixon, Sharon M. Scapple and Donna R. White. New York: Peter Lang, 2002. 79-95.

Wrigley, Christopher. *Return of the Hero.* Lewes: The Book Guild Ltd., 2005.

Zettel, Sarah. "Hermione Granger and the Charge of Sexism." *Mapping the World of the Sorcerer's Apprentice.* Ed. Mercedes Lackey. Dallas: Benbella Books, Inc., 2006. 83-100.

Zipes, Jack. *Sticks and Stones: The Troublesome Success of Children's Literature From Slovenly Peter to Harry Potter.* New York: Routledge, 2001.

INTERNET SOURCES

Anelli, Melissa and Emerson Spartz. "The Leaky Cauldron and MuggleNet Interview with Joanne Kathleen Rowling: Part Two." *The Leaky Cauldron*. 16 July 2005. n.pag. 7 Jul 2011 <http://www.accio-quote.org/articles/2005/0705-tlc_mugglenet-anelli-3.htm>.

Audrey. *Chock Full O' Sevy*. 27 June 2011. 7 Jul. 2011 <www.sevysgal.com/home.html>.

Baker, Katie L. "Harry Potter: A Hero of Mythic Proportions." Thesis. Buffalo State College, Dec. 2011. 6 Sept. 2012 <http://digitalcommons.buffalostate.edu/cgi/viewcontent.cgi?article=1000&context=english_theses>.

Bloom, Harold. "Can 35 Million Book Buyers be Wrong? Yes." *Wall Street Journal* 7 Nov. 2000. 14 June 2011 <http://1xn.org/softspeakers/PDFs/bloom.pdf>.

Bronski, Michael. "Queering Harry Potter." *Z Magazine Online* 16.9 (2003): n.pag. 5 Jul 2011 <http://www.zmag.org/zmag/viewArticle/13675>.

Dahlén, Nova. "Severus Snape and the Concept of the Outsider: Aspects of Good and Evil in the *Harry Potter* Series." Thesis. Karlstad University. 2009. 7 Jul 2011 <http://kau.diva-portal.org/smash/record.jsf?pid=diva2:224466>.

Godfrey, Esther. "'To be Real:' Drag, Minstrelsy and Identity in the New Millennium." *Genders* 41 (2005): n.pag. 16 Jul. 2011 <http://www.genders.org/g41/g41_godfrey.html>.

"Henry." *Behind the Name: The Etymology and History of First Names*. Ed. Mike Campbell. 10 May 2011. 7 Jul. 2011 <http://www.behindthename.com/name/henry>.

Joomla! "The True Story of Severus Snape." 2011. 8 May 2011 <severussnape.org>.

Lady Claudia. "Why Snape." 9 June 2002. 7 Jul. 2011 <whysnape.tripod.com>.

Lucas, George. Interview with Bill Moyers. "Cinema: Of Myth and Men." *Time Magazine* 26 Apr. 1999. 16 Jul. 2011 <http://www.time.com/time/magazine/article/0,9171,990820,00.html>.

"Mace Windu." *Wikipedia*. 2011. 5 May 2011 <http://en.wikipedia.org/wiki/Mace_Windu>.

Matril. "'The Chosen One:' Prophecy, Destiny and Free Will in *Star Wars* and *Harry Potter*." *Saga Journal* 2.8 (2006): n.pag. 5 Jul. 2011 <http://www.sagajournal.com/mthechosenone.html>.

mechayamcha. "Jar Jar Binks Must Die." *YouTube*. 2 Aug. 2011 <http://www.youtube.com/watch?v=LFcs9hIn_Qs>.

Munro, Erin. "Myth and Magic in the *Harry Potter* Series." *Xchanges* 2.1 (2002): n.pag. 7 Jul. 2011 <http://infohost.nmt.edu/~xchanges/old_xchanges/xchanges/2.1/munro.html>.

Professor-Snape.com. 11 Aug. 2005. 8 May 2011 <professor-snape.com>.

Richter, Siegfried G. "Gnosis und Manichäismus in Ägypten: Eine kleine Einführung." Arbeitsstelle für Manichäismusforschung. Institut für Ägyptologie und Koptologie, Westfälische Wilhelms-Universität Münster. 2009. 15 Aug. 2012 <http://www.uni-muenster.de/IAEK/forschen/kop/mani/>.

Schoefer, Christine. "Harry Potter's Girl Trouble: The World of Everyone's Favorite Kid Wizard is a Place Where Boys Come First." *Salon* 13 Jan. 2000. 10 June 2011 <http://www.salon.com/books/feature/2000/01/13/potter>.

"School Bans Harry Potter." *BBC News* 29 Mar. 2000. 25 Jul. 2011 <http://news.bbc.co.uk/2/hi/uk_news/education/693779.stm>.

"Severus Snape: Data." *The Harry Potter Lexicon.* 2012. 30 Aug. 2012 <http://www.hp-lexicon.org/wizards/snape.html#name>.

"Severus Snape." *Harry Potter Wiki.* 2012. 30 Aug. 2012 <http://de.harry-potter.wikia.com/wiki/Severus_Snape>.

The Death to Jar Jar Binks Home Page. 2 Aug. 2011 <http://www.mind spring.com/~ernestm/jarjar/deathtojarjar.html>.

Treneman, Ann. "J.K. Rowling, The Interview." *The Times* 30 June 2000. 5 Jul. 2011 <http://www.accio-quote.org/articles/2000/0600-times-treneman.html>.

Usborne, David. "US Parents Want 'Evil' Harry Potter Banned." *The Independent* 14 Oct. 1999. 25 Jul. 2011 <http://www.independent.co.uk/arts-entertainment/books/news/us-parents-want-evil-harry-potter-banned-743511.html>.

Valdez Moses, Michael. "Blockbuster Wars: Revenge of the Zeitgeist: What Bruce Wayne and Anakin Skywalker Can Tell Us About America's Political Mood." *Reason* (Sept. 2005): n.pag. 15 Jul. 2011 <http://reason.com/archives/2005/09/30/blockbuster-wars-revenge-of-th>.

---. "Back to the Future: The Nostalgic Yet Progressive Appeal of Wizards, Hobbits, and Jedi Knights." *Reason* (July 2003): n.pag. 7 Jul 2011 <http://reason.com/archives/2003/07/01/back-to-the-future>.

Whitton, Natasha. "Me! Books! And Cleverness!: Stereotypical Portrayals in the Harry Potter Series." *WomenWriters* 15 May 2004. 10 June 2011 <http://www.womenwriters.net/summer04/reviews/HarryPotter.htm>.

Williams, Patricia J. "Racial Ventriloquism." *The Nation* 5 Jul. 1999. 15 Jul. 2011 <http://www.thenation.com/article/racial-ventriloquism>.

13. Appendices

APPENDIX 1

Episode III

Fig. 3: Anakin's fall from grace

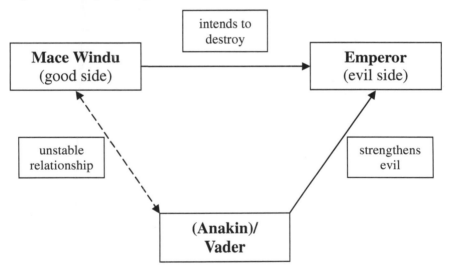

Episode IV

Fig. 4: Vader's redemption

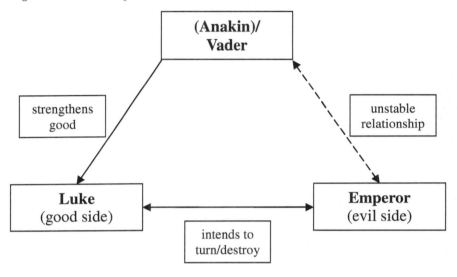

APPENDIX 2

Episode III

Fig. 5: Obi-Wan's sinning

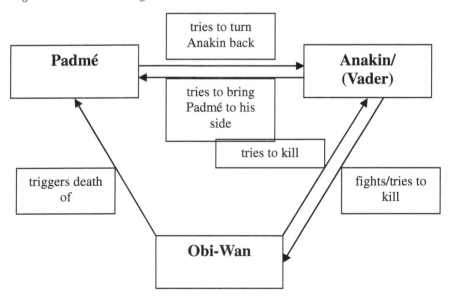

Episode IV

Fig. 6: Obi-Wan's redemption

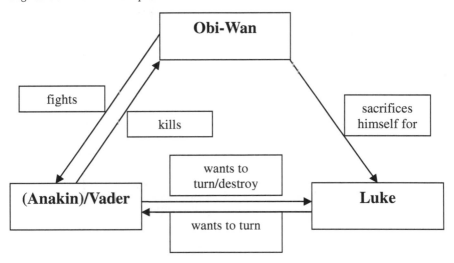

APPENDIX 3

Before the Start of Novel One

Fig. 7: Snape's sinning

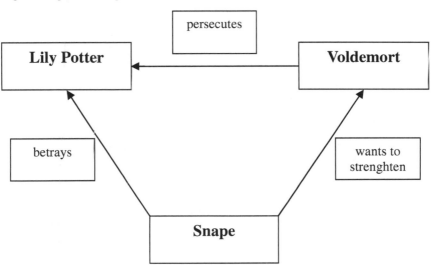

The End of Novel Seven

Fig. 8: Snape's redemption

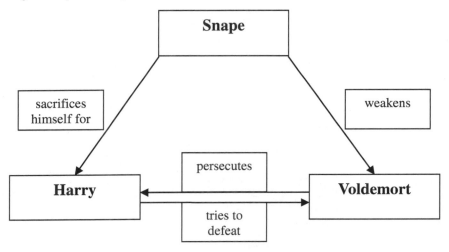

APPENDIX 4

Novel Five

Fig. 9: Kreacher's betrayal

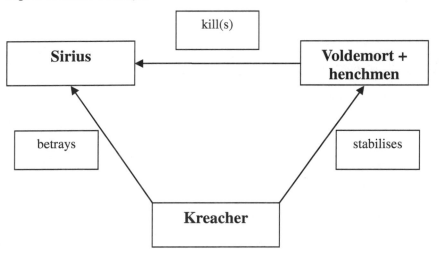

Novel Seven

Fig. 10: Kreacher's redemption

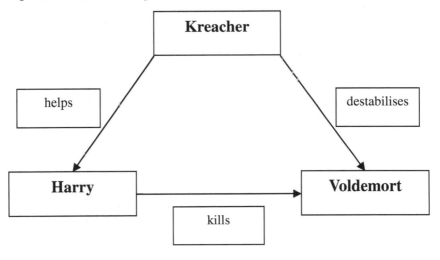